Public & Nonprofit Marketing

Public & Nonprofit Marketing

Christopher H. Lovelock
Formerly, Harvard University

Charles B. Weinberg
The University of British Columbia

SECOND EDITION

▲ *The Scientific Press* • 507 Seaport Court • Redwood City, CA 94063-2731 • (415) 366-2577

PUBLIC & NONPROFIT MARKETING, Second Edition
(First edition titled *Marketing for Public and Nonprofit Managers*)
by Christopher H. Lovelock and Charles B. Weinberg

Published simultaneously in Japanese by Hakuto Shobo Ltd., Tokyo

Printed in the United States of America

10 9 8 7 6 5 4 3 2 1

ISBN 0-89426-134-7

Publisher: The Scientific Press
Text design & production editor: Gene Smith
Cover design by Rogondino & Associates
Cover photograph by Robert Wagoner © 1988

To Molly, Timothy, and Elizabeth

&

To Joanne, Beth, and Amy

About the Authors _____

Christopher Lovelock and Charles Weinberg have been working together since they first met on the faculty of Stanford Graduate School of Business in 1972. Although now living on opposite coasts of North America (in Massachusetts and British Columbia, respectively), they have continued their collaboration through numerous articles and a total of seven books.

Christopher H. Lovelock is principal of Christopher Lovelock & Associates, a consulting and educational firm specializing in management issues in large service businesses, government agencies, and nonprofit organizations. He was a professor at the Harvard Business School from 1973 to 1984 and has also taught at Stanford and the University of California at Berkeley. He is author or coauthor of more than fifty articles and twelve books. A native of Great Britain, he obtained a BCom and an MA in economics from the University of Edinburgh. After working in advertising in London and in corporate planning in Montreal, he went on to obtain an MBA from Harvard and a PhD from Stanford. In 1984, he received the *Journal of Marketing*'s Alpha Kappa Psi Award for his contribution to advancing marketing practice.

Charles B. Weinberg is Alumni Professor of Marketing at the Faculty of Commerce and Business Administration, University of British Columbia. Previously, he taught at Stanford University, the London Business School, and New York University. He won the U.B.C. Commerce Alumni Teaching Award in 1987 for innovations in teaching and the Killam Research prize in 1986. A widely published researcher, he also serves on the editorial boards of the *Journal of Consumer Research* and *Marketing Science*. He has been actively involved in managing and advising nonprofit organizations and has served as vice president of marketing for the Vancouver Symphony Orchestra. He grew up in New Jersey and earned an ScB from Brown University, an MBA from Harvard, and a PhD from Columbia.

Contents

PREFACE

Five years have passed since the first edition of this book, titled *Marketing for Public and Nonprofit Managers,* was published. In the preface to that edition, we wrote:

> A decade ago, the formal use of marketing was at an embryonic stage of development. . . . Today public and nonprofit marketing can be said to have come of age. Although much room remains for improvement, as in the private sector, many examples now exist of a high level of skill and professionalism in developing and executing nonbusiness marketing programs.

The trend continues toward greater professionalism in public and nonprofit management. Many public agencies and nonprofit organizations are more skilled and more successful in their marketing efforts than numerous for-profit companies. And yet we constantly encounter organizations lacking any real orientation to customer needs or competitive dynamics, where marketing (if the term is used at all) is equated with advertising and publicity, and is viewed tactically rather than strategically. Many of these organizations will undoubtedly fail within the next few years unless senior managers and board members take steps promptly to develop a strong marketing orientation.

Marketing is essentially a proactive function: planning for a future environment that will quite certainly be different from today's; working to make sure that things go right; anticipating those things that might go wrong and either finessing them or making contingency plans for how to deal with potential problems.

This book takes a broader perspective of marketing than many managers or board members are accustomed to considering. Anything that impacts the customer falls within the province of marketing, regardless of whether that activity is the nominal responsibility of the board, the executive director, or of managers in such departments as operations, human resources, and accounting, or in marketing, advertising, sales, public relations, and development.

Although we recognize the importance of advertising, sales, and other commmunication activities—indeed we devote three full chapters to these topics—they are simply elements of the broader marketing mix. Developing a service or program is a marketing task; pricing it is a marketing task; selecting or creating delivery systems is a marketing task. Marketing must begin at the top, with the board and the chief executive, when they develop or restate the organization's mission and work to create strategies to achieve that mission. We have yet to encounter a successful organization whose chief executive lacked all sensitivity to the marketplace.

Good marketing programs take time to develop: they cannot be built around reactive "fire-fighting" activities nor around opportunistic, short-term tactics. Strategy should drive tactics, not the other way around. Similarly, an organization's strategy should flow from its mission statement. Our goal for this book is to provide a framework for looking at marketing issues and to help public and nonprofit organizations to develop strategies to achieve their objectives.

As authors writing on marketing management we have one major advantage over our colleagues in such fields as finance, accounting, or human resource management. For every one of our readers is also an expert consumer. Each person reading this book knows what it is like to be a customer and has had years of experience in selecting and purchasing goods, using a wide array of services, and being exposed to numerous fund-raising and advocacy campaigns.

This experience provides an excellent starting point for developing an understanding of the customer's perspective. However, one word of caution is necessary: don't assume that your individual needs and your approach to purchasing and using a service (or deciding whether to adopt or reject an advocated behavior) can be generalized to everyone else in the marketplace.

In its second edition, this book continues to be directed at managers of public and nonprofit organizations, board members or trustees of such organizations, and students interested in learning more about improving marketing management practice in the public and nonprofit sectors. Recognizing the differing levels of marketing expertise among readers, we've sought to make this volume relevant and interesting both to newcomers to the field and to experienced managers.

Acknowledgements

We're delighted that this new edition is being published simultaneously in both English and Japanese. For the English language edition, we return to The Scientific Press, with which we have been publishing books on public and nonprofit marketing since 1977; we appreciate the hard work of Paul Kelly and Gene Smith at the Press. Translation of the book into Japanese has been directed by Professor Yoshiaki Watanabe of Josai University, and our Japanese publishers are Hakuto Shobo, Ltd. of Tokyo.

Many individuals and organizations have contributed significantly to both the first edition and this new second edition titled *Public and Nonprofit Marketing*. Over a period of more than 15 years, students and colleagues at Stanford, Harvard, the University of British Columbia, and other institutions have shaped our thinking and given us many important insights. Another key input has been our experience in working with individual public and nonprofit organizations as consultants, teachers in executive programs, and board members.

We are particularly grateful to Katherine Botman for her influential suggestions in preparing this edition of the book. Special acknowledgements are also due to Gerald J. Gorn of the University of British Columbia, Mel E. Moyer of York University, and Molly Lovelock of the Cambridge YWCA for their assistance and insights. We thank Rosalie Dennie for her expert secretarial assistance. We appreciate, too, the feedback provided by instructors and individual readers of the first edition. Their comments helped us to develop a significant restructuring of the book, resulting in addition of new topics and updating of information within the context of a more concise volume.

January 1989   CHRISTOPHER H. LOVELOCK
                                                      CHARLES B. WEINBERG

PART 1

An Overview of Public & Nonprofit Marketing

Chapter 1
The Role of Marketing

During the Second World War, it is said, the workers who packed parachutes were occasionally chosen to take a test drop with their own products. What better motivation could there be, after all, for keeping the customer's needs in mind than letting workers know that they might have to play the role of customer themselves? Not every public or nonprofit organization deals with life and death issues, of course. But no organization can hope to succeed if it takes a cavalier attitude towards those it seeks to serve.

This book is addressed, of course, to managers rather than workers or customers. Managers may not get involved directly in parachute packing—or whatever the organization's business may be. Yet managers, right up to the chief executive, must take responsibility for the quality of services and programs that their organization provides. One manager we know likes to describe the marketing department as "the conscience of the organization," since its work includes determining the needs and concerns of the various constituencies served by the organization, and ensuring that those concerns are addressed in the design and delivery of programs.

Public and nonprofit organizations play a vital role in maintaining and enhancing the quality of life in modern society. Their activities are extraordinarily diverse, including the arts, conservation, education, health care, human services, postal service, public transportation, and social causes, as well as such basic local services as fire departments, public libraries, and trash removal. The organizations themselves range from struggling volunteer-run groups to major public corporations. But few among them, in our view, could not benefit from better planning and execution of marketing activities.

Managing such organizations is difficult and complex in today's world. Few can support themselves entirely from revenues based on the sale of services. And those institutions that can are being urged to transform themselves into for-profit corporations. Two management experts recently generated a storm of controversy when they concluded, on the basis of research into the U.S. hospital industry, that nonprofit hospitals could perform more efficiently and productively if they operated on a for-profit basis.[1]

Our primary focus in this book will be on organizations that require tax-based financial support or donations of volunteer funds and time. There are challenges on several fronts. Government funding for a broad range of public agencies continues to be inadequate to support human services and other important programs. Managers of nonprofits worry that future donations will be insufficient to cover operating deficits or to finance needed capital improvements; they are also concerned about their ability to recruit volunteers to help with fund raising, administrative tasks, and service delivery. And finally they worry that successful efforts to generate income from gift shops, catalog sales, and other ventures will result in taxation of that income, on the grounds that it is unrelated to the organization's main activity.[2]

Both taxpayers and donors want to see their monies wisely used. The latter, of course, have more discretion over which organizations receive their funds. One large donor, businessman Ross Perot, has given more than $100 million to charity over the past 20 years. He has learned that while good causes are easy to find, good management is not. Says Perot:

> The whole trick is to figure out which [organizations] deliver results, which have leadership, and which are using the money for the people who need it. . . .[3]

Marketing Challenges

Some sense of the scope of nonbusiness marketing—an umbrella term that we'll use to include the marketing activities of both public and nonprofit organizations—is provided by the following real-world examples.

- Challenged to create a more relevant curriculum for high school students who are not interested in going on to college, a major school district has developed a pilot vocational education program that has been very successful in placing graduates in jobs and apprenticeships with good career prospects. The program is offered at a refurbished school which is easy to reach from many parts of the city. But enrollment figures have proved disappointing. Research shows that although eligible students and their parents are aware of the program, the latter worry that the neighborhood around the school is unsafe. School district officials have evidence that the school itself is quite safe and that the neighborhood is becoming more secure as a result of redevelopment. Pressured to improve "voc ed" enrollment, they wonder whether to wait another year and hope that enrollments will rise, to develop a new and more persuasive informational campaign—perhaps accompanied by additional security measures, or to move the program to a new location.

- The newly appointed executive director of a YWCA inherits an organization that is running a substantial deficit. One of her first actions is to improve financial record-keeping so that she can determine which programs are costing more than they attract in revenues and grants. Meanwhile, she works with board and staff members to clarify the organization's mission, so that each program can be evaluated in terms of its contribution to that mission as well as its financial performance. Staff members also look at the prices charged by each program and at how YWCA prices and service features compare with those of similar programs offered by other local institutions. The findings from these analyses are threefold. First, over half of the YWCA programs are losing money and several have the capacity to serve more customers than they presently attract. Second, there is room to raise prices on several programs which are cheaper than competing alternatives. And last, although all programs are viewed as socially worthwhile, several are only tangentially related to advancing the mission of the YWCA. With this information in hand, the board votes to close several programs and to raise prices on most of those remaining. Two programs, the pool and daycare, are targeted for promotional campaigns to increase utilization. As a longer run strategy, fund-raising efforts will be beefed up to seek more grants and donations.

■ A small, struggling chamber orchestra faces a dilemma. After reviewing ticket sales and trends, the general manager has concluded that audience size is stagnant and may even be declining. The artistic director suggests offering a new concert series in one of the outlying suburbs, hoping to attract people who can't or won't make the hour-long trip into the city. The general manager does not think that this strategy offers enough potential. In addition, it will be costly. She thinks that resources should be devoted to increasing the number of fully sponsored special events, such as the civic Christmas tree lighting, fund-raising galas for the Art Gallery, and large formal events such as medical and professional conventions. Such special events would raise awareness of the orchestra, and their costs would be fully covered by the sponsor. The general manager thinks that this type of exposure will eventually increase audience size at the orchestra's regular concerts. But the artistic director doesn't like special events. He resents the artistic restrictions imposed by programs tailored to specific audiences or occasions.

■ An anti-smoking organization, dedicated to achievement of "clean indoor air," is trying to establish directions for the next several years. Progress has been achieved on several fronts but many challenges remain and the organization's financial resources are limited. Proposed legislation to restrict smoking and promotion of tobacco products has been blocked by key legislators, allegedly at the behest of the tobacco lobby. A variety of courses of action is available to the group to maintain its momentum. These include: programs to discourage school children from starting smoking; campaigns to pressure law enforcement officials to require retailers to obey laws forbidding sale of tobacco products to minors; offering support and advice to employees interested in curtailing or eliminating smoking in their workplaces; publicity stunts to get media coverage of colorfully dressed pickets protesting tobacco company sponsorship of sports activities; participation in lawsuits against tobacco firms to force them to produce self-extinguishing cigarettes in order to reduce risk of fires; and continued efforts to build coalitions powerful enough to bring about legislative action at city, regional, or national levels. Since almost almost all the group's funding comes from member pledges and donations, the board decides to present members with a list of possible actions and to ask them to vote their priorities to help the board in its decision making.

■ A popular aquarium has expanded its offerings with the opening of a new indoor gallery devoted to the aquatic life of a large river basin. With increased capacity to serve visitors, the management would like to attract greater attendance during the winter months, traditionally the weakest season of the year. One suggestion is to schedule more time for school groups to visit. However, there's concern that such a strategy may alienate families and individuals who prefer to avoid large, noisy groups of schoolchildren and might choose to visit competing attractions instead. A possible compromise involves blocking time for school groups and then extending the afternoon schedule by an additional hour to allow more time for the public to visit. The anticipated opening of a new science museum in a year's time complicates the decision.

These examples illustrate some of the breadth of management issues covered by marketing. Essentially, any decision that affects an organization's users or other constituencies should involve marketing input. Deciding what services and programs to offer—as at the YWCA and the anti-smoking group—is a marketing issue. Decisions on pricing are central to marketing management. Considering the needs and concerns of different customer groups—as at the aquarium—is a marketing task. The schedule and location of service delivery should never be established without reference to their marketing implications. Using advertising and publicity is, of course, a very visible part of marketing. And finally, no organization can make marketing decisions without reference to the strategies pursued by competing organizations.

ORIENTING THE ORGANIZATION TO THE MARKETPLACE

In many public and nonprofit organizations, especially those offering services, management attention is focused on operational issues. Often, one finds a product-oriented culture in which managers develop and operate programs without much regard for how well they meet the needs of prospective customers. Marketing, if it exists at all in such organizations, is seen as an "add-on" activity, centered around advertising and promotions designed to increase revenues by pushing existing offerings. Yet the real problem may be that there needs to be a radical rethinking of those offerings and how they are delivered.

The Non-Marketing Oriented Organization

Institution of a formal marketing function is a relatively recent event in most nonbusiness organizations (and also in many service firms in the private sector). Many organizations still lack such a function altogether.

What does a non-marketing oriented organization look like? Some never look like anything because they quickly fail. But being big and well-established is no guarantee that the organization has the sensitivity to its users and the general public that is needed for long-term survival.

Several clues provide warning signs that management's thinking is product-oriented rather than market-oriented. Consider each of the following indicators[4]:

1. Managers and board members are so enamored of their organization's programs and services that they believe these must be what the public needs.

2. Marketing activities tend to center on stimulating awareness through advertising and publicity, and on developing promotions that will give prospective users an incentive to act.

3. When prospective users fail to respond to the organization's offerings, this disinterest is ascribed to ignorance or inertia, rather than to shortcomings in these offerings and the way they are priced and distributed.

4. Little or no use is made of marketing research, and such research as is conducted fails to assess the needs and concerns of people whom the organization is trying to serve. Findings that conflict with management beliefs tend to be ignored.

5. Distinctions in market segments are ignored or played down in preference to development of "one best strategy" to serve everyone.

6. Marketing managers and staff members are chosen for their product knowledge or communication skills, rather than for their marketing expertise and sensitivity to the needs of the people the organization is trying to reach.

7. Management and board members assume that the only form of competition comes from organizations similar to their own: they ignore the presence of "generic" competitors that offer alternative solutions to similar consumer needs.

What creates the mindset underlying these attitudes and behaviors? Managers moving to a new organization are sometimes struck by the apparent insularity of the existing management, staff, and board. Current employees and volunteers may be so convinced that they are dealing with socially important issues and services that they assume that the public views these topics with equal concern. It's easy to forget that there are literally thousands of issues and services competing for public attention, and that the great majority of citizens may not consider any given activity relevant to their own situations—if, indeed, they are even aware of it.

This commitment to a cause is often what keeps public and nonprofit managers going. Many are underpaid and work extended hours under trying conditions. For those managing cause-related organizations and human service agencies, their work may be literally a labor of love. Managers in the public sector sometimes enjoy more job security than their counterparts in nonprofit organizations, but salaries, bonuses (if any), and office amenities usually fail to match those found in large companies. An added frustration for public employees is the seemingly constant carping of journalists and politicians.

The new manager may be frustrated to find that staff members have an uncritical view of the value of the organization's products, regardless of whether they cover their costs or not (even with the aid of donations). When every program has its own advocate, who may enjoy the status of a professional qualification or the "protection" of a board member, what's the end result? All too often, the collective offerings of that organization fail to represent a coherent whole with clear links to a well-defined institutional mission.

Additional problems resulting from a product-centered mindset include the assumption that potential customers will go to great lengths to obtain information about the organization's activities and to use its services. But just making a service available does not guarantee that it will be used. Neither does a minimal announcement of availability suffice to attract interest from a public bombarded all day long with sophisticated messages that are disseminated through every possible medium of communication.

There's also a real risk that customers may be seen as tolerant and forgiving. After all, if the service (or cause) is so important, won't the customers or audience forgive a few shortcomings in delivery, such as a delayed schedule, missing materials, substitute personnel, canceled exhibit, or changed location? Unfortunately, the answer is often "no." Numerous nonprofit organizations have discovered to their dismay that consumer expectations are higher than management had anticipated, and that users demand quality service from public and nonprofit organizations just as they do from private firms.

Finally, an insular, product-centered organization may tend to dismiss or even ignore competition. When management wakes up to the fact that other institutions are "trespassing" on their turf and "stealing" their clients and donors, it is sometimes too late to recoup the situation.

THE RISE OF NONBUSINESS MARKETING

Until the mid-1970s, the distinctive problems of managing nonbusiness organizations went largely ignored. But then practitioners and scholars began turning their attention to the challenge of improving management practice in public agencies and nonprofit institutions. Marketing became a buzzword of some significance in government agencies, hospitals, universities, transit systems, arts organizations, and social action groups—to name just a few. Some administrators resisted the very notion of marketing. They regarded the concept as inappropriate for their type of organization, seeing the terminology as unseemly and arcane, and viewing marketing strategies as intrusive, manipulative, and unprofessional.

A different group of nonbusiness managers felt immediately at home with the basic philosophy of marketing, since it was akin to their existing approach to management. Like Moliére's Monsieur Jourdain, who discovered to his amazement that he had been speaking prose for 40 years without being aware of it, managers of some of the better-run and more responsive nonbusiness institutions found that they had been practicing a form of marketing without being conscious of it. They recognized that it made sense to understand the needs and concerns of one's users or clients. They sought to develop programs targeted at specific groups within the population, tailoring delivery systems, prices—if any—and communication efforts to the characteristics of these groups rather than trying to be all things to all people. These managers looked to see if other organizations were offering similar or substitute services to the same target group and, if so, considered what might be the most appropriate response to make. They sought to coordinate all programmatic activities to ensure consistency, to leverage efforts through third parties when this resulted in greater effectiveness or lower costs, to evaluate program performance on an ongoing basis, and to modify the program and its execution in the light of this evaluation.

Managers with this instinctive grasp of fundamental marketing principles had—and have—the most to gain from reviewing the tools, concepts, and strategies of marketing with a view to developing greater expertise in the field. They do not need to be convinced of the appropriateness of marketing as a management function within their organizations (although they may recognize the need to convince some of their colleagues of this). They are also likely to recognize that while the technology of marketing is neutral, it can be employed for both ethical and unethical ends depending on the values and goals of its user.

Marketing as a Management Function

The practice of management requires skills in several different functional specialties. The chief executive (or general manager of a division within a larger organization) needs to coordinate the planning and execution of these functions so as to ensure a balanced, smoothly operating organization.

Figure 1.1 highlights the eight key management functions typically found in larger public and nonprofit organizations; in smaller organizations, several of these may be combined or incorporated in the responsibilities of the general manager. Only a few organizations maintain separate development and government-relations functions; typically, nonprofit institutions pursue voluntary donations through a development department, while public agencies maintain a government-relations function to ensure receipt of tax-based government financial assistance. In small and medium-size organizations, finance is often combined with control; similarly, operations may have responsibility for purchasing. In really small nonprofit organizations, the general manager may perform many of these management functions in person, relying on part-time employees, volunteers, or outside specialists to provide technical assistance in areas such as bookkeeping or fund raising on an as-needed basis.

Marketing is concerned with the process by which people adopt, maintain, or discard patterns of behavior—or accept ideas and beliefs that are often precursors of behavior. For private-sector firms, the behavior patterns of interest relate to how prospective customers purchase and use specific goods and services. Although many public and nonprofit organizations are also concerned with purchase and usage behavior, others focus on people's adoption of a wide array of different behavior patterns, ranging from voting in elections to acceptance of preventive health measures, and from conservation of resources to use of free public services. Still others see their role as facilitating organizations, seeking to promote awareness and acceptance of ideas and issues that range from energy conservation to employing the handicapped, or from promoting abortion rights to outlawing abortion.

As a management function, marketing is more than just a set of activities concerned with research, planning, program development, and implementation. It is a bridge linking

Figure 1.1 The key management function in public and nonprofit corporations.

the organization with its external environment, providing orientation toward customers and other constituencies, and helping management to position its efforts against those of competitive forces.

Exploring and Pursuing Marketing Opportunities

Organizations should exist with a specific purpose or mission. Ultimately, all private firms seek to make money for their owners and investors. No such common purpose unites public and nonprofit organizations, which exist to achieve a variety of different goals. Most nonbusiness organizations begin life with a reasonably explicit mission, but all too often this becomes blurred over time. There's a natural tendency for managers to become overwhelmed with day-to-day decisions and to lose sight of longer-term objectives. This tendency becomes almost inevitable when there is no explicit definition of mission and no strategy for fulfilling it.

In this book, we emphasize the importance of defining (or redefining) the mission of the organization and then developing a marketing strategy that is consistent with this mission. But managers cannot realistically make decisions on future marketing strategy unless they know where their organizations stand at present. Hence the need to conduct what we term a "Marketing Audit" (discussed in depth in Chapter 3). This systematic review of an organization's current situation can be immensely helpful in identifying problems and opportunities—indeed, some managers prefer to call it a marketing opportunity analysis.

A key aspect of strategic planning involves determining where the organization and its programs should stand in the future relative to competing or complementary organizations. Transforming a chosen strategy into real-world marketing activities requires creation of a specific plan of action against which progress can be measured. The process of planning includes setting up a schedule of activities to be performed at specified times by designated individuals, and then measuring the results. In this way, the marketing plan serves to guide organizational action.

FOUR KEY CONCEPTS IN MARKETING

Marketing is the management function that most explicitly links an organization to its external environment—not only to its current and prospective customers, but also to its funding sources and other relevant constituencies. A key task for any nonbusiness manager is to understand the nature of the organization and how to balance the needs and concerns of its many different constituencies.

Although marketing is most commonly perceived in terms of its tactical actions in the marketplace—a new product introduction, a price promotion, a display in a retail store, an advertising campaign—effective marketing strategies are rooted in understanding of a series of key organizing concepts. We'll look briefly now at four of the most fundamental concepts in marketing: exchange, market segmentation, the marketing mix, and competition. These and other concepts will be discussed in more depth later in the book, with explicit links being made to developing and implementing appropriate marketing strategies.

The Concept of Exchange

At the core of modern marketing thought is the concept of exchange involving transactions of value between two or more parties. More directly, marketing is concerned with how transactions are stimulated, created, facilitated, and valued.[5] The importance of this concept is that it focuses our attention on the quid pro quo of any given marketing activity: what is in it for marketer and customer, or for marketer and donor? Instead of thinking simply about who purchases what product at what price, it's often more revealing to ask: what benefits do consumers seek to obtain and what costs (of all kinds) they are prepared to incur to get them?

In nonbusiness marketing, the transactions that take place between the organization and its various customers are often more subtle than those taking place in the private sector. The products offered may be harder to define and the costs incurred by consumers may involve no financial payments at all. This situation places a premium on understanding the needs of customers and other constituencies with whom transactions must be made—the topic of Part 3 of the book. The difficulty of this task is compounded by the fact that consumers are sometimes asked to take actions, such as conserving resources, that benefit society as a whole much more than they do the individual.

Market Segmentation

There are often wide differences between one consumer and another in terms of needs, behavior patterns, and other characteristics. Not everyone is a prospective customer for a given organization; in fact, the target audience for most nonprofit programs is, realistically, just a tiny fraction of the total population. Government agencies tend to serve larger populations, but they still need to think carefully about the varying requirements and priorities of different subgroups within their frame of reference. Further, some prospects are much more significant than others in helping an organization to achieve its mission. This recognition calls for a strategy of singling out. certain subgroups or market segments, and focusing on them. Market segmentation (discussed in depth in Chapter 7), is a key organizing concept underlying the development of effective marketing strategies.

Managers cannot rely on casual encounters, gut feel, or anecdotal information to guide development of marketing strategy. Segmentation, in particular, must be based on detailed, specific information gathered in an objective manner. Marketers need data about the size and structure of the market; they need to know about trends in the environment that may influence demand from a particular segment; they need to learn about the nature and extent of competitive activities. Further information requirements concern how different kinds of consumers make choices, what benefits they are looking for, what problems they seek to avoid, and what factors or individuals influence their decisions. This information can sometimes come from existing sources, such as published reports, government statistics, or the organization's internal records. At other times, new research studies may be needed to obtain the desired insights.

The Marketing Mix

Executing a marketing strategy requires the use of a broad array of marketing tools. Many people mistakenly equate marketing with the advertising and sales functions of an organization. In practice, marketing's scope is much broader. The organization's efforts to facilitate transactions with its customers require that decisions be made in four broad areas, collectively referred to as the "marketing mix." These are (1) the characteristics of the *product* that is offered in the marketplace; (2) the *price* that is charged in exchange—both the amount and how it is to be paid; (3) *distribution*—where, when, and how the product is delivered to the customer; and (4) *communication,* which involves the nature of the messages directed at prospective customers and influencers about the organization and its products, as well as the means by which these messages are transmitted.

People have been buying and selling from each other for thousands of years. Not until the beginning of the twentieth century, however, did researchers and teachers begin formal study of marketing activities. Their interest was initially spurred by the geographic separation between producers of agricultural commodities or manufactured goods and their ultimate purchasers. Hence, early marketing studies emphasized the distribution systems (and intermediaries) linking producers and consumers. Later, marketing came to be seen as an array of interrelated elements involving decisions such as what products and models to offer, what prices to charge, whether or not to give credit, what distribution channels to use, what to say about the product to both consumers and intermediaries (such as retailers), whether or not to employ a sales force, what types of advertising media to use, and whether or not to supplement these communication efforts with public relations and in-store sales promotions.

The marketing mix concept is valuable because it recognizes the interdependence of the different elements within a marketing program. A change (or failure) in any one ingredient can influence the effectiveness of the overall program because, as in a cooking recipe, the different ingredients should be chosen to reinforce or interact with one another. Interdependence between elements requires that senior marketing managers understand the role played by each element (or subelement) in the marketing mix and work to ensure that consistency is achieved between each of the subcategories. Figure 1.2 summarizes the principal functions embraced by the marketing mix and adds marketing research, which aids in the design of marketing mix strategies, and marketing control, which is needed to monitor their subsequent effectiveness.

We recognize three different types of "products" that may be offered in the marketplace by nonbusiness organizations: goods, services, and social behaviors.

In goods marketing, the manufacturer produces a product that is sold to customers who subsequently generate benefits from consuming or using it. In services marketing, the service product is created by interaction between the service environment (usually including one or more service personnel) and its customers, who consume or use the service as it is created; the benefits may be derived immediately (as in the case of attendance at a symphony) or later (as in the case of surgery). In both instances, the aim of the marketer (or marketing intermediary who stands to benefit as well) is to encourage and facilitate behavior by the consumer that will result in consummation of a desired exchange transaction.

But social-behavior marketing is different, presenting a series of seeming paradoxes. First, the marketer advocates a particular behavior pattern but frequently does not sell the product that is the object of that behavior. For instance, traffic-safety organizations neither sell cars nor operate highways; agencies promoting nutritional eating habits are not themselves marketing the foodstuffs whose consumption they advocate; and national metrication boards that seek to facilitate adoption of the metric system are not in the business of selling foods, weather forecasts, measuring equipment, or any of the items or practices affected by the changeover.

The behavior advocated often seems to offer few benefits for the customer; indeed, it may seem to offer more short-term costs, frustrations, and self-denials than any apparent

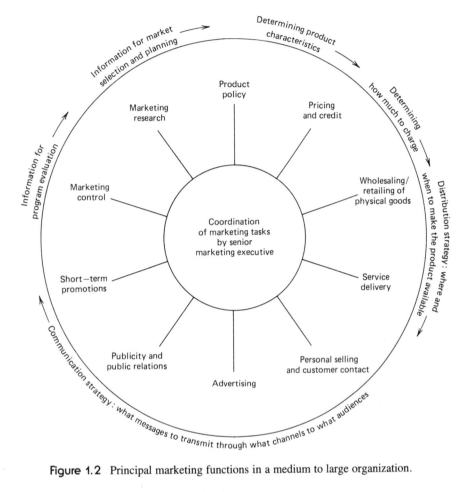

Figure 1.2 Principal marketing functions in a medium to large organization.

prospect of personal benefits. In many instances, the individual benefits (where they exist at all) are both small in nature and long-term in achievement. Frequently, these benefits take the form of *not* having something bad happen to you rather than having something good happen—as in undergoing regular medical checkups.

The real benefits from compliance with the behavior advocated are often societal in nature, reflecting the external economies of compliant behavior. For instance, use of the metric system may offer long-term cost savings for the economy and export competitiveness; nutritional eating habits may reduce health-care costs and job absenteeism; avoidance of drinking among drivers may reduce not only highway deaths and injuries, but also property damage; use of public transportation may reduce air pollution and traffic congestion.

In a sense, we can say that by their behavior, "customers" create the product at the behest of the marketer. This phenomenon raises the question of what motivates (and rewards) the marketer and the customer for their action. It also raises the question of how to develop effective strategies that bring about the desired behavior. The problem is compounded in situations where the customer must engage in the desired behavior not once (as in an inoculation) but continuously (as in flossing teeth daily).

Competition

Business corporations have always been competitively oriented. Even those that have achieved monopoly status usually fight to maintain that status. But few of the older public agencies or nonprofit organizations were conceived with competition in mind. Some, such as publicly owned postal services, enjoyed legal monopoly status from the outset. Many government agencies were formed to ensure delivery of free "public goods"—national defense, police protection, lighthouse services, and education for children of school age. With few exceptions, institutions such as colleges, hospitals, and art museums were formed to fill gaps in the existing social fabric or to supplement and extend the offerings of existing institutions—not to compete with them.

In many instances, profits were seen as an inappropriate goal. Generous benefactors made it unnecessary to charge users prices that would cover the full costs of serving them—if, indeed, any charge was made at all. Senator and Mrs. Leland Stanford endowed the university they founded in their son's memory in 1885 with land and financial assets worth $21 million; they anticipated that no tuition would need to be charged (and indeed none was until 1920). Major Henry Lee Higginson founded the Boston Symphony Orchestra in 1881, and until his death 40 years later he personally covered the annual operating deficit. Teaching and nursing religious orders organized colleges, hospitals, and other charitable services, relying on their members to work without financial remuneration as part of their dedication to a life of service and prayer; donations from lay people paid for capital costs and covered any shortfall between fee revenues and the relatively modest operating expenses.

For decades, even generations, few of these organizations were run by administrators who thought and planned in terms of competition. Nor did they need to. But the world has changed, and in consequence a competitive posture has become necessary for survival.[6]

In higher education, the demand from traditional consumer segments has shrunk relative to supply, so institutions that once competed only on the football field are now fighting among themselves for a larger share of the shrinking supply of 18-year-olds. More than 200 private colleges in the United States closed between 1965 and 1979. In health care, new delivery systems, such as health-maintenance organizations, have sprung up to challenge the traditional hospital/doctor's-office "partnership."[7] Many hospitals now find that overexpansion between the 1950s and the 1970s, coupled with declining birthrates and a reduction in the average length of hospital stay for maternity care, has led to regional surpluses of obstetrical beds.

Changes in both technology and consumer needs have resulted in new products that often represent attractive substitutes for existing public and nonprofit services. Just as telecommunications (including facsimile machines) challenge the mails and render the letter monopoly protection accorded to national postal services largely meaningless, so do home entertainment systems—spurred by cable "narrowcasting"—threaten the traditional cultural and educational offerings of libraries, colleges, and arts organizations.

Not all nonbusiness organizations have had competition thrust upon them. Some, such as health-maintenance organizations, have deliberately sought and achieved a competitive position in the marketplace. Still others were conceived by their founders as feisty advocacy organizations and were brought bawling, competitively, into the world. "Pro-choice" and "pro-life" groups at both national and local levels combat each other directly on the emotional issue of abortion Administrators of such organizations view the market-place of ideas as crowded and the supply of financial grants, donations, and volunteer time as limited and even declining. So they adopt strategies designed to publicize their goals, to develop interest in their ideas, and to build a strong base of financial and partici-pative support.

The achievement of competitive status is exemplified by public and nonprofit organi-zations that have added new product lines to make better use of their existing resources and achieve a positive cash flow. Books, magazines, and other publications, mint stamps and proof coin sets, consulting services, and the enormous array of merchandise sold through museum gift shops and catalogs are all examples of expanded product lines. Not only are most of these potentially profitable, but they often compete directly with private-sector offerings (as well as with those of other public and nonprofit organizations).

Competition is now a fact of life for most nonbusiness organizations. Adjusting to competitive realities is a difficult task for public and nonprofit managers, but not necessar-ily an impossible one. An understanding of marketing is essential, however, to develop a strategy for countering or deflecting the threats posed by competition in an intelligent and ethical manner. Occasionally, competitive analysis will lead an organization's manage-ment to the realization that the future holds no prospects for the organization in its present form, and that the only alternatives left are to redirect its energies to new fields or to dissolve itself. Bleak though the latter prospect may be, it is far better for an organization to have the time to plan for an orderly and compassionate closure operation than to collapse into unexpected bankruptcy at short notice.

WHAT IS DISTINCTIVE ABOUT PUBLIC AND NONPROFIT MARKETING?

An underlying thesis of this book is that there are sufficient differences between business and nonbusiness marketing to justify a separate treatment of the latter. We make no claims that the practice of marketing in the public and nonprofit sectors is—or should be—uniquely different from marketing management in business firms. If it were, we would have serious doubts as to the coherence of marketing as both a professional management function and an academic field of study. Our concern, as noted earlier, is that mainstream marketing is still centered on the marketing of physical goods in the private sector of the economy. For a marketing text to be useful and relevant for public and nonprofit managers, it must recognize the distinctive nature of the environment in which these managers operate and the nature of the products with which they deal. Nonbusiness marketers face some constraints that are absent (or less significant) for their private-sector counterparts. At the same time, they also enjoy some advantages not usually available to business managers. Some authors believe that these differences make the practice of marketing inherently more difficult in nonbusiness organizations. On the other hand, it is important to emphasize that some of the constraints facing marketing managers of such organizations simply reflect the relative newness of marketing in the public and nonprofit sectors and may thus become less of a problem as marketing becomes better accepted and more expertly practiced.

Nature of the Products

As we saw earlier, products or market offerings can be categorized into three broad group-ings: physical goods, services, and social behaviors. Most public and nonprofit organiza-tions are primarily concerned with services and social behaviors. Although the private sector contains both manufacturing and service firms, most marketing expertise has been developed from studying how to market manufactured goods, especially consumer pack-aged goods. Formal study of services marketing is a relatively recent development, as is that of marketing social causes or behaviors. Generalizations based on goods marketing are of only limited value to public and nonprofit managers, because services and social behaviors require a distinctive approach to marketing strategy and implementation.

Dominance of Nonfinancial Objectives

By definition, nonprofit organizations do not seek to make a profit for redistribution to owners or shareholders.* Most public agencies also operate on a not-for-profit model, although some public corporations are expected to be profitable (and a few actually achieve this distinction).

Because most nonbusiness organizations neither seek a financial surplus nor expect operating revenues to cover full costs, their mission statement invariably gives priority to nonfinancial objectives. In a very real sense, the primary "bottom line" for nonbusiness entities is basically some form of "social profit." This objective makes it hard to measure success or failure in strictly financial terms. How can we tell if one university or nonprofit hospital is more successful than another, or if the transit authority in city X is better than that in city Y? More difficult still, how can we compare the performance of a university, a hospital, and a public transportation service? Successes in fund raising or in obtaining tax revenues can be measured and compared, but these are means to an end, not an end in themselves.

From a strictly marketing standpoint, the absence of even a theoretical goal of profitability for an organization makes it harder for managers to set objectives, to choose among strategic and tactical alternatives designed to achieve those objectives, and to evaluate performance after the fact. The problem is at its toughest when no monetary price is charged for the organization's product. When consumers do make a direct payment, sales revenue goals can be set and performance measured in terms of the proportion of total and incremental costs covered by customer-derived revenues.

Any shortfall between sales revenues and costs must, of course, be made up by voluntary donations or tax subsidies. The justification for either is that in the perception of donors or the government, the social profit generated by the organization matches or exceeds the financial cost of obtaining it. This notion requires development of nonfinancial measures that can be used to document performance.

Need for Resource Attraction

All organizations need resources to function. Business firms expect to pay for the resources they use—labor, materials, land, and expertise. Public and nonprofit organizations are sometimes able to get these resources free (volunteered labor, services in kind, donated

---

*Some organizations that incorporate under the nonprofit form do generate surpluses but undertake to reinvest them in the operation or to use them for philanthropic or research purposes.

facilities, exemption from property taxes) or at a reduced rate (discounted postal rates, tax concessions, and so forth). In most instances, business firms expect the sales revenues received from customers to equal or exceed operating and relevant overhead costs—although they may occasionally seek funds from the financial markets to underpin research and development, working capital, and expansion. By contrast, the majority of nonbusiness organizations cannot cover costs from sales revenues and must devote continuing efforts to seeking new donations and tax revenues, or to preserving the flow of such revenues from existing sources.

Public and nonprofit marketers, then, are dealing with two interrelated marketing tasks, one involving programs to attract needed resources and the other concerned with programs to allocate these resources in pursuit of the organizational mission.

Multiple Constituencies

The need for nonbusiness marketers to engage in both resource attraction and resource allocation activities means that they must deal with two sets of "customers." Balancing the needs and expectations of both groups can sometimes be a difficult task. Some donors or taxpayers may demand that money be used to serve a different population group or to supply a different type of product from those that management feels are most appropriate for the organization.

The number of constituencies faced by public and nonprofit organizations is often further increased by the presence of third-party payers (such as health-insurance firms and parents who pay college tuition for their children), politicians and regulatory agencies, former consumers (such as college alumni) with a continuing interest in the performance of "their" institution, and the mass media. Although some companies do have a continuing high public profile among financial markets, politicians, and the press, few private-sector marketing managers have to juggle the interests of as many constituencies as do their public and nonprofit counterparts.

Tension Between Mission and Customer Satisfaction

The marketing concept suggests that marketers will do best if they are attentive to their customers' needs and wants. While not all companies adhere rigorously to a philosophy of "the customer is always right," most do seek to satisfy consumer needs. This model breaks down in the case of nonbusiness organizations, where consumer sovereignty may be seen as alien to fulfillment of the institutional mission. The declared objective of many social-behavior marketing programs is to stop people from doing things that appeal to them (like driving fast, smoking, or using drugs), or to do things that do not, initially, appeal (like volunteering time to help a charitable or political cause). Nutritional foods are not necessarily tastier than "junk" foods; the withdrawal symptoms resulting from giving up drugs, smoking, or drink are often quite unpleasant; putting one's litter in a trash can, fastening a safety belt, or recycling bottles can be a nuisance; driving at 65 miles per hour on an empty highway or performing physical exercises can be tedious and time consuming.

The mission of nonbusiness organizations often requires that they take a long-term view rather than pander to current popular tastes. Medical treatments must consider the long-term needs of the patient, not how he or she would like to feel or act tomorrow. A university seeks to transmit skills, knowledge, and ways of thinking and reasoning that will have extended value to students—not simply to amuse and inspire them for the duration of the course in question. Art organizations frequently feel they have a mission to educate their patrons to appreciate new art forms. Robert Brustein of the American Repertory Theatre specifically addressed the role of the nonprofit organization in an interview with *Boston Magazine*.

> *Brustein:* We live in a pluralist society, but what's not commonly recognized is that pluralism is in danger of breaking down when the profit motive becomes the overriding impulse. The profit motive requires an appeal to the lowest common denominator for the widest possible audience.
>
> *Boston:* Is your concept of "minority" theater inescapably tied to a nonprofit subsidized base of operations?
>
> *Brustein:* Inevitably, because the more serious artist does not always make his or her appeal known immediately. It takes some time before the audience catches up in some cases. In other cases, the audience is ahead. But what do we do about our James Joyces and our Stravinskys and our Picassos and our Ibsens and our Brechts until they've become absorbed into the culture and become more popular? We have to service them, we have to subsidize them, we have to support them. And that's why some institutions exist.[8]

Public Scrutiny

Most public agencies are subject to ongoing public scrutiny reflecting either the political process or media interest, or both. There is a healthy desire today for openness in government and in publicly funded activities, and a wish to prevent abuses of natural or legislated monopoly power among both public agencies and regulated public utilities. On the other hand, public agencies are often an easy target for aspiring politicians eager to seize on real or imagined shortcomings with which to lambaste the administration of the day.

Nonprofit organizations tend to attract more public attention than do private firms of comparable size. Larger nonprofit organizations, in particular, often play pivotal roles in the communities they serve. Fund-raising campaigns are usually highly visible, and large gifts may be widely publicized. The activities of politically oriented social-action groups are, by nature, quite contentious, thus inviting journalistic scrutiny. Organizations advocating certain behaviors, such as fluoridation of water supplies, quitting smoking, or practicing family planning, often have as one of their goals to stimulate public sensitivity to the issue in question. Sometimes their activities also provoke counterstrategies by organizations espousing contrary views, thereby provoking even broader awareness of the issues.

The net effect of this greater exposure to public view is that the marketing activities of public and nonprofit organizations are more likely to attract public attention than might be the case for most private firms. Related to this issue is the greater extent to which external forces are able to shape or constrain marketing activities in the nonbusiness arena.

Nonmarket Pressures

Except for firms in highly regulated industries, marketing managers in the private sector are generally guided by market forces in deciding what segments to serve, what products to market, how to distribute them, what prices to charge, and what communication strategies to employ. Marketing activities in the public and nonprofit sectors, by contrast, usually face ongoing regulation or direction from one or more sources.

Political directives may be designed to make a public agency conform to the dictates of a particular political platform or, as periodically happens in the United States, to constrain a tax-funded agency from engaging in "unfair" competition with private firms. Such directives can be given teeth through changes in legislation or the use of the budget weapon; budgetary actions, for instance, might comprise additional funds for adding new services or a line-by-line item analysis that results in cutting the funds budgeted for advertising and communication efforts.

Government regulatory agencies may seek to constrain changes in prices and terms of service; in the area of health care, both federal and state policies in the United States constrain a hospital's ability to expand or contract specific services, such as increasing or reducing the number of obstetrical beds. The actions of legislative and regulatory bodies have often severely impeded the ability of a public agency to pursue a focused segmentation strategy. They may also require service to segments that management would prefer not to serve. Transit authorities, for instance, are often required to retain service on routes with very limited ridership when greater patronage could be obtained by transferring the buses and drivers to more popular routes.

Industry associations exercise policing power over nonprofit organizations. For instance, most U.S. colleges and universities seek endorsement of the quality and scope of their educational services from one or more accrediting bodies; in other countries, such as the United Kingdom, this quality control role may be played by the Ministry of Education.

A final constraint on marketing practice is exercised by *professional associations,* whose power has traditionally lain in their control over individual professionals working at a particular institution, rather than over the institution itself. For many decades, the American Medical Association's professional code of ethics sharply limited doctors and the institutions they worked for from engaging in any form of overt marketing. Since effective competition is based on an organization's ability to inform prospective customers about its products, such "ethical" restrictions on marketing communications minimized the extent of competition that could take place in the health-care market and effectively discouraged the development of innovative new delivery systems. In recent years, however, the AMA and other professional associations have modified their stand on the use of media advertising.

Ability to Obtain Free or Inexpensive Support

In conducting their marketing efforts, managers of public and nonprofit organizations are often able to draw on donated labor and services to help them stretch their resources. Consider the following.

- Each year, the Advertising Council provides hundreds of millions of dollars worth of free advertising space and broadcast time for public-service messages by public agencies and nonprofit organizations in the U.S.
- Volunteers play key roles in helping universities raise money from their alumni, providing nonmedical services to hospital patients, operating retail stores in

> museums, and serving as guides in many of the stately homes maintained by Britain's National Trust.

- Some professional marketing-service firms—such as consultants, advertising and public relations agencies, and market research firms—make a point of accepting a small number of public or nonprofit clients, which would normally be unable to afford their services, and of offering these services free or at greatly reduced cost.

These benefits do compensate for some of the disadvantages under which nonbusiness managers must frequently operate. Wisely sought and carefully used, they can provide powerful leverage. But as we will see, free or discounted resources need strong (yet sensitive) management just as much as those purchased at market prices.

Management in Duplicate or Triplicate

A final factor distinguishing the development of nonbusiness marketing programs from those in the private sector concerns the large number of fingers in the managerial pie. As noted by a former national executive director of the Girl Scouts U.S.A.

> In many nonprofit enterprises, boards assume management responsibilities and volunteers occupy places in the management hierarchy. Seldom do they have a direct reporting relationship with the paid administrative staff.[9]

A comparable situation is found in those public agencies that have an elective board (or an appointed board composed of elected officials) whose members constantly feel the need to demonstrate their prowess to their respective constituencies. A good illustration is provided by the Southern California Rapid Transit District, responsible for transit services in the greater Los Angeles area. Among other actions, the board has taken the initiative on introducing lower fares (and obtaining the revenues to finance this move), directed that special bus services be operated on particular routes, and insisted on supplementary promotions for park-and-ride services beyond those originally proposed by management. Most of these efforts were actually quite constructive. The involvement of politicians in marketing management decisions can sometimes be very damaging for a public agency, however, particularly when patronage appointments are made to the management ranks.

The problems of "duplicate management" are compounded in situations where the service is planned and delivered by professionals who outrank the managers responsible for running the operation. The arts, higher education, and health care have all been battlegrounds for disputes between management personnel on the one hand and curators, faculty members, and doctors on the other. Although the balance of power is shifting in favor of the former, the latter still dominate in most instances, and the top slot in such organizations is usually still occupied by an administrator-professional instead of by a "career" manager. Professionals have not always been willing to accept the introduction of a stronger marketing orientation in their organizations, although a growing number now do.

Perhaps the worst situation of all is when a strong political or volunteer board (with accompanying volunteer organization in the latter instance) seeks to exercise management control over an organization composed of both professionals and managers. In such instances of "management in triplicate," the chances of developing a coherent marketing strategy are likely to be very slim indeed.

SUMMARY

A key factor underlying the trend toward a greater marketing orientation among non-business managers has been the increased competition facing their organizations. Non-profit organizations now compete among themselves to enhance their shares of what are sometimes declining markets, while both public and nonprofit organizations often find that they face direct or generic competition from the products of private firms. In an effort to improve their revenue positions, many nonbusiness organizations have developed new products and entered new markets; this has placed an even greater premium on the acquisition and development of marketing skills.[10]

The importance of marketing as a management function to both business and nonbusiness organizations lies in the fact that it links the organization to its environment. Success in raising funds from donors, in selling services to individual or institutional customers, and in encouraging people to adopt new patterns of behavior requires, in each case, an understanding of the characteristics and current behavior patterns of those in the target group. Gaining this knowledge may require marketing research projects, although sometimes existing information will provide the needed answers. Key issues in marketing strategy development include understanding the nature and size of the market, determining alternative ways of dividing the market into segments, and deciding which of these segments to serve. The strategy selected should reflect an assessment of the degree of competition (if any) within each market segment and the ability of the marketer to develop a competitive advantage there.

The elements of a marketing program are basically fourfold. They comprise: the product benefits that are offered (in the form of a physical good, a service, or a recommended social behavior); the price to customers of obtaining these benefits; where, when, and how the product is distributed; and the means employed to communicate information about the product to prospective customers. Collectively, these four strategic elements are referred to as the marketing mix.

Although it is useful to look at marketing activities in the private sector, there are limits to the transferability of marketing tools and strategies from business to nonbusiness organizations. The rest of this book is devoted to helping public and nonprofit managers to identify and take advantage of the marketing opportunities facing their organizations.

REFERENCES

1. Regina Herzlinger and William Krasker, "Who Profits from Nonprofits?" *Harvard Business Review* (January–February 1987). (See also,"Letters to the Editor" in subsequent issues.)
2. See, for example, Laura Saunders, "Profits? Who, Me?" *Forbes*, March 23, 1987; and "When Should the Profits of Nonprofits Be Taxed?" *Business Week*, December 5, 1983.
3. Gwen Kinkead, "America's Best-Run Charities," *Fortune*, November 9, 1987, pp. 145–50.
4. These indicators are based on those developed by Alan R. Andreasen, "Nonprofits: Check Your Attention to Customers," *Harvard Business Review*, (May–June, 1982).
5. Franklin B. Houston and Jule B. Gassenheimer,"Marketing and Exchange," *Journal of Marketing*, 51 (October 1987) p. 318 See also Philip Kotler, "A Generic Concept of Marketing," *Journal of Marketing*, 36 (April 1972), pp. 46–54.
6. Peter T. Johnson, "Why I Raced Against Phantom Competitors," *Harvard Business Review* (September–October, 1988), pp. 106–112.

7. Jeff Charles Goldsmith, *Can Hospitals Survive?* Homewood, IL: Richard D. Irwin, 1981.

8. "The Boston Magazine Interview: Robert Brustein," *The Boston Magazine*, September 1979, p. 67.

9. Cecily Cannan Selby, "Better Performance from Nonprofits," *Harvard Business Review* (September–October 1978), p. 93.

10. A good overview of strategies to increase revenues is provided by Edward Skloot (ed.), *The Nonprofit Entrepreneur*. New York: The Foundation Center, 1988.

Chapter 2
The Context of Public & Nonprofit Marketing

In their operettas, Gilbert & Sullivan loved to poke fun at individuals who owed their exalted positions to accidents of birth or to careers of self-serving expediency. One such personage was the First Lord of the Admiralty—equivalent to Secretary of the Navy—in *HMS Pinafore*. The First Lord sings of his rise from office boy to cabinet minister, during which career he had no connection at all with the sea. He concludes by admonishing his listeners:

> *Stick close to your desks and never go to sea,*
> *And you all may be rulers of the Queen's Navee!*

We don't think this is very good advice for would-be managers and board members. Ignorance of the operating environment is not a recipe for success. Often, working as a manager or serving as a board member in a nonbusiness organization is more complex than in a for-profit company. As we've already seen, goals and performance measures are sometimes ill-defined, there are more constituencies to worry about, and the costs and benefits of the services and programs being marketed are often highly subjective. To the extent that marketing is a bridge between the organization and its environment, marketing strategists need to know the territory on both sides of the bridge.

How does an organization get started on developing and implementing an effective marketing strategy? How might a marketing manager from the private sector approach a new position with a government agency or nonprofit organization? What does the board and the executive director need to know in order to run a marketing-oriented organization?

Understanding the context within which marketing strategy is created and executed forms the starting point. Board members, the chief executive, marketing managers, and all senior members of the management team must be willing to take time to study this context. They need to clarify for themselves the nature of their organization; to be able to articulate its mission clearly; to recognize the different types of competition that it faces; and to understand the variety of constituencies that it serves or is dependent upon.

Above all, managers and board members need to appreciate the customer's perspective: why do individuals or other organizations patronize or ignore our programs and services? What benefits do they seek? What concerns do they have? And what costs are customers prepared to incur in order to satisfy their needs?

Scope of the Chapter

Marketers cannot function effectively unless they understand the environment in which their organization is operating. The first task of this chapter is to explore the constantly evolving public and nonprofit sectors. In the process, we'll see that certain industries or applications are sector specific, while others extend into the private sector, too. However, the scope of these sectors varies widely from nation to nation, and within each country continuing shifts are taking place.

Next we will briefly compare the public sector with the nonprofit sector. To what extent are there differences in the managerial environment of each sector? Are there any criteria that determine whether particular types of institutions or activities should be organized on a public or nonprofit basis? And within each sector, can we group organizations into categories that reflect different marketing requirements?

Third, we discuss the breadth of competition facing most public and nonprofit organizations. Competition may be both direct and indirect; in the latter instance, a seemingly different type of organization may offer consumers an alternative way of meeting the same basic needs. The key is to understand each institution's competitive posture as the market sees it.

From here we turn to a review of the various constituencies to which a marketing organization must be responsive—not only consumers, but also suppliers of financial, labor, and physical resources; influencers and information providers; facilitators and other intermediaries; external communities; and regulators.

Finally, we'll examine the costs and benefits inherent in all marketing transactions. Each transaction involves an exchange of value between two or more parties. Marketers need to understand both the benefits that their customers stand to receive and the costs—in money, time, and "hassle"—that they will be willing to incur in turn. At the same time, marketers must also understand what benefits their own organization will obtain from completing any given transaction and what costs it will incur in the process. Certain transactions involve third parties or intermediaries and the relevant costs and benefits to these parties must also be determined.

THE EVOLVING PUBLIC AND NONPROFIT SECTORS

Technology, resources, the rate of economic development, social needs, international conditions, and political values all play a role in determining the scope and structure of the economy. The division of the economy into private, public, and nonprofit sectors represents a continuing compromise between past traditions and present realities. Opinions often differ widely on which activities should be the responsibility of which sector. Our concern, however, is less with whether a particular industry (or societal endeavor) should be assigned to one sector or another than with how organizations in that area of activity can best be managed.

Multisector Industries

Some industries run across all three sectors of the U.S. economy. Health care is a good example, with health services being distributed by both nonprofit and for-profit organizations and by public agencies at the federal, state, and county or city levels. In the field of postsecondary education, public and nonprofit colleges and universities often coexist in the same city with profit-seeking proprietary schools that emphasize development of vocational skills. Although culture and the arts are frequently thought of as falling within the province of the nonprofit sector, private-sector arts activity is widespread. If one considers all arts-related activities—including both "high" and "popular" culture distributed live and through broadcasting, films, and publishing—then nonprofit arts activity constitutes only a small proportion of the total.[1]

The competitive implications of this situation are important, because at times a similar product may be available from both for-profit and not-for-profit institutions: a patient may be able to have the same operation in a public, private, or nonprofit hospital; a Shakespeare fan may be able to attend *Hamlet* at a public, nonprofit, or commercial theater—or watch the play on television or at the movies; a student may be able to take a course in computer programming at a state college, a nonprofit college, or a proprietary school owned by a major industrial conglomerate.

Another way in which more than one sector can be involved in the same industry is when government agencies finance activities executed by private and nonprofit organizations. Universities and other research establishments often rely heavily on government grants for conducting scientific research. A trend is developing for public-service agencies to contract out the actual management and delivery of their services to a private firm. Public hospitals, transit operations, and fire departments are among those that have entered into management contracts with specialist firms.

Shifting Boundaries

Not only do the boundaries dividing the three sectors vary by industry among different countries (and sometimes among different political jurisdictions in the United States), but also they are changing over time. Governments espousing a conservative political philosophy often seek to "privatize" profitable publicly owned businesses. Sometimes this action takes the form of outright sale of state assets; at other times it involves selling a substantial share of the equity to private investors.

Nowhere has the trend to privatization been more pronounced than in the United Kingdom, under the government of Prime Minister Margaret Thatcher. For instance, the British Railways Board was ordered to sell off its hotel and ferry subsidiaries; shares were sold in British Airways; and the natural gas and telephone utilities were transformed into public companies. In 1987 the government announced plans to privatize electricity and water utilities. Other European countries, Canada, and Japan are among the nations considering or implementing similar strategies for selected public corporations.

In the United States, there has been a marked trend to privatization in the hospital industry, with investor-owned chains either buying public and nonprofit institutions outright or assuming long-term management contracts. The contractual approach is also of interest to local government agencies, some of which now employ for-profit firms to provide such services as trash disposal, school meals, and even fire-fighting.

The tide may flow the other way for institutions seen as having strategic, social, or economic significance. It's not only socialist governments that nationalize individual companies or entire industries. Even governments that favor free enterprise have been forced to take key private businesses into public ownership to prevent their financial collapse. In the U.S., Amtrak at the national level and urban transit systems at the local level are examples of significant transportation services taken over by the public sector when it became clear that private owners could no longer continue to run them. Over the years, many countries have seen a significant shift from the nonprofit to the public sector, with government agencies assuming responsibility for social welfare services previously delivered by voluntary charitable organizations.

Finally, both public and for-profit organizations sometimes seek nonprofit status. Legoretta and Young discuss case histories of a hospital, a gallery, and an elementary school which converted from for-profit to nonprofit status; and of a management training agency and a mental health service which were transformed from local government agencies to private nonprofit organizations.[2] The reasons included an evolving mission, financial realities, and a need for a new form of governance.

CATEGORIZING THE PUBLIC AND NONPROFIT SECTORS

Clearly, there is considerable overlap between the types of activities in which public and nonprofit organizations engage. The blurring of sector boundaries is compounded in situations where government grants form a significant portion of a nonprofit's income, since it shifts the organization's posture from one of relative independence to that of a contractual supplier of services for the funding agency. Some publicly owned organizations have turned to voluntary donations as a revenue source, further blurring the distinction between public and nonprofit sectors. The University of Minnesota, for example, ranked among the top ten universities in funds raised during 1986–87. At the local level, parent's groups at elementary and high schools have raised money for such "extras" as band uniforms, microwave ovens for home economics classes, and personal computers. Nevertheless, there are still some important distinctions between the sectors.

An important historical trend has been the assumption by government agencies of activities previously performed by nonprofit organizations. Among the reasons for this are that a government's taxing power ensures more revenue security than do voluntary donations and that government organizations have traditionally had more dependable access to new capital. Financial failure or inability to improve services and facilities has frequently been a reason for public takeover of a nonprofit organization. In many educational, medical, and charitable organizations run by religious orders, taxation has eroded the giving power of traditional donors at the very time that paid lay staff were being hired to supplement the dwindling pool of inexpensive labor provided by religious personnel. Another reason for public takeovers is the perception that government-run organizations provide greater accountability and accessibility.

On the other hand, there are good reasons for some types of services to continue to be operated by nonprofit organizations. These include situations in which the service is desired by only a small proportion of the population, or where few of those who contribute the needed tax revenues benefit personally from the service, and no good argument can be made for subsidization on the grounds of income redistribution or external economies. Many cultural, religious, and special-interest groups fit these criteria. Finally, since nonprofit organizations are less likely than public ones to be subject to external political interference, more scope is left for market discipline.

Because the deficits of unprofitable nonprofit services must be met by grants and donations, the service must touch some responsive chord in the donor—the concept of exchange that is central to marketing. Socially essential but economically unprofitable services provided by private enterprises rarely shift to nonprofit status; instead they tend to be taken over by the state and funded from tax revenues. One reason is that however necessary these services may be for social, economic, or environmental reasons, few groups or individuals would be willing to make voluntary donations toward their upkeep. Public transportation is one such example.

Public enterprises are usually associated with a particular level of government and their geographic sphere of operations defined in terms of political boundaries—national, regional, state or provincial, county, metropolitan, or city or town. Nonprofit organizations typically have more freedom of choice in selecting which geographic areas to serve.

Government Departments and Public Enterprises

Apart from the level of political unit with which a public agency is associated, two other broad classifications exist: organizations that are an integral part of a department of government and those that are quasi-independent public enterprises. As shown in Figure 2.1, agencies that sell their services at a price and cover a high proportion of their expenditures from user-based revenues are more likely to fall into the latter category. The

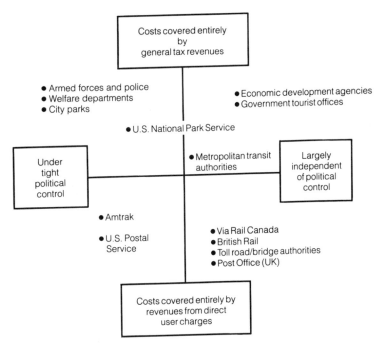

Figure 2.1 Categorization of public organizations by source of funds and nature of control. (Note: Organizations in the upper left quadrant are generally government agencies, closely supervised by elected or appointed political figures, whereas those in the lower right quadrant are more likely to be independent public corporations or authorities run by professional managers.)

significance of this distinction is that public enterprises tend to be more insulated against political involvement and are able (in many instances) to appoint managers drawn from outside politics and the civil service. For instance, national postal services were historically run by government departments; in each instance, the postmaster-general held cabinet rank in the government of the day and was automatically replaced when the government changed. But the trend has been to reorganize postal services as public corporations (the British and Canadian approach) or as independent agencies of the executive branch of government (the U.S. approach). In general, the development and implementation of marketing programs is somewhat easier for public enterprises that can maintain a modest distance from day-to-day political activities and avoid significant management shake-ups with every change of government.

Four Categories of Nonprofit Organizations

Within the nonprofit sector, Henry Hansmann identifies four categories of organizations.[3] First, he distinguishes between those that are "donative" (receiving most of their income from grants and donations) and those that are "commercial" (receiving the bulk of their income from the prices charged for their services). Second, he distinguishes between organizations controlled by their patrons ("mutual" nonprofit institutions) and those where management is able to operate independently of directives from users (these he terms "entrepreneurial" nonprofit institutions). When these divisions on the basis of income source and locus of control are linked, four categories of nonprofit institutions result. As in many such classification schemes, some organizations may effectively straddle categories—such as universities and symphony orchestras that rely heavily on both donations and sale of services. A slightly restructured version of Hansmann's scheme is shown, with examples, in Figure 2.2.

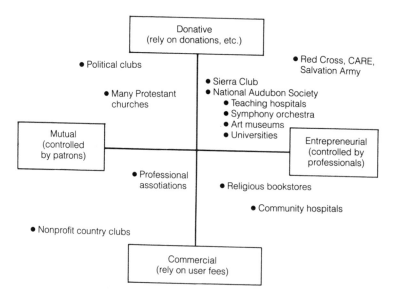

Figure 2.2 Categorization of nonprofit organizations by source of funds and nature of control. (Adapted from Hansmann, see reference 3.)

Donative-mutual organizations are primarily concerned with marketing social behaviors. Their effectiveness is based on their ability to attract donations from members; the money finances communication and lobbying efforts, while the size of the membership base provides political clout. Many members never even see the central organization (which often operates out of a relatively small office), and keep in touch primarily through letters and bulletins sent through the mails. The marketing task requires success in identifying, recruiting, and retaining members and also in developing and monitoring social-behavior programs. Members often elect board members and so can exercise some control over the organization's activities.

Commercial-mutual organizations exist primarily to serve their members directly in return for the fees they pay. Success reflects the ability of the organization to recruit new members in the first instance and to retain them by providing services that meet members' needs. Members are more likely to visit the organization's premises or to come into contact with its other facilities (such as AAA tow-truck services). The concept of membership provides a more stable consumer base than might otherwise be the case; it also means that at any given time management knows exactly who its members are. Such organizations often generate a surplus and therefore do not need to engage in fund raising. Legally, nonprofit organizations are usually allowed to make a surplus or profit but are restricted as to how that profit can be employed or distributed.

Donative-entrepreneurial organizations are characterized by a relative lack of control by donors over management, which usually reports to a self-perpetuating board of trustees. The products of such organizations are more likely to be services than social behaviors. In some instances, such as the Red Cross or the Salvation Army, most donors are neither past users nor planning to use the services themselves (although they may be motivated to give by the thought that they or someone close to them could conceivably be helped by the organization at some future time). In other instances, such as museums and symphony orchestras, donors are usually also customers and may receive special privileges not available to nondonor users of the service. In an effort to be responsive to donors, such organizations often develop parallel volunteer and professional management organizations.

Commercial-entrepreneurial organizations are often similar to private-sector firms, selling services at a price that usually more than covers costs. In many instances, the organizations are run by professionals such as doctors or scientists. The operating surpluses, if any, are plowed back into the organization or devoted to educational, research, and philanthropic purposes. Their customers may be regular or one-time users, depending on the nature of the service; hence there is greater need to continue attracting new customers than with commercial mutual organizations.

In summary, donative nonprofit organizations must engage in two types of marketing activities, which Benson Shapiro has termed *resource attraction* (obtaining donations and grants) and *resource allocation* (using these resources to develop services or social-behavior programs—most often to a different set of target markets).[4] Commercial nonprofit organizations, by contrast, are much closer to private firms since their marketing efforts usually represent a direct transfer of products in return for payments between the marketer and the customer or member. Our primary focus in this book is on those nonprofits that have traditionally fallen into the donative category. As we will see, however, many are now developing a more commercial orientation.

The Search for New Revenue Sources

Traditional funding sources—donations, grants, and tax revenues—cannot keep up with the rising costs that have beset most public and nonprofit organizations in recent years. In fact, foundation grants for nonprofit institutions and tax subsidies for public agencies have been cut in many instances. This situation forces the organization either to cut back the scope of its activities or to search for new revenue sources.

The most popular route today involves a search for increased product-derived revenues. With existing products this usually takes the form of instituting prices if the product was previously free, of raising existing prices, or of asking purchasers to add a voluntary donation to the price of their ticket. The last approach can be likened to a form of voluntary taxation, with those who both value the product more highly and can also afford to pay more increasing their payment accordingly.

The demand for existing services may not support substantially increased prices, however. Indeed, demand may even be falling for the organization's traditional services. Many organizations are therefore expanding their product lines—adding new goods and services that can be sold at a profit and thus help the organization balance its books. Expertise in marketing is needed to decide which market segments to serve with what new products. Possible competitors must be identified and evaluated. Finely developed skills will be required to develop a pricing strategy and to make retailing and mail-order distribution decisions. Communication strategies must be designed to promote the new products to both existing customers and (where appropriate) new market segments.

The search for increased revenues from existing markets and from entirely new revenue sources is changing the orientation of many nonbusiness organizations. Certain public enterprises are developing a corporate structure closer to that of private firms than of government departments. Donative nonprofit institutions are becoming more entrepreneurial and more commercial. As a result, managers of these organizations are increasingly interested in the insights to be obtained from the study of marketing practices in successful companies. Certainly, public and nonprofit managers can obtain many valuable insights from private-sector practice—and we will discuss some of them in this book. But a word of caution is in order, too. Attempts to transfer marketing techniques directly from a business to a nonbusiness context may flounder if those responsible fail to take into account the distinctive differences between the two.

COMPETITION

Although many people do not generally recognize the fact, both public and nonprofit organizations often participate in active, competitive markets.[5] Some organizations face direct competitors that offer similar products—and presumably product benefits—with a near-identical production technology. A notable example of this direct form of competition occurs among colleges and universities that clearly compete in the first place for individuals to apply and second for accepted applicants. In fund raising, many nonprofit organizations compete directly against each other for charitable contributions.

Competition is not limited to organizations that offer similar goods and services; it can be indirect as well. "Generic" competition can come from organizations offering different products but similar benefits to consumers. For example, in many countries, passenger railroad companies have been nationalized and joined together to form one national company. From a narrow product viewpoint, the railroad is a monopoly and faces no competition; however, from the passenger's side, the desired benefit in most cases is not the journey itself, but transportation from one place to another within a desired time frame. As such, the potential competitors for the rail journey include buses, airlines, boats, and driving or riding in an automobile, possibly as a hitchhiker. The relative appeal of these competitors, of course, depends on the nature of the trip, the availability and quality of the alternatives, and other factors. In Chapter 11, we discuss how these factors affect the pricing strategies used by British Rail.

The scope of competition can be broadened still further when customer needs are examined at an even more generic level, as can be illustrated by the nature of competition in the performing arts. There may be only one symphony orchestra in a city, but many potential audience members would consider the opera, ballet, and the theater acceptable alternative ways to spend an evening. Beyond other types of live professional performing-arts events, viable alternative ways to spend an evening include attending a professional hockey game, watching a movie, dining at a restaurant, or staying home to look at television or read a book (maybe even this one!). When the benefits are defined broadly—in the last example, as entertainment or diversion—the range of potential competitors is wide indeed.

An organization can examine its position as compared to competition to see how distinctively the market perceives its offerings. Some organizations may find that the market views their products as near-commodities—perceiving only minimal distinctions between the offerings of the different organizations. For example, one community center offering preschool day-care programs thought that it was differentiated in the marketplace because of its religious affiliation. A survey of parents showed that this affiliation made little difference, however. Parents felt that about five or six day-care centers were roughly equivalent on all important service dimensions, and therefore chose on the basis of price or location. The day-care program did not draw particularly well from any one religious group. At the other extreme, some organizations are positioned in a manner so that users perceive them as being relatively distinctive. To continue the day-care example, parents believed that one preschool program in the area had a particularly effective educational program and consequently positioned that organization separately. It attracted children from a wider geographic radius and at higher fees than did any of the other schools. Moreover, it had a waiting list while other programs had space available. By developing a unique competitive position, this center prospered while others were barely surviving. In general, organizations may find their position perceived as anywhere from unique to commonplace, depending on whether they are seen to provide a distinctive offering or a mere commodity.

Product-Market Boundaries

Once the notion of competition is seen to go beyond that of direct, product-form competition, the issue of determining market boundaries arises; that is, what products compete with each other in which markets? Because markets are sometimes defined by the range of alternative products that are available, the phrase *product-market* is often used to describe the competitive setting an organization faces. All market boundaries are ultimately arbitrary, but they exist to help understand and impose order on complex market environments.[6]

Definitions of market boundaries vary partially because of the range of decisions for which particular definitions may be useful. Market and product-class definitions appropriate for tactical decisions tend to be narrow, reflecting the short-run concerns of marketing managers. The short-run definition of competition tends to focus on organizations offering similar products and/or appealing to similar markets. A longer-run view, reflecting strategic planning concerns, invariably will define a larger market to account for (1) currently unserved but potential markets, (2) changes in technology, price relationships, and supply that broaden the array of potential substitutes, and (3) the time required by present and prospective buyers to react to these changes, including modifying existing behavior patterns, production systems, and so forth, in order to adopt the substitute.

Any single definition of a product market represents a compromise between the long-run and the short run and between consumer and producer perspectives. Consequently, it is quite reasonable to develop different definitions of markets for different purposes. Thus for some strategic planning purposes, a university may treat its law, graduate business, dental, and medical schools as part of the professional-school market, appealing to bachelor-degree holders who are willing to enroll in full-time postgraduate programs. For other purposes, an evening MBA program may be looked at as a separate product competing with part-time programs at other local colleges and with publicly funded night-school classes.

Defining Market Boundaries. One approach to defining market boundaries is to identify the degree of substitutability among alternatives. One such measure is the cross-elasticity of demand—the extent to which one product would lose or gain use in response to a change in another's price. Of course, the cross-elasticity concept applies not only to price but also to other aspects of the marketing mix. Thus, for example, a commuter bus may not attract automobile riders when the fare is dropped from 50 cents to 25 cents, but the addition of new buses and improved schedules can result in people switching from driving. There are serious problems in estimating cross-elasticity in practice, but it is useful conceptually as a means to define market boundaries.

Market boundaries can also be defined by the similarity of alternative products. In other words, a market can be defined in terms of products that appear to be similar in terms of physical or technical characteristics, distribution channels, retail outlets used, function, or performance. Of course, some products that are objectively similar (in terms of measurable performance, function, or technical characteristics) may not be readily perceived as substitutes by customers. For example, as some publicly funded medical programs have discovered, doctors and patients are not all willing to substitute generic versions of branded prescription drugs for physically similar advertised brands. Measurable performance characteristics are often not sufficient in themselves to define market boundaries.

Probably the most useful and generally applicable criterion for identifying members of a product category that compete in a market is the customers' perception of substitutability in use or function. In other words, a market consists of products that are perceived by present or potential users as satisfying the same needs, solving the same problems, or being appropriate in the same usage contexts. For some strategic planning questions, however, it will also be desirable to know whether organizations not perceived as supplying substitutes could potentially offer a substitute because of, for example, similarities in operations or distribution systems. To illustrate, a symphony orchestra might be concerned that a nearby opera house could become the host for touring orchestras. Or the orchestra manager might ask whether a televised series such as "Live from Lincoln Center" is a forerunner of videotaped competition.

The *usage situation* provides a useful concept around which to organize thinking about markets and to identify competition. As an example, consider the mass-transit system in a metropolitan area. In analyzing the competition, several usage situations (submarkets) might be identified: (1) the daily commuter with a standard 9-to-5 work schedule who has a single origin and destination, (2) the daily commuter who sometimes works late at night and makes several trips during the day as well, (3) a central-city resident who does not own a car, and (4) a person living in the suburbs who occasionally goes shopping in the downtown area. Each of these users requires a different type of transportation service. As the usage situation changes, so also may the set of competing alternatives and the bases on which they compete.

Competition and Behavior Change

Social agencies that are primarily concerned with persuading people to change their attitudes or behaviors (e.g., to use metric measures or to use birth control) often encounter competition even though they are not marketing products. The competition these agencies face can be subdivided into two broad types. One form of competition, passive in nature, is the reluctance of individuals to alter established attitudes and behaviors. In many social-change programs, the short-term inconvenience of adopting a new behavior is seen to outweigh the benefits that may be long-term. The status quo is often an effective competitor that appeals simply because people are used to it.

Beyond inertia and lethargy, some social-change agencies face another type of competition: direct, active opposition, as in the case of family planners who are often opposed by organized religion in addition to having to fight cultural taboos. Similarly, in the United States, antimetric organizations have slowed the conversion to a metric measurement system. Such competitors often appeal successfully not only to those who are strongly opposed to the change but also to people who are just peripherally involved in the issue but who are generally reluctant to change or to see changes made. Many conservative groups have successfully challenged the efforts of public schools to teach classes on sexuality by appealing to a broad range of people.

Competitors to social-change programs usually have two broad positioning strategies available. One is to compete essentially on the "price" dimension; that is, the status-quo group argues that the cost of the changeover is not worth the benefits to be obtained. This can often be an effective approach because, as we discussed earlier, the short-term costs are often immediate and apparent whereas the benefits may be long-term and diffuse. In anticipating this competition, agencies promoting change must be wary of aspects of their program that can be portrayed as particularly burdensome to all or even some of the population. A metrication program, for example, should be careful to ensure that its implementation strategy pays special attention to the elderly and other groups who would have particular difficulties in adapting to a new measurement system.

An alternative positioning strategy for a competitor to a social-change program is to move the basis of competition away from the costs and benefits of the immediate program to another dimension. The new dimension would presumably be one that the opponent believes the public would view favorably. Take the case of motorcycle-helmet laws. Groups opposed to the passage and enforcement of these laws do not concentrate on the argument that these regulations do or do not improve a motorcyclist's safety (they do!); instead, they argue that the issue is one of freedom of choice. According to these groups, an individual should have the right to take whatever risks he or she wants as long as nobody else is harmed. This has turned out to be an effective strategy, and pro-helmet groups appear to have had limited success attempting to counter this "freedom" or individual-rights strategy.

An agency planning to introduce an attitude-change or behavior-change program should attempt to assess beforehand the likelihood of different types of competition and develop strategies to limit the effectiveness of the competition, be it passive or active. As with public and nonprofit organizations that market products, no agency should assume it is free of competition.

MARKETING ORGANIZATIONS AND THEIR CONSTITUENCIES

All managers spend time balancing the concerns and interests of different constituencies. The task can be tougher for those working in public and nonprofit organizations, since there are more constituencies and thereby more risks of conflict. Figure 2.3 portrays the principal constituencies surrounding the organization (but without showing the inter-relationships between the constituencies themselves). Let's look at each group in turn and consider the role that it plays.

Consumers and Clients

Understanding the individuals who buy an organization's products, use its services, or are the primary target audience for its advocacy and informational campaigns forms the foundation for marketing strategy. Many organizations express pious sentiments about

Figure 2.3 Marketing organizations and their constituencies.

their present and future customers but make little effort to understand them, let alone tailor their programs to meeting customer needs and preferences.

Suppliers of Financial Resources

Few public and nonprofit organizations generate sufficient revenues from sale of goods and services to cover their full costs. Hence, donations and grants must be sought from individuals, corporations, foundations, government agencies, and other sources. Although few managers wish to have donors determining the organization's mission and strategy, successful fundraising programs are based on identifying prospects who are likely to be interested in the organization and then highlighting issues and programs that may be particularly appealing to them. Developing a long-term relationship with a donor or granting agency requires maintaining their interest and involvement, and being sensitive to the needs and concerns of individual decision-makers.

Influencers and Information Providers

Consumers' decisions often reflect advice or information from third parties. Theatergoers, for example, often seek out the opinions of other people who have attended a particular performance; they may also look for media reviews. When choosing a college, would-be students are often influenced by high-school guidance counselors and by their parents. In the case of health care, doctors may tell patients directly which hospital they should go to for treatment.

Part of the marketing manager's task is to identify these sources of influence and to understand their role in the consumer's own decision-making process. It's often necessary to contact such influencers, either in person or through impersonal communications, to ensure that they are well-informed about the institution. Although one can't hope to build favorable opinions among everyone, it is important to dispel erroneous beliefs and, perhaps, to minimize or neutralize criticism.

Specialist Intermediaries

Certain marketing tasks may be designated to outside intermediaries or facilitators. Examples include ticket or travel agencies that make reservations, banks that sell passes for transit authorities, advertising agencies that create and implement advertising programs, and contractors who manage a specific part of the operation, such as a cafeteria or restaurant.

A particularly important form of facilitation is performed by third-party payers, as when insurance companies pay certain medical expenses incurred by policyholders. A hospital that fails to conclude and maintain the appropriate agreements with health insurers may find patients bypassing that facility in favor of other hospitals where their treatment costs will be fully covered.

Suppliers of Labor and Skill Resources

Every organization requires physical labor and mental expertise to create and market its goods, services, and programs. In addition to employees working for wages and other employment benefits, many nonprofits rely heavily on volunteers. Both employees and volunteers engage in exchange transactions with the institution. Although an employee's first concern may be with financial compensation, psychic benefits such as fellowship, challenge, security, and a pleasant working environment may be important, too. Since volunteers, who may range from trustees or directors to people helping with mailings or refreshments, receive no wages, the benefits they seek tend to be primarily psychic: a sense of community service, intellectual stimulation, even social prestige.

If the organization fails to offer a satisfactory package of "benefits" to either of these groups, employees and volunteers may terminate their service or else provide it grudgingly and indifferently.

Suppliers of Physical Resources

Commercial purchases of physical goods and raw materials are needed to operate the organization, including such basics as fuel, stationery, and office equipment. When these products are purchased, rather than donated, the organization itself becomes a customer. Well thought-out purchasing strategies and good negotiating skills help to keep down costs as well as avoiding the risk of running out of supplies that are crucial to customer satisfaction—such as medicines in a hospital, books for a course, or materials for staging a museum exhibit.

Regulators

Every organization today is subject to some degree of regulation by government. In addition to basic laws applying to buildings and to their occupants—such as health, fire, and occupational safety, there may be other controls of a more situational nature. Consider the college or hospital that seeks a zoning variance to build a new extension on a site previously zoned "residential." Whether or not the local council will grant permission may well depend on how good relations are between the institution and the community. In many cases, an institution's plans for capital improvements or expansion into new activities have been thwarted because of misunderstandings, suspicion, and poor communications with public regulatory bodies.

Occasionally, an organization's activities may be constrained by the rules of private professional associations. Only recently, for instance, have "medical ethics" been reinterpreted in the United States to allow hospitals to engage in paid advertising. Meantime, the strategies of American colleges and universities are influenced by their need to obtain (or retain) the "seal of approval" conveyed by accreditation agencies.

Local Communities

Most organizations have a physical presence in the form of an office, retail outlet, or service delivery center. The more substantial this presence, the greater its impact on the local community. Museums, hospitals, and colleges usually occupy large building complexes; some have significant landholdings. Often they offer important benefits to the community by providing employment, stimulating the local economy, generating prestige and recognition for the area, and—especially in the case of universities—staging cultural and sporting events that are open to all.

But there are often costs associated with these benefits, including traffic congestion, parking problems, and need for increased city services without accompanying tax revenues from the tax-exempt organization. Sometimes, local residents are actively hostile towards the clients served by the organization, such as residents of half-way houses for mental patients or paroled prisoners. No marketing plan can afford to ignore the needs and concerns of these external communities, because they often have the power to block execution of a proposed strategy. Reaching out to these communities at the outset, however, may generate good relationships that will yield support and understanding when it is most needed.

UNDERSTANDING TRANSACTIONS

In order to be able to develop a marketing strategy, marketing organizations must first understand the nature of the quid pro quo in transactions between themselves and their consumers.* Consider the following 12 situations and ask yourself, in each instance: Who are the parties involved in the transaction? What things of value are they exchanging?

1. An office manager pays by check for a roll of 100 first-class postage stamps for use in a small business firm.
2. A passenger deposits coins in the fare box upon boarding a transit-authority bus in a large city.
3. A hiker purchases a copy of a Sierra Club trail guide before setting out on a backpacking expedition.
4. A theatergoer pays a bill from a credit-card company; the statement includes the cost of theater tickets purchased and used during the previous month.
5. An elderly couple is persuaded by a community-health worker to obtain free flu inoculations from a public clinic.
6. After some soul searching before an election, a citizen decides to vote for a newcomer to the political scene instead of an incumbent.
7. A worshipper spends an hour attending a religious service.
8. Instead of watching television, a suburban resident decides to go to the local library on a winter evening and spend an hour or so reading magazines.
9. A married couple makes a donation of used but still serviceable clothes and furniture to the Salvation Army, receiving a receipt for their estimated value.
10. Parents send a check to their son's university to pay his bill for tuition and board. Meanwhile, his elder sister, a graduate of the law school at the same university, is sending a much smaller check as her donation to the school's annual fund-raising drive.
11. Before leaving a hospital after an operation, a patient signs a release form testifying to the treatment she received; the bill will then be sent to her employer's insurance company for payment.
12. Having just seen a televised message from the Department of Energy urging people to reduce energy consumption, a homeowner gets up to switch off unneeded lights in the house and turn off the airconditioner.

In each instance, a transaction is taking place. These transactions all involve exchanges of value, although the values are not necessarily exchanged simultaneously. To

---

*We use the terms *consumer* or *customer* here to designate individuals who engage in a transaction with a marketing organization (or have the potential for doing so), regardless of whether they are consuming physical goods, using services, or simply behaving in ways desired by the marketer.

clarify the nature of these transactions, we will group them into different categories and look at some of them in diagrammatic form.

Two-Party Monetary Transactions

Several of the transactions cited in the preceding list represent the exchange of money for goods and services. Each of these instances involves a user (or consumer) who is giving up money (cost) in exchange for a product (benefit) offered by the marketer in question.

This type of exchange transaction is easy enough to understand, being similar to most commercial transactions between two parties. But it is important to distinguish between the physical product delivered to the customer in three of these instances (the bus trip is pure service) and the *benefits* that are actually received. The office manager, for instance, buys stamps; unless he is a stamp collector purchasing the stamps as a long-term financial investment, however, the stamps themselves are of no intrinsic interest. What he acquires is a prepaid receipt for use of the mail service; the benefit he seeks is the transportation and delivery of letters. Likewise, unless she is a bibliophile or book collector, the hiker is probably less interested in the physical appearance and feel of the trail guide than in the information and advice its pages contain—although she would probably not purchase a guide that was printed illegibly or bound so badly that it was likely to fall apart within a week. Finally, theater tickets are simply a receipt for payment and a reservation for specific seats. The benefits to the theatergoer come from seeing the show presented at the theater. These benefits might include such psychic rewards as entertainment, thrills, or learning; the convenience and comfort associated with visiting the theater; and the social pleasure of going out with a group of friends.

Note, too, that costs and benefits are not necessarily exchanged simultaneously, and not all payments are made in cash. The office manager pays for stamps by check before using the mail service. The theatergoer acquires the tickets before the play, but through use of a credit card delays actual payment until the following month. Only the passenger and the hiker pay cash in the examples given and receive something in exchange almost immediately (although it could be argued that the real benefits desired are not fully delivered until the passenger reaches his destination and the hiker sets out on the trail).

Finally, note the presence of intermediaries. The bookstore is acting on behalf of the publisher (and receives a commission for its role in delivering the physical product into the consumer's hands). Similarly, the credit-card company is acting as a financial intermediary for the transmission of payment from the theatergoer to the theater.

Nonmonetary Transactions

Many transactions do not involve monetary payments by customers, as shown by examples 5 through 9 from our earlier list. In four of these examples, time was an important cost and may have been central to the customer's decision-making. Allocation of time, like that of money, involves what economists term an *opportunity cost*: time spent doing one thing is no longer available for another activity. Moreover, time availability has a fixed upper limit: nobody, however wealthy, has more than 1,440 minutes per day.

There are other costs to the consumer, too, in several of these examples. Notwithstanding the admonition of Boston's late Mayor Curley to "Vote often, vote early, for James Michael Curley," the principle of democratic government is one person, one vote. Since the voter has only one vote to "spend" on each political office or referendum item, this vote—like time and money—has a scarcity value.

Physical or mental costs are things that people normally try to avoid, unless the resulting benefits are perceived as exceeding the discomfort. The elderly couple (example 5) contemplating the flu inoculation may worry about the pain of the injection and be fearful of the overall procedure: hence they associate both psychic and sensory costs with inoculation (as well as the time costs). The suburbanite (8) may have to go out in the cold (sensory cost) to walk to the local library (time cost).

There are limits to the nonmonetary costs that people are willing to incur in return for perceived benefits. One of the tasks for marketing managers is to understand consumer preferences and perceptions in making such trade-offs.

Lastly, example 9 involves a reversal of the usual flow of physical goods: a couple donates furniture and clothing (which are presumed to have some residual monetary value) to the Salavation Army. In return they receive such psychic benefits as feelings of generosity, and association with a respected organization that they wish to help. Depending on the tax laws, they may also be able to offset their taxes by the value of the gift—a monetary benefit.

Incorporating Nonmonetary Costs Into Strategy

Classic economic theorists—and even many marketing practitioners—consider only monetary price in examining the quid pro quo of a transaction. In practice, we can divide costs into four categories: monetary, time, psychic (or "hassle"), and sensory.[7] We'll look briefly at each below. A key point for marketers to note is that consumers perceive costs in very subjective ways.

1. *Monetary costs* represent the financial outlays involved in purchasing or using the product. These costs may extend beyond the purchase price to include such costs as transportation to and from the location where the product is available, phone calls to get information or make reservations, and other associated costs such as getting a babysitter, buying a meal, or taking time off from work.

2. *Time costs* represent time spent in obtaining information, purchasing, or using the product, or behaving in ways advocated by the marketer (for example, exercising). Time wasted in waiting is generally viewed as more onerous than time spent doing something useful, such as receiving service.[8]

3. *Psychic costs* stem from negative states of mind generated by the product itself or the manner in which it is sold or delivered. Anger at being kept waiting, unhappiness at being treated rudely, shame at being in need of certain medical or counseling services, irritation at being treated poorly, or fear for one's personal safety are all examples of psychic costs.

4. *Sensory costs* consist of attributes related to the product or its delivery system that offend the customer's senses: unsightly facilities, uncomfortable seating. distracting noises, unpleasant smells, or nasty tastes.

It is not difficult to see the need for managers to develop pricing strategies that take into account the monetary costs to consumers, and we discuss such strategies in depth in Chapter 11. Managers need to recognize, however, that the customer is likely to consider other costs in addition to financial expenditures.

Time costs are particularly important for consumer services such as the performing arts, transportation, health care, and education, where delivery and consumption take place simultaneously. Both scheduling (the hours when the service is available) and duration of the service (delivery or performance plus associated access and wait time) assume major importance in consumer choices.

In the case of transportation, speed is a key product attribute. Travel is a derived demand; people travel to get to another location where they will do something else. Few travelers, other than vacationers and sightseers, would agree with Robert Louis Stevenson that "to travel hopefully is a better thing than to arrive." Transportation studies show that there is a negative relationship between level of demand and travel time on many routes, especially those widely used by business travelers: the shorter the trip time, the more people want to make the journey. At issue for the transportation operator is the feasibility of increasing travel speed (reducing the time cost) to stimulate demand, and the level of additional capital and operating expenditures that would be incurred in doing so. An alternative or complementary strategy is to lower fares on slower services, so that travelers can trade off time and monetary costs.

For other types of products, time may represent both positive and negative costs. On the plus side, people may want to spend a couple of hours at a concert or play. Here, the task is to determine the right time duration—not too short and not too long. Time costs may be associated with obtaining information, making reservations, buying tickets, and getting to and from the location of the performance, however. Here, the marketing challenge is to minimize the incidence of "wasted" time—for example, by printing detailed information about ticket prices and locations in advertisements and making it easy to buy tickets by phone.

Psychological studies of transportation behavior have shown that travelers perceive that the time spent waiting for a transit vehicle passes from one and a half to seven times more slowly than the time spent actually traveling in it.[9] Similar studies might well reveal comparable findings for such activities as waiting to receive medical services or standing in line for an arts exhibition. If it is not possible, for operational reasons, to reduce the amount of waiting time, then the marketing manager should explore creative ways of making this time pass less tediously. Possible strategies might include: providing seating, shelters, and mounted transit information at bus stops so that travelers can study transit maps or just sit and read comfortably while they wait; setting up a health fair in a hospital waiting area with display panels, booklets, and audiovisual presentations on health-related topics to inform and distract waiting patients; and hiring street performers to amuse a line of museum patrons and distribute brochures about the exhibition in advance. Although all of these strategies cost money, they may prove worthwhile investments in terms of goodwill, repeat purchases, and better-informed customers. Sometimes it may even be possible to find a donor or commercial sponsor to pay all or part of the costs.

Multiple-Party Exchange Transactions

So far, discussion of the examples given has been restricted to only two parties to each exchange transaction—the consumer and the marketer (although intermediaries may have been involved). In the private sector, the price of a product is generally assumed to cover its full production, distribution, and marketing costs, and to leave some surplus funds beyond these as profits. In public and nonprofit organizations, however, this is frequently not the case. Hence it may be necessary to involve third parties to supply the needed revenues. Even when a monetary price is charged, it may not cover the full costs of providing the service. For instance, fare-box revenues in North American transit systems rarely cover more than 25–50 percent of total operating costs. In many other cases, recurring user charges are rare; few libraries charge admission, and religious services are usually free (although worshippers may be asked to make a donation). In addition, selected services such as inoculations may be made available free of any charge to certain needy groups such as children or the elderly.

To cover the difference between the revenues received from customers and the costs associated with supplying the product, nonbusiness organizations must attract resources from third parties. In the public sector, such resources come through taxation. In the United States, it is necessary to obtain voter approval of new taxes, which raises the marketing problem of how best to promote the social benefits of the service the tax is designed to support. Even where direct voter approval is not required, lobbying may still be needed in the relevant legislative body to persuade legislators of the benefits to be gained from allocating needed funds out of general revenues.

In the nonprofit sector, resources may be attracted from individual and corporate donors, foundations, or government granting agencies. Fund raising for nonprofit organizations is explicitly a marketing activity, often involving competition against other institutions for the same funds. Another important resource is the donation of time by volunteer workers, which can save expenditures on wages and benefits. Here, too, there is a marketing task in persuading people to give up their time.

In each instance, those who donate (or approve the use of) the necessary resources are themselves engaged in exchange transactions, since they are looking for some benefits in return.

As a result, nonbusiness organizations that require charitable donations or tax subsidies to cover their costs are really engaged in multiple-party transactions. Figure 2.4 shows three examples. In the first instance, a patient is receiving hospital treatment that is 100 percent covered by a health-insurance policy paid for by his company. There is still a cost to the patient in return for improved health—namely, the time lost and the discomfort and anxiety often suffered during a stay in the hospital. What does the company get in return for paying its employee's health-insurance premiums? On the one hand, it hopes to minimize the impact of employee illness through hospital care; on the other, it can offer an attractive package of both wages and benefits in return for employees' work.

In the case of the university, we can see that the purchasers of educational services (the parents) are not always the same people as those who "consume" them (the students). Here, the parents are paying on their child's behalf, and the student is putting in the time and effort to take the courses and pass the exams needed to graduate. The lengthy amount of time invested does, in fact, have a significant financial opportunity cost, representing the income lost by not taking a full-time job instead of studying. Unfortunately for the university, tuition payments do not cover the full costs of supplying a college education, so it must make up the deficit through other means. Fund raising from former students, friends, and foundations is one. (Public universities receive tax-based funding from the government.) But what benefits do the donors receive in exchange for their gifts? Benefits are likely to be mostly psychic, representing such emotions as a sense of participation, the prestige of recognition, or good feelings from helping others. There may be monetary benefits, too, such as protecting the value of one's own degree by maintaining the quality of the institution. (We discuss fund raising in depth in Chapter 18.)

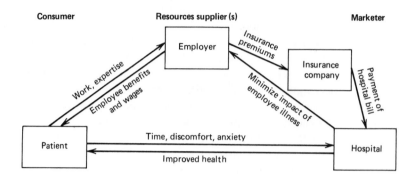

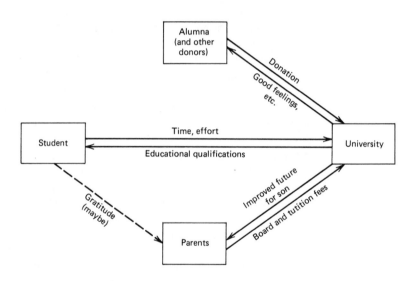

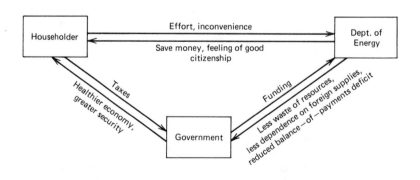

Figure 2.4 Multiple-party exchange transactions.

The third example shows a government agency that is marketing not a service or physical good but a new kind of behavior—namely, less wasteful use of energy. This behavior puts the householder to some effort and inconvenience, but offers some benefits that include modest financial savings for the individual, derived from reduced fuel consumption. If enough people conserve energy, the resulting national benefits will justify tax-funded government expenditures on the Department of Energy. The loop is completed when the government passes on such benefits as an improved currency exchange rate and a more self-sufficient economy to individual citizens.

Obviously, these examples simplify complex processes. What holds in the aggregate may not hold for individual citizens; for instance, someone who fails to save energy may still enjoy the nationally generated benefits brought about by the conservation efforts of large numbers of other people; someone who does not pay taxes may also benefit; and so forth.

The value of this type of analysis is that it draws attention to some of the tasks and problems facing managers in public and nonprofit marketing. In particular, it raises such questions as:

1. Who are the parties to any given transaction? Are they providing needed resources, are they prospective consumers, or do they play some facilitating role?

2. What benefits are sought by those who consume the goods and services offered by the marketer, or those whose behavior is in some way the target of the marketer's efforts? What choices do they have? What competitive offerings or alternative behaviors are available?

3. If the user-consumer is not making a payment that covers the marketer's costs, who is? Where do *these* funds come from?

4. What are the motivations of these third-party payers? What are they looking for in return? Are they price sensitive? Do they care about the quality of service provided by the recipient organization, and if so, how do they measure performance?

SUMMARY

Our focus in this chapter has been on understanding the environment of public and nonprofit management. A good starting point is to consider the relative division of control over the organization exerted by elected officials (in the case of public organizations) or its customers (in the case of nonprofits versus professional management. Another important consideration is the proportion of revenues that come from grants and donations versus user fees. Many nonbusiness organizations are moving towards greater control by professional managers and towards more reliance on earned income. In the process, they are becoming more "businesslike" and some are even being transformed into profit-seeking corporations.

Most nonbusiness organizations face increasing competition either from similar institutions or from seemingly different organizations that can meet the needs of the former's customers in a different way. These two forms of competition are termed *direct* and *indirect* (or *generic*) respectively. The key to understanding competition is to determine how prospective customers define their needs and perceive alternative ways of meeting these needs.

Other than competitors, what external individuals or institutions do management and the board need to understand? We looked at eight constituencies, beginning with consumers and suppliers of financial resources, and then continuing through information providers and influencers, specialist intermediaries, suppliers of labor and skill resources, physical resource suppliers to regulators and finally the local communities within which the organization operates. Failure to direct attention to each of these groups may limit the organization's ability to succeed.

The chapter concluded by examining the transactions that underlie all marketing activity. We looked at the exchanges of value that take place between the marketer and any given customer. In the process, we sought to identify the benefits that specific customers expect to obtain from a given transaction and examined the costs—monetary, time, sensory, and psychic—that they might perceive themselves as incurring in return.

We now move to Part 2 of the book, "Exploring and Pursuing Marketing Opportunities." This section begins with a chapter on "Conducting a Marketing Audit," which continues the theme of understanding the organization and its environment. We will present a formalized approach for determining what is going on both outside and inside the organization that might have an impact on the planning and execution of marketing strategy.

REFERENCES

1. Dick Netzer, *The Subsidized Muse*, Cambridge, England: Cambridge University Press, 1978.
2. Judith Manfredo Legorreta and Dennis R. Young, "Why Organizations Turn Nonprofit: Lessons from Case Studies," in Susan Rose-Ackerman (ed.), *The Economics of Nonprofit Organizations*, New York: Oxford University Press, 1986, pp. 190–204.
3. Henry B. Hansmann, "The Role of Nonprofit Enterprise," *The Yale Law Journal*, Vol. 89 (April 1980), pp. 835–901; and "Economic Theories of Nonprofit Organization," in Walter W. Powell (ed.), *The Nonprofit Sector: A Research Handbook*, New Haven, CT: Yale University Press, 1987, pp. 27–42.
4. Benson P. Shapiro, "Marketing for Nonprofit Organizations," *Harvard Business Review* (September–October 1973), pp. 124–132.
5. An insightful discussion of competition in the public and nonprofit sector may be found in Ellen Greenberg, "Competing for Scarce Resources," *Journal of Business Strategy* (Winter 1982), pp. 81–87.
6. See George S. Day and Allan D. Shocker, *Identifying Competitive Product-Market Boundaries: Strategic and Analytic Issues*, Cambridge, MA: Marketing Science Institute, 1976, whose discussion we follow in this section.
7. For a slightly different conceptualization of nonmonetary costs, see Seymour H. Fine, *The Marketing of Ideas and Social Issues*, New York: Praeger, 1981 (especially Chapter 5, "Beyond Money: The Concept of Social Price.")
8. For a detailed discussion of the importance of time as a variable in both decision-making and marketing strategy, see Douglas K. Hawes, "Time and Behavior," and Justin Voss and Roger D. Blackwell, "The Role of Time Resources in Consumer Behavior," both in O. C. Ferrell, Stephen W. Brown, and Charles W. Lamb, Jr., *Conceptual and Theoretical Developments in Marketing*, Chicago: American Marketing Association, 1979, pp. 281–311. See also the special issue on the consumption of time in the *Journal of Consumer Research*, 7 (March 1981).
9. Jay R. Cherlow, "Measuring the Values of Travel Time Savings," *Journal of Consumer Research*, 7 (March 1981), pp. 360–371.

PART 2

Exploring & Pursuing Marketing Opportunities

Chapter 3
Conducting a Marketing Audit

How well is an organization serving its clients? Are the right goods and services being offered, and are they being delivered in an efficient manner? Are the organization's personnel sufficiently sensitive to customer needs? Does the organization have a marketing strategy, and is it appropriate in light of changing markets and competitive activities? To help ensure its vitality, an organization should periodically answer questions such as these. A marketing audit, to be described in this chapter, is one approach to performance appraisal that is increasingly used in both the business and the public and nonprofit sectors.

A marketing audit is a broad-based, systematic, independent review of an organization's programs and activities and covers strategic, tactical, and operating aspects. The goal of a marketing audit is not only *to review and evaluate current performance,* but also *to identify and suggest current and future opportunities and threats*. To emphasize the positive aspect of an audit, some refer to it as a *marketing-opportunity analysis*. This is an appropriate name, because audits almost always result in the identification of new, previously unknown opportunities for the sponsoring organization.

Scope of the Chapter

Although the notion of an audit is generally well known to managers, many confine their audits to financial and accounting activities and to making an inventory of the organization's physical assets. In this chapter, we will show the relevance and value of a *marketing* audit. We will describe a detailed format for such an audit, provide examples from successful marketing audits, and discuss some ways to carry out an audit.

NATURE AND PURPOSE OF THE MARKETING AUDIT

Managers often review and appraise the effectiveness of such individual marketing activities as advertising programs, the product line, and fund-raising campaigns, but they usually evaluate each element separately and at a different time. What is lacking is an integrated appraisal encompassing a broad range of marketing issues and executed in accord with a planned program and schedule. The marketing audit is designed to meet this need.

A marketing audit is a systematic, critical, impartial review and appraisal of an organization's total marketing operation—of the basic objectives and policies of the operation and the assumptions that underlie them, as well as of the methods, procedures, personnel, and organizations employed to implement the policies and achieve the objectives. While a marketing audit should examine important operational issues, it should emphasize the overall strategy and structure and context in which tactical marketing decisions are made.

The marketing audit is potentially an important input to the process of forming a marketing strategy. The introduction to an audit of a West Coast museum highlighted this point in the following way.

> The purpose of this audit is not so much to find solutions to specific questions such as "where should we distribute our flyers?" or "what price should we charge for lectures" but rather to examine and comment on the framework from which such questions are answered. The process of decision-making is germane to the success of "museum marketing" as a whole and should be addressed before answering specific operational questions.
>
> This audit seeks to provide an objective look at how the museum functions and whether the programs undertaken and marketing activities match the stated strategic goals and objectives of individual units and of the museum as a whole. A situational analysis of the general environment and the organization's general position in the market and a look at the key players leads to a discussion of key problems or opportunities. A set of suggestions for future marketing activities follows the analysis of the success or failure of current programs.

Problem identification and definition comprise only one aspect of a marketing audit. The positive side should also be remembered. An audit is concerned with identifying the particular strengths of the marketing operation and opportunities to which those strengths can be applied.

The capability of an audit to indicate future opportunities that take advantage of an organization's strength is well illustrated by the following remarks of Thomas Hoving, former director of New York City's Metropolitan Museum of Art, who was discussing the development of retailing at the museum. Hoving discusses the audit, the steps taken in response, and the results of these actions. As can be seen, one strength of the museum was having a director who not only had a Ph.D. in art history, but also had worked in retailing and come from a family with a retailing business.

> The audit suggested: "It may prove fruitful to examine what may be potential sources [of revenue] from increased sales of museum products, both in renovated or new shops and possibly in an expanded and refined mail-order mechanism."
>
> A couple of bells went clang in my head when I read and re-read that orderly statement. You see, I had come to the Metropolitan with a secret. For years, mostly summers, I had worked in retailing. . . . I had been a coat and suit salesman at a men's store while in college. . . . So when I became Met Director I knew at least a modicum about retailing. And I liked it.
>
> And another not so secret weapon I had was knowing one Walter Hoving, Chief Executive of Tiffany and Co., the Merchant Prince of New York City, the man I call "Dad." One of the first things I did was to go down and talk to him about energizing the merchandizing aspect of the museum. . . .
>
> "If you do it right," he said, "you can expect an annual increase of 20 percent." And what were the essential how to's? The boss must be intimately involved in everything— product line, copyrighting, choice of photography, interviewing and pep-talking the sales staff—in short, be the backbone of the business. "You must insist upon quality, accuracy, taste, elegance, uniqueness and diversity," he instructed. "You can't go

wrong." "Study this," he told me at last. It was the Tiffany mail-order catalogue, so thick, so glowing with color, so marvelously written. . . .

In time we recognized that the essential point was to market, in the best sense, the entire Metropolitan Museum. Then the specific product line of reproductions would follow. But it was always a deliberate, calculated hand-in-hand relationship. We had to get word out about the museum to a whole new audience. There was no better way of doing that than by a combination of renovating the entire physical plant including expansion to the exterior, *and,* at the same time, beefing up the exhibition schedule. The key thing was to generate activity, excitement, enhancement. . . .

[The results for direct-mail and museum-shop operations] are sound. From an $85,000 net in '67 to . . . $1.5 million in '76. Grosses? From $3.5 million in '73 to $16.8 million in '78 [and $35 million in '85] . . . half the total operating budget of the museum.[1]

The marketing audit has several purposes. It should reveal potential as well as existing strengths and weaknesses in an organization; possibilities for capitalizing on organizational strengths and eliminating critical weaknesses should be identified. The marketing audit is a tool that can be of value not only to the less-successful, crisis-ridden agency, but also to the highly successful one. No marketing operation is ever so good that it cannot be improved. Long-run success requires continual adaptation to a constantly changing environment. It requires, therefore, regular scrutiny of the environment, with the aim of spotting cues that indicate a need for modifying a marketing program and the direction such modifications should take. If the marketing operation is to remain successful, a continual search for emerging opportunities and threats is needed. The marketing audit, an independent review of an organization and its environments, is one way to help maintain the vitality of a successful organization and restore strength to a struggling one.

DESIGN OF A MARKETING AUDIT

A marketing audit should follow a four-step structure, as shown in Figure 3. 1. The audit starts with the *external environments* that affect the organization either now or in the future. From there, the audit moves internally to identify and evaluate the organization's resources and limitations. The *internal environment* also includes the strategy the organization has adopted and the goals or objectives it seeks to reach.

Next the audit moves to the *marketing system* that the organization has built over time to implement marketing strategy and to manage tactical marketing activities. In this portion of the audit, the concentration is not on the marketing activities themselves, but on the structure for management: it includes the role of marketing in the organization; the marketing organization itself; and the planning, control, information, and new-products systems. For example, a review of the U.S. Postal Service indicated that during the 1970s the scope of marketing responsibilities was gradually reduced so that at the end of the decade neither pricing nor retailing was located within the marketing area.[2]

The last major portion of an audit is *activity analysis,* which examines such traditional marketing areas as products, pricing, distribution, and communication and also can include areas such as fund raising and enrollment (for membership organizations). Continuing the basic marketing concepts being stressed in a marketing audit, the analysis of each activity needs to reflect the relevant target groups, which may include current and potential donors and volunteers as well as clients, customers, and users.

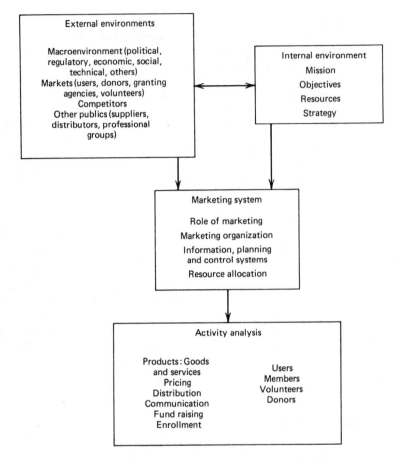

Figure 3.1 A Marketing Audit Structure

Time Frame

A marketing audit should examine an organization's past, its current position, and where it will be in the future. An audit needs to be more than just a snapshot of an organization. An audit should capture significant trends in the internal workings of the organization and the environment with which it interacts.

To be more specific, an audit's primary focus should be the organization's current condition. But the audit often needs to look as far forward as three to five years, occasionally even more, and a similar time backward into history. For the more strategic parts of the audit, the time horizon is usually longer than in the tactical and operating steps.

The appropriate time frame will also vary according to the nature of the organization and its environment. Such factors as the length of time to develop and implement strategy, the regulatory environment, capital requirements, and responsiveness of competitors can influence the time frame to use.

Who Should Conduct a Marketing Audit?

An audit is an independent, objective appraisal and review of an organization. This means, ideally, that some person or group not affiliated with the organization should conduct the audit. The present management and board members may have biases about how the organization should be and is being operated. Moreover, personnel and volunteers in the organization may not be as open and candid with their own colleagues as they would be with outsiders with whom a long-term relationship need not be maintained. An outside auditor may have special skills in interviewing people about sensitive issues. Finally, an audit is a time-consuming task, and management may not have the required time available. Completion of an audit requires considerable effort in data collection, analysis, and thought; a management faced with daily operating pressures will frequently be tempted to postpone devoting energy to the marketing audit. The completion of an audit can easily become so delayed that its value diminishes greatly. Nevertheless, although time is a factor, the main reason for using outside auditors is to preserve independence and objectivity.

Of course, managers can also use the audit framework as a checklist to appraise the organization's market position. While the same level of depth and impartiality should not be expected as when external auditors are used, considerable insight can be obtained. When a self-audit is done, management should be particularly careful not to set the scope so broad that only a superficial analysis is conducted.

A number of consulting organizations have considerable experience in conducting marketing audits in both business and nonbusiness organizations. Of course, fees may be substantial and possibly only affordable by larger public and nonprofit agencies. At times, a consulting organization may be willing to do the audit at a reduced fee, as a charitable contribution or as a stepping-stone to future engagements, either with the organization or from people who become aware of a successful audit. The audit of the Metropolitan Museum of Art, described earlier, was donated by a large consulting firm as an outright gift on the occasion of the selection of a new executive director.

Smaller organizations may only need one or two people to conduct a marketing audit. Some agencies that cannot afford professional marketing consultants may find it useful to encourage marketing students at a local university to do an audit. Students are independent and often creative, sometimes providing insights that might not come from more seasoned auditors. Students will not have the same experience and background as the outside consultant might, but can use the framework suggested in this chapter as a guide. The authors have supervised several successful marketing audits conducted by graduate students in management. Of course, the organization should be careful when asking relatively unskilled auditors to make highly subjective judgments.

Conducting an Audit

The actual conduct of an audit can be divided into four steps.

1. Determining the scope of the audit (with relevant senior administrators).
2. Preliminary review of situation and redefinition of scope, if necessary.
3. Data gathering and analysis.
4. Report writing and audit presentation.

Table 3.1   Audit Questions About External Environments

Macroenvironment
1. What are the significant, relevant, short-run and long-run developments and trends in the organization's external *environments* (political, regulatory, economic, social, cultural, technical, others)?
2. What are the likely impacts of these factors on the organization (users, targets, donors, etc.)? What opportunities and constraints will emerge?

Markets—Users, Targets, Donors, Volunteers, etc.
1. Describe (size, growth rate, national and regional trends, etc.) each of the organization's major markets: users, donors, etc. Where do the major growth opportunities seem to be?
2. In each public what are the major segments? How can these segments be characterized and how are these segments changing over time? Which segments have the most potential?
3. What benefits does the organization offer to each segment? How does this compare to the benefits offered by competitors to users? To private and public benefactors?
4. How much of the consumer volume is repeat versus new business? What percent of consumers can be classified as light users? Heavy users?
5. How do users find out about and decide to try and/or use the organization's services? When and where?
6. What is the organization's reputation, and how does it compare to that of its competitors?
7. Apply these questions to all relevant markets.

Competitors
1. Who are the organization's direct and indirect competitors, both current and potential? Describe them in terms of size, growth rate, market share, and other important factors.
2. For the important competitors, what are their strengths and weaknesses? What strategies have they pursued and how are they likely to proceed in the future?
3. What is the positioning structure in the major markets in which the organization competes?
4. What competitive threats are posed by clients, suppliers, and other facilitators?
5. Competition should be examined in both the user and donor markets.

Other Publics
1. Describe other important publics (e.g., distributors, suppliers, professional groups) and their present and future interactions with the organization. What trends and changes are taking place?
2. What are the alternative sources of the services or resources provided by these publics? What advantages and disadvantages would these alternatives offer?
3. How critical are each of these publics to the organization? Are there alternatives if current ones were no longer available?

The first step, *setting the scope of the audit,* is a crucial one that is sometimes overlooked. The overeager auditor will sometimes plunge into the middle of an organization without clarifying management's concerns. An audit cannot probe all issues in equal depth, nor are all aspects of the organization of equal interest to management. Priorities need to be established at the outset.

This first step is also the point at which to make sure all parties agree on what is expected from the audit: how much time the audit will take, what the involvement of management personnel will be, what type of data will be provided, and what form the final report should take. For example, the final report can vary from a lengthy, detailed review of all aspects and details of the audit to an outline report of major findings, plus recommendations for future action.

Most audits can be conducted within two to three months. Audits that consume too much calendar time pose problems because the "current" situation is often changing and not a constant. Parts of the audit may then be inconsistent. Audits of large organizations are completed within this time frame by increasing the number of people on the audit team. Although an audit can sometimes be completed in less than a month, this usually is not sufficient time to gather and analyze data.

The second step in the audit, *the preliminary review,* allows the auditor to confirm that the originally conceived framework for the audit is sound, before moving on to undertake extensive data collection. Audit teams have often found that the views of senior management who commissioned the audit are at variance with operating realities. For example, one auditor of a theater company was told that extensive data were available on the subscribing patterns of its audience. It turned out that the information system only had a record of whether an audience member had a current subscription, not even whether the subscription was a new one or a renewal. At times, the preliminary review may suggest unanticipated areas to investigate or planned areas that it will not be fruitful to audit in depth.

Data gathering and analysis can often be the most time-consuming step. The auditor usually has to collect both primary and secondary data, but the audit is not the place to conduct an extensive market-research project (although some of the techniques discussed in Chapter 8, "Marketing Research," may be useful in designing the audit instrument). On the other hand, the auditor may find it useful to interview users and members of other external publics; at times this is necessary because those affiliated with the organization may have a biased view of outsiders' perceptions. Often the audit team will need to supplement written data with personal interviews of organizational members and with telephone and personal interviews of outsiders. In both cases, a considerable degree of tact and good interviewing skills are required. Internal people may feel threatened by the audit, while outsiders may see the audit as a sign of weakness. The audit team must be able to deal with problems such as these.

Of course, data gathering is not the end purpose of the exercise; careful, sound, creative analysis is required to generate managerially useful insights.

The final step is *report writing and presentation.* As we mentioned earlier, the auditor and management should agree at the first stage on the appropriate format for these steps. In the usual audit, perhaps two to three months have passed since the audit was begun; it is the auditor's task to ensure that both the oral and written presentations are designed so that management and board members will understand the significance of the findings and take appropriate action.

A marketing audit is a major undertaking for an organization. To provide a better understanding of what is involved and to demonstrate some of the potential benefits from doing a marketing audit, we now describe in some detail a format for a marketing audit.[3]

EXTERNAL ENVIRONMENTS

A marketing audit usually begins by examining the external environments that are currently or potentially important to an organization. These include the macroenvironment, markets, other publics, and competitors. Table 3.1 indicates typical questions that a marketing auditor may ask about the external environment.

The Macroenvironment

The term *macroenvironment* includes those forces that can affect, influence, or constrain the organization but over which management has little influence. For example, the political and economic factors that led to gasoline shortages and higher fuel prices significantly affected the short-term demand for passenger rail travel in some areas, but the railroads had little control over gasoline supply and cost. Similarly, developments in electronic communication promise (some might say "threaten") to have major impact on postal services; postal services can anticipate and respond to these developments, but not control them. It must always be kept in mind that environmental factors include social and cultural trends that are sometimes overlooked in concentrating on technical and economic factors. For example, nonprofit organizations that depend on free volunteer labor are having increasing difficulty staffing programs as more women enter the paid labor force.

The macroenvironment is, by definition, vast and any audit needs to be selective. The audit should attempt to establish what macroenvironmental trends are relevant, set priorities, and then gather information in sufficient detail to be meaningful. For example, a marketing audit for a national postal service should probably be more concerned with electronic communication technology than with energy supply, although both are important; the opposite priorities would likely hold for a commuter railroad; both might be equally relevant for an educational institution. In the selection and analysis of the macroenvironmental factors, it is critical to remember that the concern should be not only with the present, but also with future opportunities and threats.

Markets—Users, Targets, Donors, Volunteers, Etc.

A marketing audit, like marketing itself, is critically concerned with understanding in detail the markets with which the organization interacts. Indeed, the key theme of marketing is to know your customer. Of course, some nonbusiness organizations are concerned with attitudes and behavior patterns—such as wearing seat belts, controlling blood pressure, and belief in racial equality—and cannot be strictly said to have customers or users. Those people whose attitudes or behaviors the organization seeks to affect are clearly the market target, however. As we discussed previously, a major characteristic distinguishing public and nonprofit organizations from business is the large number of "markets" or "publics" with which the organization interacts.

People new to doing marketing audits are often surprised at the number of markets that nonbusiness organizations face and may be somewhat reluctant to examine all of them. This is generally a mistake; while priorities need to be established, a major contribution of an audit can be the result of rigorous questioning of the type suggested in Table 3.1 applied to multiple markets and publics. For each identified market, constituency, and benefactor, the audit should examine such items as its size, growth rate, segmentation bases, and benefits sought. It is also helpful to look at the process of information gathering, adoption, and subsequent behavior—particularly when studying volunteers. Public agencies may find it instructive to consider the "market" of legislators who vote budget appropriations and establish policy directions.

The following introduction to the audit of an extension program at a church-affiliated university—call it Trinity Northern—indicates the multiplicity of markets that can be identified and analyzed.

> Trinity Northern's extension program has at least seven significant markets and/or publics: (1) student, (2) faculty, (3) institutional, (4) church, (5) philanthropic, (6) administrative, and (7) academia.
>
> The student market consists of present and potential students for the extension program. The faculty market is comprised of those faculty members both at the main campus and near extension locations who could provide the necessary instruction. The institutional market includes the various members of the university community who can exert either supportive or destructive influence on the extension program. The church market represents local churches that can provide both student and financial support. The philanthropic market is composed of the diverse group of individuals and organizations who may take a charitable interest in the extension program. The administrative market is the group of individuals who are potential members of the administrative team responsible for the supervision of the local extension program. The academia market is the amorphous collection of individuals and organizations (i.e., accrediting agencies, academic societies, etc.) that constitute the American educational scene. This market is significant because it can render opinions as to the worth of the educational credentials gained through extension education programs. The market is included as a major one because there is considerable and growing skepticism about the educational value of extension programs.
>
> It is clear that these markets are not discrete. That is, a constituent of one market may simultaneously be a constituent of one or more other markets. Nevertheless, it is helpful to distinguish between the various markets because they represent various needs and suggest different marketing strategies. Additionally, it is clear that the markets are highly interdependent. For example, a highly satisfied student may talk positively about an experience with the pastor of a church, leading the pastor to recommend the program to other students and perhaps motivating church members to give financial assistance to the program.

The remainder of this section of the audit analyzed each of these markets in substantial depth, examining their size and growth rates. Various segmentation plans were examined. For example, ministers who were graduates of Trinity Northern might be more receptive to the extension program than others. Trinity Northern graduates might serve as lecturers, be supportive of having neighborhood churches provide classrooms, and refer students to the program. In fact, the existence of a Trinity Northern alumni presence appeared to be related to the enrollment success of a site.

Competitors

As discussed elsewhere in this book, virtually no organization is free of competitors. Even organizations such as the U.S. Postal Service which is protected from direct *product-form* competition—as in the first-class letter-mail monopoly—often face intense generic competition. For example, the growth rate in the number of messages transmitted by telephone far exceeds that of letter mail. Indeed, one of the difficulties of legislated product-form monopolies is that managers in such organizations may develop a monopoly mentality in which they ignore generic competition and believe that the customer has no alternative but to use the offered service. Rarely is this true in the long-run.

An organization must look out not only for present competitors, but also for new-comers not now in the market. Existing suppliers and customers may become competitors. For example, one medical center had a considerable drop in patient volume when a nearby university decided to open its own clinic to serve student needs. The university believed that the outside medical center was too large and impersonal and did not recognize the special concerns of students.

Competitors exist not only in the user market, but also in other markets. The most obvious is in the fund-raising market where, at times, organizations that serve very different user markets are competing for the same donor. For example, foundations often have to choose among grants to educational institutions, medical-research programs, social-service agencies, and others. Think for a moment of all the organizations to which you have been asked to donate money or your time as a volunteer, and try to visualize the degree of competition in these situations.

The marketing audit should identify the important present and potential competitors in different markets. Usually only a few major competitors need to be studied in depth to understand the threats they pose, but the organization must be sure to analyze its overall competitive position very carefully. Although competitors are often a threat, they may also be a valuable source of ideas. Such hospital innovations as outpatient surgicenters, allowing the father (or other companion) to join the expectant mother in the labor room, and adding social workers to the staff have all been copied by other hospitals following their successful introduction.

Other Publics

Most organizations deal with a variety of other publics such as suppliers, distributors, and agencies that assist the organization in the preparation and production of a service or its delivery. These other publics can range widely, from suppliers of goods and services to accrediting agencies and community centers that lease space to other social-service organizations. Key publics may need to be intensively reviewed at times. For example, performing-arts organizations often sell their tickets through ticket agencies using computer-based systems.

Organizations using such an agency often give up direct point-of-sale contact with their customers. Consequently, it is necessary to ensure that the electronic ticket system provides such desired benefits as easy exchange of tickets and exact seat locations and is staffed by personnel knowledgeable about the performances.

When an organization offers services that are delivered by professionals, such as doctors, professors, or social workers, the auditor needs to consider both internal group-ings of these professionals and outside associations to which they belong and possibly have great allegiance to. One hospital, for instance, introduced a comprehensive health care clinic for seniors living in the surrounding area. In developing this innovative clinic, hospital management had to consider the reactions of hospital medical committees which were organized by functional specialty and the local medical association, which questioned the role of nurses and paramedics in providing certain types of health care. As another example, the artist and the intellectual can have a sense of creative integrity that overrides all other allegiances.

Table 3.2 Audit Questions About the Internal Environment

Mission
1. What is the organization's mission? What business is it in? What changes, if any, are contemplated in the organization's mission over the next five years?
2. How was this mission developed and why was it chosen?
3. How well is its mission understood throughout the organization?

Objectives and Goals
1. What are the stated objectives of the organization? Do they lead logically to clearly stated marketing objectives?
2. Are the organization's marketing objectives stated in a hierarchical order? Are they quantified so that progress toward achievement can be measured? Are they reasonable in light of the organization's resources? Are they selective and devoted to important issues?
3. Is there a set of performance measures that allow the organization to track its progress in key result areas?

Resources
1. What are the major resources and limitations (human, financial, technical, etc.) of the organization? What abilities does the organization possess? Does the organization have any distinctive advantages?
2. How do the resources compare to those of competitors? Are the resources appropriate for the objectives of the organization?
3. Describe any plans for major changes in the organization in the next five years (e.g., new central facility, divestment)

Strategy
1. What is the organization's core marketing strategy for users, donors, and others? What are the critical success factors for this strategy? Is the strategy appropriate in light of the previous analysis of external and internal environments?
2. Are major resource-allocation decisions consistent with the chosen marketing strategy?

INTERNAL ENVIRONMENT

If the first rule of marketing is to "know your market," the second must be to "know your organization." Successful marketing programs are based on matching the abilities and aims of the organization to the needs of relevant external publics; the purpose of this section of the audit is to review and evaluate the internal environment of the organization. As shown in Table 3.2, there are four major subdivisions here: (1) the organization's core mission or purpose, (2) objectives and goals, (3) resource analysis, and (4) marketing strategy.

Mission

In examining an organization's internal environment, among the first questions to be asked are "What is the purpose of this organization?" and "What mission does the organization seek to accomplish?" Although seemingly simple questions, the answers are often not so simple. Many an organization has simply evolved over time without a clear understanding of its basic mission. For example, one community center offered a broad variety of programs, chosen on the basis of what seemed appropriate at the time. Eventually, two of the programs were well accepted by local residents—day care for children aged 2 to 5 and afternoon activity programs for senior citizens. The vast majority of staff, volunteer, and financial resources and space in the facility were devoted to these two programs. The community center, unintentionally, had become de facto a provider of care services to the oldest and youngest segments—leaving out most of the community.

Frequently, an auditor will find lack of agreement on the mission of an organization. This occurs when the organization has not attempted to develop a statement of mission, or if one is developed, has not communicated it throughout the organization. This lack of consensus can severely limit the long-term impact and success of an organization and often leads to dissipation of resources.

While an organizational mission is a long-term concept, the mission of an organization can change over time. Harvard College, for instance, held to its initial mission to prepare young men for the ministry—for more than a century. Later, in keeping with the growth of the country, the mission was broadened and Harvard expanded its classical curriculum and added professional schools (and apparently invented the placement office). It is useful to examine, if possible, the historical developments leading to the current mission definition and determine if there are different aspirations for the future.

Objectives and Goals

At times, there is semantic confusion between the terms *objectives* and *goals*. Some authors distinguish these terms in the following way: objectives—what the organization wishes to achieve; goals—the measurement instruments that indicate the degree of objective achievement. Others define these terms in precisely the *opposite* way. In this book we use the terms interchangeably to include both meanings. We find that this leads to the least amount of confusion and debate because the meaning is usually clear from the context.

In a marketing audit, the prime concern is with the marketing objectives of the organization. Some of the major organizational objectives may actually be marketing objectives as well. For example, the objective of a highway safety council—to persuade people to use seat belts all the time—is both an organizational and marketing objective, although further refinement would be needed before such a goal would become operationally meaningful and measurable. Not all organizational goals, of course, have a direct bearing on marketing. A critical question to ask is whether the marketing objectives logically follow from and are consistent with organizational objectives. In examining objectives, the auditor should continually keep in mind the distinction between the financial "bottom-line" measures of for-profit organizations and the nonfinancial objectives of nonprofit organizations.

When asked, organizational members can usually generate a long list of vague, high-sounding objectives that have little operational meaning. An organization must be selective in choosing objectives, and the objectives should be subject to a number of tests. Marketing objectives should be specific, either stated in or transformable into measurable terms so that progress toward attainment can be assessed. The seat-belt usage objective cited earlier would need to be translated into such terms as, for example, "75 percent of all drivers and 50 percent of passengers always use seat belts within five years" before providing real direction for the marketing program. The long-term objectives are the basis for setting short-term goals; in this way progress toward accomplishment of long-term goals can be assessed. The goals should have some priority ranking. Of course, all the objectives should be important ones, but not all goals are equally important. It is often useful to subdivide objectives into those that are critical and those that are merely desirable. Finally, the marketing objectives should be realistic in light of the organization's current position and available resources (see the next section). Of course, if either short-term or long-term objectives are to be useful to an organization, they must be communicated to and understood beforehand by those responsible for formulating and executing marketing plans.

The objectives should lead to a set of performance measures that allow the organization to track its progress toward achieving success in key result areas. In this way, objectives are translated into terms that guide management action and allow for deviations from the plan to be identified and acted upon.

Resource Analysis

It is one thing to have lofty goals, but quite another to have the means to achieve them. For example, a local family-planning clinic is not going to be able to change societal beliefs about birth control; nor should a small liberal arts college expect to become a world-famous center for nuclear physics. In the resource-analysis stage of an audit, the primary purpose is to identify the major strengths and weaknesses of the organization and assess them relative to its marketing strategies and programs. Elsewhere in the audit, the status of the organization's external environment is reviewed. Here, the auditor examines the financial, technical, physical, human, and other resources of the organization. An important resource is the organization's image and reputation. Financial resources are obviously important; many a sound marketing program has failed because an organization has run out of funds. In evaluating human resources, the auditor is concerned not only with the number of people, both paid and volunteer, available to the organization, but also with their management ability, professional skills, future potential, and so on. Rarely does the public or nonprofit organization receive uniformly high marks in all areas.

The relevant physical resources can vary from organization to organization. For a national postal service, the vast distribution system represented by local post offices is an important physical resource. As another example, compare the relative strength of a community center that owns a large building near bus and subway lines and with ample convenient parking to one with small rental quarters, without nearby parking, and without access to the local transit system.

Sometimes, a marketing audit will reveal that the organization has capabilities that may not have been recognized as relevant for marketing. For example, a review of the U.S. Postal Service listed the following resources that could be relevant in forming a marketing strategy.

- A collection network, consisting of widely dispersed pickup posts located throughout the nation.
- A nationwide retail network of almost 40,000 post offices.
- A series of sorting offices for both letters and packages, utilizing varying degrees of automation and mechanization.
- A transportation fleet of some 200,000 motor vehicles.
- A delivery system that reaches every business and household in the nation (and also feeds into international mail distribution systems).
- An experienced labor pool of more than half-a-million full-time employees.[4]

In addition to its own labor force, facilities, and physical distribution systems, USPS also has the potential to pool its resources with those of other organizations—either public or private—possessing complementary skills and resources. One example already exists: the cooperative Mailgram venture between USPS and Western Union.

Of course, a marketing audit needs to identify and evaluate weaknesses as well as strengths. Management inability and financial limitations must be recognized. Some limitations may be overcome, but the goal of an audit is to provide an objective appraisal. On the other hand, the auditor should remember that the evaluation of resources should be matched against the size and nature of the organization. The fund-raising ability of a local boys' club should not be compared to that of the Red Cross. Resource evaluation should be carried out relative to the strategies that the organization is contemplating and the resources of other organizations with similar targets. Typical questions are: "Does the organization have the resources to reach its goals?" and "Can the limitations be overcome?" For example, one university found that it could not compete nationally for students for a daytime MBA, but that it had a faculty and other resources of such strength that it could become the dominant regional school for evening MBA students who wished to continue full-time employment while studying for a degree.

Strategy

Strategy is the means by which the organization seeks to reach its objectives. Depending on the scope of the audit, the fund-raising strategy as well as the strategy for major markets may be reviewed in depth. The first step in this component of the audit is to identify the organization's core strategy and to determine, if possible, the critical factors for success of this strategy. The earlier portions of the audit may help assess the soundness of the strategy. The auditor would like to determine the appropriateness of the strategy for the organization, given the earlier review of the internal and external environments. For example, a country's tourist bureau may wish to answer inquiries in the visitor's own language, but the counter clerks may not speak a sufficient number of languages to carry out the task. As another example, a transit system with insufficient buses and rapid-transit cars to serve current commuter needs cannot hope to displace the automobile without first expanding its capacity.

Some organizations have elegant, written strategies (perhaps to satisfy the requirements of granting agencies) that do not have much impact on the organization. The final task of this portion of the audit is to determine whether major resource-allocation decisions are consistent with the organization's claimed strategy. What evidence is there that written and oral strategies actually affect decision making in the organization?

MARKETING SYSTEMS

An audit of an organization's marketing system (Table 3.3) is needed because successful marketing over time requires the utilization of a disciplined approach to the design and implementation of marketing programs and the execution of marketing tactics. Although organizations can occasionally prosper for a while under innovative leaders and the inspirational development of programs, extended success usually requires an ongoing system. One of the most serious errors an organization can make is to assume that the strategy that launched the organization will remain appropriate over time. This is particularly true for governmental programs, which often are launched with a wave of publicity

Table 3.3 Audit Questions About Marketing Systems

Role of Marketing
1. Is there a senior-level marketing officer in the organization? What is the level of this official's authority? Who in the organization works on marketing problems?
2. What is the role of marketing in the organization? What range of activities falls under marketing's purview? Are sufficient resources devoted to marketing?
3. What is the organization's marketing philosophy? Is it formalized in writing? Is it well thought out and internally consistent? Who determines the philosophy and how is it changed?

Marketing Organization
1. Is the marketing organization structured along functional, product, or market lines? Is this the appropriate structure? Is there sufficient marketing expertise in the agency or available to it?
2. How does the marketing organization for users interrelate to those parts of the organization concerned with funders and other publics?
3. What are the relationships within the different parts of the marketing organization? Are there good working relationships?
4. How effectively does marketing interact with other functional areas, particularly operations? Is there mutual support and understanding? Is the overall organization designed for better service to customers or for internal convenience?
5. Does the organization have a formal new-product-development (old-product-deletion) system? Is the system effective at generating, developing, analyzing, testing, and introducing new products?

Information, Planning, and Control Systems
1. Does the organization have a marketing planning and control system? Are annual marketing plans developed, implemented, and used as the basis for a control system?
2. Is there a market-information system that produces timely, accurate, relevant information? What information does the organization have about its markets and other publics?
3. How is marketing research being used? What market research is available? How does it affect decision making?

Resource Allocation
1. Are the objectives and roles of each element of the marketing mix clearly specified? Do resource-allocation decisions reflect these objectives and roles, and are these decisions based on sound analysis?
2. Do marketing resource allocations reflect the importance of different segments, services, and territories, and different marketing activities as specified in the marketing philosophy and plan? Do these allocations make sense on an economic basis?
3. Does the organization carry out periodic reviews of the efficacy of its operations and evaluations of its resource allocation decisions? How and with what results?

and strong commitments from talented and motivated people. For example, when the Peace Corps was launched in 1962, a major problem was how to cope with the excess demand of Americans wanting to be volunteers and host countries who wanted volunteers. A decade later, the Peace Corps had difficulty filling its quotas and getting countries to accept volunteers. It received little mention in the press, and the Advertising Council no longer considered the Peace Corps to be a priority account.

Role of Marketing

A particular problem in analyzing the marketing system, especially marketing's role in the organization, is that many public and nonprofit organizations either do not acknowledge that they have a marketing function or refer to it by other names. For example, a performing-arts organization may have an audience-development director, a blood bank may have an officer for donor recruitment, and a museum may have an education director; all may carry out marketing activities. Moreover, some organizations merge public relations and marketing without recognizing that most businesses treat these as distinct areas. There are some dangers in using an alternative name because it fosters a narrow definition and role of marketing within the agency and limits management's ability to learn from others who openly acknowledge their use of marketing, as is discussed more fully in Chapter 16, "Organizing the Marketing Effort." Nevertheless, it is not the word *marketing* that is critical; *organizational practice* is the key.

The first stage of the marketing-systems portion of the audit is to define the role of marketing in the organization. Is there a senior officer of the organization—who may not have the word *marketing* in his or her title—who is formally responsible for marketing activities? Unless such a senior appointment exists, the marketing function will not have sufficient impact on the agency's key strategic decisions. Moreover, only a senior officer can insist that the entire organization, and not just the marketing department, adopt a customer orientation.

Perhaps more revealing is an examination of what the responsibilities of the marketing function are. For example, a review of the U.S. Postal Service in 1980 revealed that the marketing function (called "customer service") had no direct responsibility for such traditional marketing activities as pricing and management of retail outlets (local post offices). Thus decisions on pricing, particularly on services marketed to commercial firms, often were based on insufficient understanding of consumer needs and competitive pressures. In contrast, postal pricing decisions in Britain are the responsibility of the marketing department, which uses price as one component of its program to compete vigorously for contract business from large corporate mailers. The British government requires the Post Office to set prices at levels that will ensure that *total* postal income exceeds total expenditure by a predetermined percentage of sales. The general approach adopted in Britain is to gear prices to individual services, so that while all services meet at least their direct costs, the contribution they make individually to overheads and profits varies in accordance with marketing and other considerations.

Marketing Organization

The marketing organization itself must also be examined to see if it is structured to meet the needs of customers and other publics while still being consistent with the necessity of the organization to produce and deliver services efficiently. As discussed in Chapter 16, "Organizing the Marketing Effort," there is no optimal structure for all institutions. The marketing organization needs to be examined from the vantage point of how it deals with functional, territorial, product, and market perspectives and how it allows expertise in areas such as advertising and market research to emerge. Nonprofit institutions need to be particularly careful to examine and determine the appropriate organizational relationships between user markets and fund raising. Direct linkages are not always ideal, and ethical questions may arise. For example, how closely should a college's fund-raising and admissions offices be linked? Should fund raisers have access to data supplied by parents in support of their children's financial-aid applications?

The audit of marketing systems should also examine the interrelationship between marketing and other departments. It is well known that the preferred policies of marketing and operations can conflict; the critical questions are: "How well are the interface functions handled?" "How are conflicts dealt with?" and "Do operating people have a customer viewpoint?" It would be of little value for a bus system to have a marketing function if the operations department and the bus drivers did not adopt a customer viewpoint. One transit management handbook states this in the following way:

> One of the most serious mistakes which can be made in operating a transit system is to associate a consumer orientation strictly with the marketing department. In actuality, if the transit marketing staff are the only people with a consumer orientation, both the marketing function and the transit system as a whole are in trouble. It is essential that the consumer approach be an integral part of every organizational unit within the system. And, because the point of view of transit leadership invariably determines the point of view of the entire system, a total commitment to the consumer must begin at the top of the management structure. This relationship provides the opening question for the study of the marketing function in transit organizational structures: does the chief executive (and, therefore, the transit system) have a consumer orientation?[5]

Survival and success in a dynamic competitive environment require that an organization generate new products and services (as well as delete old ones). The audit should try to establish whether an organization has a formal new-product-development process and, in any case, how new products are developed. The audit should evaluate the effectiveness of the new-product system with regard to the generation, analysis, development, testing, and introduction of new products. A number of organizations stagnate because of their failure to have a system of new-product development.

Information, Planning, and Control Systems

The marketing audit should examine both the planning and control systems in use by the organization. These systems may exist formally, and managers may fill out required forms, but the critical test is whether these systems actually affect decision making, and, of course, the quality of the planning and control that occurs.

Marketing managers need a continual flow of information to carry out their functions and to be able to identify and respond to environmental threats and opportunities. An auditor should see if a marketing-information system exists and examine whether it provides managers with timely, accurate, relevant data that can be used for strategic and tactical problem identification, understanding, and resolution. In some advanced organizations, a marketing information system will include a set of computer-based statistical and analytical tools to help the manager deal with the mass of data that is available; however, this will not be the norm. Even in the presence of these systems, the key issue is the usefulness of the information, not the glamor of the hardware.

In addition, as discussed extensively in Chapter 8, "Marketing Research," the use and availability of market-research projects to help make decisions should be examined in an audit.

Resource Allocation

An important aspect of planning and control systems concerns the manner in which resources are allocated to different programs and marketing-mix elements. Each marketing-mix element and program should have a set of clearly specified objectives. A key question, then, is whether the resources are allocated in accord with the marketing objectives. The resource-allocation decisions should be based on careful analysis, not just on custom, history, and convenience. Also, the auditor needs to examine the integration of the marketing-mix elements to see if synergies are recognized and whether each of the elements is directed toward accomplishing planned objectives. An economic evaluation should also be made. In the next section of the audit, each marketing activity is examined in more detail.

ACTIVITY ANALYSIS

The last major section of the marketing audit is a detailed marketing-activity analysis. In this section, a detailed study of the elements of the marketing mix is carried out in terms of the different publics and markets that the activities impact on. In general, as can be seen by looking at the suggested questions listed in Table 3.4, this section of the audit concentrates on two main areas for each activity: (1) documenting the current operating procedures and (2) evaluating the effectiveness and efficiency with which that activity is carried out. The questions themselves logically follow from the material in this book. Organizations often do not ask themselves questions that appear obvious in hindsight. For example, the Metropolitan Museum audit, discussed earlier, discovered that "for every membership of a certain category which we were working hard to sign up in order to gain revenues, the museum was actually losing a dollar and a half apiece."[6]

Documenting Current Operating Procedures

The reader should not underestimate the value of documenting the current procedures of an organization. Often policies develop over time without any real attention being paid to them other than by the manager who first made a decision in response to an immediate problem. In other cases, it may turn out that few people know how decisions are made and what the operating procedures are. A marketing-activity audit can reveal logical flaws in operating procedures. At times, the lack of existence of systems in certain areas may be revealed, but it is more likely that an activity is being given minimal attention. For example, the "personal contact" section of the Trinity Northern marketing audit discussed earlier revealed the following.

> Apart from an occasional visit from the director, the "sales force" responsible for the recruitment of students, adjunct faculty, church, and other support consists of the local steering-committee members and an administrative assistant. While the effectiveness of this sales force will certainly vary from location to location, it is hard to imagine that a part-time administrative assistant and a volunteer committee will have sufficient time to devote to essential "sales" activities. There are no stipulated sales performance expectations for these individuals, and it does not appear that regular evaluation is conducted.

It may be noted that the person doing this audit was careful to consider personal contact as a function dealing with more than just the user market.

An audit is often useful because it may reveal preconceptions that differ from the organization's operating procedures. For example, the manager of a Canadian orchestra was asked how the organization determined the discount it offered season subscribers. This seemingly simple question turned out to be difficult to answer for reasons that became apparent only after a review of the decision-making process for price. More than 70 percent of the seats sold were bought by subscribers, so the organization first determined

Table 3.4 Audit Questions About Activity Analysis

Products—Goods and Services

1. What are the major services offered by the organization? Do they complement each other or is there unnecessary duplication?
2. For each service, what are the volume, trend, and future expectations in terms of (a) dollars (number and share of market), (b) users (number and share of market), (c) costs, etc.
3. If the organization has multiple facilities or branches, answer the previous question for each of the major subdivisions.
4. What does an economic analysis of each program reveal?
5. What are the market and nonmarket pressures to increase or decrease service volume? Service quality?
6. For each service, what are the weaknesses? (a) What goes wrong most often? (b) What are the major complaints? (c) How are complaints handled?

Pricing (If Fees Are Charged for Services)

1. What are the procedures for establishing and reviewing pricing policy?
2. Is pricing demand oriented, competition oriented, or cost oriented? Are there variations by market segments, time of use, number of services used? What are the economics of the pricing policy?
3. Are cost-of-service estimates available and used in pricing decisions?
4. What methods of payment are accepted (e.g., credit cards, credit accounts, and checks)?
5. What discounts to the basic fee structure are offered and with what rational?
6. What are the refund agreements?
7. What short-term promotional pricing policies are used and with what effect?

Distribution—Time and Place of Service Delivery

1. What geographic areas are now served?
2. How are various geographic service areas ranked in terms of priority of need and best return on investment of resources?
3. Is service delivery decentralized (outreach)? Are information, reservation, and payment for services decentralized?
4. What are the economics of the distribution system?
5. How are the service-delivery centers identified by the public? Are the centers easy to find? Easy to give directions to? How good is public-transportation access, parking for bicycles and cars? What is the access for the physically handicapped?
6. When are services made available to users by (a) season of year; (b) day if week; (c) time of day?
7. How frequently are services offered? Are there multiple offerings?
8. Are the timing decisions made in the two previous questions based on analysis of users' preferences? To what extent do the choices made reflect staff and/or volunteer convenience? Inertia from the past?

Communication—Advertising, Personal Selling, Direct Mail, Promotion, and Public Relations

1. Are there clear objectives for each element of the communication mix? How are the activities related to these objectives?
2. How is the budget for each element determined? Does it appear to be at the appropriate level? How does the organization decide on which program or markets to concentrate promotion?
3. Are the advertising themes and copy effectiv e? What do users, funders, volunteers, and organizational members think about the advertising?
4. Are the following media currently being used: (a) newspapers and magazines; (b) radio and television; (c) alternative media (e.g., church bulletins, newsletters, school catalogs); (d) telephone directories; (e) exhibitions, billboards, posters; (f) direct mail?
5. Does the organization have a paid or volunteer advertising agency? What functions does the ad agency perform for the organization?
6. What system is used to handle consumer inquiries resulting from advertising and promotion? What follow-up is done?
7. Is there a paid or volunteer personal selling force for either fund raising or increasing service utilization? If so, how is this sales force organized and managed?

*(**continued next page**)*

Table 3.4 (Continued)

8. On what basis does the organization measure the effectiveness of its various communication programs (e.g., number of people aware of its services, knowledge about the services, attitudes toward the organization, program enrollment, financial contributions)?
9. How are public relations activities normally handled? By whom?
10. How is promotion designed for and directed to different markets?
11. Are catalogs and instruction booklets easy to read and understand (without being patronizing)? Might a prospective user find the wording ambiguous or misleading? Are graphics effectively used to facilitate understanding?
12. What do the annual meeting and annual report say about the agency and its services? Who is being effectively reached by those two vehicles? Do the benefits of these publications justify the costs?

Fund raising
1. What are the target markets for the organization's fund-raising efforts?
2. What fund-raising programs does the organization have? What benefits are offered to potential donors?
3. For each fund-raising program, what are the current trends, past trends, and future expectations in terms of absolute numbers and market shares?
4. What does an economic analysis of the rund-raising programs reveal?
5. As appropriate, apply the communication section of the audit to fund raising.

Enrollment
1. Who enrolls or becomes a member of the agency? How does a potential enrollee find out about the organization? When and how does a user or nonuser become a member?
2. How is it determined which new prospects will be called on by whom? How is the frequency of contacts determined?
3. Who has the responsibility for enrolling service users? Have they had any sales training? Are there regularly scheduled and held reporting meetings where results are measured and suggestions for improvement are made?
4. How much professional staff time is spent on encouraging people to enroll? What incentive does the staff have to enroll more people?
5. How much of a typical program director's time is spent promoting more enrollments as compared to serving those already enrolled?

the price to be charged to subscribers, and then the premium to be charged to single-ticket purchasers.

Evaluation of Effectiveness

Of course, as the questions in Table 3.4 indicate, the activity audit is also concerned with evaluation. The reader should not think that the evaluations carried out will always be negative, however. An auditor should be alert for parts of the organization that are doing well, as the following section of an audit of a family-planning agency indicates.

> The agency currently has two locations: the main center, where all examinations and surgical procedures are completed, and a satellite, where only counseling is done. Given the service area targeted, the main center is convenient to all clients. Hours are 9 A.M. to 5 P.M. Monday through Friday, plus two weekday nights until 9:30 P.M. and alternate Saturday mornings. Next month, however, the main location will be open Monday through Thursday from 9 A.M. to 9:30 P.M. and from 9 A.M. to 5:30 P.M. Friday and Saturday to accommodate more clients.
>
> The expansion of these office hours reinforces the agency's philosophy of being client centered. The main office is located in a modern office park with an abundance of parking spaces. The waiting room is large, uncluttered, with many pleasant, colorful

posters, as well as literature explaining the agency, birth-control information, and other health-related pamphlets.

The staff is cordial and pleasant. The receptionist greets clients, arranges for them to fill out a preliminary history, and also answers questions. Overall, there is a warm, sensitive atmosphere, which is apparent in the staff as well as in the decor.

In Table 3.4, typical audit questions are shown for six different marketing-mix elements or activities: products, pricing, distribution, communication, enrollment (for membership organizations), and fund raising (for organizations that seek donations). Other subdivisions are possible, and the important marketing-mix activities, of course, may vary by organization. While the questions in Table 3.4 focus on each of the market-ing-mix elements separately, it is also necessary to examine the interrelationships among them. In the audit structure presented in Figure 3.1, the overall analysis is carried out at the marketing system level. In summary, the purpose of this section of the audit is to document and evaluate, in detail, the marketing activities of the organization.

SUMMARY

The marketing audit is a carefully programmed procedure for carrying out a broad, systematic, objective review and appraisal of an organization's marketing strategy and performance. An audit can cover the organization's external environment, internal envi-ronment, marketing systems, and marketing activities. Besides being a diagnostic tool in which weaknesses in the current marketing structure are uncovered, the marketing audit can both reveal future threats and opportunities and be a source of recommendations for change. The marketing audit therefore helps to identify opportunities and means to exploit them, as the history of retailing at the Metropolitan Museum illustrates.

We hope we have made it clear that a marketing audit is not a casual undertaking. The person or team carrying out the marketing audit will need to devote considerable time to the task, as well as requiring managers to take the time to provide needed information. The gains, however, can be quite considerable, both for organizations that are new to marketing and those with established, but unaudited, marketing functions. Quite simply, a properly carried out marketing audit can produce information worth far more than its cost; the audit establishes a benchmark from which strategic and operating problems can be identified and decisions taken. When audits are carried out on a periodic basis, they also help the organization to evaluate its progress over time.

REFERENCES

1. Thomas Hoving "Direct Marketing Speech," London, 1980. See also "Mixing Class and Cash," *Time* (December 9, 1985), p.56.
2. Christopher H. Lovelock and Charles B. Weinberg, "The Role of Marketing in Improving Postal Service Effectiveness," in Joel Fleishman (ed.), *The Future of the Postal Service,* New York: Praeger, 1983.
3. Alternative frameworks for a marketing audit are discussed in Philip Kotler, William Gregor, and William Rodgers, "The Marketing Audit Comes of Age," *Sloan Management Review* (Winter 1977), pp. 35–43; and Douglas B. Herron, "Developing a Marketing Audit for Social Service Organizations," in Christopher H. Lovelock and Charles B. Weinberg (eds.), *Readings in Public and Nonprofit Marketing,* Palo Alto: The Scientific Press, 1978, pp. 267–271.

4. As in reference 2.

5. *Transit Marketing Management Handbook.- Marketing Organization,* Office of Transit Management, Urban Mass Transportation Administration, U.S. Department of Transportation, November 1975.

6. As in reference 2.

Chapter 4
Competitive Strategy

The long-run growth and success of an organization depend on developing and implementing a strategy that carries the organization to its goals. Although the formulation and implementation of strategy can be viewed as the fundamental responsibility of management, managers typically find their days filled with short-run operating decisions and often trivial, time-consuming responsibilities. Strategic thought, planning, and action tend to get put aside. Too often organizations fail to achieve their goals because they are overwhelmed by day-to-day operating problems. Consequently, strategic plans are inadequately developed in the first place and not revised as market, competitive, and environmental circumstances change. Kotler provides an instructive example.

> The American Lung Association came into existence at the turn of the century to fight the dreaded disease of tuberculosis, which at that time was the major killer of Americans. Various chapters of the American Lung Association raised money to help the victims of tuberculosis by selling Christmas Seals to the general public. In the 1950s new miracle drugs were developed that effectively prevented the spread of tuberculosis, and for the first time, tuberculosis became a minor disease. Nevertheless, the organization continued to collect money for this disease while neglecting other lung diseases that were becoming more serious, such as lung cancer, emphysema, and asthma. Even in the 1970s, when the American Lung Association started to help the victims of these other diseases, it continued to raise money by selling Christmas Seals instead of considering new donor groups and new ways to raise money. In less than a decade its market share of all the money raised by major national health agencies has fallen from a high of 13 percent to a current level of 8 percent.[1]

Strategic planning involves defining the organization's mission or purpose, setting objectives, and formulating strategy. The larger the organization, the more layers of strategy are necessary. A group organized to teach handicapped youngsters to swim would have a much simpler marketing strategy than a regional community college that serves a large and varied constituency. The college's strategy would have many layers, each providing more detailed operational guidance, and coordinated with the levels above and below.

Scope of the Chapter

Drucker has succinctly summarized the fundamental role of strategy by contrasting effectiveness—"doing the right things"—with efficiency—"doing things right."[2] Although a well-designed strategy can fail because of poor tactics, rarely will good execution of an ill-conceived strategy lead to success. This chapter is concerned with formulating strategy.

We begin the chapter by examining the strategic process that generates a strategy. The strategic process includes defining the organization's mission or purpose, setting objectives and goals, formulating strategy, and specifying tactics. Each stage supports the previous one; goals, strategies, and tactics can be developed at many different levels within an organization.

This chapter will discuss strategy at four levels: organizational strategy, subunit strategy, positioning strategy, and functional-area strategy. These levels are interdependent. For example, the subunit strategy is subordinate to the organizational strategy and should be designed to meet goals that are derived from objectives and strategy at the organizational level. Marketing concepts, as we will see, are important components of strategy development at all levels.

Organizational strategy, discussed in the second section, focuses on two major issues or questions: (1) What is the scope of activities to be undertaken by the organization? (2) How should the organization's resources be allocated to the chosen activities? The phrase *scope of activities* is broadly understood to mean the range of clients, users, or markets that the organization serves and the ways of serving them. Will the organization achieve its aims by dealing with only one market or market segment with a very limited product line, or will the organization develop a diversified strategy involving a wide range of activities and participating in many markets? This course is taken by the Red Cross whose broad scope includes providing immediate disaster relief, operating the United States' largest blood-bank system, and teaching water safety and lifesaving. Organizations operating multiservice, multimarket strategies, once having chosen to participate in these activities, usually are faced with limited resources and must make allocation decisions that reflect both present and future needs, The organization needs to decide which activities to continue—with expanded, decreased, or constant levels of support—and which to eliminate. At the same time, the organization may identify new areas of activity requiring expansion. Organizational strategy focuses on such investment decisions as those just described.

In the third section of the chapter, we examine subunit strategy, which is concerned with how an organizational subunit plans to participate in a limited set of markets or to manage a related set of products. The structure of an organization will determine the scope of a subunit's activities, but for the purpose of this chapter it will be helpful to examine strategy for a subunit that is restricted to serving a single market, which may consist of several distinguishable and important market segments. As at any level of strategy, one of the key questions is: "How will resources be allocated within the subunit?" Subunit strategies are distinguished from the organizational strategy by their focus on how the organization will participate in chosen markets. How will resources be managed so that the subunit is particularly effective in fulfilling user needs and meeting subunit goals? For organizations that participate in competitive markets, this aim can be expressed more sharply. The organization should attempt to use its resources to develop a "distinctive competence" in providing goods or services that will make the organization uniquely effective as compared to its competitors over an extended period of time.

In the fourth section of the chapter, we show how useful positioning strategy can be in managing an organization. We also suggest a set of steps for an organization to follow in choosing the position it wants to hold for itself and its services.

The last section of this chapter briefly examines functional-area strategies but concentrates on marketing strategy. Functional-area strategies need to support the subunit strategy; furthermore, the different functional-area strategies must be coordinated to the extent that they overlap. Organizations offering services need to be particularly concerned with the interaction between marketing and operations. Not all functional areas are equally important, and strategic development should concentrate on the critical ones. Functional-area strategies can, of course, be further subdivided, so the marketing strategy may integrate specially formulated advertising and pricing strategies. At each level, management must decide which areas are critical enough to warrant distinct strategies.

THE STRATEGIC PROCESS

The strategic process can be divided into four major areas: (1) mission or purpose, (2) goals and objectives, (3) strategy, and (4) tactics. These are, of course, traditional subdivisions and are closely interrelated. Most readers are probably familiar with these notions, at least informally, but the fact that managers consistently push aside strategic development to deal with day-to-day concerns requires that we formally examine the strategic process. In this section of the chapter, we will examine the first three steps of the strategic process.

Mission or Purpose

An organization's mission or purpose is a basic long-term statement of what the organization seeks to do and the rationale for its existence. An organization's mission is the fundamental definition of the organization and its role in society.

Peter Drucker has probably been the most articulate proponent of the need for both business and nonbusiness organizations to establish a clear understanding of what their purpose is. An organization's mission is determined by answering such basic questions as what business are we in, who are our customers, and what value do we provide to our customers? In the case of businesses, profit making itself is not the purpose of a company, but the result of successful fulfillment of its mission. Thus VISA, best known for its credit cards, defines its purpose as:

> [To] enable customers to exchange value—to exchange virtually any asset, including cash on deposit, the cash value of life insurance or the equity in a home, for virtually anything anywhere in the world.[3]

Just as it is a mistake to say the purpose of a business is to maximize profits, it is a mistake to say that the purpose of a nonprofit organization is "to better society." As with profits, bettering society is an outcome of fulfilling a mission, not a definition of the mission itself.

Development of an effective mission statement is a difficult task. A danger to avoid is writing a statement that, on the one hand, is so general as to be operationally meaningless —as when a hospital says its purpose is to improve the health of the community—but, on the other hand, is so specific and inwardly focused as to provide little long-term guidance as to how to make choices in a changing environment—as when a hospital defines its purpose as providing facilities for kidney dialysis treatment. A sound mission statement provides guidance to an organization and helps it to make difficult decisions.

Probably the most important test for a mission statement is that it be both externally and internally oriented. As Levitt pointed out in his classic article, "Marketing Myopia," many organizations define themselves solely in product or technological terms, not in market terms.[4] Thus he ascribed the difficulties of many railroad firms in the United States in the first half of the twentieth century as being the result of defining themselves in just that way—as being in the railroad business, not in the transportation business. For several decades following the creation of the Interstate Commerce Commission, U.S. railroads found it impossible to define themselves more broadly, since ICC regulations prevented their diversification into other transportation activities. In contrast, the two major Canadian railroad companies, one private and one a government entity, have defined themselves more broadly and operate steamship companies, trucking firms, and airlines. Of course, in using a market definition, an organization must be careful not to move too far away from its resources, abilities, and interests. Thus defining a railroad as being in the transportation business does not mean that it is either desirous or capable of being a bicycle manufacturer.

Public and nonprofit organizations are particularly susceptible to narrow mission statements that confine them to offering a limited set of goods and services to, for some, restricted markets. For example, a government agency may be allowed to market only one kind of flood insurance for a home and may also be proscribed from offering a variety of other insurance and security services that might be valued by homeowners. As the quote about the American Lung Association at the start of this chapter indicates, nonprofit organizations may impose unnecessarily narrow strictures on themselves.

New organizations should be particularly careful of overly narrow constraints. When Canada Post was restructured from a government department to a crown corporation in 1981, it deliberately sought a charter that did not confine it to collecting, sorting, and delivering physical materials but instead sought and obtained a broad definition of its mission.

Finally, a mission statement should be motivating. It should be prepared in a manner that inspires the employees, volunteers, and others who work with the organization to help the organization fulfill its mission.

Objectives and Goals

Once defined, the organizational purpose should be translated into a set of goals and objectives that indicate the specific accomplishments to be attained in fulfilling it. Objectives and goals can be subdivided in several ways. Objectives need to be set for different functional areas of the organization and in the context of different markets or publics being served. The time frame utilized can vary as well; an organization needs to have both short-term and long-term goals, for example. Objectives are necessary in all important phases of the organization.

An organization should have a multiplicity of objectives with varying degrees of interrelatedness. Objectives with regard to marketing may require the development of new services; this, in turn, implies that certain objectives are required for operations—and perhaps finance as well. Not all objectives are equally important. There should be some priority ranking; the achievement of some may be more critical than the achievement of others. Within each priority level and within each functional area there may be several objectives, but an organization should be careful not to have too many objectives.

Objectives are both performance measures and targets. Without specific, measurable objectives, the organization's mission cannot be translated into action, and it becomes merely a statement of good intentions. Objectives should provide specific direction and guidelines for management. By serving as targets, they indicate what should be accomplished. By serving as performance measures, the objectives allow others both inside and outside the organization to judge which individuals and components are accomplishing their goals.

Some writers have observed that public and nonprofit organizations seem to be reluctant to be judged on a performance standard, For example, Barnhill and Shapiro, after a review of the marketing programs of Canada Post and the Northern Native Cooperative Program, note that some managers claim that they are doing their best given the difficult environmental conditions faced.[5] Consequently, neither performance deficiencies nor failure to achieve targeted objectives should be held against them, provided that they made a good effort. At an operational level, the fund-raising staff of Stanford University's Annual Fund Program reacted to targets for average gift levels and participation rates in a similar manner.[6] Some staff members felt that such targets were difficult to set and relate to because, in any event, they would be trying their hardest to maximize the total dollar value of donations.

In examining a set of organizational objectives we look for them to be:

- Important to the organization.
- Hierarchical (prioritized).
- Attainable (within the organization's capability),
- Internally consistent.
- Measurable or quantifiable.

Goals that do not meet these criteria usually do not provide guidance for managerial decision making or a target for performance measurement. These difficulties can be illustrated by examining the goals for a performing-arts series, as stated by the director of the office of public events at an institution near New Orleans that we'll call Mardi Gras University.

Mr. Williams, the director, had set a number of objectives for the program, although he had not weighted them in terms of importance. Among these, Mr. Williams included the following.

- Present a self-supporting series of top-quality professional performing events.
- Keep prices as low as possible in order to make performances widely accessible.
- Augment academic offerings in the theory and practice of the arts.
- Contribute positively to the extracurricular educational experience of the Mardi Gras students.
- Contribute to the university's position within the New Orleans community as a cultural and intellectual resource.
- Contribute to Mardi Gras's national and international prestige by presenting a program qualitatively commensurate with other offerings of the university.
- Help solidify the importance of the arts in social development and, it is hoped, thereby ensure the future of the arts.[7]

As is readily apparent, this listing of unordered goals does not meet the five criteria we just discussed. For example, if Williams attempts to build a student audience, he sacrifices his self-sufficiency goals because students pay less than community residents for tickets. Or more avant garde offerings may be of particular interest to students majoring in the arts, but not the community in general. Self-sufficiency may not be a viable goal, and it is doubtful that much can be done, by this series, "to help solidify the importance of the arts in social development." The reader can surely add other failings to this list of goals.

A well-conceived set of goals provides a means for uniting an organization toward the achievement of a common purpose. The goals for individuals and subunits in the organization provide direction for each component and a means for measuring achievement of desired performance.

Strategy

Simply stated, strategy is the plan by which the organization attempts to reach its objectives. Just as objectives are set for different units of an organization, so are strategies set at different levels. There can be an organizational strategy, a service strategy, a financial strategy, a market strategy, and so forth. In most cases, there are alternative ways to reach an objective. The strategy is the chosen way; it indicates the short-term and long-term actions that need to be taken. In other words, if the objectives specify *what* is to be accomplished, the strategy specifies *how*.

Vancil suggests that there are two main tests of a strategy.[8] First, of course, is whether the strategy is right for the organization. To answer that question, we must examine environmental forces, market opportunities, and organizational capabilities all within the context of organizational mission and societal expectations. Later in this chapter, we turn to the issue of strategy formulation and these criteria of validity. Vancil's second test of a strategy is whether the strategy is constructed so that it facilitates the management process of the organization by (1) providing operational guidance, (2) generating personal commitment, and (3) anticipating change.

ORGANIZATIONAL STRATEGY

Organizational strategy, like strategy at all levels, is concerned with the allocation of limited resources. Similarly, the organizational strategy must be directed toward achieving organizational goals; further, the chosen strategy depends on both the external environment the organization confronts and its own strengths and weaknesses. In choosing a strategy at this level, an organization must be particularly sensitive to societal expectations for it. Although businesses must conform to societal norms, public and nonprofit organizations are more likely to depend on public goodwill and benefaction and to be perceived as fulfilling a public purpose. As we have indicated, nonfinancial objectives are more important here.

Organizational strategy differs from all other levels of strategy because the focus is on the organization as a whole. It concerns all functions and activities of the organization and encompasses strategies and objectives at subordinate levels; organizational strategy is the ultimate statement of the organization's ability to match its capabilities and resources to the opportunities and risks in the external environment to reach organizational goals. In particular, organizational strategy focuses on deciding where to *invest* organizational resources and the level of resources to commit to each major activity.

There are, of course, many ways to classify the activities of an organization. We find it particularly useful to specify activities in terms of the products—be they goods, services, or social-change programs—offered and markets in which the organization participates. Of course, at the organizational level, both products and markets need to be defined broadly enough to be worthy of senior management attention while still possessing enough internal linkages to be managed and analyzed as a unit. For private corporations, such a grouping is sometimes termed a *strategic business unit* (SBU), but we prefer the more generic term *strategic management unit* (SMU). As we will discuss shortly, an important insight into organizational strategy is obtained by viewing the organization as a portfolio of SMUs, each of which can be managed to achieve different objectives. The SMUs in combination then meet the organizational objective.

An important objective for many organizations is growth. The desire for growth is driven by the dynamics of the external environment as well as the natural predilection of management to achieve more. Indeed, aside from some political appointees who are specifically chosen to preside over the "orderly disbandment" of an agency, rare would be the senior management not concerned with growth. A very useful organizing framework for examining growth opportunities is the product market-growth matrix noted by Ansoff and others.[9] We begin our discussion of organizational strategy by looking at the product-market matrix (Figure 4.1).

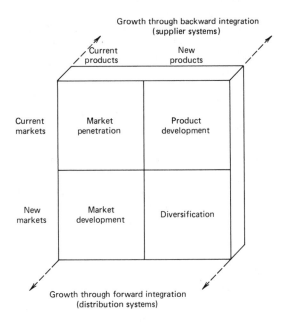

Figure 4.1   Product/Market/Integration Growth Matrix. (*Source:* Adapted and expanded from Ansoff, and Johnson and Jones, as in reference 9.)

Product-Market Growth Matrix

The product-market growth matrix is a useful way to identify and summarize the growth alternatives facing an organization. It indicates five discrete alternatives, but finer gradations can be made. The five major alternatives are the following.

1. Market penetration.
2. Product development.
3. Market development.
4. Diversification.
5. Integrative growth.

We will examine these alternatives in the context of the 4-H clubs of Alberta, Canada, whose position in 1979 can be briefly described as follows.[10]

The 9768 4-H members in 561 4-H clubs throughout the province are almost all between 10 and 19 years old. Fifty-eight percent of 4-H members are female, and 80 percent are from "rural farm communities." The 4-H clubs attract 18 percent of rural farm youth, 2 percent of rural nonfarm youth, and 17 percent of urban youth in Alberta. Total membership has declined 15 percent from the peak achieved in 1977 despite a continuing increase in Alberta's youth population.

   The overall mission of 4-H is to develop the abilities of rural youth so that they will realize their personal potential and act as responsible members of society. The means to achieve this mission are expressed in the 4-H motto, "Learn to Do by Doing." Members complete projects in any of 30 areas, including swine, beef, grain, crops, clothing, photography, home design, and small engines. The three most popular projects were beef (47 percent of all enrollments), light horse (17 percent), and clothing (17 percent). No other project had more than 5 percent enrollment. Activities included weekly club meetings, participation in local, provincial, and national fairs, and completion of projects.

Market penetration involves seeking increased use of the organization's current goods and services by the same types of users to whom it currently appeals. In the case of 4-H, a penetration strategy might focus on persuading current members to participate in more projects or to remain members for a longer period of time. At present, although the age restrictions allow a youth to belong for more than 10 years, the average tenure is just under 3 years. Alternatively, a penetration strategy could focus on trying to attract more rural farm youths, the major current market, to join in the current list of projects. With a penetration of less than 20 percent, there still appears to be room for growth here. Because the long-term projection for rural farm youth is declining numbers, however, this approach may not be sustainable.

Product development focuses on growth achieved through adding new products that appeal to the market segments currently being served. This strategy has been continually used by the 4-H in response to changing needs. Fifteen of the 30 projects available in 1979 were introduced in the 1970s, but none of these projects accounted for as much as 5 percent of the total project enrollment. The light-horse project introduced in 1966 accounts for 17 percent of enrollment, however, and is the second most popular project.

Market development consists of offering the same products, services, and programs to new markets. The basis for such an expansion is often geographic. An organization founded in one local or regional area, achieving success with its programs in that geographic market, may try to expand to adjacent markets or other areas with similar needs. The first 4-H clubs were begun in rural Manitoba in 1913, and their early success led to the formation of the first 4-H club in Alberta in 1917. In the more contemporary time frame, 4-H has divided Alberta into seven regions and found that its penetration of the youth population, excluding that in large cities, varies from 4 to 9 percent. One approach to expansion is to increase participation in the regions with lower enrollment rates.

Market development is not confined to "near-identical" populations. Sometimes an organization may identify other markets that will find its current services attractive with only minor modifications. For the 4-H clubs, the obvious new market to examine is rural nonfarm youth. The definition of rural includes all people living in communities with fewer than 1000 people. At present, only 2 percent of rural nonfarm youths belong to 4-H, yet it would seem that many of the existing 4-H programs and the 4-H philosophy would appeal to these youths. Furthermore, the rural nonfarm population in Alberta is growing.

Diversification refers to growth strategies that encompasses both new markets and new products for the organization. In examining diversification strategies, however, an organization should look for a common thread linking the diversification to the resources and capabilities of the organization.

For the 4-H clubs, a particularly interesting opportunity is to develop programs for urban youths, who currently account for less than 2 percent of membership. Because 4-H fulfills a variety of functions aimed at personal and social development through positive learning-by-doing experiences, targeting urban youth appears to be viable. This is the fastest growing segment of the Alberta population, because of the influx of people from other parts of Canada and the movement of people off the farms. Many of the programs directed toward farm children would not be viable, of course, but the increasing concern of the general population with the environment and ecology suggests that many 4-H programs could be adapted for city dwellers.

Integrative growth occurs when an organization expands by carrying out activities that either precede or follow the delivery of its current services. We discuss this notion in Chapter 12, "Distribution and Delivery Systems," where we examine how some hospitals are coping with changing health needs and practices by constructing medical offices adjacent to their premises, adding freestanding emergency rooms, and operating emergency air and land transportation systems. Backward integration occurs when an organization seeks greater control over its "supply systems." For example, a ballet company may open a school in order to ensure the availability of young dancers familiar with its choreography. Forward integration occurs when an organization develops increased control over its "distribution system" for delivering goods and services to its users. When a ballet company moves from renting space on an occasional basis in several halls to owning and operating its own auditorium, it can be said to be following forward integrative growth. Generally, the motivation behind integrative growth is to increase efficiency or control. However, integrative growth often exposes the organization to the risk and challenge of managing operations unlike its basic ones.

The product market-growth matrix is a systematic method of identifying growth opportunities. It would be a mistake, however, to pursue only the most individually attractive strategies. They have to be put into a larger context, ensuring synergy between current and future operations.

Portfolio Strategies

In the 1970s, the concept of portfolio management as an aid to making strategic resource allocation decisions gained increasing popularity (see the accompanying box, "Portfolio Analysis"). The underlying notions are quite straightforward. First, the organization should be subdivided into what we have called SMUs. Second, the institution should evaluate each of its SMUs based on the opportunities present in the markets it participates in and how effective a competitor the SMU is or can become. Third, based on this evaluation, the organization can decide how much of its resources should be devoted to that SMU.

As will be discussed in Chapter 9, "Product Offerings," some SMUs in nonbusiness organizations can be classified as net generators of resources and others as net consumers of resources; the parent organization's task thus becomes one of deciding on an appropriate balance between resource-generating and resource-using SMUs. At the most obvious level, governments run lotteries primarily to raise money that can be used to finance other programs. It has been claimed that universities have been ready to increase the size of their business and law schools not only because of the increasing demand for this type of education, but also because these academic areas usually generate more funds than they utilize; unlike the physical and biological sciences, for example, expensive laboratory equipment is generally not needed for research and teaching in business and law.

An organizational strategy specifies the resource allocations to be made to major subunits, SMUs, or product markets. A portfolio perspective often provides a useful framework for considering financial options by locating SMUs or products on the two dimensions of attractiveness of markets and strength of competitive position. In Chapter 9, "Product Offerings," we will show how this approach can be modified for public and nonprofit organizations to help managers evaluate the trade-offs between product profitability and goodness of fit with the institutional mission.

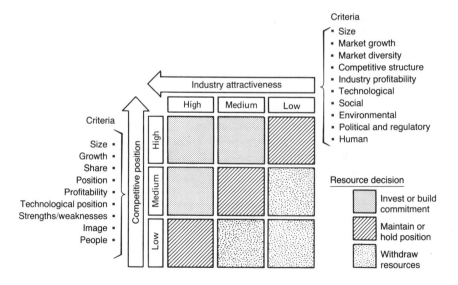

Figure 4.2 Competitive Position/Industry Attractiveness Matrix

PORTFOLIO ANALYSIS

Portfolio analysis is a technique for graphically arranging organizational subunits along two dimensions, the overall attractiveness of the subunit's market, and the relative strength of the subunit in the market. The categorization of the organization along these two dimensions has implications for resource allocation and aids in deciding whether to invest, maintain, or withdraw resources from a subunit.

In one version of the portfolio matrix, growth represents industry attractiveness and market share, the relative strength of the organization or product. Growth and share are the main dimension because, presumably, there is more opportunity to enhance an organization's position in a growth market, and the greater the subunit's relative share, the better it is already positioned to take advantage of opportunities.

Another portfolio approach, often divided into a three-by-three matrix, uses two more broadly defined or composite dimensions of market attractiveness and strength or competitive position of the unit. Each of these dimensions is based on a set of criteria such as those illustrated in Figure 4.2. A subunit's location in the matrix depends on its evaluation on these subcriteria and how they are combined to form the two overall axes. The location then suggests whether the appropriate resource-allocation strategy is to invest resources to improve or hold a position, to maintain resources at current levels to hold a position, or to harvest or withdraw resources. As with the growth/share matrix, the organization can attempt to utilize these results to offset resource generation and resource consumption in order to achieve overall portfolio balance and to ensure a mix of mature and developing units.

As compared to the growth/share matrix, the market-attraction/unit-strength matrix allows for a fuller range of factors to be taken into account at the price of requiring more information, and perhaps more subjectivity as well. As with the growth/share matrix, an accurate definition of the relevant market must be made. Furthermore, management must be satisfied that the indicated investment strategy is appropriate and the particular subunit is not an exception.

We have taken a static look at an organization's own portfolio. It is often useful to examine past and future as well as present portfolios for the organization and competitors. Furthermore, portfolio analysis can be used to portray the outcome and balance that will ensue if different investment strategies are pursued and realized.

The investment alternatives are summarized in Figure 4.2. The broad strategic options are to invest, maintain, or withdraw resources, but the amount of resources required also needs to be specified. Of course, at the subunit level, the strategic issue is how to use those resources. Advice to invest or maintain an SMU is not sufficient in itself, obviously, to guide managerial action. In allocating resources and developing an organizational strategy the organization must do more than consider each SMU individually; it also must examine the interdependencies or interrelationships among the SMUs. Only at the organizational level can these interrelationships be fully examined, although the strategies formulated at the SMU level can and should recognize important interdependencies. Moreover, at the organizational level, individual strategies must be examined to see if they provide a coherent whole. Do the strategies fit together in a way that provides a total strategy that meets organizational objectives while utilizing the unique abilities and general capabilities of the organization to meet environmental opportunities and challenges? The success of an organizational strategy depends on the subunit strategies it encompasses. Although the strategies to pursue are chosen and the level of resource commitment is made at the organizational level, the quality of subunit strategies is critical. We now turn to this area.

SUBUNIT STRATEGY

The distinguishing characteristic of subunit strategy is its focus on how the unit intends to compete or participate in a market or set of markets. Subunit strategy is distinctly concerned with identifying the critical factors necessary for success in a market and then choosing the few select ones in which the organization will excel. The key success factors can be based on abilities in marketing, operations, finance, management, or other areas. Marketing ability is not always the key factor, but market analysis is always required to identify the key factors. Subunit strategy not only identifies and defines the key success factors, but also specifies how the subunit will be managed and coordinated so that success can be achieved. Of course, one aspect of this process—as with strategy at any level—is to allocate resources among the components of the subunit. Finally, the subunit strategy sets objectives and provides strategic guidance for functional areas and other components of the subunit. In this way, functional-area activities can be planned to meet the requirements for strategic success.

In choosing a subunit strategy, the following steps should be taken.[11]

1. Select opportunities and threats to examine carefully.
2. Identify success factors and isolate critical success factors.
3. Evaluate organization's ability as compared to that of others.
4. Develop strategic thrusts.
5. Evaluate strategies.

We will examine each of these five steps in turn.

Opportunities and Threats

Opportunities and threats can arise from either the external environment or the internal capabilities. Earlier in this chapter, we showed how the product market growth matrix can be used to generate opportunities. Elsewhere in this book we discuss approaches to analyzing external environments as well as internal strengths and weaknesses.

Often an organization can generate more opportunities than it is capable of handling. It needs to select those it will analyze carefully. Of course, some "opportunities" may be forced on the organization by the basic nature of its mission. For example, it would be difficult to imagine the 4-H clubs deciding not to offer programs for farm youths. Instead, 4-H must pursue strategies that allow it to continue to dominate the farm youth segment. More generally, however, organizations need to identify the most promising opportunities and the most significant threats. Those that meet these tests should be examined more carefully.

Sometimes, an environmental analysis will indicate that several different factors all point to the same opportunity. Such a condition is important. For example, the concentration of 4-H clubs on farm youth is threatened not only by the decrease in farm population itself, but also by the decline in the number of family farms, the mechanization of tasks, and the rise in popularity of Girl Scouts and Boy Scouts. Live professional performing arts in smaller cities are threatened not only by rising labor costs and televised events, but also by the availability of video cassette tapes, videodisks, and cable television.

In examining opportunities, the question of timing can be important. Opportunities, even when long-term strategy is involved, are often available for only a short period of time. Some writers use the phrase *strategic window* to denote the time when an opportunity is available. For example, in British Columbia, forestry companies have traditionally been allowed to log pretty much where they want to. Recently, however, native groups have challenged in court the right of logging outfits to harvest timber in areas that fall within aboriginal land claims. A ban on logging has been imposed on some disputed lands. Environmentalists have taken advantage of some of these bans—and the publicity surrounding them—to press the federal government to declare areas with particular environmental significance national parks. The environmentalists believe that if they fail to have these areas protected by park status before the ban is lifted and logging proceeds, the environmental damage will be irreversible.

Recognizing—or better, anticipating—strategic windows is important. Once the time is up, the opportunity is gone. Fortunately, they often present themselves quite plainly. For instance, a charitable foundation may offer a performing arts organization a "challenging grant." If the arts group undertakes a major fund-raising drive and raises the targeted amount, the foundation will match or double the contribution. The entire sum is deposited to the group's endowment fund, building long-term financial stability.

Critical Success Factors

For each major opportunity identified at the previous stage, what does it take to succeed? For each major threat, what does it take to reduce or eliminate that threat? The answers to these questions indicate the critical success factors in a market for any participant. After identifying the key success factors, the organization must ask whether it has or can obtain the requisite factors and how it stands in this regard as compared to current or potential competitors. The key success factors can arise in a number of areas.

Operations and Production. What special operations, abilities, or production capabilities are required to participate successfully? If a medical center wishes to become an international center for cardiac treatment, millions of dollars of equipment and a large staff of outstanding medical personnel are required. A teaching facility is probably necessary as well. On the other hand, the requirements for becoming an obstetrical center are not nearly as demanding and are likely to be possessed by many hospitals.

Political and Regulatory. At times, particularly in the public and nonprofit sector, political and regulatory factors may be critical for success. The most obvious, of course, is the grant of monopoly status for offering a particular good or service. As we discuss elsewhere in the book, such monopoly status can be ephermeral.

Conceive and Design. Are any special research or creative talents required to compete or participate in a market?

Financial. Some opportunities require the ability either to invest a large amount of money or to wait a long time for a return on the investment made. An organization must identify the financial requirements of participation in any market and determine whether these are critical for success. A university would probably find that building a successful medical school is a major financial challenge that will divert a large portion of the organizational resources, but that building a business school is not nearly as severe a financial challenge. (On the other hand, there may be more of a shortage of faculty at business schools than at medical schools.)

Management. Some opportunities may demand difficult management skills that are in short supply. Organizations advocating social causes that run counter to those of entrenched interests must ask themselves if they have the ability to compete in all areas. The Sierra Club, which has been successful in protecting a number of geographic areas, has also had some notable failures.

Fund Raising. When products either are not sold for money or are sold below cost, a requirement for success may be the ability to raise funds for that activity. If the opportunity consumes a large amount of resources, fund-raising potential needs to be considered. Some opportunities have more fund-raising appeal than others. Universities often find, for example, that research programs in health-related fields are easier to fund than programs in the social sciences. Fund-raising requirements may be subsumed under the financial-success factors, but it is sometimes necessary to recognize the marketability on the resource-attraction side of different programs.

Marketing. Success factors in the area of marketing are closely linked to past, current, and future customer and market characteristics. As we stress throughout this book, understanding consumer needs and competitive offerings is vital.

Critical marketing success factors can arise in many areas, and throughout this book we discuss in depth the different functional areas of marketing and their importance. It is easy to generate a long list of success factors. The difficult management tasks in this regard, however, are (1) to ensure that all the critical success factors are identified and (2) to screen the list carefully so that only the few truly critical factors are specified.

Evaluate Strengths and Weaknesses

Once the critical success factors are identified, the organization must evaluate its capabilities to meet those requirements as compared to that of present and potential competitors. In doing this analysis, the organization needs to be objective in assessing both its own and competitors' capabilities. It is easy, and perhaps natural, to overstate the abilities of one's own organization and underestimate those of competitors. To do so is dangerous. Likewise, in the face of a seemingly attractive opportunity, the temptation to do only a superficial analysis must be avoided.

A review of strengths and weaknesses should indicate the ability to meet the critical success factors. If the organization is weak in many of the relevant factors, the wisdom of pursuing the opportunity should be questioned. Even so, the opportunity may still be worthwhile, either because the rewards are so great, in terms of organizational objectives, as compared to the risks, or because no competitor appears to be better positioned. Alternatively, the organization may believe that it has the creativity necessary to meet the challenge. Of course, in the case of threats, failure to respond may mean the loss of position in a market.

In examining critical success factors, an organization may identify new opportunities. These should be carefully considered as well. At times, the combination of several closely linked opportunities may justify a strategic thrust that otherwise would not be worthwhile.

Develop Strategic Thrusts

At this stage, the organization should be ready to specify the strategy it will use to take advantage of the opportunities and to meet the challenges it faces. For each, it will have identified the critical factors for success. Now it must decide how it will compete. How can the organization combine its distinctive competencies and internal skills and resources to obtain a long-term differential advantage to meet the requirements of specific product-market opportunities?

Within each product market, the organization looks for strategies that build on its strengths and either correct or limit the impact of its organizational weaknesses.

In appraising organizational strengths, it should be recognized that strength is usually based on accumulated experience and substantial success. Occasional flashes of brilliance are rarely dependable in the long-run, and more than a year or so of experience is usually required before a strength can be reliably dependable. In general, organizations will have different internal strengths and capabilities. Some may have greater financial resources, others more political clout, still others more marketing skills, and so on. The strategic issue is to determine whether these internal differences can become important in the product-market opportunities the organization chooses to pursue.

> Because of the strategic relevance of organizational strengths and weaknesses, it is always worthwhile for an organization to ponder what distinctive skills and capabilities it can bring to bear that will allow it to draw business away from rival organizations. Some organizations excel in manufacturing a "quality product," others in creative approaches to marketing, still others in innovation and new product development. An organization's distinctive competence is thus more than just what it can do—it is what it can do especially well as compared to rival competitors. The importance of distinctive competence to strategy rests with the unique capability it gives an organization in developing a comparative advantage in the marketplace.
>
> Typically, a key element in successful business strategy formulation is the ability to build into the strategic plan a product-market approach that will set the organization apart from others and give it some kind of strategic advantage. Generally, this means (1) following a different course from rival firms, (2) conceiving a plan which will have quite different (and more favorable) consequences for one's own organization than for competitors, and (3) making it hard for other organizations to imitate the strategy should it succeed. Obviously enough, these guidelines are easier to follow when an organization has some kind of distinctive competence around which to build its strategy. It is always easier to develop strategic advantage in a market where the success requirements correspond to the organization's distinctive competence, where other organizations do not have these competences, and where potential rivals are not able to attain these competences except at high cost and/or over an extended period of time. But if an organization has no particular distinctive competence on which to try to capitalize, the next best bet is to focus on ways to exploit existing differences between the organization and those of its competitors.[12]

Dimensions of Strategy. It would be convenient if we could prepare a short list of generic strategies and suggest that all the manager has to do is choose the most appropriate one. While we can review possible bases for strategy, strategy formulation is a creative process; no analyst can really claim to offer a complete list of strategy types.

Porter's book on *Competitive Strategy* suggests that there are three potentially successful strategic approaches: (1) overall cost leadership, (2) differentiation of goods and services offered by the organization, and (3) focus on a particular user group, geographic market, or portion of the product line.[13] As is readily apparent, the options of differentiation and focus can take on many forms and overlap as well. Indeed, the next question to ask is what are the bases for a differentiation or focus strategy. Porter provides a listing of some of the major strategic options, which we have adapted for a public and nonprofit setting.[14]

- *Specialization*. The degree to which effort is focused in terms of the diversity of services offered, the target customer segments, and geographic markets served.

- *Service level*. Reliability of service, degree of individual attention and adaptability to individual needs, uniformity of service over place and time.

- *Product quality*. Level of quality, in terms of raw materials, specifications, adherance to tolerances, features, and so on.

- *Technological leadership*. The degree of technological leadership versus following or imitation. A technological leader may (deliberately) not produce the highest-quality product in the market; quality and technological leadership do not necessarily go together.

- *Ancillary services*. The degree of ancillary services provided, such as financial aid, an in-house service network, and so forth.

- *Organization identification*. The degree to which it seeks organization identification instead of focusing on the generic product. The March of Dimes probably has greater organizational identification than does the American Heart Association.

- *Push versus pull*. The degree to which it seeks to develop a standing with the ultimate customer directly versus using distribution channels in support of a product.

- *Channel selection*. The choice of distribution channels ranging from owned channels, to specialty outlets, to broad-line outlets.

- *Vertical integration*. The extent of value added as reflected in the level of forward and backward integration adopted.

- *Cost position*. The extent to which it seeks the low-cost position in operations through investment in cost-minimizing facilities and equipment.

- *Price policy*. Its relative price position in the market. Price position will usually be related to such other variables as cost position and product quality, but price is a distinct strategic variable that must be treated separately.

- *Relationship of subunit with parent organization*. Requirements on the behavior of the unit on the relationship between a unit and its parent.

■ *Relationship with national or local government.* A public organization can be an agency of the executive or legislative branch at several levels of government or be semiautonomous. The nature of the relationship with government will influence the objectives with which the organization is managed, the resources available to it, and perhaps the future of some operations or functions that it shares with other units.

As is readily apparent, many of these strategic options depend on marketing. Later chapters in this book explore in detail the development of these strategic options. Of course, not all these options apply in every situation, and the manager must determine which are applicable and how to position the organization on the selected dimensions. Even casual observation shows that organizations differ widely in their choices. Finally, it should be noted that these dimensions are often interrelated, so an organization with a low-price policy often has a low-cost position as well, but a reliable service policy may accompany a variety of pricing policies.

Evaluating Subunit Strategies

Subunit strategies should be evaluated on at least three sets of criteria: (1) meeting the objectives set, (2) degree of risk involved as compared to the desirability of the likely outcomes, and (3) external and internal consistency. Economic analysis, of course, is a part of the evaluation, as it is at all levels of strategy.

The first criterion is whether the specified strategy *meets the objectives*. It is often useful to divide the objectives into those that are critical and those that are desirable. If a strategy cannot meet the critical objectives, it should be eliminated. For example, if a city is committed to providing mobility for handicapped citizens, among its options might be a personalized taxi service, specially equipped buses, and a rail rapid-transit system. If some of the rail stations are on raised platforms without elevators, however, that option alone would not meet the critical objectives. In practice, of course, such obvious situations would probably not develop; critical objectives sometimes serve to eliminate strategies that are otherwise attractive.

Often a strategic option will meet some but not all of the desirable objectives and do so at varying levels above or below the specified standard. Assuming that no dominant strategy meets all the objectives, the different objectives need to be traded off against one another. Often the subunit will negotiate with its senior management to help determine which objectives are more important. Frequently, the subunit will have generated several alternatives, none of which achieve all the objectives. Because resources are usually limited, this is a typical management problem and can be resolved by attempting to generate new options, by changing some objectives, or by combining both approaches.

Strategic decisions, by their very nature, involve *risk*. Rarely is the outcome of an alternative certain, given the dynamic competitive environment of most real-world organizations. The organization must decide how much risk it is willing to take and how much it will allow for each of its subunits. Organizations that are "risk-averters" lean toward strategies where external threats are minimal and internal resources are clearly ample. Such organizations tend to avoid major financial commitments and usually do not pioneer new services, technologies, or markets. However, it must be noted that the pace of change in some fields is so great that such conservative strategies become risky. As the example of the American Lung Association at the start of the chapter illustrates, continuing old practices can result in organizational decline.

As an organization develops greater tolerance for risk, its strategies tend to become more innovative and opportunistic, but the pitfalls of risk are real and should not be overlooked.

Given the degree of public scrutiny invoked in public and nonprofit organizations, managers in this sector may be less inclined to be risk takers than their business counterparts. Moreover, the internal reward structure in the private sector, where a manager's remuneration can be based on the profitability of the strategies designed and implemented, may reinforce a manager's inclination to take risks.

Risk and uncertainty have two additional major implications for evaluating the strategy. A strategy should contain contingency plans in case important assumptions prove invalid or results are not achieved for other reasons. Second, a strategy may be tested for *robustness*—that is, how much impact will changes in major assumptions have on the attainment of objectives. For example, consider a performing-arts organization committed to expanding its season in order to broaden its audience and give its artists a full year's work. Its alternatives are to build a performing-arts center in a summer resort area or to sign a long-term contract to tour several such existing centers. While the first alternative is more desirable if the economy in general is strong and the chosen tourist area prospers, the second strategy will meet the organizational objectives under a variety of environmental outcomes. Consequently, the second strategy is more robust.

Finally, strategies need to be reviewed for their *internal and external consistency*. Six major pitfalls can result in the failure of strategies (see Table 4.1). The first pitfall is basing strategy on faulty or erroneous assumptions. As we stress, strategy formulation requires careful analysis, but the organization must be careful of both its explicit and tacit assumptions. For example, many organizations concerned with changing people's health-related behavior, such as physical fitness, blood-pressure control, and medical checkup, start by assuming that health is a highly salient issue to most people. Behaviors that have only a long-term benefit appear to be neglected by many people, however. While strategy cannot avoid assumptions about the future that may turn out not to hold, assumptions about the past and present should be valid.

The second pitfall in strategy is failing to anticipate the competitor's response. At times, organizations become overconfident and assume that while they are making changes, their competitors are not. Or that the competitors, when challenged, will not respond actively. Strategic choice often involves deciding which competitors will be challenged, avoiding others, and anticipating competitive response.

Table 4.1 Strategic Pitfalls

---

1. Using faulty or erroneous assumptions
2. Not anticipating competitive response
3. Not anticipating response of internal and external publics
4. Underestimating deviation from the past
5. Attempting too much too soon
6. Mismatching human resources and strategy

Source. Adapted from William E. Rothschild, *Putting It All Together,* New York: AMACOM, 1976, pp. 202–214.

The third pitfall, and of particular concern to public and nonprofit organizations, is not anticipating the reaction of concerned internal and external publics. The public visibility of nonbusiness organizations and the many groups concerned with such organizations can intensify the reaction to strategic change, as the following example illustrates.

> Suppose a national organization decides to become more selective in the groups it serves or begins to concentrate on a specific geographic region to the exclusion of others. In a sense this is what many Catholic religious orders did when they recognized that they couldn't staff all of their schools. Thus, they chose to close some schools and to concentrate their declining resources on others.
>
> Regardless of the orders' reasons and whether their decisions were correct, many stakeholders became upset and reacted negatively. Certainly parents with children in the affected schools became unhappy. This is always the case with a retrenchment strategy. But other stakeholders—investors of two types—were also disturbed. The first group included those who contributed to the schools and the Church, some of whom stopped giving. The second group consisted of the banks and lending institutions involved, which were concerned because empty buildings meant further financial drains on already declining assets. The members of the religious orders also were affected and responded in various ways, some leaving the order and some leaving teaching entirely. And not only did the orders lose those members but, because of the adverse publicity, [they] also found it difficult to attract new members [15]

A fourth pitfall is underestimating the deviation from the past—a real challenge to the objectives of the organization. Quite often strategic statements have bright, rosy projections of what will be accomplished a short time into the future. Is this realistic? A simple technique called *gap analysis* is useful here. In gap analysis, an organization projects the future assuming it will continue its current programs and then measures the size of the gap between its objectives and the present trend. Then the organization examines the size of the gap and decides if the specific strategies designed to close that gap have a realistic chance of being successful.

Closely related to the preceding danger is the fifth pitfall of attempting too much too soon. Most readers are probably familiar with organizations that, after a period of stagnation, burst forth with a broad range of new services that overwhelm the organization's capacity to serve. New managements, in particular, must be careful to ensure that the organization can deliver on its promises.

The final pitfall is mismatching human resources and strategy. It is useful to ask, "What kinds of people are required to implement this strategy, and are they available?" This question is particularly important for organizations that depend on volunteers, but this pitfall applies to paid employees as well. In the case of volunteers, an organization may not be able to recruit people to carry out unpleasant tasks. Or some health centers have had difficulty in recruiting a medical staff that delegates traditional activities of doctors to paraprofessionals.

Once a subunit strategy is favorably evaluated and adopted, it provides a guide to how a subunit will utilize its resources to achieve its set objectives. Organizational strategy both sets the objectives for subunits and is dependent on the subunits for alternatives. Thus, as at other levels, we should expect strategic formulation to be a cyclic process involving interaction at both senior and junior levels. In the next section, we examine briefly the functional area strategies that support the subunit strategy.

POSITIONING STRATEGY

Most organizations and their products have positions. You can see this by thinking about such questions as: "What does the Red Cross mean to you?" "Or the FBI and the CIA?" "The March of Dimes?" "Amtrak's Metroliner service between Washington, D.C., and New York?" The images or positions generated in the minds of people can be based on perceptions of physical and performance attributes—such as the Red Cross's dominant position as the primary disaster-relief agency, derived from its long record of successful service in this area. Other factors can be important in establishing a position as well. For example, some colleges appear to have images based primarily on the prowess of their football and basketball teams, not on the quality or type of education provided. Positions may be based primarily on contrast with other services; some observers suggest that the best way to categorize public television in the United States is not by its programming but by its lack of commercials.[16]

The positioning of an organization and its products should be the result of a carefully planned program. Consider, for example, the introduction of Mailgrams, which are both much faster than letters and cheaper than telegrams. A choice had to be made as to whether a Mailgram should be positioned as a high-speed letter or a low-cost telegram. After market testing, the Mailgram position of low-cost telegram was chosen because it generated greater understanding and volume.[17]

Sometimes positions are unplanned; such unplanned positions are often undesirable. Some transit agencies have found themselves positioned by the public as unreliable, inexpensive providers of transportation for people who cannot afford cars. Even if such a position is not supported in fact, the agency can be saddled with an unfortunate position that limits both its ridership and its tax support by voters. Establishing a more favorable position in the public's mind is more difficult when an organization starts with a negative image.

Of course, an organization that does not consciously seek to establish a position for itself may find that it holds a position so vague that no one really knows what it is particularly good at. Such an organization can easily become no one's first choice for any task. Finally, some organizations (or products) have no position because no one has ever heard of them.

Positioning strategies involve (1) selection of target market segments on which to concentrate, (2) identification of the positions held by competitive offerings in the relevant markets, and (3) choice of a position that is (currently or potentially) important to the relevant markets. Positioning plays a critical role in the formulation of marketing strategy. It brings together market analysis, internal analysis of organizational resources and constraints, and competitive analysis. Once chosen, a positioning strategy forms the framework on which to build and coordinate the elements of the marketing mix. The product, pricing, and distribution elements of the marketing program create the chosen position, while communication efforts convey this position to the relevant target market.

Positioning has three major uses in organizational and product management: (1) as a diagnostic tool for defining and understanding the relationship between products and markets, (2) as an aid in designing and managing the product line, and (3) as a means to help formulate communication and other marketing-mix programs to preempt (or respond to) competitive actions and to meet the needs of targeted market segments. After reviewing these uses, we will suggest a procedure for choosing a positioning strategy to adopt.

Managerial Uses

Diagnosis. A positioning analysis helps an organization to understand how it and its products are serving market needs. In particular, positioning analysis allows an organization to see how it is perceived relative to the competition and to determine how well it is meeting the demands of the market. At times an organization may be serving a market well, but so are many competitors. To illustrate, one hospital found that although it was perceived as a good provider of maternity services, so were several other competitors. There did not appear to be an opportunity to expand use of the hospital services in this area.

In other cases, users may not be aware that the organization competes in a given market. The hospital just mentioned was thought to offer only limited emergency-room services. Consequently, it was not thought of as a primary source of emergency medical care, despite having a fine, fully staffed emergency room. If the hospital wanted to establish a position in this market, it would have to undertake a marketing communication program, so that consumer perceptions would match the organizational reality.

The last example illustrates another important point. At times, managers may have a biased view of the market positions held by their organization. For example, hospital personnel know of the quality of the emergency-room facilities and may therefore believe that people are aware of them. Market research is required to determine whether management's perception is accurate.

It is frequently useful to illustrate a positioning strategy graphically. To do this, a map of a market is drawn. Unlike an ordinary highway map, a product or market map may have more than two dimensions, although it is often necessary to use only two or three dimensions when displaying a map pictorially. The location of each product or organization on a map is based on how it and other entities are perceived by customers. The boxed material on perceptual maps shows one map for a transit system.

Some organizations may find from a positioning study that they are not serving the needs of the market at all. For example, one university in the eastern United States offered elective courses for an MBA program in the late afternoon. The underlying notion was that this timing could satisfy both full-time day students and part-time employed students, but the outcome was perverse. The full-time students saw the school as positioning itself away from their needs, and part-time students did not perceive this program as being as conveniently scheduled as other evening MBA programs.

An understanding of how an organization meets market needs as compared to the competition can help in forecasting demand for its services. In general terms, better-targeted positions lead to larger market shares.

Product-Line Management. Positioning analysis can help an organization identify opportunities in the marketplace for *introducing* new products, *redesigning* existing ones, and *eliminating* products that do not satisfy consumer needs or face very strong competition. Positioning's use in product-line management follows from its use as a diagnostic tool. For example, a positioning analysis that leads to a better understanding of a market will also help suggest, in the introduction of new products, the target segments and product attributes to emphasize as compared to the competition. In redesigning or repositioning existing products, similar issues arise. Should the organization appeal to the same segments that are currently served or to different ones? What attributes should be added, dropped, or modified? In considering whether or not to reposition a service, an organization should be careful not to make a change because of a short-term fluctuation in consumer needs or competitive activities. Positioning provides long-term direction, and at times success can come from better exploiting an existing position than from attempting to change a position.

PERCEPTUAL MAPS

Transit

Perceptual maps represent the positions of organizations and/or their products on a set of evaluative dimensions. The maps are based on people's perceptions of products, but eventually the manager must relate these perceptual characteristics to product features and performance dimensions. Figure 4.3 shows a three-dimensional map of consumer perceptions of transportation services. Speed and convenience reflect the ability of a mode of travel to provide on-time service that gets consumers quickly to their destinations with no long wait, is available when needed, and allows consumers to come and go as they wish. Ease of travel includes lack of problems in bad weather, little effort needed, not tiring, and easy to carry packages or travel with children. Psychological comfort includes attributes such as relaxing, not worrying about assault or injury, and not being annoyed by others.

If you were a transit manager or community planner trying to increase utilization of public transportation, Figure 4.3 suggests that you would need to improve the consumers' perception of public transportation drastically with respect to both ease of travel and speed and convenience. You might try to modify the existing bus system or introduce a new type of service that is quicker, more convenient, and easier to use.

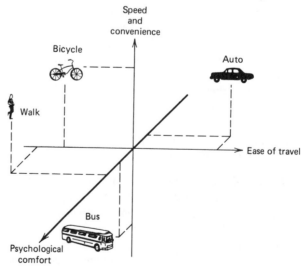

Figure 4.3 Perceptual map of transportation services. (Adapted from Alice M. Tybout and John R. Hauser, "Marketing Audit Using a Conceptual Model of Consumer Behavior: Application and Evaluation," *Journal of Marketing,* Volume 45, Summer 1981, p. 91. Copyright © American Marketing Association. Reprinted by permission.)

Sometimes, even after identifying a market opportunity, an organization may choose not to offer a product to fill that position. An opportunity may not fit within the organization's charter or long-run objectives, as might be the case when a hospital emphasizing the sophisticated treatment of major illnesses chooses not to develop a maternity facility, despite the existence of an unsatisfied local need for one. Also, some opportunities may be uneconomic. For example, a number of universities have chosen not to open medical schools because of the substantial demands a medical school places on the institution's financial and human resources.

Marketing Mix. Positioning is helpful in determining elements of the marketing mix, particularly with regard to the major themes of the marketing communication program. In some cases, the market's perception of a product may differ from its actual characteristics, and the role of a communication strategy may be defined to correct that misperception. Alternatively, consumers may be unaware or confused about the characteristics of a product. This suggests that the communication message may need to be designed to achieve awareness of the product's characteristics. For example, market research revealed that potential members of a new health-maintenance organization (HMO) in California felt that the opportunity to choose a personal physician was an important attribute in comparing health plans, but believed, mistakenly in this case, that an HMO member would not have this choice at present. Thus a communication campaign might be designed to convey this information. At times a positioning study may reveal that a characteristic that is potentially important to consumers is not valued highly by them. Then the communication task may be to attempt to convince consumers to place more emphasis on this characteristic. Usually this approach is taken when the organization believes that its product has a competitive advantage on that dimension. To continue the example, this HMO found that a certain segment of the market was concerned about what happens in the case of rare, but very costly, long-term illnesses that can exceed $1 million or more in fees that is the upper limit for some insurance plans. In response, the HMO might develop an attribute called "assured care" and differentiate itself on this dimension.

Advertising may play a particularly crucial role in positioning nearly identical products. In these cases, it is often very difficult for consumers to distinguish among goods and services on physical, perceptual, or performance dimensions. Consequently, advertising may be the principal means for establishing a product's position. At times, the ingenuity of the creative personnel in the organization and its advertising agency may be largely responsible for identifying a perceptual dimension that distinguishes a product from its competition and that also appeals to consumers. Even in these cases, the product and its performance must meet consumer expectations as built up by advertising.

Although advertising often plays a key role in communicating an organization's position, other elements of the marketing mix need to support the positioning strategy as well. Consider the role of price, distribution systems, and payment mechanisms. As an obvious example, if the attribute emphasized is value for money, the pricing strategy and product quality should support that value. If a bus system emphasizes convenience of use, schedules should reflect the times that people want to travel, stops should be located in easily accessible places, and ways to buy monthly passes should be designed so that commuters do not have to wait in long lines at the start of each month.

The positioning strategy helps set the framework within which the marketing mix is formulated. The marketing mix then supports the chosen market position.

Choosing a Positioning Strategy

The determination of a positioning strategy is based on analysis of three areas: competition, market, and internal resources and limitations (see Figure 4.4).

In *competitive analysis,* the organization should determine who the competitors are and how they are currently perceived by customers. In this analysis, the organization needs to be concerned not only with direct product-form competitors, but also with more broadly defined generic competitors. The organization should take care not to define the market too narrowly in terms of product form while simultaneously recognizing that such factors as usage situation and geographic location may narrow the range of competition that should be considered.

Once competitors are identified, the next step is to determine how they are positioned on the relevant attributes and with respect to each other. Various market-research techniques are available to develop this understanding of market positions.

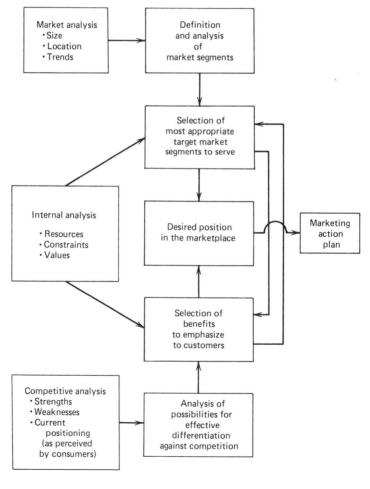

Figure 4.4   Development of a market positioning strategy.[18]

Market analysis provides an understanding of the markets in which the organization competes. The analysis is concerned with the overall size of the market and changes in demand and customer needs and preferences. Most important, alternative ways of segmenting the market should be examined, and the size and potential of different segments should be estimated. Consumer research may be needed to generate insights into the needs and preferences of prospective users within each of the different segments, as will be discussed in detail in Chapter 7, "Market Segmentation."

Finally, *internal analysis* is required to make sure a realistic understanding of the organization's resources and limitations is available. As has been emphasized at several places in this chapter, the position adopted must be one that the organization is capable of and committed to supporting over an extended period of time.

After conducting these analyses, the organization should be ready to choose a positioning strategy for itself and each of its major products. These analyses have probably resulted in a narrowing down to a limited set of potential target-market segments and major attributes, benefits, or other elements on which to base a positioning strategy. There is no simple rule for choosing a positioning strategy, but the following factors should be considered: (1) economic analysis, (2) viability of the segmentation strategy, (3) realism in terms of the organizational and product strengths, and (4) longevity of the strategy. The positioning strategy chosen must be one which aids the organization in fulfilling its mission.

An economic analysis is required to evaluate the soundness of the positioning strategy. What are the cost and revenue implications of the project? If the costs are expected to exceed revenues substantially, the organization should either have the reserves to support the chosen positioning strategy or satisfy itself that the positioning strategy chosen will be sufficiently attractive to donors as well as to users. Obviously, the risk is much greater in the positioning or repositioning of the organization as a whole than in the positioning of just one of its product lines. At times, it may turn out that retaining the present positioning is a better strategy than moving to a new one.

Positioning usually involves the choice of particular market segments, which implies that certain market segments will be neglected or ignored. As discussed in Chapter 7, choosing to serve only a limited number of segments helps to provide focus for the organization. However, public and nonprofit organizations have to ensure that they can legitimately serve only some parts of the market while receiving financial support from the general public.

A number of regional transit agencies that are partially supported by areawide sales taxes face precisely this dilemma. If the agency positions itself to meet the needs of suburban commuters, central-city residents and their political leaders may complain about the sales tax. The reverse is likely to happen when the transit agency positions itself for the central-city market. Unfortunately, it appears that the needs of the two segments are so different—in terms of pricing, type of buses used, and routings as well as overall image—that the choice of a position to occupy is a difficult dilemma.

Before adopting a positioning strategy for itself or one of its product lines, an agency must ensure that it is realistically capable of fulfilling that position. In other words, do not try to be what you are not. A new orchestra in a major city, with an already well established symphony orchestra, attempted to position itself as the city's other major classical orchestra. It soon failed, perhaps because its performance did not live up to its positioning claims. In contrast, a chamber music society, being positioned differently, might have succeeded.

Repositioning

Although a positioning strategy is designed for the long-term, sometimes an organization may find it necessary to reposition either the organization itself or some of its major products. The need for repositioning may arise from several sources.

In some cases, the market the organization serves may decline in size or importance. The March of Dimes faced just this problem. For years it devoted considerable effort to battling polio, both by supporting scientific research and by providing treatment facilities for victims of polio. With the discovery of first the Salk and then the Sabin vaccine, the March of Dimes found that it no longer had—fortunately, in this case—a sufficiently large market to which to devote its efforts. Instead of disbanding, the March of Dimes transferred its attention to birth defects and has now become a major organization in this field.[19] One reason, perhaps, for this successful repositioning was that the primary victims of polio are children, and the change in focus in many ways appears to be natural, both to those who work for the organization and those who support it financially.

A change in the competitive environment may also cause an organization to examine its current positioning strategy and attempt to reposition the services it offers. After Federal Express introduced overnight door-to-door delivery throughout most of the United States, the U.S. Postal Service (USPS) had to reexamine the position held by its mail services. One response was the introduction of Express Mail, which is the USPS's overnight delivery service. Meanwhile, priority mail (which is first-class mail for small packages) is positioned in some advertisements as slightly slower than Express Mail and other overnight delivery services, but much cheaper.

As discussed more fully in Chapter 10, repositioning can be a positive step. An organization may develop a new product or be able to capitalize on changes in the environment that allow it to improve its position significantly in the marketplace. As libraries increasingly utilize computer-based information retrieval systems, many should be able to change their position from one of merely storing and making available books to one of providing information on a wide range of topics.

The same criteria that are important in choosing a positioning strategy are also critical when contemplating a change. Thus, a decision to reposition should be tested economically, evaluated against the market segments the agency is expected to serve, examined to see whether the organization has the ability to fulfill the desired position, and analyzed for its longevity. In addition, two other criteria need to be considered. First, is the new position compatible with the public's, volunteers', and employees' current perception of the organization? As we noted, the March of Dimes' new focus on birth defects appears to be compatible with its previous position. A switch to wildlife protection, although a worthy cause, would appear to be incompatible. Second, has the organization recently changed its position? If positions are changed too frequently, the market tends to become confused and unclear as to what the organization represents. Consequently, the organization may be considered second rate. Moreover, changes in position can consume a considerable amount of human and financial resources, and frequent changes can dissipate organizational strength.

In addition to planned changes in an organization's position, sometimes alterations in an organization's programs can result in inadvertent repositioning. Such unintended changes should be guarded against. Two factors that can change an organization's position are modification of the product mix or moving a facility's location. An example of the first factor occurred in a northern California birth-control clinic that had successfully developed a strong position as a nonjudgmental, helpful service among young women. The position of the clinic was more one of providing a social service than being a medical facility. Clinic staff considered adding Pap tests for cervical cancer to its product line, but eventually decided not to add this service because of the threat it posed to the clinic's current position. The staff believed that adding the new service would detract from the agency's current position as a nonjudgmental counseling center. The second factor is exemplified by a theater moving from a site in an area containing good restaurants and pleasant shops to a new auditorium with better acoustics, sight lines, and seating, but in an office building that closes at night. Although the new facility may be more suitable, the theater's position as a source for an evening's entertainment may suffer dramatically.

Organizations also need to guard against "position drift"—the gradual, unintended change in an organization's position.[20] As consumer memories of an agency's position fade, other factors may come into play and the institution's position may subtly change in undesirable ways. The organization should use market research to keep track of consumer perception of its positions and take appropriate action when necessary.

In summary, an organization's position can be a valuable asset; an organization should appraise carefully any proposal to change its position and guard against unintended changes in its present position. While an organization's position is long-term, it is not immutable. Repositioning can be a desirable strategy, but it should be seen as a long-term decision and not one that is frequently made.

FUNCTIONAL-AREA STRATEGIES

To this point, we have examined organizational strategy (where resources should be invested), subunit strategy (how the component parts will compete in selected markets), and positioning strategy (choosing a position in the mind of users or other important publics). Now we narrow the focus further—to functional area strategies. These specify how the key functional areas are going to support the subunit and positioning strategies.

It is difficult to generalize about the scope of functional-area strategies because they depend on the particular organizational structure utilized to manage the organization and the particular subunit strategy chosen. If a performing-arts organization owns its own facility, the administrative and financial strategies needed to manage the facility may become important activities requiring careful attention. Another performing-arts organization that only rents space may not find such activities to be worthy of extensive attention. The organizational structure helps determine the scope of the functional-area manager's task. A manager may be responsible for a geographic area, a product line, a market segment, an operational area such as sales, a traditional functional area such as marketing or operations, or a staff function such as finance, law, or market research. Of course, some of these different activities may be hierarchically organized as well.

As Vancil points out, the first thing to be said about what he calls the "activity manager" is that his or her job is where the action is.[21] Although the scope of the activity manager's position is narrower than that of an SMU manager and the strategy devised is more specific, it is the activity manager who must design and execute the set of actions that will implement the subunit and organizational strategy. As at the more senior levels, the activity manager must identify opportunities and threats and allocate limited resources in order to achieve specified objectives.

The importance of functional-area strategies should not be minimized. Although they occupy the bottom rung in the hierarchy of strategies, they are in some ways the most important. While a subunit strategy may call for the development of new products or new service facilities, unless a functional area can successfully mobilize resources and accomplish these aims, the plans are merely paper.

Chapter 5, "Building a Marketing Plan," illustrates the range of activities for which a marketing manager might be responsible. As will be seen, such issues as environmental analysis, target-market selection, market positioning, and marketing-mix determination can all fall within the scope of a marketing manager's responsibility. Similarly, broad and challenging sets of activities need to be managed by operations, financial, and other managers.

In summary, functional-area strategies involve many similarities to strategies at other levels, although the scope of responsibility is more narrowly defined. On the other hand, functional-area managers are often "closer to the action" and need to design strategies that are more specific and in some senses more "real." Functional-area strategies are vital and if not well designed and executed will negate the effectiveness of otherwise sound subunit strategies.

SUMMARY

"If you don't know where you're going, all roads lead there." Strategy formulation is the vital management function that permits an organization to control its destiny instead of merely being swept along by the tide of events. It is an easy, but serious, mistake for an organization to become so caught up in dealing with day-to-day issues that strategic formulation—which is time consuming, often not concrete, and long-term—is postponed or superficially done. To prevent this, senior management needs to put a high value on strategic planning by devoting serious attention to strategic issues and by allocating resources and making decisions in accordance with accepted strategy.

The strategic process is concerned with defining the organization's mission or purpose in a generic sense, setting organizational objectives that follow from the mission definition, designing strategies to meet goals, and specifying tactics. Of course, the process is not as unidimensionally linear as the preceding description suggests but instead evolves cyclically. Furthermore, strategy is required at several levels. In this chapter we have stressed four levels of strategy formulation: organizational, subunit, positional, and functional area. At all levels, strategy involves the basic issues of identifying opportunities and threats, allocating limited resources, and specifying and selecting courses of action that lead to long-term success in achievement of objectives. Strategic choices should be based on careful, detailed analysis of alternatives, a difficult task given the uncertainty of the future. Consequently, strategy must allow for risk and uncertainty, and management may wish to test for the robustness of a strategy in a dynamic, competitive environment.

Organizational strategy should not be so sacrosanct that it is rarely reviewed or changed; it should be designed to serve as a long-term guide for the organization.

REFERENCES

1. Philip M. Kotler, *Principles of Marketing*, Englewood Cliffs, N.J.: Prentice-Hall, 1980, p. 69.
2. Peter F. Drucker, *Management: Tasks Responsibilities, Practices*, Harper & Row, 1974.
3. George S. Day, *Strategic Marketing Planning: The Pursuit of Competitive Advantage*, St. Paul, Minn.: West Publishing Co., 1984, p. 17.
4. Theodore Levitt, "Marketing Myopia," *Harvard Business Review*, Sept.–Oct. 1975.
5. J. Alison Barnhill and Stanley J. Shapiro, "Comparative Public Sector Marketing: Contrasting Two Canadian Programs," in M. Mokwa and S. Permut (eds.), *Government Marketing: Theory and Practice*, New York: Praeger, 1981.
6. Christopher H. Lovelock, "Stanford University: The Annual Fund," in C. H. Lovelock and C. B. Weinberg, *Public and Nonprofit Marketing: Cases and Readings*, New York: John Wiley and Sons, 1984.
7. Patrick Hanemann and Charles B. Weinberg, "University Arts Program," in C. H. Lovelock and C. B. Weinberg (as in reference 6).
8. Richard F. Vancil, "Strategy Formulation in Complex Organizations," *Sloan Management Review* (Winter 1976), pp. 1–18.
9. H. Igor Ansoff, *Corporate Strategy* New York: McGraw-Hill, 1965, p. 109; Samuel C. Johnson and Conrad Jones, " How to Organize for New Products," *Harvard Business Review*, Vol. 35 (May–June 1957), pp. 49–62.
10. Data are derived from Shirley Myers and Barbara McEven, "Report of Phase I of a Study of 4-H in Alberta" (October 1979) and Gail Stinson and Yvonne McFadzen, "Phase II—A Study of 4-H in Alberta" (May 2, 1980), unpublished documents.
11. The approach in this section follows that of William E. Rothschild in *Putting It All Together*. Copyright © 1976 by AMACOM, a division of American Management Associations, New York. All rights reserved.
12. A. A. Thompson, Jr., and A. J. Strickland III, *Strategy Formulation and Implementation*. Copyright © 1980 by Business Publications, Inc., Dallas Texas, pp. 70–71. Reprinted by permission.
13. Adapted with permission of Macmillan Publishing Co., Inc. from *Competitive Strategy: Techniques for Analyzing Industries and Competitors* by Michael E. Porter. Copyright © 1980 by The Free Press, a division of Macmillan Publishing Co., Inc.
14. As in reference 13, pp. 127–8.
15. As in reference 11, p. 217.
16. In 1982, this distinction began to disappear as the Public Broadcasting System (PBS) tested the selling of advertising. See "How PBS is Planning to Stay on the Air," *Business Week* (March 15, 1982), p. 34.
17. Al Ries and Jack Trout, *Positioning: The Battle for Your Mind*, New York: McGraw-Hill, 1980.
18. This diagram is adapted from an unpublished schematic developed by Michael A. Pearce.
19. William A. Mindak and H. Malcolm Bybee, "Marketing's Application to Fund Raising," *Journal of Marketing*, 35 (July 1971), pp. 13–18.
20. Alan Andreasen, personal correspondence, January 25, 1982.
21. As in reference 8.

Chapter 5
Building a Marketing Plan

Successful marketing programs are usually based on an explicit marketing plan to guide the organization's actions toward achievement of desired objectives. In this chapter, we will focus on the steps involved in building a marketing plan.

Planning, at any level for any organization, is a difficult task for management trying to cope with ongoing tactical responsibilities and a dynamic, competitive environment. Public and nonprofit managers face at least two additional difficulties as compared to their private-sector counterparts. First, nonbusiness managers often need to generate plans that place heavy emphasis on nonfinancial objectives. Financial requirements may act as a constraint, but the main focus may be on service or social objectives that are not easy to set, quantify, and measure. Consequently, it is difficult to compare alternatives objectively. Second, public and nonprofit managers often need to develop plans that meet the needs of at least two major markets or publics—the market of benefactors and donors and the market of clients or users. These additional complexities, although making the development of marketing plans more difficult, make the use of these plans more vital if the organization is to manage its marketing efforts effectively.

Scope of the Chapter

Not all organizations have formal marketing plans, so we start the chapter with a section discussing the advantages of having such a plan. In the second section of this chapter, we discuss different types of marketing plans, keeping in mind that the overall plan usually integrates a series of subordinate marketing plans and should be the result of interaction among several levels of management. To help answer the question of what comprises a marketing plan, we next present a framework for an organization's marketing plan. This guide can be adapted to the specific needs of individual organizations. Marketing plans can encompass the organization as a whole or be confined to a single product or market segment. Their time horizon is usually for one year, often with a brief reference to future years. In the fourth section, our topic is marketing control. Once a plan is accepted, it is vital for an agency to monitor performance and take corrective action when appropriate. The targets set in the plan are frequently used as the basis for a marketing-control system.

In the fifth section of the chapter we summarize an actual plan developed for the Hillside Association for Learning Disabled People (a disguised name).[1] This Association, staffed by five professionals, has been attempting to serve all age ranges of learning disabled people with a variety of programs in a limited budget. In this first ever marketing plan for the Hillside Association a new approach based on concentrating on one market segment—school aged children— is suggested. Not all marketing plans involve such radical changes, but it is important to recognize that even small organizations need to think carefully about choosing markets and serving them effectively.

THE RATIONALE FOR PLANNING

Organizations often do not have formal plans. Managers working for small and very new organizations frequently argue that they are too busy coping with day-to-day survival to have the time and resources required to formulate a plan. Other reasons given for not having a plan include claims that the market changes too quickly for a plan to have relevance or that the plan is only a written document that does not translate easily into action.

These objections merit some discussion. In the smallest organizations, the mission of the organization may be so narrow and the range of choice in action so limited that a detailed marketing plan may indeed be superfluous. On the other hand, some new organizations may find a plan valuable just because they lack a history and their options are so wide. Developing a plan is a way to help an organization choose wisely among alternatives. Some people believe that they have an internalized plan "in their heads," but most of these are probably just kidding themselves. Of course, it is necessary to avoid plans that are mere paperwork. Plans must be based on a sound analysis of the external and internal environments that the organization confronts.

To be more than just words, a management-approved plan must serve as the basis of resource allocation and performance evaluation. If a plan for a regional health center calls for developing a new distribution channel to serve people in outlying communities, the funds needed should be provided. When managers see that resources follow plans and that results are monitored against planned targets, plans are carefully built and become relevant.

What about the argument that plans become too quickly outdated? As we will show, plans actually help an organization to anticipate change and to generate questions requiring research. While there is always the possibility that an entirely unanticipated event may happen, in most cases careful analysis can identify trends and precursors. In other instances, the planning process can identify the major uncertainties so that contingency plans can be built for alternative outcomes. Different plans can also be tested against alternative scenarios.

Benefits of Planning

Well-designed formal plans that guide management actions and resource allocations offer a number of benefits for the organization. Among these are the following.

1. *Coordination of the activities of many individuals whose actions are related over time*. Some decisions must be made before others or simultaneously with others. A marketing plan can be the means to coordinate these activities. In the discussion of Robert Drinan's election campaign in Chapter 7, "Market Segmentation," we show how important it is to coordinate the activities of many people and to make sure actions take place in the proper chronological order.

2. *Setting a timetable.* A marketing plan anticipates the timing of needed activities and thus sets a timetable. For example, the opening of a new suburban branch of a community center may require a marketing communication campaign. Thus it might be useful to conduct a focus group ten months before the opening, to generate two campaign themes six months before, to test them five months before, to generate final copy four months before, to test it three months before, and then finalize and implement the campaign. Without a marketing plan, many necessary steps are rushed and market research is often not conducted, so decisions are made without adequate information.

3. *Better communication.* Because of the inevitable compartmentalization of management, it is essential that there be some integrating form of communication so that each executive will know, at least generally, what other managers are trying to achieve and how likely they are to accomplish their tasks. Communication is among the primary functions of a marketing plan.

4. *Identification of expected developments.* Many administrators can easily perceive the nature of future developments if they make a disciplined effort to look ahead. By forcing themselves to plan, they often can place future events fairly accurately in time and can better understand their relationship and serial nature. For example, nonprofit organizations that depend heavily on female volunteers are threatened by the increased participation of women in the paid labor force. Presentation House, a Vancouver organization that sponsors both visual and performing-arts events, found one way to cope by redesigning some volunteer tasks to appeal to couples with spare time in the evening instead of to women who had time available during the day.

5. *Preparation to meet changes when they occur.* Through planning, executives are forced to think through the actions they would take if certain events occurred. Furthermore, the planning systems can help to reduce nonrational responses to the unexpected by placing obstacles in the way of those executives who would respond hastily and emotionally to surprises.

   For example, in 1977 when many California communities found they needed to conserve water after two consecutive years of drought, much effort and money was wasted in initial confusion as to how much conservation was needed and how to motivate Californians to conserve. In one two-month period, the director of water resources in San Francisco first announced that no reduction was needed, then asked for a 10 percent reduction, and then demanded 25 percent.[2] Later, when that goal was exceeded, with an accompanying sharp drop in the revenue from water-bill payments, he asked people to use more water so that the city could meet its revenue targets!

6. *Focusing of efforts.* Managers generally have more problems and opportunities than they have resources available to devote to them. Successful planning systems provide a means for the organization to choose the problems and opportunities to which it may most effectively devote its limited resources. In addition, a well-designed planning process should result in a systematic procedure for generating and evaluating alternatives. Too often, administrators only consider one course of action.

   For example, a San Francisco area organization that we'll call Technological Aids for the Blind (TAB) had difficulty in raising funds. TAB's main purpose is to assist blind people in obtaining and using new electronic sensory aids as a means to increase their independence and employability. TAB sought donations from a wide variety of individuals, social groups, and corporations but unfortunately did not meet its financial goals. A consultant suggested that this shortfall was partially because of the diffuseness of the effort and recommended a more focused strategy. After considering several alternatives, the consultant advocated that TAB focus its fund-raising efforts on the successful high-technology companies in the so-called Silicon Valley south of San Francisco. These companies formed a good target segment for TAB because they appreciated the advantages to be gained from new technologies and their success had generated profits from which to make donations. This approach allowed for a more concentrated effort and helped to conserve the limited time of TAB's management.

7. *Basis of a control system.* A marketing plan not only is a guide to action but also can be the basis of a control system. The marketing plan can be used to monitor deviations from assumptions that underlie the plan as well as results that do not meet targeted goals.

Managers of performing-arts organizations, to illustrate, often have a target level of attendance for each event and intermediate goals of what percentage of that forecast should be sold on subscription by a specified number of months and weeks ahead of the date the event is to occur. When actual sales to date are below the intermediate goal, the cause is investigated. If, for example, low sales are the result of lack of awareness or ineffective advertising copy, a revised promotion campaign may be undertaken or the event may be featured more prominently in general press releases. If, on the other hand, sales are above expectations, management may reduce promotional spending or add an additional performance of that event.

8. *Maintenance of organizational integrity.* Marketing plans, by clearly specifying the strategies the organization will pursue and rooting those choices in a thorough understanding of the organization's goals, help prevent a series of ad hoc decisions that carry it farther and farther away from its true concerns, as the executive director of one social-service agency recognized.

> This year there is a lot of money available for programs for pregnant teenagers. But the most pressing problem in this neighborhood is senior citizens, which is not a sexy program this year. My Board of Directors would be pleased if we received any grant, but I have other things to think about. If we took on a teenage pregnancy program, it would take up some of our facilities, staff time, and administrative resources, all of which could be put to better use in trying to find money for senior citizens' programs. Our agency is now in a position of strength, and can refuse to back into funding that would deplete our other resources.[3]

Without a planning process to define its actions, whatever the organization does can become the definition of what it is.

TYPES OF MARKETING PLANS

Planning can be carried out at many different levels of aggregation. There can be a plan for the organization as a whole, a set of plans for the organization's different types of offerings ("product" plans), and a set of "market" plans for the individual markets that the organization wants to serve. For example, a symphony orchestra might have one marketing plan for its regular season in its main hall, another plan for a tour over a wide geographic area, and a third plan for a summer season. The marketing strategy for each alternative might be radically different—for example, the regular season may appeal primarily to upper-income subscribers who have a strong interest in the arts, the summer season to those new to the arts who are willing to spend very little but are looking for an enjoyable experience. There may also be a separate marketing plan for an important segment, as when one arts organization decided to build an audience among the elderly. To do this, the organization offered concerts on Sunday afternoons, since market research had indicated that many old people would not attend at night. This diversity of plans indicates why distinctive marketing plans are needed; yet these activities must be coordinated as well. Thus the organization's general plan is an integrated set of subplans.

Effective planning requires communication among an organization's members. Often the senior executives and staff specify the major environmental threats and assumptions to be considered and goals to be achieved; the operating management asks for resources and develops plans based on these assumptions. This is sometimes referred to as a "top-down bottom-up" approach but, more specifically, planning is viewed as a cyclic process eventually converging on a set of targets and plans for which consensus is achieved. Senior officers need to set realistic objectives that can be modified, when appropriate, by colleagues and junior staff. In turn, senior executives can suggest revisions in plans that are too ambitious or not sufficiently aggressive. Subunits of the organization may be able to develop sound marketing plans in isolation, but the need for coordination or the scarcity of resources may require modifications to their plans. At the end of the planning process, a set of plans should emerge that have general support among organizational personnel.

Formal Planning Systems

Relatively few public and nonprofit organizations have formal marketing plans that actually influence resource allocation and managerial decision making. Recognition of the value of marketing planning appears to be growing, however, and some organizations have devised effective marketing-planning systems.

Of course, the mere presence of formal written plans is not sufficient. Some organizations develop such plans to meet the request of funding organizations or board members, but these plans have no impact on management decisions. Consider the following example of how planning evolved in one large firm.

> In the company's early days of planning, divisions were mainly required to submit numerical estimates of profits, growth rates, sales, etc., over a five-year horizon. Naturally the division managers provided numbers which were set at levels which would justify their desired resource allocation or gain the approval they were seeking. The company now requires statements of the actions necessary to achieve results and assumptions about the external environment upon which the projections are based. That is, the logic necessary to achieve a numerical goal is given. Consequently, corporate officers can challenge a division's plan.[4]

This example represents the typical evolution from no plans, to budgets, to formal plans of increasing rigor. Terminal City Dance in Vancouver went through just these stages. It began as a small dance company that wished to develop and present modern dance to Vancouver audiences. Little was done in the way of formal planning as artistic vision and drive carried the organization. Later, as the organization achieved some success, it added a management staff—as well as more artists—and began to develop financial plans and targets. In the early 1980s, as Terminal City Dance expanded its scope, more formal planning for audience development and fund raising took place as well. Of course, the system is not as well developed or formalized as the planning system of a large public agency, but the system is appropriate for a small organization.

The length, detail, and format of the marketing plan can vary considerably according to the needs and capabilities of the organization. A useful set of standards for judging the adequacy of a plan is provided by a U.S. Army staff manual (see Table 5.1). How long should a plan be? Short enough to be read and understood, long enough to show people what their tasks are without bogging everyone down in a morass of detail. Organizations will vary in their ability to digest plans of various lengths.

The question of how much flexibility an individual manager is to be allowed in developing a plan arouses much discussion. A Conference Board study cites four arguments for a prescribed format and coverage.

1. Ensures completeness of a plan's coverage.
2. Helps novice planners to build initial plans.

Table 5.1 Characteristics of a Good Plan

The essential element of a plan is that it offers a definite course of action and a method for execution. A good plan does the following.
1. Provides for accomplishing the mission (Does it accomplish the objective of the planning?)
2. Is based on facts and valid assumptions (Have all pertinent data been considered? Are the data accurate? Have assumptions been reduced to a minimum?)
3. Provides for the use of existing resources (Is the plan workable? Are there any resources organic to the organization that are not being fully utilized? Are there any resources available from higher headquarters that should be used?)
4. Provides the necessary organization (Does the plan clearly establish relationships and fix responsibilities?)
5. Provides continuity (Does the plan provide the organization, personnel, material, and arrangements for the full period of the contemplated operation?)
6. Provides decentralization (Does the plan delegate authority to the maximum extent consistent with the necessary control?)
7. Provides direct contact (Does the plan permit coordination during execution by direct contact between coequals and counterparts on all levels?)
8. Is simple (Have all elements been eliminated that are not essential to successful action? Have all elements been reduced to their simplest forms? Have all possibilities for misunderstanding been eliminated?)
9. Is flexible (Does the plan leave room for adjustment to change in operating conditions? Where necessary, are alternate courses of action stipulated?)
10. Provides control (Do adequate means exist, or have they been provided, to ensure that the plan is carried out in accordance with the manager's intent?)
11. Is coordinated (Is the plan fully coordinated? When appropriate, has the manager been informed of nonconcurrence or noncoordination?)

Source. U. S. Army, "Staff Officers Field Manual: Staff Organization and Procedure," FM 101-5, 14 June 1968, by permission of the Department of the Army.

3. Facilitates review and control.

4. Upgrades the quality of the average plan to "textbook" levels of completeness.[5]

In other words, the uniform format ensures that all plans in the organization cover the critical areas as well as providing a means for communicating the aims and methods of each organizational subunit. However, making planning formats fit a textbook model risks the flexibility managers need to be able to respond to their markets. In addition, if the required data are not available in the specified format, reorganizing information can be time consuming and costly.

In general, planning systems should be matched to the organization's individual style and capabilities. All planning systems, to be effective, require substantial involvement by key personnel. To generate meaningful involvement, the plan must be seen as an important part of the organization's decision process. Smaller organizations will tend to have plans of narrower scope and possibly less formality than those of larger organizations. The goal in every case is a pragmatic plan that specifies a course of action designed to produce concrete results.

DEVELOPING A MARKETING PLAN

The marketing plan is a systematic way of organizing an analysis of a market, an organization's position in that market, and a program for future marketing activities. All marketing strategies should be conditional on such analysis. The elements of a marketing plan are not discrete; they are interrelated, so that developing a plan may involve cycling through its components several times before satisfactory results are achieved.

Table 5.2 lists important issues that should be included in a marketing plan. The following discussion amplifies portions of this suggested format, but because other sections of the book will discuss the individual components in depth, these comments will be brief. The format is stated in terms of a marketing plan for the organization as a whole; a marketing plan for specific programs, markets, or organizational subunits will obviously reflect the concerned area's particular needs.

Executive Summary

Most marketing plans begin with a brief summary of the main elements of the marketing plan. Usually, the summary covers just the major threats and opportunities faced by the organization, its key objectives, and the highlights of the recommended course of action. Such a summary helps to communicate the major aspects of the plan to other managers in the organization, particularly those who are not closely linked to the organizational subunit building the plan. For others, the executive summary provides a guide to use in reading, analyzing, and understanding the plan.

Situational Analysis

Situational analysis, the first step in a marketing plan, examines the organization's external and internal environment. The situation analysis should identify the threats, opportunities, and problems to which the marketing plan will be responsive. A marketing audit, discussed in the previous chapter, covers many of the issues included in the annual plan's situational analysis, although the audit will usually be broader in coverage and more strategic in

Table 5.2 Marketing-Plan Format

EXECUTIVE SUMMARY

Situational Analysis (Where Are We Now?)
External
Environment (political, regulatory, economic, social, technical, etc.)
Consumers
Employers
Funders
Distributors
Competition
Internal
Objectives
Strengths and weaknesses

Problems and Opportunities
Momentum forecast
Identify gaps

Marketing Program Goals (Where Do We Want to Go?)
Specific (quantifiable)
Realistic (attainable)
Important
Prioritized

Marketing Strategies (How Are We Going to Get There?)
Positioning
Target segments
Competitive stance
Usage incentive
Marketing mix
Product
Price
Distribution
Marketing communication
Contingency strategies

Marketing Budget (How Much and Where?)
Resources
Money
People
Time
Amount and allocation

Marketing Action Plan (What and When?)
Detailed breakdown of activities for each goal or strategy
Responsibility by name
Activity schedule in milestone format
Tangible and intangible results expected from each activity

Monitoring System (Are We Getting Where We Want to Go?)
Are planned activities taking place on schedule?
Are these activities yielding the results expected?
Do we need a course correction?

---

nature. The marketing plan, unlike the audit, is primarily developed by the managers who are responsible for implementing it. When available, a summary of the audit can be an important input to the plan's situational analysis—the elements of the audit that are more immediate and actionable will be emphasized. Not surprisingly, therefore, the reader will find that some of the areas covered in a marketing plan were discussed in the previous chapter's marketing-audit framework and will only be briefly mentioned here.

The situation analysis includes a historical summary, an analysis of the present situation, and an assessment of future trends. It can also include an evaluation of the impact of previous marketing efforts, although this is infrequently done in practice.[6] We will briefly discuss some of the areas typically covered in a situational analysis.

Environment. For purposes of analysis, the external environment can be usefully subdivided into the political, regulatory, economic, social, and technical environments. How does an organization's external environment affect the marketing operation? For example, local libraries need to examine the availability of computerized, time-shared information-retrieval systems that might influence the range of services they offer. This technology also calls into question traditional lending policies and free reference services. Similarly, analysis of the social environment indicates that the increasing number of women in the work force and the decline in numbers of women willing to work as unpaid volunteers may render certain marketing strategies obsolete or impractical. Working women, on the other hand, may constitute a segment that provides new opportunities for the organization.

Consumers. Marketing research plays an important role in helping managers to understand current, potential, and former consumers. A safety council, to illustrate, in seeking to understand why automobile drivers and passengers do not use seat belts as required by law, might want to know whether low usage occurs because enforcement is incomplete, penalties are not severe enough, or the belts are too inconvenient or uncomfortable. Will these people also disconnect passive restraint systems? Of course, one wants to know the size of the current and potential market, possible segmentation bases, and consumers' awareness of and attitudes toward the organization and its offerings. The information gathered here is one of the key influences on the choice of product markets.

Employees. Employees and their unions are a part of the environment and have a significant impact on marketing programs. For example, the transit consumer's satisfaction with a bus ride can be dependent on the courtesy and knowledge of the driver who is answering questions and collecting fares. In the performing arts, the quality and reliability of the product depend fundamentally on the talent of the artists presenting it.

Funders. Just as consumers need to be understood, so do funding sources. Familiar marketing concepts that help to explain the behavior of users often can be applied to funders as well. For example, university fund raisers claim that a trial-and-repeat pattern exists, that donors of small amounts after graduation are a likely source of substantial donations later. In the United States, both private and public universities now actively seek financial support from graduates and others. The existence of brand loyalty is suggested by the continued success of the March of Dimes, which holds the third leading position in fund raising for national health organizations, after changing its original focus from the problems of polio to birth defects. Some government agencies, such as public school systems, have to appeal directly to taxpayers for financial support to provide services to users. For other government agencies, the market may consists of the legislative body that allocates funds. The British Columbia Provincial Museum has become internationally recognized for its exhibits of local and environmental history. It has been suggested that its location in Victoria, immediately adjacent to the Parliament Building of British Columbia, has helped it obtain government support.

Distributors. Does the organization deal directly with consumers or does it use agents? For example, the U.S. government mandated the 65-mph speed limit, but enforcement is "delivered" by local police agencies. The success of the national strategy depends on the behavior of the "wholesalers" and "retailers." As another example, federally funded social programs, such as youth employment, are often designed and delivered to the public by local governments. Federal government sponsors need to understand the local government's needs and priorities in translating planned systems to operating ones. As we will see later, the USPS tries to convince moving companies, real-estate brokers, and others to act as "distributors" for its change-of-address kits.

Competition. Organizations usually face both direct and indirect competitors. For example, mass-transit marketing planners need to recognize that for many consumers the automobile is a superior competitor. In the consumer's mind as well as the funder's, different types of transit can compete with each other. In New York City, buses, subways, taxis, and walking are all competitors on certain trips. For those offering new preventive health-care services, the range of competitors is vast, including existing providers and, in a sense, individual habit and inertia. Public and nonprofit organizations should be on the lookout for competition from business as well as nonbusiness organizations.

Internal. Analysis of the internal environment is critical as well. What are the organization's objectives? What does it want to achieve? What are the strengths and weaknesses, honestly appraised? What distinctive competences distinguish this organization from others and will allow it to succeed in the face of competition and a possibly hostile environment?

Problems and Opportunities

This analysis of the external and internal environments should lead to the specification of a set of problems (or threats) and opportunities. The identification of threats and opportunities is the key output of the situational analysis. A momentum forecast of year-end position, which assumes that the organization is operated as usual, can be constructed based on the situation analysis. This forecast is then compared with the organization's desired year-end position, and the gaps between the forecast and the desired position identified. Such so-called gap analysis helps stimulate the creation of marketing program goals and strategies and motivates the people in the organization.

For instance, the National High Blood Pressure Education Program's original goal, when founded in 1972, was to increase awareness of hypertension (high blood pressure) and its consequences. Initially half of all Americans with high blood pressure were undetected. By the end of the decade, awareness was much improved, but about a third of hypertensives who were supposed to take daily medication did not do so. Consequently, the goals of the program shifted to persuading hypertensives to maintain their treatment regimens. Moreover, a situation analysis suggested that the problem is quite difficult because there is no immediate benefit from daily treatment. Symptoms are not reduced and patients do not feel better physically. In fact psychologically they may be worse off since the pills can become a daily reminder of the sickness itself. In addition hypertensives who continue therapy and those who drop out are about equally well informed about the consequences of the disease and that it can be controlled.[7]

Marketing Program Goals

A well-articulated set of meaningful goals plays a critical role in guiding effort at all levels of the organization. Too often, organizations flounder because objectives are not set. In this section, we are particularly concerned with the goals set for the marketing program, which should be derived from and supportive of the organization's long-term goals.

Goals should be specific and quantifiable. "Increasing the number of blood doners" is very hard to use as a motivating device, because it is not known when the goal has been achieved. A goal of "increasing awareness of adult-education programs offered in the community" raises a number of questions. Is the object to increase the awareness of students, senior citizens, or new residents, and by how much? A more meaningful goal is "40 percent of the new residents know the programs exist."

Goals should be challenging, but not set so high that they cannot be achieved. If the goals are achieved, the organization will enjoy a sense of accomplishment; if not, at least there should be a way of determining why not—an analysis that will be useful in determining goals and setting plans for the next year.

Finally, all goals should be tailored to the situation, ranked in order of priority. Goals should be few in number so that they can serve as a useful focus and be ranked so that managers have guidance if it is necessary to make trade-offs among alternative plans or tactics.

Marketing Strategy

Marketing strategy is the means by which the organization (or its components) achieves its marketing goals. Of course, in building a marketing plan, several different strategies usually must be constructed before the best one is chosen. Indeed, forcing decision makers to devise and evaluate various courses of action is one of the key benefits of an effective planning system. These alternatives must be tested against the conclusions drawn from the situational analysis done earlier.

Moreover, different markets require different marketing strategies, although eventually they must be coordinated. Salt Lake City, for example, developed a marketing plan for city residents based on improving customer service through employee excellence and city accountability programs. The marketing plan to attract new businesses focused on the cost effectiveness of the city for western markets, the efficiency of city government, and the many cultural and recreational opportunities in the area.

Positioning

Positioning is the fundamental statement of what the organization and its services represent to chosen market segments. Successful positioning is a three-step process. First, who are the target segments? To which groups is the organization striving to appeal? The organization may try to appeal to more than one group at a time, although programs attempting to do so may fail to satisfy any segment sufficiently. If a university, for example, tries to develop one program for both day students and part-time adult evening students, problems of coordination will need to be considered. Second, the manager should set the organization's competitive stance in each of the target segments. Depending on the segment, the competition can vary considerably. The final step in positioning is to establish the usage incentive. What are the primary benefits that the organization is going to offer its current and potential users in each segment? The positioning strategy is vital not only for reaching the consumers, but also for directing the organization's management; it provides a focus for management efforts and ultimately channels the efforts of the entire organization.

Marketing Mix

The marketing mix (product, price, distribution, and communication) is a convenient way of summarizing a set of activities that support the marketing goals of the organization. People new to the field often consider these activities, especially advertising, to be all of marketing; on the contrary, they are just one part of marketing.

The elements of the marketing mix are discussed extensively later in the book and will not be specifically covered here.

Contingency Strategies

A marketing plan should include contingency strategies. Because it is difficult to predict the future precisely, the manager should anticipate major surprises and be prepared for them. One theater group has three plans for the second half of the year, each based on different attendance revenues in the first half. A major company will not allow managers to cite unexpected events as an excuse for missing their annual plan goals. If a manager protests, "I never expected that to happen and as a result my sales are down by 20 percent," senior management replies, "A good manager should at least be aware of possible surprises." Knowing the possible surprises provides a big advantage, because well-thought-out and timely contingency strategies that were prepared beforehand are available immediately. For example, the marketing plan for the opening of the Monterey Bay Aquarium in California included a program designed to generate media coverage. While this coverage was realized and the aquarium was launched successfully, a contingency budget with a paid media advertising plan was developed in case the desired free publicity was not obtained.

Marketing Budget

The next step in the marketing plan is the marketing budget. There are three critical resources in running an organization: money, people, and time. Because most public and nonprofit organizations do not have enough money, people, or time, the question in budgeting is usually how to use or allocate these scarce resources. In allocating resources, it is essential to consider the relationships among marketing elements and the relative cost effectiveness of investments in each one. For each element in the plan, it is useful to examine the resources required to operate at different levels and the results at these different levels. Trade-offs must often be made. For example, a health clinic may need to choose between additional advertising to increase awareness of its services or extending its operating hours so more people can use its services. If services are paid for, increased usage could generate additional funds.

Changing the budgetary allocation for one element can sometimes have a ripple effect on others; for example, cutting funds used for advertising and printed information may cause usage to fall or lead to an increase in telephone calls requesting information. Resources can be increased by contributions—not only of money but also of volunteer time. Because many diverse organizations are increasing their fund-raising efforts, the market for donations and volunteers is extremely competitive. Fund raising, moreover, is difficult and can divert key members of the organization from other activities without commensurate return.

Marketing Action Plan

The marketing action plan is a detailed breakdown of the strategies that achieve each of the goals and an assignment of responsibilities by name of individual or office. It indicates the tactics to be implemented. The activity schedule should be in *milestone* form, so that all concerned can know what actions have to be accomplished by when if the plan's goals are to be accomplished. To illustrate, if the goal in a bicycle-licensing program is to increase registration from 60 percent of bicycle owners to 75 percent at the end of the year, registration should rise to 65 percent, for example, at the end of three months. If the goal is to introduce a new bicycle-safety program in a year, after three months some specified activities—such as distribution of posters listing rules for safety—should have been completed.

Planning without implementation is worth little, as one experienced manager and consultant points out.

> The best strategy in the world may be close to worthless if it isn't implemented adroitly. This seems so obvious; yet in case after case, leaders in all walks of life who do have carefully prepared strategies fail to make them operational. As a closing, I would like to specify some important aspects of the move toward implementing plans that will increase the probability of successful execution.
>
> 1. *Proper organization.* Look at the type of organization you have now and determine whether it fits the strategy you have adopted. An inappropriate organization structure is likely to cause failure.
>
> 2. *Measurement.* Do the current measurement systems encourage personnel to execute the strategy, or will they actually work against implementation?
>
> 3. *Rewards.* How do the rewards received for performance relate to the strategy? As is true of organization form and the measurement system, they can either support or distract.
>
> 4. *Understanding.* Do the key operating managers and professionals understand what has changed and why? Do they agree with the change, or will they only give it lip service? Do they know what is expected of them to make it work?[8]

Monitoring Systems

The monitoring system is concerned with whether assumptions about the external environment are valid, whether the organization is carrying out the plan in the desired manner, and whether the specified milestones and goals are being achieved. Deviations from anticipated happenings must be discovered and acted on; unanticipated new opportunities and problems must be recognized. Depending on the findings, the organization should be prepared to make readjustments in the original plan, substitute a contingency strategy, or, in rare cases, develop a new plan, as we discuss more fully in the next section on marketing control.

MARKETING CONTROL

Marketing control is designed to help the organization achieve its short-run and long-run goals.[9] The marketing plan often serves as the basis of a control system, although the marketing audit (see Chapter 3) is an element of a long-run strategic control system. The marketing plan is often a good basis for a control system because it is based on the best information available at the time and represents management commitment.

Marketing control is needed because results seldom go exactly according to plan. Changes may occur in users' attitudes or willingness to act, in donors' priorities, in competitors' actions, or in other environmental factors. Or the organization's personnel may not perform the prescribed activities, or these activities may use more time or money or be less productive than expected. All these factors and more can cause deviations from the plan. Early detection of these deviations is required if management is to make changes on a timely basis.

When the marketing plan is used as the basis of a control systems, the control process can be subdivided into five steps.

1. Set targets and standards.
2. Determine acceptable deviations.
3. Monitor performance and compare to targets.
4. Identify reasons for deviations.
5. Make modifications, if necessary.

Set Targets. The marketing plan should set well-defined targets for managers as to what should be achieved and what actions should be performed. In general, the emphasis in these targets should be on output measures (e.g., number of users, usage volume, and share of market), but there may be some critical input factors for which only limited output measures are available. In addition, it may be necessary to set target levels on resource expenditures, such as for volunteer time and monetary costs. To be useful for control purposes, targets need to be set for monthly, quarterly, and other relatively short time periods. Waiting to the end of the year to examine deviations is too late.

Determine Acceptable Deviations. As we discussed earlier, it is unrealistic to expect every target to be met exactly. The targets, as is the entire marketing plan, should be based on the best available information at the time, but the future is never certain. Not every deviation is equally serious, however, and a meaningful decentralized management system must allow managers some degree of discretion. By setting limits on tolerable deviations beforehand, operating managers know what range they can operate in, and senior management has a guide or "trigger" to spot exceptions to planned performance. Overachievement as well as underachievement should be signaled. A theater company that exceeds its target of selling 50 percent capacity on subscription by actually selling 70 percent can reduce its efforts to sell single tickets and increase the production budgets for its shows.

Monitor Performance. Unless there is a sound marketing-information system to monitor performance on a timely basis, the control system can achieve little. For an annual marketing plan, the review period should be on a monthly or quarterly basis if the appropriate corrective action is to be taken, as we pointed out earlier. But the review period must also be long enough to be meaningful; a library undertaking a communication program to increase usage of its computer-based information-retrieval services should not expect immediate changes in user behavior.

The targets to be monitored should depend on the marketing plan. In general, the areas typically examined include number of users, amount of usage, share of usage as compared to competitors, relationship of expenses to usage, and market perceptions and attitudes. It is particularly useful to examine market-share results to see if an organization is losing or gaining ground as compared to its competitors. Thus while one Vancouver theater had a decline in attendance of 10 percent in the first quarter of 1982, this number compared to a citywide decline of 20 percent. Changes in market perceptions and attitudes, which can be measured by some of the techniques discussed in Chapter 8, "Marketing Research," are a useful precursor of future changes in usage and behavior.

Identify Reasons for Deviations. Once a significant deviation is detected, diagnosing its cause is most important. One possible explanation is a poor forecast, perhaps because of an overly optimistic estimate by management. Deviations in usage can have many external causes such as changing market conditions, competitive actions, and other environmental factors, but ineffective or poorly implemented marketing programs are also possible explanations. The reasons for the deviations may be discovered through usage of the organization's existing marketing information and interviews with key managers, staff, and users, but special studies may also be required. When deviations occur on the expense side, such explanations as unanticipated price increases by suppliers, inadequate estimates of the resources required to reach targets, and faster (or slower) achievement of performance targets must be investigated. Before corrective action, if any, is taken, the probable reasons for significant deviations must be found.

Make Modifications, if Necessary. Depending on the extent and nature of the deviation, various corrective actions are called for. If the deviations are minor, merely calling attention to them may be sufficient to overcome the problem. If the deviations are large, it may be necessary to revise targets (upward or downward) for the rest of the planning period. In some cases, as discussed earlier, a contingency strategy may already be in place for dealing with the problem. Otherwise, new alternatives must be quickly developed, evaluated, and implemented. An agency does not always want to operate in a crisis management phase, but it must be prepared to do so at times. A sound marketing plan that is carefully monitored by a marketing control system should lead to early detection of significant deviations so that modifications can be made to limit potential crises.

AN EXAMPLE OF A MARKETING PLAN—HILLSIDE CENTER

The non-profit Hillside Center for Learning-Disabled People seeks to advance and improve the general well-being of people who possess a learning disability, regardless of age. The Center, located in a major midwestern city, began operations in 1972.

Broadly speaking, the Center offers information, counselling, referral services and educational programs *pertaining to* the various problems encountered by the learning disabled. Each summer, it runs a 4-week summer camp for learning-disabled children in a national forest 100 miles away. Located within the office is a small library of books, articles, films, and tapes concerning learning disabilities. The Center also publishes a

Table 5.3 Hillside—Present Activity Structure

I. Core Products

1. *Summer Camp*—Offered in country for four weeks/year. Cost to parents is $800.
2. *Free Tutors*—for LD kids/adults.
3. *Adult Support Group*—meets weekly to discuss members' problems, concerns with employees/manager.
4. *Preschool Program*—Intercepts and diagnoses LD children before problems arise in school.
5. *Adult Literacy Program.*
6. *Socialization Program*—for LD adults and children—to aid in adapting to new environments.
7. *Student Tracking Program*—provides feedback on how LD children fare during and after school.
8. *Learning Workshops*—for corrections personnel, adult special educators, classroom teachers and social service agencies.
9. *Counseling.*

II. Supplementary Products

1. *Referral Services.*
2. *Publishing of regular monthly newsletters.*
3. *Guest Speakers.*

III. Resource Attraction Products

1. *Memberships* ($10.00/year).
2. *Casino, Bingo.*
3. *Annual "Walk For Literacy"*—to raise public awareness and funds for illiteracy program.
4. *Direct Mail Campaign.*

regular newsletter and presents guest speakers at general meetings. Table 5.3 contains a detailed listing of present programs, subdivided into (1) *core products*, made up of services and other activities that are central to the organization's mission; (2) *supplementary products* that enhance and facilitate use of the center's core products; and (3) *resource attraction products*, representing programs designed to generate additional revenues for Hillside. (We will discuss this three-part approach to grouping an organization's products in more depth in Chapter 9, "Product Offerings.")

The Hillside Center for Learning Disabled People has five full-time professional staff and two part-time staff, as well as volunteer help. In addition, staff is hired seasonally to run the summer camp program.

At present there is effectively no marketing program at the Center, although considerable money is spent in advertising, direct mail, and fund raising. The following are selected portions of a marketing plan developed by a volunteer consultant.

SITUATIONAL ANALYSIS

External Environment

While the Hillside Center for Learning Disabled People does not consciously compete with other organizations on an enterprise-specific level, competition does exist on many other levels:

1. *Generic Level* . Many people confuse the Hillside Center with another organization in the same city, the Mentally Handicapped Foundation. (The distinction is that learning disabled people typically possess average to above-average intelligence levels.) Since the Mentally Handicapped Foundation enjoys a higher profile, it is possible that many of the donations it receives were actually intended to help learning disabled people!

   The Hillside Center also competes with the myriad of other charities for donors. In addition, Hillside, along with many other social service agencies, would like to have more volunteers, especially those who are willing to stay with the agency for a number of years. [Volunteer activities are not addressed in this plan.]

2. *Competition from the Status Quo.* Because the Center is also involved in trying to alter people's attitude toward learning disabilities, people must first be convinced to change long-standing ideas and beliefs. Inertia is a powerful force, and often those intimately involved with the organization do not appreciate that others simply do not care as much about the well-being of the learning disabled.

3. *Funding.* The external funding receipts received are comprised of government grants (25% from the City of Hillside), United Way contributions (30%) and donations (10%). This places the Center in a precarious position if either of the two major sources decides to withdraw support. The summer camp program accounts for 25% of revenue but also 35% of total expenditures.

   A related issue involves the alarming trend of government grants—down 5% in the most recent year. This reflects a national trend in governmental circles of encouraging self-reliance on the part of not-for-profit organizations. Moreover, there are no indications that donations will be increasing substantially in the future.

In a small random sample telephone survey ($n = 25$) regarding awareness of the Hillside Center for Learning Disabled People, only two respondents could give an accurate description of the organization, and only three respondents knew of its existence. There is clearly a lack of awareness about what the Center does. On the other hand, given the Center's limited annual budget (approximately $400,000 this year), it may be unrealistic to expect much more. Facing this financial situation it is difficult to mount any appreciable research effort directed toward segmenting the local learning disabled population that the Center serves. Statewide, 20% of the population is affected with some form of learning disability including 2% with dyslexia and 6% with hyperactivity. About 10% of all learning disability cases are severe; the remainder are about equally divided between mild and moderate. Other relevant data are that 35% of people with learning disabilities are 18 years old or less, up to 80% of delinquent youngsters have undetected learning disabilities, and more than 50% of the young drug addicts have a learning disability.

Internal

The Hillside Center's stated objective is ". . . to advance and improve the educational opportunities and general well-being of children and adults."

Two questions arise from this objective. First, with resources of $400,000+/year, is the organization trying to serve a user market too large for its means—resulting in few benefits accruing to anyone? Second, should allowance be made for *awareness creation* of what learning disabilities are and of what the Hillside Center for Learning Disabled People does?

With respect to the first question, it appears that the Center is trying to spread a small amount of money over a wide area, the net effect of which is less than what would be desired. One of the primary recommendations will be to alter the fundamental objectives, from an orientation involving the treatment of kids *and* adults to one concentrating *solely* on children (school aged and under). The plan argues for this approach, but recognizes the need for organizational commitment to it before implementation can proceed.

With regard to the question of awareness creation, if the Center ever wants to generate more than a minimal awareness level, it must make awareness generation a top priority. Awareness must come before widespread donations, and without financial support in the form of donations the Center will continue to run the risk of shutdown in the event that either of its two major sponsors pulls out.

MARKETING PROGRAM GOALS

The primary marketing goals to be achieved are listed in Table 5.4. A time frame for their accomplishment is given as well.

Children aged 18 and under are the focus of the student target program for four reasons. First, early detection and treatment of learning disabled children costs far less in dollars and in wasted years than does the treatment and rehabilitation of learning disabled adults. It is only prudent that the Center's limited funds be directed toward areas which will benefit the greatest number of people for the longest period of time. Second, this strategy attacks the problem where it *originates* rather than treating adult symptoms long

Table 5.4 Marketing Program Goals

Fundraising	Time Frame
1. Increase *net* donations in both corporate and private sector by 20% per year.	Each of next five years
2. Increase amount of 1987 United Way funding by 20% over previous year—due to high 1987 collections expectations; maintain real value of donations thereafter.	Foreseeable future
3. Lobby to obtain government funding increases equal to the rate of inflation—thus preserving real value.	Foreseeable future
4. Establish a contingency fund—allocating $10,000 initially, may be able to get this from a local foundation if treated as an endowment fund.	Until fund at $50,000, real value maintenance thereafter
Awareness	
Increase public awareness of the Center to the 25% level.	Two years, intermediate targets to be set
Market Served	
1. Alter the goal of old and new HCLDP programs—from helping adults *and* children to that of helping "school aged and under" children (18 and under) only.	Three months
2. Introduce new programs for children.	Six months

after the destructive process of the learning disability has taken its toll. Children aided early in life will not consume the Center's scarce resources in later life. Third, our society is very child-centered, and people tend to become more concerned about issues involving children. And fourth, while many adults suffer from the effects of learning disabilities, and programs could benefit many of them if the resources were available; it comes down to the question of directing available dollars to places where they will do the greatest amount of good.

A separate plan to demarket services to adults has been developed, but is not included here.

MARKETING STRATEGIES

Positioning

Following from the previous section, it is recommended that the Hillside Center for Learning Disabled People position itself so that its primary *target segment* consists of children aged 18 and under. The implications of this choice for fundraising are discussed below.

To meet the needs of this segment, Hillside Center should continue all existing programs for this age group, particularly the summer camp. In addition, a major innovation will be a program directed towards children attending public schools, *the school target program*.

Because of limited funds and the need to achieve success early in the life of the program (to reinforce its value), a single school will initially be targeted. Presentations will be made first to the principal (in an attempt to get an internal opinion leader on the side of the Center) and then teachers, followed up by school board/trustee presentations. The presentations will emphasize that learning disabled children possess average to above average intelligence levels. The potential nonmonetary benefits to be emphasized include lower delinquency levels, fewer dropouts, more productive students, decreased teacher stress levels, and upgraded teacher training in diagnosing learning disabilities. (Benefits must be presented to school personnel and others in terms that *they* can relate to.)

There are also potential monetary benefits in reduced taxes, such as fewer long-term funding requirements to support delinquency programs, prison systems, the welfare structure.

Once the Center has one success it can point to, other schools will be more easily convinced. Ideally, a "snowballing" effect will occur. Choosing a progressive school for the initial project is of great importance. It is paramount that the first attempt be successful.

The Hillside Center with its new focus on kids and school target program has to be repositioned in the minds of present and potential donors. As mentioned previously, awareness must come before potential donors evolve into present donors. However, the themes used to increase awareness and generate donations will be similar: tax savings and crime prevention. The corporate and private sectors require somewhat different but related approaches.

For the *corporate sector* the tax savings aspect will be emphasized, pointing out the tax costs of funding delinquency programs, prisons, and centers like Hillside, that try to rehabilitate the adult victims of learning disabilities. For the *private sector*, crime prevention will be emphasized. A special program will be developed for people living near the selected school. An alternative is an emotional appeal, based on a theme of "what if your child had a learning disability." These themes are tentative.

The Center should also try to determine what similar organizations in other cities are doing—refinements in positioning may be necessary following such observations.

Marketing Mix

Product. The Hillside Center will still have no tangible products; the new product mix can be divided into social behavior products and services.

The new core product and supplementary product lines will be geared toward kids 18 and under, via the school system. Resource attraction products will also be altered to some extent.

In the long-term it would be preferable to extend the summer camp over a period longer than four weeks, but this will ultimately depend upon funding availability.

Price. Not many Center products have a price tag attached to them; however those that do have been analyzed. The most significant is the summer camp. A fee of $800 for four weeks represents a significant outlay to many families, but doesn't quite cover camp costs. The program is one of the most successful in getting learning disabled children to interact in a group environment. From that standpoint, the Center's mission is being promoted, so increasing prices to generate revenue would be counterproductive if children were to be turned away for financial reasons, which seems likely. Corporate sponsorships may help defer costs.

The membership fee is currently $10. Consideration was given to doubling the membership fee to $20, but small fees in the $10 range encourage more membership, a priority at this time. New members can learn from the newsletter they receive, and ideally will be moved to contribute on their own.

Government regulations allow the Hillside Center, as a nonprofit organization, to run casino/bingo programs. Prices are comparable to competitive establishments. No changes are recommended.

Distribution. The *school program* represents a major innovation for Hillside. The efficiency of reaching many children at once, combined with the cost efficiency of treating children instead of adults, makes the distribution of this program through the schools the logical choice.

This program will initially target one school only. The Hillside Center will then approach other schools, using past successes as a part of the sales presentation.

Because the Center has no tangible products, the *facility* in which it operates is likely to be used to judge the quality of the organization. It is best to have a well-furnished but not opulent office that clients and donors alike find inviting, but again financial constraints intervene. It is simply a fact of life that the Center will be situated in very modest quarters for the foreseeable future.

The *campsite* is in very good condition, due to receipt of funds from an estate directed to this purpose.

Communication. Communication strategies should ideally be targeted toward well researched consumer segments. The Center has not done and cannot afford to do extensive research on this issue. Consequently the strategy outlined is based on what is presently known.

Some points to bear in mind when implementing this strategy are worth mentioning. The key to success is to have the Center's messages delivered in a consistent manner. They must be mutually reinforcing and directed toward achieving clearly specified objectives.

The recipient may not (and probably will not) share the view of the Center and its cause with those actually working there. Consequently the offerings may not initially be

Table 5.5 Suggested Communication Strategy

Awareness Building

- *PSAs* on radio and television. A local ad agency is willing to produce these as a donation; television stations say they will run them for free.
- *Billboards* are a relatively inexpensive, effective awareness builder. Not commonly used for this kind of organization, billboards could be highly effective *because* of the unusual application.
- Explore the possibility of donated *co-op advertising*. A local food chain might be persuaded to give out donation cards, also using them as advertising.
- *Radio talk shows*. The executive director has good speaking ability. This is a relatively easy (and free) way to build awareness of broad and specific topics related to Center. These communications will carry messages dealing with the school programs, other programs, and statistics demonstrating the high correlation between juvenile delinquency and learning disabilities, as well as the cost of rehabilitation that society must incur if children are allowed to reach adulthood before the diagnosis of a learning disability is made and treatment begins.
- An easy to remember phone number should be obtained and placed in these forms of communication—to allow people to reach the Center.
- Serious consideration should be given to *changing the Center's name*—for two reasons. First, the focus is now on kids and the name should reflect this. And second, the "Hillside Center for Learning Disabled People" is tough to fit on billboards and even more difficult to remember. One possible alternative is: *SKO*—Special (or Super) Kids Organization. The first letters of the title words flow well together, thus aiding recall. Also the full name has a *positive* tone.

School Program

- The communication strategy will initially be targeted to one of the large public schools in Hillside. "Personal selling" of the program will be used almost exclusively. A full set of criteria for choosing a school needs to be specified. The minimum requirements are a school in which the principal appears to be progressive and innovative, at least ten children with learning disabilities are enrolled (two or more having attended Hillside's summer camp), and a stable school district population. Teacher attitudes are also critical.

Effective ways of gaining initial support include:

- Convince the principal of the school of the program's benefits. It is much easier to win final support with the backing of an internal opinion leader.
- Identify the teachers likely to become involved in the program and meet with each one personally.
- Try to get information on the Center's proposal included in the package that is sent to parents by teachers. This information would push the statistical evidence of learning disabilities and may even aid in obtaining donations.
- Objective: to try and get a "Demand-Pull" effect working on the school board.

    Once the first school success is achieved, remaining schools should be more easily convinced, and a "snowball" effect should occur.

Fundraising

Twenty-five target employers in the city have been identified and will be approached on a personal basis by a volunteer committee. Residents of the selected school district will be approached through a direct-mail campaign, school notices, and door-to-door campaign.

seen as inherently desirable. This part of the message must be outlined clearly (broad, socially abstract appeals like "support the Hillside Center for Learning Disabled people" invite people to say to themselves "let someone else do it").

The communication strategy has been divided into (1) awareness building, (2) school target program, and (3) fund raising. These are detailed in Table 5.5.

Contingencies. Allowances for contingencies must be made. The two primary risk areas are funding cuts and failing to get the chosen school to adopt the program.

If the United Way or the City of Hillside withdrew their support, the Center would be forced to curtail the majority of its activities. The only real weapon against this contingency is to try to diversify the Center's funding sources to reduce dependence upon these two organizations.

The chance that the first school chosen does not adopt the program is a possibility, no matter how much care is taken in choosing a likely school. Back-up schools must be identified. Once a school is chosen, it is imperative that the first attempt succeed—this kind of program cannot be tried at another school having failed the first time.

MARKETING BUDGET

The marketing budget, expressed as percentages, is summarized in Table 5.6 for dollar expenditures, staff time, and volunteer time. The anticipated dollar level is $100,000.

A breakdown of expected marketing communication expenditures (across all programs) is given in Table 5.7.

Table 5.6 Marketing Budget

	Percent of Dollar Budget	Percent of Paid Employees' Time	Percent of Volunteers' Time
I. Core Products			
1. Summer Camp	10	5	5
2. Free tutors	5	15	10
3. School Target Program	30	20	15
	45%	40%	30%
II. Supplementary Products			
1. Monthly Newsletter	5	5	10
III. Resource Attraction Products			
1. Membership Program	5	5	5
2. Casino/Bingo	10	10	10
3. Annual Walk for Literacy	5	5	5
4. Personal Solicitation (Corporate Organizations)	15	20	—
5. Public Awareness/Fundraising	15	15	35
	50%	55%	55%

Table 5.7 Communication Expenditure Plan

Activity	Percent of Budget	Expenditure Plan Notes
Personal Selling	45	Relatively large portion of expenses devoted to School Target Program, corporate solicitations and volunteer door-to-door work.
Paid Radio/TV	5	Not much being spent as it is anticipated that the majority of air time will come via the PSA route.
Billboard Advertising	10	As previously explained.
Printed Items	30	Used in conjunction with personal selling— i.e., to follow up school target presentations or to be presented while door-to-door canvassing. Also includes cost of printing newsletter.
Miscellaneous	10	
	100%	

MARKETING ACTION PLAN AND MONITORING SYSTEM

A time-based outline of activities is shown in Table 5.8. Within one month of approval of the marketing plan and activity schedule, a performance monitoring system based on actions required to implement this plan and expected outputs will be established.

Table 5.8 Activity Schedules

Activity	Time Period
1. "Sell" marketing and consumer orientation concepts to manager, staff, volunteers	Continual
2. Develop performance monitoring system	January
3. Name change, obtain easy to remember phone number	February
4. School Target Program	
▪ Develop program plan	January
▪ Choose school (likely will have looked at 5 or 6)	February
▪ Public awareness advertising: PSA's—radio/TV, Billboards (located near school area)	April
▪ Presentations to school	May/June
▪ Program startup	September
5. Phase out adult activities (adult literacy program, learning workshop, adult support group, guest speaker program)	January–July
6. Launch of summer camp marketing campaign	March
7. Corporate Fund Raising Campaign	
▪ Begin planning	April
▪ Implementation	October/November

SUMMARY

Many public and nonprofit organizations carry out some of the elements of a marketing plan. There is a distinct advantage to conducting a thorough analysis of the organization's marketing situation and using that analysis as the basis for establishing a coherent marketing plan, which is then used as a guide for action and a standard for measuring achievement.

In this chapter, we offered a framework around which to build a marketing plan, indicating, in general, the analyses to be done and the areas to be covered in a plan. Although neither our framework nor the Hillside marketing plan presented can claim to be perfect or universally applicable, these materials provide a useful guide and help to demonstrate the nature and advantages of a marketing plan.

REFERENCES

1. A number of nonprofit industry associations have begun to publish books and pamphlets containing sample marketing plans. For example, plans from West Hollywood, Shreveport, and Salt Lake City are summarized in Jeffrey P. Davidson, *Marketing Your Community,* Washington, D.C.: Public Technology, Inc., 1986, pp. 53–68.

2. See Peter T. Hutchinson, Don E. Parkinson, and Charles B. Weinberg, "Water Conservation in Palo Alto," in C. H. Lovelock and C. B. Weinberg, *Public and Nonprofit Marketing: Cases and Readings.* New York: John Wiley & Sons, 1984.

3. As quoted in Ellen Greenberg, "Competing for Scarce Resources," *The Journal of Business Strategy,* 2, (Winter 1982), pp. 81–87.

4. David B. Montgomery, and Charles B. Weinberg, "Toward Strategic Intelligence Systems," *Journal of Marketing* (Fall 1979).

5. David S. Hopkins, *The Marketing Plan,* New York: Conference Board, 1981, p. 12.

6. As in reference 5, p. 10.

7. See Pamela W. Gelfand and William D. Novelli, "National High Blood Pressure Education Program" in D. Cravens and C. Lamb, *Strategic Marketing: Cases and Applications,* 2nd ed., Homewood, Ill.: Richard C. Irwin, 1986.

8. Excerpted, by permission of the publisher, from *Putting It All Together.* by William E. Rothschild, p. 255. © 1976 by AMACOM, a division of American Management Association, New York. All rights reserved.

9. Useful discussions of marketing control may be found in Joseph P. Guiltinan and Gordon W. Paul, *Marketing Management: Strategies and Programs,* 3rd ed., New York: McGraw-Hill, 1988, on which this section is partially based.

PART 3

Understanding Customers

Chapter 6 _____
Consumer Behavior &
Decision Making

A sound marketing plan is built on a knowledge of consumer behavior that allows a manager to understand how and why individuals, families, organizations, or other groups decide to use (or not use) offered products or to adopt (or not adopt) advocated behaviors.[1]

Consumer behavior is a complex subject. Consumption behavior patterns not only differ among individuals (and among organizations), but they also vary across products. Deciding to conserve energy by installing home insulation generally requires more thought and attention than deciding whether or not to buckle a seat belt. Yet the former action needs to be performed only once (if done properly), whereas the latter should be performed each time driver and passengers take a drive. As we will see, an important determinant of consumer behavior is how *involved* people are with the good or service being offered. A critical lesson for all to learn is that the service provider usually considers the product to be much more important than the user. Thus, while highway-safety organizations view wearing seat belts as vital, the great majority of the population is indifferent to this behavior.

This chapter concentrates on individual behavior, but a study of consumer behavior often needs to include the interactions among individuals. For example, the decision to lower the temperature setting on the home thermostat may involve the agreement (or, at least, not disagreement) of all members of the household. When marketing to organizations, such as when asking a corporation to donate money or offering services to a governmental agency, the procedures of the organization and the roles of different organizational personnel often need to be carefully understood. For example, a corporate-support officer's approval may be required for a large donation, a general manager may influence what requests are considered by a donation committee, but only the committee can decide which of the approved requests are actually to be funded.

Scope of the Chapter

This chapter is divided into five major sections. The first section offers examples of four decisions ranging from enlisting in military service to disposing of waste in a litter basket. We use these examples throughout the chapter.

In the second section, we examine the role of involvement of consumer decision making. We show that the steps a person goes through in making a decision depend on the importance of that decision to the individual and the frequency with which similar decisions are made.

The next section considers external and internal characteristics that have an impact on consumer behavior. We examine how such external factors as culture, social class, and reference groups (peers, family members, and others), as well as situational characteristics, influence what people decide to do and how they make decisions. In this section, we also examine the impact of life-style and other personal characteristics on consumer behavior.

One personal characteristic, attitudinal structure, is so central to many aspects of consumer behavior that the fourth section is devoted to just this topic and related issues. In particular, we look at the relationships among beliefs, attitudes, and behavioral intentions.

The fifth and last section of this chapter examines organizational buying behavior. We show that organizational buying decisions can be arrayed on a continuum ranging from a straight repurchase to a new task. The last category often becomes quite complex and can involve several people with different organizational positions and responsibilities. In such a case, in addition to understanding the people involved as individuals, it may be necessary to consider both their formal and informal roles and interactions in the organization.

FOUR ILLUSTRATIVE CONSUMER-CHOICE SITUATIONS

Understanding how people make choices can contribute greatly to making marketing more efficient. Yet decision making appears to be too complex to reduce to a simple rule, and people often have difficulty in reporting how or why they made decisions. Nevertheless there has been some progress in generating theories about consumer behavior in different settings. More and more, consumer researchers have come to accept the notion that the choice process depends on situational factors. The goal of much research has been to establish which situational contingencies are relevant and to understand decision making in these contexts. In this section we examine the nature of these settings and the theories that have emerged. First, in order to show the diversity of choice situations that can arise, we present four vignettes of different decision processes.

Timothy Turner Joins the Navy

As Timothy Turner neared completion of his fourth year of high school, he began to think of what he would do after graduation. He knew his grades were good enough for him to go to college, but neither he nor his family had the money to pay for a full-time college education. Besides, most of his friends were not going to college, and he did not really like school that much, anyway. He wanted a job where he could earn some spending money now and learn a trade for the future. Watching television one afternoon, Timothy saw an ad for the "new, modern volunteer army." Timothy had seen such ads many times before, but he never had paid much attention to them. But the ad's emphasis on learning a skilled trade while getting paid for it attracted him.

On the bus to school, he saw a sign that gave the address of the navy recruiter's office downtown. A week later, Timothy visited the recruiter, who told Timothy that he could train in lots of different fields, and still have a taste of adventure on ships that roamed the world. Meanwhile, he spoke with an army recruiter who came to the school and learned that the army had similar training programs. One of Timothy's friends enlisted in the air force and hoped to become a pilot, but Timothy knew that his eyesight was too poor for him to be a pilot.

At the same time he started looking for jobs around the city, but the few jobs available did not appeal to him. He could be a clerk in a hardware store or work at a filling station. More and more, he liked the idea of joining the army or navy. His father, who had served in the Korean War, was somewhat skeptical about the promises of career training—"the only thing 1 learned was to peel potatoes"—but both parents thought it would be "okay." Meanwhile, Timothy had had many conversations with the recruiters from both the army and the navy. He had decided he wanted training as an electrician, and both services would guarantee that in advance. Although some of the kids in school did not think too much of the military, his close friends thought it was okay if you didn't mind living in barracks. When one of his friends decided to join the navy, Timothy also enlisted so they could go to training camp together.

Beth Handel Contributes to the United Way

On Friday, January 15, Beth Handel, a marketing manager at a consumer goods firm, received an envelope with her semimonthly paycheck. Also in the envelope were a letter and form asking her to contribute by payroll deduction to the United Way. As she had for each of the past five years, she checked off the appropriate box to have a contribution deducted from each paycheck.

Robert DeMille Saves It for the Litter Basket

Robert DeMille had just finished a chocolate bar and was about to throw the wrapper on the sidewalk. Just in front of him he saw a new sign that said "Save It for the Litter Basket," and he threw the wrapper in the adjacent basket.

Amy Jordan Rides the Bus

For the past three years, Amy Jordan had been driving her own car downtown to the camera shop where she worked. She liked the convenience of her car, especially when she worked late or shopped after work. Occasionally, when she had to bring photographic equipment home, she could load the car right outside the shop. Lately, however, she had begun to notice the increasing rates in parking lots downtown, and, although she did not keep track, she knew that gasoline prices were rising. In addition, rush-hour traffic was frequently snarled and the 20-minute drive was a "hassle."

Recently, the local transit company had been taken over by a government agency. One of the first steps was to add a fleet of new buses and develop new schedules. Amy knew it was a 5-minute walk to the bus stop and a 25-minute ride to her store. Bus service was frequent until 10 P.M., so it was unlikely that she would have to wait for more than 10 minutes, but she wondered if she would get a seat. The bus fare was 75¢ each way, but she could buy a monthly pass for $25.

She really did not spend much time thinking about all this, but the next sunny day, she decided to take the bus to work. The ride was comfortable, as she expected, but she could not get a seat in the middle of the rush hour. She did get to glance at the morning paper, however. Her ride home was just after the rush hour, so she had a chance to sit and relax. The next day it rained, and Amy drove her car, but as time went on, she rode the bus to work more and more often, until she was taking it about half the time.

THREE DECISION-MAKING SITUATIONS: COMPLEX, LOW INVOLVEMENT, AND REPETITIVE[2]

We will now discuss and elaborate on three categories of decision making: complex, low involvement, and repetitive or habitual. Timothy Turner's enlistment decision and Amy Jordan's trial of the bus service would be classified as complex. On the other hand, Robert DeMille's antilittering behavior would be classified as low involvement; he was not particularly concerned with either the behavior or its outcome. Finally, Beth Handel's contribution to the United Way and Amy Jordan's regular ridership of the bus (in her case subsequent to a complex decision process) illustrate repeat or habitual behavior.

Complex Decision Making

Some decisions, such as deciding to join the navy, are the result of a complex thought process that extends over a period of time and involves interaction with both mass media and personal information sources. For purposes of analysis it is convenient to divide such complex decision making into five stages.

1. Problem recognition.
2. Information processing.
3. Evaluation of alternatives.
4. Choice.
5. Outcome of choice.

These five stages are diagrammed in Figure 6.1 and discussed below. Of course, as with any general model, such a structure tends to highlight the main features common to a wide class of decisions, and the specifics of each choice situation will vary. It is often useful to construct a flowchart of the steps involved in choosing, acquiring, and using a particular product.

Problem Recognition. The first stage of the decision process is for the consumer to recognize that he or she has a set of needs to be fulfilled. This arousal of needs can occur as a result of external or internal stimuli. For example, Timothy Turner's impending graduation from high school sparked him to look for job options. Perhaps advertising or news coverage of the new transit system first started Amy Jordan thinking about using the bus. The need for novelty or desire for change may sometimes be important in problem recognition. Performing-arts groups may attract people who are simply bored with television.

Need arousal starts the decision process. In retrospect, it is often difficult to specify precisely when problem recognition and the subsequent decision process start because people are continually facing many choices and alternatives at varying levels of consciousness and thought. Thus Amy Jordan was not constantly thinking about whether she should ride the bus or not, but she did go through some of the steps that we will discuss.

At any given point in time, individuals may have a set of needs to be fulfilled and attitudes toward alternatives. A key notion in the complex decision-process model is that the individual proceeds through a deliberate period of information search and processing and of evaluation of alternatives. An individual's needs set the parameters for the search

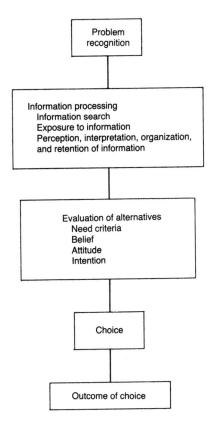

Figure 6.1 Diagram of a complex decision process.

process as well as the criteria to be used in evaluating alternatives. Needs are fundamental; ultimately, products are judged on their likelihood of satisfying needs.

Information Processing. In complex decision making, information processing involves the search for information, the exposure to information, and the mental processes related to the perception, interpretation, organization, and retention of information. In other situations, as when Beth Handel contributed to the United Way, information processing can be very limited and quite different from that in complex decision making.

Information search can be both incidental and deliberate. Timothy Turner was not watching television to learn about military training, but because he was concerned about this as a career option, he paid attention when he saw the advertisement. In contrast, his visits to the military recruiters were quite deliberate. Information search is carried out throughout the decision process, when alternatives are first being identified and when final choices are being made. In many cases, consumers do not engage in extensive deliberate information search. Casual observation suggests that few people do comparison shopping for such seemingly vital products as medical services. Marketers need to be concerned with providing information both for active and passive information seekers. The kind of information needed, as well, can vary according to the stage of the decision process the consumer is in.

Attention, comprehension, and retention of information follow exposure to a message. *Attention* is the process of taking note of all or part of a communication message or other stimulus. *Comprehension* concerns the interpretation that an individual places on a stimulus or message. *Retention* refers to the storage of information in memory.

Consumer exposure to information—and other stimuli—is *selective*. People tend to avoid information that is counter to their beliefs or past experiences. This is of particular concern to managers of behavior-change programs. For example, cigarette smokers may not "see" the Surgeon General's health warning on a pack of cigarettes, and "out of shape" people may not "hear" commercials advocating physical fitness. Stimuli are most likely to be perceived accurately when they:

- Conform to past experiences.
- Conform to current beliefs.
- Are not too complex.
- Are believable.
- Relate to a set of current needs.
- Do not produce excessive fears and anxieties.

Selective perception has two aspects. One is *perceptual vigilance* in which the user seeks and pays attention to information that is useful for decisions that he or she is concerned about, and that screens out unnecessary or irrelevant information. The other aspect is *perceptual defense,* whereby people distort information to conform to their beliefs and attitudes and thus protect themselves from threatening or contradictory data. For example, one study found that 80 percent of nonsmokers believed the link between lung cancer and cigarette smoking was proved, but only 52 percent of heavy smokers believed this.[3]

Perceptual vigilance and defense help to provide consistency between the information received and an individual's needs, attitudes, and behavior. *Before* a choice is made, conflicting information may be deliberately sought to help decide. Afterward, however, the focus may be on confirming the correctness of the chosen alternative.

Evaluation of Alternatives. Prior to making a choice in complex situations, the user evaluates the different alternatives, including that of doing nothing.

Since users often find it difficult to compare numerous alternatives, they simplify their evaluation task in several ways. First, they seldom consider the entire set of all possible choices. Instead, they focus on a limited set of options (usually referred to as the *evoked* set) which offer promise for satisfying their needs and with which they are familiar from past experience or information gained from personal or media sources.

Next, the user evaluates each alternative in the evoked set on a limited number of *product dimensions* or *attributes*. These attributes or characteristics may be the physical or performance dimensions of each alternative, as perceived by the user, or a benefit that the user expects to gain. To emphasize that an individual's viewpoint is crucial, the term "belief" is often used to represent the extent to which the alternative possesses each characteristic or attribute. For instance not everyone believes that attending college improves one's job prospects and of those who do, the belief about the amount of gain resulting varies as well.

The user also makes judgments about the *relative importance* of these attributes, or about the minimum level of performance he or she is willing to accept on each dimension. Amy Jordan's most important criteria in choosing between bus and car may be convenience and speed, but other criteria such as economy may be relevant as well. These need criteria are related to specific features of the alternatives under consideration, so that both parking charges and gasoline prices may be used to judge the economy of car travel.

Both the set of attributes used in evaluating alternatives and the relative importance attached to these attributes represent the individual's *choice criteria*. These choice criteria, in turn, reflect the benefits the person wishes to receive from the option being considered in order to effectively satisfy his or her needs and wants.

Finally, the user arrives at an overall evaluation for each alternative by combining evaluations of attributes, weighted by the relative importance of each attribute. This multi-attribute assessment results in an overall *attitude*, or preference, toward each alternative. The most favorably judged option is the one he or she will be most likely to want to use, adopt, or acquire.

Different people may use different sets of attributes for evaluating alternatives. But even when two people employ the same set of attributes, they may arrive at different attitudes because they attach different levels of importance to specific dimensions. A person's personal characteristics and social influences—his or her needs, values, personality, social class and reference groups, among other things—help determine what attributes will be considered relevant and important in making evaluations. Environmental and situational factors can also impact the perceived importance of various product benefits. For example, a symphony concert goer may be less inclined to want unreserved rush seats when going out with a date than when attending alone.

Intention, the action predisposition toward the alternative, is an intermediate step between preference and action. A person may well prefer a certain course of action but have no intention of behaving in that way, possibly because the cost of doing so is too high. For example, a high-school student may be unwilling to devote the time and effort required to obtain good grades, yet admire those who do.

Lack of availability of a preferred alternative or an unexpected price rise may result in a behavioral intention not being realized. Someone may decide to enlist in the navy but find there are no openings or that the minimum commitment is three years, not the two years previously counted on. The longer time between forming an intention and acting on it, the less likely the action is to be done due to changing circumstances. Accurate and valid measurement of preferences and intentions can be difficult, and measurement problems may also account for the lack of agreement sometimes reported between expressed attitudes and subsequent behavior.

In complex decision making, one important assumption is that beliefs, attitude, and intention operate sequentially: beliefs are formed about the characteristics of the alternatives, attitudes are developed toward the alternatives, and then a behavioral intention is set. This sequence of "learn-feel-do" is referred to as a hierarchy-of-effects model. We will later see that this same hierarchy does not hold in many other situations, such as repeat or habitual behavior and in low-involvement decision making.

Choice. Choice, of course, includes the decision not to adopt any of the available alternatives and to postpone making a decision, as well as to choose an alternative. In complex decision making, the actual choice may be better described as a series of choices. For example, a person deciding to start an exercise program must decide whether to exercise at home, at work, or at a community center or private facility; what type of exercise program to follow; what kind of exercise to do; and how often to exercise.

Implementing a choice in a complex decision-making situation often involves a number of actions and possibly a considerable time span. During this time, incidents may occur that shape or alter the decision. Timothy Turner's choice of the navy was influenced by a friend's enlistment decision. A service provider may sometimes change a person's mind; for example, a physical-education instructor may warn a prospective jogger about knee injuries. Or perhaps a music lover's resolve to attend concerts regularly may evaporate when an unexpected stress situation emerges at work.

Some choice situations involve a one-time situation and others require a repetitive change in behavior. Maintaining a behavior pattern over time requires that the marketer pay attention to methods for reinforcing that behavior, as is evident in the vignettes of Beth Handel's contribution to the United Way and Amy Jordan's use of the bus.

Outcome of Choice. If the service utilized or behavior pattern adopted meets the user's expectations, then he or she is likely to be satisfied. Overstating the favorable aspects of an alternative beyond its true worth increases the likelihood of consumer dissatisfaction. Thus, if Amy Jordan had been told that there were always seats in rush hour, her inability to obtain a seat when going to work might have discouraged her from further usage. Dissatisfied triers of a service are unlikely to become regular users. The first few uses of a product or a new behavior are best viewed as *trials,* not as firm commitments to long-term usage.

Even in the case of choices involving one-time actions, such as installing insulation to save energy, consumers are still likely to make postpurchase evaluations. If the insulation does not reduce heating bills to the extent expected, then the user will be dissatisfied. Aside from seeking redress from the sponsoring organization, the disgruntled user is quite likely to tell friends and acquaintances about this unhappy experience. Such negative comments may be important to others who are forming attitudes about insulation—and may lead them to develop a negative evaluation. This type of person-to-person, "word of mouth" communication is known to be particularly important in establishing preferences. In addition, dissatisfaction by users may eventually influence public opinion in general and thus reduce government appropriations and private contributions to the organization that provides the service or advocates the behavior in question.

Low-Involvement Decision Making

Obviously, complex decision making does not occur in all situations. In this section, we examine low-involvement decision making, such as Robert DeMille's antilittering behavior.

Although the term *involvement* is difficult to define technically, its common-sense interpretation as degree of importance or level of concern generated by the product or behavior is appropriate. In addition, some people may be more involved in a particular situation, and each person's involvement may vary over time.

Low-involvement situations are relatively unimportant to the user; the financial, social, psychological, and other risks are not high. Consequently, it is not worth a person's time and effort to search extensively for information or to evaluate a wide range of alternatives. Mere availability of a reasonable alternative may be sufficiently satisfying and consequently result in its selection. In a low-involvement situation, a person will receive information passively and, from that individual's standpoint, almost at random. If the information and the behavior are closely connected, such as having the sign "Save It for the Litter Basket" located next to the litter basket, then the low-involvement response can be immediate. In such situations, no attitudes or feelings may develop. Afterward Robert DeMille may begin to feel that antilittering is a desirable behavior, but that preference may only form after the behavior has taken place on, perhaps, several occasions.

In the low-involvement case, awareness or belief can lead directly to behavior. Table 6.1 contrasts high-involvement and low-involvement decision making. Marketers of frequently purchased goods such as soap and cereal aggressively seek display space in supermarkets to exploit the linkage between "point-of-purchase" display and behavior.

Table 6.1 Contrasting the High-Involvement, Active Consumer and the Low-Involvement, Positive Consumer

High-Involvement View of an Active Consumer	Low-Involvement View of a Passive Consumer
1. Consumers process information systematically.	1. Consumers learn information at random.
2. Consumers are information seekers.	2. Consumers are information gatherers.
3. Consumers represent an active audience for advertising. As a result, the direct effect of advertising on consumer behavior is weak.	3. Consumers represent a passive audience for advertising. As a result, the effect of advertising on consumer behavior can be strong.
4. Consumers evaluate alternatives before acting.	4. Consumers act. Favorable attitudes may develop afterward.
5. Consumers seek to maximize expected satisfaction. Hence they compare alternatives to see which provide the most benefits related to needs and buy based on multiattribute comparisons of alternatives.	5. Consumers seek some acceptable level of satisfaction and may choose based on a few attributes. Familiarity is the key.
6. Personality and life-style characteristics are related to consumer behavior because the product is closely tied to the consumer's identity and belief system.	6. Personality and life-style characteristics are not related to consumer behavior because the product is not closely tied to the consumer's identity and belief system.
7. Reference groups influence consumer behavior because of the importance of the product to group norms and values.	7. Reference groups exert little influence on product choice because products are unlikely to be related to group norms and values.

Source. Adapted from Henry Assael. *Consumer Behavior and Marketing Action.* (Boston: Kent Publishing Company, 1987) p. 96. © 1987 by Wadsworth, Inc. Reprinted by permission of Kent Publishing, a division of Wadsworth, Inc.

Similarly, public and nonprofit organizations should be particularly attentive to information displays, signs, and the characteristics of the service delivery site itself.

It is not always possible for behavior to follow awareness or knowledge directly. A person without litter has no need to deposit anything in a waste container. Or someone watching television at home cannot act on a suggestion to use a seat belt. (The use of such advertisements as a reminder in a repeat-behavior situation is discussed in the next section.) In many low-involvement situations, an alternative will be chosen because of familiarity. Repetitive advertising, or other regular communication campaigns, may serve primarily to produce familiarity. Then when need arousal does take place, the individual will recall the existence of the alternative without having any (strong) favorable or unfavorable feeling toward it. In low-involvement situations, of course, mere recognition of the alternative may be sufficient to result in behavior when a need arises.

Repeat or Habitual Behavior

Many consumption decisions can best be characterized as representing repeat or habitual behavior. Such decision situations have occurred many times before and probably do not generate much thought on the part of the individual. It is important to recognize that repeat behavior can occur in both high- and low-involvement situations, especially as repetition may lessen involvement. The contribution of Beth Handel to the United Way may involve a substantial sum of money; she may have previously gone through a careful evaluation of several alternative causes to support as well as of sums of money and ways to contribute, but her present behavior appears to have become habitual. Repetitive or habitual behavior does not mean that a person is limited to only one alternative; Amy Jordan uses either her car or a bus to get to work. Often, however, the choice in repetitive behavior is limited to a small subset of all available alternatives. Thus Amy Jordan does not even consider riding to work in a taxi or participating in a carpool.

Many people settle into a regular pattern of behavior because it is simpler and more convenient than constantly changing their behavior. Assuming that the chosen alternative is satisfactory, repeating that behavior helps to reduce the risk that would otherwise occur if a different alternative were to be adopted.

Three main aspects of habitual or repeat behavior appear to be of prime importance to the manager. First, how are repetitive behaviors established when none existed previously? What does it take for Beth Handel to become a consistent United Way contributor and for Amy Jordan to become a frequent transit rider? The beginning of repetitive behavior may be characterized as a high involvement decision. Second, once a behavior is established, what factors support or limit its repetition over time? Third, how are new behaviors established and substituted for old ones? These three questions are, of course, interrelated. For example, convincing people to donate blood regularly or persuading alcoholics to quit drinking and not start again can be viewed either as encouraging them to adopt new behaviors or as persuading them to replace old behaviors by new ones—and then maintain them.

Basic to the notion of habitual behavior is the assumption that behavior is a function of previous actions and the satisfaction obtained from them. Satisfaction leads to reinforcement and to increased likelihood of choosing the same alternative again. Eventually, the behavior becomes ingrained, with the result that information search and alternative evaluation decrease.

To ensure regular use, the marketer needs to make sure that the product or behavior *consistently* fulfills the needs or provides the benefits that generated usage in the first place. Yet, marketers of services and behavior patterns find it much more difficult to maintain consistent quality than do manufacturers. Although defective goods are occasionally shipped to users, quality control can usually ensure that the product meets established standards. On the other hand, consumption of a service often coincides with its final production and requires interaction with one or more employees and other users as well. For example, the bus driver, traffic conditions, and other passengers all influence the satisfaction that a passenger derives from using public transit. This potential lack of consistency makes it difficult to establish the *reinforcing benefits* that help first-time customers to become regular users.

In a competitive, changing environment, habitual behavior cannot be taken for granted: people may forget the behavior in question, due to lack of product use or absence of reminders, or lack of stimuli. For example, suppose a regular seat-belt user borrows a car without belts or goes on holiday. When she returns to her own car, she may "forget" to use seat belts. Intensive communication campaigns are often employed to help prevent forgetting of previous usage after a strike (for example, by an orchestra's musicians or a theater's stage hands) or other event has interrupted service. Organizations that achieve adoption of their products or advocated behaviors should not neglect the need (1) to preserve a market environment that helps to reinforce that behavior, and (2) to remind people of the situations that generated usage of the product and of the appropriate product or behavioral responses in these situations.

Changing Behavior Patterns. Existing behaviors are not immutable. Behavior may change because of a change in circumstances, an individual's desire for variety or novelty, or actions that deliberately focus attention on the repetitive behavior and question its appropriateness.

Marketers seeking to change behavior should be on the lookout for situations which can lead to consideration of new alternatives. If, for example, local private physicians provide limited evening or weekend service, then a health-maintenance organization (HMO) may emphasize its provision of a broad range of services on a 24-hour basis, particularly the availability of "off-hours" services to people who do not regularly use the HMO. In marketing frequently purchased consumer goods, an opportunity to convert loyal users of another brand occurs when that competitor's brand is out of stock in local stores, and the customer has to choose an alternative brand instead. Should the customer find this new brand satisfactory, the competition will lose a loyal user. Public and nonprofit organizations should be sensitive to analogous "out-of-service" situations among their competitors as well as in their own operations.

In addition to waiting for and taking advantage of opportunities, active steps can be taken to change regular behavior patterns, by focusing the consumer's attention on a specific behavior. In brief, there are two main alternatives: (1) introduce a new product or (2) communicate to the consumer that the issue is too important to be treated as a habit. Often these two approaches work together. Amy Jordan's decision to use the bus indicates the first type of situation. A consistent automobile commuter, she began to question her usage of the car after the city took over and revitalized the bus system. She presumably moved from habitual behavior to complex decision making and then on to a new habitual behavior of mixed car and bus use.

If habitual behavior results from a belief by consumers that it is either less risky to maintain established patterns or not worth the time or effort to consider alternatives, then one approach to changing established behaviors would be to demonstrate that the behavior is more important than recognized. One explanation for why previously sedentary people have adopted regular physical fitness and exercise programs in recent years may be the publicity about research findings concerning the link between physical fitness and health. In other words, marketing communication can be used to persuade people that the issue is important. Communication by itself is not enough, however; a complete marketing program to support the adoption and maintenance of the desired behavior must also be developed and implemented.

Sometimes organizations place too much stress on programs to change behaviors and give insufficient focus to maintaining that behavior. For example, in 1977, the Province of British Columbia passed a law making seat-belt usage mandatory for all automobile occupants and supported the law with a substantial communication program and extensive enforcement efforts. As can be seen in Table 6.2, established patterns of nonuse were dramatically reversed. In the ensuing years, however, seat-belt usage received less advertising attention, and traffic enforcement efforts were focused elsewhere. Consequently, seat-belt usage, while substantially above its prelegislation level, has declined (sporadically) over time.

EXTERNAL AND INTERNAL INFLUENCES ON CONSUMER BEHAVIOR

Behavior is influenced by a wide range of external and internal factors. Not all people behave in the same way, and their behavior varies by situation. This section reviews the

Table 6.2 Seat-Belt Usage in British Columbia, 1977–82

	Proportion of Usage, %	
	Drivers	**Passengers**
March 1977[a]	29	24
August 1977[b]	33	24
November 1977	72	66
March 1978	73	58
March 1979	54	43
October 1979	58	42
March 1980	62	55
October 1980	54	49
March 1981	52	47
March 1982	54	46

Source. Based on Western Analysis, Ltd. "A Study of Seat Belt Usage in British Columbia during March 1982," unpublished report, April 1982

[a]Prior to announcement of seat-belt legislation.
[b]After enactment but prior to effective date (October 1, 1977) of seat-belt legislation.

impact of cultural characteristics, reference groups, and personal characteristics. A more detailed discussion of these topics may be found in texts on consumer behavior.[4]

Culture

Culture describes the basic set of norms, beliefs, and customs that are fairly standardized throughout a society. Broad cultural values are passed down from generation to generation and are relatively stable over time. However, cultural values can change; for example, the previous norm of the North American household of a nuclear family with the husband as the wage earner and the wife as homemaker and child raiser has been supplemented by the recognition that households also consist of families where both the husband and wife are wage earners or where a single parent heads the family, of unrelated individuals who live together, and of individuals who live alone.[5] (See Figure 6.2.) Although cultural values vary greatly in their influence, they can sometimes be quite strong, especially when encompassed in religious beliefs or institutional structures.

The importance of cultural values can be seen by comparing attitudes and behavior patterns across nations. Nonbusiness organizations marketing internationally need to be particularly sensitive to these issues. One family-planning agency decided to focus on persuading people to use condoms as a means to limit population growth. It quickly recognized that a single, uniform international program could not be used. Instead, the program had to be carefully adapted to the cultural values of each individual country. For example, in some countries condoms are bought by women, in others by men. Although cultural norms in many nations supported the use of condoms as a legitimate means of birth control, in a few countries condoms were associated primarily with prostitutes. Elsewhere, the organization had to cope with religious beliefs and attitudes about birth control. In some countries the focus would be on spacing the number of children that a married couple would have; in another country the focus was on preventing undesired pregnancies among married or unmarried couples. While cultural values do change over time, most marketers are better advised to adapt their programs to cultural norms than to attempt to change these norms significantly.

Within countries, moreover, different cultures and *subcultures* exist. Not all individuals in a society share the same cultural values; some segments are distinguished by a set of cultural values that set them apart from others in society. Among the many subcultures in the United States are those based on ethnic background, age, and geography. In Canada, French Canadians primarily living in Quebec form a group distinct from what is sometimes called "English Canada." Scotland, Wales, and Northern Ireland are all, like England, part of the United Kingdom, but again their populations represent distinct national subcultures within the broader British culture. Some marketing programs can transcend subcultures, but others need to be varied to reflect linguistic differences, values, historical traditions, religious beliefs, and so forth.

Social class refers to the position of an individual (or family) on a social-status scale based on criteria that are important to that society or culture. In the United States, for instance, social class seems to be based on amount and source of income, education, occupation, and type and location of home.[6]

Social class can affect media exposure, shopping patterns, and purchase behavior. Often, however, an underlying variable, such as educational background, may be a more powerful consumer description, particularly as greater modility blurs class lines.

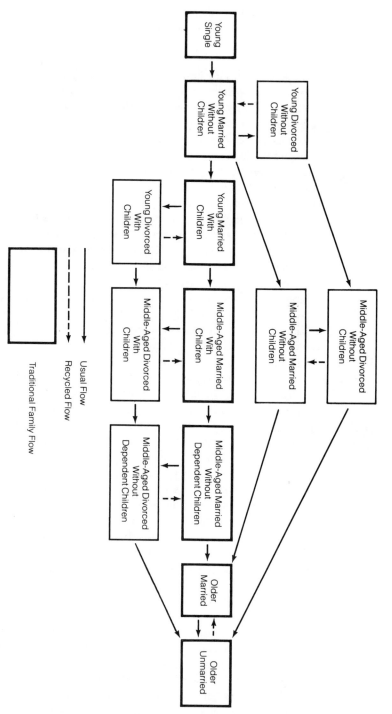

FAMILY LIFE CYCLE FLOWS

Usual Flow

Recycled Flow

Traditional Family Flow

Source: Patrick E. Murphy and William A. Staples, "A Modernized Family Life Cycle," *Journal of Consumer Research* (June 1979). Reprinted by permission of the *Journal of Consumer Research.*

Figure 6.2 Family Life Cycle Flows

Reference Groups

An important influence on a person's attitudes and behavior is the reference group or groups to which he or she belongs, aspires to, or seeks to avoid. Face-to-face groups, such as family, friends, neighbors, and work associates, are often of primary importance, but the perceived values of other groups can be significant, too. Thus agencies attempting to curb drug abuse among teenagers seek endorsements from star professional athletes who are willing to indicate that they do not use drugs. Reference groups include those a person hopes to join, as when a young manager stops riding mass transit because senior management uses private automobiles. Reference groups also include those to which someone symbolically aspires, as when physical fitness programs utilize Olympic champions to promote exercise.

Probably the most influential primary reference groups are families and peers. As most parents would testify, the relative power of these two groups is controversial. The family plays an enduring role in influencing a person's attitudes, values, and behaviors in many fundamental areas. On the other hand, peer pressure can also be a powerful force. Timothy Turner might not have enlisted in the military if *either* his family or friends had spoken strongly against it.

Reference groups influence behavior through their norms, roles played in the group by members, and an individual's status within the group. If most members of a work group jog during the lunch hour, then a new employee is quite likely to jog as well. Each member has a role and status within an organization. Sometimes these can be based on formal arrangements, as in the status of a doctor in a hospital or a curator in a museum. Roles can also be developed informally based on the expertise, age, appearance, or other valued characteristic that allows some group members to have more influence than others. In the section on organizational buying behavior later in this chapter, we see that a number of people (called the "buying center") participate in the buying decision based on their formal and informal roles in the organization. Some people authorize the buying; others may choose which suppliers are qualified to submit proposals; still others may participate in the screening of alternative proposals and develop a short list from which a choice is finally made.

Family members can significantly influence an individual's behavior, even if the behavior only affects that person. Other family members may also have needs that preempt or otherwise alter an individual's choice. We can define up to six roles that one or more individual family members can take in decisions.

1. *Information gatherers* have the most information and the greatest expertise in a particular area. Sometimes this is the consumer, as in the case of Timothy Turner joining the navy, but not always. For example, an older sister may know more about college choices than a younger brother who is choosing which college to attend.

2. *Influencers* are those who establish the means by which alternatives are evaluated and decide which alternatives come closest to meeting the decision criteria. Often the influencers will be the same as the information gatherers. Children can be important influencers in many situations. In the case of college choice, parents may restrict the geographic area considered and set the financial parameters.

3. *Deciders* are those who make the final decision. Confounding traditional cliches—the husband decides to buy the car, the wife chooses the color—changing family structures challenge simple-minded generalizations. So it is important for marketers to determine whether a decision is made by a specific individual or jointly by several people.

4. The *purchaser* is the person who actually purchases the product or, more generally, arranges for usage of the product.

5. The *payer,* who is not necessarily either the purchaser or the user, provides the necessary funds for the transaction. Common examples include a parent paying for a child's tuition at college or adult children paying for a parent's health-care expenses.

6. The *user* is the family member or members who uses the product or adopts the behavior. In the case of seat belts, this might be the entire family or each person individually; in the case of joining the military, it would only be the individual.

As should be clear, the role of family members varies from family to family and within a family, across products. The key point is to determine the role and influence of different family members in the decisions that matter to the organization. The Marine Corps advertisement reproduced in Figure 6.3 recognizes the mother's critical role as an influencer in a young man's choice of which military service to enlist in.

Personal Characteristics

Consumer behavior is undoubtedly influenced by a broad range of such personal characteristics as age, education, family status, life cycle, income, occupation, life-style, and personality. However, the relationships are not as clear or straightforward as one would imagine beforehand. For example, antismoking groups can sharpen their marketing strategies through the information that teenage girls are increasingly becoming cigarette smokers. Not all teenage girls smoke, however, and many smokers come from other demographic segments. Personal characteristics often serve to identify target markets because of their general tendency toward a behavior of interest; we discuss this issue more fully in the next chapter, "Market Segmentation."

Unlike many businesses, some public and nonprofit institutions have to focus their attention on less advantaged groups in society. For example, agencies concerned with prenatal care must develop programs for poorly educated, low-income segments as well as for the middle and upper classes. Transit systems often draw disproportionately from lower-income groups. Almost by definition, many social-service organizations serve disadvantaged and socially alienated groups.

Life-style. Life-style reflects the overall manner in which people live. Life-style can describe the nature of a society as a whole—such as the "American life-style." At a less aggregate level it can be used to describe or distinguish groups and individuals. Life-styles are generally characterized and measured by the *activities, interests* and *opinions* (AIOs) of the population of concern. The use of life-style to supplement traditional demographic and socioeconomic measures has become widespread in marketing.

Identification of specific types of life-styles pursued by different groups of people usually requires lengthy surveys involving large sample sizes. Some of the major dimensions investigated in typical AIO studies include the following:

Activities—work, hobbies, social events, vacations, travel, sports, entertainment, and shopping behavior;

Interests—family, home, job, community, recreation, food, fashion and media;

Opinions—about themselves, social issues, politics, economics, education, the future, culture, organizations, and products

An open letter to a mother whose son is facing manhood...

Now comes the time—as you knew it would—when your son must make his own way in life. It's a time of anticipation for him. A time of hope for you. With all your heart, you want things to go right for him. If you are surprised that the Marine Corps is saying this to you, please don't be. Our mothers were just as concerned about our futures as you are about your son's. And as long as we have been Marines, we have never heard of a mother who wasn't proud of her son becoming one of a few good men.

If your son *is* considering the Marine Corps, we feel there are several things both he and you should understand about us. First—and very important—we are *not* looking for quitters. If he is in high school, he should *finish* high school. If he has the chance to go to college, he should seize the opportunity.

Second, our training is demanding. If it weren't, we wouldn't be the Marines. But your son will be in good hands during his eleven weeks of recruit training. Graduation will be one of the proudest events of his life. And yours.

Lastly, there are many options open to him in the Marine Corps. Even before he enlists, he can choose between regular service or hometown reserve service. He may also qualify to choose the direction his training will take him—into aviation, for instance.

We could go on about the good pay your son will earn, the many educational opportunities open to him, or the scores of other things which would rightfully interest you...but a booklet we have for you is more complete. It's called "Facts Parents Should Know About the United States Marine Corps." To obtain your copy, simply call 800-423-2600, toll free. In California, the number is 800-252-0241.

The Marines

Figure 6.3 Marine Corps advertisement. Copyright © 1975 U.S. Marine Corps. Reprinted by permission.

In each of these topic categories respondents are asked to agree or disagree with specific statements such as, "I like to go camping," "I usually dress for fashion, not for comfort," or "There is too much violence on television."

In any particular study, the first step is to formulate a large number of questions concerning user AIOs and then to select those that best represent different consumer groups. One popular classification of life-style groups has been developed by SRI International's "Values and Life-styles" (VALS) program.[7] As Table 6.3 indicates, the VALS program identifies nine life-style groups in the U.S., each describing a way of life defined by an array of values, beliefs, needs, and points of view.

Due to the expense of collecting such large amounts of information, most life-style studies are conducted by advertising agencies, consulting firms, or collective associations (e.g., the Association of College, University, and Community Arts Administrators' study of performing arts audiences[8]) who can spread the costs and share the results across a number of organizations. From a marketer's point of view, however, a primary objective is to identify one or more lifestyle patterns associated with people favorably predisposed to the organization's products. (see Chapter 7, "Market Segmentation.")

Table 6.3 Characteristics of VALS Life Style

Consumer Group	Percentage of U.S. Population	Selected Characteristics of Typical Group Members
Need Driven		
Survivors	4%	Old, poverty-stricken, poorly educated people who tend to be despairing, depressed, withdrawn.
Sustainers	7%	Low income, high unemployment, large families, young people struggling to get out of poverty and angry, distrustful.
Outer-Directed		
Belongers	33%	Middle age or older, middle income, people who tend to live in small towns and are conventional, conservative, nostalgic, and would rather fit in than stand out.
Emulators	10%	Young, urban, fairly successful people who are ambitious, upwardly mobile, status conscious, and want to "make it big."
Achievers	23%	High income, middle age, own homes, professionals and managers, successful people who work within the system.
Inner-Directed		
"I am me"	5%	Young, single, affluent backgrounds, self-engrossed, and faddish.
Experimentals	7%	Young to middle age, well educated, people with good incomes who want to experience directly what life has to offer.
Societally conscious	9%	Very well educated, middle aged, sophisticated people who have a high sense of social responsibility.
Combined Outer- and-Inner-Directed		
Integrateds	2%	Middle age, high income, very well educated, psychologically mature, people who combine inner- and outer-directedness.

Source: Based on Arnold Mitchell, *The Nine American Life Styles* (New York: Macmillan Publishing, 1983).

Life-style research has been used to segment markets and to help managers position products. Because it provides a richer description of consumers than a demographic or socioeconomic profile, an AIO profile is sometimes used to guide the writing of advertising copy and in preparing promotional programs.

ATTITUDES

Attitudes are one of the most thoroughly researched concepts in marketing and social psychology.[9] Therefore, we devote this section to a further discussion of the concept, measurement, and usage of attitudes in marketing.

An attitude is a feeling—either positive or negative—about an alternative which predisposes a person to behave in a particular way toward that object (e.g., to visit or not visit a museum). Attitudes are formed on the basis of a person's evaluation of the likelihood that a given alternative will provide the benefits necessary to help him or her satisfy a particular need. Such evaluations are multidimensional; each alternative is judged on a number of different dimensions or attributes, and each judgement is weighted by the relative importance of the attribute to the consumer.

Our primary concern in this section is with high-involvement, complex decision-making situations in which attitudes are likely to be important in predicting future behavior—using the service, following the recommended behavior, making suggestions to others, and so forth. When we use the phrase *attitude toward an object,* the reader should recognize that the term *object* can represent a good, a service, a person (political candidate), an issue (pro or con abortion), or a behavior (exercising regularly).

How is this overall evaluation formed? This question turns out to be very difficult to answer, but recent research focuses on the following elements.

1. Goods, services, behaviors, issues, and organizations are conceived of as *multi-attribute* or *multidimensional* objects. Some attributes are objective and easily documented, such as seating capacity of a bus, but others are subjective (e.g., comfort) and more difficult to define and measure.

2. Consumer needs generate a set of *importance weights* that indicate the value placed by consumers on each attribute. These importance weights are based on underlying consumer needs, such as how important speed versus economy is to a commuter.

3. *Attribute beliefs* represent the extent (if any) to which an object possesses each relevant attribute. Beliefs, of course, are based on perception and may differ from objective reality. The beliefs may be based on an absolute standard or compared to an "ideal" object.

4. An *evaluation function* combines the importance weights and beliefs to develop an overall preference of feeling toward the object. If there are several alternatives being considered, the evaluation may result in a ranking of the objects or the selection of one (or several) most or least liked.

While this is a simplified version of the process of alternative evaluation, it allows us to examine some of the issues of most importance to managers. We start by looking at different evaluation functions in the context of the following example.

A commuter can drive her own car, ride a regional rail system, or take a bus to work. In choosing among these three alternatives, the commuter ranks the most important attributes as safety, punctuality, speed, economy, and status. On these five attributes, her perceptions of the three alternatives are as follows (where 10 = outstanding and 1 = highly unsatisfactory).

	Rating of Alternatives		
	Car	**Bus**	**Train**
Safety	9	9	9
Punctuality	7	3	7
Speed	6	6	7
Economy	3	9	7
Status	9	3	6

It is readily apparent that evaluating multiattribute objects is complex, rarely yielding obvious choices. So it is helpful to know how important each of these attributes is to the individual, and how the information is processed. Compensatory and noncompensatory models of evaluation represent two alternative ways of structuring the evaluation process.

In *compensatory* models, all attributes that are important to a consumer are considered simultaneously, so that being low on one attribute can be compensated for by being high on another. In addition, each attribute is weighted by its importance to the consumer, based on the consumer's needs.

To illustrate, suppose a commuter gave these five dimensions of transit service importance ratings (on a scale of 1 to 10, where 10 = most important) as follows:

	Importance
Safety	10
Punctuality	8
Speed	8
Economy	5
Status	5

A compensatory model assumes that the consumer's overall attitude is based on the weighted sum of his or her ratings of each alternative. Thus, the three alternatives would be evaluated (first multiplying importance weights by the attribute rating and then adding) as follows:

$$\text{Car} = (10 \times 9) + (8 \times 7) + (8 \times 6) + (5 \times 3) + (5 \times 9) = 254$$
$$\text{Bus} = (10 \times 9) + (8 \times 3) + (8 \times 6) + (5 \times 9) + (5 \times 3) = 222$$
$$\text{Train} = (10 \times 9) + (8 \times 7) + (8 \times 7) + (5 \times 7) + (5 \times 6) = 267$$

For this commuter, the train would be the most highly evaluated alternative.

This model is "compensatory" because it assumes that, since the consumer's overall attitude toward a service is determined by the *weighted sum* of his or her ratings of that service on all relevant attributes, a poor evaluation on one attribute can be *compensated* for by a strong evaluation on another attribute. It also assumes that the service with the highest total score is the one the consumer will be predisposed to use.

Although safety is easily the most important attribute, it doesn't affect the final ratings at all. This result illustrates how necessary it is to distinguish between important and determinant attributes. If the consumer rates all competing services on an important attribute at the same (or very similar) levels, then the attribute remains important but does not determine choice.

Noncompensatory models of choice suggest that consumers evaluate an object based on one attribute at a time. In a *conjunctive* model, alternatives are evaluated favorably if they meet a minimum standard on all or some of the attributes. For example, if a commuter requires that any transport alternative rates at least 5 on speed and 6 on punctuality, then car and train—but not bus—would be viewed favorably. In a *disjunctive* model, alternatives are evaluated favorably if they at least meet a criterion level of one of a set of attributes. For example, if a rating of 8 on either status or economy is required, then the train would not be considered favorably in this instance. Both conjunctive and disjunctive models are noncompensatory because high ratings on other attributes do not compensate for low ratings on the critical attributes. In a *lexicographic* model, attributes are ranked in order of importance, and the most favorably viewed alternative is the one that does best on the most important attribute. If one attribute is not sufficient, then the second most important attribute is used, and so on. In other words, objects are ranked attribute by attribute. To illustrate, if economy is the most important attribute, then the bus is preferred because it scores highest among the three alternatives being considered.

These functions are only models of how a consumer forms attitudes. They seek to capture the essence of attitude formation, but may not exactly describe the process itself. In addition, consumers may use a combination of models to evaluate an object. Noncompensatory models are often used to screen out undesirable alternatives. For example, Timothy Turner might be described as using one model to eliminate the air force from further consideration, and another to evaluate the army and navy.

In this section, we have described these functions as models of attitude. To the extent that behavioral intention and choice follow attitude, these become models of choice as well, and they are frequently used that way. In the previous chapter, we suggested that a person evaluates the benefits and costs before deciding to make an exchange. The models we have just discussed suggest different ways to evaluate these benefits and costs: the positively and negatively valued attributes, respectively.

Although these models only approximate attitude formation, they still provide some valuable insights. First, they confirm the necessity to start with the needs a person is concerned with, because these generate the importance weights or criteria. Generally, it is more difficult to change needs than importance weights, and these are more difficult to change than beliefs, especially if there are inaccurate perceptions about the attributes.

Although these attitude models suggest different ways to evaluate competitive offerings, their marketing implications are similar. They suggest that in order to design appealing products and effective marketing programs, marketers must have some knowledge of (1) the kinds of attributes or decision criteria that people use in evaluating alternatives, (2) the relative importance of those attributes to different individuals, and (3) how users rate their own and competitors' offerings on important attributes.

Suppose an organization is considering entering a market or changing an existing product that is not viewed favorably. The multiattribute approach to modeling attitudes suggests the following approaches to obtaining favorable evaluations of an object.

1. Alter beliefs about the object. For example, if the bus is, in reality, as punctual as the car, but is perceived as less reliable, then attempt to change that perception. If the bus is not punctual and that attribute is important to travelers, then improve the operating system so that required schedule standards can be met.

2. Change beliefs about competition. If the car is subject to rush-hour traffic jams and is less reliable than the train, this can be pointed out.

3. Change attribute importance. For example, a bus company might suggest that people pay more attention to economy and perhaps less to status.

4. Raise the importance of neglected attributes, If bus riders arrive at their destination more relaxed than car drivers, the focusing on this difference may call attention to an attribute that most people overlook.

5. Change the existing product or add a new one. An analysis of existing alternatives and the attribute beliefs and importance weights may indicate the opportunity for a new product. For example, a bus company may find that a premium express bus service possesses attributes that are favorably evaluated by suburban commuters who would otherwise drive rather than ride a crowded local bus that makes frequent stops.

As can be seen, these models can help in diagnosing reasons for existing attitudes toward an organization and its current products as well as stimulating new directions. Favorable evaluation does not always result in usage, however, as we saw earlier. Nevertheless, in high-involvement, complex decision-making situations, attitude is often a precursor of behavior.

ORGANIZATIONAL BUYING BEHAVIOR

Public and nonprofit organizations often offer products to (and attract resources from) corporations, associations, government agencies, and other nonbusiness organizations. If transit agencies want to change the timing of the workday in order to cope with extreme peaks at rush hour, they must appeal not only to workers but also to their employers. In the United States, substantially more than half of hospital charges are paid by other institutions or organizations (Blue Cross, federal and state Medicaid programs, insurance companies). The prices paid and the service contracted for vary by institutional client. To illustrate, at the private, nonprofit Roger Williams General Hospital in Providence, Rhode Island, approximately 90 percent of revenues comes from three organizations—Medicare (50 percent), Medicaid (10 percent), and Blue Cross (30 percent). Each has its own "cost formula" so that, for example, for one hour's anesthesiology, Medicaid pays $25, Medicare pays $36.80, and Blue Cross $40. A fee of $68.25 is billed to the remaining patients, who are usually reimbursed by private insurers.[10] A hospital must be able to understand these organizational buyers in considerable depth if it is to obtain attractive terms.

There are many similarities between consumer and organizational buying behavior, but there are at least three important distinctions, too. First, organizational as well as personal needs motivate organizational buying behavior. An organization buys goods and services primarily to be used, in turn, to produce its own goods or services (for consumption by its customers), and also to satisfy the needs of its employees or volunteers or to meet legal obligations and social concerns. For example, the Royal Life Saving Society of Canada (RLSSC) markets its lifesaving and swimming instruction programs to community centers, local governments, and other pool operators throughout Canada, who then provide instruction to individual swimmers. Pool operators adopt the RLSSC program if they believe it will enhance their overall offerings to the community. When purchasing products, businesses are frequently motivated by profitability, but all organizations are concerned with reducing costs. Sheltered workshops (institutions that employ handicapped people) often secure industrial contracts on the basis of performing, at a low cost, tasks for which their employees are particularly suited.

Organizations also buy goods and services to increase the well-being of their own personnel. Health-care services, tickets to art events, and transit passes—whether offered by the employer free or at a price—represent such occasions.

The necessity to meet legal constraints or the desire to meet social obligations also motivates some organizational decisions. Some employers offer payroll savings plans to purchase savings bonds as a public service. The purchase of advertisements in brochures and magazines published by local nonprofit organizations may be primarily motivated by social concerns. On the other hand, the publications of some nonprofit organizations, such as the *National Geographic Magazine* and *Smithsonian,* appeal to advertisers on the same basis as commercial publishers—advertising effectiveness among chosen market segments for a given dollar expenditure.

In marketing to organizations, it is important to remember that while economic reasons are important, social and personal factors also come into play. Organizational buyers are humans and react to the image of potential suppliers, their own needs (to avoid risk and to enhance their own self-esteem, for example), and interpersonal concerns. In some instances, when alternative products or suppliers are essentially equivalent, personal considerations may be dominant. At other times, a particular offering may be so superior that personal or other considerations are irrelevant. In most cases, organizational buying decisions involve both task-related and other factors.

A second distinguishing characteristic of organizational buying behavior is the influence of formal organizational structure and procedures on the decision process. For example, the University of British Columbia has a rule that all equipment purchased above a certain dollar amount must be subject to competitive bid; individual researchers cannot conclude contracts with suppliers on their own. More generally, the authority structure of an organization sets the limits within which individuals can act and the procedures that are required. In some organizational buying situations, it is important to understand the internal management information or control systems under which individuals work. Thus, a city trying to persuade a manufacturer to locate within its boundaries may need to know whether tax packages that reduce the cost of acquiring a site are more or less valuable to a company than those that emphasize lower costs once the plant is operating. There is not a general answer to this question; it depends on the management system within each company.

The third, and perhaps most important, distinguishing aspect is that organizational buying behavior is generally a group decision process. A particularly useful concept is the "buying center," which suggests the roles played by members of the organization at different stages of the buying process. Before looking at the buying center, however, we will study the decisions themselves.

Characteristics of Organizational Buying Decisions

Type of Decision. As with individual buying decisions, it is necessary to recognize that choice processes vary by situational context. A particularly useful categorization is: (1) new task, (2) modified rebuy, and (3) straight rebuy.[11]

The *new task* represents a buying decision that has not occurred before. New-task decisions are important either because they require a considerable amount of organizational resources to be committed or because they set a precedent for future decisions. A performing-arts center that is attempting to convince a symphony orchestra to use its facilities to hold a summer festival would represent a major one-time commitment and possibly a continuing relationship as well. Another example of a new task would be persuading an employer to sell transit passes on a payroll deduction plan for the first time. Generally, a new-task buying decision involves extensive information search and alternative evaluation. In many ways, new-task buying parallels high-involvement, complex decision making on the individual level.

Straight rebuy, the opposite extreme from new-task buying, represents recurring purchasing requirements. For example, once an employer has agreed to sell transit passes, then each month's sale is essentially a straight rebuy. Generally, little information search or alternative evaluation takes place in this type of buying situation; it shares many characteristics with habitual buying behavior at the individual level.

Modified rebuy is an intervening stage between new task and straight rebuy. It often arises when the basic buying situation is itself repetitive, but some aspects of the context have changed. Factors that need to be considered are changes in the overall environment as well as changes in the needs of buyers or the services provided. For example, one community center rented space in its building to a number of different local service organizations. For almost a decade, rents were raised annually to cover an estimate of overall inflation and each of the renting organizations renewed; essentially they were engaging in a straight rebuy. However, when a center-wide cost study revealed that many of the renters were not even paying the marginal costs of providing them with office facilities, new lease terms were offered to the renters. These terms, in turn, generated more attention than usual to the lease renewal decision. More generally, a modified rebuy involves a moderate amount of information search and alternative evaluation.

Steps in the Buying Process. The organizational buying process can usefully be subdivided into a number of steps. A typical model consists of the following five stages.

1. *Identification of need.* Needs can include supplies or services for resale, for facilitating operations, or for consumption as well as capital investments to house the organization or improve the efficiency of its operations.

2. *Establishment of specifications.* Specifications can refer both to the product required and to the supplier. Frequently, public-sector organizations are confined in choice of supplier—for example, U.S. government employees only fly U.S. airlines when on government business.

3. *Identification of alternatives.* Determining a list of acceptable suppliers and/or products that meet the required specifications.

4. *Evaluation of alternatives.* As in the case of individual complex decision making, evaluation typically requires assessing each alternative against multiple

criteria. However, the evaluation procedure generally includes several people who may have different criteria, importance weights, and evaluation methods.

5. *Choice*. Selection of product and supplier alternatives.

This five-step model is more applicable to new-task and modified-rebuy decisions than to straight rebuy. Since many organizational buying decisions involve continuing relationships, postpurchase satisfaction and evaluation of subsequent service should also be considered.

Buying Center

Organizational buying is a group process, especially in new-task situations. The buying-center concept represents the different people in an organization and their roles in the buying process at different decision stages. As shown in Table 6.4, the buying center encompasses five roles.

1. *Users*. Organizational members who use the goods or services to be acquired.
2. *Influencers*. Those who influence the decision process directly or indirectly by providing information and criteria for evaluating alternative products and suppliers.
3. *Buyers*. Those who have formal authority and responsibility for contracting with suppliers. In some cases, a purchasing agent may have authority to negotiate terms and may also be a decision maker; at times, a buyer may only have responsibility for implementing a purchase decision.
4. *Deciders*. Those with authority to choose among alternative buying actions. In large or significant investments, decision-making authority may rest with top management or the board of directors.
5. *Gatekeepers*. Those who control the flow of information into the buying center. For example, a purchasing agent may specify a set of acceptable suppliers and limit access to sellers to buying-center members.

One person may occupy several roles in the buying process. The user and influencer may be the same person, for example. In addition, each of the roles may be filled by several people. For anyone attempting to market to organizations, it is crucial to recognize that these five roles often exist, and that it is not sufficient to satisfy the individual or

Table 6.4 Roles of Buying-Center Members by Decision Stage

	User	Influencer	Buyer	Decider	Gatekeeper
Identification of need	X	X			
Establishment of specifications	X	X	X	X	
Identification of alternatives	X	X	X		X
Evaluation of alternatives	X	X	X		
Choice	X	X	X	X	

Source. Frederick E. Webster, Jr., and Yoram Wind, *Organizational Buying Behavior*. © 1972, p. 80. Adapted by permission of Prentice-Hall, Inc. Englewood Cliffs, N. J.

organizational needs of just one person occupying one role in the buying center. Nonbusiness organizations that are marketing to other organizations need to develop sophisticated marketing programs that recognize the complex, multiperson nature of organizational buying behavior.

SUMMARY

Sound knowledge of consumer and organizational buying behavior should be the underlying basis for all marketing decisions. In this chapter, we have attempted to illustrate the type of factors that need to be considered in understanding buyer behavior and to indicate the major aspects involved in consumer and organizational decision processes, No universal model of buyer behavior exists, but there are situational contingencies and environmental factors that help categorize some regularities in behavior. In any particular marketing program, the organization needs to establish a valid model to use in order to achieve understanding. To paraphrase an old saying, the warning for the marketing manager who does not have an adequate understanding of the market is "caveat venditor"—let the seller beware.

REFERENCES

1. For simplicity, we use the term *consumer behavior* to embrace behavior by all types of purchasers, users, and actors targeted by a marketing organization. As appropriate, the discussion will focus on such topics as the behavior of individuals, households, groups, and institutional buyers. See also, Michael L. Rothschild, "Marketing Communications in Nonbusiness Situations or Why It's so Hard to Sell Brotherhood LIke Soap," *Journal of Marketing,* Vol. 43 (Spring 1979), pp. 11–20.
2. This development is adapted from Henry Assael, *Consumer Behavior and Marketing Action*, third edition, Boston: Kent Publishing Company, 1987.
3. Harold H. Kassarjian and Joel B. Cohen, "Cognitive Dissonance and Consumer Behavior," *California Management Review* (Fall 1965), pp. 55–64.
4. See, for example: Henry Assael (as in reference 2), James F. Engel, Roger D. Blackwell, and Paul W. Miniard, *Consumer Behavior*, 5th edition Chicago: Dryden Press, 1986; William L. Wilkie, *Consumer Behavior*, New York: John Wiley & Sons, 1986; Gerald Zaltman and Melanie Wallendorf, *Consumer Behavior.: Basic Findings and Management Implications*, 2nd edition, New York: John Wiley & Sons, 1982.
5. Patrick E. Murphy and William A. Staples, "A Modernized Family Life Cycle," *Journal of Consumer Research* (June 1979), pp. 12–22.
6. See, for instance, the classic categorization developed in W. Lloyd Warner, Marchia Meeker, and Kenneth Eells, *Social Class in America,* New York: Harper & Row, 1960.
7. Arnold Mitchell, *The Nine American Life Styles,* New York: Macmillan Publishing, 1983.
8. *The Professional Performing Arts: Attendance Patterns, Preferences, and Motives,* Madison, Wisc.: Association of College, University, and Community Arts Administrators, 1984.
9. Martin Fishbein and Icek Ajzen, *Beliefs, Attitudes, Intention and Behavior: An Introduction to Theory and Research,* Reading, Mass.: Addison-Wesley, 1975.
10. William M. Bulkeley, "Federal Cost Cutting Pushes Up Deficits of Nonprofit Hospitals," *Wall Street Journal,* Vol. 106, No. 27 (February 9, 1982), pp. 1, 2.
11. Frederick E. Webster, Jr., and Yoram Wind, *Organizational Buying Behavior,* Englewood Cliffs, N.J.: Prentice-Hall, 1972.

Chapter 7 _____
Market Segmentation

The last chapter has emphasized the perspectives of individual consumers. But most marketing organizations find themselves operating in "mass markets" of thousands or even millions of customers and prospective customers. How can managers reconcile the need to be attentive to the concerns of individual consumers with the constraints of running an efficient operation, which tends to dictate similar treatment of all customers?

Even more problematic for many public and nonprofit organizations is how to identify prospective customers within a large mass market and then develop a cost-effective way of reaching them. What strategy should the British Royal Mint employ to market proof coin sets to American coin collectors? How should a hospital, faced with a decline in the number of its obstetrical patients, go about increasing its market share? What is the best way for a transit authority to help meet a city goal of improving mobility for the elderly? How can candidates for elected office, each espousing particular political philosophies, maximize their chances for success at the ballot box?

The answer to such questions generally involves adopting a strategy of market segmentation, which can be described as the development and pursuit of marketing programs directed at specific groups within the population that the organization could potentially serve. Segmentation is one of the key concepts in marketing and serves two basic managerial purposes. The first is *market definition*—helping an organization to identify and select those segments within the overall population that are most closely related to fulfillment of institutional objectives, and therefore represent an appropriate target for marketing efforts. The second is *target marketing*—helping managers direct marketing activities effectively at the chosen segments. This may require making further subdivisions in the target population and developing several coordinated marketing programs tailored to each of these separately.

Public and nonprofit organizations have come to recognize the value of adopting a segmentation approach. Some have chosen to adopt a strategy of *concentration*, focusing on a single group within the population and developing a marketing strategy tailored to the needs and behavior of that group—for instance, an agency providing home care for elderly people confined to their homes in a specific town. Other organizations, exemplified by the YMCA and YWCA, have adopted a strategy of *differentiation*, selecting two or more segments from within the population and developing distinctive marketing programs for each. Some organizations have been less focused, ignoring the varying needs and characteristics of different groups and attempting to direct a single marketing program at the entire market. Examples of this third approach (which sometimes reflects the absence of a well-thought-out strategy) include the broad-based "Don't Be Fuelish" campaign of the U.S. Department of Energy during the middle 1970s, and public transit agencies that make no attempt to tailor their services, fares, routes, schedules, and communication efforts to reflect variations in either travelers' personal characteristics or in their travel needs by time of day, purpose of trip, availability of alternatives, home and work locations, and so forth.

Constraints on Segmentation Strategies

Unlike their private-sector counterparts, managers of nonbusiness organizations may not always have the luxury of being able to pick and choose the segments they would like to serve. The problem takes two forms: being too narrowly constrained to certain segments and being unable to focus the organization's activities as tightly as management desires.

Some public agencies are required by their charters to direct their efforts at specific segments—the elderly, former military personnel, children in a particular school district, immigrants, and so forth. Without a change in legislation, it may be impossible for those organizations to broaden, narrow, or otherwise refocus their efforts, however appropriate that might seem to management. Nonprofit organizations are likely to be somewhat less constrained legally (although they must be careful not to engage in activities that might endanger their tax-exempt status). They may still face strong opposition from traditionally minded donors, trustees, existing users, and other relevant supporters if they attempt to extend their current services to new segments or add products designed to appeal to new segments.

Public agencies may also be constrained by the activities of political pressure groups who do not want to see these agencies serving market segments that they could profitably serve themselves. Many public transit agencies, for instance, have been able to reduce their deficits by offering charter services, using buses and drivers that would otherwise go unutilized outside the commuting hours. In some cities, however, opposition from privately owned bus charter firms has led to rulings restricting the public authority from most charter operations.

The problem of too broad a focus is most commonly encountered among public agencies with a broad mandate to serve the general population. More than once, the U.S. Postal Service has been rapped on the knuckles by congressional critics for providing faster service to certain large commercial or industrial customers, and then has been forced to offer a similar level of service to all users of a certain class of mail, regardless of their potential profitability or importance to the success of USPS.[1] Similarly, public transportation agencies—from Amtrak down to local city bus lines—often find themselves forced to operate routes that management would prefer to discard. Sometimes there are good external social or economic reasons why these routes should be maintained; at other times, the reasons are purely political (such as the desire of politicians to demonstrate their clout to local constituents served by the routes in question).

Scope of the Chapter

We begin be examining how segmentation concepts were used in a political campaign to analyze the situation and bring focus to a specific candidate's strategy. This case history, and the insights it provides, will then provide a base for discussing segmentation objectives and strategies in greater depth, using illustrations from a variety of public and nonprofit organizations. We emphasize the rationale for segmentation, identify the criteria for effective use of segmentation, show how market definition and targeting relate to institutional objectives, and conclude with a discussion and appraisal of alternative bases for segmenting a market.

CAN A SEGMENTATION STRATEGY HELP A POLITICAL UNDERDOG?[2]

Few people gave the Rev. Robert F. Drinan much of a chance in his attempt to win election to the U.S. House of Representatives in 1970. Drinan, a Jesuit priest and dean of the Boston College Law School, faced a major hurdle in the Democratic primary election.[3] He and a third candidate were challenging Representative Philip J. Philbin for the Democratic nomination in Massachusetts' Fourth Congressional District, just west of Boston. Drinan was a political "unknown"; Philbin was a 28-year veteran of Congress.

Drinan's campaign manager, John Marttila, knew when he started work on the campaign in March that it would be an uphill fight. In early May, a private opinion poll taken solely among the district's Democrats showed that had the election been held at this time, 48 percent would have voted for Philbin, 16 percent for Drinan, and 7 percent for the third candidate, O'Hanian. The remaining 29 percent was undecided. Equally disturbing was the fact that fully 48 percent of the Democrats—few of whom had heard of Drinan—opposed the idea of a priest running for Congress. Offsetting these problems were two important resources. Drinan's outspokenness against the Vietnam War and his strongly liberal position on many social issues had attracted a substantial number of volunteers (including many students) as well as strong financing for his campaign.

As Marttila pondered the situation, he began to form a strategy based on the fact that voter turnout tends to be low in the primaries—rarely exceeding 30 percent of all registered voters. If sufficient Drinan supporters could be identified and encouraged to go to the polls, while Philbin's supporters stayed home, Drinan might win despite the apparent preference for his principal opponent.

For such a strategy to be successful, several things needed to happen. First, the campaign organization would have to identify which of the Democratic voters in the district favored Drinan. Second, Drinan would have to win over some of the currently uncommited voters. Third, a high percentage of these Drinan supporters would have to be "pulled" to the polls on election day. Fourth, Philbin and his supporters would have to be lulled into a false sense of security, so that the congressman would make little effort to campaign and many of his supporters, believing their candidate to be assured of reelection, would not bother to vote.

Marttila began by canvassing the district to identify Drinan supporters. Volunteers were assigned areas to canvass, typically consisting of a few blocks each. With the aid of lists of registered voters and street directories that indicated the names of residents at each address, file cards were prepared for each residence in the canvass area.

The technique of canvassing involves calling at every residence personally and asking each registered voter at that address how she or he intends to vote in the election. Typically, code numbers are used to indicate on the file cards the strength of feeling evidenced by each respondent (e.g., "Strong for candidate X," "Leaning toward candidate

Y," "Won't say," "Not sure," etc.). The canvass can also be conducted by telephone, but that approach tends to yield higher nonresponse rates. Obviously, not even the best canvass can reach every voter, despite repeated attempts to reach people who are not at home on the first call.

Since the initial efforts showed that very few people had heard of Drinan, canvassers were instructed to ask how each voter felt about several major issues, including the Vietnam War. Those opposed to the war were classified as potential Drinan supporters, even if they did not know the candidate at that time. As soon as the canvassing results were computed, leaflets were delivered to current or prospective Drinan supporters stating his position on those issues that were known to be of concern to the voter in question.

The canvassing and leafleting continued throughout June and July. One districtwide mailing was sent out to supplement the selective, target mailings. In late July, with two and a half months to go before the primary, an in-house opinion poll showed Drinan closing in on his key opponent, with 48 percent still favoring Philbin but Drinan's support now at 30 percent. Uncertain of how to handle the issue of Drinan's priesthood, Marttila simply downplayed it. Campaign literature showed photographs of Drinan wearing a clerical collar but referred to him simply as Robert F. Drinan, and described him as a "Jesuit scholar."

The appearance of a low-key campaign was accentuated by Marttila's decision to avoid using radio, television, or billboard advertising on Drinan's behalf—traditional signs of a well-financed campaign in high gear. During the late summer, in-house polls showed continued gains for Drinan. But just one week before the election, Marttila was delighted to see the *Boston Globe* publish a poll that showed Philbin leading comfortably, as well as newspaper articles predicting no difficulty for the incumbent congressman. Philbin himself did not make his first campaign appearance in the district until 10 days before the election.

In the last few days of the campaign, Marttila placed a single television spot that was repeated many times on local stations; this showed Drinan speaking his mind on the issues. By election day, fully 75 percent of the district had been canvassed and the final in-house poll showed Drinan and Philbin tied. The campaign manager now played his trump card, the "pulling" operation. This involved telephoning or calling on those people whom the canvass had identified as Drinan supporters to remind them to vote. Where needed, the campaign organization was able to offer transportation to the polling places and even babysitting, thanks to its extensive force of volunteers.

When the 5 P.M. news that evening reported an unusually heavy turnout in the Fourth District, Marttila knew that the pulling operation had succeeded and felt confident that his candidate had won. The final tallies, late that night, proved him right. Drinan had obtained 46 percent of the votes cast, Philbin 36 percent, and O'Hanian 18 percent. Subsequent analysis showed that three out of every five Drinan supporters had voted in the primary, as opposed to fewer than two out of five Philbin supporters. As Marttila later remarked, commenting on the disparity between published polls and the election outcome, "Polls measure public opinion, but election results measure votes."

In the ensuing general election, Drinan won a narrow victory over the Republican candidate in a three-cornered fight that the previously defeated Philbin had entered as an independent. (Drinan was subsequently reelected to Congress for four terms but reluctantly stepped down in 1980 in deference to a Vatican ruling that priests should not run for elective office.)

Defining Drinan's Target Market Segments

Like all political campaigns, Drinan's had to consider the interests of multiple publics—voters, volunteers, donors, and sources of influence such as the media. Each of these publics lends itself to segmentation, but we focus here on the voters, who ultimately determine a politician's fate at the polls.

As can be seen in Figure 7.1, the Drinan campaign involved several sequential segmentation steps, each using a different criterion for dividing a mass market into progressively smaller groupings. The end result was the definition of two relatively small market segments of prospective voters whose support at the polls would be critical to Drinan's success.

Geographic Segmentation. For the purpose of electing members to the U.S. House of Representatives, the United States is divided into 435 separate congressional districts, each covering a distinct geographic area. Although Drinan and his opponents could not afford to overlook the rest of the Greater Boston area—because it represented a potential source of donations, volunteers, and influential media opinion—their campaign efforts

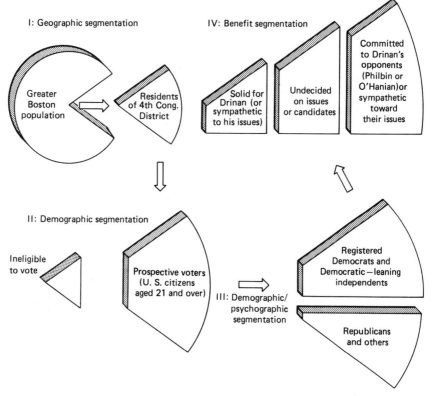

Figure 7.1 Segmenting the market in the Drinan primary campaign.

obviously had to focus on the geographic area known as the Massachusetts Fourth Congressional District.

Demographic Segmentation. Not everybody in the Fourth District was a voter. Demographic variables have long been used as determinants of eligibility to vote. At one time or another, criteria in different countries have included age, sex, religion, race, nationality, and property ownership. In 1970, any adult citizen of the United States could register to vote, with adulthood being defined as 21 years or older (in 1971 the minimum voting age was lowered to 18). Residents of the district who either were under the age of 21 or did not hold U.S. nationality represented a segment of lesser interest to the candidates, although they could be important to the campaign as volunteers, donors, and influencers of voting intention among voters. (The same was true of some nonresidents of the district.)

Psychographic Segmentation. The term *psychographics* refers to ways of describing people based on their life-styles, values, attitudes, and personalities, each of which may have an important bearing on a person's political-party affiliations. (Political-party loyalties may also be related to such demographic characteristics as income, education, and social class.) Since Drinan was running as a candidate in the primary election, his campaign manager needed to focus on those people who were likely to ask for a Democratic ballot on entering the polling place; in the strongly Democratic Fourth District, this meant a majority of voters. At this point, those committed to candidates from the Republican Party did not constitute a relevant segment for Drinan.

Benefit Segmentation. Grouping people according to who they are and where and how they live does not exhaust the range of segmentation variables available. Since marketing is concerned with offering *benefits* to consumers as part of an exchange transaction, and different people seek different benefits, it follows that segments can be created by grouping consumers (or in this case voters) according to the benefits they seek and the costs they seek to avoid. One of the benefits derived from voting for a particular candidate lies in the anticipated outcome of that individual's proposed political platform. As a liberal, antiwar candidate, Drinan promised that, if elected, he would support legislation to end the Vietnam War and introduce innovative social programs. This platform distinguished him sharply from his principal opponent, Representative Philbin. Those voters who sought the benefits offered by Drinan's political philosophy could therefore be defined as his primary market segment. Even within this segment, smaller subsegments could be distinguished, reflecting the varying priorities they placed on the several different issues espoused by the candidate. Inasmuch as some "undecided" electors could be convinced of the importance of the issues espoused by Robert Drinan and persuaded to vote for him, they constituted a second key segment.

Of course, in any election there is an enormous range of different motivations for voting for (or against) any specific candidate. Benefit segmentation was of particular significance in this instance, however, because of the campaign manager's decision to focus on the issues.

Target Marketing Strategy

It was simple enough for Drinan's campaign manager, John Marttila, to identify those people who lived in the Fourth District because its geographic boundaries were a matter of record. Identifying who was eligible to vote, who would probably be voting in the Democratic primary, and who was sympathetic to Drinan's positions was a much more difficult task. The only way to find out was through research. A starting point was provided by lists of registered voters in the district that told who the registered Republicans, Democrats, and Independents were and where they lived. Such a list excluded recent arrivals in the district and other residents who had not yet registered to vote; they had to be identified by canvassing, and those sympathetic to Drinan then encouraged to register. Canvassing was also, of course, used to determine the issues of concern to individual electors within the Democratic and Democratic-leaning Independent segments. The resulting findings made it possible for the campaign organization to send out personalized mailings, containing brochures on those issues that were of greatest interest to each recipient.

The final, and most subtle, aspect of the campaign strategy involved the use of personal telephone calls on election day to get pro-Drinan electors to the polls. The great advantage of this medium was that it only reached households containing known Drinan supporters, and thus did not stimulate those voters preferring the other two candidates.

In view of the careful targeting of such communication media as direct mail and telephone solicitation, why did Marttila bother to make last-minute use of a wide-area, high-profile medium such as television? One reason was that the canvassing had only covered 75 percent of all homes in the district, so the television commercial was needed to reach out to the balance. This advertising also served to reinforce the points made by Drinan in direct mailings, at a time when it was effectively too late for Philbin to counterattack.

WHY SEGMENT?

The Drinan campaign clarifies the value of segmentation as a marketing strategy on several different counts.

Spotlighting Relevant Segments

First, relatively few organizations realistically expect to reach out to the entire population. In some areas, such as the arts, the benefits offered appeal to only a limited group, reflecting such factors as tastes, education, and prior exposure. In other instances, only people meeting predefined criteria are eligible to participate in the transaction process. For example, a high level of intellectual potential—as measured by standardized tests and prior academic performance—is required to qualify for admission to leading universities; certain transit services are reserved for handicapped people; borrowing privileges at a public city library are often confined to residents of the city in question; and only pregnant women—most of whom fall within the age range 15–45—use the maternity ward in a hospital.

Of course, some public agencies have a charter requiring that they provide service to all citizens. Thus the Postal Service is required to provide letter service to all residents of the country, no matter what their geographic location. Yet even here, segmentation strategies are called for, as the needs of a large corporation posting literally millions of letters a month differ from those of an individual living in a remote area.

Development of Responsive Strategies

Market segmentation allows organizations to develop finely tuned marketing strategies designed to meet the needs of their chosen segments, as well as to serve those segments in a responsive manner. Segmented marketing strategies can be designed with such objectives as:

- Tailoring the product offering to appeal to the needs and preferences of one or more specific segments.
- Offering pricing alternatives that are responsive to people's ability and willingness to pay, or their need for credit.
- Providing a range of alternative times and locations for distribution of the product, so as to be responsive to people's different schedules and home or job locations.
- Selecting alternative media to communicate with the target market about the product, reflecting the fact that people's media habits (e.g., the newspapers they read, the television programs they watch, the radio stations they listen to) may vary sharply.
- Preparing different messages tailored to the interests, education, and native languages of various groups.

Efficient Allocation of Resources

Selecting target markets helps an organization to allocate its limited resources. Few public and nonprofit organizations have the capabilities to offer an entire market the same level of service, nor is that likely to be necessary. One of the principal benefits of market segmentation, in fact, is to identify those portions of the population that are not users at all, or that make only limited use of the product. For example, 30 percent of the U.S. population does not visit a doctor in any given year, and 22 percent of the population accounts for 76 percent of annual out-of-hospital visits.[4] In the performing arts, 60 percent of the U.S. population does not attend a paid professional performance in a given year.[5] Often a small portion of the population accounts for a substantial portion of the usage; a study in Canada found that the 100 largest postal customers accounted for 25 percent of total Canada Post revenues.[6] In most fund-raising campaigns, a small percentage of donors is responsible for a high percentage of the total value of all gifts. As we discuss later, not every organization chooses—or should choose—as its target market the largest customers. Understanding how large customers (or prospects), small customers (or prospects), and nonprospects are distributed within the broader population helps an organization to make conscious choices about the allocation of its resources.

Effectiveness in Attracting Funding

A fourth advantage of market segmentation for public and nonprofit organizations is that it enhances their ability to attract funds from donors and government agencies. A clear specification of market targets and institutional mission allows an organization to identify the donor segments that are most likely to be responsive to fund-raising appeals or the political interest groups who are most likely to support continued or increased tax funding of programs. In addition, successful meeting of goals by segment probably enhances the likelihood of receiving donations and the level of funding achieved.

Efficiency in Media Selection

Another advantage concerns efficiency in media selection. For instance, it is wasteful to buy advertising time on a major television station with an audience of millions when you only need to reach a small number of people. The key is to look for a communication medium that reaches out specifically to the group of interest.

Reducing Competitive Impact

A segmentation strategy may also help to reduce the impact of competition. There is often less competition in a specialized segment than in the market as a whole. For instance, Hood College, a liberal arts college for women, elected to remain a single-sex institution in the middle 1970s, at a time when many women's colleges felt that they would be able to compete more effectively by becoming coeducational. Hood succeeded in establishing a leadership role for itself among the declining number of women's colleges, attracting female students who valued this concept of education.[7]

There may also be occasions—as in the Drinan campaign—when a marketer does not wish the competition (or perhaps potential customers who are ineligible) to learn of a specific marketing program. By not using broad-reach media, the campaign manager avoided letting Drinan's opponents (and their supporters) learn what an intensive campaign Drinan was waging.

Focusing Organizational Efforts

Finally, some argue that the major advantage of a targeted market-segmentation strategy is that it provides a clearer focus for the organization and for the people who manage and work in that enterprise. When a public-transportation agency concentrates its efforts on several carefully defined segments, including those who travel by car outside peak commuting hours, this provides a degree of focus that a goal of "increasing ridership" does not. Commitment to the off-peak-drivers segment, for example, will help a transit manager to specify the information needed to understand and identify these potential users, thus putting the agency in a better position to spot opportunities for new programs and identify threats to existing ones.

MARKET DEFINITION AND TARGETING

How should an organization go about developing a marketing strategy, and where does segmentation fit within this process? The approach followed in a successful program, such as the Drinan campaign, may sometimes seem obvious after the fact, but how should a manager get started? Figure 7.2 outlines the basic procedures, beginning with definition of institutional objectives and setting priorities. Agreement on objectives and priorities leads into the issue of market definition: within the overall population, which markets are central to successful achievement of these objectives and which are peripheral or unimportant? Once these markets have been identified, and one or more target markets selected, the manager should be in a position to undertake a detailed analysis of their needs, characteristics, and current behavior patterns in a search for possible ways to segment each target market. The next task is to develop marketing strategies tailored to each segment. Once these strategies have been implemented, their performance should be monitored, evaluated, and, where necessary, modified for future periods.

In evaluating a market and developing appropriate programs, three broad alternative strategies are available: market aggregation, total market disaggregation, and market segmentation. We will look briefly at each from the perspective of managing an urban

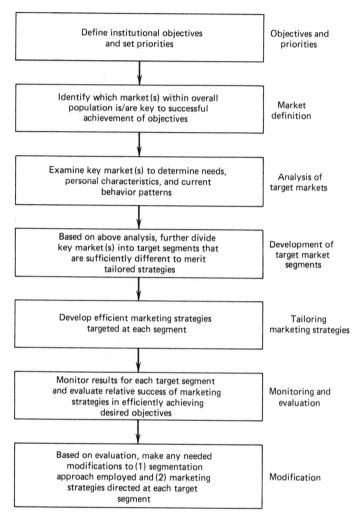

Figure 7.2 The process of market targeting to achieve institutional objectives.

public transportation system in a particular metropolitan area, where the target market is essentially all travelers making trips within this geographic area.

Market Aggregation

The market-aggregation approach, which can be termed an "undifferentiated" strategy, consists of treating all potential consumers as similar and offering a standard product for everyone. Historically, "mass transit" followed this approach, under the assumption that everybody's urban travel needs can be satisfied by the same type of public transportation service. This has largely proved to be a fallacy. Consider the scheduling implications of the different travel behavior of three commuter groups: (1) those who have regular daytime working hours, (2) those who have irregular hours, occasionally leaving work late at night, and (3) those who not only commute but also travel elsewhere during the business day. Unless the last two groups are assured of frequent, reliable service during the off-peak hours, they are likely to rely on private cars instead of public transit. Even if scheduling is adequate, transit systems need to be concerned about dealing with the psychological drawbacks of riding at night in nearly empty trains and waiting in large, cavernous stations after dark.

Total Market Disaggregation

The approach of total market disaggregation is at the opposite end of the scale from market aggregation and means that each consumer is treated uniquely. In the last analysis, each individual may be thought of as a separate market segment, on the grounds that each person is slightly different from everybody else in personal characteristics, behavior patterns, needs, values, and attitudes. There are limits as to how far disaggregation can be carried in planning, marketing, and managing an enterprise such as an art museum, a university, a political campaign, or a public transportation system. After all, to take the last of these examples, planners have to develop transportation systems for populations that may run into the millions, and there are limits to the ability of transit managers to provide personalized service in buses designed to seat 50 people and trains that may carry as many as 1500 travelers at a time.

It is usually impractical to consider individual consumers as separate segments for all elements of the marketing effort, although it may be necessary and desirable to "customize" certain aspects of service delivery, as in grading student papers, providing medical treatment, weighing a parcel at the post office, or responding to a traveler's inquiry about train schedules and reservations. If each transaction or donation has a very high value (or accounts for a substantial portion of the organization's total volume), however, it may be appropriate to develop a comprehensive understanding of each major customer so that a tailored marketing program may be developed.

A good example of this approach comes from the Canadian postal service. In the early 1970s, it developed a service called "Postpak," primarily to meet the needs of two of Canada's largest retailers, Simpson-Sears and Eaton's, for a small parcel-delivery system.[8] The new service was responsive to the decline in Canada Post's traditional parcel-post business, in the face of competing distribution systems. Postal executives collaborated with Eaton's to do a feasibility study of a new form of parcel-post service. The findings showed that Canada Post could be competitive in distributing consolidated shipments of parcels weighing up to 66 pounds, the traditional limit for fourth-class mail packages. Once these consolidated shipments reached their destination point, the individual parcels would be distributed by the consignee. Later, the Postpak service was established in five major centers—Halifax, Montreal, Toronto, Winnipeg, and Regina—offering approximately 60 destinations, mostly catalog sales offices operated by Eaton's and Simpson-Sears. Competitive pricing and the absence of paperwork for users were strategic aspects of Postpak that generated a growing demand. Subsequently, this new service went national.

In short, public and nonprofit organizations should seek to isolate any customers or donors who merit individual treatment. While such an approach cannot be used for all, it is important to recognize that it can be justified for some.

Market Segmentation

Obviously, there has to be a middle ground between complete aggregation of the population on one hand and total disaggregation on the other. This is where a strategy of market segmentation promises to be of value. It calls for grouping consumers or institutional customers into segments, so that those in each segment share some relevant characteristic distinguishing them from those in the other groups.

Essentially, market segmentation is a managerial strategy of adaptation to the existence of different demand patterns in a market. As such it consists of three stages.

1. Dividing the market into meaningful groups for purposes of identification.
2. Selecting those groups that are most relevant to fulfillment of the organization's mission.
3. Creating specific "marketing mixes" to appeal to each of these target market segments.

Management can select one of two different types of segmentation strategy—a *concentrated* strategy of focusing on only one segment within the population or a *differentiated* strategy of selecting several segments to serve and developing tailored marketing programs for each. The former strategy is exemplified by a women's liberal arts college whose admissions office recruits only female highschool students in their teens. An example of differentiation would be a university with both undergraduate and graduate programs, plus an extension division, where different strategies had been adopted to recruit undergraduates from high school, graduate students for each of the graduate schools, and working-age adults for the part-time extension program.

DEVELOPING CRITERIA FOR EFFECTIVE SEGMENTATION

The basic problem in segmentation is to select one or more segmentation variables that will be appropriate for use in a specific context. In any situation, there is an almost infinite number of potential ways of segmenting the market. Which should the manager select? The following criteria offer useful guidelines for evaluating alternative segmentation schemes: size and importance of the segments, compatibility with the institutional mission, and accessibility of the chosen segments within the overall population.

Segment Size

The segments must be large enough and/or sufficiently important to merit the time and cost of separate attention. In the business sector, where the chief concern is to generate high market response relative to program cost it is usually sufficient to define importance in terms of the size of the target market. At present, the definition is inadequate in the public and nonprofit sector, where importance is sometimes defined by those who provide the organization's funding. For example, in the United States federal legislation requires transit operators that receive federal funding to devote special attention to serving handicapped people. As a result, even though the handicapped represent a very small market segment and the costs of serving them are extremely high, they have become an important market segment for public transportation. In other cases, the premise for attracting funds is that certain market segments are to be served. Thus, most donors to Father Flanagan's Boys Town expect it to provide services to orphaned and wayward boys, although the organization now also serves other segments.

Compatibility with Mission and Resources

The skills and equipment required to serve a specific segment effectively must be compatible with the organization's mission and its resources. Private firms usually have some choice over the segments they serve; public agencies, as we have already noted, are often mandated to serve a variety of segments with widely differing needs and are not always provided with sufficient funds to do so effectively. The search for new revenue sources often encourages nonprofit organizations to go after new and more profitable segments only loosely related to the organization's primary mission. The opportunity cost of gearing up to serve these new segments may be a deterioration of service quality for the core segment.

Accessibility: Self-Selection Versus Controlled Coverage

Management must be able to identify chosen segments within the overall market and develop marketing strategies for reaching these segments. Two main approaches can be used for targeting marketing efforts: *customer self-selection* and *controlled coverage*. In both instances, the product is designed, priced, distributed, and promoted to a specific market segment. When the customer self-selection method is used, however, the product is marketed broadly, and it is expected that the target customers will self-select. For example, the U.S. Army may buy advertising on telecasts of the Super Bowl for recruitment of high-school graduates, recognizing that while not all viewers are potential army recruits, the audience does include a substantial number of high-school graduates who might potentially be encouraged to explore the possibility of joining the army. Similarly, the British Royal Mint and Royal Canadian Mint have taken advertisements in the *Wall Street Journal* to market proof gold coins to investment-oriented collectors. Controlled coverage of marketing means just what it says: the organization focuses its marketing efforts to reach the target market only. A strategy of advertising proof gold coins only in numismatic magazines would be an example of the latter approach.

At first glance, it would seem that no manager would ever want to use customer self-selection as a targeting approach, but some benefits may make this strategy reasonable. First, it may be the most economical approach. For example, the cost per reader in a mass magazine such as *TV Guide* is a fraction of the cost in more specialized periodicals. Thus even if a substantial portion of the readership of *TV Guide* is not in the target market, *TV Guide* may still be the most economical magazine available. Such a result, of course, requires a careful specification of the target market and a thorough cost analysis of the alternatives. A second reason for customer self-selection is that the mass media may reach a larger portion of the target market than do specialized media. *Time* magazine, for example, claims that it reaches more business executives than does *Business Week,* even though the latter's audience is largely composed of managers, Third, a customer self-selection strategy offers opportunities to build primary demand by winning new consumers for the product who had not previously been strongly interested in it. Finally, other alternatives may be inferior. For example, suppose an energy-conservation program includes a demonstration of how to turn off the pilot light on gas furnaces in the summer. Television, because of its superior ability to demonstrate "how to" through visual images, might be the preferred communication medium, even though many television watchers are not homeowners with gas furnaces. So the marketing director of an energy-conservation program might select television in the expectation that the homeowners with gas furnaces will self-select from the larger audience.

The choice between customer self-selection and controlled coverage may vary by elements of the marketing mix. For example, a public-transportation agency may advertise its services broadly to the community but, by its choice of routes and schedules, only distribute transit service to target market segments that are defined geographically and in terms of the timing of their travel demands.

RELATING MARKET DEFINITION AND TARGETING TO OBJECTIVES

As shown in Figure 7.2, the task of identifying target markets must be preceded by a careful definition of the organization's objectives arranged in order of priority. These objectives, of course, should flow from the organization's mission or statement of purpose. Each target market selected for marketing treatment should be derived from the institutional mission, not the other way around. Once the key target markets have been identified, analysis may demonstrate the need for further subdivision of these groups into target market segments.

Developing Target Markets and Subsegments for a University Arts Program

If a university maintains a performing-arts program primarily to enhance the extracurricular experience of its students, these students constitute a key target market. There may be supplementary objectives, too, such as reaching out to graduates in the metropolitan area and serving residents of the immediate local community. Already, therefore, three key target markets—students, local residents, and graduates in the area—have been defined within the overall mass market of people living in the entire metropolitan area. Of course, there also is an implicit geographic market definition that recognizes the constraints imposed on attendance by travel time and cost.

There may be sufficient differences among the people in each of these three target markets to warrant some further subdivision. Analysis may show that some represent a higher potential than others. For instance, although students in the music department already have some commitment to and interest in classical music, other students may have little prior exposure and require more persuading to attend a concert. In the local community, there may be many people who would come to a performance once a year as part of a group outing but not make individual visits (and the same may be true of some of the "alums"). Individuals within these segments may also differ according to their ability and willingness to pay, their programming preferences, and their exposure to different communications media (e.g., radio, newspapers, posters, etc.). As a result of this analysis, the following segments might be defined within each of the three target markets.

1. Students at the university.
   - Music and theater majors.
   - Other students.

2. Local residents.

- Those working for major employers in the immediate vicinity—(1) faculty and staff of the university, (2) others.
- Elderly people affiliated with the local senior-citizen center.
- Members of other local social and church organizations.
- Other local residents who are subscribers to the local community newspaper.

3. Graduates.

- Those who work for the university.
- Those who are dues-paying members of the alumni association and who are living in the metropolitan area.
- Other alumni resident in the area for whom the alumni association has a current mailing address.

Each of these segments would have to be evaluated against the criteria discussed earlier. For instance, with regard to substantiality one (or more) of the segments might be dropped if found to have very low potential—it might not be worthwhile to make a special selling effort to "local social organizations" if it turned out that there were only two small clubs, both oriented toward people who enjoyed hunting. On the other hand, even if "other students" were not a large segment, they would still be an important segment because of the university's educational mission.

Should these segments constitute the limit of the marketer's efforts in this instance? Not if it is projected that there will still be additional seats in the auditorium for many of the performances. In this instance, efforts might usefully be made to reach out to other prospective patrons who, although not important to achievement of the organization's educational and community service objectives, might contribute to reducing the deficit. Even here, though, a segmentation approach would yield better insights for marketing strategies and greater cost effectiveness than a shotgun approach aimed at the "remainder" of the mass market. Perhaps selling efforts could be concentrated on nearby colleges or at social and employee organizations elsewhere in the metropolitan area. Alternatively, perhaps there might be an identifiable segment of people oriented toward the performing arts who could be reached through purchase of a mailing list, advertising on a classical radio station, or announcements in the programs distributed at other local arts events.

An Example of Segmentation Strategies to Achieve Specific Objectives

By way of concluding this review of market definition and targeting, we return to the example of public transportation. If you were to ask the general managers of many transit authorities how they saw the broad objectives of their operations, you would probably be given a number of high-sounding goals that were used to justify the last request made for an increase in public funds to meet the projected operating deficit. Such goals would probably include:

- Improving mobility for elderly and low-income persons.
- Reducing air pollution.
- Saving energy.

- Reducing traffic congestion.
- Improving the quality of urban life by avoiding the need for new highways and parking lots.

If you were to ask the managers what specific marketing strategies they were taking to achieve any of these goals, you would probably receive some rather vague and general answers from many of them.

Table 7.1 provides a hypothetical example of how a market-segmentation approach might be applied to two of the objectives listed—improved mobility for the elderly and reduced pollution—as well as to the operational problem of vandalism (which, of course, has important implications for both service quality and cost containment). In each instance, the process involves identifying target market segments (within the broad target market of residents of city X) and proposing a series of marketing efforts, including research activities, to achieve the desired objectives.

ALTERNATIVE BASES FOR SEGMENTATION

No discussion of market segmentation is complete without a look at alternative methods of segmenting a market. We have already mentioned a number of different ways of breaking down a market into separate groups, beginning with the example of the Drinan campaign. It is not always obvious *which* segmentation variables to use in a specific situation, however.

Nor, of course, should a marketing program necessarily limit itself to use of just one segmentation variable. For example, if a health agency was attempting to launch a physical-therapy program at a local hospital, costing $250 per enrollee, to improve participants' heart function, its target market segment should consist of people who had medium to high incomes, lived or worked within a reasonable distance of the hospital, and perceived themselves as being "out of shape" and perhaps susceptible to heart disease. For most programs, in practice, the development of market segments involves the use of multiple dimensions.

User Characteristics Versus User Responses

Broadly speaking, segmenting bases can be subdivided into two categories—user characteristics and user responses (see Table 7.2). In establishing a segmentation strategy, management needs to establish a link between the user characteristics selected and user responses. It is generally not sufficient just to focus on user responses. Suppose, for example, a government agency wanted to target an energy-conservation program at people who waste a lot of energy. Without information about these high energy users, developing a targeted program would be extremely difficult—hence the need to identify consumers in terms of user characteristics that are also related to the user responses of interest. Analytically, a marketer can group people by various combinations of characteristics and then see if any of these groups are similar in terms of response, or vice versa.

Enabling Versus Distinguishing Characteristics of Users

User characteristics can be further subdivided into enabling and distinguishing characteristics. Enabling characteristics—usually demographic, socioeconomic, and geographic

Table 7.1   Segmentation to Achieve Specific Objectives for Public Transportation

Objective	Target Market Segments	Possible Strategies
• Improve mobility for the elderly in city X	• Persons aged 65 and over plus other persons eligible for retirement benefits	• From census data, identify residential locations where elderly persons are concentrated • From surveys of elderly and interviews with appropriate agencies and representatives of senior groups, identify major destination points to which they travel (or would like to travel) and when • Review present services to see if they match key routes desired by elderly at times desired • Consider introducing new services during off-peak hours using equipment and drivers that would otherwise remain idle • Evaluate signs and informational materials for legibility for those with weak eyes • Evaluate suitability of equipment for use by frail older persons; put most suitable equipment on key routes • Give special training to drivers on these routes • Review fare policies to see if suitable discounts can be/ are being given; clarify eligibility criteria, identification required • Publicize services and fares through media directed at elderly and through senior-citizen organizations
• Reduce pollution in city X	• Car drivers traveling in locations or corridors with densest traffic	• Improve frequency of transit services in dense, congested areas • Seek priority for transit vehicles and other measures to improve transit speed in key corridors • Use geographically specific media (billboards, direct mail suburban newspapers, posters at retailers and employers) on key routes • Lobby for increased car parking rates at locations with high congestion
• Reduce vandalism to the transit system in city X	• Parents, youths, and children living close to stations and routes where vandalism has occurred • Teachers in schools serving these areas	• Increase surveillance in worst-affected areas, publicized through press releases to local newspapers • Retrain drivers/station personnel on affected routes to help them better handle aggression or conflict situations and improve communications with passengers • Present programs in selected schools designed to improve awareness of transit benefits and generate interest and and pride in system • Advertise in selected local newspapers seeking cooperation of parents and other adults in combating problem • Promptly repair and clean vandalized vehicles and facilities (especially on key routes)

variables—are the ones that make a consumer eligible to use the product or to participate in the activity being marketed. For example, in the Drinan campaign, being a registered Democrat and living in the Massachusetts Fourth Congressional District were enabling characteristics. Not all such people could be expected to vote for Drinan, however. One distinguishing characteristic was agreement with his position on the Vietnam War. The difference between enabling and distinguishing characteristics is illustrated well by surveys of people holding season subscriptions to the opera. Findings of a 1974 Ford Foundation study showed that almost all opera subscribers had family incomes above $25,000 annually, yet only a small fraction of families in that income category actually subscribed to the opera.[9] Opera-house management needs to know what variables distinguish those who can afford to go to the opera and do from those who can but do not. One characteristic, with some predictive value, is attendance at other performing-arts events; this information may suggest a strategy of using the mailing lists of other performing-arts organizations.

Although relatively straightforward procedures will sometimes suffice, developing segmentation bases that distinguish among groups in a managerially useful way often requires use of sophisticated analytical techniques. Insights from use of these techniques have been obtained in such diverse fields as tourism, fund raising,[10] public transportation,[11] and politics.

In the remainder of this section, we look at six major segmentation variables, each of which can be broken down into a variety of subcategories. Some of these were introduced earlier when we discussed the Drinan campaign, and the reader may find it useful to refer to their application in a specific context. Table 7.2 provides a useful summary (although we do not discuss each subcategory here). We also look at the role of segmentation when marketing to institutional customers as opposed to individuals.

Demographic and Socioeconomic Segmentation Variables

Demographic and socioeconomic variables have the advantage of being relatively easy to recognize and measure. They form the basis for a great many census statistics and can often be readily linked to geographic variables.

Many social services in the public and nonprofit sectors are explicitly linked to demographic and socioeconomic variables. Thus some programs are directed at specific age or income groups. Many health programs are concerned with people in particular physical categories (such as the handicapped, those suffering from high blood pressure, the blind and partially sighted, and so forth).

Church and social organizations often focus on serving a particular ethnic or religious group. The traditional offerings of most arts organizations tend to appeal to people with a higher level of educational achievement (although some arts organizations make a special effort to appeal to nontraditional market segments). Colleges and universities have traditionally targeted their undergraduate recruitment efforts at 16- to 18-year-old high-school students, but are coming to recognize that this target market definition may be too narrow and thus excludes many mature prospects in their 20s and 30s (or even older age groups). Fund-raising efforts often involve efforts to assess the giving potential of prospective donors, based in part on "guesstimates" of their disposable-income levels; more time and effort will then be spent trying to raise money from prospects with a perceived higher potential than from those with less potential.

Table 7.2 Major Segmentation Variables and Selected Subdivisions

1. User Characteristics

Demographic and
Socioeconomic Segmentation
Age
Sex
Marital status
Family size
Composition of household
Household or individual income
Occupation
Education level
Religion
Race or ethnic background
Language spoken
Physical characteristics
State of health

Geographic Segmentation
Nation
Region of country
Specific political jurisdiction (state/province,
   county, district, city, town)
Neighborhood/community
Size of city or metropolitan area
Urban versus rural
Population density
Type of Climate
Nature of Terrain

Psychographic Segmentation

Personality factors
Life-style
Values
Quality of marital and family relations
Attitudes
Interests and avocations
Personal ambitions
IQ level
Level of motivation
Loyalty, commitment

Benefit Segmentation
(a) *Benefits sought*
   Sensory
   Psychic
   Place
   Time
   Monetary
(b) *Costs avoided*
   Sensory
   Psychic
   Place
   Time
   Monetary

2. User Responses

Segmentation by Product-Related Behavior
Frequency of use
Amount used on each occasion
Method of use
Expenditures on related products
Taking of prior qualifying steps
Timing of use
Location of use
Circumstances or purpose of use ("occasion
   segmentation")
Attitudes toward use
Perceptions of product characteristics
Knowledge of product features

Sensitivity to Marketing Variables
Response to product modifications
Price sensitivity
Access to retail locations
Access to telecommunications or
   electronic delivery systems
Response to communication variables

Demographics alone usually do not provide sufficient specificity for developing target-marketing strategies, because these variables are primarily enabling variables. Thus it is often useful to combine demographic and socioeconomic segmentation variables with those from some of the other categories.

Geographic Segmentation Variables

Like demographics, geography often represents an important enabling characteristic in target-market definition. Many public agencies serve a specific political jurisdiction, such as a state or province, county, city, or township. Eligibility to use the service may be confined to residents of that area. Some public programs are oriented toward citizens resident in particular types of locations—such as inner cities or rural areas.

Another type of target-market definition concerns the accessibility of a particular service. There is a limit as to how far most people will travel to attend a symphony or a play, or to visit a health clinic, or to take evening classes at a university. Tabulating the postal codes of an organization's customers offers a quick way to determine the current regional boundaries of the market.* This knowledge helps in developing marketing strategies, including identification of weak areas and evaluation of existing distribution points. The most important target-market segments for any fixed-facility service are, of course, those people who possess the appropriate demographic (and other) characteristics but also are located within relatively easy reach of the service.

The geographic location of prospective customers is particularly important in determining marketing communication strategy. If the target market is clustered in a limited geographic area, it may make more sense to use geographically specific media such as direct mail, billboards, and suburban newspapers than to use wide-area media such as radio, television, or metropolitan newspapers.

Demographics can often be linked to geography through a study of census statistics, which provide certain data for areas as small as a city block. If an organization is serving the elderly, census data can tell which neighborhoods in a city have a high proportion of residents over a given age. The same is true of data on family size, racial origin, and type of housing—to cite just a few instances.

Benefit Segmentation

Instead of looking at the personal characteristics of current or potential consumers, the benefit segmentation approach focuses on the *benefits* they are looking for from the product category in question. Like product-usage behavior, this approach to market segmentation tries to link customers with the product in a meaningful way. As discussed earlier, benefits can be categorized into five groups of utilities: sensory, psychic, place, time, and monetary. The same five groupings can be used to describe costs (or disutilities) that consumers may be seeking to avoid or minimize; these, too, may form the basis for segmentation. Benefit segmentation is appealing in that it can help explain (and even predict) behavior instead of just describing it. Consequently, it may provide insights for future managerial action, not least in the area of designing the product offering.

For instance, some hospitals that offer maternity care have recognized that increasing numbers of women view birth as a natural, healthy process, not a medical "problem" requiring extensive intervention through administration of drugs and surgery, These hospitals have moved to set up "alternative birth centers" that try to create a homelike atmosphere, emphasize the role of midwives instead of doctors during delivery, avoid drugs, anesthesia, or surgery unless absolutely necessary, and encourage participation by the father (or other companion) throughout labor and delivery.

In the field of public transportation, many transit managers now recognize that some people want to travel at speed, in the company of others like themselves, free of crime

---

*British and Canadian postal codes are precise enough to identify a specific city block. If the new nine-digit Zip Code in the United States is widely adopted, it will offer a similar level of precision.

risks, and with a reasonably high level of comfort; moreover, they are prepared to pay extra for these benefits. In the New York City area, comfortable, nonstop commuter buses run parallel to subway routes in some instances; despite this competition and the fact that they charge much higher fares than the subway, these premium bus services have been very successful in attracting patrons.

Several factors are necessary for success in benefit segmentation. First, the marketer must undertake research to determine consumer needs and preferences; second, distinctive segments of sufficient size must be developed based on desired benefits; third, the characteristics of product offerings must be tailored toward one or more of these segments; fourth, the product must be made available in appropriate locations at appropriate times; finally, prospective customers in the target segments must be informed about it.

Psychographic Segmentation Variables

The concept of psychographics has attracted considerable attention from marketing researchers in recent years as a means of explaining differences in consumer behavior that could not be explained by factors such as demography or geography.[12] The term has been somewhat loosely used; we use it here to refer to life-style variables such as values, attitudes on specific topics, and personal interests—and also to personality traits such as self-confidence, aggressiveness, and conservatism.

It is not difficult to see how many of the psychographic variables listed in Table 7.2 might be relevant in helping certain social-service agencies define their market; the real problem lies in identifying and reaching the target segments. Although IQ measures are sometimes suspect, variables such as intelligence (important to universities) tend to be easier to measure than values and may be connected to such identifiers as media habits ("highbrow" versus "lowbrow" publications and programs) and high schools attended.

Psychographics may be particularly useful in many other nonbusiness marketing contexts as an input to communication strategy. If research shows that certain life-styles—as reflected in people's attitudes toward eating, drinking, the need for exercise, etc.—are bad for health, an intensive advertising program directed at the segments at risk might lead some people to change their views and thereby their behavior. It may be difficult to find media specific to these segments, thus requiring use of a self-selection strategy employing messages in the mass media.

As discussed in Chapter 6, life-style groups are often compiled from information on people's activities, interests, and opinions. SRI International's "Values and Life-Styles" (VALS) is just one of several such frameworks that are available and used for segmenting markets.

Product-Related Behavior

How consumers behave relative to the product in question (or to competing alternatives or substitutes) is obviously a central dimension in formulating marketing strategy. It is helpful to segment prospective consumers along this dimension if the relevant information can be obtained from research and observation.

As discussed earlier in this chapter, a high proportion of total product use is often accounted for by a relatively small proportion of customers. This holds true in nonbusiness organizations, too. For instance, in fund raising it is quite common for 90 percent of the value of the gifts received to come from only 10 percent of the donors. The bulk of passenger trips on public-transportation vehicles are made by a core group of riders who commute to and from work each day. Although in some cities a high proportion of residents and visitors may claim to have ridden the transit system in any given year, the great majority of these people are likely to have used it on only a few occasions. Marketers need to pay careful attention to big donors or heavy users, because if they are lost the organization may quickly find itself in trouble.

The purposes for which the product is used are also significant. Surgical patients in a hospital tend to have different expectations and needs than do those in obstetrics. Doctoral students are likely to make different demands on a university library than undergraduates. Art lovers buying for themselves are likely to make different purchases at a museum shop than visitors seeking souvenirs of a particular exhibition or people who use the shop for buying Christmas cards and presents.

Combining Segmentation Variables

In the increasingly competitive markets that businesses and nonprofit organizations face, it is often not sufficient just to use one or two segmentation variables. Several need to be combined for accurate targeting of markets. This approach is probably the most refined in the area of direct marketing, where demographic and life-style information is combined with geographic data to define appropriate lists.[13] Major direct marketing service bureaus compile lists of millions of names and combine them with information gained from census data and market research surveys, overlaid with existing data on occupation and income, purchasing patterns, and results of VALS or other life-style surveys to produce highly refined definitions of market targets. While the computer service bureaus producing such lists are large companies, small nonprofits have been able to successfully use such firms when they can define their geographic markets tightly. For example, one performing arts organization conducted a survey of its current subscribers to understand their life-style better. It then hired a direct marketing company to provide a list of census tract areas with a life-style profile similar to that of its current subscribers, located nearby to its auditorium, and with moderate to high income. Working within these parameters, a manageable list was obtained at reasonable cost and a successful mailing was completed.

Sensitivity to Marketing Variables

Consumers may also be segmented by their sensitivity or responsiveness to marketing variables. For example, price is often more important to one market segment than it is to another. The challenge for management is to find a way of offering a price discount to the first segment but not to the second. Transportation agencies, for instance, struggle to develop a strategy for offering discounted fares to people who are traveling for pleasure trips or other personal reasons, without making these easily available to business travelers who can afford to pay more.

Another example concerns a performing-arts organization that presented performances of classical music. Research showed that a substantial portion of its potential audience actively sought out the information available about each event, especially the particular works being played. Previous advertising had emphasized the performer's name and an excerpt from a laudatory review about the performer, but to meet the needs of this "program-sensitive" segment, the organization developed a new information campaign, using small space advertisements in local newspapers.

Segmenting Organizational and Institutional Customers

Organizational markets can often be usefully segmented. When dealing with major institutional purchasers, each customer alone may be substantial enough to justify a distinct plan, as in the case of a home nursing service which treats separately each of three hospitals accounting for more than 15% of its annual referrals. Not only large customers, however, are worthwhile pursuing. Statistics Canada, for instance, which collects census and other data in Canada, has successfully marketed a series of booklets targeted to the needs of small businesses.

Kotler and Fox, as another illustration, suggest a number of ways that a business school providing training programs to companies might segment the market.[14] These include geographic location (the market for an evening program is more tightly defined than the market for a Saturday program), size, as large companies are more likely to have in-house programs than small firms (although larger companies may want more advanced programs), and resource or expenditure level for training. Useful ways to segment the market may also include a company's buying criteria—does the company emphasize the prestige of the school giving the program, the faculty teaching it, or the specifics of the course itself—and the buying process—how long does it take to make a decision and who is involved in it. According to the results of segmentation analysis and the skills available to the university, it may choose to offer short courses to local companies that can make quick decisions, residential programs featuring famous professors, or another alternative.

SUMMARY

This chapter has clarified that segmentation serves two basic purposes: (1) to define markets within the total population or "mass market" that an organization wishes to serve, and (2) to break down these target markets into segments that merit development of tailored marketing strategies.

A basic challenge in market segmentation is to select segmentation variables that would prove useful in a specific operational context. Three basic criteria have to be satisfied if useful segments are to be developed: the chosen segments must be (1) compatible with the organization's mission and resources, (2) accessible within the total population, and (3) substantial or important enough to merit special attention. There are a number of different ways of segmenting a market. These include demographics, geography, psychographics, benefits sought, and product-related behavior. Each offers different types of insights, and its appropriateness for segmenting any given market will depend on the objectives of the organization, the characteristics of the market, and other situational factors.

The concept of market segmentation is based on three propositions: (1) consumers are different, (2) differences in consumers are related to differences in market behavior, and (3) segments of consumers can be isolated within the overall market. Market segmentation is a great improvement over undifferentiated mass marketing, because it requires a focused effort rather than an attempt to be all things to all people.

REFERENCES

1. Christopher H. Lovelock and Charles B. Weinberg, "The Role of Marketing in Improving Postal Service Effectiveness," in Joel Fleishman (ed.), *The Future of the Postal Service*, New York: Praeger, 1983.

2. This section has been adapted from: (1) Eric Rudman and Richard Neustadt, "John Marttila and Campaign Management," 9-578-747, Boston: Intercollegiate Case Clearing House, 1975; (2) James L. Heskett, *Marketing,* New York: Macmillan, 1976, pp. 370–373. See also, Gary Mauser, *Political Marketing,* New York: Praeger Publishers, 1983.

3. Elections to the United States Congress take place in two stages: the primary election and the general election. When registering to vote, prior to an election, electors declare themselves as Republicans, Democrats, or Independents. The primary election is held first. In Massachusetts, on entering the polling place, registered Republicans receive a Republican ballot and registered Democrats receive a Democratic one, but voters who have registered as Independents may choose either. Both ballots generally feature several candidates for each of a variety of local, state, and federal elective offices. The primary thus serves as a preliminary selection procedure, with Democratic and Republican voters each choosing, separately, their preferred candidates for the general election later in the year. The winners in the primaries automatically become their respective party's candidates in the upcoming general election (although Republicans and Democrats may still find themselves opposed by Independents and candidates of minor parties). Thus, to become the Democratic candidate for Congress in the general election, Drinan first had to win the Democratic nomination in the primary.

4. Based on data in *Physician Visits: Volume and Interval Since Last Visit, United States—1971.* In *Vital and Health Statistics,* ser. 10, no. 97. Washington, D.C.: U.S. National Center for Health Statistics, 1975.

5. Derived from data in National Research Center for the Arts, *Americans and the Arts,* New York: Associated Council of the Arts, 1976, pp. 77–80.

6. J. Allision Bamhill, "Developing a Marketing Orientation—A Case Study of the Canada Post Office," in Ronald C. Curhan (ed.), *Marketing's Contributions to the Firm and to Society,* Chicago: American Marketing Association, 1975, pp. 293–298.

7. Christopher H. Lovelock, "Hood College," in E. R. Corey, C. H. Lovelock, and S. Ward, *Problems in Marketing,* sixth edition, New York: McGraw-Hill, 1981, pp. 46–61.

8. Stanley J. Shapiro and J. Allison Bamhill, "The Post Office in the Marketplace, A Ten-Year Retrospective," in D. N. Thompson et al., *Macro-Marketing: A Canadian Perspective,* Chicago: American Marketing Association, 1980, pp. 50–76.

9. *The Finances of the Performing Arts,* New York: Ford Foundation, 1974.

10. See, for example, Christopher H. Lovelock, "Stanford University: The Annual Fund," in C. H. Lovelock and C. B. Weinberg, *Public and Nonprofit Marketing: Cases and Readings,* New York: John Wiley & Sons, 1984.

11. See, for example, Frederick R. Dunbar and Christopher H. Lovelock, "The State of the Art in Urban Travel Consumer Research," in R. K. Robinson and C. H. Lovelock, *Marketing Public Transportation: Policies, Research Needs and Strategies for the Eighties,* Chicago: American Marketing Association, 1981.

12. William D. Wells, (1) *Lifestyle and Psychographics,* Chicago: American Marketing Association, 1974; (2) "Psychographics: A Critical Review," *Journal of Marketing Research* (May 1975), pp. 196–213.

13. Gillian Teweles, "Direct Appeal," *Madison Avenue* (January 1985), pp. 55–56.

14. Philip Kotler and Karen F. A. Fox, *Strategic Marketing for Educational Institutions,* Englewood Cliffs, N.J.: Prentice-Hall, 1985.

Chapter 8
Marketing Research

Successful marketing management is based on a good understanding of the markets in which the organization competes. This understanding requires that the organization have accurate, timely information and a means to analyze and communicate this information to relevant decision makers. In this chapter we concentrate on marketing research, the form of marketing information primarily concerned with special purpose research projects.

Decision makers should recognize the limitations as well as the potential rewards of research and begin every investigation with a clear understanding of their organization's specific needs for information. Given the uncertain, dynamic, and competitive nature of the markets and publics with which most organizations must deal, no manager can hope to gain perfect understanding. The goal of marketing research is to reduce uncertainty to tolerable levels at a reasonable cost.

Not all marketing research involves expensive, large-scale, sophisticated surveys. Tightly directed studies are often helpful to managers trying to make sound decisions. Kotler and Andreasen identify five myths that result in nonprofits doing insufficient marketing research:

- Big-decision only
- Survey myopia
- "Big bucks"
- Sophisticated researcher
- Research is not read[1]

Although some research problems do demand "big bucks" and sophisticated researchers, the uncertainty in many problems can be resolved by inexpensive projects using commonsense approaches. Even "small" decisions may benefit from market research input. For instance, one performing arts organization found in an audience survey that less than 10% of attenders preferred its present starting time of 8:30 P.M. to an earlier time of 7:30 P.M. or 8:00 P.M. The next year it switched to an 8:00 P.M. time (which was also more convenient from a production viewpoint).

Surveys are but one source of data: there are many alternative ways of gathering needed information. Organizational records, library materials, information from governments, and interviews with individuals and groups are generally readily available at low cost. Generally there is a lot of knowledge within an organization that can be tapped to provide useful information.

Why are research reports sometimes not read? Often because they don't address a clearly defined information need. This may occur because (1) the need was not defined in the first place, (2) improper execution of the project has allowed it to drift away from its original purpose, or (3) the research purpose was inappropriate, e.g. an excuse to delay a decision, an attempt to prove someone wrong, or merely an exercise to confirm a decision already (tacitly) made.

Scope of the Chapter

To begin this chapter, we will briefly review a research project that had a substantial impact on management decisions. This project, involving a combination of donated time by consultants and local students, involved minimal cost to the organization beyond printing and mailing questionnaires.

Following description and discussion of this example, the chapter develops a 10-step *process* for carrying out market research: (1) definition of research purpose—why is the information needed and how will it be used? (2) statement of research objectives—what specific information is required? (3) review of existing data—is the information we need already available elsewhere? (4) value analysis—will the value of the information exceed the cost of getting it? (5) research design, embracing exploratory, descriptive, and causal studies; (6) methods of primary data collection; (7) research tactics—sampling procedures and instrument design; (8) conduct of field operations; (9) data analysis; and (10) interpretation and presentation of data.

THE AMERICAN CONSERVATORY THEATRE SURVEY[2]

After some difficult early years, the American Conservatory Theatre (ACT), a major repertory theater in San Francisco, achieved substantial artistic recognition and a strong audience following. Although most performances were not sold out, tickets were generally difficult to get. Management, however, was facing some difficult decisions with regard to maintaining high subscription sales. Consequently, ACT's management decided to conduct research on the nature of the subscription-buying process, both to help make decisions on some specific pricing issues and to identify any previously undetected problems.

Subscribers were sent a six-page survey by mail. Even though the theater did not pay return postage, a 45 percent response was obtained. The key to the high response rate was a convincing cover letter that explained to subscribers the benefits of completing the questionnaire ("to better serve you in the future"). Only a few of the results from the questionnaire will be discussed here.

The issue of why people subscribed to ACT was addressed by asking them about the benefits they sought to obtain. One possible benefit was the price discount of seven plays for the price of six. Another reason why people might buy a subscription was that it gave them more impetus to attend. If a person already had tickets for Saturday night, he or she would probably go. If, on the other hand, a decision to buy tickets had been postponed until Saturday afternoon, there was a greater chance the theatergoer would stay home. Other potential benefits of a subscription included priority seating and a guarantee of obtaining a ticket.

One significant finding was that price discounts were not one of the major benefits that ACT subscribers sought. (This did not imply that ACT could charge subscribers a premium price.) Because the preliminary findings from this survey supported management's prior beliefs, ACT decided to stop offering subscribers the "seven for six" price discount. In the years immediately after this change, the renewal rate remained at or rose above its previous level.

Generalizing from this result to other pricing strategies can be tricky, however; it would be wrong to conclude that subscribers were indifferent to any rise in prices, as ACT discovered when it surveyed reaction to its programs. At every performance, ACT distributed a glossy, lavishly designed program that described the play and other current cultural events in San Francisco. As printing costs increased, ACT management felt that the only way it could afford to continue the program (even with advertising), would be to charge 25¢ a copy. ACT then asked its subscribers whether they wanted to pay 25¢ for the traditional program, or whether they preferred something less elaborate. Despite their willingness to pay $50 or more per subscription and their relative indifference to the subscription discount, 80 percent of the respondents said no to the 25¢ charge, perhaps stating, in effect, "Charge what you want for the subscription, but I want to enjoy my night out and I don't want to be bothered searching for a quarter when I get to the theater." ACT consequently printed a simpler program.

Another unexpected finding concerned how people first become subscribers. The decision involves spending $100 to $150 for a pair of subscriptions (the usual purchase) to seven plays. The hypothesized pattern for this decision was a gradual one in which a couple first go to one or two plays, then gradually increase their attendance to three or four plays a year, and finally buy a seven-play subscription. This is a logical model that makes a lot of sense, and, in fact, 30 percent of new subscribers follow that pattern. However, about 25 percent of the subscribers had no contact with ACT for up to five years before suddenly subscribing. Socioeconomically and demographically, the sudden subscribers are not very different from the other subscribers, but they do participate less frequently in cultural activities. The response to the survey raises an important question: if a large fraction of subscribers have never been to ACT before, what should be done to persuade that fraction to become loyal supporters of the theater? Perhaps special "orientation" booklets or "evenings with the actors" should be arranged for this new audience. Such discoveries raise some very real questions as to what ACT's product is—entertainment, intellectual benefit, social status—and what should be offered to the different segments that comprise ACT's audience.

In summary, as is often the case, the results of the survey confirmed some of management's preconceptions—and contradicted others. Both types of information are essential to decision making. What is especially notable in this case is that the survey was designed with such decision making clearly in mind; thus, its results had a measurable impact on managerial actions.

THE RESEARCH PROCESS

Market research is properly viewed as a sequence of steps that can be termed the *research process*. A summary of the research process is presented in Table 8.1. When beginning a study, it may be tempting to go straight to instrument-design and data-collection stages,

Table 8.1 Marketing Research

The Market Research Process

1. Purpose of research—why is information to be gathered?
2. Statement of research objectives—what information is needed?
3. Review existing data to discover what is already known
4. Value analysis—is the research worth the cost?
5. Research design—How are the data to be collected?
   (a) exploratory
   (b) descriptive
   (c) causal
6. Methods of primary data collection
   (a) communication
   (b) observation
7. Research tactics—sampling procedures and instrument design
   (a) universe
   (b) sample selection
   (c) sample size
   (d) instrument design
   (e) pretesting
8. Field operations—collection of the data
9. Data analysis
10. Completing the project
    (a) interpreting the data
    (b) recommendations
    (c) report writing

without thinking through the prior steps. This is a serious mistake, and often leads to market-research reports that are not useful because the wrong questions were asked or the data collected turn out to be unreliable and inaccurate. The temptation to leap ahead to data gathering before the real purpose of the study has been directed must be resisted.

In this chapter, we go through the steps of the research process in sequence, presenting some of the major issues in the field. Market-research texts and handbooks provide a fuller treatment of these topics.[3]

PURPOSE OF THE RESEARCH

The primary questions to be asked before beginning any market research are "why is this information needed?" and "what will the implications of this research be?" If no possible finding or outcome is expected to have an impact on management decisions, the research should not be carried out. Of course, not all discoveries will lead to changes. For example, if a sample of mass transit riders believe that schedules are clear, no changes will be made. If a negative result is obtained, however, further research presumably will occur to determine the reasons for rider dissatisfaction and to test alternative designs for schedules. In any research project, at least some outcomes should have implications for management decision making. From the outset, ACT's market-research project was designed to be used by management in planning a marketing strategy.

The reasons for conducting marketing research can be categorized by examining the process of decision making. A useful three-stage model is (1) recognizing and defining problems, (2) generating and selecting alternative courses of action, and (3) monitoring performance. Although it is often overlooked, the first stage of any decision is recognition that a need for a decision exists.

Initial signals that managers receive are often only vague indications or symptoms of a problem; but once the problem is detected, market research can be very useful in defining and understanding it. A rise in complaint letters, an increase in vandalism, a sudden falloff of patronage for a service (for no obvious reason), a sudden increase in staff turnover or a difficulty in filling positions, even an increase in press coverage—each may indicate problems that market research can help an organization understand.

Once the need for a change is recognized, market research can help the manager search for and evaluate alternative courses of action. Although at times the process of generating alternatives can be relatively informal and may even be part of the problem-definition stage, much of the work done in this area is characterized by formal research procedures. Indeed, the careful gathering of descriptive data and the evaluation of specific alternatives through questionnaire and observational studies is the stereotypical conception of market research—and probably is the area in which the most money is spent. Even here, the availability of secondary information should not be overlooked.

Once a decision has been made and a marketing plan implemented, progress should be measured against the original purpose through performance monitoring or evaluation research. The questions to be asked after a program has begun include: To what extent is it reaching its objectives? What other impacts, both anticipated and unanticipated, is the program making? What accounts for deviation from the predicted results? Because marketing deals in such a highly uncertain and competitive environment, deviations can result from changes in the environment as well as improper execution of the plan. Consequently, evaluation research must examine both inputs and outputs of the marketing program as well as external factors (such as weather) outside the marketer's control. Performance monitoring is important not only because it can indicate a need for changes in a plan or its execution, but also because it enables managers and other personnel to learn from their mistakes—as well as their successes—and to redirect the organization accordingly.

STATEMENT OF RESEARCH OBJECTIVES

After establishing that the research will serve a useful purpose, the next step is to state explicitly the research objectives—what information is needed? This statement of research objectives should lead to a listing of specific information requirements. In other words, this stage involves going from the general to the particular. The person doing the marketing research will often find that the manager has not thought through the specific information requirements and will need to be "pushed" to make a careful statement about the information needed. Too often, at the *end* of a research project, managers say that the research has not provided them with the information they really wanted. That is too late!

A useful first step is to state the information requirements in writing. These requirements can then be reviewed to see if they are specific enough to provide guidance to the research, set forth the issues to be investigated, and include all the relevant questions to be asked.

Some find it useful to determine information requirements by stating their beliefs about the market as a set of hypotheses. For example, a library director trying to determine the building's best operating hours may be interested in a test of the hypothesis that opening the library two evenings a week will increase traffic on the days selected by 10 percent. A second hypothesis could be that the particular day chosen will have no impact on the percentage increase in traffic. These hypotheses are then used to generate data requirements. For the library, information about use by time of day would be required, but data about payment of overdue fines and length of time books are held would not be necessary.

Another fruitful approach is to prepare samples of possible outputs from the project and see what questions the sample report raises. Are other data needed before the results can be used? For example, in preparing a draft report the library director may also see a need to determine staffing requirements by asking, say, what types of materials evening users are likely to want. Will evening users want to have access to the children's book section, or can that section be closed? Will evening users require the services of a fully trained reference librarian? Careful examination of the sample output will also reveal whether the report contains data that will *not* be useful and can be eliminated from the study. As this library example illustrates, it is often useful for a manager to determine

---

ELECTRONIC RETRIEVAL OF SECONDARY DATA

Secondary data have always been a major information source for marketing managers. However, the difficulties involved in finding a complete data base and then searching through it often overwhelm managers. The advent of widespread computerized data bases has helped overcome many of these problems. In addition to commercial information brokers, many public libraries have added electronic data base searching to their capabilities and offer it at little cost to users. Four main types of data bases are available:

Bibliographic:	Indexes of articles from newspapers, magazines, trade journals, government reports, press releases, etc. Relevant articles can often be accessed through the use of *keywords* identifying the topic of interest. Abstracts and complete copies of the original can often be obtained, at an additional fee.
Statistical:	Demographic, economic, and other numerical data series for a variety of time frames and geographical areas.
Corporate Financial:	Detailed information about public corporations.
Directory/Encyclopedia:	Facts about people, organizations, associations. Often these are on-line versions of well known reference works. Names and addresses of key personnel are included.

Most on-line services are kept current (to within three months).

Some organizations now employ information specialists to codify their own internal information so it can be accessed by the same electronic data base approach that is used on outside data. In brief, organizations have realized that their information has value only if made easily accessible to their own managers.

beforehand what information will be needed if each of the alternatives being studied is adopted. This information may possibly be gathered at low cost initially, saving both time and money later when a course of action is decided.

Alternatively, a manager can start by working backwards from the stage of how the research results will be implemented. In the main, the central theme of all the approaches is that by starting with a focus on the output of the research, relevant research is likely to be produced.

REVIEW OF EXISTING DATA

Before going out and gathering new data to resolve a well-specified research problem, researchers should investigate the possibility of using data that already exist. Market researchers divide information into two classes, primary data and secondary data. Primary data are new information collected especially for the research project being undertaken; secondary data have previously been collected separately for other purposes. People often underestimate the amount of secondary data available. An organization's own internal record keeping system, the observations of staff, published statistics, books and articles, and other information can often be readily assembled to give a good deal of valuable marketing information not requiring field surveys. A good general rule to follow is not to gather primary data until it becomes clear that no satisfactory secondary data are available. Even then, it is best to start with secondary data and only collect primary data for questions that remain unresolved.

Secondary data have the advantages of lower cost (sometimes free) and immediate availability. On the other hand, because secondary data rarely solve the exact problem specified, they have several potential disadvantages. They may not be current or cover the right time period; they may be measured in units different from those desired; they may be subdivided into inappropriate classes; or they may omit critical variables.

VALUE ANALYSIS

Is the research worth doing? To answer that question, we must compare the cost of the research to its value. In general, cost can be estimated fairly closely. An estimate of value is much more difficult to make. Because the outcome of the study is not known, we can, at best, only make probability estimates of the likelihood of different results. Moreover, unless we are using the research to choose among a set of predefined alternatives, specifying the value of any particular outcome is very difficult. Thus value can only be approximated.

Not all information is worth its cost, either because it is unlikely to have an impact on management decisions or because its anticipated cost exceeds its expected benefits. For example, one transit agency planned to undertake an expensive study of commuter traffic, but closer analysis of the situation revealed that the agency's major problems were lack of capacity and poor operating performance, not customer behavior. In other cases, an organization may not be able to afford a particular research project even if its cost is low relative to its value. Before devoting scarce resources to the design of an overly ambitious project, managers should develop a rough estimate of the size of the studies they can afford. In addition, the value and cost of alternative research designs should be estimated.

Before carrying out a research project, the manager should be satisfied either (1) that its cost is so low relative to the magnitude of the problem being studied that no formal analysis of the project's value is required, or (2) that the expected value of the project exceeds its cost.

We have made value analysis an early step in the research process. This analysis should be updated periodically as the research process unfolds. Depending on the particular project, a full-scale value analysis may be most appropriate at a stage earlier or later than is suggested here.

Few market-research projects will produce findings conclusive enough to eliminate all doubt about the course of action to be taken, A good project is one that reduces uncertainty to a degree that allows a manager to make an informed decision—even if only to do more research.

At times, researchers are called on to gather market information on an issue that arouses strong opinions on opposite sides, Frequently, such views may be based on little or no acquaintance with reality ("I've made up my mind; don't bother me with facts"). In such situations the goal should not be to change anyone's opinion, but to make the participants in the debate take notice of the research. To achieve this goal, the research project must be truly relevant to the question that originally initiated it; moreover, its reliability and accuracy must be such that the results cannot be dismissed out of hand. In hotly debated issues, this standard can be a very demanding one.

RESEARCH DESIGN

A research design is the plan that guides the collection and analysis of data. The research design attempts to develop an economical means through which to achieve the project's objectives. Although each study has a specific purpose, it is useful to classify market research into three broad groupings of studies: (1) exploratory, (2) descriptive, and (3) causal.

Exploratory Studies

Exploratory studies are most often used in the problem-discovery and problem-definition phases of decision making.[4] Their purpose is to outline the dimensions of a problem more clearly by helping researchers to become more familiar with it and to learn the vocabulary and perceptions of the users. Often an exploratory study will be instrumental in developing hypotheses about a problem; sometimes it will be used to discover the practicality of doing research in the problem area.

As one might imagine, exploratory studies are more informal and less rigidly controlled than standardized questionnaire interviews, Although only a small number of respondents are typically contacted, the interview is less structured and more intensive in order to provide an in-depth understanding of the situation. The methods employed to conduct exploratory studies include: (1) review of related literature, (2) survey (usually by an unstructured personal interview) of people who have had practical experience with or have special knowledge of the problem being studied, (3) in-depth interviews of small samples of typical consumers, either in groups or individually, and (4) intensive analysis of a few analogous situations. The last method usually consists of developing relevant case histories and then investigating them in detail. This approach is particularly useful in complex situations in which many variables interact.

Exploratory research often involves the basic qualitative methods of in-depth or group interviews, as in the following examples.

> A social-service agency wanted to prepare a public-information pamphlet for teenagers about venereal disease. In group sessions, teenagers discussed venereal disease in their own terms and areas of confusion. The text of the pamphlet was based on these discussions.
>
> Focus groups are often used to help assess different creative themes in commercials. In 1977, the Baptist General Convention of Texas prepared an extensive marketing campaign to increase membership in its church. As a test, four commercials were shown to separate groups consisting of active Christians, nonactive Christians, and non-Christians. All three segments gave their highest rating to testimonials in which the speakers indicated how important their faith in Christ had been in overcoming their own problems. In one, the speaker said that he had been a revolutionary, but his life had been changed by another revolutionary and closed with the statement: "My name is Eldridge Cleaver. I'm living proof." This "living proof" campaign was later widely used throughout the United States. Focus groups were also used to help set criteria for acceptable spokespersons.[5]

Exploratory studies often use semistructured individual interviews. While the interviewer may have a preplanned list of areas to cover, the timing, exact wording, and depth of coverage depend on the discretion of the interviewer during the interview. Unexpected but important issues that arise can be covered. The success of this approach depends critically on the skill of the interviewer. He or she must be able to establish rapport with the subject quickly, to clarify and extend important responses, and to keep the discussion on the main topics without seeming to be overbearing. Individual interviews of this type are often the only way to get the cooperation of powerful people, and the session must be interesting to the respondent if it is to be successful. Record keeping is a difficult problem in such studies; although a tape recorder is ideal, many times respondents will be uncomfortable or not allow a recording to be made.

Focus-Group Interviews. In a focus group, a small number of people (typically six to ten) are brought together to discuss a particular topic under the guidance of a skilled moderator. Although the organization of the group interview often seems to be loose or casual to the participants, in practice the group leader closely follows a topic guide prepared in advance. Typically, the early discussion is quite broad as the moderator tries to establish a friendly tone, making sure that everyone shares in the conversation and reacts to the comments made by other participants. Group interaction is an important part of focus-group interviews. The opportunity to be stimulated by others and respond to their comments distinguishes the group from the individual interview. This can lead to more spontaneous and perhaps more honest comments. Sometimes the sessions are conducted in rooms with one-way mirrors so that concerned executives can observe them; more frequently they are taped (audio and/or video) and transcribed for later use.

Cautions and Limitations. Exploratory research is just that, and the danger managers face is overgeneralizing from the results. Qualitative studies are compelling because they show real people talking in their own words about the organization's products. But caution is necessary. First, the results are not based on a representative sample of the population and consequently cannot be projected to the entire market. Second, the semistructured nature of the research, the role of the interviewer in directing the responses, and the subjectiveness of the answers do not usually allow for a clear, unambiguous interpretation of the results. Qualitative research should be used to gain insights into the consumer perspective and suggest hypotheses for further testing and alternatives to pursue. Quite often, such studies will generate, and even answer, questions that researchers would never have even thought of beforehand. This information, of course, is exactly the type needed at the exploratory stage.

Descriptive Studies

Descriptive studies are used for the following purpose.

1. To portray accurately the attitudes, behavior, and other characteristics of persons, groups, or organizations and their frequency of occurrence.
2. To determine the extent of association among two or more variables.
3. To draw inferences about the relationships among variables and to make predictions. Although descriptive studies do not provide definitive proof of causal relationships, such proof is not always required to make inferences and to formulate predictions.

The ACT study, discussed at the start of this chapter, is descriptive research and was used to satisfy all three of these purposes. The survey results described the characteristics of various categories of ACT subscribers. In addition, ACT was able to examine the extent of association between number of years subscribing, contribution behavior, income, and years resident in the San Francisco area. The finding that even long-time residents could become "sudden" subscribers led management to institute a direct-mail campaign to charge-account holders at prestigious stores. Finally, the survey suggested that there would be only a limited reduction in the number of subscriptions sold if the price discount were discontinued.

Unlike an exploratory study, a descriptive study must be based on a detailed research plan, as we discussed earlier. Both the data-collection and the data-analysis strategies should be carefully thought out before the field research is begun.

In general, descriptive studies can be subdivided between cross-sectional and longitudinal studies. The cross-sectional study is most familiar and involves, as in the ACT study, an examination of the population of interest at one point in time, A longitudinal or panel study investigates a fixed sample of people who are measured at a number of points over time. A panel allows researchers to monitor a separate individual's behavior over time. For example, if we want to know whether someone who reduces energy consumption as the result of a marketing communication campaign persists in that behavior after the campaign is concluded, panel data are required. Cross-sectional or aggregate data will only tell us whether consumption is reduced. They will not reveal the use pattern behind that reduction—that is, they will not show whether many people each conserve for a short period of time, or whether a few people conserve consistently.

Causal Studies

Although descriptive research is often used to estimate relationships among variables and to make predictions, managers often want stronger evidence that a causal relationship exists. Although we can probably never prove that X causes Y, we can often build a very strong case.

In order to establish a causal relationship, the data must pass at least three tests. First, there should be a concurrent variation between the variables and changes in the variables. Suppose we wanted to investigate whether increased enforcement of traffic laws influences the speed at which people drive. If the proposition is true, we would expect a change in the speed of driving as well as a change in the strictness of law enforcement. Of course, such changes are not in themselves sufficient evidence; there should be an expressed or implied relationship between the variables such that a change in one might logically have an impact on the other in a reasonably direct manner. (A rise in births in Massachusetts may parallel a rise in the use of London buses, but it's unlikely that the first increase *caused* the second, or vice versa,) A second test in establishing causality is that of sequence. The causal agent (here, increased enforcement of traffic laws) should precede the resultant change (reduction in driving speed). The third test is the absence of other possible causal factors or the elimination of plausible rival hypotheses, We would have to make sure, in the case cited, that road repairs in the area had not slowed traffic or that a large segment of the population—say, college students—had not left town for summer vacation.

Experiments. The best means for establishing a causal relationship is an experiment. In an experiment, various levels of the causal factor—the treatment—are assigned on a statistically random basis to subjects. Then differences in response between those receiving the different treatments and those receiving no treatment—the controls—are measured and analyzed to see if there is evidence of a causal relationship, In the traffic study, highway patrols might be placed on one road but not on another of similar location and usage. Differences in the speed of traffiic flow would then be measured and compared.

There are two types of experiments: laboratory experiments and field experiments. In lab experiments, the researcher develops a similated environment in which some variables are manipulated and others are controlled. Here the researcher has great control, and the impact of other relevant variables can be kept to a minimum. Field experiments, in contrast, are much harder to control and may require the cooperation of employees, consumers, or even the weather. Yet by the same token, field experiments are conducted in much more realistic situations, and managers often place more trust in field results.

A test market, one form of field experiment, is frequently used in introducing new products, and both field and lab experiments are employed in designing advertising campaigns. The time required and monetary costs involved, however, limit the number of true experiments that are actually run. Nevertheless, whenever any new program is introduced or a major change is made, it should be viewed as a quasi-experiment. In attempting to measure the impact of the change, the principles of experimental design, particularly of comparing treatment to control and controlling for errors or threats to validity, can be used.

Threats to Validity. In interpreting the results of experiments (as well as other research designs that attempt to assess causality), researchers speak of internal validity and external validity. Internal validity addresses the question, "Is the effect we are observing actually caused by the experimental treatment or is it caused by some other factors?" External validity is concerned with whether the results of the experiment can be generalized to other persons, settings, and times. Of course, the researcher attempts to achieve high levels of both internal and external validity.

What are the threats to *internal validity?* That is, what other factors might have caused the effect we are observing? Several possibilities immediately come to mind. *History* refers to other events, external to the experiment but occurring at the same time. For example, a study of the effects of a price reduction on museum attendance would be confounded if a local newspaper published a major story on the museum's exhibits. *Maturation* refers to processes that are internal to respondents and happen to occur at the same time as the behavior being studied. For example, children who have been exposed to commercials on television for a year may be better able to differentiate between commercial and program material simply because, in the year that the test ran, their cognitive processes developed further as part of normal growth. A *testing* effect threatens internal validity because those who are observed or who complete a survey at one time may show changes when observed or questioned a second time, simply because they were tested before. *Selection bias* occurs when the subjects selected are already different from each other at the outset of the experiment. Suppose we were testing people's desire to seek health care after they have been exposed to information describing the dangers of high blood pressure. We might set up two groups, expose one to television commercials, and then observe the behavior of all subjects over the next month. If one sample happens to be dominated by middle-aged executives under stress and the other mostly young college students, the results will have no validity. Matched samples and random assignment of subjects to samples are attempts to overcome this bias. Finally, *statistical regression* refers to the tendency of extreme responses to move toward the average. It operates when experimental subjects are chosen because of extreme behavior—behavior that may be only a temporary aberration. For example, if a state decides to impose a crackdown on speeding drivers because the number of highway fatalities has suddenly risen, any decrease in deaths in the next year may be due as much to chance as to the increased enforcement of the speed limit.

What are the threats to *external validity?* A major one is *interaction between selection and the experimental treatment variable.* Is it possible that the results only apply to the population that was studied? Difficulty in recruiting subjects for the experiment is a warning signal; in this case, the results may only generalize to this type of volunteer, As Cook and Campbell waggishly point out, "Whenever the conditions of recruiting respondents are systematically selective, we are apt to have findings that are only applicable to volunteers, exhibitionists, hypochondriacs, scientific do-gooders, those with nothing else to do with their time, etc. . . . An experiment involving executives is more likely to be ungeneralizable if it takes a day's time than if it takes only ten minutes, for only the latter experiment is likely to include busy persons with little free time."[6] A second major external threat is a *reactive* effect, Does simply knowing one is participating in an experiment change behavior? If so, the results cannot be generalized to other populations.

Instead of cursing or ignoring these and other threats to validity, the experimenter must develop a design that will control and possibly eliminate them.

METHODS OF PRIMARY DATA COLLECTION

The two major methods of data collection are communication and observation. *Communication* requires the subject to participate actively in the research process and provide either oral or written data, *Observation* involves only the recording of behavior, and in some cases the subjects may not even be aware that they are being observed. The bases of choice

Table 8.2 Issues in Sample Design

1. Who is to be studied? The target population.
2. Who should be sampled? Sample selection.
   (a) Probability samples.
   (b) Nonprobability samples.
3. How large should the sample be? Sample size.
4. What about nonrespondents? Response rate.

between the two general methods are (1) capability of providing the required data, (2) time and cost required to collect the data, and (3) objectivity and accuracy of the data. Of course, the two methods can be combined, as when someone first completes a questionnaire and then is observed in a lab experiment.

Observational data are generally limited to behavior and some readily observable characteristics, such as sex. Other characteristics such as a person's awareness and attitudes, or even past behavior, can only be obtained by communicating with the person. In general, the communication method is more versatile; it is usually cheaper and faster to ask people about their behavior than it is to observe it. When communication methods are used, it is unnecessary to wait for events to happen and to set up sometimes elaborate procedures for observing behavior. Think of the complexity of observing the number of doctors a patient visits before choosing a personal physician.

Why, then, are observation methods used? Because they do not depend on the ability or willingness of the respondent to provide data, nor do they induce a reactive effect simply because the respondent is being questioned. For example, a woman may be unwilling to admit that she did not read the energy-consumption data on an appliance; on the other hand, she may want to impress an interviewer by appearing to know a great deal about the subject. Thus observation data are potentially more objective. The respondent does not frame her answers in a manner to suit the interviewer. Of course, she may behave differently if she knows her behavior is observed, but observation techniques can be unobtrusive. Some, like hidden television cameras or people posing as participants in an event, are well known. Other unobtrusive techniques show real cleverness. For example, a Chicago automobile dealer who wanted to know which radio stations he should use for advertising instructed his mechanics to make a note of the buttons that were set on radios in cars that came in for repairs. In another case, a museum that wanted to know which exhibits were most popular kept records of wear on tiles in different locations.[7]

Good questionnaire design can do much to deal with the problems of objectivity and accuracy, and we discuss some approaches to these problems later in this chapter.

RESEARCH TACTICS—SAMPLING PROCEDURES

After all the work setting up our research project, we now are ready to move on to research tactics: the specific decisions with regard to who is to be studied, how they are to be studied, and what they are to be asked. We focus on sampling procedures, specifically the issues listed in Table 8.2.

The Target Population

The first question is, "Who is to be studied?" It is important to distinguish between the population or universe, the sampling frame, the sample, and the respondents (see Figure 8.1). The *population of interest* is the group we wish to study. For example, if we are

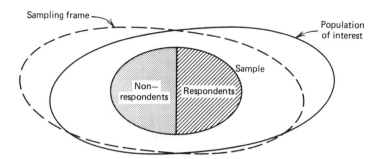

Figure 8.1 Who is studied?

planning a social-services program for people over 65 living in a particular community, that is the population of interest. If the population is relatively small or the costs of error are very high, we might wish to conduct a census of the population. In the ACT study, all subscribers were surveyed because management felt the survey had public relations value and did not want some subscribers to feel that their opinions were unimportant.

It is not always easy to identify the members of the population to be surveyed. For the senior-citizen program, one might compile a list of all those who receive Social Security checks and sample from that list, Such a list is called the *sampling frame*. The frame may not be a perfect representation of the population, however;, in this case, not everyone who is over 65 receives Social Security payments. On the other hand, some people who are not in the population of interest, such as disabled workers less than 65 years of age, may still be included in the sampling frame because they also receive Social Security payments. A sampling frame is needed whenever we wish to conduct a survey of people who are preselected by name. If we are willing to send an interviewer to a shopping center to question every fifth person who enters, a list of preselected names is not needed.

Sample Designs

A *sample* can be chosen from the sampling frame in many different ways. The first and most fundamental decision is the choice of sample design.

In *probability samples,* every person in the frame has a known chance of being selected; the actual choices will be made probabilistically. (A *random sample* is one kind of probability sample in which each person has an equal chance of being selected.) The great advantage of probability sampling is that this known chance of selection allows us to make a statistical estimate of the size of the sampling error—that is, we can make a reasonably accurate guess as to how far the findings in our sample differ from findings obtained from a study of the entire population. For example, if 80 percent of the respondents to the ACT survey said they preferred a free, somewhat plain brochure to a more lavish one that costs 25¢, statistical techniques allow us to say that we are more than 99 percent sure that the actual percentage preferring the free brochure is in the range 80 percent + 5 percent (i.e., 75 percent to 85 percent).

In practice, most probability samples are drawn using a combination of stratified sampling, cluster sampling, and random sampling, In *stratified sampling,* a population is divided into mutually exclusive and collectively exhaustive strata or segments, and a random sample within each segment is taken. For example, a medical study might divide its population into government, nonprofit, and privately owned hospitals. Stratified sampling ensures that all important segments are represented in the final sample, In *cluster sampling,* the population is first divided into subgroups, and a random sample of subgroups is selected. For example, suppose we were conducting a study of attitudes toward family planning among newly married men and women in large urban areas. To do cluster sampling, we might first make a list of all cities with more than 1 million population, randomly select four cities, and do a field survey in each one. The primary justification for cluster sampling is economic. It is far cheaper to do field surveys concentrated in cities than to interview the same number of people nationwide,

In *nonprobability samples,* the choice of respondents is partially left to either the researcher or the interviewer. The probability of any given respondent's being chosen is not known, so that we cannot calculate the sampling errors. On the other hand, such precision may not be the primary objective of an investigator who wants to get a sense for a trend or attitude before deciding to begin a complex study. A college dean who wanted to know what bothered students about dormitory living and who was more interested in *collecting* opinions than determining their exact proportions might be satisfied with a nonprobability sample.

The three major types of nonprobability samples are convenience samples, judgment samples, and quota samples. In *convenience samples,* the subjects are people who volunteer or are readily available to the researcher: men and women walking through a shopping center, church groups, students in class. In *judgment sampling,* someone, usually an authority in the field, decides who the representative units are to be. For example, in contrast to the four-city cluster sampling described earlier, a judgment sample in the same project might require an expert to specify the four cities to be studied, in an effort to make sure they were most representative of the nation.

Quota samples are designed to ensure a desired number of respondents on a set of prespecified control characteristics. For example, we might specify that our sample is to be split equally between men and women. Of course, it is more difficult to set quotas for other characteristics, such as age and income, which cannot be determined at a glance. In addition, striving to fulfill certain quotas may result in biased sampling of other characteristics. An interviewer attempting to fill a quota of high wage earners may oversample white males.

A danger exists whenever an interviewer has control over the choice of respondents: namely, the interviewer will tend to choose those who are easiest to interview—those who look friendly, appear to have spare time, or live in convenient locations, such as apartment houses in "good" neighborhoods. People who meet these criteria are not necessarily representative of the population as a whole, even though they may share some of that population' s readily measurable characteristics.

In summary, only through probability sampling can respondents be chosen in such a way as to allow us to obtain an estimate of sampling error. In practice, however, researchers use nonprobability designs quite frequently. Such designs are the logical choice for informal exploratory research and are also used to save time and money in other studies. And, importantly, nonprobability samples may provide better control of error because of factors other than sampling.

Sample Size

"How large should the sample be?" is one of the most frequent and seemingly simple questions asked in planning market-research studies. Unfortunately, the answer is complex; it depends on the purpose of the research, the sampling design used, the characteristics being studied and their variation within the population, the precision desired from the estimate, the desired level of confidence in the accuracy of the estimate, the cost of the study, and the time available.

In exploratory research and in cases when precise estimates are not required, sample sizes tend to be small. Researchers emphasize the information each respondent gives instead of the number of respondents in the study. When seeking the answer to a simple yes or no question—will you vote for candidate A, did you buy a subscription to a dance group, do you have a library card—a rule of thumb is that a sample of 100 respondents will allow you to be 95% confident that the percentage answering yes is within ±10% of the true proportion of the sampled population who would answer yes. A sample of 400 would be required to be 95% certain within ±5%.

When a respondent has more than two choices (University A, B, or C) or needs to estimate a value (how many opera performances did you attend this year) or we are interested in subgroups of people (men vs. women, users vs. nonusers), sample size calculation is more complex and the reader should see one of the market research books cited earlier.

Response Rate

Once a sample is chosen, the researcher seeks to achieve a high response rate in order to limit nonresponse bias, which may be defined as error resulting from the differences between those people who respond to a survey and the population of interest (see Figure 8.1). People fail to respond to surveys for two reasons: either they are not reached by the researchers (not at home in personal or telephone interviews, wrong address in mail surveys), or they refuse to participate. Response rates vary depending on the way interviews are administered, Mail questionnaires typically achieve response rates in the 10–50 percent range; personal and telephone interviews (with three or four callbacks) reach 50—80 percent of subjects. Nonresponders to personal and telephone interviews are probably equally divided between not-at-homes and refusals.

Responders and nonresponders generally differ. Women who never respond to morning telephone calls, for example, may be employed outside the home, in contrast to homemakers, who are easier to reach, The researcher needs to determine how significant these differences are for interpretation of the data and make adjustments where appropriate. In addition, early responders to a survey may differ from those who respond late.

Some typical nonresponse and early-response biases are exemplified by a California Department of Public Health survey about knowledge and use of the Papanicolaou (Pap) test to detect cervical cancer.[8] The sampling plan consisted of a letter notifying subjects of the survey, followed by up to three mailings of the questionnaire. The data were tabulated by groups according to which questionnaire was returned. As can be seen in Table 8.3, 61 percent of the women who responded to the first mailing had had a Pap test, compared to only 36 percent of those responding to the third mailing. Using only one mailing would have seriously biased the results.

Table 8.3 Marketing Research—Response to Health Survey

Mailing to Subject which Responded	For Each Mailing, %		
	Fraction of Sample Responding	Had Heard of Pap Test	Had Taken Pap Test
First	50	88	61
Second	20	77	50
Third	10	66	36

Source. Joseph R. Hochstim, "A Critical Comparison of Three Strategies of Collecting Data from Households," *Journal of the American Statistical Association* (September 1967), 976–989. Reprinted by permission.

Large sample sizes do not in themselves compensate for biases resulting from low response rates. Often, greater validity is achieved by increasing the response rate than by increasing the number of people sampled. The researcher should view the survey as the marketing of a product. Completion of the survey or an agreement to be interviewed, which is analogous to use of the product, must be related to specific benefits to be obtained. In mail surveys in particular, a cover letter that explains why the survey should be completed is important in encouraging subjects to respond. Special incentives, prior mailings, a well-designed questionnaire, and a combination of interview methods can also lead to higher response rates. For example, at the end of a telephone interview, the respondent might be asked to commit herself to completing a mail questionnaire.

Nonresponse error is not subject to statistical testing. Instead, researchers attempt to compensate for it by measuring whether the responding sample accurately portrays the total population. In the ACT survey, for example, 78 percent of the respondents said they definitely or probably would renew their subscriptions the next year; this finding corresponds well with the actual renewal rate, which ranges from 70 to 75 percent.

RESEARCH TACTICS—INSTRUMENT DESIGN[9]

Figure 8.2 outlines a procedure for designing a questionnaire. Although the procedure appears very neat and straightforward, it is, of course, an iterative process with frequent cycling back and forth between the steps. We concentrate in this section on questionnaires, not on forms for recording observations, because the design of questionnaires is more complex. In observational studies, the observer can be trained to provide consistent observations; the exact wording and structure of the form, although still important, are not as critical.

Methods of Administration

Telephone and personal interviews and mail questionnaires designed for self-completion are the three major ways of collecting information, although various combinations of these methods can be used as well.

One of the key criteria for choosing among these methods is cost. It is difficult to generalize, but mail is usually the cheapest of the three methods, followed by telephone and then personal interviews. Even with mail surveys, the cost of data collection,

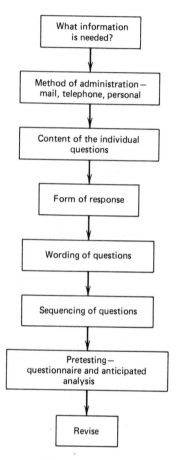

Figure 8.2 Questionnaire design.

keypunching, and computer analysis usually exceeds $5.00 per each completed survey. Telephone can be two to four times as expensive, and personal interviews even more so. The actual costs incurred will depend on a number of factors, such as the amount of information required, the length of the questionnaires, the number of callbacks or follow-up mailings needed, and travel time. Public and nonprofit organizations can lower the costs of personal and telephone interviews by using volunteers, but, as we discuss in the Field Operations section of this chapter, training and managing volunteers can be time consuming and difficult.

Mail questionnaires offer lower costs and have several other advantages. A major one is uniformity of administration. The interviewers themselves may add variation to personal and telephone surveys, although training and performance-monitoring systems try to minimize this problem. Another plus for mail questionnaires is that respondents may have greater confidence in their anonymity (when it is promised) than they feel when being interviewed. This protection, plus the absence of any need to communicate directly with another person, may lead to more honest answers. (Professional interviewers, more adept than volunteers at putting subjects at their ease, can partially compensate for this disadvantage in personal surveys.) On the other hand, mail questionnaires do have a number of drawbacks. The time allotted to carry out a mail survey must be long enough to allow for the sending out and return of questionnaires as well as follow-up and repeat mailings. Rarely can mail questionnaires be used to probe a subject in great depth.

Although *personal interviews* are costly, they usually result in very high response rates if several callbacks are made, Conversations can go into a topic in greater depth and provide the researcher with greater flexibility and control than the other methods offer. A great disadvantage of written questionnaires is that many respondents are simply incapable of addressing complicated issues or questions because of limited ability to read or write. In addition, it may be difficult to sustain a respondent's interest in a long questionnaire. A skilled interviewer should be able to help a person understand and answer the questions and maintain interest throughout the interview. Interviews are required if many of the questions in a survey are conditional on previous answers.

The interview is particularly appropriate for revealing information about complex, emotional subjects and for probing the sentiments that underlie expressed opinions, Because mail questionnaires are usually rigid in structure and require answers to be written out, they work against full discussions of issues.

A new trend is to do interviewing with the aid of personal computers. In one method of administration, people in a shopping mall are asked to participate in a survey. After a limited explanation, people are usually able to respond to questions on a screen by typing on a computer keyboard. The advantages to the researcher are that the particular questions asked can be adjusted according to the responses of subjects (e.g., users of a service are asked different questions than non-users) and data analysis is available almost instantly after interviewing is completed.

Telephone interviews are generally inexpensive and quick to complete and obtain high levels of response. For example, in the last weeks before an election, political candidates' staff often use telephone interviews to monitor the changing opinions of the voters. Telephone interviews combine many of the advantages of the mail and personal methods: detail, complexity, a certain degree of anonymity. Of course, telephone interviews cannot use graphical materials and cannot be as rich in content or as long as personal interviews, but well-designed telephone interviews of up to 20 minutes are feasible.

A major problem with telephone surveys is the limited representativeness of the population frame. In many countries, less than half the households have their own telephones, although nearly all do in Canada and the United States. In these countries, however, many telephone numbers are unlisted (more than 25% in California, for example). With the increased prevalence of homes with either two telephones and/or telephone answering machines, an unbiased, accurate telephone sample is sometimes hard to achieve, even with random digit dialing.

In choosing the most suitable method of administration, the researcher should start by determining the information required, the time available, and the budget. Choices should be made from a systems perspective; it is important to remember that decisions here will affect other parts of the market-research process, For example, money saved on the method of administration may be used to obtain a large total sample size, to generate a high response rate, or to expand the data-analysis and report-preparation stages.

Content of the Individual Questions

There is no scientific guide to the design of individual questions. Nevertheless, researchers have developed a set of questions that can be used as a checklist.

1. Is this question necessary? The temptation to ask questions just for curiosity's sake should be avoided. The researcher should make sure the same information is not available elsewhere or asked for in another part of the questionnaire.

2. Are several questions needed instead of one? For example, the question "did you read the EPA gas mileage ratings when you last bought a car?" presumes, first, that the subject bought a new car and, second, that the car was bought after 1975, when the requirements were first posted.

3. Does the respondent have the necessary information, and will he or she be able to remember it or provide it without too much time and effort? In general, respondents will provide answers to questions, but not always as accurately as researchers like. For example, in one general public-opinion survey that asked people about the Metallic Metals Act, the following responses were obtained:

21.4%   It would be a good move on the part of the United States.
58.6%   It would be a good thing, but should be left to the individual states.
15.7%   It is all right for foreign countries, but should not be required here.
 4.3%   It is of no value at all.
 0.3%   No opinion.

Unfortunately, there is no such thing as the Metallic Metals Act!

4. Will the respondents provide the information? Responses are especially unreliable when embarrassing or socially sensitive questions are asked. For example, in one study in which actual data were available, 40 percent of respondents responded inaccurately to a question about whether they had contributed to the United Fund; 25 percent to whether they had registered and voted; but only 4 percent to whether they owned a house.[10]

5. Is the question sufficiently specific and close to the respondent's personal experience? For example, instead of asking whether someone uses mass transit, a questionnaire might ask how many days in the past week mass transit was used.

Form of Response

In general, questions can require either open-ended responses or selection from a set of fixed alternatives (multiple choice). Open-ended questions provide the respondent a chance to reply in his or her own words and at length, but the answers are difficult to code. In contrast, responses to multiple-choice questions can be coded easily; moreover, the very range of answers available helps convey the meaning of the question to the respondents. In attempting to measure a respondent's opinion, a closed-form question can employ a rating scale that might indicate strength of opinion, degree of satisfaction, or extent of agreement or disagreement. Market-research texts should be consulted for the details of constructing rating scales.

Wording of Questions

A critical, though often neglected, step in instrument design is the specific wording of questions. Researchers should keep the following principles in mind.[11]

1. Use simple words. The vocabulary skills of most seventh-graders are greater than those of many adults.

2. Use clear words. Researchers have found that the words *regularly, usually,* and *frequently* can be ambiguous.

3. Avoid leading questions.

4. Refrain from asking biased questions such as: "Don't you agree with the President that . . . ?"

5. Avoid implicit alternatives; state them explicitly. For example, an answer to the question "Should the transit system buy 100 new buses?" depends on whether the alternative is to buy no buses—or to buy 200 buses.

6. Avoid implicit assumptions. For example, in asking a subject whether she is "in favor of laws requiring the use of air bags," an interviewer assumes some knowledge of what air bags are and the economic and public-safety implications of their use.

7. Avoid double-barreled questions. For example, many people might answer yes and no to this question: "Does reducing the speed limit make driving safer and more relaxing?"

Sequencing of Questions

In general, the questions that deal with the basic information desired should appear early in the questionnaire, and classification questions about age, income, and socioeconomic and demographic characteristics should appear at the end. The opening questions should be interesting and involving; they are analogous to a trial purchase of a new product, If respondents "like" the trial, they will "repurchase"—that is, complete the questionnaire, Questionnaires should be logically organized, moving from the general to the particular, but care should be taken to minimize the chance that the answer to one question will be affected by the answers to preceding questions.

Pretesting

The researcher should never expect that the first draft of a questionnaire will be usable, Thus, after completion, it must be reexamined as a whole and revised. Even then the design is far from complete; the key test of a questionnaire is how it performs in practice. Two types of pretesting are required. The first is conducted through personal interviews with a convenience sample to identify major errors, More critical is a pretest that simulates the actual administration of the questionnaire. Those who design a questionnaire are much closer to a problem than the respondents will be, and the pretest identifies problems that arise because of these vast differences in perception. Additionally, the researcher should attempt to tabulate the data from the pretest to see if, in fact, the analyses that were planned can be carried out.

Pretesting is a *must*. The manager should always insist that any questionnaire and its analysis be pretested.

FIELD OPERATIONS

Field operations include those parts of the research process during which the questionnaires are actually administered and the data collected and coded.[12] Since a number of professional market-research firms specialize in these tasks, many organizations contract out all or part of the fieldwork.

In planning a schedule for field operations, managers should remember that personal and telephone interviewers must be recruited, selected, trained, and supervised. One objective of the training program is to eliminate as much variation as possible among interviewers or observers, particularly when volunteers are used. Consistency requires that the interviewer ask *every* question in the *order specified, exactly as worded*. The interviewers should also know whether they are to prompt the respondent ("Can you think of any more reasons?") and to probe in depth ("Why do you prefer that?"). If open-ended questions are asked, should the interviewer record answers verbatim or paraphrase them? Verbatim records are usually preferred in order to control interviewer bias. Finally, rules for when and how often the not-at-homes should be called back must also be specified. Since household interviews carried out during the day may produce results biased against people who work, interviewers are frequently instructed to call back the daytime not-at-homes at night.

A schedule for a mail questionnaire would not need to provide time for the hiring and training of interviewers, but time for a second and third mailing might be required. All interview methods should allow time for a subsequent verification by the project supervisor that the interview was, in fact, conducted (and not fabricated by the interviewer). Projects vary markedly in their time requirements; a common error is to underestimate the time required for field operations.

In this chapter, we do not discuss the operations involved in response coding and data processing; nevertheless, they are extremely important. In one study of how frequently people went to a theater, 35 percent of the nonsubscribers were falsely classified as new subscribers because the analysts interpreted no reply to a question as equivalent to a check by the number 0—an answer that represented a new subscriber.

DATA ANALYSIS

Data analysis is a vast subject, often involving complex, sophisticated techniques. The reader should not reject data analysis just because it is complex; at times it can make a valuable contribution to understanding the phenomena underlying a data set. On the other hand, useful analysis techniques need not always be complicated. We will briefly discuss some basic concepts of data analysis, and refer the reader to the market-research texts we cited earlier for a more complete review.

In general, we can classify data analysis techniques according to (1) the number of variables being analyzed simultaneously, and (2) whether we merely want to describe the sample from which we have collected data, or whether we wish to make inferences about the population from which the sample is drawn.

In most cases, analysis of a single variable is concerned with measures of central tendency—the mean, median, and mode—and measures of dispersion or variation of the range of observations. At times, we only tabulate the data in terms of frequency of occurrence.

When we have two or more variables to examine simultaneously, we usually try to see if there is a degree of association between them. Often a simple cross-tabulation between two variables can provide useful insights into the data. For example, in the ACT survey discussed at the start of this chapter, a table comparing a respondent's subscription status with a preference for a price discount showed no substantial difference, Thus the decision to eliminate the price discount could be taken without special concern for sudden subscribers.

Although data analysis is one of the last steps in the market-research process, its impact appears much earlier. For example, the type of analysis to be done often influences the content and form of the questions. As we discussed previously, it is often a good idea to create dummy versions of the tables that are expected to appear in the final report and to make sure that the questions included (and their format) lend themselves to the sort of analysis required to complete those tables.

INTERPRETATION OF DATA, RECOMMENDATIONS, AND REPORT WRITING

Each manager should decide individually how involved to be with the final stage of the research project. Depending on their skills, interests, and organizational policies, researchers and managers may share a good deal of the writing and interpretation, or none at all. In many cases, two cautions are in order. First, the interpretations of the data should be based on an analysis of what the survey actually discovered, not on what the manager and researcher hoped would be found. Second, the report should be written clearly and concisely so that the newly discovered information and insights are communicated to the relevant decision makers.

Effective communication of the findings to the users of the research is a vital component of the research process embracing both the written report and the oral presentation (if any). Aaker and Day list five guidelines to making effective presentations.[13]

1. Communicate to a specific audience.
2. Structure the presentation.
3. Create audience interest.
4. Be specific and show data in visual form.
5. Address issues of validity and reliability.

The written report should include an executive summary that provides an overview of the key findings and conclusions and an introductory guide to the contents of each chapter or section. Graphs and charts are often an excellent way to communicate clearly a mass of data. Research design issues that could affect interpretation of the results, and thereby the conclusions drawn, should be clearly identified. The presentation should also provide some feel for the reliability of the results, particularly if the sample size was small.

SUMMARY

Market research is not a simple matter of asking questions, It is a process that provides a disciplined approach to data collection—a process designed to help a manager make decisions. Many market-research projects are carried out in public and nonprofit organizations, but because of weaknesses in planning, execution, analysis, and presentation, their findings often fail to influence policy. By following the market-research process outlined here (or a carefully constructed variation of it), both managers and researchers are more likely to obtain findings that will be useful for decision making.

REFERENCES

1. Philip Kotler and Alan R. Andreasen, *Strategic Marketing for Nonprofit Organizations*, Englewood Cliffs, NJ: Prentice-Hall, 1987, p. 202.

2. This section is based on Adrian B. Ryans and Charles B. Weinberg, "Consumer Dynamics in Nonprofit Organizations," *Journal of Consumer Research,* Vol. 5, No. 2 (September 1978), pp. 89–95. In summarizing some of the results from the ACT survey, we emphasize that research findings for an individual organization may not be generally applicable. Thus, although these results suggested changes for ACT management, they should be treated as hypotheses at most by other performing-arts groups.

3. There are a number of excellent market research books including David A. Aaker and George S. Day, *Marketing Research,* New York: John Wiley & Sons, third edition, 1986, Gilbert A. Churchill, Jr., *Marketing Research: Methodological Foundations,* 4th edition, Hinsdale, Ill.: Dryden Press, 1987, and Thomas C. Kinnear and James R. Taylor, *Marketing Research: An Applied Approach,* 3rd edition, New York: McGraw-Hill, 1987. User-oriented guides to individual topics in market research are provided by chapters in Robert Ferber, *Handbook of Marketing Research,* New York: McGraw-Hill, 1975; and Robert M. Worcester and John Downham, *Consumer Market Research Handbook*, 3rd edition, New York: Elsevier, 1986.

4. A more detailed discussion of the methods of exploratory research may be found in Aaker and Day, *Marketing Research,* reference 2. This section is partially based on that discussion.

5. William Martin, "The Baptists Want You," *Texas Monthly* (February 1977), pp. 83–87; 149–157.

6. Thomas D. Cook and Donald T. Campbell, "The Design and Conduct of Quasi-Experiments and True Experiments in Field Settings," in Marvin D. Dunnette (ed.), *Handbook of Industrial and Organizational Psychology,* Chicago: Rand McNally, 1976. This chapter is an excellent guide to the full range of potential threats and ways for dealing with them.

7. These and other examples may be found in Eugene J. Webb, Donald T. Campbell, Richard D. Schwartz, and Lee Sechrest, *Unobtrusive Measures: Nonreactive Research in the Social Sciences,* Chicago: Rand McNally, 1966.

8. Joseph R. Hochstim, "A Critical Comparison of Three Strategies of Collecting Data from Households." *Journal of the American Statistical Association* (September 1967), pp. 976–989.

9. An excellent reference, which we follow in our discussion, is the chapter "Questionnaire Construction and Interview Procedure," in Claire Selltiz, Laurence S. Wrightsman, and Stuart W. Cook, *Research Methods in Social Relations*, New York: Holt, Rinehart, & Winston, 3d edition, 1976.

10. H. T. Parry and H. M. Crossely, "Validity of Responses to Survey Questions," *Public Opinion Quarterly,* Vol. 14 (1950), pp. 61–80.

11. Adapted from Kinnear and Taylor, as in reference 3.

12. A good guide to the management of field operations is found in Ferber's *Handbook of Marketing Research,* as in reference 3.

13. Aaker and Day, as in reference 3, chapter 15.

PART 4

Planning & Pricing the Product

Chapter 9
Product Offerings

The output of public and nonprofit organizations varies enormously, not only in quantity but also in terms of the characteristics of the end product. Most produce services, ranging from health care to higher education, from public transportation to the performing arts, and from museum operations to municipal utilities. Others market causes or social-behavior patterns; their goals range from saving sea mammals to saving souls, from banning handguns to banning abortion, and from promoting highway safety to promoting racial harmony. Although few produce goods as their primary activity, a growing number, as we will see in Chapter 20, are getting into the business of marketing physical goods as a profit-making sideline.

Nowadays most public and nonprofit institutions are multiproduct organizations, providing a portfolio of different offerings. Unfortunately, new products are often added without regard for their impact on the organization as a whole or for their interrelationship with other products in the portfolio. Old products sometimes continue to be offered, long after they have ceased to be useful to fulfillment of the institutional mission or to match the needs and concerns of potential customers.

Earlier, we emphasized that two of the most critical decision areas for an organization's management are which products to offer and which market segments to target. Other strategic marketing-mix decisions should flow from decisions in these first two areas. Although pricing, distribution, and communication concerns may occasionally constrain or require a modification in product-market strategies, each should be seen as facilitating tools in a nonbusiness marketing program—not the driving force behind it.

Scope of the Chapter

We have already raised product-related issues in several prior chapters. Chapter 4, "Competitive Strategy," showed how important it was for organizations to design their products with reference to the needs of specific market segments and also with a view to distinguishing these products from competitive offerings. We build on these insights in this chapter and the next one.

Most books on marketing equate products with physical goods and make only passing reference to services. As we stressed earlier, however, the public and nonprofit sectors are primarily concerned with services and social-behavior marketing. When nonbusiness organizations market physical goods, this is usually a means to an end—such as making profits from selling items in a museum shop—instead of an end in itself. Because marketers need to understand the differences between physical goods, services, and social behaviors if they are to develop effective strategies, the first concern of the chapter will be to review the nature of each type of product, including how they are produced and how they are consumed. We will identify some basic implications for marketing strategy in each instance.

Our second concern is with determining the composition of the product line. We recognize that most nonbusiness organizations market multiple products. Many offer one or more *core products* that are central to advancing the institutional mission, plus some *supplementary products* that complement—or facilitate consumption of—the core product(s), and one or more *resource-attraction* products designed to generate funds and other donated resources.

Although it is relatively easy to distinguish between different products in a manufacturing organization, product distinction in services and social behaviors are sometimes more subtle. Hence, our third area of focus in this chapter is on defining the product line.

Finally, we recognize that an organization offering multiple products needs to think in terms of its product portfolio. This approach entails studying the interactions between different products and the relative emphasis given to each product—as opposed simply to examining each product in isolation. To help in this analysis, we propose a portfolio model tailored to the objectives of public and nonprofit organizations.

PHYSICAL GOODS, SERVICES, AND SOCIAL BEHAVIORS

The word *product* is one of the key terms in the marketer's lexicon. It is relatively easy to understand in the context of a manufacturing organization, where it refers to the physical good that emerges from the production process and is subsequently sold or given away to consumers. Marketers have long recognized, of course, that this physical good is often only part of a broad bundle of benefits offered to the customer; the term *augmented product* was coined to describe this bundle, which includes packaging, supplementary services, and imagery.[1] Nowadays the term *product* is also widely used to describe both the output of service organizations and the programmatic activities designed to advance a particular cause or social issue. The term is not entirely satisfactory, since by definition it emphasizes the producer's perspective, not the customer's. Successful marketing entails building bridges between the production (or operations) function and the purchase and usage behavior of consumers, who are interested less in operational procedures than in what the marketer has to *offer* them.

Recognizing these dual perspectives, we'll periodically use the term *product offerings* to emphasize the different yet linked concerns of both marketers and customers.

How Different Are Physical Goods, Services, and Social Behaviors?

In Chapter 1, "The Role of Marketing," we discussed some of the characteristics that distinguish physical goods, services, and social behaviors from one another. Conventional marketing wisdom, as handed down by academics, is still strongly slanted toward consumer-goods marketing. Consequently, it is important for managers to recognize ways in which good marketing practices may differ for each of these three product types.

Physical goods account for a relatively small proportion of public and nonprofit marketing activities. Although product design and development are important issues for museum shops and other profit-seeking retailing activities that create, commission, or select new items for retail or catalog sales (see Chapter 18), some public and nonprofit organizations find themselves selling secondhand manufactured goods over whose features they have relatively little control. Examples of the latter include public agencies responsible for disposing of surplus government equipment, police forces selling confiscated or unclaimed goods, and thrift shops selling donated clothing and furniture. Workshops for the handicapped often fall into the trap of deciding to manufacture products that provide good therapy for their clients without first determining whether a market exists for these items. A more realistic approach, followed by some workshop organizers, is to act as a subcontractor, producing or assembling components that will form part of another manufacturer's product.[2]

Table 9.1 summarizes some of the key marketing-relevant characteristics of physical goods. This type of product has been studied and discussed extensively in the marketing literature; hence most marketing textbooks will provide useful insights into the management of all elements of the marketing mix as they relate to physical goods.

Services account for the majority of public and nonprofit market transactions, where the product is sold at a monetary price. In addition, many government agencies and numerous religious and charitable organizations provide services free of cost to deserving users. Among the largest nonbusiness service "industries" are health care, performing arts and museums, public transportation, education, postal service, and human or welfare services. In many instances, of course, private-sector firms compete in the same industries. Since these firms seek to make a profit, their products are often positioned somewhat differently in the marketplace from those of nonbusiness organizations, but head-on competition may also exist.

Only during the past few years have academic marketers started to turn their attention to marketing in the service sector.[3] In general, the study of service marketing has lagged behind that of nonbusiness marketing, but as the field matures, there should be important opportunities for cross-fertilization of marketing ideas and practice between business and

Table 9.1 Marketing-Relevant Characteristics of Physical Goods

- The product is physical and subject to investigation and evaluation by each of the customer's five senses
- Since the product is manufactured first, then consumed later, it can be subjected to quality control after production, before the user comes in contact with it.
- Manufacturing can be centralized: products can be shipped to multiple distant locations and stored for sale at a later date.
- Marketing and production personnel are jointly concerned with determining core-product characteristics, but marketing tends to take full responsibility for the product once it leaves the factory gates, including decisions on product augmentation.
- The marketer needs to be concerned with the design and operation of physical distrubution channels.
- The producing organization can choose to leave customer contact and some or all of the customer marketing activities to autonomous retail intermediaries, but it must still be concerned with marketing to these intermediaries.
- Production, distribution, and selling costs are relatively easy to identify if good records are kept (although some cost-allocation problems may occur). This facilitates monetary-pricing decisions and profitability analysis.

nonbusiness organizations. Table 9.2 summarizes some of the key marketing-relevant characteristics of services.

Social behaviors are, in many respects, the most difficult to define of the three basic product categories. In most instances, it is not the marketer who creates the product but the consumer, acting at the behest of the marketer. Performing a social behavior sometimes carries psychic and other costs for the individual that exceed any apparent personal benefits; the real benefits may be received by other people or society in general. For instance, obeying speed limits wastes the driver's time but may save lives and reduce highway injuries; likewise, refraining from smoking is difficult and frustrating for many smokers, but doing so may improve the health of others as well as that of the smoker.

In many respects, social-behavior marketing is a major growth area. The past 20 years have seen a substantial increase in the marketing of political candidates and referenda items (voting is a social behavior), in sophisticated fund-raising efforts, and in the promotion of social causes ranging from many forms of conservation to advancing the concerns

Table 9.2 Marketing-Relevant Characteristics of Services

- The product contains less tangible elements; being primarily experiential, the characteristics of services are often difficult for the consumer to evaluate and for the marketer to communicate.
- Unlike physical goods, finished services cannot be inventoried (although the equipment and personnel required to produce them can be held in readiness, they remain nonproductive until the service is used).
- Most services must be produced locally through "factories in the field," where customers are often directly involved with the service producer.
- Distribution decisions tend to center around where to locate service outlets and what opening schedules to maintain. Customers often place a premium on convenience, reflecting the time costs of traveling to the service outlet and waiting for service delivery.
- Since the customer often enters the "service factory," the physical facilities and the behavior of the customer-contact personnel frequently become integral parts of the production process and the product offering.
- Other customers may become part of the service product, and the marketer may need to manage customer behavior to ensure that it is consistent with what other customers find acceptable.
- The operations and marketing functions are more closely intertwined than in manufacturing organizations. Yet operations, with its concern for efficiency, has historically tended to overshadow marketing, with its concern for customer satisfaction.
- Some potential exists for customers and service providers to deal at arm's length through mail, telephone, or electronic media in situations where the physical presence of customers is not required. But personal service is usually quite important.
- Management of demand over time assumes greater importance for services than for goods, since services cannot be inventoried, and there is a tendency for demand to show daily/weekly/monthly/seasonal peaks and valleys, resulting in potentially inefficient utilization of capacity.
- Pricing, communications, and product modification can each play important roles in smoothing demand.
- Since a high proportion of costs are often fixed—or tied to the level of capacity rather than directly to usage—allocating costs to different services may be a difficult process, thus complicating pricing decisions.

Table 9.3 *Marketing-Relevant Characteristics of Social Behaviors*

- The marketer does not create the product as such, but instead advocates that target customers adopt a specific behavior (or an attitude that will trigger a desired behavioral response under certain conditions).
- The product offering is no more than a concept until customers create it through their actions. However, the marketer needs to provide a blueprint for action and ensure that facilitating mechanisms are in place.
- The effects of social-behavior programs are frequently second order in nature, with benefits accruing over the long run to the broader population as a result of customers' actions. In the short run, the costs to individual customers of adopting a particular social behavior sometimes outweigh the immediate benefits (if any).
- Many social-behavior programs require the presence of facilitating goods or services for implementation (examples include insulating materials for energy conservation and medical diagnostic services for preventive health maintenance). This may require the marketer to coordinate efforts with providers of such products.
- Social-behavior programs can often be leveraged through formal or informal coalitions with other organizations engaged in parallel or complementary activities.
- In certain programs promoted by public agencies and supported by legislation, legal sanctions may be used to complement marketing efforts to encourage the desired behavior. Examples include observance of highway regulations and prevention of child abuse.
- Some social behaviors are controversial. In such instances, marketers must be prepared to compete against groups espousing contrary views and attacking their own organization directly. Examples include campaigns for and against abortion rights in many countries, handgun control in the United States, political referenda, nuclear-arms control, and so forth.
- Social-behavior programs are often directed at changing deeply ingrained habitual patterns—such as drinking, smoking, sedentary life-styles, or use of familiar weights and measures that are to be replaced by metric units. These changes are particularly difficult to bring about because they require extinction of the old behavior and replacement by a new one that often has to be maintained in the face of cues that remind the consumer of the old behavior.
- Some social-behavior programs require compliance or change by the entire population, including individuals or groups that are difficult to reach or vigorously resist adopting the advocated behavior. Reaching and seeking to persuade 100 percent of the population raises costs and increases the chances of political controversy; this task requires the use of both broad-based and highly segmented marketing strategies.

of innumerable special-interest groups. The volume of published work in this area is still relatively small, although progress has been made in developing a better understanding of how to plan and execute social-behavior programs more effectively.[4] Table 9.3 summarizes some key marketing-relevant characteristics of social behaviors.

In summary, there are clearly some important marketing-relevant distinctions among the three types of product offerings. The task for marketers is to decide which marketing concepts and strategies are generalizable to all types of product offerings and which need to be tailored to the special characteristics of physical goods, services, and social behaviors (this caveat also applies, of course, to differences among products *within* each category).

DETERMINING THE PRODUCT LINE

Few public or nonprofit organizations market only a single product; the great majority market two or more. At a minimum, most nonbusiness organizations not only market a core service or social-behavior program, but also engage in fund-raising or lobbying activities to maintain their financial solvency. Recent years have witnessed a broadening of the product line for many nonbusiness organizations: additional *core products* have been created to advance the institutional mission; *supplementary products* have been added to broaden the appeal of the core products or to facilitate their use (examples in the case of an art museum might include presentation of chamber-music concerts in the galleries, creation of a restaurant, and construction of a parking lot for museum visitors); and new *resource-attraction products* have been developed to tap additional sources of funds, volunteers, and donated resources.

To illustrate the diversity of product lines found in the public and nonprofit sectors, we'll look at five different multiproduct organizations. Subsequently, we'll categorize their product offerings as physical goods, services, or social behaviors, and also group them into core, supplementary, and resource-attraction products.

The Vancouver Public Aquarium (VPA), in Vancouver's Stanley Park, is dedicated to "the preservation and enhancement of aquatic life." In pursuit of this mission, it attempts to educate and entertain the public by offering the opportunity to visit its collection of aquatic animals. The animals are grouped into a number of different exhibits, each of which emphasizes a group of related species. At no extra fee, all can enjoy the killer whale and the beluga whale shows. In addition, there is a newly opened, unique gallery depicting the varied plant and marine life in the Amazon River region (the Graham Amazon Gallery, named in honor of the major benefactor). Periodically, special exhibitions are mounted for a limited duration. The admission fees charged do not cover the full costs of operating the aquarium, so an active membership and fund-raising program is maintained; it includes special events for members. In addition to more than 40 employees, VPA depends on the approximately 200 volunteers. The VPA also operates the Clamshell Gift Shop, which sells aquarium-related merchandise, books, souvenirs, and postcards; rents its facilities for business meetings and social activities; and offers film and lecture programs. Separately, VPA also maintains an active research program.

Transition House runs a residential shelter for battered women and their children in Boston; it also provides child care for the children while their mothers are looking for housing, jobs, and legal and financial assistance. To advance public understanding of the problem of battering and to encourage actions designed to prevent it, Transition House has established a speakers' bureau that provides speakers (sometimes at a fee) for meetings sponsored by other organizations, plus an educational program for high-school students. Finally, a film on the problem of battered women is available for sale or rental and has been shown widely in the United States, Canada, and Europe. To finance its programs, whose costs are only marginally covered by fees for service, Transition House has obtained state contracts, corporate and foundation grants, and individual contributions.

GASP (Group Against Smoking and Pollution) promotes the rights of nonsmokers to live and work in an environment free of tobacco smoke. Active in several countries, it is organized into regional chapters whose efforts include filing legislation at all levels of government, initiating and pursuing lawsuits to protect nonsmokers, picketing promotional programs by tobacco companies, and presenting medical, environmental, and economic evidence of the problems caused by smoking to smokers and nonsmokers alike. In addition, some GASP chapters are now working to develop fee-based consulting services for large employers to assist them in planning and implementing no-smoking policies, especially as these relate to the creation of smoke-free areas in the workplace. GASP leaders hope that these efforts will assist nonsmokers and also generate additional income to supplement the funds obtained from individual contributions.

Britain's *Post Office* operates three major businesses: national and international Royal Mail services, the banking facilities of the National Girobank, and a retail network of post offices (a fourth business, telecommunications, was spun off in 1981 as a separate corporation called British Telecom). The Royal Mail comprises a diverse group of postal services, characterized by such features as size of item to be mailed, speed of delivery, location of delivery, and volume of usage (individual versus bulk). The National Girobank offers a wide range of financial services, including checking and savings accounts, loans, and transfer of funds. It serves individuals, commercial customers, government departments, and local authorities, using local post offices as its retail branches. Britain's 22,000 post offices represent the nation's largest retail chain. These offices are used not only for mail and banking transactions, but also for retailing a wide variety of services on behalf of government agencies and nationalized industries. Unlike postal services in many countries, the Post Office makes a profit and so requires no government subsidies.

The *Red Cross* is a group of organizations operating in numerous countries around the world. The scope of Red Cross services varies somewhat from one country to another and even from chapter to chapter within a large nation such as the United States. The basic thrust of American Red Cross activities in the United States is fourfold. First, it provides disaster-relief services (including medical aid, emergency shelter, and provision of medicine, food, clothing, and other supplies) as the need arises. Second, blood-collection efforts are conducted on an ongoing basis, with periodic blood drives in different locations and special appeals when supplies of a particular blood group are dangerously low. Third, the Red Cross provides first-aid services at events attracting large numbers of people. Finally, the organization offers a variety of courses grouped around two themes: safety (especially in the water) and medical help. Although fees are charged for participation in most of these courses, the American Red Cross needs substantial donations to help cover the cost of its other services.

Table 9.4 summarizes the products offered by each of the five organizations, classifying them as physical goods (PG), services (S), or social behaviors (SB). In a few instances, as we discuss later, a product is classified jointly both as a good or service and as a social behavior.

As we can see, each organization is engaged in a broad array of activities. All of them —except the Post Office, which is self-sufficient—need to engage in resource-attraction efforts to help cover the expenses associated with offering the core products that advance their respective institutional missions. Some product offerings are a little difficult to categorize. For instance, in Table 9.4, we have categorized GASP's consulting service as a resource-attraction product because it is designed to yield a positive cash flow; however, if it were offered at cost it would be categorized as a supplementary product. Either way, the consulting service helps to advance the institutional mission, but it represents a second-stage effort that is dependent on previous successes in marketing the core products. Similarly, the Post Office's counter services are classified here as a supplementary product, although they do attract additional income for the organization.

Table 9.4 Examples of Component Business and Product Categories/Programs[a]

Vancouver Public Aquarium	Transition House	GASP	Post Office (U.K.)[b]	American Red Cross

Core Products
Exhibits
  Animal displays (S)
  Aquatic shows (S)
  Special exhibits (S)
  Regional exhibit (e.g., Amazon River Gallery) (S)
Research program (S)
Supplementary Products
Film and lecture program (S/SB)
Resource-Attraction Products
Membership program
Newsletter (PG)
Evening lectures and special events (S/SB)
"Behind-the-scenes" tours (S)
Fund raising (SB)
Rental of facilities for social functions (S)
Gift shop
  Aquarium-related merchandise (PG)
  Souvenirs (PG)
  Post cards (PG)
	Core Products
	Residential shelter
	  Bed and board (S)
	Speakers' bureau
	  High school (SB)
	  General (SB)
	Resource-Attraction Products
	Film
	  Sales (PG/SB)
	  Rental (S/SB)
	Supplementary Products
	Child care for residents
		Core Products
		Advocacy program
		  Legislation (SB)
		  Picketing (SB)
		  Education (SB)
		Resource-Attraction Products
		Consulting services (S)
		Fund raising
			Core Products
			Royal Mail
			  Letters (S)
			  Parcels (S)
			  Express services (S)
			  Philately (PG)
			National Girobank
			  Checking accounts (S)
			  Savings accounts (S)
			  Loans (S)
			  Money transfers (S)
			  Foreign exchange (S)
			Supplementary Products
			Post Office counter services
			  Telecommunication transactions (S)
			  Transit pass sales (S)
			  Pension disbursements (S)
			  Post bus transportation service (S)
				Core Products
				Disaster relief (S)
				Blood collection (SB)
				First-aid services (S)
				Educational programs
				  Safety (S/SB)
				  Health (S/SB)
				Resource-Attraction Products
				Fund raising
				Volunteer programs

[a](PG) = physical good; S = service; SB = social behavior.
[b]Because of the breadth of the product line within each business, only a few examples are shown in each instance.

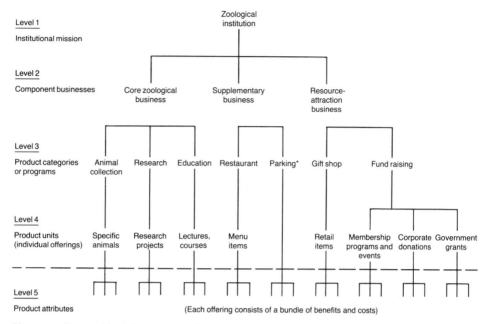

Figure 9.1 Structuring the components of a multiproduct organization:
a hypothetical example for a zoo.

Levels of Marketing-Management Activity

In most organizations, we can distinguish up to five levels of marketing activity. Figure 9.1 outlines a hypothetical example for a zoo. The first level concerns the entire organization, which in most instances is headed by a chief executive officer* (although in some nonprofit organizations, such as Transition House, the management responsibility is centered in a coordinating committee instead of in a single individual). At this level, the tasks are to advance the mission of the organization within certain predefined financial constraints by maintaining an appropriate balance between its various activities, and to achieve and maintain a favorable image of the organization among each of its constituencies.

The second level of marketing activity concerns the principal areas of activity—or businesses—in which the organization is engaged. In a medium to large organization, there may be one or more *core businesses* that are central to advancing the institutional mission, one or more *supplementary businesses* that complement the core activities but that are not the central focus of the organization's efforts, and one or more *resource-attraction* activities designed to keep the organization financially solvent. For instance, the core activities at the Vancouver Public Aquarium are maintaining the aquatic-animal exhibits as a public museum and running the research program; supplementary activities might be defined as the film and lecture series; the gift shop, volunteer program, and fund-raising efforts constitute the resource-attraction business. Some public and nonprofit organizations (such as the British Post Office) are able to achieve break-even status or

---

*The title given to this executive varies widely. Common titles include chairman, president, general director, director-general, general manager, executive director, and administrator.

better without government subsidies or voluntary donations; hence they do not need to engage in resource-attraction efforts.

The degree of independence accorded to managers of these businesses should reflect the size of the organization, the nature of the skills required to run each business, and the extent to which the organization's control systems allow separate evaluation of each business's financial performance. In certain organizations, such as the Post Office, each business is run as a strategic management unit (see Chapter 5) and its managers given a high degree of autonomy. In smaller organizations, such as GASP, the chief executive may run each business personally.

At the third level of activity come the specific programs or product categories marketed by each business. Responsibilities at this level may be assigned, in a large organization, to a product (or program) manager who reports to the general manager of the strategic management unit. At this level, there are opportunities for product specialization within the business, with the product manager making recommendations on product features, pricing, distribution, and communication decisions. We discuss issues relating to product management in depth in Chapter 16, "Organizing the Marketing Effort."

Examples of different product categories are shown in Table 11.4. In each instance, we have identified the product offering as a physical good, service, or social behavior. Sometimes a physical good or service can also be jointly categorized as a social behavior; this situation occurs when using that good or service will lead consumers to change their future behavior. For instance, Transition House's film, *We Will Not Be Beaten,* can be purchased outright (a physical good) or rented (a service). The pricing structure is sufficient to recover all costs, but the ultimate goal of the film is to change behavior. The film has a powerful effect on nearly all who see it, making the audience aware of the extent to which women are beaten by men and leading many individuals to make donations in support of shelters for battered women or to volunteer to help attack this social problem.

The fourth level represents units within a product package (such as the specific animals exhibited at a zoo or aquarium, menu items in a restaurant, or individual book titles in a gift shop). Not all organizations have to make decisions at this level.

The fifth level represents product attributes and requires that management address the issue of what characteristics or features each product should possess. Decisions in this area relate directly to the benefits obtained by customers, as well as to some of the costs they incur. Failure to consider these characteristics from the customers' perspective may lead to lack of success in terms of persuading prospective customers to buy the product or adopt the recommended behavior.

DEFINING THE PRODUCT LINE

What constitutes a separate product? When should we say that an organization markets a line of products instead of just a single product? Each market transaction between an organization and a customer involves at least one product, but multiple transactions may involve either an array of different products or repeated purchases of the same product.

Manufactured Goods

The distinction between individual products and a line of products is relatively simple to understand in the case of manufactured goods, where differences and similarities can be perceived directly. For instance, the Sierra Club markets a number of different books;

each title represents a separate product and may be priced, distributed, and promoted somewhat differently from each of the other titles. Underlying these marketing-strategy distinctions is the publisher's belief that each title has a distinctive appeal that, in all probability, will make it more appropriate for sale to some segments than to others. When there are considerable commonalities among the individual products, a product line can be established. Thus the Sierra Club also has several product lines of books. The "Exhibit Format" product line consists of large-size, hardbound, photographic-essay-type books, such as *The Rockies* and *In Wildness*. Another product line, the "Tote" book series, includes small-size, inexpensive, paperbound books designed to be taken on hikes, such as *Hiking Tetons* or *In the Smokies*.

Services

In the case of services, product distinctions may be based as much on how customers *use* the product offering as on how it was created. For instance, urban public-transportation agencies are in the business of moving people in transit vehicles. An operational definition of the service might divide it into three products, categorized by type of vehicle—rail, bus, or ferry. This would not be a very useful way of defining the product line if research showed that many travelers used at least two modes—say, bus and train or bus and ferry—to complete a single journey. Of more interest to the transit marketer is who is using the service, when, where, and for what purpose. Looking at the business in terms of customer-use behavior may suggest opportunities for marketing the service to different segments in different ways. For instance, a line of different transportation offerings could be created around operational distinctions that are meaningful to travelers, such as express versus regular service. Further distinctions could be based on routes that serve key destinations: airport service, shoppers' shuttle, sight-seeing special. Still another point of differentiation might reflect timing and frequency of use, such as weekday commuting versus occasional midday, evening, or weekend travel. Finally, distinctions could be made between different types of travelers—say, children, students, adults, and the elderly.

At what point do these distinctions lead to creation of a separate product? Splitting a broadly defined product into several more tightly defined products requires a degree of differentiation in the marketing programs employed. If a transit agency singles out express service for special marketing treatment, charging premium prices and promoting it separately from "regular" service, we can reasonably say that express service is now a separate product. The same would hold true for the airport service, shoppers' shuttle, and sight-seeing special if tailored marketing programs were developed specifically to boost ridership on any one of these.

Many organizations sell services in advance of use. In such situations, the ticket (or other receipt) can become the symbol of the product offering and the focus of a distinctive marketing effort targeted at a particular market segment. Thus a public-transportation agency might devote special advertising efforts to monthly transit passes and sell them to commuters through convenient locations such as banks or large employers; meanwhile, the availability of discount tickets for the elderly might be advertised to social-service organizations and tickets sold at senior drop-in centers; similarly, sight-seeing trips on city buses could be promoted in tourist brochures and tickets sold at visitor centers as well as at transit terminals or on the vehicles themselves. Symphony orchestras, repertory theaters, and other performing-arts organizations typically offer a season of performances extending over a period of months. Tickets may be sold for single performances, for the entire season, or for each of several performance series composed of subsets of the season's offerings. Marketing efforts might be further subdivided into sales to individuals and bulk sales to groups or to ticket brokers. As a result of these separate marketing efforts, the audience at any one performance might be divided among those who had purchased a ticket for that performance alone, those who had chosen to buy tickets for a series, those who had bought the entire season, and those who came in a group whose organizers had packaged the performance as part of a broader product that included (say) transportation and a meal.

Social Behaviors

What about social-behavior products? When should a cause or idea be divided into separate products? Three factors drive product decisions in social-behavior marketing: (1) opportunities for segmentation; (2) the importance of extending performance of the desired behavior across as many specific situations as possible; and (3) the need for resource-attraction efforts to fund the social-behavior program.

Segmentation strategies recognize that different programmatic efforts may be needed to reach different groups to achieve the same broad end. Thus a goal of helping the handicapped may require (1) lobbying for changes in legislation designed to outlaw job discrimination against handicapped persons and to require barrier-free access to buildings and transportation vehicles; (2) efforts directed at business firms and other institutions to hire the handicapped; and (3) efforts to get individuals and corporations to make donations to train and rehabilitate handicapped people. Each of these three thrusts might realistically be treated as a separate product.

Situation specificity recognizes the varying circumstances under which the desired behavior might be performed. For example, energy conservation involves undertaking a large number of conserving behaviors, such as turning off lights, installing insulation, driving more slowly, turning thermostats down in winter and up in summer, and buying energy-efficient appliances. These behaviors could be promoted collectively or separately, with each behavior being treated as a distinct product. In practice, a middle course may be the more appropriate, with energy-saving efforts being categorized into groups by situation or area of application. For instance, among individuals and households, conservation efforts could be direct at influencing (1) day-to-day behavior in the home, (2) installation of home insulation, (3) new-appliance purchases, (4) transportation behavior, and (5) new-car purchases. Each of these activities might, in a national conservation campaign, be treated as a separate programmatic effort (or product offering). A separate set of programs would need to be developed to encourage energy conservation among institutions.

Resource attraction becomes necessary because social-behavior marketers are not usually able to sell their product offering at a price and therefore need to raise funds to finance the core business. Public agencies can often obtain direct government funding, although this may require lobbying. Nonprofit organizations usually need to develop resource-attraction programs to finance their educational and advocacy efforts, as well as to recruit volunteers who will help staff these efforts. Many fund-raising efforts involve creating and marketing a line of potentially profitable goods and services—ranging from souvenirs to consultancy—that are designed to generate a positive cash flow as well as to advance the cause itself. Another approach is to develop membership programs for donors and volunteers, offering a periodic newsletter and other benefits as an incentive. Each of these categories of resource-attraction efforts can be thought of as a product.

No Universal Answers on Product Definition

In summary, there are a number of useful guidelines for identifying distinctive product offerings and separating them from a broader product line of related yet different products. These guidelines can be helpful to managers in organizing marketing efforts and in developing tailored programs.

In Chapter 4, "Competitive Strategy," we noted that there are no universal answers to the problem of market definition. The same is true of product definition. Each organization must decide for itself how far to disaggregate the product line into separate and identifiable products. This decision should reflect customer needs, competitive realities, and organizational resources.

SHAPING THE PRODUCT PORTFOLIO

What is the most appropriate mix of products for an organization to offer? In Chapter 4, we discussed the concept of portfolio analysis, which suggests that an organization should look at its *mix* of business (or strategic management) units and their constituent products, instead of treating each product independently of the others. In a for-profit organization, the goal of portfolio analysis is to seek a balance between high returns and security of profits, and between established products that are currently profitable and those that may require a period of nurturing before they achieve profitability. Existing business-oriented portfolio models emphasize long-term and short-term profitability but ignore the concern of nonbusiness managers to meet the nonfinancial goals inherent in their missions.[5]

Figure 9.2 proposes a portfolio model tailored to the objectives of public and non-profit organizations. The horizontal axis addresses the issue of the profitability of each product (or product category, or business, depending on the level of aggregation selected), while the vertical axis concerns the product's contribution to advancing the institutional

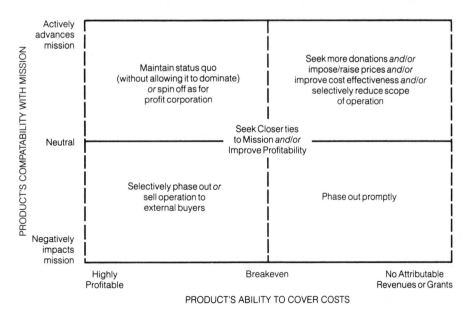

Figure 9.2 Analyzing a nonbusiness organization's product portfolio.

mission. Each product should be evaluated simultaneously against both criteria. By definition, we would expect to find core and supplementary products contributing to advancement of the mission and resource-attraction products contributing to profitability. The profitability of a product should take into account both sales revenues and grants or donations earmarked specifically for support of that product. Revenues from general fund-raising campaigns should be excluded from this analysis, being used to offset overhead costs not attributed to specific products.

By definition, this type of analysis requires accurate and detailed cost data and the ability to assign costs to specific products or areas of activity. Historically, many nonbusiness organizations have lacked the capability to identify and record exactly how costs are incurred. But this situation is changing in response to both internal management needs and external requirements (such as tax reporting and pressure from funding sources). The availability of modestly priced accounting software has made the tasks of cost recording and analysis much easier.

In Figure 9.2, we have identified five product locations within the matrix, together with possible strategies for future action. (In reality, of course, a product might be located anywhere within this diagram.)

As a generalization, the overall goal for public or nonprofit organizations that are operating in the red will be to move the institutional center of gravity within the portfolio matrix in a "northwesterly" direction—that is, toward more actively advancing the institutional mission while also improving the relative profitability of each product. Unfortunately, however, these two goals are not always mutually compatible.

An Example of Portfolio Analysis

As an illustration of how this portfolio analysis might be presented, let's consider an art museum with 10 separate businesses (excluding general-purpose fund raising). Table 9.5 shows its performance during the most recent fiscal year.

What information would the museum's managers need to position each of their products (or businesses) on a chart similar to that in Figure 9.2? Positioning of businesses on the vertical axis, relating to mission advancement, is a subjective task that is probably best

Table 9.5 Operating Results for a Large Museum

Business		Annual Operating Results		
		Revenues[a] ($ millions)	Costs ($ millions)	Revenue/Cost Coverage
Core businesses	Maintenance and exhibition of core collection	3.83	5.12	75%
	Research program	0.16	0.47	34%
	Museum school	0.76	0.53	143%
Supplementary businesses	Special exhibits	1.72	1.08	159%
	Film and lecture series	0.08	0.09	89%
	Concert series	0.31	0.30	103%
Resource-attraction businesses[b]	Museum store	6.16	5.92	104%
	Restaurant	2.85	2.48	115%
	Annual auction	0.29	0.09	322%
	Function rentals	0.90	0.53	170%

[a]Including the net proceeds of grants, donations, and membership fees specifically earmarked for this purpose.
[b]Excluding general fund-raising efforts.

done through group consensus. The viewpoints of curators and other managers, museum-board members, and representative visitors should all be considered in making these qualitative evaluations, which require agreement on the basic mission statement as a benchmark.

By contrast, calculating the relative cost coverage of each product is straightforward, once the data have been collected. Although obtaining accurate data can be difficult, the calculation itself involves simply dividing revenues by costs. In our example, cost coverage ranges from only 34 percent of the museum's research program to 322 percent for the auction. The resulting percentages enable us to position each product or business on the horizontal axis of the chart; the mid-point on this axis, 100 percent, represents a break-even position.

To be really useful, the chart must incorporate one other piece of information: the relative size of each product, in terms of the total costs incurred by the museum. In order to give greater visual impact to the presentation, the analysis can be depicted in the form of a bubble chart. In Figure 9.3, each product or business is depicted as a circle, whose area is proportional to its associated financial costs.

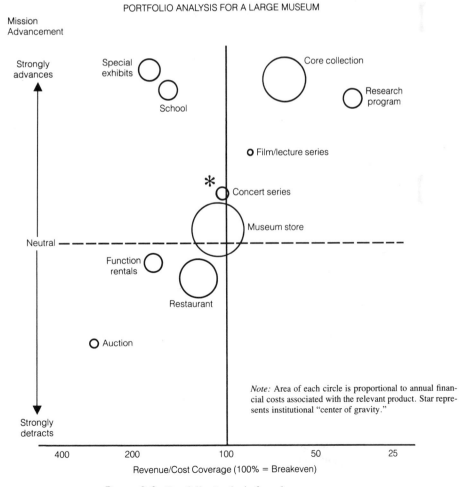

Figure 9.3 Portfolio Analysis for a large museum.

We can now see at a glance the relative size of each business and the extent to which it contributes positively or negatively to both overhead costs and advancement of the institutional mission. By overlapping a similar analysis from the previous year, we could see how each business had changed, over time, in terms of both size and positioning. An institutional "center of gravity" can also be computed and is represented here by a star. In this example, it is apparent that the institution's financial position (before considering the impact of unrestricted funds and unallocated overheads) is marginally above break even, but this may have been achieved at the expense of a shift away from strong advancement of the institutional mission.

An interesting aspect of this analysis is that it presents more useful insights for marketing decision making than the operating data in the annual report, which must be organized to conform with financial accounting requirements.

As with all portfolio models, the analysis in itself is not prescriptive: it doesn't indicate what the organization should do in terms of establishing and achieving goals. Instead, it suggests some of the trade-offs that must be made by management in designing the product portfolio for their organization. In short, the contribution that portfolio analysis can make is to stimulate careful management thought by highlighting key issues in an integrated format.

SUMMARY

The two most important decisions faced by marketers are what products to offer and to which markets. The public and nonprofit sectors are distinguished from the private sector by their emphasis on marketing *services* and *social behaviors*. Marketing *physical goods* is relatively less important and is primarily undertaken as a means to an end, such as attracting resources to help cover deficits.

Most nonbusiness organizations offer multiple products that can usefully be grouped into three categories: (1) *core products* that advance the institutional mission; (2) *supplementary products* that facilitate or enhance customers' use of the core product(s); and (3) *resource-attraction products* that help attract the resources needed to run the organization in situations where the sales revenues (if any) derived from core and supplementary products are insufficient to cover operating outlays.

Organizations offering multiple products need to think in terms of their *product portfolio,* as opposed to simply examining each product in isolation. A useful form of analysis for public and nonprofit organizations is to evaluate each product simultaneously against two criteria: (1) the net financial contribution it makes, and (2) its ability to advance the institutional mission. Because many core products lose money (even after allocating earmarked grants and donations), resource-attraction products such as sale of gifts or rental of facilities for social functions may be needed to cover the deficit. However, it is sometimes undesirable to offer products that are largely unrelated to the institutional mission.

Over time, changes in the environment may require adjustments to the product portfolio. In Chapter 10, which follows, we examine decisions on adding, deleting, and modifying products.

Although product policy is the most central element of the marketing mix, but decisions in this area cannot be planned and executed in isolation from distribution, communications policy. In Chapters 11 through 15, we will look at each of the other elements of the marketing mix. But readers should continually ask themselves how strategic decisions in these other functional areas of marketing are influenced by product-policy considerations and, in turn, how distribution, pricing, and communication issues serve to shape and constrain the nature of the product.

REFERENCES

1. Theodore Levitt, "Marketing Success Through Differentiation—of Anything," *Harvard Business Review,* January–February 1980, pp. 83–91.

2. See, for example, "C. Roland Christenson and Molly Lovelock, "The Fernald Workshops" in C. R. Christensen, K. R. Andrews, and J. L. Bower, *Business Policy: Text and Cases,* Homewood, Ill.: Richard D. Irwin, 1978, pp. 331–356.

3. See, for example, John E. G. Bateson, "Why We Need Services Marketing," in 0. C. Ferrell, S. W. Brown, and C. W. Lamb (eds.), *Conceptual and Theoretical Developments in Marketing,* Chicago: American Marketing Association, 1979, pp. 131–146; J. H. Donnelly and W. R. George (eds.), *Marketing of Services,* Chicago: American Marketing Association, 1981; and Christopher H. Lovelock, *Services Marketing,* Englewood Cliffs, N.J.: Prentice-Hall, 1984.

4. Karen F. A. Fox and Philip Kotler, "The Marketing of Social Causes: The First Ten Years," *Journal of Marketing,* 44 (Fall 1980), pp. 24–33; and Seymour H. Fine, *The Marketing of Ideas and Social Issues,* New York: Praeger, 1981.

5. For a good discussion of conventional product portfolio analysis as it relates to health care organizations, see Philip Kotler and Roberta N. Clarke, *Marketing for Health Care Organizations,* Englewood Cliffs, N.J.: Prentice-Hall, 1987.

Chapter 10
Adding, Modifying, &
Deleting Products

$\mathbf{I}$n nearly all successful marketing organizations, the composition of the product portfolio is slowly but continuously evolving. Likewise, the characteristics of the individual products making up that portfolio are themselves undergoing change. Both processes reflect the need to be responsive to the dynamics of the marketplace. As we noted in Chapter 3, "Conducting a Marketing Audit," external factors in the environment—the economy, technology, government policies, social structures and values, and competitive forces—are constantly changing.

As each planning cycle begins—and sometimes more frequently if sudden external changes occur—the marketing manager needs to consider the following issues.

1. Are we offering the appropriate mix of products in our portfolio or is a shift in emphasis needed? Should new products be added or existing ones deleted?

2. Are we currently offering (or planning to introduce) products with the right characteristics to appeal to our target market segments, or are changes needed in product attributes?

3. Do the other elements in the current marketing-mix strategy for each product—distribution and delivery systems, monetary prices and nonmonetary costs, and communication efforts—reflect a cost-efficient (and, where appropriate, competitive) approach to marketing the product to our target market segments? If not, what changes should we be making in our marketing mix?

Scope of the Chapter

We've already considered the issue of managing the product portfolio. Our focus in this chapter will be on decision making for individual products. In later chapters, we consider each of the remaining three elements of the marketing mix. It is important to remember that no decision can be taken on product strategy without reference to how that product should be priced, delivered, and communicated to its target market segments. Effective marketing strategy requires consistency and synergy between each element of the marketing mix; hence decisions concerning any one element must be evaluated against their impact on—and must fit with—the other three.

Product decisions are driven by a variety of forces, including changes in the external environment, evolving customer needs, and new or anticipated competitive developments. We begin by considering theories of product evolution and the product life cycle concept. Although the latter has its limitations, it provides a framework for discussing creation of new products, subsequent modification, and product deletion.

Our review of the tasks involved in adding new products to an existing portfolio is complemented by a brief discussion of starting a nonprofit organization from scratch. We follow with a look at the diffusion of innovations, a field of study that provides valuable insights into how marketing strategies can influence the speed and extent of new product adoption.

The balance of the chapter addresses decisions on whether or not to modify or delete an existing product, and development of appropriate strategies.

Product Evolution

Marketing theorists are constantly looking for conceptual frameworks that will help practicing managers better understand the nature of the problems and opportunities they face.

One intriguing approach is to consider the evolution of species, as described by the theory of natural selection, as a model for the evolution of products in a competitive marketplace.[1] Appraising this analogy, Yoram Wind remarks:

> The basic concepts of the Darwinian natural selection theory and marketing concepts are strikingly similar. The individual organism in the evolution theory is analogous to a product (not product class . . .). The concept of *variation of species* is analogous to the differences among products and brands. The concept of *overpopulation* relates to the tremendous production capacity for most products. The *struggle for existence* and *survival of the fittest* are quite descriptive of the product marketplace in which only few new products ever make it.
>
> The result of overcapacity (overpopulation) is competition among species (products). In this competition, those best suited to the *environment* (the marketplace) have the best chance for success (survival and growth).[2]

A number of useful managerial insights are suggested by this analogy. For instance, specialization (typically entailing a carefully designed product-positioning strategy) undoubtedly offers an advantage under conditions of strong competition. However, as the environment changes, the characteristics that determine suitability also change, requiring evolutionary development of the product so that it may adapt; this emphasizes the need for long-range product planning. When the environment changes suddenly—reflecting such factors as significant technological, economic, or political developments—highly specialized products that were well adapted to the old environment may be less capable of adjusting to the change than less specialized products. "This conclusion," says Wind, "suggests the intriguing hypothesis that products aimed at narrow market segments or very specialized applications have shorter 'life cycles' than more broadly-based products."[3]

Recent rethinking of Darwinian theory suggests that evolution may have been less gradual than Darwin believed, consisting more of a series of sudden, discontinuous spurts in response to dramatic environmental changes. This is also, perhaps, a better model of the marketplace for the products of public and nonprofit organizations, faced as they are with sudden shifts of the political pendulum, the ups and downs of the economy, and the periodic advent of new technology. The key difference between animal species and product species lies in the fact that animals can only *react* to change. Managers, however, can *anticipate* change and take proactive steps to enhance their products' prospects for future survival. The sum of all the products offered by an organization is the organization itself; that, too, must evolve and change over the years if it is to survive as an entity.

The Product Life Cycle

Complementing the product-evolution model is another conceptual framework, the product life cycle (PLC), which is based on the biological life cycle of birth, growth, maturity, decline, and death. It can be applied to an individual product or to an entire class of related products produced by a number of different competing organizations.

Most marketing theorists divide the PLC into four stages.

1. *Introduction.* A period of typically slow growth in sales volume following the launch ("birth") of the product. At this point, an innovative organization that is the first to market the product may have the field to itself. However, extensive communication efforts are often needed to build consumer awareness.

2. *Growth.* Demand for the product begins to increase rapidly, reflecting repeated use by satisfied customers and broadening awareness among prospective customers who now try the product for the first time. Competition develops as other organizations introduce their own versions, transforming a single product into a product class of competing brands.

3. *Maturity.* This is often an extended period during which sales volume for the product class stabilizes and astute marketers seek to position their own product offerings in ways that will differentiate them from those of competing organizations. However, fad and fashion products may be characterized by a very short product life cycle in which demand grows extremely rapidly, peaks briefly during the maturity stage, and then goes into sudden and precipitous decline.

4. *Decline.* Sales volume for the product class declines as a result of environmental forces such as changing population profiles, changing consumer preferences, new legislation, or competition from new types of products that meet the same generic need. Some competitors, anticipating the death of the entire product class, kill off their own entries in the market.

The appeal of the PLC concept to marketers is that it provides a marketing-strategy prescription tailored to the stage in the life cycle that the product has achieved. It is based primarily on the experience of private-sector firms that market consumer packaged goods.

The PLC concept has some serious problems, and it should not be employed uncritically.[4] The life cycle of a product class often seems so extended as to be meaningless. Further, in evaluating the relationship between marketing strategy and the PLC, it is often an open question whether the life cycle for a particular product or product class is an inevitable, independent force to which organizations must adopt their marketing efforts, or whether marketing strategy can change the course of the life cycle.

An interesting characteristic of public and nonprofit organizations is that they are often involved with a product for only a limited portion of its life cycle. Here are some examples:

- Passenger rail services and urban public transportation developed, grew, and matured in the private sector. Only after they had gone into decline were private systems rescued by the public sector. The mission of making profits has been replaced by that of achieving the social and environmental benefits offered by promoting alternatives to travel in individual cars or commercial aircraft (or not traveling at all).

- Many social causes, such as protection of the environment or hiring the handicapped, are initially championed by nonprofit advocacy groups that raise public awareness of the issues. As the product passes a certain point in the growth stage, sufficient political clout becomes available to ensure passage of legislation mandating the behavior advocated. At this point, primary responsibility shifts from the nonprofit to the public sectors, although the originating groups may remain active in a watchdog role and in seeking out related issues for resolution.

- Occasionally, it becomes necessary for an entire nation to change its way of doing things. Thus Sweden switched in 1968 from driving on the left to driving on the right; Britain replaced pounds, shillings, and pence by a new decimal currency between 1968 and 1971; and by 1980 Australia had virtually completed a multiyear program to replace customary units of measurement—such as feet, pounds, and gallons—by metric measures. In each instance, a public agency was formed to facilitate the difficult process of killing off a mature product and replacing it by a new one.

Figure 10.1 summarizes these kinds of examples graphically.

In order to manage its product portfolio effectively, every organization needs to have a sense of where its individual products stand in terms of their respective life cycles. It is particularly important to understand the life cycle of the product class in which individual offerings compete. Failure to do so can result in such mistakes as launching a new product at a time when the product class is moving into decline or introducing an innovative product without sufficient communication support.

Because they are less directly subject to the economic discipline of the market than profit-seeking firms, public agencies and nonprofit organizations are often slow to spot and respond to the symptoms of the decline stage of the PLC. Periodic marketing audits, as recommended in Chapter 3, can provide early warnings to managers and policymakers of a declining product. Appropriate corrective actions can then be taken. In some instances, these may take the form of scaling back or consolidating programs; in severe cases, it may be necessary to delete the product in question.

The PLC concept also provides an important insight to nonbusiness organizations launching new products: success requires effective marketing at each stage in the process. At the outset there is often a great deal of enthusiasm, drive, and publicity, serving to get the product off to a good start. But if a product is to move beyond introduction and achieve growth and maturity, sustained commitment and appropriate shifts in strategy are needed. Unfortunately, many public and nonprofit organizations drop the ball at this point, resulting in a slow fizzle. Politicians, board members, and volunteers often have short attention spans, and their interest may shift to other activities unless the initial planning for the project took a long-term perspective and ensured that support would be provided at each stage to supply the resources and skills needed.

In all but monopoly situations, the mature phase of the PLC is typically characterized by the presence of numerous competing organizations. Where goods and services are concerned, this imposes constraints on the number of customers and the revenue or volume

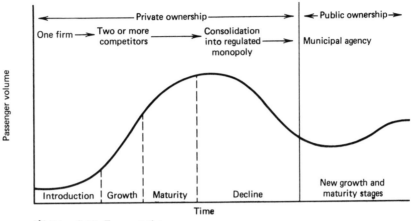

(A) Urban Public Transportation

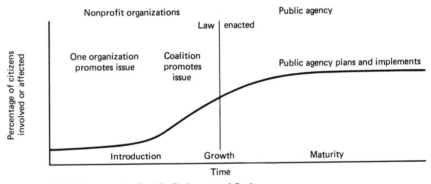

(B) Achievement of a Specific Environmental Goal

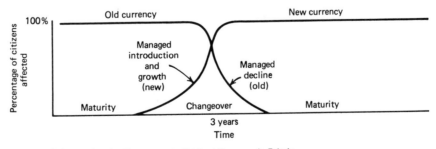

(C) Managing the Changeover to Decimal Currency in Britain

Figure 10.1 Public and nonprofit involvement in specific stages of product life cycle.

that each organization can expect. In the case of social-behavior programs, however, the presence of numerous "competitors" can be turned to advantage. Although consumers cannot simultaneously use two or more competing goods or services, they can join two or more organizations advocating related social-behavior programs. Further, these organizations can band together in a coalition to maximize their clout when seeking to broaden awareness of a specific concern that they share or to encourage passage of new legislation. The environmental movement provides a good example. As interest in environmental issues has grown, new environmental organizations have been founded, often with quite specialized objectives. Under certain conditions, they have found that it is to their mutual advantage to exchange mailing lists and to work together.

Coalitions often bring together disparate groups that agree on a particular issue, but for different reasons. Frequently the introductory stage of a social-behavior program is marked by one organization bringing a problem to the attention of a particular market segment; for instance, a fishing club may oppose damming a wild river because it will spoil the fishing. As awareness of the issue develops, other groups may join in opposing the project for *other* reasons, such as that it will drown historic artifacts, eliminate whitewater canoeing, or burden taxpayers with excessive costs. The competition in the mature stage of the PLC for this issue will not come from other organizations advocating the same behavior, but from groups or coalitions advocating the contrary view—namely, approval of the dam. These might include electrical utilities, construction interests, boating enthusiasts, land developers, and certain labor unions.

PRODUCT-LINE ADDITIONS

Few organizations face a static, unchanging market for their products. Most marketplaces are dynamic—changes in customer needs and behavior and in the number and mix of customers occur; competitors enter and exit; technological changes influence product features and delivery systems. Products that advanced the institutional mission well 10 years ago may be outmoded, uncompetitive, or even irrelevant today. And to fulfill the mission well 10 years (or less) from now may require development of new product offerings that will be attuned to the needs and opportunities of the times.

Developing New Products

Public and nonprofit organizations may perceive a need or opportunity to develop new products in several areas. Advancement of the institutional mission in a changing environment may require adding new *core products*. For instance, government agencies launch new services to resolve social, economic, or political problems. Hospitals add new forms of treatment, perhaps reflecting advances in technology and scientific knowledge, or a better understanding of the human needs of their patients. Performing-arts organizations introduce new works into their repertoire. Social-change organizations identify causes that are currently overlooked—such as the need for research into a rare disease, maltreatment of the elderly, or a new environmental threat to a fragile piece of land. Occasionally an entirely new organization is founded to launch a new product that no other institution offers.

A second category concerns new *supplementary products,* introduced to facilitate use of the core product. Examples include development of a parking lot to encourage attendance at a museum or creation of a day-care center for children of parents attending a government-sponsored retraining program.

Finally, in recent years we have seen the introduction of a large number of innovative new *resource-attraction products,* designed primarily to raise money through innovative forms of fund raising or sale of goods and services at a profit. Such profits include merchandise sold through gift shops and catalogs, raffles and auctions, magazines and books, consulting services, and rental of facilities.

Many new products prove to be a disappointment to their sponsors, failing to advance the institutional mission, diverting management time and attention, generating a net cash drain on the organization's finances—or perhaps all of these. Managers who have had bad luck with new products in the past often become averse to risk as a result. But no organization can afford to stagnate, and not introducing any new products at all may prove as damaging to the institution's health as selecting the wrong new products or botching the introduction process.

New-Product Development

The issue of designing and marketing new products has attracted great interest from both managers and academics.[5] There is general agreement that the new-product-development process should proceed systematically through a series of steps, beginning with a review of corporate (institutional) objectives and constraints and continuing through to product introduction. Figure 10.2 summarizes these steps in diagrammatic form. As can be seen, there are three major sets of inputs:

1. Corporate and marketing objectives.
2. The organization's strengths and weaknesses (assessed by conducting a marketing audit).
3. Information on the current and anticipated market, the competitive situation, and other environmental factors (also assessed via the marketing audit).

From these inputs, management can derive an indication of what the desired product portfolio for the organization should look like. By comparing this "ideal" with the current portfolio, gaps and opportunities can be quickly identified. Objectives can then be set for new-product development and suitable criteria established for evaluating prospective candidates.

New products can be developed entirely in-house or through external acquisition. Thus a merger might take place between two organizations with complementary products, or a government department might take on new responsibilities transferred from another public agency. In either case, a carefully managed process is needed, first, to ensure that good ideas are not overlooked and, second, to subject the ideas that are generated to a rigorous screening process. Ideas that pass the initial screening can then be more formally conceptualized and developed into a specific product proposal.

As shown in Figure 10.2, stage 6 in the new-product-development process involves generation and evaluation of the final product *and its associated marketing strategy* (our emphasis). This stage is critical, since it represents the point at which a concept is transformed into reality. Part of that reality is how the product will be priced, distributed, and communicated to prospective customers.

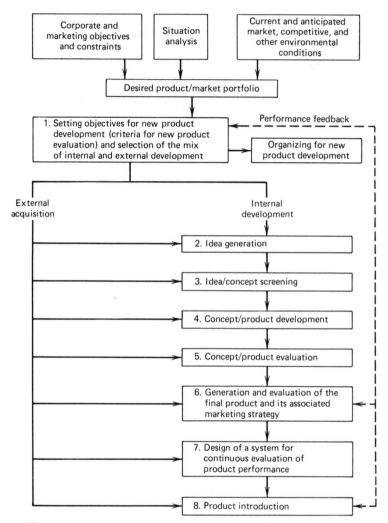

Figure 10.2 New-product-development system. (From Yoram J. Wind.[6])

A mock-up or prototype can easily be made of a physical good, but a service or social behavior can really only exist in *blueprint* form until the concept is made operational. Essentially, the marketer must understand what processes must take place for the service to be performed or the advocated social behavior to be executed by prospective customers in each of the segments targeted. Figure 10.3 shows a blueprint for a simple service such as a corner shoeshine. It shows the four basic steps required to complete a shoeshine, standard execution times for each step, the customer's estimated tolerance for delays in execution, and specification of the facilitating goods and services required. Describing this model, Shostack writes:

> The basic requirements of a service blueprint are three. First, since processes take place in time, the blueprint must, like PERT charting, show time dimensions in diagrammatic form.

(A) Process of Product Execution

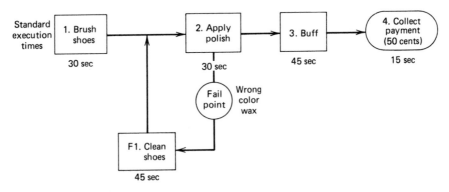

(B) Facilitating Elements

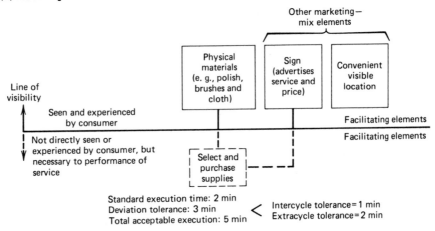

Figure 10.3 Example of blueprinting a simple service: a street-corner shoeshine operation designed to raise funds for a small nonprofit organization. (Adapted from G. Lynn Shostak.[7])

Second, like methods engineering, the blueprint must identify all main functions (and subfunctions) of the service. Where these are performed by people, a work chart should be constructed. All input and output of functions must be shown. Like systems design, the blueprint must identify and handle errors, bottlenecks, recycling steps, etc.

Finally, usually after research, the blueprint must precisely define the tolerance of the model, i.e., the degree of variation from the blueprint's standards that can be allowed in execution without affecting the consumer's perception of overall quality and timeliness.[8]

The last two stages in the new-product-development process involve design of a system for continuous evaluation of product performance and, finally, product introduction.

Evaluating Product Fit

Throughout the new-product-development process (and even after introduction), the product must be evaluated in terms of how well it fits the marketing environment. There are two basic dimensions to product fit:

1. Product-organization fit.

2. Product-market fit.

Product-organization fit raises such questions as how well the product matches the institutional mission and what its impact will be on the organization's financial situation. There are also questions relating to the fit with other existing resource inputs, including labor, management skills, and physical facilities. Finally, the product can be evaluated against each element in the organization's current marketing mix.

- Is it a logical extension of the existing product line? Will it complement existing products or "cannibalize" them by eating into their sales?

- Are the monetary price and payment terms compatible with those for existing products? What are the implications for a public or nonprofit organization of introducing (say) a fee-based service when previously all its services have been offered free of charge?

- Can existing channels of distribution or delivery systems be used, or will it be necessary to add new outlets and new intermediaries?

- What communication strategies will be needed to inform prospective customers about the product? Is it possible to "piggyback" information about the product on existing sales calls or advertising messages, or must new communication programs be developed—perhaps requiring use of unfamiliar media and communication techniques?

Product-market fit is concerned with how well the product matches customer needs, interests, and purchase/adoption procedures. Can the organization reach prospective customers with the information they need about the product? Can customers afford the cost in terms of money and time? Will they be turned off by perceived psychic and sensory costs associated with the product? Are customers likely to patronize the locations in which the product will be made available? Even if the product appears to fit well with prospective customers, do competing products fit even better? Will introduction of the product result in a competitive retaliation to which the organization cannot adequately respond?

Starting a New Organization

Not only products and product classes go through life cycles; organizations do, too. Just as many new products are launched, only to fail, so do many organizations quickly fall by the wayside. Existing institutions are often reluctant to add new goods, services, or social-behavior programs to their existing product line. Hence the only way for an individual or group inspired by missionary zeal to introduce a new product may be to create a new organization designed to achieve just that.

Government agencies are usually created by the passage of new legislation (sometimes an executive order may suffice). Intensive lobbying or campaign efforts may be needed to elect officials with the necessary commitment, to obtain the agreement of those already holding political office, or to pass a referendum. However, starting a new nonprofit organization is often the work of a single dedicated individual who is able to find or convince others to share the same vision.

Table 10.1 Key Factors Contributing to Success or Failure in an Organization, as Identified and Rank Ordered by Founders of Nonprofit Organizations

Success Factors	Failure Factors
1. Clear goals	1. Unclear or contradictory goals
2. The will to succeed	2. Lack of the will to succeed
3. Focus on a limited number of goals	3. Conflict of interest
4. Plan and timetable to reach goals	4. Boring programs
5. Tangible victories	5. No plan or timetable to reach goals
6. Exciting programs	6. Out-of-date or inaccurate bookkeeping
7. Fun	7. Too little money
8. Strong board of directors	8. Too many goals
9. Dependable income	9. Lack of dedicated leaders
10. Up-to-date bookkeeping	10. Lack of paid staff

Source. Joan Flanagan, *The Successful Volunteer Organization,* Chicago: Contemporary Books, 1981, pp. 5–6.

An excellent guide to starting a nonprofit organization is provided by Joan Flanagan's book, *The Successful Volunteer Organization.*[9] She asked founders of nonprofit organizations to think about the most successful organization they knew and to identify the factors contributing the most to its success. She also asked them to identify the factors most likely to cause the failure of an organization. Table 10.1 lists 10 success factors and 10 failure factors, in order of their perceived importance. As can be seen, these factors cover the full spectrum of management functions, but high among them are such marketing-related issues as product definition (goals), planning and implementation, attraction and retention of human and financial resources, and clear evidence of progress in achieving goals.

Underlying specific goals is the purpose of the organization, or mission statement, about which Flanagan has this to say.

The statement of purpose, sometimes called a mission statement, gives you a chance to say exactly what this group wants to do. The statement may also include what the group will not do. For example, the Metropolitan Milwaukee Fair Housing Council (MMFHC) states its purpose as: "The purpose of the MMFHC is to promote fair housing throughout the Milwaukee Metropolitan Area by guaranteeing all people equal access to housing opportunities and by creating and maintaining racially and economically integrated housing patterns."

The Parent and Childbirth Education Society (PACES) says, "Our mission is to promote good parenting from prenatal through the preschool years through an expanding program of educational and supportive services."

Keep the statement of purpose as short and simple as you can. This is the group's reason for existing. Your tactics, whether filing lawsuits or running a lending library, are means to an end and should be left out of a statement of purpose. Leave yourself room to grow and change. Your job is to write a clear, simple statement that will reflect the goals of the group and still allow healthy diversity within the group. If one person thinks "good parenting" is mothering twenty-four hours a day, and another person thinks it is affordable, quality child care for working parents, both can belong to the same organization in good faith.

The statement of purpose allows everyone, including newcomers, to share the ideals that inspired the founders. Especially if your group is growing quickly or is very busy with many activities, the people involved must sometimes be reminded of why you are doing this work.[10]

From here, an initial plan can be developed for the organization. At a minimum this should address the following topics.

- What benefits will be created by the organization and which other people will wish to join?

- Who might oppose the organization and for what reasons? What strategy should be adopted for dealing with opponents (who may already offer, or decide to introduce, competing goods and services, or opposing social-behavior programs)?

- In pursuit of its goals, what specific products should the organization offer and to which market segments?

- Where will the organization operate and what will be the geographic scope of its activities?

- How should the organization communicate with the target market segments?

- What is the time frame for conducting specific tasks and achieving specific goals?

- Which other organizations can be recruited for building coalitions or assisting in an intermediary role?

- What financial outlays will be incurred for salaries, building expenses, operating costs, and so forth? How might the money to cover these costs be obtained (fund raising, fee for service, etc.)?

DIFFUSION OF INNOVATIONS

Important management insights into obtaining market acceptance of new products, ideas, and behaviors can be gained from studying the field called *diffusion of innovations*. This area of study concerns the process by which an innovation is communicated and adopted (or rejected). The notion of an innovation is a broad one and refers to any good, service, idea, or behavior pattern that is perceived as new by an individual. Thus sterilizing water by boiling it, metric measurement, heart transplants, and marijuana have all constituted innovations in particular locations at a given point in time. Marketing strategies and actions can influence the speed and extent of new-product adoption, as we will see throughout this book. Several findings from diffusion of innovations research are particularly relevant for marketing management; they include the characteristics of each innovation (as perceived by prospective adopters), how quickly people adopt an innovation, stages in the adoption decision process, and the role of personal influence in encouraging (or discouraging) innovative behavior.

Characteristics of Innovations

Not all innovations are the same, and the rate and level of adoption depend on the ability of a specific innovation to fill a market need. Six factors are often related to the success of an innovation: (1) relative advantage, (2) compatibility, (3) complexity, (4) trialability, (5) observability, and (6) perceived risk.

Relative advantage concerns the extent to which an innovation is superior to the products or behaviors it supersedes. The nature of the innovation generally determines what specific types of relative advantage are important to consumers. Products should be designed with consumer needs in mind in order to enhance their relative advantage. Consumers are often faced with a trade-off to make between an innovation's relative advantages and disadvantages over existing alternatives. A new rail service might involve higher costs than car travel, but offer shorter travel time and be more relaxing. It is important to remember that people's perceptions of the relative advantages of an innovation are not necessarily fixed but may change over time. Promotional efforts and interpersonal communications represent two ways in which such perceptions may be influenced.

Compatibility represents the degree to which an innovation is consistent with consumers' existing values and past experiences. The greater an innovation's compatibility with (1) cultural norms and (2) previously adopted ideas, goods, and services, the better its chances for adoption and the faster this is likely to take place. Examples of incompatible innovations are the use of birth-control pills and IUDs (intrauterine contraceptive devices) in areas where religious beliefs discourage the use of birth-control devices or social norms encourage large families.

Complexity is the degree to which an innovation is perceived as relatively difficult to understand and use. More complex innovations, requiring the user to develop new skills, usually take a longer time to diffuse than simpler ones.

> For example, the rhythm method of family planning is relatively complex for most peasant housewives to comprehend because it requires understanding human reproduction and the monthly cycle of ovulation. For this reason, attempts to introduce the rhythm method in village India have been much less successful than campaigns to diffuse the loop, a type of IUCD, which is a much less complex idea in the eyes of the receiver.[11]

This example also illustrates the point that complexity, like the other characteristics, reflects the perceptions of the intended user, not management. Like relative advantage, part of marketing's role can be to reduce the perceived complexity of the product in the customer's eyes.

Trialability, (or "divisibility") denotes the degree to which an innovation may be tried initially on a limited basis—being a function of the size, cost, and/or frequency of purchase or usage of a product. New ideas that can be tried on the "installment plan" will generally be adopted more rapidly than innovations that are not "divisible" in this way. To some extent, a product's trialability can be enhanced by free trial periods and rental schemes, but this is impractical or even impossible for some innovations. On the other hand, many behavior patterns, such as exercising or attending class, can be tried a few times before a long-term commitment is made. Managers should beware of mistaking short trial periods for long-term commitment.

Observability (or "communicability") refers to the extent to which the innovation and its results are visible to others. The results of some ideas are easily observed and communicated, but it may be difficult for people to describe other innovations to their acquaintances. Where the product or service has low visibility, it may be necessary to generate "excitement" by packaging, product design, and the nature of advertising and promotion. Blood-donor groups, to illustrate, often give pins to donors not only to show appreciation but also to communicate with nondonors that some do give.

Risk in adopting a new product or behavior can arise from financial, social, psychological, or other sources. Increased risk decreases the likelihood of adoption. Unfortunately, many programs of planned social change, such as education, conservation, and welfare, generate a high degree of risk. Often marketers need to find ways to reduce the risk; for example, new education curricula may be introduced on a voluntary basis or only in selected sites in the school system. More generally, developing trialability in an innovation is a way to reduce perceived (and actual) risk.

The Innovation-Decision Process

The innovation-decision process is the mental process through which a person goes, starting from knowledge or awareness of the product to a decision to adopt or reject and to confirmation of the decision. Rogers and Shoemaker describe the process as consisting of four stages.

1. *Knowledge.* The individual is exposed to the innovation's existence and gains some understanding of how it functions.

2. *Persuasion.* The individual forms a favorable or unfavorable attitude toward the innovation.

3. *Decision.* The individual engages in activities that lead to a choice to adopt or reject the innovation.

4. *Confirmation.* The individual seeks reinforcement for the innovation-decision he or she has made, but may reverse the previous decision if exposed to conflicting messages about the innovation.[12]

This model is similar to the complex-decision model discussed earlier in this chapter. The three stages of that model—problem recognition, information processing, and alternative evaluation—are aggregated into the two steps of knowledge and persuasion. A more detailed description would find the two models very similar. Both models stress that individuals go through a sequence of steps in making a choice. The Rogers and Shoemaker model starts by focusing on becoming aware of and learning about an innovation; the complex-decision model is more general and looks at problem recognition as the first step.

Particularly noteworthy, however, is the stress placed on the confirmation stage in the innovation model. Continued information seeking often recurs throughout the confirmation stage. Individuals generally seek to reinforce their decisions by looking for favorable information or approval by peers. At times discrepant information or dissatisfaction with the adopted innovation may lead to discontinuance; examples include declining seat belt usage, failure to maintain preventive health measures, and dropping out of drug abuse programs.

The innovation-decision model is most appropriate for optional decisions made by individuals. A more complex model is required to describe *collective decisions*—for example, a voter referendum on whether to fluoridate a city's water supply—which require that the individuals in the social system reach agreement by some form of consensus. Once consensus is achieved, each individual generally has little choice but to go along with the collective decision.

Another type of decision is an *authority decision,* where an individual or group can make a decision and impose it on the whole social system. Organizational buying behavior for new products, represents one example of this situation.

PRODUCT MODIFICATIONS AND DELETIONS

Few products remain unchanged for extended periods of time. Most evolve in response to changes in the environment, with various features being added, modified, or deleted. A majority of products eventually reach the end of their life cycle and are removed from the marketplace.

Even a national historic site that is hundreds or thousands of years old may be modified by the agency responsible for its upkeep to improve the quality of the visitor experience. Thus a twelfth-century cathedral may have its stone frontage cleaned or a new organ installed inside, new trails may be developed at a national park, or a new interpretive center may be opened at the site of a historic battle to improve visitor understanding of the event and its underlying circumstances. For its centennial in 1986 the Statue of Liberty underwent a major renovation.

Evaluating Product Performance

Responsive organizations regularly evaluate the performance of each product in the portfolio. We proposed two key criteria for the products of public and nonprofit organizations: ability to advance the institutional mission and net financial impact on the organization. This evaluation process should reflect both current and projected performance, assuming a continuation of existing or planned marketing strategies and market conditions.

Factors that should be seen as indicators of the need to modify or delete a product include the following:

- Decline in sales volume or deterioration of the product's financial impact on the organization.
- Declining ability of the product to advance the institutional mission.
- Declining market share in an expanding market for this product class.
- Changes in attitudes of consumers, intermediaries, volunteers, or donors/granters toward the product. (While public and nonprofit managers should not allow themselves to be blackmailed by individual donors, a broad-based loss of support may be indicative of perceived deficiencies in a specific product or program.)
- Dissatisfaction with product quality.
- Introduction of new competitive products or changes in current or expected activities. (In the case of social-behavior programs, new activities by opponents may signal the need for changes to the current program).

■ Introduction of new products by the organization that threaten the viability of existing offerings or require a repositioning of the latter for maximum synergy.

■ A change in government regulations or passage of new laws that either close off certain marketing options or open up new opportunities.

■ A change in the availability of suppliers, intermediaries, or other facilitating organizations.

■ Technological changes that might affect the characteristics of a physical good, the execution of a service, or the customer's ability (or need) to perform a social behavior.

■ Changes in institutional mission or in the resources available to the organization.

The outcome of this performance review should be assignment of each product to one of three categories.

1. Acceptable current and projected performance that requires no change in strategy.

2. Acceptable current and projected performance, but the product would improve its performance if some change in strategy were made.

3. Unacceptable current or projected performance requiring a change in strategy or deletion of the product.

Poor performance against key *internal* criteria is not the only reason for modifying or deleting a product in a nonbusiness organization. Indeed, as Figure 9.2 suggests, excellent performance on the criterion of profitability but poor performance on institutional mission advancement may be grounds for selling off or transferring a product (or strategic management unit) to another organization; this outcome also serves to illustrate that there are more ways of deleting a product than just killing it! Managers who are not well attuned to the dynamics of the marketplace may feel quite content with their product's performance, but they may be overlooking opportunities for doing much better if the market is expanding rapidly or other competitors are withdrawing their own product entries in the market.

Repositioning

Changes in strategy may, of course, refer to any element in the marketing mix. Our primary concern here is with changes in product features, but it should be recognized that a product can be *repositioned* to compete more effectively by changing the price, the delivery system, or the communication program (or all three) without necessarily changing the features of the product itself. However, the greater the changes in other elements of the mix, the more likely it is that some aspects of the product will need to be modified, too.

There are a variety of different bases for establishing a positioning (or repositioning) strategy. These bases, while tied to the reality of what the organization stands for and the services that it can deliver, also provide the platform for building a communication program. Possible bases for a positioning strategy include:

1. Specific product attributes, performance dimensions, and/or price.

2. Benefits.

3. Usage situation.

4. User category.

5. Competition.

The Appendix to this chapter shows how the use of positioning maps can aid in formulating a positioning strategy.

One frequently used strategy is to position by product attribute, performance dimension, and/or price—a strategy that can be termed *attribute positioning*. For example, some public transit agencies have developed a positioning strategy for express-bus services for suburban commuters. In some cities, special lanes in freeways are reserved for rush-hour buses that speed by traffic jams. Using names such as "The Flyer," these agencies have positioned their services on the speed and reliability dimensions (often in contrast to ordinary bus services as well as cars).

It is often useful to distinguish between *important* and *determinant* attributes, as discussed in Chapter 6, "Customer Behavior and Decision-Making." An important attribute on which users perceive all competing alternatives to be alike will generally not influence the choice of alternatives. Thus commuters generally do not choose to use rapid transit or an automobile because of the safety of either mode. It is assumed by most people that both these forms of transportation are just about equally safe. Determinant attributes, on the other hand, are not only important, but are those on which significant differences are perceived among the alternatives. Thus a commuter may choose to ride rapid transit because it provides a faster way to get to work during the rush hour.

The major difficulty with attribute positioning strategies is that they focus on the product and not the consumer benefit. Although the translation may sometimes be easily made—new buses are more comfortable, but not necessarily faster or more reliable—the emphasis should really be on benefits to the consumer. Thus pure "attribute-positioning" strategies are rarely seen; they are usually combined with benefit positioning or another positioning approach.

Benefit positioning is similar to attribute positioning, but it is expressed in terms directly related to the market. For example, one express bus service focused on the benefit of how relaxed a commuter felt when arriving at work. It attempted to position bus commuters as more relaxed than automobile commuters.

In examining benefit positioning, it is important to remember the critical role of market segmentation. In developing a benefit positioning strategy, an organization will often choose to focus on benefits that others have not emphasized. The organization does not expect that the entire market will find the benefit emphasized an attractive and meaningful one, but that a segment will.

The reader should not worry too much about making fine distinctions between benefit segmentation and benefit positioning. The major distinction here is that positioning strategies tend to place more focus on competition, but some analysts would suggest that the process involved in choosing a benefit segment to pursue involves such considerations as well.

The armed-forces recruiting campaigns present an interesting example of a benefit positioning strategy. Why, after all, should someone commit two or more years of life to enrollment in a military service? In the days of the draft, there was no choice. Now some benefits must be provided that offer competitive advantages over civilian jobs. In recent years, the major benefit has appeared to be vocational training. The armed forces do not appear to be positioned as fighting forces or defenders of a country but as a way to learn a trade. This positioning strategy puts the armed forces in competition with civilian employment and technical schools, but less so with police forces. In contrast, examine the benefit positioning strategy adopted by the Peace Corps, at least initially. Here the main benefit was self-fulfillment. Both the Peace Corps and military services offer patriotic ways to spend several years of one's life, but they are positioned very differently.

Another way to position a product or an organization is to associate it with certain uses or occasions. Thus, some counseling agencies have developed particular positions connoted by such names as "Suicide Center" and "VD Hotline." Instead of offering a broad range of services, these agencies seek to serve only a limited market defined by a particular *usage situation*.

A number of universities have adopted this strategy with respect to part-time professional degree programs. One business school decided to position itself as *the* metropolitan-area business school for evening students. To achieve this position, the school rented classroom facilities in a downtown area, ensured that popular courses were offered frequently and that all electives were offered in the evening, and gave priority to part-time students in registering. The school enforced a rigorous admission policy and did not relax academic standards, so a quality program was built. In all, if a student wanted to pursue an MBA degree in an evening program, this university became the preferred choice.

For historical reasons, a number of community organizations find themselves with names and user category positions that somewhat limit their ability to serve wide markets.

- League of Women Voters.
- YMCA (Young Men's Christian Association).
- YWCA (Young Women's Christian Association).
- JCC (Jewish Community Center).
- Boys Clubs.
- Girls Clubs.
- Family Planning Services.

When people read this list, they associate these organizations with limited user markets. In these examples, the names seem to restrict the organization's market by religion, age, sex, and marital status. Yet many of these organizations, and certainly their local facilities, do not wish to be so restrictive. Breaking out of firmly established positions is difficult.

At times, people incorrectly position an organization as dealing with an inappropriate or limited user group. Arthritis, for example, is frequently perceived as a disease that only strikes the elderly, but in fact, even teenagers suffer from arthritis. To change this perception, the Arthritis Foundation conducted a campaign that seemed to say, "arthritis, a disease of all ages."

Positioning with respect to the competition is a potentially powerful strategy. If the competition already has a strong, established position in the user's mind, that image can be used as a reference point in establishing another agency's own image. The competition's position can be used as a base to show how the agency is better on certain dimensions, how the agency differs on other dimensions, or how the agency is the same as the competition, but offers better value.

The famous line of Avis Rent-a-Car that "We're number two, so we try harder" suggested that Hertz was so big that they did not need to work as hard for the customer as Avis. At the same time, the theme positioned Avis as a major rental car company along with Hertz, and thereby positioned Avis away from National, which was at that time a close third to Avis. Thus the theme positioned Avis as being a major company just like Hertz, but better.

New organizations or products in established fields often try to position themselves relative to a well-known institution. When a competitor to Zero Population Growth (ZPG) arose, its name of Negative Population Growth immediately conveyed the major differences between it and ZPG..

In summary, there are many possible bases in which to reposition an existing product as well as to position a new one. As nonbusiness organizations adopt segmentation strategies, they often develop several variants of the basic product, each targeted at a different segment.

Once the decision has been made to modify a product, a process similar to the new-product-development process can be set in motion. Managers should remember that as much or more may be at stake when an existing product is modified—especially if it is being sold to a large number of customers—as when a new product is launched. Following the sequence shown in Table 10.2, new objectives will need to be set, ideas generated and screened for how best to modify the product (existing customers and intermediaries may be a good source), and the modified product developed, evaluated, and integrated with a revised marketing strategy.

Product Deletions

Product deletion may become necessary under any of three conditions: (1) the product is not performing at a satisfactory level and modification is impossible or not worthwhile; (2) the product is performing at a satisfactory level but is being replaced by a superior substitute; or (3) the product is performing at a satisfactory level but the organization lacks the resources to continue offering it. Deleting a product can be a painful process in any organization, especially if the decision is being taken by those who earlier developed and nurtured the product in question. The deletion decision is particularly hard when the product appears to be meeting important societal needs but the funds or volunteers needed to support it are no longer available. If all avenues for new resources have been exhausted, management should review the possibilities for transferring the product (and its associated marketing effort) to another organization with compatible goals, or for merging two or more distinct product offerings into a single programmatic effort. The risk with these approaches is that too much may be lost in the process, with the result that certain market segments will either cease to be served or else receive in the future a service that no longer matches their needs.

Some public and nonprofit products must be uprooted because they have reached the end of their life cycle in terms of meeting individual or societal needs; some must be pruned out because they have become technologically, economically, or politically obsolescent; some are bulldozed by sudden political shifts or severe recession. A significant number of worthwhile public and nonprofit offerings wither on the vine because of lack of

Table 10.2 Integrating Product Policy with Other Elements of the Marketing Mix

	Marketing Program			
Elements of the Marketing Mix	Compulsory Use of Seat Belts	School-Lunch Program	Screening Program, High Blood Pressure: Interaction with Health Care Provider	Exercise Program: No Interaction with Health System
Product policy	Define standards for seat belts by vehicle type and usage (shoulder or lap straps); whether usage is mandatory for passenger as well as driver	Define minimum nutritional standards for single meal or sequence of meals; supply menu guidelines	Design screening procedure to minimize apprehension and maximize convenience; screening personnel are included in the product concept	Define appropriate levels of exercise for groups varying in physical condition or demographic profile. May be included in information pamphlet
Pricing policy	Impose penalties for non-compliance, perhaps graded according to number of offenses	Determine whether lunches are to be provided free, subsidized, or at full cost, and whether price should vary according to parental income	Decide whether screening is to be free, subsidized, or at full cost, and whether price should vary according to income or size of risk population. Consider price of follow-up treatment for those screened as "positive"	Distinguish programs that involve only equipment costs from those that involve a participation fee. Consider whether costs should be borne by users or by the general tax fund
Distribution policy	Deploy enforcement personnel. Determine applicability of regulation by vehicle type, geographic area	Set eligibility requirements for individuals and school districts; list schools and times at which lunches are available	Select types of facility, locations, and times for screening. Deploy screening personnel to minimize waiting time	Parks, recreational facilities, bicycle paths, should be readily accessible, be open at convenient hours, be relatively uncrowded
Communications policy	Make consumers aware of the regulations, their reason, enforcement procedures, and penalties	Make parents aware of program availability, cost, nutritional value of meals. Persuade children to attend, eat the food provided, inform the institution if dissatisfied	Inform populations at risk of the existence of high blood pressure, its lack of symptoms, the need for checkups, availability of screening procedures, cost of screening (if any), nature of the procedure	Inform target groups of benefits of varying types of exercise; warn against overexertion; indicate where and how more information can be obtained. Ensure continuation of exercise program as well as trial

Reprinted from *Millbank Memorial Fund Quarterly/Health and Society,* 58, No. 2 (1980), John A. Quelch, "Marketing Principles and the Future of Preventive Health Care," by permission of the MIT Press, Cambridge, Mass.

forward planning on the part of management—typically reflecting lack of attention to the need for periodic product modifications and insufficient cultivation of the resources required to support creation and delivery of the product.

PRODUCT POLICY AS AN ELEMENT IN THE MARKETING MIX

It is an axiom of marketing that no product offering can meet its full potential unless: (1) it is appropriately priced for the segment(s) at which it is targeted (pricing policy); (2) it is made available at times and in locations these segments find convenient (distribution policy); and (3) information about its characteristics and availability is effectively communicated to the target market (communication policy).

The elements of the marketing mix must be designed so that they are consistent with one another. All four must be tailored to match the needs and characteristics of the target market segment(s). An integrated marketing program creates synergy because the various elements of the marketing mix mutually reinforce each other. Without this synergy, the marketing effort is likely to fail (or at least the results fall below their potential), even though the basic product is soundly conceived.

Table 10.2 shows four examples of integrated marketing programs in the public and nonprofit sectors: compulsory use of seat belts (a social behavior); a school-lunch program (a physical good with service elements added); a high-blood-pressure screening program operated by health-care providers (a service); and an exercise program for individuals to undertake on their own (a social behavior) involving no direct interaction with the health care system.. Note the attention given to facilitating and enforcement mechanisms: enforcement of seat-belt regulations by special personnel, with fines for non-compliance; choice of schools for distributing school lunches and of facilities for conducting screening programs; and the need for special equipment and accessibility of specific recreational facilities for exercise programs.

SUMMARY

Over time, changes in the environment may require adjustments to the product portfolio. Some existing products may have to be dropped; perhaps they have reached the end of their life cycle and are outmoded and unprofitable, or perhaps they no longer advance the institutional mission in useful ways. Sometimes, redesigning and repositioning the product may be a feasible option. Consideration should also be given to the identification, development, and introduction of new products—a process requiring rigorous evaluation of possible alternatives and careful attention to detail.

In this book, the chapter on product policy precedes those on pricing, distribution, and communications. The development and implementation of a marketing program does not necessarily proceed on a sequential basis through each element of the mix, however. Program development involves an interactive process. Managers should recognize that decisions on one element of the mix may require modifications to one or all of the other elements in order to adapt to constraints on marketing-program design, ensure consistency, and maximize opportunities for mutual reinforcement between the elements.

REFERENCES

1. I. Gross, "Toward a General Theory of Product Evolution: A Rejection of the Product Life Cycle Concept." Marketing Science Institute Working Paper, September 1968.
2. Yoram J. Wind, *Product Policy.: Concepts, Methods, and Strategy*, Reading, MA: Addison-Wesley, 1982, p. 64.
3. As in reference 2, p. 64.
4. A good critique is provided by Nariman K. Dhalla and Sonia Yuspeh, "Forget the Product Life Cycle Concept," *Harvard Business Review*, January–February 1976, p. 104.
5. See, for example, Glen L. Urban, John R. Hauser, and Nikhilesh Dholakia, *Essentials of New Product Management*, Englewood Cliffs, N.J.: Prentice-Hall, 1987, and Wind, as in reference 2, Chapters 8–16.
6. As in reference 2, p. 229. Reprinted with permission.
7. G. Lynn Shostack, "How to Design a Service," in J. H. Donnelly and W. R. George, (eds.) *Marketing of Services*, American Marketing Association, 1981. Copyright © American Marketing Association.
8. As in reference 7, pp. 8–9. Reprinted by permission.
9. Joan Flanagan, *The Successful Volunteer Organization*, Chicago: Contemporary Books, 1981.
10. As in reference 9. Reprinted with permission of Contemporary Books.
11. Everett M. Rogers with F. Floyd Shoemaker, *Communication of Innovations*, New York: The Free Press, 1971, p. 22.
12. As in reference 11, pp. 103–104.

Appendix   Positioning Maps

A positioning map, or product space, is a geometric representation of users' perceptions of available products. (See Figure 4.3 in Chapter 4 for an example.) A map is usually confined to the most critical two or three dimensions. When more dimensions are needed to describe a market, a series of graphs needs to be drawn.

How many separate maps are required to represent adequately the perceptions of all the respondents? At the extreme, each respondent might require a unique map. One of the main advantages of a positioning map is that it summarizes a large amount of data in a compact, readable form. Allowing a totally different map for each respondent would destroy much of the value of this result. On the other hand, one map for the entire market might be too great an aggregation and might destroy useful information about variation. A useful compromise would be to recognize that respondents fall into a relatively small number of subgroups or segments with different product perceptions. For example, colleges seeking to attract students might draw separate maps for local residents, state residents who are not within commuting distance, other domestic applicants, and international applicants.

Positioning maps can also be used to indicate customer preferences. Starting with a product space either for all respondents or for all respondents in a market segment, differences are accounted for by locating each individual's preferences on the map. Sometimes this approach involves having a person describe the ideal product, based on the same attributes and rating scales used for existing products. Instead of mapping each individual's preference separately, it is often more useful to approximate the distribution of preferences by clustering respondents into a small number of groups. Preference for a product is related to the closeness of the product to the group's ideal point.

DEVELOPMENT OF A POSITIONING MAP

The development of positioning maps can be subdivided into three stages.

1. *Determination of relevant product markets.* Submarkets are defined in terms of the major types of usage situations or other segmenting variables for which concepts are to be developed or evaluated. A set of relevant existing organizations or products and customer subpopulations are identified as appropriate for each submarket.

2. *Identification of determinant attributes.* For each submarket, identify the set of attributes that are probable determinants of product preference or choice.

3. *Creation of a perceptual map of each submarket.* Existing products and descriptions of products appropriate to each submarket are represented abstractly as locations in a perceptual product space.

Many of the approaches to developing positioning maps involve the use of complex statistical procedures, which will not be discussed here.[a]

Determination of Relevant Product Markets

The opening step, determining relevant product markets, is often one of the most critical, because the positioning map that is eventually produced will depend on the initial definition of the product market. Specifying the product-market tends to involve three major areas. First is determining the market segment with which the organization is concerned. For example, a health-maintenance organization may find it useful to treat individuals and families at different stages of the life cycle separately. Young families might find the availability and quality of pediatric care to be the most significant factor in choice of health-care provider; elderly people have other concerns. Second are the situational factors on which the positioning map is to be based. Probably the most important situational factor is usage. For example, a positioning study for hospitals considered separately (1) surgery with a rapid recovery period and (2) major surgery that requires a long hospitalization. Or the choice among transportation alternatives might depend on the length of the trip. As an obvious illustration, meal service would be less important on a one-hour than on an eight-hour trip. The third factor is the range of competitive offerings to be considered. For example, if a university were to conduct a study of its position in the minds of high-school seniors, it would probably not wish to consider all existing colleges as competitors. The university officials might generate a list of who the relevant competitors are. Another approach is to ask consumers, in this case the students, what schools they know about or are familiar with and then define the competition as all schools mentioned by at least some given proportion of the students. This type of approach seems particularly useful when a large number of potential alternatives are available.

Identification of Determinant Attributes

Determinant attributes are those that distinguish among the alternatives in the relevant market and also can be reliably associated with current or potential user perceptions, preference, or choice. Some attributes may be important to users but not determinant because they are presumed to be present at the desired level in all the alternatives. For example, in choosing among hospitals, the prospective patient probably assumes that they all have sterile facilities and a competent, certified nursing staff. If this assumption does not hold, these important attributes could become determinant.

Determinant attributes are, in principle, related to the benefits and costs customers seek through their purchase and use of various goods and services. They may be psychological as well as physical in nature. Attributes should be specified in terms meaningful to consumers. The marketer's concerns, however, are often with controllable factors—physical properties, price, and so on. Thus the manager must develop a way to transform the controllable variables into perceptual characteristics. In some cases, the link between controllable variables and user perception is difficult to make. For example, if a transit manager finds that potential riders say that frequency of service is important, this does not provide a direct guide on how the buses should be scheduled. Even more difficult to transform would be an attribute such as comfortable seating.

A variety of techniques are available to generate the determinant attributes. Easiest, of course, is for the manager to specify them. The manager's view, however, as we have frequently discussed in this book, is often not the same as that of the consumer. For example, an exploratory study of hospital choice among physicians and hospital administrators suggested six factors as possible determinants of the hospital-selection decision—the type of hospital affiliation, the physical appearance of the hospital, the proximity of the hospital to the patient's home, the reputation of the attending physician, the familiarity with the attending physician, and the cost per day. Interviews with potential patients found an additional factor—quality and speed of nursing care—that was emphasized most frequently by those who had been previously hospitalized.

Consumers can be asked directly to list the determinant attributes, but this sometimes proves to be inadequate. One alternative is to list a wide range of characteristics of the market offerings and then ask the respondent to describe the offerings on each of the characteristics. This information is summarized in terms of a small number of discriminating factors. Some indirect techniques are also available. One approach, which has the formidable name of metric or nonmetric multidimensional scaling, asks the respondent to judge the degree of similarity (dissimilarity) among products. The analytical routine develops a map (in two, three, or more dimensions) in which the distance between products represents the degree of similarity. The analyst then attempts to identify the discriminating dimensions.

In summary, identification of determinant attributes usually requires information from consumers that allows the manager to determine what attributes are not only important but also serve to distinguish among alternatives. In addition, the manager should also search for attributes not currently offered, but that could become determinant.

Creation of Perceptual Maps

Once we have ascertained what the determinant attributes are, the next step is to represent the product on a perceptual map. A critical assumption, as we indicated earlier, is that all consumers within a market (or a segment) have the same perceptual map. While it is theoretically possible to have individual maps for each consumer, the approach loses much of its advantage as a means of summarizing data if each respondent generates his or her own map. Depending on the situation, it may be useful to create a map for the market as a whole, for each predefined segment, or for segments defined after examining the data and grouping people with similar perceptions.

In most approaches, the creation of a perceptual map begins with users giving a rating for each existing product (and perhaps some fictitious ones as well) on each attribute. The set of attributes may be all those thought possibly to be important, or just the set of determinant ones. If the number of (potential) determinant attributes is greater than two or three, something of a dilemma arises. Although theoretically a map of a product space can include as many dimensions as necessary, graphic illustrations are usually more limited. Consequently, statistical approaches such as discriminant analysis and factor analysis may be employed to reduce the number of dimensions used to describe the product market—with, obviously, some loss in accuracy. So far there is no universal answer to the problem of what is the right number of dimensions to represent a market. The best approach varies by the purpose for which the perceptual map is to be used and how much information is lost by reducing the number of dimensions.

In this appendix, we have looked primarily at perceptual models of a market as a means to identify the current positioning of market offerings. As we pointed out, this does not preclude the possibility that new attributes, not currently available, will be created or identified. When a map is used to help assess the viability of repositioning a product or developing a new product, the map can include both hypothetical dimensions and products.

After a perceptual map is developed, it may be used to represent preferences of individuals or segments either for existing products or for new products. If a sound model relating preferences to behavior can be formulated, the next step could be to make predictions about a product's relative success or failure. Examination of both the organization's or product's own position and that of its competitors relative to preferences can then be used as the basis for forming marketing strategies.

Appendix References

a. Our approach draws from an excellent review by Allan D. Shocker and V. Srinivasan, "Multi-Attribute Approaches for Product Concept Evaluation and Generation: A Critical Review," *Journal of Marketing Research* (May 1979), pp. 159–180. We do not attempt to review the mechanics of these processes; a useful reference in this regard is Glen L. Urban, John R. Hauser, and Nikhilesh Dholakia, *Essentials of New Product Management,* Englewood Cliffs, N.J.: Prentice-Hall, 1987.

Chapter 11
Developing Monetary Pricing Strategies

When marketing managers ask themselves, "How much shall we charge?" and consumers inquire, "How much does it cost?" both groups have in mind the *monetary* price of the product. This is the most obvious type of price, although the terms used to describe prices often vary according to the context—universities charge tuition, hospitals a fee, turnpikes a toll, public-transport services a fare, museums an admission charge, and local utilities a rate.[1] These monetary prices are particularly important to marketing organizations that rely on receipt of revenues from customers for a significant portion of their incomes.

There are other costs—what Seymour Fine describes as the "social price"—that customers may have to take into consideration when presented by a marketer with a product offering.[2] *Time* is a precious commodity for many people, and one whose supply for each individual has a fixed upper limit; there is an opportunity cost to the time spent traveling and waiting in pursuit of a good or service, or in trying to behave in ways urged by a social-behavior marketer. There may be disadvantages attached to a product's physical characteristics *(sensory* costs) or to the location where a service is available *(place* costs). Finally, there may be *psychic* costs attached to the use of a particular service—feelings of discomfort, inferiority, social disapproval from others, or even fear. In short, as discussed in Chapter 2, the bundle of benefits presented by the product must be traded off against the bundle of costs associated with using it. These nonmonetary prices assume greater prominence in the case of free services, where one might at first assume there would be no barriers to access.[3]

Scope of the Chapter

As its title suggests, this chapter is principally concerned with the monetary aspects of pricing. Careful attention to pricing strategy is essential to the survival of any public or nonprofit organization that depends on user fees or third-party reimbursement for even a small portion of its revenues.

In the private sector, the role of pricing is typically fairly explicit: to recover all costs and enable the firm to make a profit. As we will see, this model holds true for some of the products of public and nonprofit organizations, but not for most of them. We'll start by introducing some of the key criteria used in pricing and discuss how these may need to be modified to take account of the special situations often facing nonbusiness managers. We will take a detailed look at the fairly sophisticated pricing strategies adopted by British Rail in recent years, using this example to introduce some key concepts and issues in pricing. We'll go on to discuss the establishment of pricing objectives, look at the interrelationship between demand and price levels, and conclude with an analysis of the steps involved in developing a pricing strategy.

THE ROLE OF PRICING IN PUBLIC AND NONPROFIT ORGANIZATIONS

The foundations underlying pricing strategy were once described by the president of General Motors as a tripod, with the three legs being named costs, competition, and market demand.[4] The costs to be recovered set a floor to the price that may be charged for a specific product; the value of the product to the customer sets a ceiling; the price charged by competitors for similar or substitute products may determine where, within the ceiling-to-floor range, the price level should actually be set.

Adapting the "Pricing Tripod" to Nonbusiness Situations

The principles developed for use in the private sector can be modified to nonbusiness pricing. Companies seek to make money, of course, so they must recover the full costs associated with producing and marketing a product, and then charge a sufficient margin on top to yield a satisfactory profit.* In a nonbusiness organization, by contrast, donations and tax revenues often cover a significant portion of the costs, thus reducing the amount to be recovered through price.[5] Many public and nonprofit organizations are unwilling to price up to the maximum level that consumers might be willing to pay—even in situations where private-sector competitors are successfully doing so—since the institutional mission may require that the product be made available to prospective customers inexpensively or even free of charge. The desired image of the organization may also influence pricing strategy. For instance, the American Repertory Theatre surveyed the prices charged by competing theaters in the Boston area to help it in setting prices for its own performances. A.R.T. management felt that it was important to have a top price "high enough to distinguish us from the church basement productions . . . but on the other hand, we do depend on outside funding and for that reason we can't be out for blood like the commercial theatres."[6]

Private firms competing with public agencies are sometimes quick to denounce "unfair competition" when they feel that such an agency is pricing services below their true cost and relying on tax revenues to make up the difference. For instance, United Parcel Service (UPS) competes directly with the United States Postal Service in transportation of small packages. Time and again, UPS has argued at postal rate hearings that parcel-post rates do not cover the full costs and should be raised (usually to levels higher than those charged by UPS in its key markets). At the root of this problem is the difficult question of how overhead costs should be allocated among the multiple products marketed

---

*An exception occurs in the case of "loss leaders," designed to attract customers who will also buy profitable products from the same organization.

by many service organizations. UPS arguments invariably center on what their lawyers claim is inappropriate allocation of overhead costs among the different classes of mail, with the case being made that parcel post is not carrying its fair share and is being subsidized instead with tax revenues intended for other classes of mail.[7] We return briefly to this issue of cost allocation later in the chapter.

Third-Party Payments

Prices are not always paid directly by those who consume the product. For instance, the medical costs incurred by a hospital in treating a patient may be reimbursed by a third party such as an insurance company or government agency. The patient may pay indirectly—through insurance premiums or taxation—but the apparent cost of consumption is zero (or just a token fee in some instances). While this system facilitates access, it may also encourage unnecessary use of a service that is expensive to provide.

Third-party payments are quite common for social services. A variant of this approach is the provision of vouchers by a public agency to eligible consumers, allowing them to choose between alternative service suppliers. One often-cited experiment concerned the use of vouchers for educational services delivered by the Alum Rock school district, near San Jose, California.[8]

When Should Products Be Sold for Money?[9]

In addition to the need to recover costs directly from those who benefit from the use of a good or service, there are a number of reasons for a public or nonprofit organization to sell its products rather than give them away and, beyond this, to sell them at a monetary price that approximates full cost.

- *Motivate the Client.* Charging clients may make them more aware of the value of the goods and services supplied and may encourage prospective purchasers to consider whether they really need the product.

- *Motivate Managers.* If services are sold, the responsible outlet or department can be treated as a revenue center instead of as a cost center, so both input and output come to be measured in monetary terms.* The manager of a revenue center thus becomes responsible for operating it in such a way that revenues cover costs (or at least a predefined portion thereof).

- *Measure Output.* When products are sold at prices that approximate full cost, the resulting revenue figure is a useful measure of the quantity of products supplied by the organization. This is of particular value in service organizations where the unit of service is otherwise hard to define and measure. Unless an organization has appropriate ways of measuring its output, it is hard to evaluate either efficiency or effectiveness.

---

*For example, retail post offices in the United States are operated as cost centers. Local postmasters are evaluated on their ability to keep down costs. If these post offices were also treated as revenue centers, the postmasters would, in addition, be evaluated on their ability to stimulate use of postal services. The latter approach would serve to deter adoption of cost-cutting measures that discouraged patrons from using postal services—for instance, reducing the number of window clerks and thereby increasing the wait to use such competitive services as parcels or express mail.

When Should Products Not Be Sold at a Price?

Despite the advantages of charging for goods and services, situations can occur in which no monetary charge should normally be made.

When Public Benefit Is Desired. Public goods are services intended for the benefit of the public in general rather than a single client, and that cannot realistically be withheld from those who refuse to pay for them. Commonly cited examples include national defense and the provision of lighthouse services. In the latter instance, "consumption" of the light by one ship does not preclude its use by others; nor, short of using a sophisticated beam-scrambling device, is there any way to deny the light to one ship while simultaneously providing it to others.

Other services offered for the public benefit, such as police and fire protection, could potentially be withheld from those who refuse to pay, but such a denial would run contrary to public policy in most communities. Hence, like the lighthouse and national defense, these services tend to be financed indirectly through taxation. Even so, situations may arise in which an identifiable user can be charged for specific services. For example, promoters of rock concerts or other events drawing large crowds may have to pay the police for the extra cost of providing security and traffic control. (Alternatively, they may choose to hire a specialized security firm.) As we note later, there is currently a trend in the United States to identify opportunities for instituting user charges as a way of reducing the general tax burden.

When Prospective Customers Are Unable to Pay. Often, it is an article of public policy that no one unable to pay for certain basic services should go without them. The availability of such free services and the extent to which eligibility for them is restricted tend to vary from one country to another and from even one local political jurisdiction to another. Examples include job counseling, certain types of health care, and legal aid.

When Collection Costs Are Excessive Relative to Revenue Generated. When numerous small payments are being collected frequently from large numbers of customers—such as a 10¢ or 15¢ toll for crossing a bridge—the costs of collection may represent a substantial proportion of the resulting revenues. If the objective is only to cover the costs of producing and supplying the service, this situation makes little sense and it may be better to make no charge at all. If, however, the purpose of pricing is other than cost coverage—for instance, if pricing is designed to ration demand when supply is limited—the policy may still be quite defensible.

Trends In Pricing by Nonbusiness Organizations

Faced with sharply rising costs and, in the public sector, a growing reluctance among taxpayers to accept higher taxes, many public and nonprofit organizations are searching for additional sources of revenues directly from their customers. The trend today is to charge for products and services often available free in the past.

Prices have been raised sharply in many instances, and the rates of increase have far outpaced the overall inflation rate. Examples include postal charges in most countries, college tuition in the United States, and ticket prices for most performing-arts events. Charges have also been imposed for services that were formerly provided free. Consider, for instance, the impact on California of the passage of a referendum to reduce property taxes.

> In the year since Californians voted themselves a deep cut in property tax payments under Proposition 13 [in June 1978], they have been increasingly confronted with new or rapidly escalating fees, charges and other costs for services and programs local governments previously paid for from general revenue. . . .
>
> [The passage of Proposition 13] has wrought a fundamental and probably irreversible change in the way Californians pay for services, programs and facilities provided by the state's 58 counties, 417 cities, and 4,750 special districts. While many have praised the new "pay as you go" approach, others fear its negative effects on such groups as low or fixed income people. . . .
>
> After lengthy debate and several changes of mind, the Los Angeles City Council recently passed a residential trash collection fee ranging from $1.50 to $5.00 per month. There wasn't any agonizing earlier when the city imposed or raised fees for such things as dog licenses, use of recreation facilities, emergency ambulance transportation, fire safety inspections, and repairs of cracks in sidewalks, to name a few. . . .
>
> A major concern of a State Commission on Government Reform . . . is the effect of new and higher fees on the quality of life, particularly that of the lower income groups that tend to use public-facilities the most. . . .
>
> "We don't want to turn paths and swimming pools into country clubs for the middle class and rich" [says one observer]. . . . "Fees may increase total revenues, but already attendance is down everywhere from the Sacramento Zoo to inner city pools and parks. . . ."
>
> Fees have been instituted at previously free museums, while charges at beaches and campgrounds are up substantially and fines for overdue library books have doubled or tripled in many cases, Community colleges . . . have started charging for formerly free classes and services. As a result, attendance at noncredit courses—mainly recreation, crafts, and courses for senior citizens—dropped almost 26 percent this past semester. Some 20 percent of 4,600 noncredit courses were shelved.[10]

At the same time, many organizations—especially in the nonprofit sector—are introducing or extending peripheral goods or services and pricing them at levels intended to generate profits that will cross-subsidize the areas of their operations that consistently show a loss. One successful example, discussed in detail in Chapter 20, is a museum shop.

An interesting trend among some nonprofit organizations concerns the increasingly fuzzy distinction between a fixed price and a voluntary donation. The Mormon Church has always expected its members to tithe (give one tenth of their incomes). Among other denominations, religious services have traditionally been considered free, with church or temple members being asked to provide support through donations and volunteered assistance. Yet many members now find themselves under strong pressure to commit themselves to a specific level of giving. Some Catholic churches even collect a small, fixed sum from each member of the congregation at Mass in addition to "passing the plate" for contributions. Other manifestations of this trend toward formalizing the donation process include stronger pressure for "suggested" donations from visitors entering free museums or architecturally significant buildings that have no formal admission charge. Finally, some nonprofit arts organizations now add a "contribution line" to season ticket subscription forms and strongly urge subscribers to pay more than the basic price.

The Special Case of Social-Behavior Pricing

What is the role of pricing for social-behavior marketing? Can monetary price be used to encourage citizen involvement in creating such products as energy conservation, highway safety, or family togetherness? The answers are mixed, with much depending on the nature of the relationship between the marketer and the target market. In the case of energy conservation, the principal advocate is often government, which has the power to increase or decrease energy taxes or otherwise regulate the prices that energy suppliers are allowed to charge their customers for consuming a unit of energy.*

Highway safety, as we saw in Chapter 9, is really a blanket term for a large number of different behaviors—including maintaining vehicles properly, obeying traffic laws, discouraging drivers from drinking, and (as a pedestrian) wearing light-colored clothing at night on roads without sidewalks. Some of these behaviors can be enforced by law, with fines (or other punishment, representing different types of costs) for those convicted of breaking the law. Thus there is a price to be paid for illegal behavior. It is not always clear in advance how much "bad" behavior will cost, however—if indeed it costs anything. Major highways in Pennsylvania have large signs, posted at regular intervals, displaying a veritable menu of speeding penalties that lets motorists know exactly how large the fine is for each speed category above the limit. In practice, the amount of the fine may be less significant as a determinant of behavior than the individual's perception of the probability of having to pay it.

Take the case of Joe Smith, who knows that the penalty for speeding on a highway he uses regularly is a flat-rate fine of $20. Joe also knows from experience that the chances of being ticketed for driving 10 mph above the limit are very low. He estimates that he ends up paying for a ticket once every 50 trips, representing an average penalty (or "expected value") of 40¢ per trip—a price he is willing to pay for the benefit of being able to drive faster. Any public manager contemplating the threat of fines as a means of achieving the desired behavior must be prepared to adjust both the level of the fine and the effectiveness of the enforcement mechanism (as perceived by the target market) in order to achieve a satisfactory level of compliance.

A concept such as family togetherness is somewhat more abstract, although specific behaviors such as "family home night" each week or hugging one's child at least once a day may be advocated. Behaviors such as these are impossible to enforce through the monetary price mechanism. At most, a psychic cost—such as guilt—can be imposed through communications messages.

Nonprofit organizations advocating changes in social behavior can hardly impose and enforce fines among nonmembers for not complying with the behaviors they advocate. What they can do is work through government intermediaries, lobbying for new legislation that will prohibit the behavior they seek to discourage, with penalties for noncompliance.

Concluding Comment

Our concern in this chapter is not with the often philosophical questions of whether a product should be offered free or fines imposed for noncompliant behavior, but with what

---

*To encourage energy conservation in Canada, the federal government at one time offered a grant of up to $500 for adding insulation to a house and up to $800 for converting from heating by oil to heating by natural gas, a more abundant fuel.

pricing strategies should be adopted once the decision to charge a price has been made. To introduce an array of important pricing issues, we now turn to a discussion of pricing policies for passenger services in Britain's nationalized rail system.

Although this is a large, government-owned organization, its product is easy to understand, and lessons can be drawn which are applicable to a wide array of services sold directly to users.

PRICING POLICIES AT BRITISH RAIL*

In an era of rapidly rising costs, many public and nonprofit organizations need to increase their revenues in order to avoid financial collapse. Yet raising prices across the board may be self-defeating, resulting in simply driving away customers. British Rail has adopted a highly selective approach to pricing that recognizes differences between market segments in their ability and willingness to pay.

The railroads of the world have traditionally charged passenger fares that are proportionate to the distance traveled. For instance, the timetable for Swiss Federal Railways states the rate per kilometer for the different classes of travel (first, second, child, etc.), so that passenger fares on any given journey can be worked out from the distance column for each route. The use of these so-called scale charges is a logical approach to pricing still followed by most railroads.

Until 1968, scale charges for rail travel were the practice in Britain, too. They ensured administrative simplicity and what was termed a "fair fare"; that is, the cost per mile for each ticket type—one-way, round-trip, or season ticket (commuter pass) was the same for everyone. Faced with rising costs, British Rail (BR) decided to abandon the old approach. Instead of an across-the-board rise in fares to cover these cost increases, BR adopted a strategy of selective changes that management believed would offer scope for deeper market penetration, as well as improved earnings.

Variables Underlying Selective Pricing by Route

BR's analysts found that selective pricing required considerably more effort and skill than a scale system. The simple variable of distance between stations had to be replaced by a complex network. Each key fare between major stations on BR's Inter-City network was reviewed in the light of three main variables: quality of product, strength of market demand, and degree of competition.

Quality of product reflects the nature of the equipment and facilities on a given route and also the speed of the service. Very often, of course, the two are related. When new diesel trains capable of speeds up to 125 mph were introduced on certain routes in Britain, passengers received a faster ride on newer and more comfortable equipment. Fares went up more on these routes in the next round of price increases than they did elsewhere, yet it was found that patronage did not decline relative to other routes. One of the reasons for this trend was substantiated by studies that showed the demand for rail travel in Britain—particularly on major business routes—to be highly time-elastic.[†] Many travelers, espe-

---

*This section is based, in part, on articles by Ford[11] and Keen,[12] supplemented by interviews with British Rail managers.

†That is, a small reduction in travel time was likely to result in a proportionately greater increase in demand for rail travel on that route.

cially business executives, were prepared to pay a higher price to obtain time savings. Clearly, it made sense to incorporate these research findings into pricing decisions.

The *strength of market demand* is basically determined by the types of industry in the area served by the trains, economic prosperity and employment levels, and related factors such as the relative attractiveness of particular destinations for business travelers, tourists, and others. For instance, demand for travel between London and the major Scottish cities of Edinburgh and Glasgow has increased in recent years as a result of the economic growth stimulated by North Sea oil. Strong markets may be able to support higher fare levels than weak ones.

The *degree of competition* is also taken into account by British Rail when setting its fares. The London–Edinburgh/Glasgow markets may be strong, but so, too, is the competition from British Airways' "Scottish Shuttles" on these two 400-mile routes. Although train travel times were down to under 5 hours by 1979, air travel was obviously still much faster, even on a city-center to city-center basis. Fare strategies on these routes therefore have had to take account of this strong competition, to avoid pricing BR out of the market.

All these factors are weighed for each major route by a committee of BR fares experts. A fare structure has to be internally consistent, or anomalies may arise that distract traffic patterns and flows, possibly driving passengers off one route onto another that lacks the capacity to support increased patronage. Fares also have to be coherent to railway staff and passengers, so that the former understand the fare structure and the latter can learn quickly what they are going to pay for a given journey.

In addition to its concern with *how much* to charge for fares, BR has also looked at *how customers pay.* Travelers enjoy the convenience of using credit cards, as well as cash or checks, to purchase tickets; meals on board the trains can also be charged to credit cards.

At British Rail the basic full fare is only the starting point in the selective pricing process. A variety of reduced fares, likewise based on selective pricing, is used to attract more people to rail travel. Understanding the needs, behavior, and ability to pay of different market segments is central to the success of the discount-fare strategy. British Rail continues to experiment with new types of fare packages, not only to attract families and other off-peak travelers, but also to make rail travel even more appealing to business travelers, who tend to be time and convenience sensitive rather than price sensitive.

In 1987, for example, BR introduced an improved InterCity Executive Ticket. With a single transaction, the traveler obtains a first-class round-trip ticket, reserved seats, snack vouchers (meal vouchers can be purchased as an optional extra), 24 hours' free car parking at the originating station, a voucher good for 15 percent discount on car rentals at specified BR stations, and—if the traveler is going to London—two tickets for travel within the inner zone of the London Underground (subway).

Assessing the Effects

BR monitors individual passenger routes carefully to determine the effects of fares on traffic and total revenues. If traffic is falling off significantly on a particular route, or if the average fare paid is declining (i.e., travelers are trading down from first to second class or from full to reduced fare), corrective action may be taken once the reason for the decline has been established. Such action could take the form of improved service, more promotional efforts, or even changes in fares.

At BR, the objectives of selective pricing are basically threefold: to be more responsive to different categories of travelers, to increase revenues without unduly discouraging patronage, and to reduce the subsidy borne by taxpayers. BR's Chief Passenger Marketing Manager has estimated that selective pricing generates 5–8 percent more in total passenger revenues than a mileage-based scale would have produced.

INSIGHTS FROM THE BRITISH RAIL EXAMPLE

A number of useful insights may be obtained from studying BR's approach to pricing. Like most public and nonprofit organizations, BR is in the business of supplying a service, not a physical good. Because services cannot be inventoried or "saved" when they are not used, it's important to try to maintain the use of a service at the highest possible level. Running empty trains outside periods of peak demand, like performing a play to rows of empty seats, represents a lost opportunity for generating revenues.

Market, Consumer, and Competitive Factors

The three basic factors influencing BR's pricing strategy—market strength, product quality, and competition—are relevant to most nonbusiness organizations and merit careful analysis.

- *Evaluating Market Strength.* How large is the potential market for a given product? This depends in part on the "catchment area." How many people live or work reasonably close to the locations at which the service is available? Within this group, how many need the service offered, and how much are they willing to pay for it? What economic or social factors determine the need for travel, and how much is transportation service worth? How will these factors change in the future?

- *Determining Consumer Response to Product Costs and Benefits.* In many instances people will pay more for a higher-quality product and less for a lower-quality one. This is because the former generates greater benefits for the user and is therefore of greater value. Hence the willingness of some travelers to pay more for first-class accommodations or to pay higher monetary costs in return for lower time costs. The challenge for the marketer is to determine which benefits are desired by which market segments. Unfortunately, managers sometimes focus on what *they* consider to be the important product characteristics (which may be irrelevant to the principal market segments).

- *Identifying Competition.* Most nonbusiness organizations find themselves in competition with alternative or substitute products. British Rail may have a monopoly on intercity passenger rail service in Great Britain, but its trains compete with air and bus services as well as private cars. A less direct form of competition is provided by mail and telephone services, which may substitute for personal travel in some instances. Understanding competitors is central not only to pricing strategy but also to the entire marketing effort. How do their products compare in terms of the benefits they offer customers? What share of the market do they have, and is it rising or falling? How much are they charging? Do they offer simpler payment methods or better credit terms?

Segmentation and Pricing

An important lesson running throughout the British Rail example is the role of *market segmentation* in pricing. Different segments within the traveling public vary not only in terms of their travel needs (and the product benefits they seek) but also in terms of when they travel and their ability to pay. Many business travelers are looking for speed and comfort in a travel mode, but they are not very price sensitive, because their employers are paying the fare. So, in common with a few affluent people traveling for personal reasons, they constitute a market segment attracted by first-class travel. Most others travel second class, which is less roomy and more likely to be noisy and crowded, especially at peak periods. In addition, business travelers and commuters have little flexibility in deciding *when* to travel, which is typically on a weekday, toward the beginning and end of each working day. By contrast, individuals traveling for pleasure (like tourists) or for other personal reasons are better able to travel outside these peak periods. They may be unable or unwilling to pay the full fare, so BR offers discounts to appeal to these segments. To prevent business travelers from taking advantage of the cheap fares, BR imposes a variety of restrictions (like the need to book seven days in advance, or to travel during the middle of the week, or to stay away for at least a week—all requirements that full-fare travelers might find too restrictive).

The principle underlying selective pricing is that of charging what each market segment will bear. The business traveler who is willing to pay £10 for the service but bought a ticket for only £7 is enjoying what economists call *consumer surplus:* she is paying less for the benefits than they are worth to her. BR's strategy is clearly designed to minimize consumer surplus by identifying different market segments and charging the members of each segment as much as possible without driving them away. Doing this successfully requires an understanding of consumer behavior, so realistic restrictions can be placed on the use of discounted fares. These restrictions do more than just prevent "trading down" by full-fare passengers; they also *shape the timing of travel* by discount travelers in order to fill empty trains running at off-peak hours. Adding extra passengers to an already full train may require the addition of extra passenger cars or even a second train, both of which are very costly. Adding passengers to an empty train costs almost nothing, and thus may be very profitable—even when fares are heavily discounted.

Similarly, theaters lower their prices for matinees and charge peak price on Friday and Saturday evenings. The U.S. Postal Service provides reasonably speedy first-class letter transmission for 25 cents, but Express Mail—a guaranteed next-day service, used primarily by the business segment—costs more than 40 times that amount. In each of these instances, price differentiation is based on differentiation in the timing or nature of the service provided, as well as reflecting the varying needs of different market segments. Many social-service organizations carry price segmentation even further by charging consumers according to a sliding scale based on their ability to pay. A community mental-health clinic, for example, may offer equally high-quality counseling, at identical times and locations, to patients representing a wide range of incomes; fees will vary accordingly. When considering this system, managers should note that in some instances it may lead to charges of discrimination.

Alternative Payment Methods

Another dimension of pricing, illustrated by British Rail's policies, is concerned as much with the *method of payment* as with *how much* the price is. In addition to accepting checks and cash, BR now accepts major credit cards—providing a convenience to customers, many of whom have come to expect this service from one of BR's major competitors, British Airways. In addition, the use of credit cards may soften the impact of a substantial bill by allowing the customer to repay the credit-card company in small installments. A second way of facilitating payment is to allow people to purchase passes good for unlimited travel on certain routes for the period of validity. BR offers season tickets for commuters, which saves both travelers and station staff from engaging in daily cash transactions. It also sells BritRail Passes to tourists (who must purchase them in their home countries), allowing unlimited train travel for periods of from one to three weeks. Another type of ticket that also provides "up-front" money to the organization is BR's Railcard, which allows senior citizens, students, and families to purchase tickets at half price: the card itself costs a little less than $20. This strategy provides a way of restricting a discount to specific market segments, while providing the greatest benefits to those who use the discount most. Interestingly, BR has found that many Railcard holders receive their cards as presents from other family members. In 1982, a major bank offered a student Railcard at half price to any first-year college student who opened a checking account at one of the bank's branches.

In summary, we can see a variety of different pricing strategies being employed by British Rail as it seeks to achieve the seemingly conflicting objectives of maximizing rail patronage (which has important social benefits for the country) while making most of its passenger services pay their own way (thereby reducing the burden on taxpayers).

ESTABLISHING PRICING OBJECTIVES

Underlying any decision on pricing strategy must be a clear understanding of the organization's objectives. As shown in Table 11.1, there are three basic categories of pricing objectives open to a nonbusiness organization: revenue oriented (profit-seeking or cost-covering), operations oriented, and patronage oriented.

Profit-Oriented Objectives

Private-sector firms are profit-seeking organizations. Within certain limits, they attempt to maximize the surplus of income over expenditures. Public and nonprofit organizations, by contrast, are more likely to be concerned with breaking even or with keeping the operating deficit within acceptable bounds. Although theirs is a not-for-profit mission (and high prices may even be at variance with the organizational mission), they cannot afford to ignore the revenue implications of a change in price. In some instances, one or more elements in the organization's product line may be priced to yield a profit that will cross-subsidize other products. Gifts and souvenirs sold by retail outlets (such as museum shops) or by direct mail are one example; others include bus charters by transit authorities, sale of proof coins by national mints, first-day cover sales to philatelists by postal services, executive programs for professionals at graduate schools, and UNICEF Christmas cards.

Table 11.1 Alternative Bases for Pricing

---

(1) Revenue

Profit Seeking
Make the largest possible surplus
Achieve a specific target profit level, but do not seek to maximize profits

Cover Costs
Cover fully allocated costs (including institutional overhead)
Cover costs of providing one particular service or manufacturing one particular product category (after deducting any specific grants and excluding institutional overhead)
Cover incremental costs of selling to one extra customer

(2) Operations Oriented

Vary prices over time so as to ensure that demand matches available supply at any specific point in time (thus making the best use of productive capacity).

(3) Patronage Oriented

Maximize patronage (where capacity is not a constraint), subject to achieving a certain minimum level or revenues
Recognize differing ability to pay among the various market segments of interest to the organization and price accordingly
Offer methods of payment (including credit) that will enhance the likelihood of purchase

---

Pricing Relative to Costs

Determining the cost side of the pricing equation can be difficult. We'll look at three different types of costs. *Fixed costs* are those that would continue (at least in the short run) to be incurred even if no services were provided or physical goods manufactured. This "institutional overhead" is likely to comprise such elements as building rent, depreciation (sometimes only in part), utilities, taxes, insurance, administrative salaries, security, and whatever repairs and maintenance are necessitated by the passage of time as opposed to wear and tear from use.

Semivariable costs are those that are related to the volume of goods and services produced by the organization. These include production and transportation, operating costs, and wages and salaries incurred in paying overtime or hiring additional personnel. Such costs tend to vary widely from one product to another, depending on the nature of the good or service provided, the number of people involved, and the extent of additional facilities required. Typically, such costs rise in stepwise fashion. For instance, it is not possible to add just one extra seat to a train; instead one must add an extra passenger car. Adding an additional train to the existing schedule would involve extra labor costs, result in additional fuel consumption, and probably lead to increased maintenance expenditure.

Finally, there are the *variable costs* associated with selling an additional sales unit (e.g., a seat in a train or theater, a copy of a book or record). In many services, such costs tend to be extremely low, probably being close to zero in the typical train or theater (unless there is a tax on each ticket, or patrons receive free souvenirs, or users are particularly prone to littering or vandalism). By contrast, the incremental costs associated with selling additional manufactured goods, such as books or art reproductions, may form a significant percentage of the final selling price.

The fact that an organization has sold a product at a price that exceeds its variable cost does not mean that the organization is now profitable, for there are still the overhead fixed and semivariable costs to worry about.

The difference between the variable cost to the seller and the price charged to the purchaser is known as the *contribution margin* (not to be confused with a donation). This contribution goes to defer semivariable costs and overhead. In the case of a seat for a performance offered by an arts organization, the contribution per ticket is the selling price less any taxes or sales commission; other incremental costs per unit tend to be minimal. The contribution to the retailer on a commercially produced book or recording sold in, say, a theater lobby or museum shop may be 30–50 percent of the final selling price—more if the item has been donated.

Determination and allocation of costs is a difficult task that falls under the province of cost accounting (and may require the marketing manager to work closely with the controller). It is particularly problematic in service operations because of the difficulties of deciding how to assign overhead costs. For instance, a hospital might assign overhead to its emergency room on the basis of the percentage of total floor space it occupies, the percentage of employee hours or payroll it accounts for, or the percentage of total patient contact hours involved. Each of these methods would probably yield a totally different fixed-cost allocation; one might make the emergency room appear a terrible financial drain, another make it seem a break-even operation, and a third make it look highly profitable.

Operations-Oriented Objectives

Some organizations want to match demand and supply so as to ensure maximum use of their productive capacity. A nonbusiness service organization cannot achieve its mission if nobody uses it. Operating far below capacity looks bad to donors; in the case of a tax-supported public service it may be cited as evidence of wasting the taxpayers' money. Performing-arts organizations like to have a full house because, among other reasons, holding a show in a half-empty theater is depressing for both audience and performers. Matching demand to the number of seats in such an instance may be achieved by pricing high so as to ration demand at peak periods (or for especially popular shows), and pricing low as part of the marketing program to increase demand in off-peak periods. The problem with matching demand to supply through price raises questions of social equity, because it may freeze out the less well-to-do. An alternative is to introduce a reservations system.

Attempts to use pricing to match supply and demand sometimes run into difficulties. For instance, the Massachusetts Bay Transportation Authority (MBTA) sought to decrease crowding at peak hours and increase it at midday by offering a 60 percent fare discount between 10 A.M. and 2 P.M. Although the MBTA attracted some new riders during these times, management eventually discontinued the experiment because only a small percentage of rush-hour commuters switched to travel during off-peak hours. The problem, it became evident, was not that the discount lacked appeal, but simply that most people traveling to and from work lacked control over their hours of employment. The moral? Understand the factors determining the timing of demand before trying to change it.[13] Administrators of the Sunrise Hospital in Las Vegas did just that. Investigating the reasons why hospital bed occupancy was invariably lower at weekends than on weekdays, they found that patients requiring nonemergency treatment preferred not to be in the hospital over a weekend if they could avoid it. So the hospital began offering a cash rebate of 5.25 percent on the total hospital bill of every patient admitted on Fridays and Saturdays. This strategy proved quite successful in increasing weekend occupancy but had to be abandoned after 11 months because health insurance companies insisted on keeping the rebates for themselves. So in its place, the hospital instituted a weekly lottery, open only to patients checking in on Fridays and Saturdays, with a prize of an all-expense-paid vacation for two worth $4000.[14]

Stimulating Patronage

Not all nonbusiness organizations suffer from a short-term capacity constraint. Many feel that their mission can best be accomplished by maximizing patronage, but must trade this objective off against the need for a high level of customer-derived revenues. For instance, environmental organizations such as the Sierra Club feel that a larger membership gives them proportionately greater lobbying clout in Congress. Yet conducting lobbying activities is also expensive. With a $20 average membership fee and 200,000 members, the Sierra Club would generate $4 million in revenues. Suppose that raising the fee by $5 (25 percent) would result in only a 10 percent loss of members (fewer new members plus some lost renewals); the club would certainly be better off financially, since membership revenues would now total $4.5 million (180,000 × $25). The "downstream" effects might be damaging, however. A drop in membership might reduce the club's perceived political clout. There would also be fewer prospects from whom to seek supplementary donations and volunteer assistance, or to encourage to participate in club programs.

Organizations wishing to maximize their appeal among specific types of customers need to adopt pricing strategies that recognize a differential ability to pay among various market segments (as well as variations in preferences among customers for alternative payment procedures). Some organizations achieve this by offering different membership categories, with reduced rates for designated groups. Professional associations, for example, may reduce membership dues for graduate students. An "honor system" is sometimes used for people on limited incomes to save them the embarrassment of having to prove their status.

In practice, pricing strategies cannot be developed with the single-minded aim of satisfying just one class of objectives. Realistically, each of the three perspectives noted earlier must be included, although the comparative importance of profits, operations, and customer preferences may vary from one situation to another.

PRICING RELATIVE TO DEMAND LEVELS

Service organizations are often eager to attract the largest possible number of customers or patrons, since high patronage not only ensures that the organization's resources are fully utilized but also increases public visibility. Customers, by contrast, often prefer to use services when they are not too busy or crowded. (The performing arts are often an exception to this rule, since a "full house" provides a more exciting and rewarding experience for both audience and performers.) Pricing to maximize *use or attendance* is not necessarily the same as pricing to maximize *revenues*. Much depends on the extent to which a change in price affects people's willingness to buy the product.

Price Elasticity

The concept of elasticity is used to describe how sensitive demand for a product to changes in its price. When price elasticity is at "unity," sales rise (or fall) by the same percentage that price falls (or rises). When a small change in price has a big impact on sales, demand for that product is said to *be price elastic*. In the situation, when a change in price has little effect on sales, demand is described as *price inelastic*. Figure 11.1 shows how the demand schedule might look for a certain type of performance at a particular auditorium (based, perhaps, on past experience or on the findings of surveys among target consumers). For simplicity we have assumed one price and open seating. We also assume that the maximum seating capacity for the auditorium is 1500. From this chart, we can read off the projected number of tickets that would be sold at any given price, from which it is quite simple to calculate the resulting gross revenues (Table 11.2).

A strategy of revenue maximization, according to this demand schedule, lead management to charge an admission price of $7.50, thus yielding gross revenues of $7125. At this price, the hall would only be 63 percent full (950 ÷ 1500). At a $3.00 price, management could expect to sell out the house and to have to turn away 500 people; but box office revenues would only total $4500. Looking at the chart we can see that to feel confident of selling 1500 admissions (the capacity of the hall), management should set the

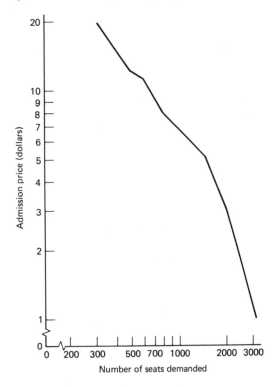

Figure 11.1 Hypothetical demand schedule for auditorium admissions at a performing arts organization. (Note: Ratio (logarithmic) scales have been used on both axes.)[15]

Table 11.2 Revenue and Occupancy Implications of Price-Demand Relationships[a]

Price ($)	Number Demanded	Potential Gross Revenues ($)	Seating Capacity Utilized (%)	Gross Revenues With 1500 Seat Constraint ($)
20.00	350	7000	23	7000
15.00	400	6000	27	6000
12.00	500	6000	33	6000
10.00	650	6500	43	6500
7.50	950	7125	63	7125
5.00	1350	6750	90	6750
4.50	1500	6750	100	6750
3.00	2000[b]	6000	100	4500
1.00	3000[b]	3000	100	1500

[a]Derived from Figure 11.1.

[b]Demand exceeds supply.

price at about $4.50, which would generate the same revenues as a $5.00 price ($6750) but attract 150 more people.

By studying the curve in Figure 11.1, we can see that at high prices, the vertical slope is fairly steep, signifying that demand is relatively price inelastic. In other words, a 25 percent cut in price (from $20.00 to $15.00) attracts only 14 percent more people. At a lower price level, the same 25 percent cut, from $10.00 to $7.50, attracts 46 percent more people, so in this price range demand is relatively price elastic. Toward the bottom end of the price scale, demand again becomes more price inelastic; a 67 percent cut in price from $3.00 to $1.00 generates only a 50 percent increase in the demand for seats. Between a $4.50 and $5.00 price, and again between a $12.00 and $15.00 price, the loss of admission is exactly compensated for by the increased price paid by each attender. Here we can say that the price-elasticity ratio is unity. The significance of this type of exercise lies in its ability to help a manager understand the trade-offs between revenue maximization and attendance maximization.

It may also be useful to group prospective attenders into *market segments,* based on their willingness or ability to pay particular prices. For instance, Table 11.2 shows that 400 more people would be attracted to the performance if the price were lowered from $7.50 to $5.00, and that another 650 would want to come if the price were dropped from $5.00 to $3.00. An important question facing the marketing manager is how to determine *who* the people are in each of these price segments.

Most theaters and auditoriums do not have a single, fixed admission price for performances. Instead, the price varies according to (1) the location of the seats and (2) the time of the performance. In establishing prices for different blocks of seats—a process known as scaling the house—it is important to identify what the demand for each price category will be, in order to determine the appropriate number of seats to offer at that price. Poor judgment on this score may result in large numbers of empty seats in some price categories and immediate sellouts (and disappointed customers) in other categories. Similarly, management needs to know theatergoers' habits and preferences as they relate to the scheduling of performances—matinees versus evenings, weekends versus weekdays, and possibly even seasonal variations. In each instance, the objective is to manage demand over time with a view to maximizing either attendance, revenues, or a combination of the two (for example, maximizing revenues, subject to a minimum attendance goal per performance of 70 percent of all seats sold).

Break-Even Analysis

Since managers need to know whether or not a new product will be self-supporting, the total *contribution margin* received from additional sales at any given price should be compared with the cost of supplying the product(s) in question.

To continue our example of ticket sales in an auditorium, suppose that the total cost (fixed plus variable) of staging a show is $4000. The contribution per ticket sold is the price of that ticket *less* any taxes or sales commissions. Dividing $4000 by the unit contribution will tell us how many tickets we need to sell at that price to break even—that is, to recover the costs of staging the show. Table 11.3 shows how break-even figures might be calculated at different prices, assuming a 10 percent tax and a 50¢ commission payable on all sales. The required sales volume can then be related to price sensitivity (will customers be willing to pay this much?), market size (is the market large enough to support this level of patronage?), and extent of competition (how strong an appeal do our competitors offer to potential customers?).

Just covering the costs of a particular show, or even making a surplus on it, does not necessarily guarantee financial solvency for the organization. There are also overheads to be covered, such as rent, utilities, and administrative salaries. Either the total surpluses achieved on all shows must cover these fixed costs, or grants and donations must be sought to bridge the gap. The value of break-even analysis is that it relates the demand characteristics of the market to the cost characteristics of the organization. It is a particularly useful tool for deciding whether or not to make an addition to the organization's product line and, if so, what price to charge.

Table 11.3 Calculating the Level of Sales Needed to Break Even

Retail Price ($)	Net of 10% Tax ($)	Unit Contribution ($) (Net of 50¢ Sales Commission)[a]	Break-Even Sales Volume (No. of Seats)[b]	Feasible?
20.00	18.00	17.50	229	Yes
15.00	13.50	13.00	308	Yes
12.00	10.80	10.30	388	Yes
10.00	9.00	8.50	471	Yes
7.50	6.75	6.25	640	Yes
5.00	4.50	4.00	1,000	Yes
4.50	4.05	3.55	1,127	Yes
3.00	2.70	2.20	1,818	No[c]
1.00	0.90	0.40	10,000	No[d]

[a]Assumes a flat rate commission of 50¢ is paid on all seats.

[b]Indicates number of seats that must be sold at that price to cover $4000 overhead (divide 4000 by unit contribution at that price). To determine how many seats must be sold to cover the overhead and, say, yield a $2500 profit, divide $6500 by the unit contribution.

[c]Capacity of hall is only 1500.

[d]Demand at that price is only 3000 (and hall capacity is only 1500).

Discounts and Subsidies

Many nonprofits have got themselves into financial difficulties by underpricing their services. Managers often argue that public and nonprofit organizations should price their services low in order to make them accessible to students, elderly people on fixed incomes, and low-income families or individuals. Laudable though this intent may be, the net result may be to set prices below the levels that other consumers are able and willing to pay.

Sentiment is growing among nonbusiness managers that, where possible and appropriate, prices should be set at levels that enable operating revenues to cover operating costs. If such an approach is seen as unrealistic in light of the target customer's ability and willingness to pay, then anticipated shortfalls should be specifically identified beforehand. Grants, donations, and tax subsidies are then targeted towards those products and programmable activities—such as research, lobbying and outreach, capital improvements, and new service development—that cannot be financed through direct user fees, as well as to cover planned operating shortfalls.

Grants and donations can also be used to subsidize the prices paid by those segments who cannot afford the full price. Scholarships, restricted discounts, and financial aid are some of the ways of reducing the price for those segments who genuinely need a "break," and whose participation actively advances the institutional mission.

Some nonprofits, which rely almost entirely on user fees for their income, use income-based sliding scales to provide a cross-subsidy mechanism. However, this approach must be used with care, as suggested by the following example of a Boston-based daycare center.[15] From its inception, the Oxford Street Daycare Cooperative in Cambridge, Mass., based tuition fees on a sliding scale. As the costs of providing daycare rose, new income categories were added at the top of the scale so that by the mid-1980s upper-income families paid more than double the tuition fees charged for the children of lower-income families. (About 20% of all places at the center were funded by grants from the Massachusetts Department of Social Security to help needy parents so that the discussion below relates to families paying their own tuition.)

During 1984–85, the Center found itself facing a serious financial crisis, with expenditures significantly outstripping revenues. A mid-year tuition increase was imposed across the board to cover the shortfall while the finance committee studied the situation. Two key problems were identified.

First, the tuition scale was the same for each of the four "rooms" in the center—infants (one year olds), toddlers (2 years), stompers (3 years), and pre-schoolers (4 years)—despite the fact that the cost incurred per child was almost twice as high for infants as for pre-schoolers. Essentially, the ratio of teachers to children decreased with age. Most competing centers set infant tuition higher than Oxford Street and pre-school tuition lower. As a result, Oxford Street's pre-school room was overpriced, especially for high income parents and there were frequently several vacancies in the room.

The problem was compounded by the fact that the annual tuition rate was set by equating the median price (on the nine-point sliding scale) to the average cost per child, assuming full enrollment.* Budgeted annual expenditures were simply divided by the number of children and by 12 months to arrive at the median tuition figure. Examination

---

*Although parents occasionally withdrew children during the year, the one-month security deposit held by the center was usually sufficient to offset tuition losses before a replacement child could be enrolled.

of enrollment data showed that the income distribution of parents was biased below the median, especially in the pre-school and stomper rooms which were not competitively priced for higher income parents.

The solutions adopted were basically threefold. First, it was decided that each room had to cover its costs (including its share of overheads) from tuition. This meant increases in fees for infants and toddlers, and decreases for stompers and pre-schoolers (which had the effect in making them competitively priced with other daycare centers). Second, the sliding scale was reduced to five income brackets, and a policy of "forced balancing" instituted. This meant that new families with below-median incomes would only be placed in one of the two lower tuition brackets for the room in question if there were another family paying tuition in a higher bracket to provide the necessary cross-subsidy.

These proposals were accepted by the parents for the following year, and Oxford Street's finances returned to stability. Because demand for good quality daycare was strong in the Boston area, especially for children under three, the center was able to fill all its slots at the new fee levels. In several instances, parents in lower income brackets enrolled their children initially at the median fee level, but were subsequently given a reduced rate because of successful balancing.

FORMULATING PRICING STRATEGY

By now it should be clear that determining pricing strategies in a nonbusiness organization requires making decisions on a range of different issues. These, in turn, must be based on both a clear understanding of the organization' s objectives and sound information on a range of relevant inputs.

Table 11.4 summarizes six major issues related to monetary pricing decisions, each of which can be further subdivided. This exhibit makes clear that although the first pricing decision is *how, much* to charge, the information needed for a complete pricing strategy extends much further.

How Much to Charge?

A realistic decision is critical for the financial solvency of the organization. First, the manager must determine what the costs are and then whether the organization is trying to cover just the variable costs associated with delivering the product or whether it is seeking to recover a share of the fixed costs, too. This decision may depend on the availability of donations or tax revenues to help cover all or part of these overheads.

Second, the manager must assess consumer sensitivity to different prices. In pricing to recover fixed costs, it is very important to be able to make an accurate prediction of sales volumes at different price levels. If a surplus is sought, an appropriate profit margin must be added on top of the costs. This step sets an average "floor" price for the product.

The level of competitive prices provides a third input. The greater the number of similar competing alternatives that appeal to consumers, and the more widely available they are, the greater will be the pressure on the marketing manager to keep prices at or below those of the competition. The next step may set a "ceiling" price in situations where competitive products are closely similar. The greater the difference between the floor and ceiling prices, the more room for maneuvering is available. If a ceiling price is *below* that of the floor price, a nonbusiness organization has two choices. One is to recognize that the

Table 11.4   Some Pricing Issues

---

1. **How Much Should Be Charged for This Product?**
   What costs is the organization attempting to recover?
   Is the organization trying to achieve a surplus by selling this product?
   How sensitive are customers to different prices?
   Does the support of donors and government agencies depend on the prices charged?
   What prices are charged by competitors?
   What discount(s) should be offered from basic prices?
   Are psychological pricing points (e.g., $4.95 versus $5.00) customarily used?

2. **Who Should Collect Payment?**
   The organization that provides the service
   A specialist intermediary (e.g., travel or ticket agent, bank, retailer, etc.)

3. **Where Should Prices Be Paid?**
   The location at which the product is delivered
   A convenient retail outlet or financial intermediary (e.g., bank)
   The purchaser's home (by mail or phone)

4. **When Should Prices Be Paid?**
   Before or after delivery of the product?
   At which times of day?
   On which days of the week?

5. **How Should Prices Be Paid?**
   Cash (exact change or not?)
   Check (how to verify?)
   Credit card
   Loan from financial intermediary
   Vouchers
   Third-party payment (e.g., insurance company, government agency)

6. **How Should Prices Be Communicated to the Target Market?**
   Communication medium
   Message content (how much emphasis should be placed on price?)
   Timing of messages

---

product is noncompetitive and either discontinue or modify it so that it becomes competitive at a higher price. The other is to seek third-party funding to cover some of the costs, thus allowing the product to be sold at a lower price.

A strategy of discounting from basic prices should be approached cautiously, since it dilutes the average price received and reduces the contribution from each sale. As the British Rail example showed, selective discounting may offer important opportunities to tap new market segments and fill capacity that would otherwise go unused. The challenge is to understand the price elasticities of different market segments and to discourage high-paying segments from taking advantage of discounts designed to lure more price-sensitive consumers.

Many social-service programs allow for discounting based on ability to pay. This raises the question of how to administer such programs once the criteria for eligibility have been selected. Willcox and Mushkin argue for the development of discount systems that will (1) carry a low administrative cost, (2) be reasonably convenient for those they are intended to benefit, (3) be sufficiently flexible to permit adaptation in the light of experience, and (4) avoid stigmatizing beneficiaries through scornful treatment by clerks or obvious segregation from full-price payers.[16]

Finally, once the approximate price level has been determined, a specific price must be set. This raises the question of whether to price in round numbers or to seek to create an impression of prices being slightly lower than they really are. Consumers may come to expect prices to be marginally lower than a round number—for instance, $3.95 or $5.75. If competitors promote such prices heavily, a strategy of charging $4.00 or $6.00 may convey an image of prices much higher than is really the case. On the other hand, rounded prices offer convenience and simplicity—benefits that may be appreciated by both consumers and salespeople.

Who Should Collect Payment?

The marketer must make it simple and convenient for the customer to obtain information, make reservations (for services), and offer payment. Sometimes an organization finds that this goal is best accomplished by delegating these tasks to intermediaries, thus freeing the organization to focus on service delivery. Examples include travel agents who make rail bookings, ticket agents who sell theater seats, banks that sell monthly transit passes, and stores that sell state or provincial lottery tickets. Although the service organization may have to pay a commission, the intermediary is usually able to offer customers greater convenience in terms of *where, when,* and *how* the price should be paid, as discussed in the previous chapter. Even after paying commissions, the use of intermediaries often offers a net savings in administrative costs to the primary organization.

Where Should Prices Be Paid?

Service organizations are not always conveniently located. Train stations, theaters, and concert halls, for instance, are often situated some distance from the areas where potential patrons live or work. In situations where consumers purchase a service before using it, there are obvious benefits to using intermediaries that are more conveniently located, or allowing payment by mail. A growing number of organizations now accept telephone reservations and sales by credit card; callers simply give their card numbers and have the charge billed directly to their accounts.

When Should Prices Be Paid?

Asking customers to pay for a product at the time they acquire or use it has disadvantages. First, customers may not be in a position to pay the full price immediately and so may desire credit. Unlike businesses, which are accustomed to providing customer credit by setting up charge accounts, most public and nonprofit organizations prefer to let other financial intermediaries take the responsibility (and the risk) of providing credit. We are now seeing growing acceptance of third-party credit cards among such institutions as passenger rail systems, universities, museum shops, and performing-arts organizations. Although the credit-card company charges a commission on each sale (typically 3–5 percent of the purchase price), the seller benefits from being able to offer greater convenience (which may attract new customers), handling smaller amounts of cash, and not having to worry about bad debts. The buyer benefits from the convenience of being able to postpone payment.

Among the nonbusiness organizations that provide credit are colleges and universities. Because tuition in the United States and Canada is so expensive, and because students often forgo full-time jobs in order to study for a degree, most institutions offer loans to needy students (although some do this with the aid of government funding). Managing student loans may not seem like a marketing task, but the availability of sufficient loans may be a determining factor in an accepted applicant's decision to attend a particular institution.

Prices can also be paid in advance of consumption. Sometimes it's inconvenient to pay each time a regularly patronized service—such as the mail or public transportation—is used; to save time and effort, customers may prefer the convenience of buying a roll of stamps or a monthly transit pass. Performing-arts organizations with limited funds and heavy up-front financing requirements often offer discounted subscription tickets in order to bring in money in advance. A different form of prepayment, involving the notion of insurance, is found in health-maintenance organizations in the United States, where members pay a fixed annual or monthly fee that entitles them to free (or minimally priced) care.

How Should Prices Be Paid?

As shown in Table 11.4, there are a variety of different ways of paying for a product. Cash may appear to be the simplest method, but it raises problems of security. One solution, adopted by most American and Canadian bus systems, is to require passengers to deposit the exact fare in a locked box so that the driver need carry no change; but this is inconvenient for customers.

Accepting payment by check for all but the smallest purchases is now fairly wide-spread among nonbusiness organizations and offers obvious customer benefits, although it may require controls by the organization to discourage bad checks. As noted earlier, there are also credit cards. In deciding whether or not to sign up with a major credit-card company, management needs to trade off the extra costs incurred (payment of commission, internal paperwork, need for working capital to finance delayed receipt of payments) against the anticipated benefits (increased sales, fewer bad debts from returned checks, better record keeping). Many business organizations offer customers the convenience of a credit account, but relatively few nonbusiness organizations do this, preferring to leave the provision of credit to third parties, through such procedures as bank loans and credit cards. Sometimes, though, it may be necessary to set up accounts for large purchasers (such as companies) who insist on monthly billing and settlements. The important thing for the marketing manager is not to allow the accounting department to dictate policy nor to force procedures on the organization that will increase costs more than it increases revenues.

Other payment procedures include using vouchers as supplements to (or instead of) cash, and directing the bill to a third party for payment (as often happens in health care). Vouchers are sometimes provided by social-service agencies to groups such as elderly or low-income people. Such a policy achieves the same benefits as discounting, without the need to publicize an array of different prices and to require those who collect the money to act as police (a role for which they may be unsuited and untrained).

Communicating Prices to the Target Markets

The final task, once each of the other issues has been addressed, is to decide how the organization's pricing policies can best be communicated to the target market(s). People need to know the price for some product offerings well in advance of purchase; they may also need to know how, where, and when that price is payable. It may be appropriate to relate the price to the costs of competing products or to alternative ways of spending one's money.

SUMMARY

Table 11.5 summarizes the questions that must be answered before a pricing strategy can be settled. Relating production and selling costs to any grants, donations, or subsidies that may be available helps to determine the net monetary cost to be recovered from customers. Time limitations are incorporated into planning by (1) evaluating capacity constraints (which may limit the number of customers the organization can serve at any one time), and (2) reviewing the organization's cash-flow needs.

If a public or nonprofit organization is to achieve its mission, it must have sufficient finances to maintain the quality of the operation. Although the revenues derived from customer payments for goods and services are not the only source of income for most public and nonprofit organizations, they are often the key to financial solvency. A good understanding of pricing theory and practice can make an important contribution to putting the organization on a sound financial footing.

Table 11.5 A Summary of Inputs to Pricing Decisions

---

1. Costs associated with the product
2. Availability of internal and external funds to subsidize operations
3. Total capacity available
4. Institution's need for up-front money
5. Extent and nature of competition in any given situation
6. Pricing policies of competitors
7. Potential market size for a specific product offering, reflecting:
   - Type of offering
   - Location
   - Scheduling
8. Additional costs (beyond purchase price) incurred by patrons or consumers
9. Price elasticity of potential customers, reflecting:
   - Different market segments
   - Variations in product characteristics
10. Purchasing behavior of potential customers
    How far in advance is purchase/use decision made?
    Preference for advance reservations, series/season tickets
    Preferred payment/reservation procedures
    - Payment made directly to originating organization versus payment through retail intermediary
    - Cash versus check or credit card
11. Alternative products offered by the organization
12. Changes in the external environment that may affect:
    - Customers' ability or willingness to pay
    - Nature of competition
    - Size of market (and segments within that market)
    - Organization's costs and financial situation
    - Ability of organization to determine preferred pricing policies without third-party "interference"

Early in the chapter, we emphasized that prospective customers can often be segmented according to their ability and willingness to pay. The challenge for marketing managers is to determine the price sensitivity of each segment and to devise ways of charging customers in each segment a price that reflects their differential ability to pay. Nonbusiness marketers in general may sometimes find themselves constrained by public expectations of a "fair" price; in the meantime, public agencies may be accused of discrimination if different segments are charged widely varying prices for what is perceived as the "same" service.

In this chapter we have shown that carefully developed pricing strategies involve much more than just setting a dollar price: they also require decisions on how, where, and when prices are to be paid, as well as how prices should be communicated to customers and who should take responsibility for collecting payment. Marketing managers should remember that the costs to a customer of making a specific exchange transaction frequently extend beyond the monetary price. Time, form, place, and psychic costs may constitute major barriers to the completion of a transaction. The possible influence of such costs cannot be ignored in any exchange, but they tend to assume particular significance when a product is offered to customers either at a nominal monetary sum or free of charge. Identifying, understanding, and trying to minimize these other costs are also parts of the marketer's task.

REFERENCES

1. David J. Schwartz, *Marketing Today: A Basic Approach,* New York: Harcourt Brace Jovanovich, 1977.
2. Seymour H. Fine, "Beyond Money—The Concept of Social Price," Chapter 5 in *The Marketing of Ideas and Social Issues,* New York: Praeger, 1981, pp. 81–90.
3. Jeffrey Manditch Prottas, "The Cost of Free Services: Organizational Impediments to Access to Public Services," *Public Administration Review* (September–October 1981), pp. 526–34.
4. A. M. Alfred, "Company Pricing Policy," *Journal of Industrial Economics* (November 1972), pp. 1–15.
5. Charles B. Weinberg, " Marketing Mix Decision Rules for Nonprofit Managers," in J. N. Sheth, *Research in Marketing,* Vol. 3, Greenwich, Conn.: JAI Press, 1979.
6. Penny Pittman Merliss and Christopher H. Lovelock, " "American Repertory Theatre," Case no. 9-580-133, Boston: HBS Case Services, Harvard Business School, 1980, p. 12.
7. Christopher H. Lovelock and Charles B. Weinberg, "The Role of Marketing in Improving Postal Service Effectiveness," in Joel Fleishman, *The Future of the Postal Service,* New York: Praeger, 1983.
8. Paul M. Wortman and Robert G. St. Pierre, "The Educational Voucher Demonstration: A Secondary Analysis," *Education and Urban Society* (August 1977), p. 471.
9. This and the following section are based, in part, on the discussion in Robert N. Anthony and Regina E. Herzlinger, *Management Control in Nonprofit Organizations,* 3rd edition, Homewood, Ill.: Richard D. Irwin, Inc., 1985.
10. Stephen J. Sansweet, "Catch-13—Californians Discover Tax Cut Mania has a Corollary: Fee Fever," *The Wall Street Journal* (June 1, 1979). Reprinted by permission of *The Wall Street Journal,* © Dow Jones & Company, Inc. 1979. All rights reserved.
11. Roger Ford, "Pricing a Ticket to Ride," *Modern Railways* (August 1977), pp. 302–305.
12. P. A. Keen, "Inter-City is a Moving Target," *Railway Gazette Internationai* (May 1979), pp. 407–411. Information updated to 1987.

13. Christopher H. Lovelock and Robert F. Young, "Look to Consumers to Increase Productivity," *Harvard Business Review* (May–June 1979), pp. 168–178.
14. Henry A. Sciullo, Eddie M. Goodin, and Philip E. Taylor, "Sunrise Hospital: A Case in Innovative Marketing Strategy,'" Case No. 9-578-691, Boston: Intercollegiate Case Clearing House, 1978.
15. Information supplied by Oxford Street Daycare Cooperative, Cambridge, Mass., 1987.
16. Marjorie C. Willcox and Selma J. Mushkin, "Public Pricing and Family Income: Problems of Eligibility Standards,'" in S. J. Mushkin (ed.), *Public Prices for Public Products*, Washington, D.C.: The Urban Institute, 1972, pp. 395–419.

PART 5

Making Contact with the Customer

Chapter 12

Distribution & Delivery Systems

Distribution is concerned with making desired goods and services available to consumers in a location and at a time that is convenient—the right product at the right time in the right place. Distribution's primary focus is on the development of time and place benefits for consumers of goods and services. Distribution strategy is relevant, too, for social-behavior programs. Efforts to facilitate and enforce desired behaviors must be made at appropriate times and locations. Similarly, supporting goods and services—such as energy-saving devices or alcoholism-treatment programs—must be available when and where needed.

Because the products of public and nonprofit organizations are predominantly services, the design of the service-delivery system assumes particular importance. In many instances, consumption takes place at the site of the service provider and is simultaneous with final production of the service. Manufactured consumer goods usually flow through physical channels from a factory to retail outlets, but in service organizations, the retail service location often *is* the producer or "factory." Hospitals, the performing arts, and transit services are examples of this. Both the site itself and the manner of delivering a service can influence the way consumers see the product and determine whether or not they are satisfied with it. Success requires that management coordinate activities from both an operations standpoint and a marketing (or user) viewpoint.

Operating schedules are of concern to service marketers because many services are perishable and cannot be stored for later use. Thus an orchestra cannot use its Tuesday-night performance to satisfy audience members who wish to attend a live concert on Saturday night, and a transit system's excess capacity at midday does not relieve congestion during the commuting hours.

The location and accessibility of sites at which services are provided—the retail outlet—are also particularly important. Numerous studies have shown that usage of many services declines as the distance of the site from the consumer's home or work location increases. Table 12.1 illustrates this decline for two organizations. In the first example, 60 percent of a community center's members come from families living within two miles of the center, although this area includes only 25 percent of the population in the five-mile area the center is designed to serve. In the second example, more than two-thirds of the subscribers to a university's performing-arts series live on campus or immediately adjacent

Table 12.1   Usage Declines as Distance Increases

(1) Membership in a Community Center in California		
Radius from Community Center (miles)	Population, %	Membership, %
1	5	15
2	20	45
3	30	15
4	30	10
5	15	5
	100	90[a]
(2) Subscribers to a University Performing Arts Series[b]		
University addresses		70
Immediately adjacent communities		400
Within 30 minutes drive		160
More than 30 minutes drive		50

[a]Ten percent of members live more than 5 miles from the site. Based on an analysis of Zip Code records of members.

[b]Total residential population increases as distance from university increases.

to it, even though a majority of the area's population lives further away. Accessibility—measured by travel time instead of by geographic distance—often proves to be a key variable in determining patronage of a service.

As the three examples in Figure 12.1 illustrate, a variety of distribution channel structures can occur. The first example shows a frequently appearing structure for the distribution of physical goods—in this case drawn from the vantage point of a museum shop. The example illustrates the variation that is seen in the length of a distribution channel; on the one hand, the museum shop is the only intermediary between local artisans and the ultimate purchaser who shops at the museum, and on the other hand, the gift shop is only one of several intermediaries between a publisher and the eventual purchaser of the book. Managing the interrelationships among different channel members and assuring an adequate supply of physical goods and their efficient movement through the distribution system (as well as the management of the retail site itself) are important concerns in the distribution and delivery of products. The second example illustrates a situation frequently present in public and nonprofit organizations: the agency—here a bus system—provides a service using its own facilities. Management must be concerned with the number and location of sites, their manner of operation, and the personnel and facilities with which the customer comes in contact. As we will see later in the chapter, the customer often interacts directly with only some of the personnel and part of the facility; the remaining portion, the "technical" core, may be at a separate geographic location and managed primarily for operational efficiency, provided that prespecified customer-service standards are met. The third example illustrates a distribution system for a social-behavior agency that has no direct contact with its market target—in this case, parents and their children who should be immunized against childhood diseases. The distribution problems are complex; if the agency is to be successful, it needs to make sure that medical services and supplies are available for the immunization to take place. In addition, the agency may need to manage relationships with government departments that enforce health regulations. As these examples illustrate, successful management of distribution and delivery systems requires coordination of a network of organizations and a variety of functional areas.

Scope of the Chapter

In this chapter, we will examine important issues that arise in the management of distribution and service-delivery systems. We will begin with an example examining the impact of recent changes in the delivery of medical care in the United States. The balance of the chapter is divided into five major sections.

The first section discusses customer-user factors that are important in the design of distribution systems. Next the chapter turns to the decisions involved in two important

Physical Distribution Channels (Museum Gift Shop)

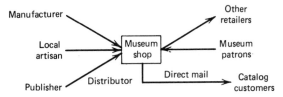

Production and Delivery System for Customer Contact Services (Bus System)

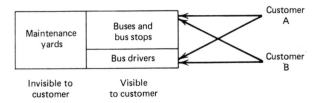

Distribution Systems for Social—Behavior Programs (Immunization of Children)

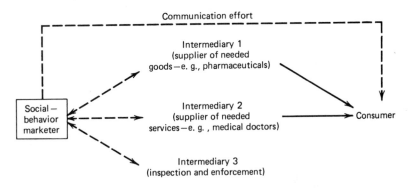

Figure 12.1 Examples of different distribution channels.

areas: choosing locations and operating schedules for the provision of services. The third section examines the nature of distribution systems for physical goods, looking at both the use of direct mail and the role of intermediaries and the functions they perform: many service organizations also market ancillary physical goods; a nation's treasury department produces coins and currency, museums sell souvenirs and reproductions of artworks, and conservation organizations market such products as books, calendars, shirts, and posters. The fourth section examines the transfer of the concept of physical distribution to service organizations and the role of intermediaries in the delivery of services. Finally, the chapter discusses distribution issues in social-behavior marketing.

HOSPITALS RESPOND TO CHANGING PATTERNS IN HEALTH SERVICES AND DELIVERY

Historically, the primary role of hospitals has been to provide inpatient acute care. Economic, technological, social, and political forces are now changing the way people obtain medical services with the consequent substitution of outpatient for inpatient care. Between 1982 and 1986, hospital admissions in the United States fell from 37.8 to 33.0 million persons.[1] Both for-profit and nonprofit hospitals are hurting. New alternative health-delivery systems, such as health-maintenance organizations (HMOs) and freestanding (physically apart from a hospital) emergency-care facilities, have achieved success. To cope with these environmental and competitive forces, hospitals need to consider new approaches to distributing health-care services.[2]

Multisite Strategies

Multihospital systems, such as the Samaritan Health Service of Phoenix, Arizona, are becoming more prevalent. Samaritan operates a nonprofit multihospital system, comprising a major hospital with sophisticated treatment facilities in Phoenix and satellite hospitals elsewhere in the state.

Emergency rooms are an important feeder system for hospitals—often accounting for a significant percentage of hospital admissions. Consequently, innovative hospitals have opened freestanding emergency rooms that offer most of the services that hospital-based emergency rooms do except for full-scale surgery that requires general anesthesia. Samaritan Health Service has established a freestanding emergency room in an eastern suburb of Phoenix to feed the easternmost satellite hospital in the Samaritan group with emergency cases requiring hospitalization.

Outreach Programs

One way to increase the size of the geographic market covered by a hospital is to develop transportation systems that make the hospital more accessible to patients. One of the most elaborate of these serves the 1100-bed University of Iowa Hospitals and Clinics, located in Iowa City, a town of approximately 60,000 people. To survive, Iowa Hospitals cannot rely on patients from Iowa City alone; consequently, the system operates a fleet of vehicles that can bring patients to the hospital from any location in Iowa. This service has made it more convenient for physicians to use the Iowa Hospitals' sophisticated capital-intensive facilities (for open-heart surgery, cancer therapy, kidney transplant, and so forth).

In addition, the hospital owns and operates an emergency helicopter service that is linked to the trauma center, which can dispatch a helicopter and put paramedical personnel into remote accident sites within minutes.

Multiservice Provider

As inpatient hospitalization costs continue to escalate, substitute methods for providing health care will emerge. One way for a hospital to cope with this change is to provide new services that use the physical facilities of the hospital. In many larger hospitals, for example, a significant portion of prehospital care is now provided in outpatient facilities operated by the hospital. For example, at the University of Chicago Medical Center, the hospitals and clinics handle more than 220,000 outpatient visits annually.

Another innovative service is outpatient or day surgery. Many patients prefer day surgery because it minimizes time away from work and is more convenient than a hospital stay. Many hospitals, as well as private physicians, have established day-surgery programs that offer all the logistical support needed for surgery. Patients are prepared in their physicians' offices in advance of the visit. They arrive at the facility in the morning for surgery, spend the day recuperating in the facility—frequently with friends or family present—and go home in the evening.

Vertical Integration

The distribution systems for many organizations are often characterized by the presence of intermediaries who provide services for the user before and/or after the organization provides service. In the case of hospitals, a patient's personal physician or an emergency room serves as intermediary. (Figure 12.2 indicates some of the organizations and people with which a potential patient might interact on entering a hospital.) Hospitals, in turn, may be a prior step for those entering nursing homes. Vertical analysis of a distribution channel includes analysis of the number of levels in the channel, what functions are performed at each level, and where the control in each channel lies. Some distribution strategies for hospitals amount to vertical integration into nonacute health care and capturing and controlling more of the hospital's patient flow. Other vertical strategies include constructing a medical office building adjacent to the hospital and developing outpatient facilities that are linked to the hospital by common medical staff, even if legally or physically separate.

Examples of these last two strategies can be found at Rush-Presbyterian-St. Luke's Hospital and Medical Center in Chicago. Rush constructed offices adjacent to the hospital that are leased to more than 200 physicians. The private practices of many of its voluntary staff are carried out in the building, which has its own ancillary laboratory and radiology facilities, as well as facilities for outpatient surgery. Rush also developed a network of community-based outpatient facilities under separate incorporation from the parent hospital. The Mile Square Health Center, Inc., named for the mile-square area of inner city around the hospital, serves 125,000 patients annually. The center is affiliated with the Medical College at Rush, which provides academic appointments and teaching opportunities for the center's salaried medical staff. After the establishment of these two organizations, Rush closed its hospital-based outpatient department, relying on these two captive but corporately independent distribution systems, its emergency room, and extensive referrals from physicians in the Chicago area to fill its hospital.

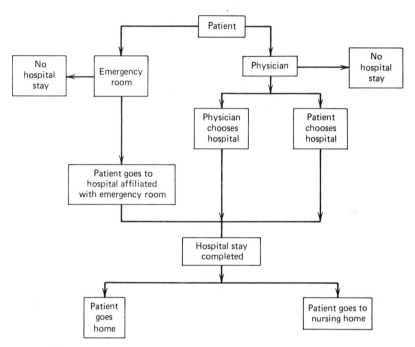

Figure 12.2   Example of alternative flow patterns for hospital patients.

New means of distributing health-care services are rapidly developing. As these brief examples show, hospitals must adapt to changing customer, competitor, and environmental conditions by altering their traditional role as providers of inpatient acute-care services. We will see that many of the principles involved in the design of distribution systems are applicable to the challenges that hospitals face.

MEETING USER NEEDS IN THE DESIGN OF DELIVERY SYSTEMS

The design of a delivery system should begin with an understanding of the consumer's needs in purchasing and using a product. Of course, this is a standard marketing approach, but it is particularly relevant here because the consumption of many services takes place at the site of the organization providing the service. In Chapter 6, we discussed consumer behavior generally. In this section we concentrate on those aspects of consumer behavior that are particularly relevant for designing and managing a distribution system in which goods and/or services are delivered directly to users.

Amount and Character of Shopping Effort

How much time and effort are consumers willing to devote to shopping for goods and services? Often it turns out to be surprisingly little.[3] For example, one energy department official proposed setting up conservation displays in a few large stores. The premise was that most appliance buyers would see these displays and then be motivated to buy energy-efficient brands and models. Survey data showed that the typical buyer visits three stores or fewer before making a purchase, however, and many go to only one store. Consequently, a great many displays would be required to reach a large proportion of appliance buyers. The plan was abandoned because the department's budget was inadequate to provide the extensive distribution that consumer analyses showed would be necessary.

Even in health-related areas, people often spend little time comparing or looking for service providers. How much time, for example, did you devote to the choice of your personal physician or dentist? Did you interview different practitioners and review their backgrounds? What type of comparison shopping did you carry out? Many patronage decisions are based on convenient location and are only minimally affected by other factors. Hence marketing managers need to examine the amount of shopping effort that users are willing to expend and use this information to locate service sites appropriately.

Consumer products can be subdivided into *convenience, shopping,* and *specialty* products, depending on the amount of time and effort the user is willing to devote to acquiring the good or to obtaining or using the service.

For *convenience products,* the consumer is usually well informed about the various alternatives and wants to acquire that product with a minimum of effort. Quite often, in response to these demands, distribution systems have grown up that are easily accessible. For example, daily newspapers are widely available in a variety of stores and in vending machines as well as by home delivery, the ultimate convenience. Many convenience services—such as retail banking—are low cost and frequently purchased; either the consumer is aware of a range of competitors and has limited brand preference or the distribution system provides extensive variety. Curing a headache can generally be dealt with by a visit to any pharmacy; formal medical care is unlikely to be needed.

Shopping products are those for which the user is willing to spend a moderate amount of effort to compare alternatives or to acquire the service. Home appliances are shopping products, and personal physicians and dentists may be as well. The consumer may not be as knowledgeable about the good or service provided as when shopping for convenience products, and may use the shopping experience as a means to become better informed. Shopping products are usually more important than convenience products to the consumer for financial, health, or other reasons.

Specialty products are those for which the consumer is willing to devote considerable effort in order to acquire the desired product. Often a consumer will forego more accessible alternatives in order to obtain the particular good or service desired. Thus a prospective college student may be willing to travel across the continent to enroll at a particular school; an opera fan may be willing to spend several hours in transit to hear a famous opera singer perform; a patient with a serious medical problem may be prepared to search and travel extensively to find the facility and medical specialists able to provide the necessary treatment.

The convenience/shopping/specialty classification system is a useful framework to apply to distribution decisions. If consumers do not classify an organization's products as "specialty" ones, the organization must either develop intensive distribution policies or recognize that some parts of the market will be lost. Of course, not all consumers classify products in the same manner; for example, not all would be willing to travel long distances away from home to acquire a college education. People devote different amounts of effort to the choice of a family physician. Nevertheless, the tripartite classification system is useful.

An organization should also realize that it can sometimes change the classification of its products by adding distinctive characteristics that compel at least some users to treat that organization's offerings as specialty products. An organization may find that one of the advantages of having distinctive offerings is that there is less need to distribute its products intensively because users are willing to travel for a longer time to acquire or use such products.

Value of Time and Place Utility

Closely related to the shopping-effort classification system is the value of time and place utility—that is, how important the time it takes to find out and obtain a good or service is in a consumer's decision to use that product. While time-and-place utility does not provide a convenient three-level classification, it covers a wider range of goods and services.

Time and place utility appears to be an important factor in the decision to utilize services that have to be consumed on the site of the provider. Patronage of performing-arts organizations, community centers, and numerous other service providers decreases among more distant prospective customers, as Table 12.1 illustrated.

In response, many organizations have attempted to use branching strategies. A community center may put on programs in school buildings or other rented facilities for those who don't live or work near the main facility. Or the center may actually own branch offices in suburban locations. Performing-arts organizations may offer concerts in suburban locations as well as in its traditional home base. The San Francisco Symphony often performs a concert several times in San Francisco, and then repeats it in Alameda or Contra Costa County to the east and near San Jose to the south. This strategy attracts an audience that enjoys the music but is unwilling to travel 20–50 miles to San Francisco to hear the symphony.

Information, Reservation, and Payment Activities

Before deciding to use a product, a consumer may want to learn more about it. Upon deciding to use a product, a consumer may need to make a reservation or pay for use in advance. Although many of these steps can be separated from the actual use of the product, some organizations traditionally have not allowed for their separation. For example, some transit systems still do not have a monthly pass system for commuters and insist on exact-fare payment at the time of use. Although many performing-arts organizations allow purchasers to buy tickets by mail or telephone, often the only way to find out specifically what seats are available is to go to the box office.

For economic or technical reasons, many services can only be provided at a single or a very limited number of sites. Consumer research often reveals that a consumer proceeds through a number of distinct steps before using the service. Management needs to determine whether any steps in this process can be redesigned so as to make the services easier for the consumer to obtain. For example, some performing arts organizations have broken the process into four steps: (1) information acquisition about the event and price, (2) reservation, (3) payment, and (4) attendance (see Table 12.2). In turn, some of these steps can be delegated either to other marketing functional areas or to intermediaries who may be more efficient operationally and/or convenient for users. To illustrate, many performing-arts groups have found that advertising and direct-mail brochures can more efficiently

Table 12.2 Examples of Decentralization Alternatives for Information, Reservation and Payment Activities

Activity Information	Performing-Arts Organizations	Local Transit Systems
Information	Brochures mailed to subscribers and others on mailing list (mailing lists may be shared with other organizations), by advertising, or by telephone answering service in operation at all hours	Schedules may be distributed with salary checks by employers on main routes, billboards can be seen by travelers, advertising, or signs at transit stops
Reservation	Retail ticket agencies, telephone service provided by outside organizations, or telephone service answered at box office	Not applicable except in special cases. For dial-a-ride services, telephone reservations for one-time or recurrent usage. For commuter buses serving a limited number of employers, employee benefits office may reserve spaces
Payment	By mail, by telephone if credit cards are accepted, at ticket agencies, or not required until time of performance	Applies primarily when multitrip tickets and commuter passes are offered. Payment by mail, payroll deduction, or at banks and other retail outlets

provide much information about upcoming events than box-office personnel can. Some arts organizations have joined computer-based ticket agencies that have capabilities identical to those of the main box office to provide ticket information, accept payments, and issue tickets. If the ticket issuer also accepts credit cards as a method of payment, the consumer can minimize time and place costs by handling the entire transaction on the telephone. In a parallel situation, the U.S. National Park Service has contracted with ticket agencies to allow campers to make reservations through these agencies.

Hospitals have seen the development of similar concepts. As mentioned earlier, the number of inpatient hospital days has declined. One reason is that a number of pre- and postsurgical steps can be performed in the doctor's office or the patient's home. There are even situations in which diagnostic equipment can be applied to the patient by paramedical personnel (or the patient in person) and the resulting data transmitted electronically to the doctor at a distant location.

In general, the focus is on discovering what portions of the usage process can be performed separately and the costs and benefits of doing so.

Timing of Demand

A frequent problem in services marketing is matching the timing of demand to service availability. The problem is compounded by the fact that services cannot be stored for later use. While providing capacity to meet demand can be clearly categorized as a distribution problem, the full range of marketing capabilities and functions is often used to deal with, and in some cases alter, the timing of demand. Distribution management can take the lead in setting such strategies.

In some instances, the timing of demand is largely under the control of the user. For example, individuals themselves usually decide when to attend a performing-arts event. In other instances, the timing of demand is under the control of a third party. For example, some transit agencies have tried to deal with morning and afternoon commuter peaks by offering discounts to off-peak riders. Unless employers change the hours of the workday, however, the program will have little impact on commuters. If the timing of demand is derived from a third party, marketing programs must be addressed both to immediate users and to these third parties.[4]

Failure on the part of some organizations to provide service when demanded can be an opportunity for others. For instance, some emergency rooms and health clinics have prospered by offering 24-hour service on a no-appointment basis. Some patients who are not acutely ill but who have no physician or other means of getting care use emergency rooms. In many underserved areas, as many as two-thirds of the visits may be non-emergency cases.

Public organizations often do not offer *opening hours* that meet the expressed preferences of users. For example, the vast growth of evening and Sunday retail shopping has not been matched by a change in opening hours of municipal, state, and federal government offices that deal directly with the public. Only a few such offices are open at times other than weekday mornings and afternoons—inconvenient hours for most working people. Similarly, many museums are open only for such regular hours as 9 to 5 on weekdays, one weeknight, and part of the weekend. To the extent that the target market is working people, "regular" hours might better be weeknights, the entire weekend, and one day a week! It should be noted, however, that one difficulty in establishing such a schedule is the willingness of the organization's employees and volunteers to work such a timetable.

Sometimes management can employ marketing strategies involving a number of functional areas to *alter the timing of demand*. Price and other incentives can be used to motivate some people to use facilities in off-peak hours. For example, many theaters offer lower-price tickets for weeknight performances. A reservation system can be used to deflect excess demands from one time period to the next. A reservation system also helps people who cannot or will not alter the time at which they use a service. Although these people may be disappointed if they cannot obtain a reservation, at least they do not have to wait in vain for a service that is not delivered. For customers who use the service, satisfaction is improved because total waiting time is reduced.

In many situations, however, the timing of demand cannot be changed. For example, hours of work still dictate the peak use of transportation systems, and full-time university students are still largely tied to a fall-to-spring academic year.

Organizations can sometimes turn to becoming multiservice providers *to fill the off-peak periods*. Some transit systems operate different route patterns—oriented toward shopping areas—during the daytime hours. Universities offer a wide variety of noncredit courses in the evenings, on weekends, and during vacation periods; in addition, some use their dormitories as "hotels" and their physical-education facilities and grounds as campsites during the summer. For example, the University of British Columbia (UBC) in Vancouver has a large campus with excellent athletic facilities. During the summer, UBC offers a variety of one, two, and three-week sports programs to appeal to Vancouver youths. Additionally UBC utilizes its dormitories to house boys from all over the province of British Columbia who participate in one-week residential hockey camps. To help meet demand by summer tourists for hotel space, rooms in the newest dormitories are rented to campus visitors when UBC is not in session.

Timing of demand is a particular concern because the costs of operating the delivery system are tied more closely to the capacity of the system to provide service than to the number of individual users. Once a system for operating—say, a 200-bed hospital—is established, then whether the hospital is serving 140 or 160 patients, the total costs of running the hospital are relatively stable. Transit systems, visual- and performing-arts organizations, and many other service providers share the dilemma of managing both excess capacity and excess demand, but at different times.

The problem is intensified in situations where it is difficult to estimate demand. Management must balance the desire to avoid the costs of excess capacity and the dissatisfaction of users who cannot obtain the service they desire. The latter can occur because potential users are turned away—as when a theater is sold out—or receive incomplete service—as when visitors are rushed through a popular museum exhibit.

LOCATING AND OPERATING SERVICE FACILITIES

Where should an organization have its facilities and how many facilities should it have? Is an organization better off having one large facility, many small facilities, or a combination of full-service and limited-service centers? Should new facilities be opened or existing facilities closed? All these are vital distribution decisions for management.

Accessibility

As was pointed out in the previous section, location—or, perhaps more properly, convenience of location and ease of access—is an important determinant of usage. Any decision with regard to location has to be considered from the vantage point of how it will affect the level of usage and the composition of users, as the following example from a marketing audit shows.

The Vancouver Chamber Choir (VCC) is a professional choir with an outstanding reputation. Despite the existence of several competitors, its concerts held in the 500-seat Ryerson Church, located in a residential area of Vancouver, are usually filled near to capacity. A downtown church with 1250-seat capacity has expressed a desire to attract cultural functions. It has offered a rental fee only slightly more than that charged by Ryerson. This would avoid VCC's having to turn people away from a concert.

There is a risk of losing part of the current audience in moving downtown. Significant portions of the audience (such as senior citizens) may enjoy the convenience of walking to Ryerson; others may value not having to travel downtown, even if they cannot walk. The possibility of a negative reaction to this move should be investigated by means of market research. If there is much dissatisfaction, an alternative would be to increase the number of performances held at Ryerson, but weekday nights would have to be scheduled. This may also be inconvenient and should be investigated.

Location is more important for some services than for others. By definition, users will generally be willing to travel longer distances and to spend more time getting to sites where specialty rather than convenience services are offered. Additionally, other product characteristics may be traded off for locational convenience. Some public school systems have found that parents are more willing to accept the closing of neighborhood schools if parents are offered a choice of school types beyond the standard one, such as schools that focus on the fundamentals ("3 Rs"), "open learning" schools, and schools that feature special programs in the arts or athletics.

As the example of University of Iowa Hospitals indicates, service providers may use specially developed transportation systems to expand the size of the geographic market that can be served within a given time period. In other words, the dedicated transportation system increases the proportion of Iowa's population that lives within one hour of the hospital.

The actual or potential impact of competition must also be remembered. As long as geographic convenience is a significant factor in the user's deciding which alternative to use or whether to utilize a service at all, organizations must think in terms of preemptive and reactive site-location strategies.

In selecting a site, a manager should keep in mind the retailer's classic statement of the three factors most critical for success: "location, location, location."

Operations Perspectives

While a user perspective argues for more convenient locations, the costs of establishing and maintaining a facility and the need for operational efficiency and control often argue for a more concentrated strategy. Additionally, the technology of providing services prevents complete atomization of the delivery system. To obtain minimum economies of scale, community centers, hospitals, performing arts halls, museums, and many others must exceed a certain size if they are to function efficiently (although the optimum size of these organizations may vary widely).

As was discussed in more detail in Chapter 11, it is useful to divide costs into three different types—fixed, semivariable, and variable.[5] Fixed costs, at least in the short run, tend to stay constant over a wide range of volume, while variable costs vary directly with the amount of usage of the service. For many organizations, the majority of operating costs are semivariable and vary with the capacity to provide services. For example, if it is decided to open a library in the evening, more of the costs will vary because of the change in opening hours than because of an increase in number of books lent. That is, a 20 percent increase in opening hours will have a greater impact on cost than a 20 percent increase in library usage.

As the number of facilities, the amount of usage per facility, and the total amount of usage increase, the service organization can realize economies of scale at the facility level, the market-area level, and the organization level.

1. *Facility level.* For a given service facility, there are some costs such as the cost of the manager and license fees that are fixed and other costs such as labor, energy, and maintenance that have a fixed component. As per facility volume increases, these fixed costs on a per service unit delivered basis decline.

2. *Area level.* For a given market area that can contain a number of facilities, there are also economies of volume available. For example, supervisory and marketing expenses on both a per facility and a per service unit delivered in the area basis decrease as the number of facilities and the usage of these facilities increase.

3. *Organizational level.* At this level, there are economies of volume in the administrative, purchasing, and financing areas. As more service units are delivered, the lower the administrative expenses per unit delivered. As the organization grows in both number of facilities in operation and number of service units delivered, it often achieves the bargaining power to negotiate lower prices for its equipment and supplies.[6]

In some regards, operating economies argue for larger service units and for one organization to manage multiple facilities. For example, there are now a number of successful multisite nonprofit (as well as for-profit) hospital organizations, such as the Samaritan Hospital system in Arizona.

Operating economies are not the whole story, however. Most critically, there must be sufficient demand to support larger facilities. Because locational convenience is such a major factor in deciding whether to use a service or in choosing among alternative service providers, one large facility may not be able to generate the same level of usage or the same amount of satisfaction among users as several smaller, more conveniently located facilities.

Additionally, as a service organization becomes larger, the complexity of managing either one large facility or multiple sites increases. In fact, the diseconomies of managing a complex multisite/multiservice organization can sometimes outweigh the economies obtained from increasing volume. Additionally, larger organizations face the danger of becoming more bureaucratic and less flexible in responding to change.

Demand Generation and Economic Efficiency

Organizations have found several ways to cope with the twin pressures of user satisfaction—arguing for convenient location—and operating economies—suggesting larger scales of operation. One approach is to examine the service-delivery process and to separate the customer-contact functions from those involving little contact with customers (this latter part is sometimes termed the *technical core*). An organization can then decouple the technical core from the customer-contact portion of the organization and manage the technical core to obtain economies of scale and the customer-contact function to provide user satisfaction and demand stimulation. For example, a blood-collection station should be "operated with the psychological and physiological needs of the donor in mind and, in fact, often takes the 'service' to the donor by using bloodmobiles. The blood itself is processed at specialized facilities (bloodbanks) following 'manufacturing' procedures common to batch processing."[7]

Similarly, postal systems can decouple their customer-contact functions from the mail-processing functions. Sometimes, however, organizations fail to recognize this distinction. For example, the United States Postal Service (USPS) initially offered its over-the-counter, overnight Express Mail service at a limited number of post offices, some of which did not seem to have been selected with customer convenience in mind. They were often main postal stations, economic from an operations perspective, but located at some distance from the types of customers most likely to use the service on a walk-in basis. This strategy may have resulted in loss of business to competitors that offered less restrictive pickup services or more convenient dropoff locations than did USPS.

Another way to cope with the dual pressure of consumer demand and operating efficiencies is to use a branching strategy in which only a limited range of services are provided at branches and a fuller range of services at major facilities. The services at the main center are usually chosen either because they are of a specialty or shopping nature, so that potential users are willing to spend more time traveling to reach them, or because the economics or capital costs involved in providing the service at a central site are so compelling. Again, the Samaritan Hospital system provides an example of this strategy. Samaritan operates both freestanding and hospital-based emergency rooms, local satellite hospitals that provide acute patient care, and major hospital centers that provide sophisticated, capital-intensive facilities.

A third approach employed by organizations is to expand the range of services offered at a facility. To take full advantage of already existing sites or to justify economically the establishment of a new facility, an organization can broaden the range of services provided. This expansion can include becoming a retailer or host for other organizations. Rental of university, performing-arts, and community-center facilities to other organizations is now commonplace. More innovative has been the effort of the British Post Office, which has developed its nearly, 23,000 post offices into retail outlets for a broad range of government services. To quote a recent advertisement, it has become:

> Not so much a Post Office, more a community centre. . . . Selling stamps, and postal orders, accepting parcels and telegrams, of course. But also handling dog, driving, and car licences, paying pensions and allowances, selling Government securities, providing information for all-comers, and branches of the Girobank, most of them open on Saturdays too.[8]

Of course, operating a multiservice site is a complex task. Counter personnel must be trained to handle a wide array of transactions, ranging from sale of a single first-class postage stamp to delivering financial services with a value equal to that of several thousand postage stamps. A broad mix of users may be in a post office at any one time, and the facility must be managed so as to satisfy these users' widely varying needs.

Tangible Characteristics of the Service Facility

The tangible characteristics and the ambience of a service facility are important for two major reasons. First, these characteristics contribute to the user's overall satisfaction with the service. This can happen even though the primary tangible characteristics may be secondary to the basic service. For example, New York City subway cars are covered inside and out with graffiti. Although the graffiti have no impact on the speed and reliability of service, they may well decrease total satisfaction on the part of the rider. Second, "customers evaluate what they can't see—i.e., the service itself, by what they can see—e.g., the location and decor of the office, the demeanor and appearance of the office staff and principal service providers."[9] The tangible aspects of the facility and its production capabilities help attract the attention of prospective users, suggest the quality and the nature of the services offered, and provide support or evidence that promised benefits will be forthcoming. To illustrate, consider this example.

> Physicians' offices provide an interesting example of intuitive environmental management. Although the quality of medical service may be identical, an office furnished in teak and leather creates a totally different "reality" in the consumer's mind from one with plastic slipcovers and inexpensive prints. Carrying the example further, [consider the change in image that would result from] painting a physician's office walls neon pink or silver, instead of white.[10]

The service facility should be designed and operated to enhance, or at least maintain, user satisfaction.

CHANNELS OF DISTRIBUTION FOR PHYSICAL GOODS

Some public and nonprofit organizations exist primarily to sell goods as opposed to services. In Northern Canada, Eskimos and Indians have established government-funded artist cooperatives to distribute native carvings and paintings to art collectors, souvenir hunters, and gift buyers throughout North America. More frequently, physical goods are ancillary to the services provided by the organization. Thus some family-planning agencies sell contraceptive devices, many museums operate gift shops, and environmental groups such as the Sierra Club sell books and calendars. Distribution costs often account for more than half the delivered cost of physical goods, and management attention to the distribution function can be vital.

Distribution management consists of two major areas: (1) logistics (or physical distribution), which is concerned with the activities involved in physically moving and storing goods, and (2) channels, the design and management of a distribution organization of perhaps independently owned and operated resellers. To the extent that intermediaries perform some of the logistical activities, the two functional areas are interrelated.

The Physical Distribution Function

Physical distribution is a complex management function involving a wide range of activities, including transportation, order processing, warehousing, and inventory management. Physical distribution needs to be managed on a systems basis and not necessarily to minimize the cost of each element. For example, a system may achieve lowest total costs by combining a limited number of warehouses and low inventory levels with frequent use of air freight to meet customer-service standards for delivery time and reliability. Another organization may find that the most efficient alternative is to have numerous depots but use inexpensive transportation. The critical cost factor is not individual elements in the system but total distribution system costs.

Beyond looking at costs, physical-distribution management must also consider the impact of service-delivery standards on customer satisfaction and demand. At the retail level, failure to have an item in stock (e.g., a Sierra Club book) can result in lost sales. In the ideal case, there should be an understanding of the relationship between demand and service levels. In this case, the concept of total distribution cost can be expanded to include the cost of customer ill will and lost sales from being out of stock and delivering late.

Functions Performed by Channel Members

A channel is the system by which the producer's output is brought to the consumer. Although the stereotypical distribution channel for consumer goods is

manufacturer → wholesaler → retailer→ consumer

there are many variants on this model. One organization can use a variety of channels. For example, in Figure 12.3, we see that the Sierra Club markets its books directly to members by mail order and to others through bookstores, which in turn are served by book distributors.

The functions performed by intermediaries are many beyond transporting, storing, and displaying the items. They include the following activities.

Selling
Promoting the product to potential customers.

Buying
Purchasing a variety of products from various sellers, usually for resale.

Assorting
Providing an assortment of items (often interrelated) for potential customers.

Financing
Offering credit to potential customers to facilitate the transaction; also providing funds to sellers to help them finance their affairs.

Storage
Protecting the product and maintaining inventories to offer better customer service.

Sorting
Buying a quantity and breaking bulk items into amounts desired by customers.

Grading
Judging products and labeling them as to quality.

Transportation
Physically moving the product between manufacturer and end user.

Market information
Providing information to manufacturers about market conditions including expected sales volume, fashion trends, and pricing conditions.

Risk taking
Absorbing business risks, especially risks of maintaining inventories, product obsolescence, etc.

These functions must be performed somewhere in the distribution channel—by the producer, intermediary, or end user. Although one person can "cut out the middleman," the entire market cannot. The critical question is not whether these functions are to be carried out, but who is to perform them.

Intermediaries are used because they increase the efficiency of the overall system. A system of four producers selling to five retailers requires a total of twenty transactions; a system of four producers selling to one multiline wholesaler who serves five retailers

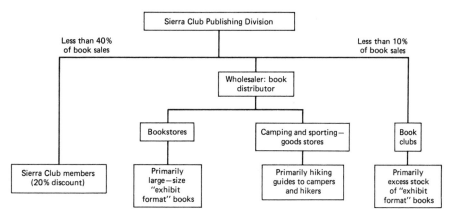

Figure 12.3   Selected channels of distribution for Sierra Club book sales.[11]

requires only nine transactions. Intermediaries may also be used because they possess abilities and strengths that producers do not; book wholesalers and distributors have established access to retail outlets that the Sierra Club cannot duplicate.

On the other hand, the use of intermediaries involves *reduced control* by the producer over a number of important functions. For example, the Sierra Club does not even control the price at which retailers sell their books; the club can only list a "suggested retail price." Few producers of physical goods have the capacity to distribute directly to the final user, however; they need to develop a channels strategy that includes independent organizations.

From the vantage point of retailers, the goal is often to move as much control as possible down the channel to the retail level. Retailers and other intermediaries who take on a greater role in the marketing of products tend to achieve more channel power. A museum gift shop that commissions reproductions of the artwork it owns can be the dominant channel member, but a gift shop that only sells postcards and other souvenirs will tend to have much less channel power. No matter where the greatest channel power lies, all members must be motivated to work jointly toward achievement of system goals.

Designing a Channel System

Designing a distribution system requires determining the number of levels and types of intermediaries to utilize and deciding on the functions to be performed at each level. Some functions will be carried out by the manufacturer, some will be left to the consumer, and others will be assigned to the intermediaries. Remember, the issue is not whether these functions are to be carried out but who is to execute them.

The design of a channel system starts at the level of the ultimate user by careful analysis of user needs relative to the acquisition and use of the product. Based on this, the organization determines the appropriate channel strategy at the lowest level, the level that links the consumer to the channel system. In this way, the organization determines how intensively the product should be distributed and what functions should be carried out by the retailer.

The producer must then seek alternative ways to meet the requirements at the retailer level. This may be difficult because appropriate retailers may not exist or may be working for competitors. Suitable retailers may be willing to carry out some but not all of the desired functions. For example, most bookstores would not be willing to offer discounts on sales of Sierra Club books to club members.

Once alternatives are generated at the retailer level, the same process is repeated at each intermediate level until the producer level is reached. Of course, at each stage the producer must ask whether a distinct level is needed to carry out certain functions.

The organization then needs to choose a channel of distribution that provides a sound method of reaching its target markets. In evaluating alternatives, economic factors are, of course, important. Additionally, the availability and capability of specific intermediaries to provide the desired market coverage and to perform desired functions need to be examined. For example, the Sierra Club contracted with its book distributor to process and collect accounts receivable. The Sierra Club had difficulty collecting from many retailers to whom the club only sold a few books; the much larger distributor was able to do this more easily. Finally, the feasibility of implementing a system of rewards to motivate the intermediaries to perform the specified functions should also be considered in selecting channels.

This description portrays the producer as the major force in designing a channel system. The leading role, however, can also be played by other channel members. For example, a retailer can be the dominant force and set up a channel system of manufacturers and wholesalers to provide the retailer with a range of products needed to service its customers.

Management of Existing Channels. Once designed, active and continual attention must be paid to the management of the channel system. Channel management is difficult because of the differing and sometimes conflicting objectives of channel members, the complexity of the channel system, the geographic dispersion of intermediaries, and the lack of direct control over independent organizations that are part of the channel. Marketing programs must be evaluated in terms of their impact not only on ultimate users but also on channel members. Special programs usually need to be developed to motivate performance by intermediaries. In addition, the producer should have a system to monitor performance and to provide ways to help a distributor improve in performance.

Occasional conflicts among channel members appear to be almost inevitable. These arise because each channel member emphasizes the concern of its own functional specialty, goals differ among channel members, channel members disagree about the actual and expected performance of themselves and others, and communications among the members breaks down. While some conflict can be a positive force that leads to adaptation and innovation, too much conflict can be destructive. In any case, a system to manage and control the conflict that occurs must be established. (n the first instance, this includes designing the channel structure to limit conflict by assigning roles and responsibilities and providing compensation and rewards in ways that support each channel member's own interests while emphasizing channel cooperation and mutual concerns. In addition, it is vital to set up communication programs among channel members so that each can understand the problems and concerns of others. Good communication among all channel members helps to limit the number of conflicts that arise and to moderate the severity of those that do occur. Regular meetings among channel members, timely and relevant newsletters, and joint participation in trade associations are examples of particular steps that can be taken. When good communication and mutual understanding among channel members exist, better individual and collective decision making can take place and fewer divisive struggles will occur.

CHANNELS OF DISTRIBUTION FOR SERVICES

Channel-of-distribution management, while less important for some services than for physical goods, is still significant in the delivery of many services. Manufacturers of physical goods, particularly in the consumer market, often are legally and operationally independent from both intermediate and final sellers. As a result, channels management has become primarily concerned with the management of *interorganizational* relationships in the distribution system. The producer of the service is often the same organization as the final seller of the service, however, and channel-management concepts remain valid and pertinent for many service providers because:

1. Many services organizations sell ancillary physical goods, such as publications marketed by the Sierra Club and the sale of reproductions by museums.

2. Service organizations may use intermediaries to generate customers for their services (as hospitals use private physicians to admit patients), or to provide information, reservation, and payment services (as theaters contract with ticket agencies to sell tickets).

3. Some service organizations never see their customers in person and use other organizations to interact with customers (as the Passport Office contracts with city and county government offices to accept applications for passports).

Managing Retail Outlets

Few products are either pure services or pure goods. Organizations are classified by their dominant product, which for most public and nonprofit entities is a service. Nevertheless, many of these organizations provide goods that are closely associated with the fundamental service offered. For example, some family planning agencies dispense a wide range of contraceptives. In other cases, the relationship is more tangential. London Transport, for instance, sells replicas of London Transport posters and other transport-related gifts and souvenirs to both retail and mail order customers.

The appropriate role of revenue-producing retail and mail order is a difficult question to resolve. As the proportion of revenue from this source increases, management must make sure it retains its proper place as an ancillary or support function. On the other hand, within its assigned role, it should be managed as an effective and efficient retail operation. In this chapter we have only attempted to highlight the need for effective management of retail operations and some of the issues that arise when retail sales become an important source of revenue. These issues are discussed in depth in Chapter 20.

Use of Intermediaries

The essence of management of channels of distribution for physical goods is to specify the tasks that must be accomplished at each level and to administer these channels in such a way that *independent* entities carry out their assigned tasks. Service organizations often deal with independent entities that are important in facilitating the use of the organization's services. A service organization should analyze, plan, and manage the efforts of its intermediaries as carefully as manufacturers do those of their wholesalers and retailers. As with physical goods, service managers should realize that they cannot dictate how independent intermediaries will operate, but a system can be designed to encourage intermediaries to perform in the desired way.

As the example at the start of the chapter suggests, the concepts a hospital uses to help manage its relations with private physicians, emergency rooms, and HMOs are similar to those a manufacturer might use to manage relations with retailers who have more immediate contact with the ultimate consumer. If the retailer does not stock a manufacturer's product and display it well, for example, purchases of the manufacturer's product will fall. Similarly, a hospital will not attract many patients if nearby physicians and other sources of referrals do not support the hospital. While hospitals deliver services directly to the final user, the user may interact with several intermediaries before entering a hospital. Successful channel management requires understanding the nature of services and information appropriate at each stage and designing and implementing a channels system to carry out the necessary tasks.

The greater the distinction between the production of the service and its consumption, the more relevant channels concepts become. Thus, as organizations are increasingly able to segregate a technical core, the possibility of establishing a distribution structure including independent channel members is greater. For example, the British Post Office, to its own staff, has become a multiservice distributor of such products as passports, monthly allowance checks, and bus passes. From the view of the British Foreign Office, which officially issues passports, the Post Office has become its retailer. To the consumer, the Post Office's role has expanded; the postal clerk may provide a form, answer questions, and a few days later deliver the passport. (Perhaps postal clerks will soon be supplied with instant cameras with which to take passport photographs as well.) The use of post offices has probably increased consumer satisfaction and convenience, as well as total system efficiency, but the Foreign Office must now deal with the management of an independent distribution channel.

DISTRIBUTION ISSUES IN SOCIAL-BEHAVIOR MARKETING

Organizations that are primarily concerned with social behavior often have no direct contact with the people whose behavior they are trying to change. Nevertheless, as we discuss in this section, certain aspects of distribution management are important for these organizations. Three major relevant areas are (1) providing goods and services that are needed if a behavior change is to be made, (2) identifying the timing and location of social behaviors and their possible change, and (3) facilitating and enforcing the change. In managing a social-change program, it is important to remember the concept of the marketing mix. The likelihood of people adopting a new behavior increases when the change program is supported by appropriate pricing, enforcement, communication, and distribution strategies.

Distribution of Ancillary Goods and Services

The provision of goods and services to support a behavior-change program can often be critically important. Family-planning agencies in underdeveloped countries must not only motivate potential parents to limit the number of children they have, but also provide medical and paramedical services and contraceptive devices so that those committed to practicing contraception can do so. The problem of distributing contraceptives is particularly difficult; in some of the first population-planning programs, contraceptives were distributed through health clinics, hospitals, medical offices, and similar channels. Millions of people, particularly the poor and those living in rural areas, however, had virtually no access to medical facilities on a regular basis, and population-planning agencies had to design and implement a highly intensive distribution system. In many underdeveloped countries, contraceptives (particularly condoms) are now distributed and prominently displayed in small general retail stores that extend to the smallest villages and supply the population with a range of what we have called "convenience" products.

There are many other examples of the need to ensure that appropriate physical goods and services are available for behavior-change programs. For example, in energy conservation, the U.K. Department of Energy found that 75 percent of homeowners had insulating jackets around their hot water heaters, but only one quarter were at least 3 inches thick, which is considered to be the minimum acceptable thickness for meaningful conservation. Consequently, several steps were taken. Jacket manufacturers were contacted and agreed to manufacture only jackets that were at least 3 inches thick. Moreover, as part of a program to convince homeowners who already had installed jackets to upgrade their thickness, the Department of Energy's representatives called on building-supply merchants to persuade them to recommend greater insulation thickness to their customers.[12]

Identifying Time and Location of Behaviors

Sound distribution management requires us to understand the time and place at which consumers want to utilize goods and services. Similarly, behavior-change programs need to be sensitive to these dimensions, to determine the best time to introduce a behavior change or reinforce a newly learned one. An interesting example of the use of timing to introduce a burglary-prevention program occurred in Palo Alto, California.

> One part of the burglary problem is the failure of homeowners to take proper precautions to protect their homes. *After* a burglary occurs, the police department's antiburglary squad arranges a meeting of neighbors in the burgled home and outlines measures that could be taken by homeowners to discourage burglars. The burglary rate in the affected areas has been reduced to 40 percent of the rate in the remainder of the city. In many cities, the same kind of information is disseminated through the media and in community meetings without comparable effect. In this case, police shrewdly determined when its audience was most likely to "buy" the idea.[13]

In attempting to encourage and support a new behavior, communication and distribution concepts may overlap to a great extent. To choose an elementary example, in order to increase compliance with antismoking regulations, signs need to be placed to direct smokers to areas in which it is permissible to smoke and to remind people not to smoke in other areas. Market research on behavior patterns can indicate where and when people are likely to light cigarettes; in a theater, for example, it may be appropriate for ushers to remind (tactfully) smokers not to light their cigarettes at the intermission unless they leave the auditorium.

The program to help Swedish drivers adapt to new traffic rules when Sweden switched from driving on the left to the right side of the road on the night of September 2–3, 1967, is particularly pertinent. The actual behavior change could not be a gradual transition; it had to occur simultaneously throughout the entire country. It was possible to get drivers used to looking to the right for road signs; a set of more than 360,000 road signs were placed on the right-hand side of roads. Through interviews with Swedish drivers who had recently driven in other European countries on the right-hand side of the road and through theoretical analyses, a list of "critical traffic situations" in which drivers would likely revert to their previous behavior in driving on the left-hand side was established. A special sign, a sloping "H" that could be seen at a long distance, was developed and set up at potential critical traffic situations to remind drivers to stay on the right. This analysis also helped to guide the kind of police supervision that was utilized at different locations. After the program was introduced, road accidents were monitored to identify accident-prone areas (or behaviors), and appropriate corrective steps were taken at these locations. In passing, it might be noted that traffic accidents in Sweden during the second six months of 1967 were lower than in any six-month period since 1957.[14]

Providing Facilitation and Enforcement

Closely related to the identification of the time and place that behavior takes place is providing a means to facilitate and enforce that behavior. The Swedish right-hand driving program encompassed both of these steps. Because successful marketing programs are usually based on careful research, this linkage should not be surprising.

Managers in behavior-change programs at times overlook the need to provide enforcement and facilitation. The reader can add his or her own favorites to such violated statutes as the 65 MPH speed limit, ordinances against marijuana smoking, 68-degree thermostat settings, and smoking limitations in public buildings. The reasonableness of these regulations is not the issue here; our concern is to point out that just passing a law is not sufficient to ensure compliance with it. Despite the seemingly widespread flouting of numerous regulations and laws, government officials often seem surprised when laws are not obeyed. A facilitation and enforcement system is required as well. Parking regulations are generally not obeyed unless parking tickets are given and procedures are instituted to collect fines. Managers of voluntary change programs must be even more concerned that a system exists to support the proposed changes.

Introducing new coins and currency has been the object of behavior-change programs in both the United States and the United Kingdom.[15] The failure to build a distribution system to support the introduction of the $2 bill and the Susan B. Anthony dollar coin in the United States was a major factor in the failure of both to achieve widespread circulation. In contrast, attention to distribution issues helped account for the smooth changeover in Britain from a system of 12 pence to the shilling and 20 shillings to the pound to a decimalized pound made up of 100 new pence.

The failure of the $2 bill is particularly noteworthy. For the $2 to achieve widespread use, banks and retail stores would have had to act as active distributors. They did not take on this role and often acted in the opposite manner. To illustrate, if a $2 bill was given to a cashier, it frequently was placed under the cash till with the $20 bills, presumably to be returned to the bank. Some store managers commented that consumers were confused by the $2 bill and that there was insufficient space for it in the cash register drawer. Yet Canada has virtually the same monetary system as the United States with only one major exception: the $2 bill is in widespread circulation.

These examples indicate the need to build systems to enforce and facilitate behavior change. In some cases, what is required is a distribution system to supply the goods and services so that those wanting to make the behavior change can do so. In other cases, a study of behavior will identify specific opportunities to introduce a change program and indicate the systems required to facilitate the successful introduction and maintenance of the change.

SUMMARY

Distribution management is an important activity for marketers of public and nonprofit organizations, whether their products be goods, services, or social behaviors. Marketers of physical goods are particularly concerned with the design and management of systems of transportation, storage, display, and information so that their products will be available at the time when and in the place consumers want to obtain usage of the product. Marketers in service organizations share similar concerns to the extent that their services are accompanied by the consumption of goods. Moreover, because the consumption of the service often takes place on the site of the service provider and is coincident with the final production of the service, marketing management must be concerned with the site itself and the manner of delivering a service. Successful service-delivery management requires dealing with inherent conflicts between marketing and operations orientations in providing service. An understanding of what consumers desire and a consistent, reliable system to provide the desired service are mandatory. As we have shown, even organizations solely concerned with behavior change need to consider distribution issues, because these relate to where and when the desired behavior takes place and the availability of supporting goods and services.

Distribution often requires the management of systems that involve independently owned and operated facilitating organizations. Even nonbusiness organizations that provide direct service to users usually deal with outsiders who either perform functions prior to usage of the service (as ticket agencies sell theater tickets) or direct potential users to the service facility (as doctors admit patients to hospitals). The producer of the good or service seeks to establish a system such that each channel member carries out assigned tasks in a manner that meets the producer's interests. While members of a distribution channel share mutual interests, they each have their own goals and expectations about the performance of others. Consequently, conflict can arise in the channel, but sound initial design of the channel structure and good communication among channel members can limit the frequency and severity of such conflicts.

Many nonprofit and public organizations conduct retail operations that are supplementary to the main service they provide. Operations such as food services or shops may contribute a positive cash flow as well as enhance the primary function of the organization. In Chapter 20, "Managing Retail and Catalog Sales Operations," we expand our discussion of retailing issues.

Public and nonprofit managers often overlook distribution and service-delivery issues. These are easily taken as a given unless examined carefully as a source of problems or opportunities. Yet, as the example of hospitals illustrates, failure to be aware of changing consumer, environmental, and competitive activities in this area can threaten survival.

Distribution—the final link between the user and the organization—deserves careful management attention as an integral part of developing, implementing, and monitoring marketing programs.

REFERENCES

1. "Prognosis: Empty Beds and Falling Profits," *Business Week,* January 12, 1987, p. 102.
2. This section is based on Jeff C. Goldsmith, *Can Hospitals Survive?* Homewood, Ill.: Dow Jones-Irwin, 1981.
3. For a discussion of prepurchase information-gathering patterns, see John D. Claxton, Joseph N. Fry, and Bernard Portis, "A Taxonomy of Prepurchase Information Gathering Patterns," *Journal of Consumer Research* (December 1974), pp. 35–42.
4. See Christopher H. Lovelock and Robert F. Young, "Look to Consumers to Increase Productivity," *Harvard Business Review* (May–June 1979), pp. I66–178.
5. Robert N. Anthony and Regina E. Herzlinger, *Management Control in Nonprofit Organizations,* 3rd edition, Homewood, Ill.: Richard D. Irwin, Inc., 1985.
6. Earl W. Sasser, R. Paul Olsen, and D. Daryl Wyckoff, *Management of Service Operations,* Boston: Allyn & Bacon, 1978, pp. 559–560.
7. Richard B. Chase, "Where Does the Customer Fit in a Service Operation?" *Harvard Business Review* (November–December 1978), p. 139.
8. The advertisement is shown in Christopher H. Lovelock and Charles B. Weinberg, "The Role of Marketing in Improving Postal Service Effectiveness," in Joel L. Fleishman (ed.), *The Future of the Postal Service,* New York: Praeger, 1983.
9. Kenneth P. Uhl and Gregory P. Upah, "The Marketing of Services: Why and How Is It Different," in Jagdish N. Sheth (ed.), *Research in Marketing,* Vol. 6, New York: Elsevier, 1981.
10. G. Lynn Shostack, "Breaking Free from Product Marketing," *Journal of Marketing* (April 1977), p. 78.
11. See Arthur Segel and Charles B. Weinberg, "Sierra Club Publishing Division," in Christopher H. Lovelock and Charles B. Weinberg, *Public and Nonprofit Marketing: Cases and Readings,* New York: John Wiley & Sons, 1984.
12. Nicholas Phillips and Elizabeth Nelson, "Energy Savings in Private Households: An Integrated Research Program," *Journal of the Market Research Society* (October 1976), pp. 180–200.
13. Adapted from Frederick 0. R. Hayes, "Interaction between Government and Citizen," unpublished paper presented at a conference in Annapolis, Md., July 13–15, 1976.
14. Anders Englund, "Changing Behavior Patterns: Sweden's Traffic Switch," *Progress* (1968), pp. 26–32.
15. Christopher H. Lovelock, "Marketing National Change: Decimalization in Britain," in Christopher H. Lovelock and Charles B. Weinberg, *Public and Nonprofit Marketing: Cases and Readings,* New York: John Wiley & Sons, 1984.

Chapter 13

The Nature & Methods of
Marketing Communication

Communication is the most visible or audible—some would say intrusive—of marketing activities, but it has little value unless used intelligently in conjunction with other marketing efforts. An old marketing axiom says that the fastest way to kill a poor product is to advertise that product heavily. By the same token, an otherwise well-researched and well-planned marketing strategy, designed to deliver, say, counseling on family planning at a reasonable price and at times and locations tailored to consumer needs, is likely to fail if people lack knowledge of the service.

Through communication, the marketer is able to inform existing or prospective customers about product, price, and distribution details; to create (where appropriate) persuasive arguments for using the service, buying the goods, or adopting the recommended social behavior; and to remind people of the product—especially at times and in locations where purchase or other desired behavior is particularly relevant or appropriate.

Much confusion surrounds the scope and purpose of marketing communication. Many managers define it narrowly as the use of paid media advertising and professional salespeople, failing to recognize the many other ways in which an organization can communicate with its customers. Moreover, the content of such communications, especially in nonbusiness settings, is more often designed to provide relevant information (which recipients can use as they see fit) than to persuade the audience to adopt a specified form of behavior.

Each of the elements in the marketing mix tends to communicate some message. The appearance of a physical product or service personnel, the way a customer is treated, the price charged, the location and atmosphere of a service-delivery facility—all contribute to a general impression that reinforces or contradicts the impression created by the specific messages the marketer communicates. A social-service agency may spend many hours and a good deal of money developing an advertising campaign built around the message "We care," but a single rude or indifferent receptionist at the agency can shatter that image in an instant.

Scope of the Chapter

We start by introducing some communication issues that are particularly relevant to nonbusiness marketers. To demonstrate that communication efforts extend far beyond the use of such mass-media vehicles as television, radio, newspapers, magazines, and billboards, we present a graphic illustration of the enormous variety of communications to which people are likely to be exposed during a short walk through an urban area. An analysis of the experiences of this walk will show how important such elements as signage and other forms of non-mass-media communication can be for marketing services and social behaviors.

Next, we discuss how communications work, including insights from communications theory and consumer behavior research. In the final section of the chapter, we identify and evaluate the different types of communication methods available to public and nonprofit marketers, indicating their strengths and weaknesses as well as their relative appropriateness for specific types of tasks and situations. This will set the stage for the next chapter on advertising and promotion, which will address the specific issues of how a marketer should decide what to say (message design and execution), to whom (which target audiences), where (through which communication channels), and how often (frequency of exposure), as well as how much to spend on the different elements of the communication program.

SOME COMMUNICATION ISSUES FACING NONBUSINESS MARKETERS

Effective design and implementation of marketing communication strategies require a clear statement of objectives (including definition of the target audience), a good understanding of the strengths and weaknesses of different communication methods, and the ability to formulate and communicate a consistent message.

Constraints and Opportunities

Marketing managers in public and nonprofit organizations often face constraints on their communication activities that are much less likely to be a problem for their counterparts in business firms. Such problems may include limited budgets, resistance both internally and externally to the use of certain media, and pressures to avoid controversial messages.

In the United States, even public agencies as large as Amtrak and the U.S. Postal Service have been criticized for their advertising expenditures despite their relatively modest use of paid media advertising. Politicians have periodically sought to reduce or eliminate the amount of funds budgeted for this purpose.[1] Such actions demonstrate either a complete misunderstanding of the role that advertising plays or a very cynical attitude on the part of individuals who have frequently spent enormous sums on advertising to get themselves elected!

Even where the need for advertising is accepted, some media may be regarded as "inappropriate" by top management or board members. For instance, billboards or advertising on the inside or outside of transit vehicles can be cost-effective ways of reaching certain target markets, but these media are sometimes regarded as "undignified" by senior administrators of institutions such as colleges or hospitals, because of the nature of some of the other products advertised through them (for instance, liquor, cigarettes, medicines, and candidates for political office).

In both of the instances described, the marketing manager faces an uphill battle to get the desired advertising program approved. The more carefully planned and documented the program, the better the chances of winning approval. It's hard to make a convincing argument for spending money on a particular campaign unless clear goals have been established, alternative strategies carefully evaluated, and measures of performance established between the cost of the proposed program and its projected results. This level of precision requires evidence of the probable effectiveness of different media in achieving the desired effects, suggesting a need either for conducting prior research or for demonstrating evidence of performance based on the experience of comparable campaigns.

Many public and nonprofit organizations worry about their ability to finance large-scale media campaigns or the communication research efforts needed to plan and evaluate them. In some instances, their operating budgets are simply too small to permit such efforts. In many cases nonbusiness organizations may qualify for free public-service advertising, whereby media time or space is donated. (We discuss this issue in more depth in Chapter 14.) Central or federal government agencies often qualify for free or discounted postal rates, while nonprofit organizations in the United States can obtain inexpensive mailing privileges. These benefits greatly reduce the cost of conducting direct-mail campaigns. Additionally, some advertising agencies may be willing to volunteer their creative or production services free or at low cost to nonprofit organizations. (Obtaining gifts of these and other services-in-kind will be one of the topics of Chapter 18.)

Communication Efforts for Services and Social Behaviors

Communication strategies extend well beyond direct mail and use of advertising in the mass media. Budgetary limitations aside, communication methods other than advertising seem to be less contentious and seem to encounter less resistance from critics both inside and outside the organization. This is just as well, since public and nonprofit organizations tend to employ a broader array of communication methods than manufacturing organizations, reflecting the former's emphasis on services and social behaviors.

As we saw in Chapter 12, "Distribution and Delivery Systems," service marketers are more likely than manufacturing organizations to manage their own distribution operations. Hence, many communication tasks that a manufacturer might leave to a retailer—local advertising,* directional signs and identification of facilities, and interactions between retail service personnel and customers—must be addressed directly by the service marketer. Furthermore, whereas instructions for using a physical good may appear on its outer package or in an accompanying leaflet, instructions for using services must be distributed at the point of consumption through either easily visible signs or the assistance of customer contact personnel.

Managers seeking to market social-behavior programs rely heavily on the communication element of the marketing mix. Although some aspects such as advertising can be planned and controlled internally, the actions of independent communication intermediaries may be even more important. For example, in a 1980 survey of 1353 U.S. households, almost two thirds reported making at least one food change in the previous three years for health or nutrition reasons. Among those making a diet change, 56 percent

---

*Although many manufacturers share the cost of local retail advertising, the specific decisions on how to spend these funds are usually made by the retailer.

cited doctors, dentists, or nurses as sources of influence, 13 percent cited dieticians or nutritionists, 8 percent mentioned government publications, and 4 percent referred to such information sources as extension workers or public health educators.[2] It's likely that other sources of information, such as magazine and newspaper articles, food packages, advertising by food companies, and remarks by friends and family members also influenced behavior but went unremembered at the time respondents were surveyed.

The key to success in any communication program is that the messages delivered to the target audience be consistent, mutually reinforcing, and directed toward achieving clearly specified communication objectives. This task is complicated by the presence of numerous intermediaries—individuals or organizations in touch with target consumers but not directly employed by the marketer responsible for the program. Such intermediaries can offer important opportunities for reinforcement of the desired message, especially for social-behavior marketers operating within limited budgets. An outstanding example of a successful effort to coordinate a national communication program across many intermediaries was provided by the work of the Decimal Currency Board (DCB) in coordinating the changeover to decimal currency in Britain between 1966 and 1971.

The DCB recognized the enormity of the communication task required in changing the national currency from pounds, shillings, and pence to a pound composed of 100 new pence. In 1967, the board outlined the role it expected to play over the four years as follows.

> Many other organizations besides the board will be issuing publicity and educational material about decimal currency. We welcome this because we alone cannot persuade over 50 million people in Britain to change the money habits of a lifetime. We are always willing to help organizations to prepare publicity and training material. . . . The publicity campaign is a team effort but we are glad to act as coordinators.[3]

Part of the success of the decimal changeover (which was completed smoothly in 1971 despite negative attitudes toward the change on the part of almost half the population) can be ascribed to the DCB's success in leveraging its efforts through intermediaries and in ensuring that the information and advice they offered was consistent with the board's own messages in advertising and brochures. These intermediaries included banks and retailers that provided decimal currency information to their customers, schools that gave decimal lessons to all their students, and even manufacturers of products with a decimal theme—such as games, dishcloths, and dress materials.[4]

AN URBAN WALK

To develop a better understanding of the many different communication methods other than advertising or personal selling that are available to public and nonprofit marketers, we will look at the numerous communications to which a pedestrian or driver in a large city might be exposed.

It is a pleasant 10-minute walk from the campus of Central University to Federal Square. Outside the campus, the street is filled with traffic. Most of the vehicles carry local license plates, but there are several out-of-state cars, too; a car from Maine has plates bearing the slogan "Vacationland," while the plates on another car read "Beautiful British Columbia." The traffic lights turn red, an almost universally recognized order to stop, but a car from Massachusetts accelerates and runs the light. The other vehicles stop, led by a taxi with an advertisement for a radio station mounted on its roof and the name and phone number of the taxi company painted on its door.

Among the pedestrians on the sidewalk is a small child who is holding her father's hand. She is wearing a T-shirt emblazoned "Virginia is for Lovers" (a recent tourist slogan for that state). The cross-street is labeled Jefferson Parkway. Mounted by the intersection is a cluster of traffic signs containing route numbers, a 35-mph speed-limit warning, and a "trucks prohibited" symbol consisting of the silhouette of a truck with a red slash through it. A blue and white sign on a separate pole indicates the direction to the Museum of Science.

Marking time as they wait for the lights to change are a couple of joggers wearing Downtown Athletic Club track suits; their shoes display the name of a well-known sporting-goods manufacturer. Two young women are shading their eyes and looking upward. They are watching a small aircraft skywriting what appears to be an ad for a local Ford dealer.

The lights change and the traffic lurches forward again. Coming in the opposite direction is a green and white bus with a destination board reading "Union Station." It has a big black M in a white circle on its side, the symbol of the Metropolitan Transportation District. Also mounted on the side of the bus is a large advertisement for a brand of low-tar cigarettes. The driver wears a green uniform cap and white shirt with a shoulder flash displaying the M symbol of the transit district. Street signs warn of two-hour parking, and a row of meters invites potential users to insert coins in the slots provided for that purpose. Not everyone is obeying the regulations, it seems, since a couple of cars are parked next to meters displaying red "violation" flags. A meter attendant is tying a parking ticket to the windshield-wiper blade of one of the cars, notifying the owner of the fine that is due and telling how to pay it.

The traffic on the street is getting steadily thicker. There are trucks and vans bearing company names on their sides. Most of the cars display, with varying degrees of discretion, their manufacturer's name, plus the model name or number, and often that of the dealer who supplied the vehicle. One car is immediately recognizable from its distinctive radiator grille: a Rolls Royce. About one car in eight has a bumper sticker. Their messages range from "Sullivan for City Council" to "'Bequeath Thy Kidneys," and from "This Car Climbed Mount Washington" to "Save the Whales." A white truck marked with the stylized eagle symbol of the U.S. Postal Service has a bumper sticker reading "Save Gas—Shop by Mail" and, on a side panel, a small poster promoting Express Mail. On the left side of the street is a big brick and glass complex, identified by a plaque as the Museum of Science; a banner strung above the entrance promotes a special exhibit on the space shuttle. Next comes an older brick building, on one wall of which someone has sprayed the slogan "No Nukes Oct. 6 Riverville"—a reference to an antinuclear rally. In smaller letters, someone has written "Joe Loves Doreen." Nearby, a directional marker clamped to a utility pole points the way to the University Lutheran Church.

Lined up on a side street marked "No Entry" is a row of buses, each parked beside a bus stop identified by a small destination sign. On the opposite corner is a Shell service station; a notice in the station forecourt orders drivers to turn off their motors and extinguish all smoking materials; a second notice advertises a tire sale. The price per gallon is displayed on the top of each pump. Beyond this is a retail complex, containing stores and a movie theater with a marqee advertising the times of the films being shown. Approaching

Federal Square, the traffic, the pedestrian volume, and the number of retail stores all increase in intensity.

Retail signs and displays are everywhere. A large travel agency has a window display by British Airways featuring one-week vacations in London; it also has a large sign above its entrance that tells passersby, "Please Go Away—Often." A drug store advertises discounts on toothpaste, a wine store promotes specials on French Burgundy, a furniture store displays its wares, several restaurants have menus outside their entrances, and another travel agent promotes Caribbean vacations in one window and scenic train journeys on Amtrak in the other. Heaped up outside a doorway is a pile of empty boxes marked with the name of a well-known brand of stereo components and the warning, "Fragile. Handle with care. This side up."

Another set of traffic lights looms ahead. The poles on which they are mounted have been pasted with flyers and small posters—as have several blank stretches of nearby wall; on one pole, the subject matter ranges from details of a forthcoming concert by a small chamber music group to a membership drive by a Marxist-Leninist organization. The flyers pasted on the wall promote a local bookstore sale, a women's march against rape, and a poetry reading at a nearby coffeehouse. Each emphasizes the date and location.

A car in the black and white colors of the city police department and bearing the slogan "Dial 911" on its trunk is nosing its way through the traffic when it suddenly turns on its siren and its set of flashing blue lights. Other vehicles pull over to make way for the police car, which accelerates away as best it can. A woman who has been using a pay telephone mounted on the sidewalk looks up as the police car passes, then returns to her perusal of the *Yellow Pages* directory.

On one corner of busy Federal Square stands an impressive stone building, its entrance up a flight of stone steps flanked by massive columns. It is the post office. Outside on the sidewalk are a pair of dark blue mailboxes, one labeled "Stamped Mail" and the other "Metered Mail." A uniformed postal employee is busy emptying the contents of one of the boxes into a large sack. A small sign on each mailbox once indicated mail pickup times, but unfortunately, the ink has faded and the times in question are illegible.

On the opposite corner of the square stands a low brick structure, topped by a sign reading "Rapid Transit to All Points." Another sign with a black M in a white circle indicates that this is a subway station. Behind the station stands a large billboard promoting enlistment in the U.S. Marines. Next to the subway entrance stands a magazine and newspaper store, surmounted by an electric message board that alternately flashes advertisements, details of forthcoming events, the time, and the current temperature in both Fahrenheit and Celsius. A 14-year-old boy, selling papers in front of the newsstand, periodically calls out "Ti-i-imes, Times Standard." A pedestrian rushes across the street to the department store in defiance of the red "Don't Walk" signs. Outside the store, a young man with a blond beard stumbles along inside a sandwich board advertising a new restaurant. A teenage girl standing on the sidewalk pushes a leaflet into people's hands as they pass by—she is promoting a discount sale at a nearby record store; the sidewalk is littered with discarded copies, despite the message on a nearby trash container to "Please Keep Our City Clean." Nearby, a young couple armed with clipboards is politely accosting passersby and inviting them to sign a political petition. Next door to the department store, a middle-aged man is pushing buttons on an automatic teller machine built into the outside wall of the adjoining bank, as he follows the instructions flashed on a small video screen. Beyond are more stores, a movie theater advertising a horror film, and then, in a surprisingly quick change of environment, an old stone church with an outside bulletin board telling of upcoming activities sponsored by the church.

A Bombardment of Messages

More than 70 different messages were noted in the 10-minute walk described here. Some are merely identifiers or informational in content, but many others are specifically designed to influence behavior.

Only an unusually observant person, of course, would note as many as 70 messages in such a short time, and even then, most would have been quickly forgotten. Someone busily chatting with a friend would probably have noticed relatively few. Yet hundreds more messages went unnoticed. If pedestrians took the time to read every license plate, bumper sticker, traffic and street sign, directional marker, retail store sign, restaurant menu board, and window display; to scrutinize all graffiti items and each poster, bus destination, and transit information sign; or to absorb the significance of every uniform, siren, or street cry, they would take about two hours to make the same trip!

Types of Communications

Among the communications encountered on this walk were, first, what can be termed *identifiers*. Such communications were provided not only through the medium of the printed word (such as the name of a company on its trucks or a sign outside a store, post office, or museum), but also through symbols, ranging from the big black M of the transit district to the stylized eagle of the U.S. Postal Service, and from the distinctive design of the Rolls Royce radiator to the paintwork and flashers on the police car. Another form of symbolism is found in uniforms—bus drivers, postal workers, police officers, and meter attendants can all be recognized by their uniforms. A caution from a police officer to a jaywalker will probably have greater impact on the recipient than it would coming from someone in civilian clothes. Furthermore, being able to identify a police officer may also be useful to a tourist needing directions.

Symbols are also prominent in *admonitory signs and cues*—such as traffic lights, sirens on emergency vehicles, or pictographs of trucks with a red slash through them. People have to be taught the meaning of such symbols, but once learned they are usually easier to identify and absorb than the printed word would be. Consider the pictographs in Figure 13.1. How many of these are familiar to you, how many are unfamiliar but self-explanatory, and how many require you to check the key at the bottom for an explanation? Problems can arise when the same symbols mean different things to different people. In Massachusetts, for instance, when a traffic signal shows red and yellow lights simultaneously, it means that cars must wait for pedestrians to cross; in Britain, by contrast, it means that the traffic lights will turn green in a second or two.

Admonitory signs and cues are particularly significant in social-behavior marketing. It is important that they be placed at the point of relevant behavior; traffic signs tell drivers how to behave at a particular point in time and place, and antilitter signs are usually located in places where people are likely to need to discard paper, boxes, cans, or bottles. People learn from experience which messages couched in an imperative tone are legal

Key: scenery, agriculture, lodging, camping, dining, fishing, swimming, boating, biking, skiing, riding, hiking, tennis, golf.

Figure 13.1 Symbols adopted by the Vermont Travel Information Council. Reprinted by permission.

warnings and likely to be enforced (such as "No Entry"), which are requests for a particular form of social behavior (for example, "Please Keep Our City Clean"), and which are simply commercial exhortations (such as the travel agent's plea to "Please Go Away").

Not all communications are admonitions or identifiers. Many are designed to provide specific *information* that will be helpful to prospective users. The bus destination board tells travelers that the vehicle can take them to Union Station (regrettably, the transit district in question doesn't bother to provide details of intermediate points on the route). The sign on the mailbox should tell postal customers the times of mail pickups (unfortunately, poor maintenance or use of the wrong ink in the first place has resulted in an illegible—and therefore useless—message). Meanwhile the *Yellow Pages* at the pay telephone helps callers identify and reach commercial and institutional phone listings, and the menus outside the restaurants let people know what types of meals are available at what prices.

The media used to convey these many different messages are very different from such media as radio, television, newspapers, and magazines. Most are location specific, although some—such as the messages on vehicles, sandwich boards, and clothing—do move around. A few may seem whimsical or even silly, but many are components in a carefully integrated communication program. Note that most of the communications recorded on the walk concerned services or social behaviors; a distinction should be drawn between retail stores, which are service organizations, and the goods that are sold there.

Some messages were designed to increase awareness (the vacation potential of certain states, the phone number to dial for police assistance, recognition of a brand of running shoes or a Ford dealership, the availability of Express Mail) without any expectation of immediate action on the part of the customer. Others were designed to stimulate interest in a particular product and promote further inquiry (vacations by Amtrak or British Airways, special deals on toothpaste or wine, enlistment in the Marines, an upcoming chamber music concert). Still others were designed to impose a particular behavior pattern there and then (drive at 35 mph, make way for the police car, put your litter in this trash container). A final group of communications was intended to assist people in executing a specific market transaction they had already decided to make (insert 50 cents here for an hour's parking; indicate the amount of money you wish to withdraw from the automatic bank teller).

An important insight to be obtained from this brief excursion concerns the proliferation of messages in modern urban life. You can throw away your newspaper and turn off the radio or television, and you will still be bombarded with messages, unless you leave town altogether and escape to the country. Even there, you may encounter billboards beside the road and come across signs such as "No Hunting" and "Prevent Forest Fires."

These messages come from public, nonprofit, and business sources (as well as from individuals, in the case of graffiti), and the competition for the audience's attention is intense. Not all, however, are expected to succeed in isolation. Some messages, using a single medium, rely on repetition and constant reexposure to get their point across. Others are part of a carefully orchestrated program by a specific organization, using an integrated series of symbols, messages, and media to create an overall impact.

Some communications are highly transitory in nature. Sirens and flashing lights (like radio and television commercials) are strictly ephemeral. Skywriting disappears within 10 to 15 minutes. Posters stuck on walls or utility poles are usually removed or pasted over by new messages within a few days. Yet signs, uniforms, and identifying vehicle color schemes may be quite long lasting, representing more of a capital investment by the relevant organization than an operating expense. Even though the capital cost may seem expensive, the cost per exposure is often very small indeed.*

Our "urban walk" example provides a perspective to marketing communication that is usually missing from textbooks, because most thinking on the topic tends to be confined to mass-media advertising, public relations, sales promotion, and formalized personal selling. Later in this chapter, we'll identify and evaluate the roles of both personal communications and such impersonal communication vehicles as television, radio, news-

---

*The term *exposure* refers to one person's being exposed to a particular communication on one occasion.

papers, billboards, and direct mail. First, we'll look at how the communication process actually works.

HOW DOES COMMUNICATION WORK?

Communication involves a sender (or "source") transmitting a message through one or more media to a recipient, with the intention of eliciting some form of response. As shown in Figure 13.2, the sender must first transform or "encode" the desired communication into a symbolic form that can be transmitted in person or through a chosen medium and will be intelligible to the recipient. If the resulting message is sent through impersonal channels such as advertising, it may not reach each member of the target audience; either it may miss some people altogether or it may get lost in the general clutter or "noise" of everyday life. Even if it reaches a specific recipient, it may not be understood correctly ("decoded") or stored in that person's memory long enough to result in the response desired by the sender. Of course, consumers are not necessarily passive actors in this drama. Their interest whetted by need or curiosity, they may be actively seeking new information. While this curiosity increases the chance of their receiving communications on the topic of interest, it does not guarantee it.

Barriers and Screens to Communication

The communication model introduced here recognizes that even if people have the opportunity to be exposed to a particular message, various barriers or screens may prevent a message from actually reaching members of a target audience and being recorded in their memories. These are represented graphically in Figure 13.2.

As we noted on the "urban walk," people are bombarded by an enormous number of messages each day. As long ago as 1957, a vice-president of General Foods estimated that a "typical metropolitan family"—which he defined for the purposes of his study as consisting of husband, wife, and two children—could *potentially* be exposed to 1518 advertising messages on a single weekday.[5] This amazing total was composed of 510 display ads in the three newspapers read by the couple, 53 radio commercials heard at breakfast, lunch, or in the car, 447 ads in two national magazines read by the wife, 216 posters and advertisements on subway stations and inside subways and buses along the husband's route to work, 178 outdoor billboards along the wife's drive route, 64 television commercials seen in the evening, and 50 ads in comic books read by the children. These figures, of course, excluded most of the types of communications identified on the trip from Central University to Federal Square. In practice, nobody can be sure how many marketing communications messages an individual has the opportunity to see or hear on any given day, but for most urban residents it is likely to be at least several hundred. Of more interest is how many messages people actually note and absorb.

Selective exposure refers to the process by which people miss or ignore the bulk of the communications they might have an opportunity to notice. Bauer and Greyser conducted an experiment to measure how many advertisements people actually notice each day.[6] A sample of 1536 individuals used a pocket counter to record each advertisement they *noticed* in newspapers and magazines and on radio and television (outdoor advertising was not included). Half the sample recorded ads noticed between the time they got up in the morning and 5:00 P.M., while the other half recorded ads noticed between 5:00 P.M.

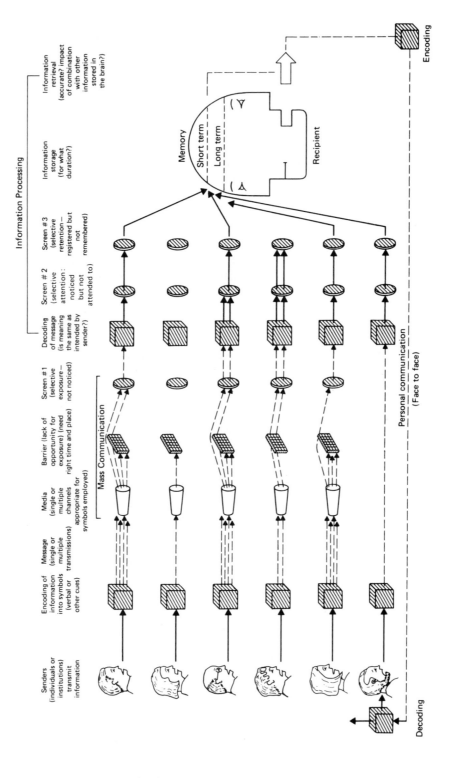

Figure 13.2   Model of communication and information processing.

and the time they went to bed. The average combined total for the full day was 76 advertisements. (This figure excludes interpersonal communications, outdoor advertising, and non-mass media communications of the types described earlier.)

Noticing an advertisement or other communication does not necessarily mean that its content actually registers. *Selective attention* is the process of screening out (or not attending to) messages the recipient has been exposed to but does not consider noteworthy. Bauer and Greyser continued their experiment by asking respondents to fill out a card for each ad that they considered especially annoying, enjoyable, informative, or offensive. Approximately 15 percent of all ads recorded on the counter were singled out for notation on these cards, representing an average of 12 advertisements per day.

People do not necessarily remember every piece of information that catches their attention. *Selective retention* is the process of forgetting some communication messages and remembering others. Some information may be retained in short-term memory for less than a minute and then forgotten. A wide variety of evidence suggests that we can keep only about four to seven immediate ideas in our minds at any given time, and that an existing piece of newly received information can quickly be displaced by another idea or information item before we have had time to rehearse the former and "file" it for retention in the long-term memory of the brain.[7] The relative importance of short-term and long-term memory retention depends on the situation. A street sign telling drivers to take the next exit for the Museum of Science does not need to go into long-term storage, whereas a highway safety message urging drivers not to combine drinking and driving does. A message reaching long-term memory is, of course, still subject to forgetting, particularly if it is not processed along with other released information in the mind to produce feelings, intentions, and actions.

Criteria for Effective Communication

What factors determine whether or not a marketing communication will be effective in stimulating an individual to behave in ways desired by the marketer? Table 13.1 lists eight conditions that must be met.

First, a communication strategist must understand the day-to-day behavior of the target audience, so messages can be delivered in places and at times likely to result in exposure. In turn, this requires an understanding of the media habits of the target audience —the specific newspapers and magazines they read (and, if possible, what sections of these they read); the times they are likely to watch televison and listen to the radio together with the types of broadcast programs they are most likely to turn to; and the routes and transportation modes they use for traveling to work and on shopping or recreational trips. Although media research can be conducted to obtain detailed answers to such questions (and will be discussed in more depth in Chapter 14), specific research projects can be very expensive. An alternative, and much cheaper, approach is to relate the characteristics of the target audience to the audience profiles of different newspapers, magazines, radio stations, and television stations. Such data are developed by most media organizations of any size and usually describe the audience in terms of demographic segments within a particular geographic area. Information on psychographic and benefit segments (see Chapter 7) usually has to be inferred from the nature of the medium or program content.

Second, the placement, scheduling, format, and content of the communication must be designed in such a way that it stands out among competing stimuli, thereby gaining the

Table 13.1 Conditions Necessary for Effective Communication

---

1. The intended recipient must have the opportunity to be exposed to the message.
2. At exposure, the message must gain the target recipient's attention, getting through the "noise" of competing stimuli.
3. The communicator must use common symbols that can be "decoded" by the recipient and thus understood as intended.
4. The message must have sufficient interest or relevance for the recipient that it is retained in short-term memory.
    (a) If the message urges an immediate action, the recipient must be able and willing to respond in the manner desired by the communicator within a very short period of time (less than one minute).
    (b) If the content of the message is directed at feelings, intentions, or actions of a less-than-immediate nature, the recipient must quickly rehearse the message so that it can be retained in long-term memory.
6. The information must be processed (integrated with other information already in the mind) before forgetting occurs or a competitive message interferes with accurate remembering.
7. The information thus recorded must stimulate or be responsive to some need, want, or concern on the part of the recipient.
8. The individual must be able to respond in the manner desired by the communicator.

---

target audience's attention. Success in this area involves skills in copywriting, design, and production. A visual ad that looks different (or an audio ad that sounds different) from other advertisements in the selected medium is one way of achieving this goal. We discuss these and related topics in more depth in the chapter that follows.

Third, the message must be couched in terms that the target audience will understand. The symbols used in communication are many; they include verbal language, body language, color, shape, typography, music, and other sounds. For communication to be effective, both communicator and audience must place similar interpretations on these symbols. Nothing demonstrates this better than the difficulties encountered by travelers in other countries in interpreting the communications they receive. Foreign languages, new currencies, and cultural differences in body language are obvious examples,[8] but others are more subtle. For instance: the "ringing" and "busy" tones on telephones vary sharply from one country to another; highway speed signs in most countries are given in kilometers per hour, but in the United States and Britain miles per hour are used; there are regional variations in the pronunciation of common English words ("route" may be pronounced as "root" or "rowt"). Some significant differences exist between British and American usage in the meanings of words (a "subway" in London is a pedestrian underpass; American. Canadians wishing to take the subway should look for a sign saying "Underground" or ask for directions to the "tube"). Schedules and opening hours throughout Europe tend to be printed in 24-hour notation; Canada and European countries make extensive use of pictographs and other symbols for signs, whereas U.S. signage is more likely to use words; police officers' uniforms vary sharply from country to country (and sometimes even between jurisdictions in the same country). French mailboxes are yellow; U.S. ones are predominantly dark blue; British "letter boxes" are bright red and a totally different shape from North American mailboxes. The list is almost endless!

The fourth through seventh conditions are concerned with ensuring that the communication imprints itself on the recipient's mind for long enough to have the desired result.

Essentially, the message must be designed to strike some responsive chord in the target audience if it is to elicit the response sought by the communicator. Effective copywriting requires an understanding of the needs, wants, concerns, and even fears of the audience. Often, as noted in the chapter on market segmentation, the marketer can divide a large group of prospective customers into market segments, based on either the benefits they seek from a particular product (benefit segmentation) or their attitudes, interests, opinions, and life-styles (psychographic segmentation). For instance, a campaign directed at getting people to eat a nutritiously balanced diet might promote the way such a diet allows people to maintain a high level of physical activity, or it might promote reduced risk of subsequent illness. Messages addressing the former theme might be addressed to physically active people who wanted to stay that way, while the latter theme might be targeted at those who worried about their health.

The final condition for effective marketing communication is that the recipient of the message must be able to respond in the manner desired by the communicator. Many of those who see or hear a message and take note of it are not, of course, prospective customers of the marketing organization. If a prospective customer is motivated by an advertisement or personal communication to take the action advocated, all the necessary follow-up mechanisms should be in place. For instance, if a phone number is listed as a source of further information, the line should be staffed or connected to a recorded message; the times and locations of service delivery should be easily obtainable (and adhered to in practice); goods advertised should be in stock at the time the advertising is run. These may sound like commonsense suggestions (and they are), but it is surprising how often there is a lack of coordination between those who plan and schedule the communication effort and those responsible for product execution.

THE COMMUNICATION MIX

The term *communication mix* is sometimes used to describe the array of communication tools and channels available to marketers. Just as marketers need to combine the elements of the marketing mix (including communication) to produce a marketing program, they also need to select the most appropriate ingredients for the constituent communication program.

The elements of the communication mix fall into four broad categories: (1) personal selling, (2) media advertising, (3) publicity and public relations, and (4) promotional or informational activities at the point of sale (or location where the behavior desired by the marketer is expected to take place).

The distinction between personal communication and the other three elements is that the former involves representatives of the marketer engaging directly in two-way communications with customers, either in person or via electronic media. The latter three elements are all one-way communications—from the marketer to the customers. The difference between advertising and public relations and publicity is that advertising messages are designed by the marketer (or an intermediary in the distribution channel) and transmitted through the chosen media in a predesigned format and at a preselected time.*

---

*Marketers who use free public-service advertising usually have to forgo some degree of control over format and scheduling.

Public relations and publicity, by contrast, involve the creation of information by the marketer for dissemination to the mass media whose editors then decide whether or not to use it and, if so, how and when to run it. "Point-of-behavior" promotion and information refers to signs, displays, and other forms of nonpersonal communication intended to attract customers' attention and motivate them to act. This element, sometimes coupled with discounted prices or even free use of a service, is often designed to promote immediate action as opposed simply to stimulating awareness and interest.

In short, communication elements can be divided into two broad groups: *interpersonal* communications that take place directly between individuals and *impersonal* communications that use a printed, broadcast, or other medium to transmit messages between sender and audience.

Interpersonal Communication

As suggested earlier in Figure 13.2, communication between individuals has a powerful advantage over mass-media communication in that the message goes directly from sender to recipient without (as a rule) having to leap the twin hurdles of lack of exposure and selective exposure. A second major advantage is that personal communications are usually two-directional, with the recipient able to ask the sender for clarification or additional information. A sender can adapt the content and presentation of the message to the characteristics of the recipient—and to that individual's needs and concerns as revealed during the interaction. In fact, communication may be initiated by a prospective customer who has learned about a product from friends, advertising, or other sources and wishes to obtain specific additional information. Such communication may take place face-to-face or by telephone.

In Chapter 6, we introduced the concept of the purchase (or adoption) decision process, whereby in many instances an individual is believed to go through several stages—including awareness, evaluation, and trial—in the process of deciding whether to purchase a product (or adopt a behavior pattern). The significance of this process for developing communication strategy lies in the fact that different communication channels may be relatively more effective in moving consumers from one stage of the process to another. At the outset, mass media are likely to be the most cost-effective channels for stimulating awareness and providing background knowledge. As consumers move toward evaluation and purchase, however, they may actively seek out two-way personal communications that will enable them to ask specific questions that will help them make their final decisions. Often, they will seek advice from family members and acquaintances—what is known as "word-of-mouth advertising."

Five types of interpersonal communication are relevant in the development of a communication strategy: proactive selling, reactive selling, customer service, customer contact, and personal advice.

Proactive selling involves the use of trained salespeople or change agents who actively seek out prospective customers or clients and attempt to encourage them to buy (or adopt the behavior pattern advocated by their organization). The term *change agent* is often used as a generic term to describe individuals whose job involves obtaining a change in their clients' social behavior (such as improved dietary habits, preventive health care, or adoption of safety procedures), as opposed to making a monetary sale to a customer. In either the monetary or the nonmonetary case, proactive agents often are involved in closing the sale—getting the client's agreement to undertake the desired activity or to buy and use the product.

Proactive selling involves going out and looking for customers, who may be acting on behalf of institutions or simply on their own behalf as individual consumers. For instance, a theater might send out a representative to obtain group bookings from a company for its employees to attend a performance; a health-maintenance organization may first need to get employers to include the HMO as a recognized part of their health-benefits package before individual employee enrollments can be solicited. Proactive selling can be a demanding job requiring creativity, staying power, and good interpersonal skills. Personal selling by telephone (one form of telemarketing) is widely used by nonprofits for fund-raising, membership renewals, and in political campaigns, as we discuss in Chapter 15.

Reactive selling, by contrast, is typified by situations in which the customer seeks out the salesperson or change agent, not vice versa. Examples might include a museum-shop attendant or a travel agent. Successful selling usually entails responsibility for closing sales (or for seeing that a specified behavior is adopted). This involves an element of persuasion—of marshaling the arguments for a particular course of action advocated by the seller.

Not all communications between the customer and representatives of the marketer necessarily involve persuasion or advocacy. A related activity, formalized in many service organizations, is the *customer service* function (described in detail in Chapter 15), which traditionally focused on giving out information (in person, by phone, or by personalized correspondence), responding to routine inquiries, and handling complaints or problems.

Nowadays, the role of customer service often embraces *customer-contact* personnel whose job brings them into contact with customers, even though the primary focus of that job may not be selling or customer assistance. Examples include bus drivers, train conductors, hospital staff, college administrators, and museum guards. The importance of these people from a marketing standpoint lies in customers' expectations of them. Someone unfamiliar with a city bus service may ask a bus driver how to get to a particular destination. A train traveler may wish to know about connecting services. Patients may need information from hospital staff and vice versa. Students may want information from college administrators about financial aid. A museum visitor may ask directions of a security guard. If these interactions are handled badly by employees, their ineptitude may reflect poorly on the entire organization. A brusque "I dunno" or "that's not my job" may be ill received by customers, as may insensitive demands from administrators or other personnel for information or payment. Hence management should offer training in communication skills to customer contact personnel and supply them with information that will enable them to respond to frequently asked questions. The use (and promotion) of distinctive uniforms may also assist customers in identifying the most appropriate employees for supplying advice or information. ("Need assistance? Ask any of our representatives in the red blazers.")

The final type of interpersonal communication is *personal advice* from individuals who are not directly involved in making a "sale," but who are in a position to influence the customer's behavior. These individuals may be family members, friends, other customers, or people whose job it is to offer objective advice—such as guidance counselors, ministers, or health workers.

Impersonal Communications

Although personal communication provides a powerful channel for messages, it is also costly and time consuming. Much information can be delivered far more cheaply through impersonal sources, particularly when the objective is to generate initial awareness.

Impersonal channels normally allow only for one-way communication between marketer and consumer. (In the future, however, we can expect to see more interactive information systems such as videotext.) The principal impersonal communication channels available to marketers can be divided into three groups—broadcast, print, and outdoor/signing/point-of-activity media. From the standpoint of the communication mix, it is important to distinguish between those communications that are controlled and paid for by the marketer and those that are ultimately controlled by the media in which the information is designed to appear (public-relations releases).

Table 13.2 shows the principal advantages and disadvantages of the two types of broadcast media, television and radio. Television is a powerful communication medium

Table 13.2 Principal Advantages and Disadvantages of Broadcast Media

Medium	Advantages	Disadvantages
Television	Impact of combining sound and moving visual images Mass coverage Opportunities for hourly, daily repetition Flexibility—a wide variety of message format and content is possible, can be used for demonstrations "Big-league" image Messages can be scheduled at specific times and within specific programs Availability of audience-research data by program	High cost of producing good-quality commercials Expensive to purchase because of audience size (not necessarily true of cable TV) Message is fleeting Message may lack authenticity of printed media Less easy to target specific market segments (easier with cable TV) Most advertisements are 30 seconds or less, limiting the content of advertisement Lacks narrow, geographic focus within a metropolitan area
Radio	Flexibility—can use any message that can be adapted to sound Production costs are relatively inexpensive Lead time for placing commercials is short Well-segmented audiences in large cities (including second-language groups) Highly mobile medium (radios go almost anywhere, including cars) Easy to be time-of-day specific Good for short reminder messages	Extensive competition from other stations in large cities Message is fleeting Hard to give out relatively specific information Limited research data available Lacks narrow, geographic focus within a metropolitan area

because it combines both audio and visual images. On the other hand, the high cost of producing good-quality commercials puts television outside the price range of many nonbusiness organizations even if donated advertising time can be obtained. Radio messages leave more to the listener's imagination because no visual images can be shown. Radio can often reach people at times and in locations where television sets are unlikely to be found—for instance, while they are driving cars or at the beach. In developing countries, where literacy rates are still low, radio is often the most pervasive impersonal medium. A key characteristic of both television and radio is that broadcast messages are fleeting; without use of recording equipment, they cannot be retained for later reference. Radio advertising is often used for short reminder advertising to encourage people to take action after previous messages, perhaps in other media, have built up awareness and knowledge of the product.

Print media may be more effective than broadcasting for transmitting messages containing a great deal of factual information. As shown in Table 13.3, newspaper and magazine ads can be clipped for future reference; direct mail not only provides a message in tangible form but also offers the advantage that the content of the message can be personalized to meet the particular situation of the recipient. Like personal communications, print media are often used to close the sale—typically, by printing an order coupon in the body of the ad, or including an order form and reply-paid envelope with a direct-mail communication. Radio and television messages sometimes include an address or phone number to contact, but are less satisfactory because this requires the audience to have pen or pencil ready to copy down the information quickly.

The third category of communication media is described in Table 13.4 under the general term of principal advantages and disadvantages of outdoor advertising, signs, and point-of-activity displays. These can carry only short messages as a rule, but many of them, such as billboards and signs, have the advantage of being geographically quite specific. This makes them useful for reminding people about social behaviors that have been advocated at greater length through other communication channels; examples include driving safely, obeying highway laws, preventing forest fires, and disposing of litter properly. At the point of purchase, signs and displays can be used to supplement personal communications in telling people where to find a service and how to use it.

In Chapter 14, "Advertising and Promotion Management," we discuss the issue of media selection in depth, including an appraisal of the opportunities for obtaining donated space or broadcast time. The first step in media selection is to recognize the wide array of communication channels available to nonbusiness marketers and to be aware of their relative advantages and disadvantages in reaching specific market segments and in communicating certain types of messages. Frequently, it is necessary to use several different communication elements so they will mutually reinforce one another, with the strengths of one complementing the relative weaknesses of another.

Marketer Control over Communication Content

As shown in Table 13.5, communication channels can be categorized not only according to their form (vertical axis) but also according to who controls their ultimate content (marketer versus intermediary versus consumer, as shown on the horizontal axis). The significance of the categories on the horizontal axis concerns the progressive loss of control that occurs over the content, format, and scheduling of the messages as other

Table 13.3 Principal Advantages and Disadvantages of Print Media

Medium	Advantages	Disadvantages
Newspapers	Metropolitan suburban papers offer intensive coverage Ads can be keyed to sections of paper with specific focus (e.g., Arts, Education, Business) Reader can control extent, duration of exposure Availability (in some instances) of zone editions and color inserts Can include high level of detail Reader can clip information or coupon Date of publication is known	Short life—soon discarded Reading is often hasty, cursory Relatively poor reproduction quality Selective reader exposure to different sections
Magazines	Audience segmented by nature of interests Good-quality reproduction Opportunities for use of color Long life before discard increases exposure potential (pass-along readership) Can include high level of detail Often used by consumers searching for information Ads can be clipped for reference, coupons	Longer lead time required Hard to make last-minute changes Variations in timing (date) of reader exposure leads to lack of immediate impact Fewer opportunities for geographic segmentation (varies by publication depending on its ability to produce regional print runs) Often skimmed quickly, resulting in selective exposure
Direct Mail	Extreme selectivity possible Opportunity to build own direct-mail list Can combine advertising messages with billing Scheduling can be controlled by advertiser at short notice Flexibility of format and reproduction quality Opportunities for personalizing messages and salutations through computerization Ability to provide complete information and reminders in controlled sequence (In United States) sharply discounted mailing rates for nonprofit organizations Availability of free franking privileges for some central/federal government agencies Ability to include envelopes (prepaid or not) for response	High unit cost per addressee Dependence on quality of mailing list Cost of updating mailing lists Customer resistance to junk mail Dependence on reliability of postal service (note problem of postal strikes and slowdowns) Inability to control delivery date with high precision (especially for discounted bulk-rate mail)

Table 13.4 Principal Advantages and Disadvantages of Outdoor Advertising, Signage, and Point-of-Activity Displays

Medium	Advantages	Disadvantages
Billboards	Location specific Highway sequencing allows high level of repetition of message Location on commute, shopping routes ensures high frequency of exposure Easy to notice and understand Can be implemented on "on-off" basis for extended period Good for building awareness and for reinforcement	Requires simple message Advertiser may be seen as contributing to visual pollution Message cannot be clipped for reference May be local restrictions on use of outdoor advertising in most desirable locations
Transit Advertising	Location specific (stations and shelters) Mobile (for external-vehicle messages) Reaches captive, traveling audience inside stations and vehicles Reaches broad cross section of population through external ads on vehicles Opportunity for tear-off response coupons on ads inside vehicles Offers high level of repetition	Risk of vandalism and weather damage Usually hard to confine to specific bus routes (train is more controllable) Association with "unsuitable" products (transit ads often emphasize cigarettes, drink, patent medicines) External vehicle ads require simple message Subject to removal or pasting over
Posters[a]	No media charges Can be time and location specific Can include tear-off telephone number Very low budget if use inexpensive printing and volunteer labor	Limited readership Subject to removal, vandalism, pasting over, or weather damage May generate image of low-budget nonprofessional organization if simply pasted on a wall
Signs	Serves as reminder Complements/reinforces personal or mass-media messages Offers high exposure in high-circulation areas Can remain in place for extended periods	May be lost in urban "clutter" Risk of vandalism to exterior signs Need for periodic maintenance, cleaning, lighting, removal of vegetation, etc. Local restrictions on use
In Store/Point of Activity Display	Serves as direct action follow-through to preselling in mass media Opportunity for association with specific retail outlet or intermediary Provides motivation and support to retail intermediaries Encourages impulse purchase and behavior Generates excitement at point of activity Opportunity for customer education to supplement sales personnel	Must compete for display space with other marketers May not be possible to guarantee scheduling and duration of display Controls may be needed to prevent misuse of display by retailer

[a]Defined as small-format ads pasted or mounted on bulletin boards or other free space (large posters, as the term is understood in British usage, are described here as billboards).

Table 13.5 Categorization of Communication Channels by Form and Locus of Control

Channel Form	Locus of Control		
	Marketer	**Intermediary**	**Consumers or Volunteers**
PERSONAL Face-to-face or telephone	Marketer's sales force or customer-contact personnel	Distributor's sales force or customer-contact personnel Voluntary efforts by third-party organization	"Word-of-mouth"
IMPERSONAL Mass-media communications (Television, radio, newspapers)	Paid or public-service advertising	Paid or public-service advertising	Critical or complimentary letters to the editor
Direct mail	Personalized mailings Brochures, catalogs, coupons, etc.	Enclosures in intermediaries' mailings	Consumer-originated mail to friends, family, colleagues, etc.
Public relations and publicity	Events and activities organized by marketer	News stories and editorials in mass media	Events at volunteers' homes
Displays, sales promotions, handouts, etc.	Displays and promotions at own or rented facilities	Displays and promotions at donated or nominally "public" facilities	Messages and symbols on clothing Bumper stickers on cars
Signage and other cues	Signs, symbols, etc., on own or rented space	Signs, symbols, etc., on donated or nominally "public" facilities.	Lawn or window posters, etc.

sources take responsibility for message dissemination. Reputable intermediaries who are paid for their services at commercial rates are generally fairly reliable, but intermediaries who undertake to execute communication tasks for a token fee or on a volunteered basis often fail to perform as the marketer had hoped. A particularly difficult problem arises with public-relations efforts designed to achieve favorable news coverage, which may be ignored, or presented in a different way than that desired by the marketer. The availability of public service advertising in the United States is particularly significant for nonprofit organizations operating on limited budgets. Editorial restrictions on "controversial" content and lack of guarantees on scheduling, placement, and format limit the value of this type of advertising. We will discuss its use in more detail in the next chapter.

Marketers exercise the least control over communications transmitted by individuals. Even with carefully trained, paid salespeople, there is no guarantee that they will communicate with customers in the manner desired by management. Volunteers present a challenging problem because management cannot always be as selective as it might wish in recruiting them and lacks the sanctions available to motivate and discipline paid employees. As we emphasize in Chapter 19, volunteers need careful training and supervision. Without this, they are likely to prove unreliable and inconsistent communicators. Consumers represent the final source of communications about an organization and its products. Their actions are very hard for the marketer to predict or control. For this reason, word-of-mouth comments usually carry a lot of weight with prospective customers; but the message content is not always favorable nor, in the marketer's view, an accurate representation of reality.

SUMMARY

Communications are used in marketing to inform, persuade or remind. Messages may be transmitted personally to existing or prospective customers through salespeople (or change agents), through customer service personnel and other employees in contact with customers, or even through consumers themselves. Alternatively, messages can be transmitted through impersonal channels such as the broadcast and print media, signage, retail displays, and so forth.

The array of communication alternatives potentially available to public and nonprofit marketers is immense, reflecting not only the diversity of their products, but also the opportunity to obtain free or discounted communication options that may be denied to commercial marketers.

A necessary prerequisite to formulation of marketing communication strategies is recognizing how communications work and then evaluating the strengths and weaknesses of different communication channels.

People are potentially exposed to hundreds of different messages each day, and even that number represents only a tiny fraction of all the messages publicly transmitted in a given city on a particular day. Through a process known as *selective exposure,* the average person sees or hears only a small proportion of the messages to which he or she might potentially have been exposed; only a fraction of these messages are actually noticed or attended to, reflecting a screening process known as *selective attention.* As a result of a process known as *selective retention,* only a few of the messages perceived are actually remembered long enough to be processed by the brain, integrated with other information already stored in the memory, and then acted on.

These screening processes make it necessary for marketers to seek ways of penetrating the screens through a combination of messages and presentation formats that are more likely to catch the attention of the target audience. Frequent repetition of a message may also increase its chances of being noticed and remembered.

An important issue for many nonbusiness marketers is that political or financial restrictions may constrain their ability to engage in expensive communication efforts. This poses a need for leveraging the impact of the funds that are available. Each communication channel has its advantages and disadvantages. One disadvantage is simply the cost of producing certain types of messages (such as television commercials) and buying time or space in the relevant media. On the other hand, a nonbusiness organization may be able to leverage its efforts through the use of volunteered services and donated media or through the use of intermediaries offering both expertise and economies of scale. The problem of relying on the services of intermediaries or individual volunteers is the loss of control over message content, format, and scheduling that may result. Marketers exercise the least control over "word-of-mouth" advertising by consumers. Precisely because it is hard to control what consumers say about an organization or its products to their families and acquaintances, this type of communication often carries a great deal of credibility among prospective customers.

REFERENCES

1. Christopher H. Lovelock, "An International Perspective on Public Sector Marketing," in M. P. Mokwa and S. E. Permut (eds.), *Government Marketing: Theory and Practice,* New York: Praeger, 1981, pp. 114–143.

2. Judy Jones Putnam and Jon Weimer, "Nutrition Information: Consumers, Views," *National Food Review,* Spring 1981, pp. 18–20.

3. Decimal Currency Board, *First Annual Report, 1967–68.* London: Her Majesty's Stationery Office, 1968.

4. Christopher H. Lovelock, "Marketing National Change: Decimalization in Britain," in C. H. Lovelock and C. B. Weinberg (eds.), *Public and Nonprofit Marketing Cases and Readings,* New York: John Wiley & Sons, 1984.

5. Reported in *Advertising Age,* May 13, 1957, and cited in Raymond A. Bauer and Stephen A. Greyser, *Advertising in America,* Boston: Division of Research, Graduate School of Business Administration. Harvard University, 1968, pp. 173–174.

6. As in reference 5, pp. 175–177.

7. Michael L. Ray, *Advertising and Communication Management,* Englewood Cliffs, N.J.: Prentice-Hall, 1982, p. 7.

8. Edward T. Hall, "The Silent Language in Overseas Business," *Harvard Business Review,* May–June 1960, pp. 87–96.

Chapter 14
Advertising & Public Relations Management

A story is told about a business executive who, on reviewing his organization's advertising efforts, observed ruefully: "I know that half the money we spend on advertising is wasted. Unfortunately, I don't know which half." It is easy to waste money on advertising and other marketing communication efforts such as publicity and public relations, since such efforts often cannot be related directly to subsequent sales. Personal selling, which involves direct customer contact, is sometimes easier to evaluate, but it is a very expensive medium of communication and does not always offer the most efficient approach to communicating with customers.

Many public and nonprofit managers are fearful of spending money on communication efforts, regarding such expenditures as "wasteful" and even "inappropriate." As a result, they may be condemning their organizations to operating far below their potential —and even risking failure in the process. Another group of managers, while reluctant to spend money, do recognize the need to inform customers about their products and to encourage them to buy (or to use a free service or to adopt an advocated behavior pattern). The latter's approach is to seek out sources of "free" communication, such as public-service advertising, public-relations activities, and volunteer salespeople. For some organizations, this approach works well; for others, it may represent a false economy.

The development of effective communication strategies must be based on a clear understanding of what role communication efforts are expected to play in the overall marketing program. In social-behavior programs, personal and impersonal communications typically play the central role; in marketing goods and services, on the other hand, communication efforts are generally designed to support and complement the product, distribution, and pricing elements of the marketing mix. In either case, the nature of the tasks assigned to communications must be defined precisely before an effective, cost-efficient program can be designed.

Scope of the Chapter

The previous chapter introduced the different types of communication tools available to marketers and discussed how communication processes work. This chapter will be concerned with development of communication strategies, including: selection of tools (and the role that each is to play); determination of target audiences, messages, budgets, and scheduling; and measurement of the effectiveness of communication programs.

We begin with a brief recapitulation of all the elements of the communication mix, emphasizing that most well-planned communication programs entail the use of several different elements designed to complement and reinforce each other instead of representing either/or alternatives. We consider, too, some ethical concerns that arise in developing a marketing communication program. From here, we turn our attention to the different steps involved in developing a communication program, proceeding from situation analysis to specific marketing objectives and the role of communication activities in meeting these objectives. To illustrate how research can help define objectives, develop an effective communication campaign, and monitor performance, we describe a program used in the Australian state of Victoria to encourage physical fitness among the population.

Specific issues in setting budgets, establishing goals, and developing and disseminating messages constitute the next topic for discussion. Because budgetary restrictions have long been a central issue for public and nonprofit organizations, many have historically relied on supposedly "free" channels of communication, such as public-service advertising and public relations in place of paid media advertising. We take a look at both public-service advertising and public relations, examining their pros and cons.

Our primary focus in this chapter is on managing impersonal communications. Customer service and personal selling, which involve fact-to-face communications, will be discussed in more depth in Chapter 15.

COMMUNICATION CRITERIA

A small nonprofit organization may spend as little as $10–15 on promoting a local event such as a rummage sale. A national public agency, by contrast, may spend millions of dollars each year on advertising and personal selling. In each instance, how carefully that money is spent—and, indeed, whether the amount budgeted is sufficient for the task at hand—will determine how successful the communication program is in meeting its objectives.

Ethical Concerns

As we noted in the previous chapter, a marketer has available a wide array of communication tools, collectively known as the *communication mix*. Figure 14.1 summarizes the key elements. Perhaps the most debated of these elements for nonbusiness organizations is paid media advertising. Many nonprofit and public agencies have long been reluctant to invest in the expense of paid advertising, preferring instead to employ the less reliable tools of either public-service advertising or public relations to transmit messages to their target audiences.

This antipathy to the use of paid media advertising is beginning to ease, but still remains significant in the U.S. public sector, where many critics regard advertising expenditures by government as wasteful or propagandistic.[1] Criticisms have also been made in Canada, where federal advertising expenditures are significantly higher as a proportion of total government outlays than those in the United States.[2] Among the concerns expressed is that the government of the day is using advertising to promote a

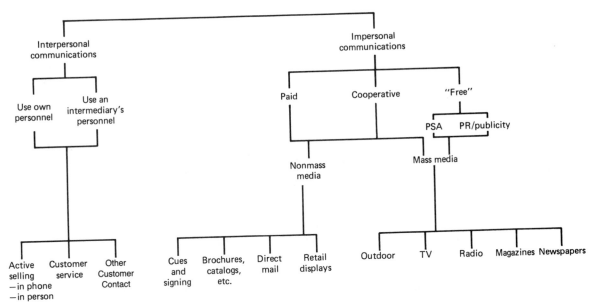

Figure 14.1 Communication-mix decisions.

partisan point of view; others worry that lucrative advertising contracts may be awarded to agencies on the basis of political favoritism.[3]

As we have emphasized before, the tools of marketing—including each element of the communication mix—are ethically neutral. It is how they are used that determines whether they merit criticism on moral or other grounds. A 1982 survey of 1000 people in four Canadian provinces showed that at least three-quarters of the sample felt that government advertising served a useful purpose. People particularly approved of government advertising to discourage such social behaviors as drunk driving, drug abuse, and alcohol abuse, as well as advertising to promote healthier living habits and safety in the workplace. This approval held especially "in cases where there is a demonstrated economic as well as social benefit from such advertising."[4]

Over 80 percent of those surveyed approved of advertising that informed citizens of changes in the law, tax exemptions, government-assistance programs, and job-training opportunities. Respondents also approved highly of government advertising that encouraged people to "buy Canadian," conserve energy, or respect the rights of others. Two-thirds to three-quarters of the sample (the percentage varied by province) believed that governments had the right to advertise their own views, even on politically sensitive issues. Only a minority of respondents (9 to 30 percent, depending on the province) mentioned the cost to taxpayers of government advertising as undesirable. Over 60 percent of the total sample agreed that there should be "regulations on what governments can say or show in their advertising." More generally, there was concern that governments state their point of view

> in a forthright, factual, unbiased way, not a manipulative way. [People] are supportive of government advertising of a factual, informative nature, but they challenge advertising that they perceive as manipulative or as image building for the government.[5]

In general, respondents believed government advertising had a place in society, but they questioned its possible use in a manipulative manner.

Other areas in the political arena also lend themselves to possible abuse of marketing communications. Chief among these is political campaign advertising, either for candidates or for referendum issues. Well-financed campaigns, involving misleading messages repeated with a high degree of frequency over a limited span of time, certainly have the potential to swing undecided voters. At least mass advertising is visible to all—proponents, opponents, and undecided voters—when it appears in outdoor, press, or broadcast media. The problem here is that political opponents may lack the funds to counter half-truths and outright distortions with large-scale advertising efforts of their own. Perhaps more insidious is the growing use of direct mail, containing a variety of subtly different messages, each targeted at a different segment. The mails are private, and it may not be possible for others to determine what messages are being sent and to whom.

Direct mail has become a major communication channel for political campaign committees in recent years, fueled in part by the use of sophisticated research to uncover the beliefs and concerns of different market segments, the availability of carefully segmented mailing lists, and the ability of modern word-processing technology to generate "personalized" letters. This same technology has, of course, been used by both scrupulous and less scrupulous political groups, and by a wide array of nonprofit organizations seeking support for a specific cause or fund-raising program. The technology is neutral, but it offers a powerful tool whose use might reasonably be scrutinized more carefully— particularly because it uses the national postal service as its distribution channel.

Other communication elements tend to receive less scrutiny than paid media advertising, but both managers and critics would do well to remember that personal selling frequently involves more significant financial outlays, even when the selling is done by volunteers. All forms of communication have the potential to be manipulative.

Sound Communication Decisions

Readers may feel that we have taken a rather jaundiced view of communication efforts so far in this chapter. Our concern, however, is simply to help marketing managers make good communication decisions and to enable nonmarketers to develop a broader perspective on the use of communication elements by public and nonprofit organizations.

Other than behaving in an ethical way, what do we mean by "good communication decisions"? There are two criteria. One is that the communication program achieve the specific objectives, in terms of measurable results, that management intended for it. Second is that the program make efficient use of the organization's resources (including management, staff and volunteer time) in achieving the desired results.

Effective, efficient communication strategies require that communication objectives be linked explicitly to broader marketing objectives and that communication budgets be set in the context of the overall marketing budget and the value of the goals to be achieved. Knowing how communications work and being aware of the wide array of communication tools available are important prerequisites to sound decision making. But much more is required. The choice and use of communication elements must be consistent with decisions on product policy, pricing, and distribution. A communication budget must be established with reference to the tasks that are to be performed and the value to the organization of the desired outcome(s). Alternative ways of spending the budget must be carefully evaluated. Finally, research inputs will probably be needed at four levels.

1. To develop the campaign objectives.
2. To set budgets.
3. To pretest the effectiveness of planned communication elements.
4. To evaluate the impact of the communication program by measuring key variables (attitudes, sales, etc.) both before and after launching the campaign.

As in the private sector, advertising campaigns by public and nonprofit organizations are often unsuccessful because of failure to use research inputs at any (or all) of these four levels.

To illustrate a successful campaign and the effective use of research in analyzing a situation, defining objectives relative to specific market segments, and developing an appropriate communication mix and message strategy, we'll review the "Life. Be In It" campaign for physical fitness developed by the state government of Victoria, Australia.

DEVELOPING A FITNESS PROGRAM IN AUSTRALIA

Responding to concerns about the social and economic impact of illness, the Department of Youth, Sport, and Recreation of the State of Victoria decided to implement a "fitness program." The initial concept called for a communication campaign to take a hard-line approach to encouraging people to "get fit"—and be quick about it, too. Some administrators, however, suggested that it might be wise to study the topic first.

A research program was therefore developed with the following objectives.

1. To better understand the factors that motivated or demotivated people with respect to physical recreation.
2. To isolate target groups as a basis for effective communication.
3. To assess how Victorians might best be encouraged to participate more in physical activities.

The initial steps in the research program involved talking to people working in the field of recreation, reviewing relevant research and publications, and conducting a series of small group discussions about activities that people undertook in their spare time. Some of the findings raised fundamental questions concerning the intended fitness campaign. From the group discussions, it was learned that people did not see health and fitness as synonymous; indeed, for many the conscious pursuit of fitness was not a concern or issue. Further, although attitudes toward fitness and recreation were quite favorable, the link between these attitudes and actual behavior was tenuous.

These insights were helpful in developing a household survey that was subsequently administered to a quota sample of 1000 subjects—800 in the Melbourne metropolitan area and 200 from five smaller towns in the state. The findings from this survey confirmed those from the earlier small-group discussions and yielded the following key conclusions:

■ Whereas favorable attitudes toward activity existed, action based on such attitudes was a scarcer commodity.

- Around 60 percent of the Victorian population was unconvinced of the need to engage in physical activity, even though they understood the arguments in favor of it. This group was referred to as the "drifters."

- Another 20 percent of the Victorian population had "tuned out" to physical activity. This group included many females and older people who lacked confidence in their physical abilities.

- The remaining 20 percent of the population was "tuned in" to physical activity, but to varying degrees and with different motivations.

- A high level of support was evident for the concept of improved health through physical activity. However, this was quite different from acceptance of the need for physical exercises as a basis for health.

- Emphasis on "keeping fit" had led to a narrow stereotyped image of the need for such activities as exercises and jogging.

- The emphasis on "working" to be fit clashed with the much wider concept of "physical activity" held by many.

- Keeping fit was generally seen to be boring, slow, and tedious and hard work.

- The concept of enjoyment pervaded viewpoints on active recreation. Even those who took activity for granted were doubtful of the virtues of doing things in the absence of enjoying the activities.

- Actual and/or potential feelings of embarrassment and/or feelings of incompetence were significant factors in causing people to "tune out" to physical activity. This was particularly true of those who did not regard themselves as having the "necessary skills" to keep fit.

Through cluster analysis of responses to the attitudinal scales, the researchers identified psychographic segments: "drifters," "tuned out," "tuned in," and "supertuned."

This analysis showed clearly that the department's original plans for a hard-hitting fitness campaign would not appeal to 80 percent of the Victorian population (composed of the two groups described as the "drifters" and the "tuned out"). The Minister of Youth, Sport, and Recreation subsequently announced that the original concept would be dropped in favor of a strategy based on the market research. The department's task was redefined: the public's concept of physical activity had to be broadened from such narrow stereotypes as jogging; people had to be shown that physical activity could be given a higher priority without pain; the inactive had to be encouraged to think about becoming more active and the already active to continue being so.

Because the department was not in the business of supplying recreational services, the project team assigned to the campaign recognized that they had to deal with two marketing tasks: (1) reaching members of the public, and (2) gaining the cooperation of organizations that were "suppliers" of physical activities.

Strategy Development for the Public Campaign

The principal objectives of the public campaign were stated as follows.

1. Target "drifters" and "tuned-out" segments, representing 80 percent of the population.

2. Emphasize activity instead of fitness.

3. Associate activity with fun and enjoyment instead of with health and fitness.

4. Show how the many forms of low-key physical activity could be built into everyday life and all life-styles.

5. Demonstrate opportunities for the family members to engage in recreation together.

Three types of activity were then identified as the basis for promotional efforts. *"Get Moving"* activities required no special facilities, equipment or organized structure. They emphasized walking, bike riding, using local parks, playing with balls or frisbees, flying kites, and so forth. *"Where You're At"* activities involved some equipment and structured use of this in places where people tended to congregate naturally, such as parks, beaches, and picnic areas. Finally, *"Learn To"* activities would provide people with opportunities to learn—or improve their skills in—a wide range of specific physical activities.

During the first 12 months of the program, priority would be given to "Get Moving" activities, with the others being introduced on a sequential basis and given greater emphasis during the second phase of the campaign. This approach would allow time for outside organizations to become supportive of the program. It also provided a logical sequence for building individual involvement.

The key communication objectives for the first phase of the public campaign were twofold.

1. Obtain acceptable levels of recognition, recall, and awareness for the department's overall campaign theme, specific campaign events, and ongoing activity alternatives.

2. Encourage public participation in a wide range of activity alternatives.

Knowing that fitness programs in other countries had taken several years to develop widespread awareness and generate the advocated behavior, the project team was cautious in its expectations for the campaign. No formal target figures were announced, but one observer suggested that attaining a 50 percent awareness level after 12–18 months would be considered a very good performance.

Strategy Development for the Organizational Campaign

To leverage the public campaign, it was important to secure the cooperation of numerous other organizations, ranging from other state-government departments, such as education and parks and gardens, to sporting associations, mass-media outlets, and commercial firms.

A total of 22 organizations (some of them federations of smaller local groups) were identified. Each was analyzed to determine the contribution that it could make to (1) the *communication* aspects of the campaign (for instance, advertising, publicity, exhibitions, literature, and films) and (2) the *supply* aspects (such as physical locations, equipment, people, funds, and programs).

These organizations were contacted personally in order to establish the credibility of the program and to encourage their involvement in the various phases of the campaign, particularly the "Learn To" and "Where You're At" activities during the second year of the program. Prior to launching the first phase of "Get Moving" activities, particular attention was given to ensuring that media organizations fully understood the objectives of the campaign and had sufficient understanding to provide supportive media coverage. To supplement personal contact, information kits were developed for both the media and other organizations.

Development of Messages

An advertising agency was selected to work with the project team on developing and transmitting specific messages. Reflecting the insights gained from the research findings, planners agreed that the thrust of the campaign should be to encourage "evolution" instead of "revolution" in individual life-styles. The task was seen as getting most citizens to do a little more, not getting a few to do a lot more.

The agency's creative director described his creative philosophy as follows.

> The Australian has a strong anti-authoritarian streak and far prefers to offer irreverent advice [as a spectator] . . . than participate in physical activity. This suggests that a sense of humour is an important ingredient in any attempt to communicate. . . . A good-humoured approach to the problem breaks down hostilities, prejudice, intellectualized resistance. A government program postulated on good humour is hard to brand as authoritarian. Therefore the approach, although very serious in intent, does not express itself in an over-serious tone of voice. It doesn't lecture, or sermonize, or harangue. . . .
>
> The programme will offer people useful but amusing suggestions as to how they can escape from their self-imposed restrictions. We will offer them life instead of mere existence, show them that life can be a little more enjoyable, and suggest that they in fact "Be In It."

The campaign slogan became: "Life. Be In It."

The nature of the campaign practically demanded the visual impressions of movement that only television could deliver to a mass audience. The agency developed four 60-second television advertisements using animated cartoon characters instead of people. This approach was not only inherently amusing but also made it easier for viewers of all backgrounds to identify with the characters (who subsequently achieved a certain celebrity status!). One commercial depicted a family taking exercise together in various low-key ways; two specifically promoted walking; a fourth gently satirized inaction. Figure 14.2 shows the preliminary storyboard for the fourth commercial.*

Several television stations agreed to provide extensive free public-service showings of these commercials. During the first 12 months of the campaign there were more than 1000 exposures of these advertisements, which were not attributed to the state government in the interest of ensuring a nonauthoritarian stance (not an easy political decision to take).

Four other communication elements—T-shirts, stickers, posters, and publications—were used to reinforce and expand the messages contained in the television advertising. They were distributed in large quantities through such channels as departmental regional offices, publicity events, schools, stores in a pharmacy chain, and organizations such as the National Fitness Council of Victoria. A number of other promotional items were also developed. More than 210,000 copies of the publications were distributed.

Complementing both the advertising and promotional efforts was a public relations campaign designed to get the "Life. Be In It" message across through news and editorial coverage in the mass media. A public-relations agency was appointed to handle this aspect

---

*A storyboard is an advertising agency's mock-up of how a completed advertisement might actually appear.

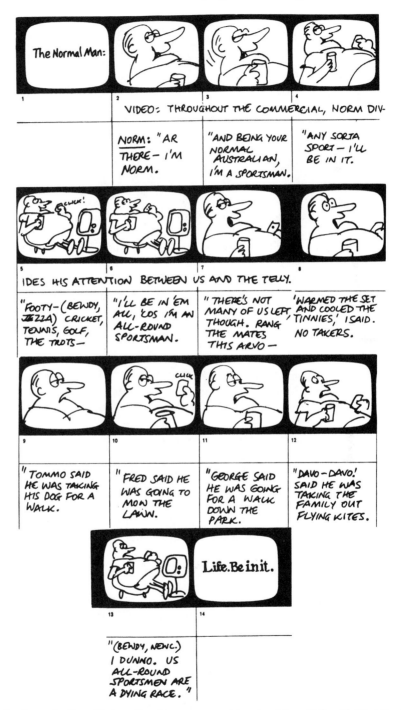

(*Note:* Readers unfamiliar with Australian slang may appreciate a translation. "Ar" = hi; "Footy" = football; "the trots" = trotting races; "Bewdy" = beautiful shot!; "Jezza" and "Newc." = nicknames of two well-known Australian sportsmen; "Arvo" = afternoon; "Tinnies" = beer cans.)

Figure 14.2 Television storyboard for the "Life. Be In It" commercial.

of the campaign and worked closely with the department to develop press and broadcast contacts. Specific efforts included a precampaign launch conference, distribution of publications and films, and a series of events that highlighted the theme of gentle exercise being good for all.

Campaign Results

As set out in the marketing plan, evaluations of the "Life. Be In It" campaign were carried out six and eighteen months after its launch. After six months, unprompted recall of the campaign stood at 53 percent and prompted recall at 79 percent. After eighteen months, these figures stood at 90 percent and 97 percent, respectively. By comparison, it took Germany's "Trimm" fitness program five years to reach these levels. Not only were Victorians able to recall specific messages disseminated in the campaign, but there also was clear evidence of behavior change. Six months after the campaign began, around 15 percent of those surveyed stated that they had become more active as a direct result of the campaign, and were able to state how they had done so. After 18 months, this figure had risen to 35 percent.

Perhaps the most significant accolade for the campaign's effectiveness came when the "Life. Be In It" campaign was expanded across the entire country as Australia's official "National Activity Programme."

An Appraisal

The "Life. Be In It" campaign is a classic example of a successful, large-scale social-behavior marketing program. Undoubtedly the most significant aspect of the program was the use of research to define the precise nature of the product, including minimization of the nonmonetary costs commonly associated with physical activity. The research findings were helpful in identifying key psychographic segments and in developing messages to communicate to the two largest segments.

Other noteworthy features of the campaign were the use of promotional elements to supplement and reinforce the television commercials, the leveraging of departmental resources through public-service advertising, the successful cultivation of the media through public relations, and the recruitment of many other organizations to assist in communication efforts or in supplying various facilitating resources. Finally, follow-up research was subsequently used twice to evaluate the performance of the campaign.

COMMUNICATION DECISION SEQUENCE

Much has been written about specific aspects of marketing-communication management. Obviously, we cannot hope to provide in-depth coverage here of all relevant issues, but we emphasize the integrated approach to communication decisions proposed by Michael Ray and briefly review its principal components.[7]

As shown in Figure 14.3, the starting point for making communication decisions is a situation analysis (see Chapter 3, "Conducting a Marketing Audit"). Marketing objectives are then set. Depending on the type of organization and situation, objectives might be specified in terms of sales value or volume, share of total votes cast, value of donations

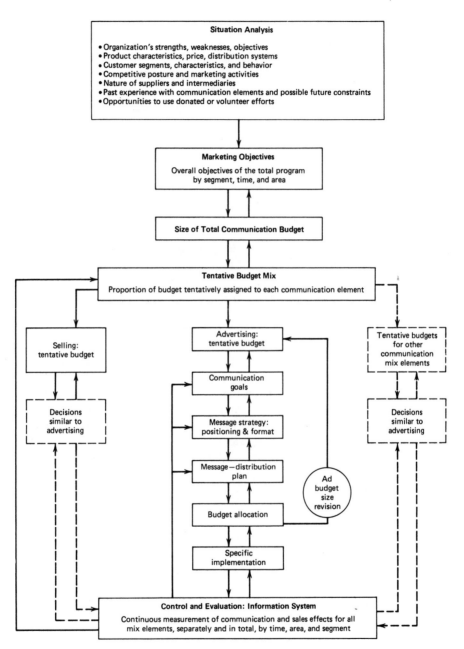

Figure 14.3 The communication decision sequence.
(Adapted from Michael L. Ray. "The Full Decision Sequence," *Journal of Marketing*.
January 1973, p. 31. Used with permission.)

received, awareness of a specific social issue, intention to use a particular service in the future, number of volunteers recruited or letters written to politicians, percentage of reduction in traffic accidents, or a host of other measures. Not every communication campaign seeks to influence behavior directly. For instance, the initial phase of a campaign may seek to develop knowledge and awareness, the second to influence preferences for a particular course of action, and the third to get the target audience to adopt the desired behavior.

Management must think not only of the desired objectives, but also of the budget necessary to reach them. As Figure 14.3 indicates, the communication decision sequence reflects a need to iterate between communication planning and economic evaluation. The manager needs to ask whether there are sufficient funds to reach the goals, if achievement of the goals is worth the cost, and whether the funds are being spent most efficiently.

Setting the Budget

As the chapter-opening quote indicated, setting the communication budget—both in total and for each element of the communication mix—is a controversial issue, posing both practical and theoretical problems. Advertising is probably the most troublesome area to set budgets for, and we will phrase our discussion in those terms, but all areas of communication pose difficulties.

Ideally, managers should use an economic model based on the marginal response to advertising. Additional funds would be devoted to advertising (or particular media, such as direct mail) as long as the response justified the expenditure. Even in the private sector where a sales response can be translated into a net revenue figure, such an approach is infrequently used. Because of difficulties in measuring the response to advertising, other approaches are usually employed. We will briefly review these approaches, but in the long-run we believe that a sound approach to advertising management requires budgeting approaches based on measurement of the response to advertising expenditures.

Many organizations appear to budget for the next year based on what they spent in the previous year. Some do this just by extrapolating the dollar level from the previous year, and others relate expenditures to sales, usage, or some other activity. Thus a theater company may spend $500 per play for publicity and set next year's budget at $2500 if five plays are to be produced. The obvious fallacy here is that the output of the organization is creating advertising budgets and not the other way around. Advertising should help build an audience for a play and the attendance estimates should be partially based on advertising levels.

A related budgeting philosophy is to spend whatever can be afforded. This assumes, at the extreme, that advertising and sales are unrelated and the value of advertising cannot be shown. As in the last approach, the dependence of usage on advertising is not recognized.

Another approach is to base expenditures on what either competitors or complementary organizations are doing. Thus one university might increase its advertising budget for continuing education in local newspapers in response to increases by other nearby colleges that are also trying to attract students. Paying attention to competition is important, and such information can play an important role in budget setting. But relying solely on matching (or relating in a fixed manner to) competitive spending levels—the "competitive parity" approach—ignores such facts as the differing goals, media efficiencies, and market segments of competitors. Moreover, this method implicitly assumes that competitors are spending optimally.

A frequently used approach is the "objective-and-task" method in which subobjectives are established for the communication program (and its constituent elements) and a budget is set and allocated in terms of the tasks deemed necessary to achieve the assigned objectives. This can be a sound approach when based on a detailed situation analysis, good understanding of the response of communication targets (e.g., awareness, knowledge, attitude) to different advertising levels, and careful evaluation of the worth of achieving different goals. Public and nonprofit organizations that do not sell products at a price (or do so below cost) may find that the correct issue is not placing a monetary value on their advertising goals, but using their funds to meet communication goals most efficiently. An objective-and-task approach, as compared to the three approaches just outlined, has the advantage of focusing attention on what advertising can do. Difficulties occur, however, when objectives and tasks are largely platitudes instead of measurable performance indicators, and no real effort is made to determine how changes in advertising levels will influence the achievement of communication goals. As we've stressed throughout this chapter, establishment of sound goals is critical in planning a communication program. The next section turns directly to goal setting and other key communication decisions.

FOUR KEY DECISIONS IN MARKETING COMMUNICATION

How can a marketing manager coordinate such varied communication activities as advertising copywriting, management of sales territories, and liaison with media outlets for publicity purposes? The answer lies in taking decisions across the entire communication mix in four key areas.

1. Communication goals.
2. Message appeals-positioning.
3. Message format.
4. Message-distribution plan.

The balancing of goals, positioning, format, and distribution must reflect the current situation and available budget and may need to be changed over time. Consider, for instance, the case of a newly constructed rapid-transit system. When the system first opens, management can probably rely on widespread publicity from stories in the mass media to build awareness but may need to augment this with an informational advertising campaign giving people specific details on using the new service and letting them know how to obtain further information. Perhaps a direct-mail campaign may also be conducted in the corridors served by the rapid-transit lines to distribute maps and schedules. As time passes and public knowledge of the system improves, special promotions may be used to boost ridership during off-peak hours. Figure 14.4 illustrates the "Bus 2 Us" promotional campaign developed for retailers by the Southern California Rapid Transit District (RTD). The RTD developed the concept, based on a slogan on a California vehicle license plate, and encouraged its use by retailers located along bus lines. Sales representatives may be hired to work with large employers, retailers, and other groups to develop public-transportation packages tailored to the needs of specific segments. In the unlikely event of a strike shutting down the system, effective use of public relations may help to minimize unfavorable publicity and to ensure that the mass media provide accurate information about transportation alternatives. When the dispute has been resolved and the system reopens, a new advertising campaign will be needed to restore public confidence and rebuild ridership.

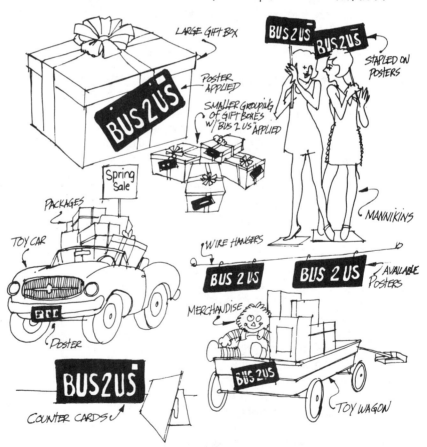

Figure 14.4   Promotional materials suggested for "BUS 2 US" campaign.

Communication Goals

In any given campaign, each communication element should be assigned a specific role to play in achieving overall objectives. Communication goals refer to the states of mind that a prospective customer may go through or the actions that a person may take in response to advertising or another communication medium. Often different elements in the communication mix are assigned different goals. For instance, a multistep process is sometimes used in which different elements move the prospective customer along a hierarchy from initial awareness to final purchase. Thus a print advertisement may seek to promote awareness of the organization and provides enough information to stimulate interest among prospective customers in writing or telephoning to request further information. The use of a *direct-response* approach such as this provides rapid feedback on the effectiveness of the campaign (the advertisement can be coded to identify the magazine, or even the issue, in which it appeared). It also helps the organization to build a mailing list.

Setting the appropriate communication goal for each element of the campaign is a difficult task; yet it must be faced. Without explicit communication goals, it is difficult to guide and control decision making in other key areas of marketing communication. Advertising is particularly susceptible to lack of control, and so we'll discuss some of the alternatives available for setting advertising goals.

Advertising objectives, like other goals, should be operational and meet the tests of specificity, importance, and challenge as outlined earlier. An obvious communication goal is an immediate action or behavior—sales, usage, or inquiries—and direct-response ads can be linked directly to a behavioral outcome although not to actual enrollment. Whenever possible, objectives should be expressed in terms of usage. Often, however, sales or usage cannot serve as operational objectives because (1) advertising is just one part of the marketing program and only one of many factors influencing usage and (2) advertising's contribution to achievement of the goal may occur primarily over the long-run. To illustrate the latter point, the impact of one year's advertisements to promote energy conservation may not have a behavioral impact until several years hence when a person buys a more fuel-efficient automobile or appliance.

If behavioral objectives cannot be used, an analysis of the thought and other processes leading to the desired behavior and an assessment of the role that advertising can play in those processes should be made. Such an analysis was well illustrated in Australia's physical-fitness campaign where objectives were stated in terms of awareness and recognition. The key is not to build awareness for its own sake, but to build awareness of a program because that is a logical precursor of behavior. Advertising goals often are stated in terms of recognition, awareness, image, and/or attitude; the material in Chapter 6, "Customer Behavior and Decision Making," provides a more complete discussion of the processes underlying behavior and the appropriate concepts to use as goals. Once established, communication goals become the guide for establishing a message strategy.

Message Appeals-Positioning

Message strategy consists of two parts: what to say (appeals-positioning) and how to say it (format). A campaign's appeals-positioning, sometimes called the "copy platform" or "message idea," should be based on the notion that each audience segment will be

Figure 14.5 Single-column newspaper public-service advertisement
for American Red Cross campaign.

motivated by specific appeals or product features.* As shown in the "Life. Be In It"
campaign, research often plays a vital role in identifying segments and determining how
best to communicate to them. The statement of appeals-positioning or copy platform
provides the framework or "blueprint" on which specific copy messages are built.

Compare Figures 14.5 and 14.6 as examples of advertisements that are loosely
versus tightly positioned. The first depicts a public-service advertisement for the American
Red Cross designed to fit in a single column of a newspaper. The ad can do no more than
create broad awareness that the Red Cross needs volunteer assistance of an unspecified
nature. Figure 14.6 reproduces a full-page magazine public-service advertisement for the
National Center for the Prevention of Child Abuse, which has been effective in dispelling
misconceptions about this problem and encouraging people to take action. Note the
combination of factual information (which people need to have to understand the nature
of the problem), an appeal to the reader's emotions and conscience, and an invitation to
write for further information.

---

*Positioning strategy, as discussed extensively in Chapter 4, is a broader concept than appeals-positioning,
although the advertising program is often the major element in communicating the desired market position. Some
of the material in that chapter can be applied to building a communication program.

No one wakes up thinking, "Today I'm going to abuse my child."

Abuse is not something we think about. It's something we do. It runs against our nature, yet it comes naturally. It's a major epidemic and a contagious one. Abused children often become abusive parents. Abuse perpetuates abuse.

Child abuse is a major cause of death for children under two. Last year in America, an estimated one million children suffered physical, sexual or emotional abuse and neglect (many cases go unreported). At least 2,000 died needless, painful deaths. And if you think child abuse is confined to any particular race, religion, income group or social stratum,

you're wrong. It's everybody's problem.

What's being done about prevention? Not enough. Preventive facilities are simply inadequate. Most social agencies deal with abusers and their victims after the damage has been done.

Child abuse doesn't have to happen. With your help, most abusers could be helped. Your community needs your aid in forming crisis centers, self-help programs for abusers, and other grass roots organizations. Please write for more information on child abuse and how you can help.

What will you do today that's more important?

Abused children are helpless. Unless you help.

Write: National Committee for Prevention of Child Abuse, Box 2866, Chicago, Ill. 60690

A Public Service of This Magazine & The Advertising Council [Ad Council]

CHILD ABUSE CAMPAIGN
MAGAZINE AD NO. CA-1188-81—7" × 10" [110 Screen]
Volunteer Agency: Campbell-Ewald Company.

CM-5-81

Figure 14.6   Advertisement for National Committee for Prevention of Child Abuse.
Used with permission.

Message Format

Given a goal and a copy platform, what form should the message take? Should the advertising be humorous, use testimonials, include a demonstration, create fantasy, or evoke concern? What types of salespeople are needed and what should be included in their presentations to customers? Should the publicity release include pictures or not? Is there a role for a short-term sales promotion to dramatize some feature of the product?

Development of a message format is a "creative process"; many managers feel out of their depth at this point and look for professional advice to help in copy execution. Suppliers of creative marketing services—such as advertising agencies, public-relations firms, and promotional specialists—can be retained to design and implement the necessary steps. It is very important, however, to ensure that each specialist understands the budget constraints to be observed, the goals of the overall communication program, and the role assigned to the specific element of interest. Managers who fail to provide this necessary guidance are unlikely to achieve effective results. On the other hand, sharing insights from research and/or past experience, clarifying goals, and working from a well-specified copy platform (appeals-positioning) will maximize the chances of success.

There are no easy ways to judge the effectiveness of an advertisement beforehand. Of course, the ad must be judged against the communication goals and the copy platform to see if it is meeting the objectives set out for it. The execution of the ad itself must also be judged—does the ad communicate the main idea in a believable way? In many instances, an advertising agency will produce several alternative executions of ads for the client organization to review. A valuable step at this point is to *pretest* alternative message formats on a sample of the intended audience. Performing this step repeatedly over time for a particular product category will result in a better understanding of what types of messages are most effective in a particular context. For instance, an analysis of more than 40 public-service announcements (PSAs) on television relating to health issues concluded that producers of health PSAs who want their messages to be effectively received, understood, and accepted by target audiences should observe the following guidelines.

- Emphasize both the health problem and the solution in the PSA.
- Use a person typical of the target audience when presenting a testimonial.
- Visualize a reward from practicing the recommended health-improving behavior.
- Communicate the psychological benefits of practicing this behavior.
- If possible, actually demonstrate the healthful behavior.
- Use an approach other than humor.
- Use a high or moderate emotional appeal.[8]

Message-Distribution Plan

Once messages have been developed, the task is to decide how they should be distributed. Should the organization use its own employees for personal selling and other customer-contact tasks or should it use the services of an intermediary? Should the advertising be run on television, radio, newspapers, or billboards—or on a mix of these media options? Should promotions be staged at the organization's own facilities or at some other location that is perhaps more visible? Should special promotions be publicized through paid advertising, public-relations releases, or both? What is the most effective use of funds and employee and volunteer time? These are complex decisions, both for organizations with large communication budgets and those with minimal budgets. Advertising agencies are often well placed to undertake sophisticated analyses of media alternatives in order to allocate the budget in the most effective way, and they typically work with management to develop a media plan.

The objective of the media plan is to reach the desired target audience most efficiently within a limited budget. Generally, a mix of media vehicles is required because achievement of communication goals usually requires that a message (or set of messages) be seen more than once and because only rarely can one medium reach all members of a segment. We will examine three aspects of media scheduling.

1. Selecting the type of medium to use.
2. Selecting specific vehicles for consideration.
3. Determining the desired reach, frequency, and continuity of messages.

Selecting the Type of Medium. As we discussed in the previous chapter, each medium has its own characteristics. The needs of the campaign may dictate that certain media be used, as the following examples illustrate. If a mass-transit agency wants to inform riders of its new time schedules, print media that can list timetables are most appropriate. If a highway-safety organization wants to provide a visual demonstration that seat belts are effective in a crash, television advertising is most appropriate. If a long message needs to be conveyed, outdoor billboards are not appropriate. If the audience target is single women, magazines that these women read should be used. If the organization's media budget is small and the organization is unlikely to be able to use public-service advertising, expensive media must be ruled out.

One of the more difficult media questions is comparing the value of advertisements in different media forms (e.g., broadcast versus print). Advertisers should try to test different media types and their cost efficiency for themselves, but organizations may often need to base their choices on an assessment of their communication objectives and budgets, and on the characteristics of each individual medium. Most important, organizations should consider how to interrelate different media and not neglect the many forms of media that are available.

Selecting Media Vehicles. A vehicle is a specific magazine, newspaper, or television or radio program. Once a medium is chosen, the choice of vehicles is based on each vehicle's ability to reach the target segment, cost, and other factors such as the editorial climate and mood that may influence the fit of the product and the advertising message within the context of the media vehicle itself. For example, a family-planning agency may find that advertising in both the *Ladies Home Journal* and *Playboy* makes sense, but different copy executions probably would be required for each magazine.

Rating organizations, industry associations, advertising agencies, and the media themselves provide information on audience size, demographic and other characteristics of the audience, and costs. Costs within a media vehicle depend, in broadcast, on the duration of the ad and the time of showing, and, in print, on the size, number of colors, and placement of the ad. After the physical characteristics of an ad are determined, the cost of each vehicle relative to the size of expected audience can be calculated. The typical measure used is cost per thousand (CPM) and is defined as

$$CPM = \frac{\text{cost of a single insertion}}{\substack{\text{number of target market members} \\ \text{in audience (in thousands)}}}$$

Although frequently quoted and a helpful guide, CPM must be used with caution. It only measures one economic aspect of a media plan. For example, it may be necessary to use more costly media, on a CPM basis, in order to reach a larger fraction of the target segment. Furthermore, magazines differ in page size, and ads in weekly magazines may have less likelihood of being seen than ads in monthly magazines. Finally, as we discussed earlier, media vehicles must be judged in terms of their overall effectiveness in meeting the goals of the communication plan.

Determining Reach and Frequency. Reach represents the number of audience members who are exposed to the advertising at least once; frequency is the average number of times members of the target audience reached are exposed to the ad. In the advertising trade, there is considerable controversy as to what is meant by the word *exposed*. To illustrate, in terms of television advertising, is someone who is sitting in a room reading a newspaper exposed to an ad shown on the screen? Should someone knitting and watching television be counted as an exposure? Print advertising faces similar dilemmas: how should someone who is casually flipping through a magazine be counted versus someone who stops to read the headline of an ad?

Definitional issues aside, it is apparent that a media planner working within a budget needs to trade off reach versus frequency. For instance, if the target market consists of 1,000,000 people, is the organization better off reaching 250,000 an average of two times each, 500,000 once each, or 100,000 five times each? The answer depends on how responsive the customer is to a different number of messages and what the goal of the campaign is. In the case of Australia's "Life. Be In It" campaign to promote fitness, one exposure was likely to have little impact on the target segments, and a media plan based on multiple exposures was needed. On the other hand, a symphony orchestra announcing that a world-famous soloist was going to appear with the orchestra would probably not be concerned with developing a high repetition rate among its subscribers. In addition, media planners have to be concerned with the pattern of advertising over time. Initial aspects of the campaign may use a high proportion of the budget, while later aspects may be more limited and concentrate on reminder advertising.

Development of a media plan is an important step in a communication program. Many public and nonprofit organizations will find that media costs are the most expensive part of their advertising program. Others will be fortunate and be able to make effective use of public-service advertising and publicity. It is to these areas that we turn next.

PUBLIC-SERVICE ADVERTISING

In many countries, there are opportunities for public and nonprofit organizations to obtain donated advertising time or space. Nowhere are these opportunities as well developed as in the United States, where the Advertising Council (see box) coordinates production and distribution of national public-service advertising campaigns. At the local level, individual publishers or broadcasters will often agree to run public-service announcements (PSAs) on behalf of organizations located in the area.

The value of public-service advertising is a somewhat controversial topic among marketers. On the positive side, there are opportunities to reach a large audience with professionally prepared advertisements (donated free of charge by an advertising agency).

THE ADVERTISING COUNCIL

The Advertising Council is a private, nonprofit organization that conducts public-service advertising in the public interest. It began life in 1941 as the War Advertising Council and throughout World War II used mass communications to inspire public support for conservation of materials, armed-services enlistment, and purchase of war bonds.

After the war, the council changed its name and voted to continue its efforts on behalf of government agencies, while also welcoming requests for assistance from philanthropic organizations. Several basic criteria are employed in evaluating the 350 plus requests for assistance received each year. To be accepted by the council, a campaign must be:

- In the public interest.
- A project that lends itself readily to advertising.
- Timely.
- Noncommercial, nonpartisan, nonsectarian, and not designed to influence legislation.
- National in scope and priority (but the message must also apply at all the local levels).

The council conducts approximately 28 major public-service campaigns each year and supports roughly 50 additional campaigns by recommending them to the media and publishing information about them in its bimonthly *Public Service Advertising Bulletin*.

Most campaigns are concerned with such topics as health and safety, education, the environment, the disadvantaged, economics, community, the arts, and international understanding. Among well-known campaigns run by the Ad Council are "Smokey the Bear" (prevention of forest fires), "Take Stock in America" (U.S. Savings Bonds), "A Mind is a Terrible Thing to Waste" (United Negro College Fund), "Double Up America" (car pooling), "Sign of the Good Neighbor" (American Red Cross), "Give to the College of Your Choice" (Aid to Higher Education), "Let's Stop Handicapping the Handicapped" (rehabilitation), and "Take a Bite out of Crime" (crime prevention).

Planning, writing, and designing of campaign materials are contributed by a volunteer advertising agency. The organization for which the campaign is being conducted reimburses the council for all out-of-pocket production costs, such as films, recordings, mats, and plates; this averages around $75,000–100,000 per campaign. The finished materials are then distributed and promoted by the council to some 20,000 media outlets nationwide. Those outlets electing to broadcast or print the advertisements do so free of charge.

On the negative side, not all organizations qualify for public-service advertising, agencies are often selective about which clients they will take on free of charge, the messages must be noncontroversial, and the marketer has little control over where, when, and how frequently the ads are run. Since the time or space allocated to PSAs is usually what the media outlet could not sell or fill with its own editorial material, PSAs are often broadcast at odd hours or buried in obscure locations in a publication. Very few PSAs are played on television during prime time.

Critics argue that Advertising Council claims for the value of free public-service advertising are greatly overstated, since many broadcasters and publishers do not run the nationally prepared PSAs that are distributed to them through the council. One study found that less than 15 percent of network-fed PSAs were actually aired in local markets.[9] The advertising campaign director of the American Red Cross has said that she receives only 15 to 20 percent of the approximately 22,000 business-reply cards sent out by the council asking media outlets about their usage of Red Cross PSAs.[10] In many instances, local media may simply be replacing nationally distributed PSAs with paid advertising or local PSAs.

Another problem with public-service campaigns is that they often must be noncontroversial in order to satisfy the sensitivities of the multiple parties involved in providing a free campaign. For example, a report on an advertising campaign developed for Planned Parenthood through the Advertising Council noted:

> It took two years to get our campaign approved. Whenever our campaign was presented to a reviewing committee (and we had more reviewing committees than I could possibly remember), some surgical action was always inevitable. . . . Our campaign falls a good deal short of the objectives . . . hoped for. But compromise is a fact of life.[11]

The lure of free advertising and the failure to understand the difference between paid advertising and PSAs have resulted in many institutions banning the use of paid advertising. The result of an advertising prohibition is that other elements of the marketing mix, such as paid donor recruitment personnel, have to bear a disproportionate share of the overall marketing communication task.

Although PSAs have their limitations, Stephen Weber notes that people do see and remember PSAs.

> Smokey the Bear, for example, is a product of public service ads from the [U.S.] Forest Service, and it is doubtful that Ronald McDonald or Tony the Tiger are better-known advertising symbols.[12]

Few public-service campaigns have run the same campaign theme for as long as the Forest Service, which has used Smokey as its symbol for over 40 years. Indeed, the tag line "Only You Can Prevent Forest Fires" is now so well known that some of the advertisements run only part of the line, relying on the reader to complete it—thereby reinforcing the message in the process (Figure 14.7).

Although few PSA campaigns are in the Smokey category, many campaigns can be successful in achieving modest, carefully selected communication goals. For instance,

- A PSA campaign can reach a large number of people, at least in absolute terms.
- PSAs can provide information.

■ PSAs can affect behavior if the reinforcement environment will support the new behavior. For target behaviors of this type, the message in PSAs can serve as a cue or reminder ("mail early" or "douse your campfire"), or the information may be instrumental for achieving desired objectives (how to reduce home-energy costs).

The use of PSAs depends on the marketing goals. If brief, largely informational messages designed to allow for somewhat irregular audience exposure can be used, PSAs can be a helpful leveraging tactic for public and nonprofit organizations.

Making Effective Use of Public Service Advertising

The choice of PSAs versus paid media advertising is generally an "either/or" decision. There seems to be a widely held belief that organizations that have been using paid

Figure 14.7 Smokey the Bear: Public-service advertisement.
Courtesy U.S. Department of Agriculture Forest Service.

advertising will find it hard to obtain donated time and space from the media. Further, once an organization that has been using PSAs starts to use paid ads as well, it may find publishers and broadcasters withdrawing the PSA option—at least for the specific product featured in paid advertising.

If a public agency or nonprofit organization needs to focus its efforts on carefully selected target segments (other than a geographically compact audience served by local media), or to reach audiences with a hard-hitting message that needs to be repeated at regular intervals for maximum impact, PSAs are probably a poor choice. Some of the shortcomings of PSAs can be countered by parallel or sequential use of other communication tools such as direct mail, personal selling, local promotions, and public-relations efforts. In fact, many campaigns use PSAs simply to generate awareness and interest, leaving the tasks of attitude change and enactment of behavior to more controllable communication tools such as direct mail and personal contact.

A number of actions can help to enhance the likelihood that a public-service advertising campaign will prove effective—assuming that the objectives of the campaign are in themselves reasonable and that the topic is not highly controversial. One of the primary barriers to effectiveness is failure to obtain airtime (or print space). Several factors encourage local media outlets to use a specific PSA. These include:

- Creating advertisements or commercials of good technical quality with an appealingly presented message.
- Using a format (broadcast duration or size in inches) that matches the media outlet's preferences.
- Adding a local tagline to the advertisements (for instance, listing a local address to visit or phone number to call).
- Identifying the message with a local sponsor.
- Delivering the advertisements in person and explaining the organization's purpose to the media outlet's advertising managers rather than simply sending the ads through the mails.

Following up afterward can often increase the chances of obtaining repeated use of current and future PSAs. Broadcast stations in the United States claim that they appreciate thank-you letters because they can be placed in the file as evidence of the station's community-service orientation on the next occasion that its license comes up for renewal.[13] Of course, each of these actions adds to the cost of preparing PSAs and serves to narrow the differences in costs between public service and paid advertising. Other factors that will improve the effectiveness of PSAs tend to be the same for all types of mass-media communications. They include issues discussed earlier in the chapter, such as prior audience research, careful message pretesting, and persistence in communication efforts. PSAs may need to be redistributed at periodic intervals in order to maximize both their reach (breadth of audience exposed to the ad) and the frequency with which individual members of the audience are exposed to the ad. Furthermore, new campaigns should generally seek to reiterate or build on the themes used in previous years (assuming research indicates that they have been effective).

Donated Advertising: An Alternative to PSAs

Not all organizations feel they can afford the cost of paid media advertising, yet many consider the public-service route inappropriate for their specific purposes—or even inaccessible.

An alternative to PSAs that is generating growing interest among nonprofit organizations is advertising space that is donated by a party other than the media outlet, such as a corporate sponsor. Typically, this approach takes the form of cooperative advertising in which the sponsor's name is also mentioned. Sometimes there is simply a statement that the cost of the advertisement was given by, say, the XYZ Corporation. Alternatively, the message is a dual plug for both the sponsor and the nonprofit.

We will return again to the topic of donated advertising and promotional support in Chapter 18, "Attracting Donations and Gifts-in-Kind."

PUBLIC RELATIONS AND PUBLICITY

People sometimes find it difficult to distinguish between the different forms of marketing communication. The *Readers Digest* once provided the following humorous clarification:

> If the circus is coming to town and you paint a sign saying "Circus Coming to the Fairground Saturday," that's advertising. If you put a sign on the back of an elephant and walk him into town, that's promotion. If the elephant walks through the mayor's flower bed, that's publicity. And if you can get the mayor to laugh about it, that's public relations.

For many nonbusiness organizations, public relations (sometimes referred to as community relations or public information) was long the only formal marketing activity conducted by management. Some organizations have employed public relations as a relatively bland—even reactive—tool, using it to respond to inquiries about the institution and to disseminate information routinely to a large mailing list via periodic press releases. Others have taken a more proactive stance, establishing formal communication objectives that identify target audiences of interest and specify particular messages to be transmitted to each. Instead of routinely mailing press releases to a long list of broadcast stations and magazine and newspaper publishers, they cultivate certain stations or publications whose audiences they wish to reach. Months may be spent working with reporters or editors in an attempt to develop an exclusive story that communicates information likely to influence the attitudes and opinions of the audience.

One of the advantages of using PR as opposed to advertising is that the former may result in more believable messages. Readers, viewers, or listeners expect advertising messages to be slanted in favor of the sponsor, and they raise their guard accordingly. However, the contents of a news story, editorial, or feature are more likely to be accepted at face value by the audience.

Stories appearing in the print media are not necessarily restricted to prose. For instance, when Boston's Beth Israel Hospital opened an "alternative birth center," offering a homelike environment for labor and delivery, the director of public relations worked with a photographer from the *Boston Globe* to create a photo essay. Describing his objectives, the public-relations director declared:

> The care and attention that our patients receive go far beyond that required for competent delivery of services, and we try to convey that idea. When I was working on a press release on the Alternative Birth Center, I applied this principle by focusing on one family's point of view, and illustrated the warm, personalized care for which we strive.[14]

The photo essay subsequently appeared across a full page in the *Globe,* clearly identifying Beth Israel in the brief accompanying text. To purchase a similar amount of advertising space would have cost thousands of dollars. On the other hand, this publicity was hardly free of cost to the hospital, since the public-relations director and other staff members devoted extensive time to working on the project.

Although public-relations efforts can sometimes pay off handsomely, for every news release or story that appears in the media, many others are ignored or discarded. Outside small local newspapers and radio stations or specialized publications with limited circulations, there is tremendous competition for the media's attention. A number of books provide detailed information on how to be successful in obtaining media coverage, and we commend them to readers who are interested in learning more about the specifics of public-relations work.[15]

It is when organizations *fail* to perform as expected that the press scents a story—and it usually portrays the organization in question in a negative light! To obtain media coverage, public-relations executives must be constantly alert to opportunities for newsworthy stories or for incidental coverage in which the organization is featured as an identifiable backdrop to some other event. Much of the time it is difficult to say anything newsworthy about an organization; hospitals are supposed to have friendly, well-qualified staff caring for their patients; colleges are expected to have erudite professors teaching their students; public-transportation agencies have a responsibility to carry travelers quickly and safely to their destinations.

The solution to lack of positive news happenings may be to engage in *publicity,* which involves creating newsworthy events that will attract the interest of the media. Frequently, there is a logical link between promotional activities designed to attract new users or donors directly and public-relations efforts intended to carry news of the organization to a much broader audience. Examples include: walks for hunger (or other causes); fund-raising efforts such as auctions, benefit evenings, and parties in unusual settings; and anniversary celebrations. Initial communication efforts attract people to support these events; subsequent communications carry news of the event to people who may use or support the organization in the future.

Another way to create news is to identify noteworthy people within the organization or interesting activities that are taking place on an ongoing basis. These may include human-interest stories about employees with unusual jobs, features on intriguing research efforts at a university or hospital, or even impressive-sounding statistics about the number of miles covered annually by vehicles in a transit agency or postal service.

News Releases[16]

To obtain coverage in the print and electronic news media, publicists use a variety of informational materials (primarily news releases and photos—although there may also be a role for audiotapes and videotapes).

News releases are the principal tool of the publicist, who may use these to build awareness of activities such as news conferences and special events. As shown below, news releases take several forms:

- *Hard news releases* are simply straight news stories.

- *Feature releases* take a news peg and give it a human interest twist.

- *Backgrounders* provide explanatory information that can be filed for use in a later story; alternatively, they may accompany a more timely news release.

- *Fact sheets* provide basic information about the organization and/or specific topics or issues. It's very important to make sure that they are continually updated.

- *Q & A sheets* are succinct fact sheets prepared in question and answer format. Some reporters prefer this format to backgrounders.

- *Biographies* need to be prepared (and periodically updated) on all the key people in the organization. If possible, they should be accompanied by a large, recent, glossy black and white photograph of the individual.

- *Media advisories* and *news alerts* serve the same purpose as a formal invitation. They are not written for publication, but should specify in brief outline form: *what, when, where,* and *who*.

- *News kits* provide all the information that editors need to write a story—a news release, summary fact sheet, backgrounder on the organization, biographies, features related to the main event but separate from the main story, captioned photographs, brochures, catalogs, etc.

The Changing Role of Public Relations and Publicity

With the growth of interest in marketing strategy across all four elements of the marketing mix—product policy, distribution and delivery systems, pricing, and communication—public relations is being seen less as an independent function and more as an element of the *communication mix*. Just as there should be a search for synergy and consistency between each of the elements of the marketing mix, each subelement of the communication mix should be designed to complement and reinforce the others.

One reason for the historical dependence on public relations and publicity in many public and nonprofit organizations is that custom, politics, or professional association restrictions prohibited the use of advertising in any form. U.S. hospitals, for instance, were constrained by "ethical" prohibitions by the American Medical Association against advertising. When these restrictions were finally lifted at the end of the 1970s, it was no longer necessary for public relations to carry the full burden of a hospital's mass-media communication program. The use of paid media advertising allows much greater precision in targeting desired audiences with a specific message in a specific format at a specific point in time—strategic considerations that may be very important to the success of a marketing campaign, yet cannot be guaranteed by use of public relations alone.

Certain communication tasks are best handled by public relations. For example, in addition to trying to place positive stories in the media about their organization and to respond to queries for information, public-relations directors sometimes find themselves coping with negative situations that might generate adverse publicity. Accidents, scandals, politically motivated attacks, staff resignations, strikes or other labor unrest, a deteriorating financial position, customer complaints, unfavorable comparisons with competing products, charges of misleading advertising or price-gouging—all these newsworthy problems (and many others) are liable to be picked up by the press and reported in ways that create a negative image for the organization. At a minimum, public-relations directors should be capable of ensuring that facts are not distorted by reporters in ways that make the situation appear even worse than it really is. If a good working relationship has been established in advance with editors and reporters, there is a chance that a spokesperson for the organization will be invited to clarify the institution's position and, where appropriate, to identify the steps that are being taken to correct the problems at hand.

Grooming key spokespersons for the organization to act as effective communicators may help establish a good working relationship with editors, reporters, and the public at large. Senior managers often must play the role of sales executives, promoting—or even defending—their organization in speeches or interviews (which may, in fact, have been organized by the public-relations department). Because many of these events are covered by the mass media, it's very important that the speaker or interviewer convey the right message in a convincing manner. Hence public-relations departments may not only assist with speechwriting, but also coach people in how to respond to specific questions, how to improve their public-speaking capabilities, and how to handle hostile reporters or interviewers.

SUMMARY

While the previous chapter showed how communication processes work and introduced the wide array of communication elements available for use by public and nonprofit organizations, this chapter discussed what is entailed in planning and managing communication strategies centered on advertising, promotion, and public relations. Communication decisions should, of course, be taken across the full array of communication-mix elements instead of being compartmentalized, element by element. This poses a need for an integrated approach to advertising, personal selling (and other customer contact services), public relations, and promotional activities, instead of treating these as unrelated tools that are independent of one another. *Interdependence* and *synergy* should be the watchwords of communication planning. In particular, marketers should note the use of different elements to move the target audience through a sequence of stages—becoming aware of (say) a problem, learning about a solution to that problem, and actually doing something to help resolve it.

A systematic approach to communication planning should begin with a situation analysis and proceed through the definition of marketing objectives, the establishment of size of a total communication budget, and the selection of a tentative budget mix for each element. Subsequent steps involve clear definition of goals for each communication element, determination of message appeals and positioning, selection of message format, and choice of message-distribution plan.

In the following chapter, we examine the characteristics of customer service and personal selling, review their capabilities, and study the tasks involved in effective management of these areas.

REFERENCES

1. Dean L. Yarwood and Ben M. Enis, "Advertising and Publicity Programs in the Executive Branch of Government: Helping or Hustling the People?" *Public Administration Review,* January/February 1982, pp. 37–46.

2. W. T. Stanbury, Gerald J. Gorn, and Charles B. Weinberg, "Federal Advertising Expenditures," in G. Bruce Doern (ed.), *How Ottawa Spends Your Tax Dollar,* Toronto: James Lorimer, 1983.

3. Peggy Berkowitz, "Government is Top Advertiser in Canada, Angering its Critics," *Wall Street Journal,* March 4, 1982, p. 31.

4. Goldfarb Consultants, "Public Reaction to Government Advertising: Executive Summary," paper presented to First Canadian Symposium on Government Advertising, Montreal, Nov. 19, 1982, p. 5. (Note: This paper is discussed in Stanbury et al., as in reference 2).

5. As in reference 4, p. 5.

6. This section is based on *The Hoover Awards for Marketing 1978* presentation by TQ Consultants Pty. Ltd. in conjunction with the Department of Youth, Sport and Recreation, Victoria Richmond, Victoria, Australia: TQ Consultants, 1978.

7. See for example, David A. Aaker and John L. Myers, *Advertising Management,* Englewood Cliffs, N.J.: Prentice Hall, second edition, 1982; Michael L. Ray, *Advertising and Communications Management,* Englewood Cliffs, N.J.: Prentice Hall, 1982; and Gilbert A. Churchill, Jr., Neil M. Ford, and Orville C. Walker, Jr., *Sales Force Management,* Homewood, Ill.: Richard D. Irwin, 1981.

8. Reported in "Study Identifies Qualities of Effective Health Public Service Announcements," *Marketing News,* April 3, 1981. For details of the methodology, see Elaine Bratic, Rachel Greenberg, and Phyllis Petersen, "HMTS: Improving the Quality of Public Service Announcements Through Standardized Pretesting," *Journal of the Academy of Marketing Science,* Winter 1981, pp. 40–51.

9. Kenneth H. Rabin, "Network Public Service Announcements Feeds: How Many Do Affiliates Really Use?" Unpublished paper, American University, Washington, D.C. [undated].

10. Jamie Talan, "Getting a Message of Help Across," *Advertising Age,* Aug. 2, 1982, p. M-29.

11. Richard K. Manoff, "The Mass Media Family Planning Campaign for the United States," *Using Commercial Resources in Family Planning Programs: The International Experience,* Honolulu: East-West Center, 1973.

12. Stephen J. Weber, "Government Marketing Through Public Service Advertising," in M. P. Mokwa and Steven E. Permut (eds.), *Government Marketing, Theory and Practice,* New York: Praeger, 1981, pp. 330–342.

13. David L. Rados, "Interviews with Public Service Directors," in *Marketing for Non-Profit Organizations,* Boston: Auburn House, 1981, pp. 139–80.

14. Cited in Terrie Bloom, Christopher H. Lovelock, and Penny Pittman Merliss, "Beth Israel Hospital, Boston," In C. H. Lovelock and C. B Weinberg (eds.), *Public and Nonprofit Marketing: Cases and Readings,* New York: John Wiley & Sons, 1984.

15. See, for example, Scott M. Cutlip and Allen H. Center, *Effective Public Relations,* Englewood Cliffs, N.J.: Prentice-Hall, fifth edition, 1978; and "The Practice of Public Relations in the Nonprofit Organization," in T. D. Connors (ed.), *The Nonprofit Organization Handbook,* New York: McGraw-Hill, 1981 pp. 5.1–5.141; and Public Interest Public Relations, *Promoting Issues and Ideas: A Guide for Public Relations for Nonprofit Organizations,* New York: The Foundation Center, 1987.

16. Based on Public Interest Public Relations, as in reference 15.

Chapter 15 _____
Customer Service & Personal Selling

The decision to use a service is often based on more than the service itself. The people delivering the service can have a profound effect on the user's satisfaction. A single unthinking or poorly motivated employee or volunteer can destroy the impact of an otherwise well designed and executed program. On the other hand, thoughtful, empathic personnel can enhance satisfaction, avoid misunderstandings, and even turn around unpleasant situations. For example, while blood donors may want to give a gift or "share life," their decisions to become regular donors may depend more on the behavior of the nurses and volunteers at the clinic than on the primary product benefit.[1]

Good customer service can make a difference. The volunteers who lead tours at the Metropolitan Museum of Art in New York City turn what can be an intimidating, overwhelming and confusing experience into an informative, enjoyable, and eye-opening encounter with art. On a more mundane level, the bus driver who avoids jamming on the brakes when someone is standing will earn the gratitude of passengers who have come to dread the unpleasant and sometimes dangerous lurches to which buses seem prone. Sometimes the difference between average and good customer service is just letting customers know they made the right decision. The theater's telephone sales clerk who says, honestly, "That was a very good choice of seats. I would have chosen the same ones for myself," leaves that customer feeling good about the transaction and, more important, about the play he will attend.

Good customer service doesn't just happen. The right people have to be in place, and they have to be supported by a management system that encourages good customer service. Nonprofit organizations may not always be able to exercise much selectivity in choosing the volunteers who will have contact with their users, so designing and managing a good customer service system is crucial.

Everyone who has contact with customers is responsible for customer service. However, the salesforce has additional tasks: finding customers and persuading them to use the service.

Some nonprofit organizations have a long history of personal selling, although the term "sales" is not always used. Blood banks, for example, have "donor recruitment departments." The recruiters convince local companies and their employees to organize and participate in blood donor drives, an assignment involving selling at both the organizational and individual levels. International development agencies employ "change agents," whose task is to convince the people of less technologically advanced societies to adopt new behavior patterns or products.

Other organizations are more reactive. They respond to inquiries and take orders, but do not actively seek out customers and sell to them. Box offices for performing arts groups respond to telephone and personal calls, but make little effort to generate the calls. Likewise, a question about a program at the local Y can be answered fully and courteously by a service representative, but this same person is unlikely to go out and "prospect" for new members.

Despite the term "personal" selling, not all selling needs to be done face-to-face. The telephone can be a useful tool. Many universities, for example, organize phonathons as part of their fundraising efforts. Innovations in telecommunications and widespread use of credit cards have led to further developments in "telemarketing." The Vancouver Symphony Orchestra spends a substantial part of its subscription marketing budget on a telemarketing campaign. Carefully screened lists of current and former subscribers, single ticket buyers, and other likely prospects are contacted by trained sales representatives, who can provide extensive information about the coming season, reserve seats, and take payment—all over the telephone.

Not all nonprofit organizations have the resources to maintain a formal sales organization. Instead, selling is included among the many other responsibilities of executives and staff. It is important that these people have enough knowledge of customer service and the selling process to take advantage of every opportunity to turn a potential user into a user, or to move current users to make further commitments to use the organization's services.

Scope of the Chapter

This chapter is concerned with the management of the customer contact functions, customer service and personal selling. Customer service cannot be isolated from other aspects of marketing; the chapters in this book on "Product Offerings," "Distribution and Delivery Systems," and "Organizing the Marketing Effort" (among others) all relate to customer service and selling. But certain topics in this area deserve special emphasis, and that is the focus here.

We begin by providing a definition of customer service that captures its multifaceted nature. We consider the elements that contribute to good customer service, both those that are experienced by the user (the so-called "front office" operation), and those with which the user has no direct contact (the "back office"). The nature of customer contact depends on the organization and its environment, so next we consider the factors that shape the tasks performed by customer service, and its place within the organization. The section ends with a set of guidelines for effective implementation of customer service programs.

The second major part of the chapter focuses on personal selling. Many aspects of sales force management are similar to advertising management. Like advertising managers, sales managers are concerned with designing messages, selecting communication targets, and meeting the communication goals of the marketing plan, all within the limits set by the budget. The difference is that personal selling involves the recruitment, training and management of people who interact directly with customers or prospects, carrying out assigned selling responsibilities.

This chapter concentrates on the aspects of sales force management that differ from advertising. We begin with a discussion of issues in planning and managing sales force activities for both paid and volunteer sales people. Because successful personal selling programs involve effective use of people, we pay special attention to how to recruit, train, supervise, and motivate an organization's sales force.

The chapter concludes with a brief discussion on telemarketing, an increasingly important communication approach that involves elements of both personal and impersonal communication.

CUSTOMER SERVICE

In many organizations, customer service is viewed as having a restricted, reactive role. The term has often been used in the context of manufacturing, where it was originally concerned with effective distribution, emphasizing inventory reliability, order accuracy, and order cycle times. In service industries, however, the concept has a much broader scope. The retailer's policy that "the customer is always right" recognizes the importance of customer service as a competitive tool. No longer is customer service restricted to providing information, processing refunds, and taking complaints:

> *Customer service is defined as a task, other than proactive selling, that involves interactions with customers in person, by telecommunications, or by mail. It is designed, performed and communicated with two goals in mind: operational efficiency and customer satisfaction.*

It is not enough simply to respond, on an exception basis, to customer problems or complaints. Each contact between a staff member or volunteer and a customer becomes part of the overall service product, even though the task may be defined in strictly operational terms. Balancing operational efficiency and customer satisfaction is important. For example, hospital cleaning staff may have nothing in their job descriptions about dealing with patients, and may not have time for long conversations, but their pleasant greetings and kind words can make a hospital stay more bearable for many patients.

The Disney amusement parks have built much of their business on customer service.[2] New employees are told that Disney is in the entertainment business. They are cast members, not staff members. Those who deal with the public are onstage; everyone else is offstage—but considered equally important. Employees are never seen in half costume; that would spoil the illusion. They never stand in line to buy food at the concessions; that might delay service to visitors. Instead, Disney has private relaxation areas for its staff.

The training program focuses on the Disney tradition of hospitality. Visitors to the parks are treated as guests, with employees acting as hosts. Hosts are trained to answer even the most "foolish" questions, which are of course anything but foolish to the guest doing the asking. For particularly unusual questions, hosts are backed up by a 24-hour information bureau.

Public and nonprofit organizations can adapt these philosophies and operating principles to their own situations. In fact, one reason for the extraordinary success of Canada's EXPO 86 in Vancouver, British Columbia, was its adoption of a visitor-oriented approach similar to Disney's. As soon as the fair opened, EXPO's hospitality was widely reported, in the media and by word-of-mouth. These reports attracted tourists and area residents, who became repeat visitors after they had experienced EXPO's friendliness. By the end of the fair, admissions topped 20 million, exceeding projections by more than 50%.

We certainly don't want to imply that a library has to become an amusement park in order to succeed in customer service. But librarians should anticipate the information and other needs of their users, and prepare to respond appropriately.

The workers and volunteers with whom customers have direct contact are not the only ones contributing to user satisfaction. In analyzing service operations, a distinction is made between the "front office" and the "back office".[3] Front office procedures are those directly experienced by the user. In some cases, they represent a very small proportion of the organization's total activities. For instance, the contact between residents of the United States and the national social security system is generally limited to regular payroll deductions. Perhaps there is an occasional phone call or letter when problems arise or a retirement decision is made. But all the remitting of deductions and data processing are done behind the scenes. In contrast, a community center is almost all front office. The user is exposed to the physical facilities, as well as to numerous personnel, including receptionists, program instructors, and locker room attendants.

Figure 15.1 illustrates the division of the service operations system into front and back room activities, the incorporation of the front room operations into the service delivery system (where the contact between users and service personnel and facilities takes place), and the inclusion of the service delivery system into the broader service marketing system (which includes all actions and reactions that affect the user in any way). The multifaceted total service offering shown in this model includes both the core product and the related supplementary products.

CUSTOMER SATISFACTION AND CUSTOMER SERVICE

Good customer service requires the integration of operations and marketing. This begins with research to determine customer needs and sources of satisfaction (or dissatisfaction). Most nonprofit organizations have some idea of their customers' needs. Monitoring customer comments and complaints can provide useful information. Not only can customer needs be inferred, customer perceptions of the organization's performance with respect to those needs may become clear. Formal research can be used to supplement this knowledge.

As with the results of any research, conclusions should be drawn with caution. Complainers may not be typical of the organization's customers, and they may not be able to articulate exactly what is bothering them. Transit users who complain about crowded buses may really be dissatisfied with scheduling or routing. Likewise, respondents to questionnaires may say that customer service is not what it should be, but may be unable to say what is missing. Once sources of satisfaction and dissatisfaction have been uncovered, effective customer service programs can be developed. A user-oriented approach does more than enhance customer satisfaction. It may result in improved efficiency and productivity,[4] as discussed in the next chapter. Moreover, focusing attention on customer needs can also improve employee and volunteer morale. In short, a competitive edge is gained.

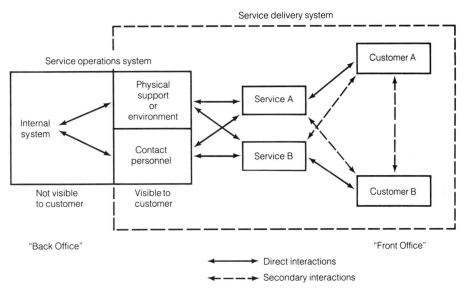

Source: Adapted from Eric Langeard, John E. G. Bateson, Christopher H. Lovelock, and Pierre Eiglier (1981), *Services Marketing: New Insights from Consumers and Managers,* Cambridge, Massachusetts: Marketing Science Institute.

Figure 15.1   Front and back office systems.

DEVELOPING THE CUSTOMER SERVICE FUNCTION

The nature and extent of customer contact inevitably varies by service industry and type of organization. Among the factors that fix the place of customer service in the organization and shape the tasks performed are:

Presence or absence of intermediaries. Some customer contact tasks may be more efficiently performed by intermediaries. Usually, these relate to initial contacts by customers prior to the delivery of the core service. Performing arts organizations, for example, use ticket agencies to provide information and advice, make reservations, and collect payment. Although this strategy weakens the organization's control over performance of some key customer contact tasks, it may result in better service at lower cost.

Number of customer contact points. The more face-to-face customer contact points, and the more geographically removed from head office they are, the more complex is the management of the customer service function. A classic example is the postal system. The large number of offices and employees means that the opportunities for mistakes or poor service are many and varied. Management's task is to produce the conditions that will prevent as many mistakes as possible, and allow for speedy resolution of problems when they do arise. Of course, it is equally important to recognize that the opportunities for good customer service increase as the number of contact points increases, and management must find ways to encourage positive encounters. In contrast, managers of low contact services with a limited number of customer contact points find it easier, but equally important, to have tight control over the quality of customer service.

Institutional versus individual purchases. Greater variability is likely to be introduced into customer service activities when dealings are with members of the general public rather than managers or employees of institutional customers. The latter are likely to purchase in greater volume and with greater frequency, but there may be multiple contact persons within the client organization. Particularly good record-keeping on the part of the service deliverer is important in this situation. For example, a charitable group organizing a "fun run" to raise awareness and money (through entry fees) will usually approach businesses to cover the costs of the event. Contacts with these potential sponsors are considerably more complex than those with the individual runners, partly because of the size of the commitments involved.

Duration of the service delivery process. The longer it takes for service delivery to be completed, the more likely it is that customers will require information on work-in-progress, such as estimated completion dates, projected costs, and so forth. Good internal monitoring systems are required to generate and communicate the needed information. Private American universities, in the face of increased competition for bright students, now pay greater attention to providing this. Application packages include detailed estimates of expenses, financial aid information, and prospects for students after graduation.

Capacity-constrained services. In most instances, this category of services—which includes performing arts, hospitals and clinics, certain types of public transportation, educational programs, and museums—should offer either a reservation system or a queuing-control mechanism. The former approach may benefit from online access to a reservations database, while effective queue management requires friendly but firm interaction with waiting customers and realistic estimates of the delay involved. Museums which offer "blockbuster" shows such as a Picasso or Renoir exhibit have realized that a properly designed reservation system can lead to improved customer satisfaction by reducing (or even eliminating) waits, lessening crowds at peak times, and increasing attendance at off-peak hours.

Frequency of use and repurchase. When the bulk of consumption is accounted for by repeat use, regular customers are a valuable asset and should be cultivated. Because proactive selling—finding new customers—is time- consuming and expensive, it is often cost-effective to dedicate specific resources to realizing the potential of the existing customer base. Moreover, simple order-taking does not service the customer or the organization well. Customer contact personnel should be able to identify regular customers and encourage them to use all the services that would benefit them, as often as is appropriate. Alert librarians make a note of the reading interests and preferences of frequent borrowers, and then draw their attention to materials that may appeal to them.

Level of complexity. Some services are simple to use and easy for the operations department to deliver. Other services are more complex, and inexperienced users require assistance. Murphy's Law can always be depended on: what can go wrong, will—and usually at the worst possible moment. Complex services simply have more things that can go wrong. They therefore need customer contact personnel who can provide information and help to educate the user. They also require contingency plans for problem resolution, necessitating training of personnel on what action to take when a particular problem arises. Superior performance by service personnel in restoring operations or providing acceptable alternatives can create a very favorable impression in customers' minds, distinguishing excellent organization from the "also rans." The more complex a service is, the more difficult it is to ensure good customer service. According to a General Accounting Office survey, for instance, 22% of taxpayer inquiries to the Internal Revenue Service are answered incorrectly.[5] Such inadequate performance is not inevitable, and the IRS has plans to improve its service.

Degree of risk. Service managers must understand the consequences for customers of a service failure. Contingency planning is often required by government regulation where personal safety is a factor. Other consequences for customers range from personal inconvenience to monetary loss. The higher the probability of a service failure, and the more serious the consequences to customers, the more important it is to employ well-trained contact personnel who behave calmly and tactfully when faced by upset customers, and can resolve problems quickly.

ASSIGNMENT OF TASKS TO CUSTOMER SERVICE

A broad array of tasks may fall under the heading of customer service. An important question for any organization that is developing or expanding its customer service function is which specific tasks should be performed. These can be divided into selling-related and non-selling activities, as well as customer-initiated and firm-initiated interactions.

Customer service personnel are primarily involved in non-selling activities. But sometimes selling-related activities improve the level of service to the customer, and should be pursued. For instance, a battered woman arriving at a shelter may only be looking for a safe haven, but the staff will encourage her to use the shelter's counseling and other services for abused women, as well. However, the same services would probably not be suggested to a teenage girl who had just run away from home. While the girl might be offered shelter for the night, another agency would be better suited to provide needed counseling services.

Both the type of service offered by the organization and the specifics of each situation determine whether contact is initiated by the customer or the service agency. A customer service audit is a systematic way of examining the tasks customer service can and should perform.

CONDUCTING A CUSTOMER SERVICE AUDIT

To determine the appropriate nature and scope of its customer service function, each service organization should review its current situation by conducting a customer service audit. Table 15.1 outlines the basic format for such an audit, although different organizations will want to go into greater detail in different areas. The findings provide a basis for planning the future scope and quality of the customer service function.

Table 15.1 Conducting a Customer Service Audit

Identify Customer Contact Tasks (Other than Sales), e.g.:
- Information, reservations
- Service delivery tasks
- Billing and Customer record transmittal
- Problem solving, complaint handling

Review Standard Procedures for Each Task
- Written standards (Procedures manual) for each Task
- Oral/written instructions (ad hoc)
- Availability (hours/days, locations)
- Interactions with other personnel

Identify Performance Goals by Task
- Specific quantitative goals
- Qualitative goals
- Contribution to related activities
- Contribution to long-term success of system

Identify Measures of Performance by Task
- Dollar-based
- Time-based
- Management/supervisor evaluations
- Customer evaluations

Review and Evaluate Personnel Elements
- Recruiting/selection criteria and practices
- Nature, content of training
- Job definition, career path (if any)
- Interactions with other employees and volunteers
- Nature of supervision, quality control
- Evaluation procedures
- Corrective actions available
- Attitudes, motivation of employees and volunteers
- Hours, extent of paid/unpaid overtime for employees

Identify and Evaluate Support Systems
- Instruction manuals, brochures, form letters
- Office facilities, furnishings, layout
- Office equipment (phones, computers, word processors)
- Vehicles and equipment for repair/maintenance
- Radio communications
- Record keeping materials (e.g., log books)

DESIGNING AND MANAGING THE CUSTOMER CONTACT FUNCTION

The customer service audit identifies the unique characteristics within each organization that affect the balance between marketing and operations. The customer service organizational structure must be designed to maintain the proper balance.

Two contrasting examples illustrate the range of issues that can arise. At one extreme is the professional service organization (PSO), such as a family-planning clinic or a university, offering a range of services tailored to the needs of individual customers and delivered by a skilled—often professionally certified—workforce. At the other extreme is the consumer service organization (CSO), such as a transit system or a postal service, which often consists of a large number of relatively standardized facilities delivering a limited range of services.[6]

Professional Service Organizations

Professional service organizations differ from other service institutions in a number of ways. Employees of a PSO are often highly educated and may be members of prestigious professions. Although many service operations involve primarily low-skill, low-pay, "undesirable" jobs, PSOs often offer desirable positions with high potential earning capacity. It might appear simple for a well-educated person to manage peers; however, the characteristics of PSOs can make the manager's task extremely difficult.

An important characteristic is that each member of the PSO can have a significant impact in many areas, including revenues, reputation, and skills "inventory." In a very real sense, the individuals providing the PSO's service form part of the product and serve to define the organization; employees may be replaceable, but every replacement alters the nature of both the product and the organization (this is true to a lesser degree in large PSOs with extensive staffs). As a result, it is difficult to standardize the characteristics and the quality of the PSO product.

The manager's task in a PSO is complicated by the fact that members can often exert considerable leverage on the organization because of their relative importance to it. A prominent surgeon, for instance, can have a substantial impact on a hospital's image, community standing, and its revenues. The same is likely to be true of a Nobel Laureate (or other prominent academician) at a university, or a world-famous conductor at a symphony orchestra. In some cases, PSO employees have a high degree of job mobility, making the management task more difficult.

PSO characteristics argue that an autocratic management style might be less likely to succeed in a PSO than in another kind of enterprise. Many PSO employees are self-motivated, requiring only an adequate salary and support systems. Others, by contrast, may have more subtle needs. To be effective, PSO managers must determine these needs and design a job environment that provides an opportunity to satisfy them.

In a consumer service organization the management objective is often to remove initiative and autonomy from the front-line staff in order to standardize and better control service delivery. A PSO usually cannot use this approach because the product itself cannot be well defined in advance but is usually developed during the course of its execution. The nature of the work is often such that it does not pay to have it checked in detail by a superior. In fact, excessive supervision may discourage initiative and lead to loss of motivation.

On the other hand, professionals do not always give adequate consideration to their customers' needs. When health-maintenance organizations first appeared in the 1970s as an alternative form of health-delivery system, some HMOs hired young doctors who felt that the traditional formal attire of doctors was unnecessary and consequently dressed in casual clothes such as sweaters, jeans, and sandals. This approach alienated some patients who felt that patronizing an HMO was innovative enough without having to contend with "mod" doctors. Another health-care issue concerns patients who criticize doctors for not explaining illnesses, diagnoses, and treatment programs in sufficient depth for them to understand. The doctors' response is typically that they are too busy examining and treating patients to spend inordinate amounts of time talking with each one. Clearly, even in PSOs, with their opportunities for personalized service, a better balance needs to be struck between operational and marketing considerations.

Consumer Service Organizations

At the other end of the spectrum, and demanding a different organizational structure, is the consumer service organization that provides relatively standardized services to a large public. Examples include public transportation, postal service, and public libraries. CSO operations are usually explicit and easy to replicate. As such they are subject to standardized routines and detailed job descriptions that facilitate the staffing at both the service employee and management levels.

Although CSO employees do not always require advanced educational qualifications, they are sometimes highly skilled in the specific tasks for which they are responsible. Training for these tasks can be accomplished relatively quickly.

Those CSO employees whose jobs call for them to interact directly with the public need good interpersonal skills. They should have a pleasant manner, speak clearly, and be dressed and groomed in a fashion consistent with the image desired by the organization for which they work. While employees sometimes resent constant inspections, managers responsible for quality control in standardized CSO operations quote the maxim that "people do what you *inspect,* not what you expect."

Changing the nature of the contact person's job is difficult in a CSO. Marketing managers who have previously worked in consumer-goods companies often do not appreciate the complexity of the operating system and are sometimes surprised to find that seemingly small changes in the way employees interact with users can have significant repercussions throughout the organization. Consider the implications of a hypothetical management decision that the public library system in Canada should always be able to provide assistance to users who speak either French or English. The chances are that it would cause considerable upheaval in existing staffing practices. New shift schedules might be required, and libraries previously staffed by a single person during periods of low usage would henceforth require either a bilingual librarian or one French-speaking and one English-speaking librarian. Even if there were no further ramifications of the change, the manager would still have to train and motivate employees to adopt new procedures. In a real sense, managers of service organizations need to practice "internal marketing" and understand the needs and practices of employees before designing and implementing new programs. In some cases, internal marketing may be as important for success as externally focused efforts.

The critical skill for the first-level supervisor in a CSO is "people management." The educational and intellectual skills required of such an individual may be less than for a PSO manager, but good human-relations skills are needed to motivate customer-contact employees in a CSO. The manager should also be capable of performing subordinates' jobs, not only to demonstrate to employees that he or she understands their work, but also to be able to intervene if a key employee is absent or a volatile situation develops between user and employee.

The nature of the service-delivery system and its workforce dictates a multitiered organizational structure with a narrow span of control containing "people managers" at all but the highest level. The primary task of these managers is to motivate, monitor, and evaluate their subordinates.

The central organization of a CSO differs markedly from the rest of the organization. Standardization of products and retail operating units across the organization makes it possible to centralize almost all the functions outside of managing people. Thus such functions as planning, budgeting, product design, site selection, facilities design, pricing, procurement, and advertising are often centralized on a regional or national basis.

These managerial characteristics can create conflict at the highest levels of management. To accomplish their individual goals of rising in the managerial hierarchy, CSO managers must develop a thinking process and operating style oriented toward implementing preset goals and standards. Unfortunately, this operating responsibility can stifle the innovative and decision-making skills necessary to function effectively at the top levels of the organization.

An expanding institution can sometimes forestall these problems by continually increasing the number of levels in the organization and the number of units to be managed. In the long run, such a policy runs the risk of reinforcing a narrow operations orientation. What is needed are policies that help managers to acquire a broader perspective. Thus rotation between field and head office or between operations and marketing positions may educate different managers about others' concerns. In-house and external training programs, as well as personal reading, may also expand the horizons of managers at all levels. Whatever approach is adopted, the organization must take positive steps to ensure that its managers appreciate the value of both the marketing and operations orientations.

GUIDELINES FOR EFFECTIVE PROGRAM IMPLEMENTATION

The balance between marketing and operations is a key factor in the design of the customer service program. No matter how well designed the program is, poor implementation will seriously impair its effectiveness. Careful consideration should be given to each of the following tasks.[7]

Recruit the right employees and volunteers. Individuals whose job requires them to interact with customers must possess not only the right technical skills and aptitudes, but also appropriate personal characteristics. Depending on the job, this may include appearance, mannerisms, voice, personality, and so forth. While the organization may not be able to be as selective where volunteers are concerned, there should be as much proper matching of task to person as possible. For example, developing a good Board of Directors is a crucial task for many nonprofit groups. The Board of a social service agency should contain a balance of fundraisers with good connections in the business community, specialists in such disciplines as accounting, law, and marketing to provide guidance to staff members, and individuals who have expertise in the agency's work.

Train personnel properly. First, the training must develop the necessary level of technical proficiency to perform specific tasks competently. Second, customer contact personnel must be instructed in such factors as personal appearance and/or telephone manner, behavior toward users, and use of correct language. The Disney example earlier in the chapter illustrates this. Finally, skills in handling a variety of anticipated situations must be acquired. Role-play exercises are often useful in building the confidence and knowledge necessary to deal with personal interactions under difficult or stressful conditions.

Educate customers. Customers need to know how to use and how not to use the service. Information in printed form is usually helpful; clear, coherent signs are important at service delivery sites and on self-serve equipment. In large service facilities, customer service desks or booths should be available to help users with questions or problems. When users and the service organization transact at arm's length, consideration should be given to using a toll-free telephone number.

Educate employees and volunteers. Organizational personnel should view customers with problems as a source of useful information for the organization, rather than a source of annoyance. Internal marketing programs may be needed to change negative attitudes and to communicate strategies for effective interactions with customers who have experienced difficulties or need questions answered. One Big Sister agency, whose volunteers devoted five hours a week to working with a teenaged "Little Sister," had certain recurring questions indicating there were problems that needed to be worked out systematically. A monthly group meeting for volunteers was added to the program to discuss these concerns.

Be efficient first, nice second. The objective of a customer service program is to serve the customer, not to provide a social outlet (unless that is the purpose of the organization, like a seniors' center). While courtesy is important to convey a caring attitude, too much friendliness can be inefficient. When other clients are waiting, the primary responsibility of the customer service representative is to serve the customer properly and quickly.

Standardize service response systems. Use of a standard form for handling inquiries and complaints provides a checklist for the customer service agent and facilitates entry of the data into a computer system. This expedites follow-through and enables monitoring of the level and mix of customer-initiated contacts. Effective response also requires timely referral of specialized issues to the appropriate personnel. At a large nonprofit financial institution in Canada, Vancouver City Savings Credit Union, there is an elaborate system for monitoring customer complaints. Each month, the Board receives a summary report of the complaints received during the month. These reports have resulted in several policy and many procedural changes to improve customer service. In fact, the Board found this information so useful that it now offers a monetary incentive to its customers who propose useful and practical improvements.

Develop a pricing policy. Quality customer service is not necessarily free; consideration should be given to levying fees for certain categories of service that have traditionally been offered at no charge. Some libraries now charge business users who want extensive information searches performed. Fees become necessary when delivery of the service costs the organization money. The introduction of a fee, an incentive for callers to look up telephone numbers, has lowered the cost of providing directory assistance. Before the charge was instituted, 60% of calls to directory assistance in some cities were for numbers already published, and 10% of customers were making more than half of these calls.[8]

Involve subcontractors if necessary. Fast response and high quality customer service is sometimes easier and cheaper to provide when certain functions are subcontracted to outside firms. Thus performing arts groups use ticket agencies. The disadvantages of this approach are that the primary service supplier loses control over the quality of customer service, and may be unable to capture the valuable marketing information inherent in direct customer contact.

Evaluate customer service. Meaningful, measurable performance standards must be set for each element of the customer service package. Actual performance should be compared to these standards, and reasons for any variance determined. In addition, users' opinions on customer service elements should be solicited at regular intervals. This may be done by distributing comment forms to all users and relying on those who experience above-average or below-average service to respond with compliments or complaints. This is the strategy used by many hotels, which leave guest comment cards in each room. Some hospitals now employ a similar approach. It can also be used quite inexpensively by organizations that send out monthly statements or newsletters: a short survey can be enclosed every year or so. Alternatively, periodic surveys of a representative cross-section of users may be conducted.

Be Proactive. Don't wait for things to go wrong and then fix them; make sure things go right from the start. Anticipating the influx of visitors to the province for EXPO 86, the British Columbia Ministry of Tourism introduced the SuperHost program several months before the fair began. Offered at nominal charge to employers and individuals, SuperHost training gave participants information on EXPO, Vancouver and the province, and taught them how to make tourists feel welcome. Thousands of Vancouver area residents took advantage of the program, including all bus drivers and most taxi drivers in the city. The result was an enthusiastic welcome for millions of visitors.

If things are going well, steps should be taken to ensure that they continue going well. Superior performance by customer service personnel should be formally and, if appropriate, publicly recognized. Initiative should be rewarded. In fact, the ambitious SuperHost program grew out of an earlier program with the same name, that encouraged tourists to complete and mail a postage-paid ballot to B.C. Tourism whenever they received exceptionally good service. The government then sent a certificate to the individual named and to his or her employer, recognizing the "SuperHost." The accompanying window stickers were displayed in hundreds of stores, restaurants, hotels, and other service establishments.

Be involved. Many service managers have so many administrative duties that they become removed from their customers and the important insights that develop from day-to-day contact with users. Employees and volunteers who do interact directly with customers should be encouraged to offer suggestions and feedback. This is standard practice in many firms in the private sector, and is often viewed as crucial to success.

Take action to correct deficiencies. Shortcomings in customer service may be overcome by making employees aware of problems and taking action to correct them. Tactics may include retraining, reassignment of employees who are unsuited for customer contact tasks but are otherwise well-motivated and proficient, and, if necessary, termination of incorrigibles. It may also be necessary to revamp support systems, restructure the work environment, and reassign responsibilities within the customer service group to improve efficiency. Finally, in order to catch problems before they become too serious, it may help to develop improved performance monitors.

Customer service is evolving from a purely reactive function, sometimes grudgingly performed, to a responsive and even proactive force designed to enhance the organization's competitive posture. Personal selling takes customer contact a step further: it seeks out new customers.

PERSONAL SELLING AND SALES-FORCE MANAGEMENT

Sales-force management is, in many ways, similar to advertising management. Both are forms of communication and must address the fundamental question of "who says what to whom." Both advertising and sales-force managers need to be concerned with designing messages, with choosing communications targets, and with working within the budget constraints and communication goals of a marketing plan. The fundamental difference is that personal selling involves people—who must be recruited and trained—to deliver the message and to interact directly with customers or prospects. In advertising, implementation (but not evaluation) concerns essentially cease once the advertisement is designed and placed in the media; in contrast, a sales force needs ongoing management to ensure that sales personnel consistently carry out their assigned tasks and roles.

Of continuing concern to a sales manager are the answers to such questions as: are sales representatives allocating time across accounts, products, and selling activities in a manner consistent with the policies and procedures established in the marketing plan? Are they delivering the intended message or are they modifying it? How is the behavior of sales representatives changed by actual and anticipated reactions of the customers and donors with whom they deal directly? The primary responsibilities of sales managers (or other supervisors) are to hire, train, motivate, and evaluate sales representatives so they will carry out their assigned selling tasks effectively.

The big advantage of personal selling as a communication or promotional tool is that it involves person-to-person contact with a potential user (or donor). This allows the sales representative to tailor the message to fit a particular customer's concerns and interests. During a sales call—which may take place in person or by phone—communication flows in both directions, allowing the salesperson to respond to immediate feedback from the customer. Questions and objections can be met and answered, and alternative approaches can be tried when the initial ones do not seem to be working. Sales representatives can also communicate a large amount of complex information in one or a series of sales calls. Visual aids and working models can also be used. By calling on the same client repeatedly, the salesperson can educate the client over time about the particular advantages of the product or organization. Regular contact over an extended period is particularly important when offering a product that can be tailored to the needs of an individual user—as when a health-care clinic provides medical services to local businesses. When the customer is a regular user of the organization's products or a frequent donor of funds, personal contact can be used to deepen and strengthen that loyalty, as well as to deal with any operational problems and concerns that may arise from time to time.

The advantages of personal over impersonal communication are often offset by the major disadvantage of cost. Heavy monetary costs are incurred when a paid sales force is employed. Even when volunteers are used, the costs of travel and salaried staff to support personal selling efforts can be considerable, to say nothing of the time expended by volunteer sales reps and supervisors. The cost of mass media such as television and magazines is usually measured in cents per contact; the cost of personal selling is measured in terms of dollars per contact.

According to *Sales & Marketing Management* magazine's 1987 survey of selling costs for industrial firms, the average direct cost per sales call exceeds $100 in many selling situations.[9] About 75% of this amount is for compensation, the rest is for expense.

In this part of the chapter, we focus on "outside" sales forces who call on present or potential clients. Among the outside sales forces commonly encountered in the public and nonprofit sectors are:

- *Industrial/institutional account representatives* such as postal-service sales personnel working with large mailers.

- *Recruiters* for the armed forces, colleges and universities, Peace Corps, and other large employers in government departments or public agencies.

- *Fund raisers* calling in person on foundations, corporations, and large individual prospective donors, and by telephone on prospects with more limited potential, as well as street-corner solicitors for charitable organizations.

- *Specialized change agents* working in such fields as energy and water conservation, agricultural extension, preventive health care, and family planning.

- *Canvassers and vote seekers* acting on behalf of referendum campaigns and political candidates.

- *Lobbyists* seeking to influence government policy by gaining the support of elected officials for their cause.

As we discussed in Chapter 6, organizational selling typically involves working with a buying organization of several people from different departments in the client organization. It's important to understand the nature of the buying process and the varying roles that different people play in an organization's decision to buy a product. The selling organization may not be able to rely on just one salesperson to reach all the people—instead needing to develop a formal or informal team to deal with the potential client and the members of the "buying center" (or institutional decision-making unit).

In this section of the chapter, we will concentrate on those aspects of sales-force management that are most distinct from advertising management; for example, we won't spend much time examining message format and positioning—what the salesperson says to the customer—because these are central issues in both selling and advertising that we discussed earlier in the chapter. Our discussion will use a three-stage model of the personal selling function—strategic, managerial, and individual salesperson—that corresponds to the major decision-making levels in sales-force management.[10] A multilevel model is appropriate because sales-force and personal selling decisions are made at several different levels in the marketing organization. In each instance, decisions are made within guidelines set by managers at higher levels. The results and feedback obtained from the lower levels in the organization provide one basis for modifying the policies and plans at higher levels. Smaller organizations, of course, may have one manager responsible for more than one level, but conceptually it's instructive to examine each level separately.

Strategic Level

As with advertising, sales-force strategy and the resources devoted to personal selling should flow from the organization's marketing objectives and the situational analysis that led to their establishment. In developing a sales strategy, it's particularly important to understand the nature of the individual or organization buying process.

Five types of personal selling or interpersonal communication (see Chapter 13) are relevant for developing a communication strategy.

1. Proactive selling.
2. Reactive selling.
3. Customer service.
4. Customer contact.
5. Personal advice.

A public agency or nonprofit organization may find it effective to use more than one approach to personal selling because of differences in the markets that it serves, the products it offers, and/or the competition it faces. Also criticial at the strategic level is determining how important personal selling should be in the marketing program as compared to advertising and other communication-mix elements.

The U.S. Peace Corps, for example, attempts to attract college graduates to serve overseas in developing countries. Although both advertising and personal selling are used to make graduates aware of the Peace Corps and the benefits of joining, the major burden of recruiting volunteers is placed on a proactive personal selling program. This approach recognizes the high personal commitment involved in joining the Peace Corps and the need to satisfy the unique concerns of each individual volunteer. In a similar vein, although advertising for the U.S. armed forces is by far the largest paid advertising expenditures of the federal government, much more money is spent on the personal selling program, which involves thousands of armed-forces recruiters.[11] In both cases, advertising and personal selling work together. In the present context, however, the crucial strategic decision is to establish the role of personal selling in the organization's marketing program: how much emphasis should be placed on personal selling versus other elements of the marketing mix? What specific objectives should be accomplished by personal selling? And what level of resources should be budgeted for the sales force? The desired role of personal selling in the marketing strategy is the major influence on decisions made at the tactical level.

Managerial Level

As shown in Figure 15.2, decisions at the managerial level involve developing both a sales-force organization and a set of policies and procedures in the area of deployment,

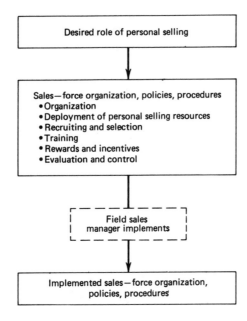

Figure 15.2 The managerial level of sales-force decision making.

recruiting and selection, training, rewards and incentives, and evaluation and control. For the personal selling program to be successful, it must be effectively implemented by the field sales manager responsible for supervising the sales force. Many nonprofit organizations use volunteers as a major component of their personal selling program, particularly with regard to fund raising or managing ancillary retail operations, as we discuss later in Chapters 18 and 20. To assume that volunteers will carry out their assigned roles merely because they are "volunteers" is a mistake—and unlikely to lead to success. A carefully designed and soundly implemented management system is needed. The issues that we discuss here are also applicable to the management of volunteers; a successful example can be seen in Stanford University's Annual Fund, which "employs" more than 3500 volunteers, coordinated by a paid staff of fewer than 25, to raise millions of dollars annually.[12]

Organization. A major decision in large agencies is whether the sales force should be organized on a geographic, product, or market basis or some combination of these. Figure 15.3 illustrates the organization chart for the Peace Corps' sales force, the Office of Volunteer Placement (OVP), in the early 1970s. Although the primary structure was geographic in orientation, there was also a focus on specific skill areas (e.g., engineering, mathematics, and education) needed by the host countries. A geographic orientation allowed recruiters to develop sound knowledge of and good contacts in the individual colleges and universities for which they were responsible. On the other hand, this geographic orientation sometimes resulted in not filling the quotas for a special skill needed by host countries. The purpose of the "skills recruiters" was to concentrate on these areas and mount special programs to attract Peace Corps volunteers with the needed skills.

A related organizational decision concerns the number of levels of sales management and the number of individuals who report to each type of sales manager—what is termed

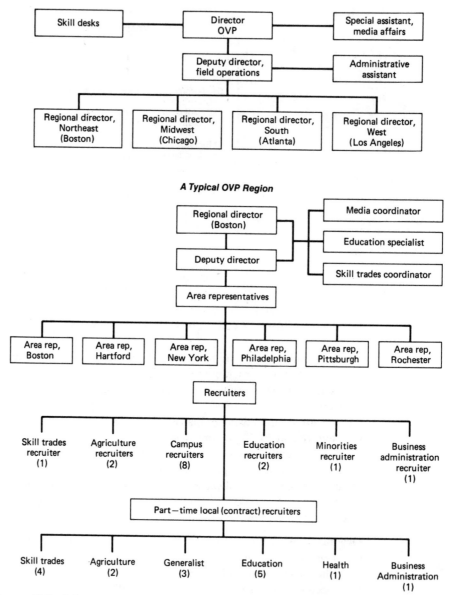

Figure 15.3 Sales organization: the Peace Corps Office of Volunteer Placement. (From Steven H. Star, "The Peace Corps," Boston, MA: HBS Case Services, 1970 (Case #9-571-035).

the *span of control*. A policy of narrowing the span of control (that is, lowering the number of sales representatives reporting to each field sales manager) provides closer supervision for each salesperson, but also reduces the proportion of the personal selling budget actually devoted to selling. There is no general rule for the optimal span of control because the span, like most sales-management decisions, depends on the nature of the selling task. When this task is complex, a narrow span of control is desirable, resulting in each field sales manager having only a few sales reps to supervise directly. On the other hand, too narrow a span of control can lead to overcontrol and decrease salesperson initiative and motivation. In addition, too many levels of management between the field salesperson and senior sales management can result in organizational inertia and inability to respond quickly to changing circumstances. Although some authors suggest that the ideal span of control is between six and eight salespeople, there is, in fact, little empirical evidence to support this recommendation. Practice varies widely; Figure 15.3 indicates that the span in the Peace Corps varies from 15 to 31 recruiters; the Stanford Annual Fund has a span as low as four for supervision of volunteers soliciting major gifts, but a much larger span for volunteers soliciting smaller gifts.

Deployment of Personal Selling Resources. Once the basic sales organization has been determined, decisions must be made about how the sales force should be deployed. The issues include the assignment of accounts to sales reps—the territory-design problem— and allocation of sales-force time to accounts, product lines, and activities such as opening new accounts versus servicing existing ones. While senior sales management usually develops general policy guidelines on deployment issues, implementation of these policies is generally left to field sales managers and individual sales representatives.

Some of these decisions, such as the emphasis on new accounts or the choice of products to emphasize, depend closely on the organization's marketing objectives and strategy. Thus if a shortage of Peace Corps volunteers with an engineering background were to develop, recruiters would be assigned to colleges with large numbers of engineering graduates. Other decisions depend on the relative efficiency of the available alternatives, so the design of a territory is partially based on the market potential available, the presence of large versus small accounts, and the geographic configuration with its implications for travel time and cost.

Fund-raising organizations typically use volunteers to make personal solicitations of prospects with a giving potential of more than $100 or so. Assignments are generally made on the basis of geographic location, with more intensive solicitation efforts being devoted to prospects who are judged to have substantial giving potential. In contrast, "phonathons" and direct-mail appeals tend to be used to solicit gifts from prospects who appear to have only a modest potential for giving. It's good practice to review sales-force activities and assignments at least once a year, and to make incremental changes as appropriate. Making major changes every year is likely to disrupt personal relationships between salespeople and their customers. On the other hand, complacency and inertia can lead to an inefficient sales force that is not attuned to current needs of the market and competitive factors.

Recruiting and Selection. Clearly defining the role that personal selling is to play in the marketing program and the specific tasks that salespeople will be assigned can suggest the types of individuals needed, likely sources for recruitment, and appropriate selection criteria. Organizational resources, sales-force size, and job requirements often determine whether the organization should try to hire experienced or inexperienced people. Historically Peace Corps recruiters were selected mainly from the ranks of former Peace Corps volunteers (PCVs). While knowledgeable about life in the Peace Corps, these individuals often had limited experience, training, or skills in personal selling. Peace Corps knowledge and experience constituted the key criteria in hiring, since being able to convey the nature of a PCV's experience was the main concern in attracting potential recruits who would prove to be successful volunteers themselves. Nonprofit organizations that rely on a volunteer sales force should recognize that they will be using people who are mostly inexperienced in selling. This situation argues for a relatively narrow span of control to supervise and guide the efforts of new volunteers.

Training. Almost all organizations must do some training. For newly hired, inexperienced salespeople, training should provide selling skills, a detailed understanding of customers and their needs, and extensive knowledge of the organization's products and its policies and procedures. Besides an initial program of familiarization, experienced sales personnel may benefit from more intensive training to improve their selling skills, inform them about new products and policies, or prepare them for more responsible positions within the sales organization.

Rewards and Incentives. Rewards and incentives include both financial and nonfinancial elements. Rewards can be subdivided into two main categories, intrinsic and extrinsic. The former, which are linked to carrying out the job, include such intangibles as feelings of competence, completion, and self-worth. Managers and researchers are paying increasing attention to the role played by intrinsic rewards within the overall incentive system. Of special concern are the factors that motivate volunteers to offer their services without any expectation of financial compensations.

Extrinsic rewards—tangible external elements controlled by the organization—include financial and other benefits. The compensation systems should be designed to encourage the types of behavior desired by the organization. Public and nonprofit organizations are often severely restricted in the use of financial rewards, such as commissions, that are tied directly to performance. Extrinsic rewards, such as distinguished-service awards for successful volunteer fund raisers, can often be an important motivator. Even in the private sector, there is a concern about too much reliance on commissions, since these may cause sales representatives to focus on the short-term and not pay sufficient attention to building long-term account relationships. The design of the compensation system plays an important role in attracting and retaining qualified people for the sales force. Unfortunately, talented salespersons sometimes find the financial rewards of the public and nonprofit sectors insufficient.

Evaluation and Control. Procedures are needed so that sales executives can monitor the performance of individuals and sales groups against certain standards. This information can then be fed back to the involved parties so that any necessary corrective action can be taken. The standards may take the form of measures of *input* (such as the number of sales calls to be made, the number of new accounts to be contacted, and the level of that salesperson's knowledge) or measures of *output* (such as sales quotas for different products, market segments, or both). Performance against some of these standards can be measured quite objectively, while performance against others must often rely on the subjective judgment of the field sales manager. A good evaluation and control system provides both the field sales manager and the salesperson with an opportunity to identify areas of strength and weakness and to develop programs to correct any deficiencies that are identified.

Field Sales Manager. The first-level field sales manager is a major factor in the success of a sales force. Figure 15. 2 positions the field sales manager as responsible for implementing the policies and procedures developed by senior sales executives. The field sales manager's responsibilities can include:

- Deploying sales resources.
- Final selection of salespersons.
- Sales training and coaching.
- Setting salaries and bonuses.
- Establishing sales quotas.
- Evaluating and motivating the sales personnel.

He or she must also be skilled in dealing with problem employees, including dismissing them when necessary. In addition, the field sales manager is responsible for tailoring the personal selling program to the particular characteristics of the local marketplace. Many nonbusiness organizations fail to recognize the importance of field sales managers for the success of personal selling programs. This oversight is serious, since good sales management in the field is critical for success in accomplishing the goals of the sales force.

Individual Salesperson Level

The third level of sales-force management examines factors that directly affect how well individuals perform their jobs. It's at this level that the selling job actually gets carried out. Hence, it's very important to spell out the specific selling task, so that each salesperson has a clear view of what is to be accomplished and the field sales manager has a sound basis for supervising the sales representatives. Some of the responsibilities that can be assigned are listed in Table 15.2. Of course, no one salesperson can be expected to carry out all these tasks, nor are all of them equally important for accomplishing the goals of a specific marketing plan. However, a salesperson can only be successful if each task to be performed is clearly specified.

How well the sales representatives accomplish their assigned tasks depends on three main factors: (1) the nature of the situation in the territory (or set of assigned accounts), (2) the sales predisposition of the salesperson—motivation, knowledge and skills, and selling strategy, and (3) salesperson-customer interactions and outcomes, including the salesperson's job performance and job satisfaction.

Situational Characteristics. The salesperson's characteristics, market conditions (including customer characteristics and competitive intensity), and sales-force policies and procedures comprise the "situational" characteristics. Personal characteristics play an important part in determining how successful a person will be in a sales job. Among the criteria frequently employed in screening candidates for sales positions are:

- Physical factors, such as appearance and age.
- Qualifications, such as education and prior sales experience.
- Mental characteristics, such as general intelligence, verbal ability, and quantitative skill.

Table 15.2   Checklist of Responsibilities that May Be Assigned to Salespersons

- Negotiating sales, including financial terms
- Selling new goods, services, or social behaviors
- Identifying benefits and applications of products
- Providing information to current users
- Training customer personnel in using the product
- Training personnel employed by intermediary organizations in reselling the product
- Managing local advertising and other promotional programs
- Administering cooperative programs in association with donors, intermediaries, or coalition members
- Representing the organization at meetings
- Monitoring competitors, coalition members, and opponents
- Handling customer complaints and product problems
- Responding to customer complaints
- Building and maintaining rapport with customers
- Developing an understanding of each customer's buying process
- Monitoring customer inquiries and sales
- Providing market information to management
- Coordinating all the organization's contacts with each customer
- Obtaining new accounts
- Collecting money or gifts in kind from customers or donors
- Being visible in the community

■ Personality, including interpersonal style, social sensitivity, and willingness to take risks.

■ (For volunteer salesjobs) willingness to devote a minimum number of hours per week to the organization.

A number of sales-management texts emphasize the importance of some of these factors. Some, for example, focus on two personality characteristics: ego drive (ability to get the job done) and empathy (ability to understand and relate to customers). In truth *very few empirical studies clearly support a general relationship between any of these characteristics and sales success*. In practice, hiring policy should be based on careful consideration of the nature of the selling task in question, from which a statement of desirable personal characteristics for that job can be derived. People unsuited for some selling jobs may be well suited for others. The stereotypical successful salesperson is a myth, not a reality! Furthermore, the organization's training program, supervision by field managers, compensation scheme, and procedures for motivating employees play a major part in determining how well a salesperson does.

Sales Predisposition of the Salesperson. A salesperson's performance is strongly influenced by three personal factors: motivation, knowledge and skills, and selling strategy.

Motivation represents willingness to devote the needed amount of effort to specific job requirements, such as calling on potential new accounts, planning sales presentations, and filling out reports.

Knowledge and skills include information about products and customers (including the consumer's decision-making process and how the product fits into the customer's operations), as well as knowledge of the organization's operations and policies. The latter is important because sales representatives are often responsible for marshaling their agency's resources and special talents to meet customer needs and solve users' problems. Also very important are *interpersonal and communication* skills. These include skills in establishing rapport with customer personnel, probing and questioning skills to uncover needs, and skills in reading a customer's reactions to ideas and proposals.

Recruiting and selection policies and the training program of the organization have a major impact on sales-force knowledge and skills. When relying on volunteers, the training program is particularly important. Good supervision, coaching, and follow-up by the sales manager can have a major impact, too.

Selling strategy involves perception of the role the salesperson is to play, allocation of effort across products and customers, and a strategy for dealing with each individual account and sales call. Since sales reps must interact with people both inside and outside the organization, they are often likely to find their roles ambiguous and even conflicting because of the pressures, demands, and expectations of others. How well a salesperson does depends in part on how clearly he or she understands these sometimes conflicting demands.

The development of an account strategy for dealing with the decision-making unit at each account is a particularly important task. It is useful to divide the sales process into five stages.

1. Developing an impression of the customer.
2. Formulating an account strategy.
3. Transmitting the selected communication.
4. Evaluating the effect of the communication.
5. Making appropriate adjustments in the account strategy.[13]

This five-step model requires more than the knowledge and skills discussed earlier. Developing an effective strategy involves taking the information gathered, synthesizing and organizing it, developing alternative selling strategies for given situations, and selecting one of these, which must then be implemented. Good interpersonal and communication skills are certainly necessary, but they are not sufficient skills for success.

In situations where the potential customer looks to the salesperson for advice and guidance, technical skills and expertise may be more important than personal characteristics. For instance, in deciding whether to install a new energy-efficient furnace to help conserve energy, the average consumer is looking for technical expertise. A trained heating engineer may be more successful than a person who is similar to the customer in many respects yet has no technical background when the sales task involves convincing a homeowner to switch from oil heating to gas heating. Unfortunately, there are no general rules about the appropriate bases of similarity or of difference. Thus we turn back to the guiding principle of sales management—establish a clear definition of the role of personal selling and the specific tasks to be carried out by the sales force—as the source of criteria for making decisions about personal selling.

TELEMARKETING

While the invention of the telephone has revolutionized communication, it is now so familiar that most of us take it for granted. That may be the reason its potential to improve customer contact has only lately received attention from marketers. "Telemarketing" uses the telephone as an integral part of the communication program. It can be used to take orders, improve customer service, and sell. Libraries, for example, may use telemarketing in all three of these ways. Borrowers can phone in to ask if a specific book is available, or to renew a book. Librarians may mention special services to callers, like interlibrary loans for the books they do not have, or extended loans to someone who renews the same book repeatedly. They may also contact frequent users of a special collection to ask for a donation to enable the library to enlarge the collection.

Telemarketing integrates telecommunications technology into the marketing program. It allows the use of personal selling, without the expense of face-to-face contact. Used properly, it may improve the effectiveness of both customer service and personal selling. However, poor planning or execution of a telemarketing campaign can annoy customers, and undo the work of the other elements of the communications program.

Calls That Come In

The simplest form of telemarketing is order-taking. Someone dials 911 to report a car accident. A weekend gardener phones the local botanical gardens to ask about the dark blemishes on her rose bushes. The S.P.C.A. gets a call from a man wanting to know how to adopt a dog. In each of these examples, customers have taken the initiative. The role of the organization is then to provide the expected service promptly. Police cars are dispatched to the scene of the accident. The volunteer at the botanical gardens diagnoses the rose problem as Black Spot, a common fungal growth, and suggests an effective treatment. The staff member at the S.P.C.A. explains the steps involved in adopting a dog and gives directions to a nearby shelter.

Often, there is an opportunity to do more than respond to questions. People answering the phone have more information about the organization's services than do the customers calling in. It is up to customer service personnel to judge, sometimes on the basis of subtle cues, whether their customers need further information. For example, the caller to the S.P.C.A. asking how to adopt a dog might mention that he wants a small, quiet dog. An alert staff member would pick up on this and ask tactfully questions about his living situation and reasons for wanting a dog. If he lives in an apartment, is only home in the evenings, and is looking for companionship, both he and his pet might be happier if the pet were a cat.

Sometimes staff who deal with customers over the phone should use a checklist to help determine the suitable combination of services for each caller. Many community centers offer fitness courses and allow telephone registration. Because so many people try to start their exercise program at an inappropriately high level, some centers ask, as part of the registration process, a few questions about the caller's current level of activity and fitness. Their responses are used to guide participants into the right classes.

It is important to remember that when people phone in to request a service, they may not be aware of everything necessary for well-informed choice. Part of the "service" in a service organization is recognizing this and taking appropriate action.

Using The Telephone To Sell

Some organizations don't wait for customers to phone them; they reach out to their customers. Performing arts groups, for instance, sometimes phone subscribers to remind them to renew. Many subscribers appreciate the reminder and like the convenience of being able to renew over the phone using a credit card, instead of having to mail in an order form.

Telemarketing is similar to personal selling in most ways. A good database is essential, as is recruiting and training the right people. However, many people find telephone selling intrusive and offensive. It is important to approach customers with this in mind and have a good reason— from their point of view, not the organization's—to call them, and a good exit line if they are not interested. For example, a wheelchair sports association soliciting new players would have to make a very careful approach to newly disabled individuals, who may see involvement in wheelchair sports as an admission that they have given up hope of full recovery, an admission they may not be ready to make.

Telemarketing has generated excitement as a particularly cost-effective way to sell. Unfortunately, it is not a magic cure for all marketing woes; it is simply an approach that can, under the right circumstances, be a useful part of a good communications program.[14]

SUMMARY

Customer contact is the base upon which service organizations are built. It encompasses both customer service and personal selling. The latter concerns seeking out new sales opportunities and new customers; the former involves all other interactions with customers.

Customer service personnel have to balance the sometimes conflicting needs to satisfy customers and maintain operational efficiency. The sources of customer satisfaction will determine the basic shape of customer service programs. Many other factors affecting the user also come into play and customer service programs must take all of them into account. This user-oriented approach enhances customer satisfaction and improves efficiency and productivity.

A wide variety of tasks, both selling-related and nonselling-related, may fall within the domain of customer service. A customer service audit can clarify the situation by systematically examining the tasks that can and should be performed by customer service. The results of the audit form the basis for planning the customer service function. Key elements in the plan should be the organizational design and provision for systems to ensure that programs are implemented effectively.

As nonprofit organizations grow larger and the number of service delivery sites increases, customer service is becoming the yarn that knits an organization together. It also ensures that operations managers recognize the need to strive for customer satisfaction, as well as operational efficiency.

The more customers are exposed to high quality execution of customer service tasks, the more they will come to expect it of all service suppliers. In the past, many organizations were able to survive in spite of the inadequate or mediocre performance of customer service activities. In the future, such organizations are likely to find themselves severely disadvantaged unless they take steps to develop and implement an improved customer service function.

As well as improving customer service, nonprofit organizations are paying increased attention to personal selling. This is an expensive activity, so effective performance is crucial. Strategic decisions flow from the organization's marketing objectives and relate to choosing the appropriate type of selling for each target market. At the managerial level, the decisions center around organizing the sales force and developing policies and procedures in a variety of areas. In the end, however, it all comes down to each member of the salesforce and how well he or she implements the organization's selling strategy.

Telemarketing is a specialized form of customer contact. Its attraction is that it combines the advantage of personal contact with costs approaching those of the impersonal media. In certain instances, it may be better than personal contact.

The importance of the customer contact function cannot be overemphasized. In many cases, it is the people delivering the service, rather than the service itself that finally determine how much—and even whether—customers will use the service.

REFERENCES

1. William R. George and Fran Compton, "How to Initiate a Marketing Perspective in a Health Services Organization," *Journal of Health Care Marketing* (Winter 1985), pp. 29–37.

2. See N.W. Pope, *"Mickey Mouse Marketing,"* *American Banker* (July 25, 1979) and "More Mickey Mouse Marketing," *American Banker* (September 12, 1979).

3. Richard B. Chase, "Where Does the Customer Fit in a Service Operation?," *Harvard Business Review* (November–December, 1978), pp. 137–142.

4. Christopher H. Lovelock and Robert F. Young, "Look to Consumers to Increase Productivity," *Harvard Business Review* (May–June 1979), pp. 168–178.

5. Rose Gutfield, "IRS Chief Talks About Refunds and Rudeness," *The Wall Street Journal* (April 14, 1987), p.37.

6. The next two sections are based on "Designing the Service Firm Organization," in W. E. Sasser, R. P. Olsen, and D. D. Wyckoff, *Management of Service Organizations*, Boston: Allyn and Bacon, 1978, Chapter 6.

7. Several of these guidelines are adopted from Hirotaka Takeuchi and John A. Quelch, "Quality is More than Making a Good Product," *Harvard Business Review* (July–August 1983) pp. 139–145.

8. J. McDonald, "Charging for Directory Assistance Service," *Interfaces* (November 1976), pp. 5–18.

9. This survey is conducted annually. See "1987 Survey of Selling Costs," *Sales & Marketing Management* (February 16, 1987), pp. 12–13.

10. Adrian B. Ryans and Charles B. Weinberg, "Sales Force Management: Integrating Research Advances," *California Management Review*. (Fall 1981), pp. 79–89 and "Territory Sales Response: Stability Over Time," *Journal of Marketing Research* (May 1987), pp. 229–233.

11. For example, in the 1978 fiscal year, the U.S. Navy spent $16 million on media advertising for recruiting and $42 million on nonadvertising recruiting. It maintained a network of over 1300 recruiting stations and more than 3200 recruiters. See Dominique M. Hansens and Henry A. Levien, "An Econometric Study of Recruitment Marketing in the U.S. Navy," *Management Science* (October 1983), pp. 1167–1184.

12. Christopher H. Lovelock, "Stanford University: The Annual Fund," in C. H. Lovelock and C. B. Weinberg (eds.), *Public and Nonprofit Marketing: Cases and Readings*, New York: John Wiley & Sons, 1984.

13. Barton A. Weitz, "Relationship Between Salesperson Performance and Understanding of Customer Decision-Making," *Journal of Marketing Research*, (November 1978), pp. 501–518.

14. For further discussion of telemarketing, see Bob Stone and John Wyman, *Successful Telemarketing*, Lincolnwood, Illinois: NTC Business Books, 1986; also Eugene M. Johnson, "Nonprofits Calling: The Many Faces of Telemarketing," *Nonprofit World,* September/October 1988, pp. 20–22.

PART 6

Organization
& Implementation

Chapter 16
Organizing the Marketing Effort

Recognition of the need for a stronger consumer orientation and adoption of a competitive market posture clearly must lead to acquisition of new skills and creation of a different management structure. The nature of the structure chosen will determine how the skills are focused and how marketing relates to the other management functions. Among the issues to be addressed are how much emphasis should be given to:

- Planning and executing the different functional tasks within the marketing mix (e.g., advertising, personal selling, pricing, product development).

- Planning and executing marketing strategies for each of several different products offered by the institution.

- Serving customers in dispersed geographic markets.

- Understanding and responding to the needs of current or prospective customers in each of several different market segments.

Organizing the marketing effort requires more than just deciding how to structure the marketing department and assigning specific responsibilities to specific individuals. It includes examining marketing's role in the overall organization, facilitating marketing's interaction with other functional areas of management, and seeking to develop a strong consumer orientation throughout the institution.

If marketing is to have substantial impact on decision making, it must be positioned as a top-management function. In other words, the senior officer responsible for marketing should have an organizational position corresponding to that of senior officers in other functional areas. Traditionally, public and nonprofit organizations have either not had a marketing function or have confined this function—often called by another name—to narrow operating activities such as public relations and direct mail. When institutions first add a marketing function, it is often at a middle-management level that limits the range of activities undertaken and thus constrains marketing's role in the overall organization. This approach does not maximize the strategic and operational contributions that marketing might make, but instead restricts it to low-level, short-term, tactical activities.

Terminology

Many public and nonprofit organizations carry out some marketing functions but do not use marketing terms to describe those functions. Consider, for example, the following short list of departmental titles used in a variety of different organizations.

Organization	Title of Department
Theater or orchestra	Audience development
University	Admissions office
Blood bank	Donor recruitment
Transit agency	Public information
Museum	Education office
Energy agency	Conservation office
Social-service agency	Needs assessment
Hospital	Referral services
Postal service	Customer service
City government	Community affairs

There are three main reasons for this approach. First, it is easier to start with an existing name and build from it than to introduce new terminology. Second, a new name or department may be threatening to some people in the organization and resisted on that basis alone. Third, many who are unfamiliar with marketing have a negative attitude toward it. For example, one consultant to a city government bemoaned

> . . . the negative conception of marketing that prevails among many in local government. It is important for me to define marketing for interviewees and dispel misconceptions of marketing as immoral, propagandistic selling. For practical reasons, therefore, the marketing function should not be called such.

Although this conclusion does have practical merit in the early stages of developing a marketing organization, we believe that avoiding use of the term *marketing* in the long-term is unrealistic. It is undoubtedly true that "marketing" has a negative connotation for some, but the benefits of using marketing terms are likely to outweigh the costs of fighting this negative image and of changing the existing terminology. For example, using the common terminology of marketing allows for greater cross-fertilization of ideas across business and nonbusiness situations and within public and nonprofit organizations. Without a common language to describe common concepts and problems, effort is likely to be wasted in reinventing ideas and in communicating. Consider, for instance, how awkward it would have been to write this book without using "marketing" terms! One danger in using organization-specific terms is that they often limit the scope of an activity. A name such as "public information department" applies to only one aspect of the communication element of the marketing mix and may allow other people to categorize the function in a similarly narrow way. Eventually, as the scope of a "public information department" expands, its name will have to be changed. So it is probably easier to adopt marketing terms earlier than later.

Scope of the Chapter

This chapter looks at alternative ways in which marketing responsibilities, broadly defined, can be organized. Our emphasis is on medium-size to large-size institutions, which are big enough to permit some degree of task specialization among different managers, as opposed to having all management responsibilities centered in just one or two individuals. We begin by showing the need for a market or customer orientation throughout the organization, not just in the marketing department itself. We contrast bureaucratic organizations, which concentrate primarily on internal efficiency, to responsive organizations, which anticipate and adapt to changing market needs.

In the second section we argue that marketing should be recognized as a major strategic function and that its role in the organization should be similar to that of other major functional areas such as finance and operations.

The third section reviews some of the special problems involved in managing a service business as opposed to a manufacturing one. How can a balance be struck between a marketing orientation and an operations perspective in institutions that have historically been dominated by operational considerations?

Next, our focus turns to the marketing area itself, with a look at a fundamental organizational dilemma. How should the organization be subdivided to take best advantage of the benefits of specialization, while coping with the problems involved in integrating diverse functions? There is, of course, no universal solution to this dilemma, and we will examine the major situational factors—both internal and external—that need to be assessed in order to design the most appropriate organizational structure.

The fifth section describes and evaluates several well-known organizational structures for marketing departments—including functional, product-manager, and market-manager systems—and examines the specific task responsibilities assigned to managers in each instance.

PROVIDING A MARKETING ORIENTATION

Marketing should provide the bridge that links the institution to its environment. As many managers will recognize, change does not come easily to public agencies, because of either the weight of bureaucratic inertia or the pressure of meeting day-to-day operating problems, especially in times of budgetary stringency. (Many nonprofit institutions find themselves similarly constrained.) One of the most significant contributions that marketing can make is through the constant pressure it exerts for change in institutions otherwise preoccupied with traditional bureaucratic ends and means.

Organizations vary greatly in their responsiveness to the external environment in which they exist.[1] As illustrated in Table 16.1, they can vary from being bureaucratic and unresponsive to being highly responsive and even proactive, in the sense of making changes that anticipate what is happening in the environment.

The Unresponsive, Bureaucratic Organization

Many institutions begin as vibrant agencies designed to fulfill a specified purpose or mission. Generally, as time passes, the needs of the market and the concerns of other interested parties change. One response of an organization to these pressures may be to focus increasingly on its internal operations and maintain traditional policies and procedures. Such bureaucratic organizations often develop rigid hierarchies and specialized operations, defining management functions narrowly so that it is difficult to respond to changing consumer needs. Internal efficiency, as defined by management, takes precedence. In this way, it seeks to justify its existence.

Table 16.1 Degree of Organizational Responsiveness

Type	Characteristics
Bureaucratic and unresponsive	Efficient in serving original market focus
	Routinizes operations, replaces personal judgment with impersonal policies, specializes jobs of employees, and interprets procedures narrowly
	Little effort made to measure needs, perceptions, or preferences of users
Casually responsive	Sensitive to expressed criticism and public dissatisfaction
	Interested in learning about needs, perceptions, preferences, and satisfaction of markets and other relevant publics
	May alter operations in response to identified problems
Highly responsive and proactive	Regularly and systematically obtains and utilizes information to assess needs, perceptions, preferences, and satisfaction of markets and other relevant publics
	Manages operations to balance internal concerns of efficiency and external market requirements
	Adjusts present and introduces new services, organizational policies, and procedures in response to and in anticipation of changing conditions

Source. Philip Kotler, *Marketing for Nonprofit Organizations,* © 1975. Adapted by permission of Prentice-Hall, Inc. Englewood Cliffs, N.J.

Such bureaucratic approaches can succeed either when the organization is a government agency providing a unique service clients find themselves obliged to use, or when demand for the service greatly exceeds supply. The first case is exemplified by practices in government immigration offices that issue visas and permits for foreign nationals. Thus, the United States Visa Office in Vancouver, Canada, will only accept telephone inquiries on selected mornings during the week. Higher education during the 1960s provides an example of unresponsive behavior in a sellers' market. With the demand for college education greatly exceeding the available space, many colleges were often insensitive to student needs. Of course, as most readers are aware, the change from a seller's to a buyer's market in the 1970s and 1980s has caused universities to become more market responsive out of necessity, if not desire.

The Casually Responsive Organization

An intermediate point on the continuum from unresponsive to highly responsive is occupied by the "casually responsive" organization, which shows sensitivity to user complaints and occasionally gathers information from users and other relevant constituencies. An important distinction needs to be made between responsive organizations and those that only make a show of gathering information but do not subsequently alter their operations in any meaningful way. In response to various pressures, for example, college administrators have increasingly opened their doors to students, participated in student events, and encouraged student suggestions. If little is actually done to meet student complaints and to respond to changing needs, however, "open-door" policies only serve to increase student frustration and demand for change.

The degree of responsiveness of an organization can be examined by looking at whether the activities modified are fundamental or peripheral. Opening the campus bookstore during weekends and evenings may be more convenient for students, but opening libraries, computer centers, and laboratories at those hours is more fundamental. Still more basic is scheduling courses in ways to eliminate course conflicts for students as opposed to scheduling for faculty convenience or simply in accordance with tradition.

The Highly Responsive Organization

In contrast to the casually responsive organization, the highly responsive organization systematically collects information about its environment and audits its activities (see Chapter 3, "Conducting a Marketing Audit"). Such an organization may be termed *proactive* because, instead of being content to react to the changing environment, it attempts to anticipate future requirements.

Responsiveness does not mean that the organization should cater to its customers' every passing whim and abandon its basic mission in the process. It means that the organization's products, methods of operations, and scope of activities are suitably adjusted in the light of both internal and external factors. Responsiveness is closely linked to the prominence of marketing in the organization. If marketing is seen only as a minor tactical activity—sending out brochures to college applicants, for example—the organization will tend to be bureaucratic. Giving marketing a more prominent role will result in the needs of the external environment being communicated internally, so that the organization's response capability is improved.

Readers shouldn't assume that government agencies alone become bureaucratic and unresponsive. Many business corporations behave that way, too. American automobile manufacturers have been widely criticized for their failure to respond to consumer desire for small, well-built, fuel-efficient cars.[2] Instead of adapting to a changing environment, General Motors, Ford, and Chrysler initially pursued a classic bureaucratic approach of doing more of what they believed they did best—in this case, manufacturing big cars—resulting in record losses. Today, competition has made them more responsive.

The difficulty of establishing a highly responsive orientation should not be underestimated, as is discussed more fully in Chapter 17, "Implementing Marketing Programs." Particular attention must be paid to the organization's culture. At times this culture may be internally focused on the services the agency provides and may not allow for change in response to, and in anticipation of, changing external environments. Successful implementation of marketing requires that such conflicts in culture be recognized and resolved.[3]

MARKETING'S PLACE IN THE ORGANIZATION

In most manufacturing firms, the senior marketing officer reports directly to the chief executive officer (CEO) of the corporation or to that person's direct deputy. This individual has the same relative rank as the senior managers responsible for finance, production, control, and other major functions. However, marketing's high standing in the management hierarchy was not always thus.

The marketing function in manufacturing business evolved to its present broad strategic mandate from an initial focus on selected tactical activities, notably personal selling. We expect a similar evolution in well-managed public and nonprofit organizations. Marketing as a functional area in such organizations frequently has its roots in the public-relations department. Distribution decisions such as opening hours are made by the operating staff, the product line is determined by the professional staff based on their expertise, and pricing is closely tied to costs and may be decided by the board of directors. Consequently, the initial role assigned to marketing is limited to building awareness of the existing product and to developing a favorable image for it. When pressures to expand demand become stronger, advertising and promotion are left as the only controllable marketing activity. If the institution has instinctively developed a sound product that meets market needs, yet has never effectively communicated its existence and benefits, such an approach can be successful. For instance, in his book *Subscribe Now!* Danny Newman lists over 50 performing-arts organizations that have more than doubled their audience by adopting an aggressive promotion campaign for subscriptions sold at a discount from single ticket prices.[4] The key point to note is that an advertising or publicity department is just a section of the organization concerned with tactical function. Such a department can become the building block for development of a full-fledged marketing group, but that usually requires upgrading its status and expanding its scope.

Consider some of the possible negative consequences of assigning the marketing function in a large city hospital to a midlevel supervisor rather than to a senior manager.

> Not only was the supervisor unable to spend adequate time analyzing the hospital's major markets and competitive stance, but also the supervisor found that he was unable to obtain support for the few (quite reasonable) marketing actions he recommended. Because no one in top management had initiated the analysis from which the recommendation came and no top level manager was responsible for the marketing function, no one with the power to implement the recommended marketing actions would support them. The result was a frustrated supervisor who spent a good deal of his over-allocated time on a nonproductive task and a hospital which missed out on two substantial market opportunities.[5]

Of course, developing a high-level marketing department does not end all conflict or guarantee the organization a market orientation. Nor should we expect that to happen, since service organizations almost inevitably suffer conflicts between marketing and operations, reflecting the important differences between these two management functions. The challenge is to balance the concerns of both areas.

The boxed material, "Things a Marketing Manager Should Do," illustrates how one consultant defined the marketing manager's job for a performing arts organization.

Important Situational Characteristics

Many public and nonprofit institutions begin life as small agencies consisting of only a few employees and/or volunteers. As long as a group stays small, many of the subdivisions that we talk about later in the chapter are not particularly relevant. When few people are involved, our primary organizational concern is that these people maintain a marketing orientation, not how tasks are subdivided and, in turn, coordinated. Often, however, success leads to growth. A difficult transition step occurs as the organization evolves from an "entrepreneurial" phase where the founders make and execute almost all the decisions to a "managerial" phase in which responsibility must be delegated. Many small institutions have foundered because the originators have not been willing to yield control and neither have, nor are willing to acquire, the managerial skills needed to run larger agencies. The remaining sections of this chapter suggest ways of subdividing a large organization; a smaller organization will not utilize such fine detail but will, in fact, combine many of these functions. A large organization, for instance, may need to develop a regional management structure to whom functional managers report. A small organization may not need this level of regional managers and have only one set of functional managers.

Not all institutions evolve the same way. Some start as single-product agencies and then evolve into multiproduct ones. Others start as local agencies and then evolve into national or international organizations with complex sets of interrelationships among local chapters, regional bodies, and national headquarters—as the history of the Sierra Club illustrates. "The small, intimate Sierra Club—[founded in 1892] to explore, enjoy, and preserve the Sierra Nevada and other scenic resources of the United States"—had become, 75 years later, a 172,000-member organization with a reputation "for political activism, expertise in hiking, camping and quality publications."[6] It had almost 50 regional chapters and more than 200 local groups. The club's first major environmental battle was to save Yosemite Valley from developers. To help accomplish this goal, John Muir, a founder of the club, accompanied President Theodore Roosevelt on a camping trip through the region; a year later Congress voted to make Yosemite a national park. Today, however, more complex organizational structures are needed to manage and implement the far-flung activities of the present Sierra Club.

What factors contribute to organizational complexity and need to be taken into account in designing an organizational structure? Beyond mere size itself, we will look briefly at the following dimensions.

> Number of sites.
>
> Presence of regional and local chapters.
>
> Number of products.
>
> Nature of products—goods, services, and behavior patterns.
>
> Presence of resource-attraction (e.g., fund raising) function.

These factors can be important in determining the nature of the marketing function, its place in the organization as compared to management functions, and the method of subdividing marketing tasks.

Number of Sites. When an agency has only one facility, the senior managers can keep a direct eye on daily operations so that control is relatively easy. As we discussed in Chapter 12, "Distribution and Delivery Systems," however, many potential users of a service value convenience highly. Thus successful service organizations often feel pressure to expand beyond their original location or facility. As an organization adds sites, at least three changes occur in its structure. First, a management function for site location and development must be established. Second, management systems for effectively operating disparate

THINGS A MARKETING MANAGER SHOULD DO

Fundamentally, the marketing manager is responsible for achieving goals of the organization which can be objectively measured, such as sales or revenue attendance or number of customers/clients to be served. Planning the marketing strategy, implementing the plan and monitoring the results are three essential aspects of the marketing manager's job. To be successful, the marketing manager should maintain effective communication with all departments in the organization, including production, finance and anyone involved with "customer contact." Above all, successful marketing requires an orientation focussed on satisfying the customers needs, even if the basic product offered cannot be changed.

Planning

1. In developing a strategy to achieve the organization's goals, the marketing manager should first carefully analyze the market. Questions to be asked include:

   a. Who are the customers? Which market segments exist?
   b. What are the benefits sought by the customer? Has this changed over time?
   c. What are the costs (in terms of time, money and effort) the customers will be willing to pay?
   d. What alternatives are available? Who is the competition?

   If this information is not immediately available, the marketing manager should take steps to improve his/her understanding, and will need to be imaginative. "Knowing the customer" is an important aspect of planning marketing strategy.

2. The marketing plan (Whether short-term or long-term) should address all aspects of "the marketing mix":

   a. the product or mix of products offered;
   b. pricing strategies;
   c. promotional and communication strategies;
   d. distribution or delivery of the product.

   While the marketing manager may only be able to directly control specific aspects of the mix, such as promotion, the other elements cannot be ignored, especially in the long-term. For each product, a set of objectives and a marketing strategy should be developed: identify the market, identify product attributes, specify goals (e.g. number of customers), specify promotional strategy (including costs

sites must be established, because the founders of the organization can no longer directly oversee the operation. Each site must be managed so that it is sensitive to the needs of its own local community, but still provides sufficient uniformity to maintain the integrity of the organization. Third, a system for coordinating and motivating management at disparate sites must be established. Managers in "branch offices" should not view themselves and their sites as peripheral; instead, their importance to the center needs to be reinforced.

If the organization grows substantially, by having either an extensive number of sites or very large sites, a difficult question arises for the marketing department—namely, which marketing tasks should be retained in central headquarters and which marketing and rationale), anticipate possible outcomes. The plan should evolve from the initial "situation" analysis.

3. The marketing manager should develop a budget to support the plan. The budget must address monetary expenditures required, allocation of time and personnel, and include projections of when expenditures will be needed.

Implementation

1. The marketing manager should ensure that everyone in the organization involved with the customer is aware of the marketing plan and its goals. Coordination of all aspects of the marketing strategy and consistency in delivering the message is a key success factor in implementing the plan.

2. The marketing manager should delegate tasks where appropriate, and ensure that specific target dates and deadlines are met. This is especially important in the timing of the promotional/communication strategies.

Monitoring the Results

1. The marketing manager should closely monitor the results of the marketing effort. Questions which should be asked include:

   a. Were target goals met?

   b. Were there unforeseen circumstances?

   c. Was the promotional strategy effective?

   d. Was there any feedback from the customer?

   e. Does anything need to be changed? How could it be improved?

2. The monitoring system should be organized to provide input into new marketing strategies. The marketing manager should ensure that an efficient, accurate information system is in place to collect data which can be used in the planning process.

    The marketing manager's job requires constant monitoring of the general environment to develop new opportunities, or explore new ways of offering customer service. The manager may be involved in market research, promotion, personal selling, advertising, product development, pricing or identifying different markets. While the marketing manager must respond to immediate crises, ultimately he/she should help develop long-term marketing plans for organization.

Source: Adapted from a report prepared by Cheryl Jansen, January 1987.

functions should be delegated either to regional offices (overseeing sites in an area) or to site management itself. No general answer exists to this question, and agencies should resist the temptation to become overly bureaucratic and centralized. A sound marketing strategy should represent the overall goals and policies of the institution, but decentralized management responsibility is usually required if the organization is to remain responsive to user needs.

Presence of Regional and Local Chapters. In many ways, an organization consisting of regional and/or local chapters is analogous to a multisite organization. In both cases, issues arise as to the delegation of responsibility and coordination of effort between area and national offices. For purposes of organizational structure, however, the critical characteristic of a chapter is the degree of autonomy possessed by the local chapter. In some cases, the national organization is only a loose confederation of area chapters. Frequently, the local chapter will have its own board of directors and locally based management, and will also have a substantial commitment to achieving national goals within broad policy mandates.

One consequence of a chapter structure is often to force a separation of the marketing planning and staff functions from the operating and execution functions. In some instances, chapters focus primarily on short-term operating problems and are essentially oriented toward tactical decision making. Meanwhile, the central organization staff focuses mainly on long-term issues and may develop policies and procedures divorced from the operating realities facing the organization. Managers at both the local and national level should be concerned with the harmful effects of such behavior and should seek to design integrating structures and procedures to limit such conflict and to promote meaningful interaction.

In any case, the strength of a chapter structure is its ability to tap local resources and to provide programs that meet local needs. From the standpoint of the national organization, it is sometimes useful to view the local chapters as the manufacturer views its distributors—as a set of dependent but somewhat autonomous units, whose needs must be carefully considered in the design and implementation of programs. The national organization, then, must be concerned with the needs not only of the ultimate users or targets of the program, but also of its "intermediaries," the local chapters.

Number of Products. As the number of products offered grows, management becomes more complex. We describe later in this chapter how organizations providing a single product or very few products can rely on an organizational structure that is subdivided by marketing specialty—for example, advertising, personal selling, and marketing research. When the product line lengthens, however, some subdivision along product or market lines is also required for at least some of the functional areas. Clearly problems of coordination arise. In agencies providing services, increasing the product line makes performance and management of operations more complex and requires even closer cooperation between operations and marketing, as will be discussed in the next section.

Nature of Products: Goods, Services, and Behavior Patterns. To the extent that agencies primarily focus on changing behavior patterns (e.g., persuading people to wear seat belts, obey the speed limits, and drive defensively), the marketing organization emphasizes the communication functions (e.g., advertising and personal selling) and support activities (e.g., market research). If the organization provides services, the distinctive organizational question that must be faced is how to subdivide responsibility between marketing and operations for the design and delivery of services and then coordinate their activities. This task is rarely easy, yet it is central; the marketing and operations nature of the customer-contact function is inherently joined. For example, the nurse who collects blood from a donor is concerned with safely and efficiently drawing the blood and with providing a positive, satisfying experience that will lead the donor to make subsequent contributions to the blood bank.

Agencies that provide goods, whether self-manufactured (as in the case of publications sold by the U.S. Government Printing Office) or purchased from others for resale, can generally separate more fully the production and marketing functions. However, lack of close coordination between these functions can be costly. Marketing information must be sufficiently accurate to allow for efficient production, and the production system must also be sufficiently flexible to be responsive to changing market needs. The marketing department of an agency providing goods must develop functional skills in the areas of the physical presentation and distribution of goods. For example, expertise in packaging and labeling may be required. Furthermore, marketing may become heavily involved in such areas as warehousing and inventory management as part of an effort to balance the costs of overstocking products against those of lost sales and user ill will from not having required products.

In summary, the nature of the products offered influences the types of expertise and functional skills to be included, or at least emphasized, in the marketing department. In all cases, however, coordination with other functional areas is required.

Presence of Resource-Attraction (e.g., Fund-Raising) Function. Many nonbusiness institutions have an active fund-raising department, although others do not. For instance, some government agencies rely largely on a budget allocation for support, as in the case of a parks board or a library, and use political skills to gain support for their programs. In other cases, user fees pay almost all of the costs of the program. Many nonprofit hospitals and health-maintenance organizations (HMOs) are self-supporting, although frequently third-party payers need to be considered. However, the majority of nonbusiness organizations must be actively concerned with attracting resources.

An important consideration in designing the organizational structure is the degree of coordination required between user and funder. Obviously, some coordination is required; donors contribute and governments provide funds based on their assessment of the need for and worthiness of the services delivered and the programs provided. If the funders and users are largely disparate, as in the case of many social and charitable agencies, the user and funder sides can be largely separated. However, many institutions rely on users to contribute funds as well as to pay user fees. Universities, for example, rely on their graduates for donations, and performing-arts organizations address funding appeals to their audience. In such cases, the institution must face the challenge of designing an organizational structure that recognizes the mutuality of interests between users and donors, while making sure that the needs of present and potential users are not made subservient to those of the donors and patrons. As we discuss in Chapter 20, "Managing Retail and Catalog Sales Operations," a similar need for both coordination and separation arises when an organization such as a museum turns to retail sales as a means to earn money.

MARKETING AND OPERATIONS

In most service organizations, an operations orientation dominates the marketing one, partly because of the historic absence of a strategic marketing function. Where a marketing department exists, it is often a staff function confined to peripheral areas such as information, promotion, and advertising. Furthermore, when public and nonprofit organizations make their services available free or at only a minimal charge, costs often become the dominant control mechanism. Such a control system puts a premium on operational efficiency, an orientation that is further emphasized by the complexity involved in the simultaneous production and consumption of services. A firm that manufactures goods can separate the production function from customer contact, but usually a firm that provides services cannot make such a separation.

When an operations orientation is dominant, both major policies and minor operating procedures are established in ways that increase the internal efficiency of the system yet may inconvenience customers. For example, the timing of university courses, the appointment schedules at hospitals, and the opening hours of public agencies often reflect greater concern for the service provider than for the user. As noted by Patrick Ryan in *Smithsonian* magazine, such a perspective can degenerate into near farce.

> Note this newspaper report from the Midlands of England: "Complaints from passengers wishing to use the Bagnall to Greenfields bus service that 'the drivers were speeding past queues of up to 30 people with a smile and a wave of a hand' have been met by a statement pointing out that 'it is impossible for the drivers to keep their timetable if they have to stop for passengers.'"
>
> It will thus be seen that the official function of a bus service is not, as popularly conceived, to carry people from A to B, but to meet its timetables. The sacred schedules must be maintained, even if the bus has to run empty. Therefore, ultimate efficiency of bus services can be achieved only if passengers are banned altogether. Such a prohibition would have the ancillary advantages of extending clutch and brake longevity and markedly reducing the wear and tear on the upholstery. Much the same attitude can be observed in the facial expressions of the staff at any airport as they handle your tickets, while longing for the day when they can be left to run the place like clockwork with their TV screens and admonitory announcements, without all those blasted, disorganized air-travel passengers milling about all over the place.[7]

Reconciling Marketing and Operational Perspectives

Marketing and operations should be seen as mutually supportive functions. Developing customer demand for a service that cannot subsequently be produced is as harmful to an organization as efficiently producing a service nobody needs and for which there is no potential to develop a demand. Successful products make sense from the vantage point of both operations and marketing.

Nevertheless, there are fundamental differences in orientation between marketing and operations that management must bridge in order to achieve competitive and market success. Marketing management is oriented externally to the needs of the customers and to threats from competition. In response, it tends to offer a wide range of services and to want to update them frequently. Success is defined in terms of customer satisfaction and utilization. Operations management, on the other hand, is internally oriented. It wants to offer a few standardized services and is reluctant to make changes. It emphasizes producing these services in an efficient manner. Operating managers tend to believe that if the system is well run according to internal standards, the public will use it; success tends to be measured in terms of cost minimization and achievement of operating standards that may have no relation to customer concerns. Often there is little recognition that the organization currently or potentially faces either direct or generic competition.

Both the operations and marketing viewpoints should be reflected in a well-run service organization. Since they are not entirely compatible perspectives, it is top management's job to reconcile the conflicting demands. In organizations that are already operations-oriented, this is best done by developing a broad understanding of customer needs and concerns among all employees. Indeed, two of the most important elements in organizing the marketing effort are:

1. Ensuring that marketing's place in the organization is equal to that of the other major organizational functions.

2. Infusing the entire organization, not just the marketing department, with a consumer orientation. In other words, a highly responsive organization requires that all areas make the user viewpoint a central concern.

It is sometimes easy for an operations manager, faced with managing a complex system, to argue that the organization cannot afford marketing, since it adds costs and complexity to an already overburdened and possibly budget-constrained system. Such an argument, as we have discussed elsewhere in this book, fails to recognize the important benefits that can result when a marketing orientation pervades the entire organization.

1. *Improved customer satisfaction* achieved by providing services that perform well on dimensions that are relevant to users. This is particularly important in government services, which are dependent on public (and thus political) goodwill as well as customer satisfaction.

2. *Improved net operating performance* achieved by tailoring services to the needs of major market segments and, where appropriate, offering sufficient value to customers so as to command commercially viable prices.

3. *Improved productivity* achieved by implementation of programs that require customers to modify their behavior. Such service innovations as the use of Zip Codes by postal patrons and payment of exact change by transit riders require gaining customers' cooperation in changing established behavior patterns so that productivity gains may be achieved.

Some managers argue that a publicity campaign will suffice to get the public to adopt a required form of behavior. It is certainly true that lack of consumer information can result in the failure of an otherwise sound program, but massive publicity by itself is not sufficient—as indicated by the widespread violations of the 55-mph speed limit in the U.S. (since repealed in many states) and the failure of many consumer energy-conservation programs. Operating managers need to be educated to realize that a marketing orientation in both management decision making and service delivery can contribute directly to the operational efficiency of their units, as well as providing other benefits.

DESIGNING THE MARKETING ORGANIZATIONAL STRUCTURE

The effectiveness of marketing efforts depends on how well matched the marketing department is to both the external environment and the institution's internal characteristics. No single organization structure can be effective in all settings, and the structure of a marketing department may have to be changed as the institution evolves.

Alternative Marketing Structures

Marketing departments are generally structured in one of three major ways (see Figure 16.1). A *functional system* groups together people who carry out similar marketing functions. Thus all those working on advertising would be in one group, those involved in field sales in a second, those responsible for pricing in a third, and so forth. By contrast, a decentralized *product-manager system* focuses on grouping together managers on the

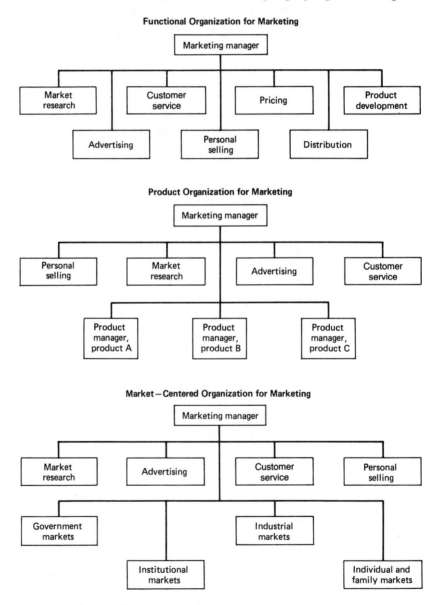

Figure 16.1 Alternative forms of marketing organizations.

basis of a series of different products. Some have found that a product-manager system provides too much focus on the product and not enough on the market segments served and have turned to a *market-centered approach*. In complex situations, combined product-market-manager systems are sometimes needed.

The choice between a functional versus a product-manager or market-manager system has long been a topic of debate in marketing. Each system has its strengths and weaknesses. Institutions rarely install one of these frameworks in a "pure" form, tending to modify the basic structure to meet their own needs. A combined product and market structure is newer and seeks to address the problems of larger organizations whose products and markets are interrelated, yet also contain important distinctive characteristics.

Functional Organization

In the functional organization, specialists in such areas as advertising, promotion, and personal selling report directly to the senior marketing officer (or immediate deputy if there are a large number of specialized functions). Functional organizations are horizontally differentiated, making them relatively simple to administer and facilitating development of expertise in such important marketing functions as advertising, market research, and promotion.

A functional structure is most appropriate when the organization faces similar markets and offers broadly similar services. When products or markets are differentiated, problems arise. In a functional organization, it is relatively difficult to undertake detailed planning for specific products or markets, because no manager has responsibility for them (this is not the case with the product-manager or market-manager system). Sometimes functional areas develop their own subgoals, which are not necessarily coincident with the marketing goals of the overall organization. For example, the advertising department may create advertising that is highly effective in developing awareness of the service, but not so effective in convincing the target group to try the service. Just as the operations department should recognize the needs of the overall enterprise rather than focusing exclusively on internal efficiency, marketing-specialist functions must be managed to achieve marketing objectives.

Despite these difficulties, the functional structure is highly effective when markets and products are relatively homogeneous. For example, the *Transit Marketing Management Handbook* recommends a functional approach for the marketing department in public-transit agencies.

> The functional organization is the most appropriate structure for the transit marketing function. Transit services are homogeneous, the transit market is relatively localized, and transit marketing resources are limited; these three conditions call for a simple and responsive organizational structure which the functional model can best provide.
>
> The recommended transit marketing organization [depicted in Figure 16.2] is strictly a line structure. The decision-making flow for transit marketing proceeds clearly upward from each functional area through the marketing manager to the general manager. Each major activity area within the marketing unit has a well-defined function to perform, thus preventing fragmentation of the marketing effort while minimizing conflicts between groups.

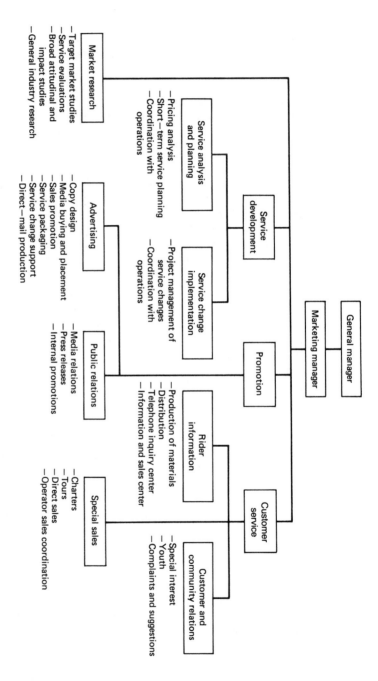

Figure 16.2 Recommended marketing organization and functions for larger public transit systems. *Source:* From United States Urban Mass Transportation Administration *Transit Marketing Management Handbook: Marketing Organization,* U.S. Department of Transportation, 1975. Reprinted with permission.

Within service development, there is a natural and logical division between "analysis and planning" activities and "service change implementation." Similarly, the promotion activity may be broken down into its "advertising" and "public relations" components. Customer services can be divided into "rider information, customer and community relations," and "special sales."[8]

Decentralized Product-Manager Organization*

The major purpose of a product-manager system is to help the organization cope with a complex, multiproduct environment. Individual product managers focus their attention on the needs of a particular set of products. Product managers are task oriented and apply the different functional abilities of the organization (including external groups such as volunteers and advertising agencies) to achieve success for their specific products (or markets).

Product managers have three main responsibilities: information, planning, and coordination.[9] They are expected to be the resident experts on their particular products. Product managers should also possess sufficient information to evaluate the effectiveness of different strategies, build market plans, monitor performance, and understand the implications of any new developments that may arise in the market.

A particularly important part of the product manager's job is to coordinate activities of different parts of the organization. In building a plan, the product manager works closely with other specialized functional areas—particularly operations in a service organization. At times, the product manager will need to use functional managers as staff or consultants concerning the feasibility of different strategic and tactical options, methods of implementation, or assessment of the likelihood of success for a particular program. At other times, the product manager seeks the commitment of functional areas to implement plans in desired ways. For instance, as part of a program to increase the sales volume of a newly opened museum restaurant, a marketing plan may require personnel at the admissions desk to mention this service to all customers entering the museum. Once the plan is accepted by senior management, the product manager must coordinate its implementation and ensure that other functional areas meet their commitments. This entails monitoring the performance of the product (are admission-desk personnel actually promoting the use of the restaurant?) and making changes when required. A major advantage of a product-manager system is the flexibility it provides to make changes.

The major dilemma of the product-manager system is that it conveys responsibility without authority. The product manager has to be successful at getting others to do the job, yet rarely has *direct* authority over all the functions necessary to implement marketing plans successfully. However, the product manager does have some levers other than "friendly persuasion" to gain cooperation and compliance. These may include budget authority to "buy" the use of certain services such as market research and the sales force. In addition, the advertising agency may be directly responsible to the product manager. An important source of power for the product manager is the authority to ask questions anywhere in the organization and to expect carefully thought out answers. In a more

---

*As will be seen, the key distinction between product managers and market managers is the basis of decentralization. Consequently, much of this section applies equally well to the market-manager system. Furthermore, some organizations use the term *product manager* to refer to what we mean by a market-manager system.

general sense, the product manager's authority derives from access to senior management and the support received from them. Table 16.2 lists the key requirements for a successful product-management system.

Pros and Cons of a Product-Manager System

The main advantages of a product-manager system derive from the focus it provides on individual products. The product manager gathers the information necessary to understand the specific market environment in which the product competes, and to design and coordinate an integrated marketing program. The product manager also provides a means to ensure that the organization does not overlook smaller markets. For example, in 1974 the U.S. Postal Service was selling more than 100 million money orders per year and generating revenues of more than $50 million. In the context of a $10 billion organization, the product had been neglected and in decline for 20 years until a newly installed product-manager system reversed the trend.[10] A third major advantage of the product-manager system is its capability for quick response to changing market circumstances.

A product-manager system also has disadvantages. There is almost inevitable conflict between the product manager and the functional and operations areas, as noted earlier. Burdened with responsibility, yet without authority, the product manager spends much time negotiating with other areas for support. These other areas may tend to treat the product manager as only a low-level coordinator and not as an executive with planning and operational responsibilities. For this structure to work effectively, top management

Table 16.2 Requirements for a Successful Product-Management System

1. Strong support from top management.

2. Competent staff specialists, especially in advertising, market research, and site management.

3. A training program for product-managers that will

   (a) Develop creative insight into the marketplace through

       (1) An understanding of consumer behavior.
       (2) An understanding of advertising.
       (3) An understanding of research and its limitations.
       (4) A sense of industry and competitive trends.

   (b) Clarify the expectations of the product-management role.

   (c) Establish working relationships with functional areas.

4. Top-management control through the use of marketing plans.

5. Product managers who are manageable, not free wheeling entrepreneurs.

6. Product managers who, because of their lack of authority, are persuasive communicators with staff and line personnel.

7. The inclusion of procedures for resolving differences.

8. Realistic measures of performance.

Source. Adapted from David Hughes, *Marketing Management,* © 1978. Addison-Wesley, Reading, MA, pp. 114–115. Reprinted with permission.

must carefully specify the limits of the product manager's responsibilities. In fact, organizations vary in seeing the product manager from primarily as a coordinator of functional efforts to being virtually a "minipresident" with extensive executive authority.

Another major limitation of the product-manager system is the amount of knowledge required to coordinate diverse functional and operational areas and to understand dynamic, competitive markets. Product managers often do not have sufficient time to become experts in areas such as advertising and site management that might be critical for product success. Consequently, they must learn when to call—on and how to judge and utilize—specialists in these areas.

Successful product managers require broad general management skills. Some organizations choose people with great product knowledge to be product managers—such as when a community center's cultural program is managed by a local artist—rather than people with the appropriate management skills. An organization must realize that a product manager needs to focus on the users of the product and how to market them.

Toward a Market-Manager Structure

A product-manager system subdivides the organization on the basis of products. Such a structure can sometimes overemphasize the technology of the institution at the expense of the needs of the market. For example, a hospital with separate departments for X-rays, laboratory tests, and medical consultations may find that such a structure neglects important but differing needs of the elderly, of expectant mothers, and of emergency patients. A transit agency with separate departments for bus services and rail services may pay insufficient attention to suburban commuters who use both bus and rail.

Some organizations have adopted a market-manager (or "market-centered") structure.[11] In such a framework, a set of user needs and not a product line or process forms the basis of decentralization. For example, a museum might define distinct responsibilities for school groups, local residents, tourists, artists, and art historians. (A separate manager is not required for each, only a definition of responsibility by market.) Such a structure matches organizational design to the market.

There are several advantages to this approach. First, in competitive situations, it may help the organization to become a more effective competitor. For example, a museum's market manager for tourists may focus attention on the same tour groups and tourist information centers that such competitors as restaurants, theaters, and retail stores solicit and thereby establish a market position that is attractive to the tourist. A market manager for school groups may be able to compete successfully with the many other available attractions. Another advantage of a market-centered approach is that it may help in identifying new product opportunities. For example, a museum may find that a good basis for adding lecture and film programs is the nature of the market addressed, not the era in which a painting was done. The main advantage, however, which subsumes all the rest, is that a market-centered approach puts the focus on the external markets, not the internal operations of the agency. (Of course, a product-manager system that is truly oriented toward the *users* of the product can achieve these objectives as well.)

The market-manager system is a complex one and not without its costs. Most important, as discussed in the section on marketing and operations, there needs to be an integrating system so that market managers do not design products that cannot be delivered or make commitments that cannot be fulfilled. Market managers, more than product managers, may lack a sense of the capabilities of the agency and the need to work within them. When several market managers are concerned with the same product, problems of coordination increase. Furthermore, a market-centered system may add direct financial costs because separate information systems, field-contact personnel, and advertising programs may be required. Despite these significant costs, some organizations may find the benefits of this approach to be worthwhile.

Other Approaches

For service organizations, geography is an important way to subdivide the market. Different geographic areas may have different needs, and the nature of service sites may vary as well. When off-track betting (OTB) was introduced by New York City, separate marketing managers were assigned for each of the five boroughs—thus recognizing the diversity of the boroughs, ranging from small, suburban Staten Island to the borough of Manhattan, whose market includes commuters as well as residents. Some policies, such as pricing and television advertising, had to be established on a citywide basis, but there was sufficient diversity among the boroughs to justify separate market managers for each.

Geography is not the only way to subdivide the organization. Any substantial basis for market segmentation is a potential framework for organizing the marketing function. In Canada, for instance, the presence of two official languages often represents an important rationale for dividing the market into French-speaking and English-speaking groupings.

Furthermore, it is sometimes useful to consider both products and markets when designing an organization. For example, fund-raising departments often subdivide their markets by size of potential gift, as well as establishing a number of separate programs, each supporting a different activity (e.g., school or athletics). The requirements for managing systems to attract donations from people or companies capable of donating large sums of money differ greatly from those directed at prospects whose giving potential is assessed at $25 or less. The Stanford University Annual Fund has instituted a complex market-manager system under which fund-raising activities are organized both by size of potential gift and by the prospect's area of interest at Stanford.[12]

SUMMARY

In organizing the marketing effort, we are concerned both with marketing's role in the organization and with how the marketing department itself subdivides its tasks.

For marketing to have a significant impact on the agency's decision making, it must be recognized and situated as a top-management concern and function. In this way, marketing insights contribute to both strategic and tactical decisions. Adoption of marketing at the top, however, is not sufficient. To be effective, a market or user orientation must permeate the organization at all levels, as the contrast between an unresponsive, bureaucratic orientation and a highly responsive orientation illustrates. Of course, marketing is not the only important concern of an agency, and the needs and practicalities of other departments need to be balanced as well. In particular, the necessity of reconciling both marketing and operations viewpoints is stressed in this chapter. A key area is the customer-contact function; personnel in direct contact with users have to reflect a customer orientation at the same time that they are participating in the production of the agency's service.

For too long, nonbusiness organizations have been dominated by an operations orientation; a more balanced view involving both marketing and operations must prevail for long-run success.

Turning to the marketing area itself, the key organizational dilemma is how to subdivide the marketing tasks and functions to gain the benefits of specialization and to provide a means of integrating diverse functions. No single organizational structure fits all situations. As our perspective moves from a single-product, single-market focus to a multiproduct, multimarket one, more complex organizational structures are needed. Such factors as the nature of the product, the growth of the agency, and the personnel involved all need to be considered in designing an organizational structure.

There are three major ways to subdivide marketing departments—functional, product manager, and market centered—and each has its own strengths and weaknesses; more complex settings may require a blend of these forms, such as the product-market systems that have emerged in some large agencies. When the structure of an agency's marketing department is well matched to the external environment and the internal characteristics of the agency, both the efficiency and effectiveness of the marketing effort are enhanced.

REFERENCES

1. The discussion of degree of responsiveness in the following section is adapted from P. Kotler, *Marketing for Nonprofit Organizations,* Englewood Cliffs, N.J.: Prentice-Hall, 1975, pp. 40–43.

2. J. Patrick Wright, *On a Clear Day You Can See General Motors,* New York: Avon Books, 1979.

3. The importance of organizational culture and the potential for conflict are issues in both the business and nonbusiness sectors. For instance, see Tom Peters and Nancy Austin, "A Passion for Excellence," *Fortune* (May 13, 1985), pp. 20–32. For a discussion in the context of health care, see Alan R. Andreasen and Jean Manning, "Culture Conflict in Health Care Marketing," *Journal of Health Care Marketing* (March 1987), pp. 2–8 and Denny R. Arnold, Louis M. Capella, and Delia A. Sumrall, "Organization Culture and the Marketing Concept," *Journal of Health Care Marketing* (March 1987), pp. 18–28.

4. Danny Newman, *Subscribe Now!* New York: Theatre Communications Group, 1977, pp. 271–276.

5. Roberta Clarke, "Marketing Health Care: Problems in Implementation," *Health Care Management Review* (winter 1978), p. 24.

6. Arthur Segel and Charles B. Weinberg, "Sierra Club Publishing Division," in C. H. Lovelock and C. B. Weinberg, *Public and Nonprofit Marketing: Cases and Readings,* Palo Alto: The Scientific Press, 1984.

7. Patrick Ryan, "Get Rid of the People and the System Runs Fine," *Smithsonian* (September 1977), p. 140. Reprinted by permission.

8. United States Urban Mass Transportation Administration, *Transit Marketing Management Handbook: Marketing Organization,* 1975. U.S. Department of Transportation. Reprinted with permission.

9. A description of a product-manager organization may be found in L. Frank Demmler and Christopher H. Lovelock, "United States Postal Service," in C. H. Lovelock and C. B. Weinberg, *Public and Nonprofit Marketing: Cases and Readings,* New York: John Wiley & Sons, 1984. See also, John A. Quelch, Paul W. Farris, and James M. Oliver, "The Product Management Audit," *Harvard Business Review* (March–April, 1987), pp. 30–36.

10. As in Demmler and Lovelock, reference 9.

11. Mark Hanan, "Reorganize Your Company Around Its Markets," *Harvard Business Review* (November–December, 1974).

12. Christopher H. Lovelock, "Stanford University: The Annual Fund," in C. H. Lovelock and C. B. Weinberg, *Public and Nonprofit Marketing: Cases and Readings,* New York: John Wiley & Sons, 1984.

Chapter 17

Implementing Marketing Programs

Implementation is concerned with getting things done, with transforming marketing plans into marketing actions. Sound strategy without good implementation results in little gain. One hospital learned this lesson well from the failure of a medical office it opened to generate referrals from a rapidly growing suburban area in which virtually no doctors were located.[1] The hospital planned to open a four-room office suite to be staffed by part-time physicians with varying specialties; the office was launched with a direct-mail campaign to every household in the community and full-page ads in the local newspapers. The results two years later were dismal—fewer than five office visits daily were being generated. The key reason for this failure was that the delivered product did not meet consumer needs. The hospital could only convince one member of its medical staff to practice in this facility and thus did not provide the range of services that the community wanted and that were offered by other hospitals with freestanding emergency rooms and doctors' office buildings serving area residents. The hospital learned from this experience and launched a large-scale communication campaign for its outpatient cancer-care center only after it had consolidated the many multidisciplinary services required by a cancer patient into one easily accessible location. This example illustrates the critical importance of implementation and execution, and also that an organization can (and should) learn from its mistakes.

Devoting a separate chapter to implementation does not mean that implementation can be separated from such other managerial tasks as analysis, planning, and decision making. Success requires that all aspects of management be integrated, as we have stressed throughout this book. This cascading effect of strategy and tactics extends throughout the organization. To illustrate this point, a community center's strategic decision to serve teenagers can be effective only if there are program personnel to design meaningful, attractive programs. In turn, these programs are worth little unless the community center's workers can actually perform the program's requirements.

Strategy and implementation form a cycle, each affecting the other. The interaction between implementation and other managerial functions is seen elsewhere in this book. For instance, conducting a marketing audit (see Chapter 3) provides the means to examine an organization's environment, organization, and past performance, thus providing a key input into strategy formulation for the future. Likewise, as noted in Chapter 5, marketing control systems monitor performance compared to targets set in the marketing plan. Finally, in Chapter 16, "Organizing the Marketing Effort," we showed that an important goal of organizational structure is to facilitate the implementation of marketing programs.

Scope of the Chapter

Implementation is a broad topic and can justify a book on its own. This chapter highlights some key issues particularly pertinent to public and nonprofit institutions.

The first section discusses ways to introduce and establish a formal marketing function in an agency that does not *explicitly* recognize marketing as a management activity. The issue is not whether the agency performs marketing activities—dealing with users and other publics per se involves marketing—but whether it possesses a formal marketing function. The section presents alternative ways to install such a function in a nonbusiness organization that currently lacks it (as many still do).

The second section examines the ethical implications of implementing a marketing approach. Some people confuse marketing with the most crass forms of advertising and personal selling and thus—mistakenly in our view—reject marketing out of hand. Others fear marketing's potential to change society and may not recognize that marketing is just one method of introducing change in a social system; other approaches range from force and legal coercion at one extreme to "benign neglect" at the other. Any attempt to induce social change can raise ethical questions. Within the field of marketing itself, different tactics vary in their ethical sensitivity, and certainly some approaches are highly questionable. As we will see, the issue is not whether marketing should be used, but how to use it in an ethically sound manner. We illustrate these concerns with examples of abuses in the field of higher education.

The third section discusses how public and nonprofit agencies can leverage their efforts through third parties. Many nonbusiness organizations do not have adequate funds to establish a fully staffed marketing function or to pay for extensive marketing activities. They often have access to free or low-cost goods and services that allow them to extend their limited resources. The United Way, for example, uses public-service advertising on televised football games where the commercial time is worth literally millions of dollars; the United Way also gets considerable amounts of management time from senior business executives at no cost. Free goods and services sometimes have restrictions on their use, however, and agencies must be careful in accepting and using such donations. Government agencies can also supplement their efforts by the imposition of laws, rules, and regulations—such as fining violators of highway speed limits—to help achieve their objectives.

All marketers need to use outside suppliers to provide some services. Market-research firms, advertising agencies, and outside consultants are frequently employed to help an organization develop and implement marketing programs. Similarly, intermediaries may be used to provide information, make reservations, accept payment, and even deliver the product to the customer. In the fourth section of this chapter, we suggest ways to select and use outside suppliers and intermediaries. If carefully managed, outsiders can make powerful contributions to successful marketing programs. When unwisely used, however, outside consultants waste valuable resources; to make the most of outside services, an institution needs to learn how to be both a good client and a good manager.

Although outsiders can help an organization develop and implement marketing strategies, ultimate success depends on the agency's own ability to execute its program. Excellence in execution is an important goal. In the fifth section of this chapter, we look at specific steps an organization can take to accomplish its task and to facilitate the transformation of marketing plans into real achievements.

The chapter concludes with a brief section on the future role of marketing in public and nonprofit organizations.

ESTABLISHING A MARKETING FUNCTION

As we have seen throughout this book, virtually all organizations engage in marketing, but relatively few public and nonprofit institutions have formal marketing departments or incur marketing expenditures comparable to those of similarly sized business counterparts. Although the introduction of marketing can benefit an organization greatly, it would be foolish to assume that adoption of a formal marketing program is a simple process. "Marketing" itself must be marketed, just as any new good, service, or idea needs to be in order to secure its usage. Nor should the marketer assume that gaining adoption is an easy task. Consider the following, perhaps overly pessimistic, remarks of two experienced consultants.

> Social marketers typically find that they must function in organizations where marketing activities are poorly understood, weakly appreciated, and inappropriately located. Social organizations have a tendency to adopt marketing in small doses. The management may decide to try marketing by hiring a few employees or consultants with marketing backgrounds. These persons are generally assigned to work with public affairs or public information offices because management generally equates marketing with communications or promotion. The results the marketers can achieve in these positions are quite limited, since they have little influence over program development and administration and must restrict themselves primarily to informing the public about the features of the program. Thus, social marketers are often programmed for mediocre performance from the very beginning. They cannot convince management to give marketing the prominence it needs to be effective, and they cannot earn their way to prominence through outstanding performance. This dilemma may continue to confront social marketers as long as physicians, lawyers, scientists, law enforcement specialists, social workers, and others who often dominate social agencies and organizations feel uncomfortable and unfamiliar with marketing.[2]

There are, of course, many successes in the establishment of marketing, as this book has illustrated. The authors of the preceding quote, for example, cite by contrast the long-term, disciplined marketing approach of "the National High Blood Pressure Education Program, which has been unerring in its positioning for eight years and has made substantial progress in contributing to hypertension control in the United States."[3]

In thinking about how to establish marketing as a formal management function, it is useful to recall the factors that the literature on diffusion of innovations suggests are related to the likelihood of success: (1) relative advantage, (2) compatibility, (3) complexity, (4) trialability, (5) observability, and (6) perceived risk. Marketing is a complex management function that can pose considerable risk to administrators, especially those who manage bureaucratically and are set in their ways. Marketing is not always compatible with established procedures, yet sensitive marketing managers must establish harmonious relationships with other management functions, as shown in the discussion of marketing and operations in Chapter 16, "Organizing the Marketing Effort." While conflicts will arise from time to time, good managers should be able to resolve them in a manner. On the other hand, marketing can provide a significant relative advantage to an organization, and successes can often be shown and made readily observable.

A critical task for newly appointed marketing managers in an organization that has previously lacked a formal marketing function is to choose appropriate *early* assignments: they should look for projects that are seen as useful by other managers, have reasonable visibility, and offer a high chance of success in a relatively short time period. One advantage of working for an organization that has neglected marketing is that there are usually a number of such projects available. Finally, the implementers of marketing should recognize that initial projects are only trials; they must continue to develop the utilization of marketing until it is fully accepted as a vital, necessary organizational activity.

Criteria for Selecting Early Marketing Projects

The choice of the first marketing projects to be undertaken is critical. In Table 17.1, we suggest five criteria that should be employed in screening early marketing projects. These criteria are drawn from the concept of "diffusion of innovations."

Early projects have to be easily judged, which is why *explicit (quantifiable) performance measures* are needed. Without measurable results, anyone not inclined to use marketing could claim a program was not successful or had no impact. That is also one of the reasons for a *short to medium time period for completion*. In addition, keeping the time period short helps retain the interest of organizational members. Because many public and nonprofit agencies face annual funding cycles, a useful rule of thumb is to look for projects that take months instead of years. (On the other hand, projects that take weeks instead of months are usually too superficial to have a lasting impact.) Staff and volunteer turnover

When marketing is new and possibly perceived as threatening by some, it is useful to choose projects that only use a *limited amount of the organization's resources*. In this way the opposition of those unfamiliar with marketing can be avoided until there is a chance for a fair trial.

Early marketing projects should be *neither peripheral nor central* to the agency. If the project is too peripheral, it can easily be dismissed as not being pertinent to the main concern of the agency. For example, early marketing efforts at a hospital that concentrated on redesigning the cafeteria facilities would be seen as irrelevant to the main concerns of the hospital by most doctors and administrators. In a similar vein, an early marketing program at the U.S. Postal Service (USPS) directed toward increasing household letter

Table 17.1 Criteria for Screening Early Marketing Projects

1. Can be evaluated by explicit performance measures
2. Can be completed within a short to medium time period
3. Uses limited portion of available resources
4. Is neither peripheral nor central to the organization
5. Is visible to key decision makers within the organization
6. Has a high probability of success

writing was seen as peripheral by the USPS's senior management.[4] Although both the cafeteria and letter-writing campaigns met the other criteria so far discussed, their contributions could be negated by their peripheral nature. On the other hand, choosing a project that is too central to the organization makes the risk unnecessarily high and encourages active opposition from skeptics. Examples of appropriate middle range projects would be for a blood bank to increase donations from college students and for the community center to improve its program for teenagers.

The fifth criterion is that the results of the project, if successful, are *visible* to the rest of the organization, and especially to key decision makers. This criterion is closely related to the first two of measurability and limited time duration. Demonstrably successful trials are generally required before marketing will be accepted as a standard management function.

Perhaps implicit, but still worthwhile stating, is the sixth criterion of having a *high probability* of success in order to build confidence in marketing.

It is difficult to specify who should have responsibility for the initial projects. An individual manager will often be the initiator when facing a problem that he or she recognizes as involving marketing issues. In nonprofit agencies, a board member, perhaps with a marketing background, might suggest that marketing approaches be tried. For instance, the president of Boston's Museum of Fine Arts, a former business school dean, initiated an in-depth marketing study of the museum. Alternatively, a manager may start the process as a result of reading an article or attending a seminar. Quite often, because of the novelty of the idea of marketing, a committee may be formed to oversee the project. The members would typically include the initiating executive, other executives either likely to be affected or thought to be sympathetic, and paid or voluntary outside marketing experts. This committee needs to have sufficient authority to get initial programs started, breadth to ensure that politically sensitive issues are avoided or handled discreetly, expertise, and enthusiasm—to get the job done.

For example, before the Evanston (Illinois) Hospital launched its first consumer advertising campaign (one of the first in the United States) for one of its satellite hospitals, it established an advertising committee to oversee the project.[5] The committee's members included medical staff and board members as well as marketing personnel. Also, before the campaign was launched, a brochure reproducing the ads was distributed to all employees, volunteers, board members, and physicians. Such a procedure built support for the advertising program before the ads were actually run. Moreover, the campaign itself appeared to be successful; unaided awareness was raised from 55 percent prior to 71 percent following the campaign, and the level of patients' visits to the emergency room increased by one-third.

Moving Beyond Initial Projects

The type of projects we have just described are short-term, tactical marketing programs. Marketing, however, is a strategic function. Hence the marketing practitioner must avoid doing too many tactical projects because, although they are necessary and useful, they also represent building blocks toward the establishment of a formal marketing function. For example, a transit agency manager who has run successful advertising programs to help introduce several new routes should realize that, in the long-run, the objective should be to ensure that marketing concepts are used to help decide which routes should be established, the type of service to be offered, and the rider segments served.

To go beyond such tactical activities, two conditions are necessary.

1. Support from the chief executive officer (CEO) of the organization.

2. Establishment of a senior executive with responsibility for marketing.

Without support of the CEO, marketing cannot become a significant strategic function. Marketing introduces the reality and complexity of a dynamic, competitive environment into an organization's planning and operations. As such, it appears to make the job of the other management functions more difficult—although in the long-run a marketing orientation makes the organization more responsive, vital, and successful. Some of the difficulties and contrasts between the marketing and operations orientations were discussed in Chapter 16. The task of financial management is made more difficult because substantial expenditures are often required to develop and plan marketing programs. Investments must often be made in intangibles, such as marketing research, service development, and personnel training, the value of which does not appear on the balance sheet along with physical assets. The accounting and control functions need to provide cost and other data on a product, market, or other basis that reflects current market structure rather than historical tradition. More generally, as one experienced marketing consultant points out, the introduction of marketing

> may require drastic and upsetting changes in organization. It usually demands new approaches to planning. It may set in motion a series of appraisals that will disclose surprising weaknesses in performance, distressing needs for modification of operating practices, and unexpected gaps, conflicts, or obsolescence in basic policies. Without doubt, it will call for reorientation of business philosophy and for the reversal of some long established attitudes. These changes will not be easy to implement. Objectives, obstacles, resistance, and deep-rooted habits will have to be overcome. Frequently, even difficult and painful restaffing programs are necessary before any real progress can be made in implementing the concept.[6]

When the CEO indicates that marketing is "here to stay" and will be an important part of the organization's future and that the organization intends to be user oriented and service minded, the framework is set for establishing marketing as a strategic management function.

The CEO, however, cannot do it all. While the CEO can set the direction, there needs to be a senior marketing executive who sits as an equal with the top executives of the other managerial areas. Only then can marketing be fully incorporated into the strategic planning activities of the organization. A senior person can also be responsible for the organization's relationship to a number of external constituencies—such as donors, governmental bodies, and trustees—as well as to users. Some organizations start by appointing a middle-level manager to a marketing position. This is one way to limit the risk in adopting a marketing orientation, but the limited clout of such a position restricts the range of problems that can be handled. An executive in such a position, without top management support, will have difficulty in getting other functional areas to implement marketing programs. Such a case was illustrated in Chapter 16 by the example of the frustrated middle-level marketing supervisor in a hospital. This manager had inadequate time and resources to analyze the hospital's major markets and was unable to get others to implement recommended marketing actions because no top-level manager was responsible for the marketing function. Consequently, little was achieved. Some organizations prefer to move from tactical marketing projects to appointing a middle-level marketing manager and later to appointment of a senior marketing executive, but the middle-level-manager stage should be recognized as a transition step. We recommend moving to the senior executive stage as soon as possible in order to realize marketing's full potential.

Some organizations already have staff people who are carrying out some aspects of marketing. As Kotler warns, however, CEOs of organizations should exercise caution in considering whether or not to assign overall responsibility for marketing to an existing staff member.

> Some organizations feel that they are not only doing marketing but that they already have formal staff positions responsible for marketing. Therefore, they don't need to add another staff position called "marketing." A college president may feel that the admissions director, the public relations director, the planning vice president, and the development vice president are the institution's professional marketers. This may or may not be correct, however. Many admissions directors are sales oriented rather than marketing oriented. They are good at "pounding the pavement" for prospective students, but not skilled in marketing research and marketing strategy which would make this selling job easier. Most public relations directors are skilled in journalism and communication, but are not trained in analyzing, researching, and planning for markets. Planning vice presidents may concentrate on developing the physical plant and on financial problems, without having much marketing knowledge or aptitude. Development vice presidents are often sales oriented and fail to put their fundraising efforts on a modern marketing management basis. Though these officers should be professional marketers handling their respective markets, they typically are not.[7]

These are valid concerns for any organization new to marketing. Part of the challenge in initiating a marketing orientation is to use the marketing abilities that the present executives have and to give them training in order to broaden their skills. In smaller organizations, of course, many of the different marketing functions will be carried out by the same individual.

Toward a Marketing Orientation

Implementing marketing entails more than establishing a separate marketing function. Meaningful implementation requires a marketing orientation throughout the organization, starting with the CEO. Managers throughout the organization must understand what marketing is and how it can contribute to the organization. Employees and volunteers must be service oriented and be prepared to act as if they were users instead of providers of the service. Approaches to achieving this type of behavior are discussed later in the chapter.

Once market sensitivity has been achieved, maintaining such an orientation is a continuous process. In the short run, it always seems easier to keep on doing what has been done before and to maintain the status quo. Long-run vitality requires change and the external perspective that marketing brings, however. An institution's management system must be directed toward keeping the organization responsive to changing circumstances.

Effective marketing implementation requires good interaction skills.[8] Much of the marketing job is to influence others, often under conditions where marketing managers lack formal authority to get their own way. Getting customer-contact employees and volunteers to devote more time to a specific product or market segment requires interacting with operations executives and other senior managers whose support is necessary to make the project successful. Good interaction or "people" skills are also needed to deal with numerous outsiders including advertising agency personnel, market researchers, consultants, suppliers, distributors, and many others—not to mention the customers themselves.

ETHICAL DIMENSIONS IN IMPLEMENTING MARKETING

Maintaining a marketing orientation throughout the organization and implementing formal marketing programs help an organization to achieve its goals effectively and efficiently. While marketing has many benefits to offer, it can also arouse considerable antagonism. As one early proponent of the use of marketing in higher education bluntly pointed out, the term *marketing*

> has become [to many] a catch-word standing for all the undesirable elements in American business: the foisting of worthless products on an unsuspecting public; the aggressiveness of Madison Avenue and its immoral manipulation of people. In short, marketing is looked upon by many as being fundamentally self-seeking and thus unacceptable by its very nature . . . . [If] anything is undesirable about marketing, it is not in the activity per se; rather it is in the motives of those guiding the activity and the manner in which it is carried out.[9]

Executives in public and nonprofit organizations need to be prepared for criticism when they use marketing techniques. To some observers, marketing has a negative connotation because of a lack of understanding of the subject, concern about the power of marketing to influence public opinion, awareness of certain distasteful marketing tactics, or other reasons. Ideally, critics should recognize that marketing itself is neutral; their concern should not be with marketing but with how managers use marketing concepts, tools, techniques, and strategies.

Marketing Styles

What might be called "marketing styles" range from aggressive or hard-sell marketing at one extreme to minimal marketing at the other. Hard-sell marketing, which is characterized by large advertising budgets, sales forces, and/or sales promotion, is found in such industries as automobiles, packaged goods, toiletries, encyclopedias, and real estate, but it occurs elsewhere as well. For example, some family-planning agencies in developing nations use hard-sell tactics, including offers of transistor radios or pots and pans to get as many people as possible to adopt family-planning practices.[10] It is common to criticize aggressive marketing, but sometimes this approach is necessary to get the attention of the market. Hard-sell marketing efforts, for instance, have contributed to increased ticket sales for a number of performing-arts institutions, as the following examples from around the United States illustrate.

> In Minneapolis, the Guthrie Theater uses highway billboards with giant pictures of Hamlet to promote subscriptions. In Wisconsin, the Milwaukee Repertory Theater Co. floods the mails with 350,000 leaflets a year and sells 10 times as many subscriptions as

a decade ago. "It's a hard-sell approach," says an official. "We bombard people with the stuff, and they finally break down and buy a subscription."

In Louisville, Ky., the Actors Theater has used hundreds of coffee kitchens to help multiply subscription sales fivefold in the last decade. Supporters of the theater invite friends for coffee, and the theater gives them the subscription pitch along with a slide show. "We call them cultural Tupperware parties," says Patricia Pugh, the theater's associate director. The Brooklyn Academy of Music (BAM) pushes ballet and theater the way other people sell television sets. To promote its first African dance series, BAM held a street fair with African crafts and an elephant ride for the children. To boost ballet sales, it held a "dance-lover's sweepstakes." Among the prizes: a trip to London, two treatments by a dancers' masseur, and a stage backdrop for Swan Lake (complete with a giant plastic swan). "We're in the business of selling a perishable product," says a BAM official. "In supermarkets, the lettuce wilts. In our case, the curtain goes up."[11]

In the 1970s, as college enrollments began to decline, some schools used (or at least proposed) a variety of attention-getting schemes to stimulate interest among prospective applicants, including distribution of monogrammed Frisbees or be-sloganed T-shirts, inserts in newspapers, release of balloons containing scholarship offers, and sponsorship of juggling acts in shopping centers.[12] Is there necessarily anything unethical in all this? We believe that from a consumer standpoint there is nothing morally wrong in strategies that serve merely to generate awareness of the institution, so long as they do not willfully misrepresent facts in the process. Some of the approaches used represent lighthearted innovations that attract attention and perhaps serve to diminish the stodgy, sanctimonious impression that some people have of college administrators. Others, however, are ridiculous to the point that they simply make the institutions look foolish and may even discourage applicants.

Both managers and observers of public and nonprofit organizations must learn to *distinguish the innovative from the inappropriate and the unethical from the merely foolish.* The marketer must learn to avoid the distasteful while bringing a fresh approach to the markets the agency serves.

At the opposite extreme of an aggressive marketing style stands minimal marketing; this usually means that the organization has no formal marketing function.[13] The premise underlying minimal marketing is that demand for the product will grow simply because the organization is offering it, or offering it well. Often this approach is present in hospitals, universities, and museums and other organizations run by professionals, who seem to argue, "Why should we have to *sell* a worthwhile service?" Such reasoning is misguided, as the reader should be well aware by now. Often such beliefs originated at a time when demand greatly exceeded supply, so the suppliers could ignore the market and still have an extensive call for their services. Such a monopoly condition usually does not last because institutions arise that better serve customer needs. The success of outpatient surgery, hospices for the terminally ill, and other health-care innovations, for instance, has forced hospitals to recognize that their concept of the desired product is not necessarily shared by the patients.[14] Minimal marketing seeks to avoid the use of advertising and other paid communication media, but failure to use paid advertising can be costly. In other words, reliance on minimal marketing, while it may appeal to one's sense of professional dignity, can lead to a loss of both effectiveness and efficiency.

In terms of the marketing mix, aggressive and minimal marketing can each be characterized as relying on only one element of the mix—promotion or product. Both can raise ethical concerns, the first by errors of commission and the second by errors of omission. What is needed, of course, is a balanced marketing program that employs a complete set of marketing tools in a sensitively designed program.

Marketing and Social Change

Marketing is one means to foster social change on such issues as nutrition, family planning, abuse of drugs, resource conservation, and many others. A wide range of methods can induce change, from physical force, legal coercion, and other severe deprivations to merely making alternatives available. Ethical concerns arise because marketing may be seen as manipulative by facilitating change, by its association with a cause that is controversial (at least to some people), or for its specific tactics.

The word *manipulative* has negative overtones, yet one undeniable outcome of a successful social marketing program is to change people's beliefs, attitudes, and/or behaviors. Any program that concentrates on social change raises potential ethical dilemmas, and we must question both the goals of the program and the methods to achieve them.[15] The family-planning literature, in particular, has devoted extensive attention to these very complex issues. Virtually any program of change involves ethical dilemmas to some degree. The ethical issues involved in whether society should attempt to change some of its members in some way and in the choice of specific goals raise complex philosophical issues well beyond the scope of this book. However, managers should be aware that those opposed to social-change programs may not distinguish between the advocated programs and the marketing tools being used to promote them.

When compared to the use of force, such as in alleged involuntary sterilization campaigns in India, marketing seems to raise few ethical issues. This is an unrealistic comparison because such severe measures are rarely employed. Manipulation of public opinion, through the use of propaganda, is a serious concern. Although not unique to marketing, it is of special concern as marketing becomes increasingly used by public and nonprofit organizations. In a sense, the argument for the use of marketing—that it is more powerful than just relying on communication strategies—is the one that heightens the ethical sensitivity and need for responsibility on the part of managers. Marketing managers should attempt to understand the ethical ramifications of their work. In doing so, they must be sure that their judgments reflect an honest assessment of the opinions of others, not just their own desire to get the job done.

Marketing Abuses: Examples from Higher Education

It would be unrealistic to believe that there are no abuses in the use of marketing in public and nonprofit organizations. After all, how marketing is used depends on the people who employ marketing approaches and the environments in which they work. To illustrate some of the potential concerns that can arise, we will draw a set of examples from the field of higher education, an area that we, as educators, know well. However, the potential for abuse exists in all endeavors and fields.

Those who mistakenly consider marketing as just another name for advertising and personal selling tend to see marketing abuses in higher education in terms of false or misleading advertising, or unreasonable pressure by college recruiters on students to enroll. Yet unethical communications are often the mechanism that makes abuses possible in the other elements of the marketing mix.

This communications view of marketing is, in certain respects, a deceptively comfortable one to adopt. The blame for abuses can be conveniently shifted to "semiprofessionals" outside the mainstream of institutional life who can be quickly excised from the organization if they cause any problems. A similar myopia exists in many other organizational settings.

Market transactions between a service enterprise and its customers involve four key elements: the product, the delivery systems employed to bring it to the customer, how it is priced (and payment made), and how it is communicated to prospective purchasers. As will be shown, many aspects of these transactions involve both faculty and administrators; hence the ethical and managerial aspects of marketing abuses are brought to center stage, and the collective decision-making procedure of academic faculties implies a shared responsibility for such abuses. We will examine examples of abuses in several marketing-mix elements.

Product issues or abuses can be separated into two types. The first represents deviations from the average consumer's fair and reasonable expectations of basic product characteristics. Colleges are expected to set reasonable standards of educational quality before awarding degree credits. There may be a benefit to an individual student in letting academic standards slip, but when it is widespread, the practice abuses both present and former students (who may see their own degrees devalued) as well as graduate schools or employers who may find themselves uncertain as to what they are getting. Other basic attributes that any student has a right to expect include minimum standards of safety, comfort, and hygiene in the institution's physical facilities and food services.

The second category of product abuses is tied to communications—when a product is different from or inferior to what students were led to expect by the institution and its representatives. Such abuses may include the following.

- Delivery of instruction programs that are different in content or standards from those promised in the institution's published or verbal communications.

- Faculty who are inferior teachers or who fail to live up to their responsibilities in meeting with students outside class and providing adequate feedback on performance.

Distribution issues include questions about the quality of services delivered at satellite or branch campuses, in evening sessions, or during the summer. Particular problems arise in satellite locations where the facilities may be inferior to those of the main campus, as manifested in such shortcomings as poor classrooms, minimal libraries, and inadequate student services in the areas of counseling, job placement, or extracurricular activities. These limitations may be compounded by product-related deficiencies; for example, unsatisfactory teaching by adjunct instructors who are not part of the school's mainstream faculty.

Pricing issues in higher education include financial aid and tuition. As with the other elements, the abuses are of two types—improper practices per se and failure to honor previously stated policies. In the former category are such ethically questionable practices as the following.

- Failure to identify all program-related costs (e.g., books, laboratory charges, parking, mandatory athletic fees) that may add substantially to the basic room, board and tuition charges.
- Inadequate refund policies in the event of either institutional cancellations or student withdrawals.

The second category of possible abuses with regard to pricing includes not living up to stated refund policies and not offering loans and scholarships advertised. It also includes inadequate warning of changes in stated pricing policies—such as a sudden hike in tuition or cut in financial aid, or the introduction of charges for previously free supplementary services without prior warning. Because students have made a long-term commitment to a school, they often face little real choice but to pay these charges, even if, given more notice, they would not have chosen to enroll in the school.

Communication issues are a traditional concern. Misleading advertising, "small-print" contracts, and false promises by high-pressure sales personnel have long been favorite targets of business critics. Misleading or fraudulent marketing communication can be found in other media. In the case of college recruiting, we would include published brochures, catalogs, and leaflets; booths at college fairs; audiovisual presentations; internally and externally distributed periodicals; press releases; and information provided by college personnel (or their representatives) by mail, by telephone, or in person. Similarly, careful examination is required of communications to currently registered students who need information to make decisions about which courses to enroll in, what types of financial aid to apply for, which types of jobs to seek through the placement office, and even whether to transfer out of the institution. Both impersonal and personal communications need scrutiny.

Impersonal communications that make false promises, present out-of-date facts, distort or otherwise misrepresent the facts, make selective omissions, or are not comprehensible to inexperienced consumers raise ethical concerns. Not only the printed word lies or distorts; photography can also misrepresent reality. Carefully posed photographs that purport to show a "typical" campus scene or selective retouching of negatives can create an image that bears little resemblance to fact, as in the case of an Indiana college whose catalog featured a young couple strolling past a waterfall that was nowhere near the campus. Subtler and more widespread distortions are perpetuated by such practices as including in the catalog numerous pictures of minority students (when there are really few such students at the institution), or showing undergraduates working with laboratory equipment that would not ordinarily be available to them.

Personal communications by college employees (or other parties formally representing an institution) who are guilty of any of the abuses noted, who apply unfair pressure on a student or applicant, who fail to counsel objectively in a manner that recognizes that individual's own best interests, or who fail to respond adequately and honestly to questions asked by a student or applicant are all examples of unethical practices, too.

Recruiters using high-pressure sales techniques appear commonly in stories of ruthless proprietary schools, but there is reason to believe that many administrators and faculty members in traditional colleges and universities are also misrepresenting, to both prospective and current students, the products offered by their institutions, the prices charged, and the quality of the facilities in which these services are delivered. This type of misrepresentation is hard to pin down because so much of it takes place in one-on-one communications; moreover, not all of it is deliberate. Yet collectively it adds up to deceptive selling.

These examples show how numerous the possibilities are for unethical practices. Sins of both commission and omission are represented. We have used higher education simply for illustrative purposes, not because we consider it to stand out relative to other areas of public and nonprofit activity. All types of nonbusiness organizations are potentially at risk.

Using Marketing Ethically

Marketing can make a positive contribution to society overall and to the organizations that adopt a marketing orientation. Marketing research and analysis help an institution to gain a better understanding of its current and prospective markets and publics and to improve its ability to serve their needs in an increasingly competitive environment. This understanding can be used to develop strategies that are ethical or unethical. A lack of such understanding will probably result in strategies that are administratively foolish rather than managerially sound.

In short, managers must be sensitive to ethical concerns in their use of marketing, since any technology that fosters social change must be carefully examined. The use of marketing is especially likely to raise questions in situations where it either represents a new approach to management or where implementation of marketing strategies is threatening to an established order. Our hope is that nonbusiness managers will use marketing intelligently, anticipating or being responsive to legitimate ethical concerns, and implementing marketing programs in responsible ways.

LEVERAGING MARKETING EFFORTS

Public and nonprofit organizations, because the services they offer are usually viewed as essential or socially desirable, can leverage their efforts by using the services and resources of others, provided at no or reduced cost. In addition, government agencies can supplement their marketing efforts through the imposition of laws, rules, and regulations.

The most familiar examples of leveraging are to use "free" public-service advertising and to employ volunteer help, but many other opportunities for leveraging are available. For instance, a transit agency's marketing manager suggests that leveraging provides

> . . . someone or something to help our marketing efforts, to share the risk of program development, and to assist in program implementation. The "someone" can be a person, organization, or company. The "something"' may be the elimination of an institutional constraint, a change in an organization's policy, a new law or administrative rule or a change to existing legislation. Leveraging is aimed at increasing transit ridership by providing our customers benefits for or incentives to riding the bus. These benefits may accrue to the customer directly or indirectly. Leveraging can take many different forms from direct monetary payments for using the bus, to assuming the administrative work of a project or program, to providing extra personnel.[16]

Leveraging is one way for an organization to cope with a limited budget. In a sense, it is a chance to obtain services at a reduced price. In creating opportunities for leveraging, an agency must look at both its own requirements and the potential contributions that others might make. This process will be discussed in depth in Chapter 18, "Attracting Dona-tions and Gifts-in-Kind." Illustrations of leveraging opportunities include the following.

- On behalf of a theater company, a department store includes inserts advertising the theater in its monthly bills to charge account customers, who can also charge tickets to their accounts.
- Savings bonds are sold by payroll deduction to a company's employees.
- Blood-donor drives are held periodically on a company's premises and or-ganized by the firm's personnel department.
- A newspaper or television station offers space or air time for free public-service announcements.
- Downtown merchants offer their customers a free bus ride home (in a sense, offsetting the lure of free parking at suburban shopping centers).
- A company sponsors a night at the symphony for its employees and/or customers.

Cooperative promotions in which a company uses some aspect of a public and nonprofit organization as part of its own promotion campaign also provide opportunities for leverage. For example, during one promotional campaign, American Express made a contribution to selected arts organizations each time its credit card was used or a new one was applied for. Not only were substantial funds raised, but the programs of several performing arts and visual-arts groups were also widely publicized. Promotions of this magnitude are available infrequently, but public and nonprofit institutions should seek out and be sensitive to similar opportunities at a more modest level.[17] Of course, as with all marketing, the institution should ensure that the promotion is tasteful and carried out in a manner consistent with its position and standing in the community.

Laws, Rules, and Regulations

Government agencies and institutions have an important area of leverage that businesses do not—use of the legal system in coordination with their marketing programs. Certain activities can be banned and fines can be imposed on violators. Only the most naïve person, however, would argue that simply passing a law will ensure compliance—as the number of speeding drivers and marijuana smokers proves daily—but regulations, laws, and fines can be an important part of the marketing mix. In many jurisdictions, health and school officials have agreed to ban kindergarten enrollment by children who do not have adequate immunization against certain diseases, but the true goal is to persuade parents to take care of immunization before that time.

This example illustrates two ways in which the legal system can be utilized: first, to extend the range of tactics or tools that can be added to the marketing mix, and second, to concentrate on those segments not responsive to voluntary programs—at the same time providing a sense of fairness to all. For example, during a serious drought, everyone may be asked to conserve water. One person's lack of conservation will have little direct impact on the total amount of water used, but others in the community might be disinclined to save if they know there are some "free riders." If the water meters are read, and "free riders" are dealt with effectively, community support can be better maintained for the water-conservation program.

Regulations can also be used in a positive manner. To promote nutrition, many schools in the United States and Canada have banned the sale of candy and drinks containing sugar in vending machines on their premises. To promote efficient use of transportation arteries, a number of highway, bridge, and tunnel authorities have set aside lanes for use only by car pools and buses, thus allowing faster travel for such vehicles. The objective is to maximize the carrying capacity of the transportation artery in question by moving as many people—as opposed to vehicles—through it as possible. If single-occupant vehicles enter the restricted lane, they clog the traffic in that lane, thus removing the incentive to car pool or use public transportation and making it impossible to achieve the objective of the program. Municipal, regional, and national governments may offer a variety of tax and regulatory benefits to attract commercial and industrial employers. For instance, cities often relax zoning regulations for new employers, and states offer reduced tax rates during the initial years of operation. In this case, however, the need to be fair to existing enterprises and taxpayers must also be considered.

CHOOSING AND USING OUTSIDE SUPPLIERS OF MANAGEMENT SERVICES

Marketing is so complex that few organizations can avoid relying on outside suppliers, advisers, and consultants for at least some services.[18] Public and nonprofit organizations that are new to marketing particularly need outside help. In some areas, such as advertising, almost all enterprises use outside advertising agencies. Similarly, firms specializing in marketing research are frequently employed to design, execute, and/or analyze surveys. In general, a sound management system is needed for successfully choosing and making use of outside suppliers. Although most guidelines sound like homilies, in practice the results of hiring outside advisers "fall fairly evenly along the spectrum from triumph to disaster."[19]

There is no simple technique for choosing and hiring outside advisers. Nevertheless, three areas deserve special concern: specifying the project, selecting the supplier, and managing the relationship. We will look at these in turn.

Specifying the Project

The first step is to specify the areas in which help is needed. At times, the specifications can be precise. For example, when designing a survey research project, a written set of objectives and specifications should be prepared, as discussed in Chapter 8, "Marketing Research." When hiring an advertising agency, the client must decide if it wants an agency primarily to design copy and buy space in advertising media or to play a major role in preparing its marketing plan. It is common, and relatively straightforward, to hire specialist firms to carry out closely defined operational tasks for which the organization lacks the requisite skills or resources. The Vancouver Symphony Orchestra, for instance, hired a professional telephone sales consultant to contact lapsed subscribers who had not responded to a mail campaign, and subsequently realized thousands of dollars of extra income.

For more strategic projects, it becomes difficult to specify the precise nature of the work. An outsider cannot be given carte blanche to pursue whatever avenues look promising. For instance, Chapter 3, "Conducting a Marketing Audit," discussed ways to specify the range of a market audit so that it meets the organization's needs, while providing useful guidance to an auditor. The terms of all projects should be put in writing at some stage. It is a distressing fact of life that unless the organization specifies its needs carefully, the outsider will often interpret the assignment in ways that suit his or her needs or areas of interest.

Finally, before turning to an outside consultant, an organization must ask itself whether it has the resources and is willing to implement sound recommendations. Unfortunately, it is quite common to spend money on surveys, reports, and recommendations—and then do nothing with them. One study found that less than 5 percent of the surveys conducted for performing arts organizations were actually used by them.[20]

Selecting the Outside Suppliers

Table 17.2 indicates some guidelines in selecting an outside supplier or consultant. The first one is to allow sufficient time to generate and evaluate alternative sources of help. In some cases, such as in hiring an advertising agency, the relationship is a long-term one so that the organization must be particularly careful. For large-scale projects, it may be useful to have someone other than the decision maker develop a short list of potential consultants—to act as a screening device and avoid personal bias.

The second suggestion is to check a variety of references. Almost by definition, an organization is hiring expertise that it cannot judge directly. It is important to ask former clients for references about the client-supplier relationship and the value of final outcomes, while other professionals or the trade press may offer evaluations of technical skills. The authors of this book, for example, have been asked a number of times to comment on the quality of work produced by different market-research firms. Both types of references are necessary inputs to a sound decision.

The third guideline is to select a supplier of the right size and experience. A supplier that is too large will often be unable or unwilling to give small projects the priority and involvement that a smaller firm would. Conversely, too small a firm may not have the resources or ability to cope with large-scale projects.

Relatively inexperienced consultants should be tried first on small, reasonably well-defined projects before being trusted with more ambitious ones. If possible, hire consultants who are experienced in the types of problems the organization faces. For example, a number of nonbusiness organizations have hired marketing consultants whose background has been in businesses that manufacture physical goods. Unfortunately, not all of these consultants know the subtleties of designing and executing marketing programs in public and nonprofit settings.

Table 17.2 Guidelines for Choosing Outside Suppliers

---

1. Allow sufficient time to choose the right suppliers

2. Check not only client references, but also trade and professional references

3. Choose a supplier of appropriate size and experience

4. Make your selection based on the people who will actually work on the project, not just the reputation of the supplier firm

5. Evaluate price relative to the value offered

Many institutions operate within a geographically restricted area. A good source of outside consultancy services can be successful organizations in other locales. Recognizing this potential, British Rail and the British Post Office each operate a group to provide consulting services to railroads and postal services, respectively, around the world.

Fourth, in selecting an outside supplier, concentrate on the abilities of the people who will actually work on a project. The name and reputation of the advertising agency, market-research house, or consulting firm can be important in setting a standard of service, but actual work and advice are supplied by people. In choosing an advertising agency, for example, the client should look at the previous commercials of the creative director and the record of the account director who will be assigned to the client's work, not just those of the agency and its new business team. In brief, base the decision on the people who will actually be working on the account, not just those selling the business.

Finally, price and its relation to value must be considered. An organization should have a full understanding of the fee structure, the cost of specific tasks, and how they will be charged beforehand.

Managing the Relationship

Once a consultant or other service supplier is selected, the focus turns to managing the relationship most productively. The first step here is to complete an agreement, preferably in writing, that includes the goals to be achieved, division of responsibilities between the consultant and client, resources (e.g., access to records, time with people) required from the organization, tentative timetable for the completion of stages of the project, a flexible schedule for review meetings, a payment schedule, and the nature of final report.

In managing a consulting relationship, it is important to distinguish between "ends" and "means." The task should be expressed in terms of the ends to be achieved, but the consultant is the expert with regard to the means.

> Express the consultant's job in terms of the end result you want to achieve. If you tell the architect you want a three-story office building, that is what he will design for you. But if you explain to him the pressures of staff or the reorganization plan or the diversification policy that led you to the idea of the three-story building, he may see a better solution than you can. Do not try to teach your adviser his own job—but do not ask him to do yours. The distinction between ends and means is at the heart of your relationship. You are the expert on ends; he is the expert on means. This is a barrier you cross at your peril, and the dangers of crossing it are greatest in areas where the client thinks he can understand what the adviser is doing. Marketing and advertising are minefields, and many a senior agency copywriter has felt his blood pressure rise to the threshold of cardiac arrest to see his granite-chiseled words "improved" by a trainee product-manager from the client company. Do not trespass on the areas of professional skill and professional judgment that you hired your advisers for.[21]

Management must always stay in firm control of the project; decision making is management's responsibility. As one experienced marketing consultant cautions:

> Consultants should never be asked or allowed to make business decisions. All too often managers abdicate responsibility and implicitly allow a consultant to make the decision. It is human nature for a consultant to want to go the next step—to tell you what to do. Consultants bring a specialized expertise, objectivity, and creativity for attacking a

problem due to their breadth of experience in working on related problems in other companies or even other industries. What they do not have is the time or commitment to be thoroughly familiar with your business and the day-to-day realities of marketing, production, competitive activity and so on.[22]

Effective problem specification, supplier selection, and management of the relationship are all necessary steps when advice and consultancy are being sought. The end goal is meaningful implementation, of course, and this is the criterion on which outside suppliers—and the management hiring them—must be judged. Many consulting projects have been unsuccessful and have wasted valuable resources, often because inadequate attention was paid at some stage of the consulting relationship. As this section has indicated, careful attention to all phases of the consultancy relationship can improve the chances of success.

ACCOMPLISHING THE TASK

The phrase *marketing implementation* can have several meanings. At one level it means designing the tactical programs to support the marketing strategy. For example, if a theater decides to build volume by selling subscriptions, one aspect of implementation concerns designing the subscription package (how many and what performances to include, determining pricing strategy, etc.). At another level, marketing implementation is concerned with the actual execution of the program (e.g., in a subscription campaign, with the writing of copy, placing advertisements, and mailing out tickets). As we have emphasized throughout this book, marketing is concerned not only with the grand design of strategy, but also with the implementation of programs and the execution of a myriad of necessary details if a strategy is to accomplish its goals. While excellent execution cannot save a misdirected strategy, only good execution can transform a sound strategy from plans on paper to reality. In this section, we examine areas that are particularly important for successful implementation at both levels of meaning.

We begin by stressing the need for the marketing function to coordinate and integrate its efforts with other functional areas. Of particular concern, especially in service organizations, is the need for customer-contact personnel and managers of service facilities to reflect a consumer orientation in their dealings with users. This requires close cooperation between marketing, operations, and human-resources management; we discuss some specific steps that can be taken to foster this cooperation. Beyond cooperating with other functional areas, successful implementation requires that the marketing function itself be well managed. So we also look at some characteristics of good practice in marketing and suggest questions that can be asked to appraise execution quality. We must recognize, however, in designing and implementing a marketing strategy that public and nonprofit managers operate under constraints that their business colleagues do not. For instance, government managers are often unable to use aggressive advertising and may have legislators questioning their advertising budgets as being either too high or too low. Successful implementation entails working within the bounds imposed by such constraints; as a result, excellence in marketing practice becomes an even more challenging goal for public and nonprofit marketers than for managers working in the private sector.

Working with Other Functional Areas

Marketing is just one of several major management functions in public and nonprofit organizations. Although the importance of these functions varies by the nature of the organization, the types of products offered, and the organization's location in the public or nonprofit sector, successful design and implementation of marketing programs require cooperation and coordination across functional areas. Table 17.3 illustrates some of the areas of overlap and interaction. For example, a marketing orientation requires that the finance and control functions provide financial information, such as costs of service and revenue sources, on a product or market basis so that decisions about changes can be made in a sound way. A performing-arts organization needs to know the difference in costs if it offers eight instead of five performances a week; a hospital should know both the incremental and allocated costs of adding outpatient surgery to the range of services it offers. One of the most difficult questions for membership organizations such as community centers to answer is how to allocate membership fees to different programs. Because financial executives often have an oversight role on (substantial) investments and expenditures, marketing managers must educate these executives as to the need to spend funds on intangibles such as market research and advertising, which are not capitalized as assets on the balance sheet and whose value is realized only after the money is spent. Marketing and

Table 17.3   Illustrations of Areas of Coordination Between Marketing and Other Functional Areas

---

General management

  Choice of products to offer and markets to serve
  Resource commitment to programs

Finance and control (accounting)

  Provision of capital
  Budgeting
  Accounting and financial information
  Credit and collection
  Economic analysis of investments
  Management control

Human resources

  Recruitment, selection, and training of new personnel
  Compensation and incentives
  Personnel policies and procedures

Development and government relations

  Fund raising from donors—and possibly users
  Demonstration projects
  Provision of funds and volunteers

Operations

  Design and delivery of service
  Meeting prespecified service standards
  Introduction of new products
  Management of facilities
  Supervision of user-contact personnel

---

financial managers have a mutual concern to see that budgets, forecasts, and cash-flow projections are firmly based on sound estimates and forecasts of user volumes, competitive effects, and market trends.

Coordination with all functional areas is important, but cooperation with operations management is of particular concern in public and nonprofit organizations, especially those primarily offering services. Although businesses selling physical goods also have problems of cooperation between marketing and production, the separation of the factory producing the good from the place where the ultimate consumer acquires and uses the good is helpful in dividing responsibilities. By contrast, many organizations providing services frequently produce the final product as it is being consumed. The orchestra concert, the transit ride, and the medical visit all exhibit this simultaneity. As a result, the marketing function in a service organization must be closely interrelated with and dependent on the personnel and operations functions and the people, procedures, and facilities administered by these functions. In brief, it is usually operations personnel, not marketing personnel, who have direct contact with users. (In universities, hospitals, and other professional service organizations, as discussed in Chapter 15, the people delivering the service have a high degree of autonomy, making management even more complex.)

Successful execution of marketing programs requires that operations management be responsive to the initiatives of marketing and that a human-resource (personnel) management system be established so that user-contact personnel perform according to user-oriented standards and procedures. Obtaining the full cooperation of operations management requires that marketing build a track record of success and that top management provide full backing for marketing by recognizing it as a senior management activity with the consequent resources and responsibilities. We discussed earlier how to reduce conflict between operations and marketing managers and how to use productively the strengths of both. Often, however, a key concern is integrating the operating and marketing viewpoints in the field—the user-contact level—and we now turn to that area and possible approaches to motivating marketing-oriented behavior.

Motivating Field Personnel

Among the approaches to making field personnel and managers of service facilities more consumer oriented are: (1) decentralizing revenue responsibility in organizations that charge for their services, (2) internal marketing, (3) control through procedures manuals, and (4) training programs. These approaches are more often used in combination than separately.

Decentralized Revenue Responsibility. Public and nonprofit organizations frequently judge their employees on the basis of cost efficiency. In cost centers, managers and staff are likely to be driven inward to focus on their operation rather than outward to reach toward their customers. Thus the manager of a post office, for example, can limit costs by operating with only a few counter clerks and letting customers wait in line for service. Although revenue is lost from industrial customers who use commercial carriers and from individuals who might use special delivery or registered mail if there was not a wait for a counter clerk to explain and determine the fee for these services, the manager's costs—on which he or she is judged—are low. Such a system leads to highly standardized products, low tolerance for change, and reluctance to serve customers, particularly those that are difficult or unusual. A more sensible system is one that emphasizes achievement of the performance goals generated by the market-planning process.

The effect of putting revenue responsibility on traditionally minded branch or unit managers can be traumatic; they are suddenly faced with a need to understand where their revenue stream comes from! The most obvious result of such a move is typically a growing awareness of the consumer and of the need for proactive marketing at the unit level. Such a change is often major and not easily done. The help of the human-resources staff is needed in orienting and training people to their new revenue responsibilities and, in the longer term, hiring people who work well under this system. The accounting and management control function needs to design a system in which revenues are properly attributed and costs are allocated in such a way that different facilities managers and field personnel are not operating at cross purposes. For example, a railroad passenger complaining about lost baggage should not be passed between origin and destination offices as a means to avoid responsibility. Of course, revenue responsibility should also be tied to controllable costs.

Even more challenging is developing a consumer-oriented measure of output in organizations *not* charging a fee for service. In some cases, actual usage—the number of people attending clinics or using a park—can be developed, perhaps on a sampling basis, but in other cases, such as the impact of drug-abuse programs, the availability and reliability of user-oriented measures at the field operating level become problematic. The use of superficial measures that are quantifiable but have little meaning should be avoided. When appropriate, however, revenue responsibility can have a dramatic impact on the user orientation of field personnel.

Another problem, particularly for government agencies, is the limited range of rewards that can be offered for excellent performance. A private company could give a substantial financial bonus to an executive who substantially increased profits or successfully managed the introduction of a new product, but this is obviously not possible for most public and nonprofit agencies. Nonfinancial rewards and public recognition can be bestowed for outstanding work, however, and management should try to use such rewards appropriately.

Internal Marketing. Internal marketing is often needed in service organizations because new procedures and services affect not only users, but also service employees and volunteers. Sometimes innovations involve just minor changes in operating procedures; at other times they may require major procedural changes and retraining or displacement of employees. In such cases internal marketing may be as important for success as externally focused efforts.

Formation of a task force is often a part of the internal marketing campaign to build acceptance of service innovations among management and staff members. For a task force to be effective in moving the project off the drawing board and into the development phase, the task force must play a meaningful role and not just be a public-relations ploy. Members of the task force should represent and interact with operating personnel in the field. Winning the cooperation of operating managers requires that they be represented on the task force. Winning the acceptance of field personnel requires that senior field management sell the project to the staff.

Organization Procedures Manual. Another approach to help implement a user-oriented approach is through control by the organization's procedures manual, which lays down detailed procedures and systems for performing virtually every operating task. This manual is the operations department's standard control document. When a service organization finds itself faced with the need to adopt a stronger consumer orientation, one of the ways to achieve this is through the medium of its procedures manual. Through research, the agency can identify what are the "key success factors" from a consumer perspective. These factors can then be incorporated into standard procedures to be followed by operating personnel.

For instance, a number of service firms in the private sector have expanded their manuals to include procedures for how service personnel should interact with customers. The new versions specify such factors as the maximum time that customers should be allowed to wait before being served, key phrases that should be used in conversing with customers (often including an attempt to cross-sell another service), and the need for service personnel to make eye contact with the customer and, where appropriate, to smile. Such manuals require a control system to ensure that the prescribed procedures are, in fact, followed. One control system takes the form of a "mystery shopper," who visits service outlets in the guise of a customer to evaluate the qualitative and quantitative aspects of the service provided to consumers. In order to score maximum points from the mystery shopper, field managers are obliged to make sure that their subordinates act in ways corresponding to the requirements of the procedures manual, thereby controlling the quality of the service they deliver.

Training. Training programs are an important part of any program to motivate consumer-oriented behavior. For customer-contact employees, even those who only occasionally serve users directly, an early orientation program that stresses dealing with people in a helpful, friendly manner and meeting consumer needs is essential. Follow-up programs are also needed. The approach to training adopted by some service organizations reflects the importance of the concept of internal marketing, just discussed. In these organizations, including some passenger railroads and airlines, training in operating tasks has been supplemented by efforts to develop appropriate *attitudes* among reservations, terminal, and on-board staffs toward their customers. A number of private-sector service firms use sophisticated training films developed with as much care as any advertisement seen by the customers.

The need for training is not limited to operating personnel. At the managerial level, a variety of workshops and seminars should be used to help develop a marketing orientation, as well as to teach specific marketing skills. Some of these can be in-house training sessions just for the organization's personnel, but participation in external education programs should also be encouraged. Training is a continuous process, and the organization should be constantly encouraging its personnel to learn more.[23]

Where possible, cross-functional assignments can help to provide broader understanding and background. Just as agencies occasionally give field-operating people assignments at headquarters, personnel in marketing, finance, operations, and other functions should rotate positions if feasible, perhaps for specific projects. Temporary marketing assignments will allow others to see the difficulties involved in effectively serving users in a competitive environment, while marketing personnel will gain a better understanding of the constraints with which other departments must contend.

Good Marketing Practice

As Thomas Bonoma has pointed out, "marketing is long on strategy, but short on recommendations for how to get the job done once strategic directions have been chosen."[23] Audience-development specialist Danny Newman's book *Subscribe Now*, one of the few available guides to execution of marketing strategy, includes examples of how subscription program sales can be harmed by inadequate execution at the box-office level.

> Often, simply for their own convenience, box office personnel may insist upon cutting off renewals or new sales long before they should. I recall the case of a harassed theatre company manager who foolishly permitted his ticket-selling staff to decide for him that they already had all the subscriptions they needed, and despite the fact that sales were coming in heavily, they stopped taking orders. Thousands of subscribers were turned away in the crucial period just before the initial season of this new project was to begin. The young and quite inexperienced box office staff's arrogant error almost closed up the theatre since single-ticket sales later did not develop to anywhere near the volume they had predicted. Those turned away subscriptions were sorely missed, and only heroic exertions on the part of the company's leadership closed the resulting financial gap and enabled the theatre to continue. In another case—a classic, I should say—a strong-willed promotional director successfully fought back the box office staffs insistence on a premature deadline date, got a last minute reprieve from the general manager, and went on to sell an additional 4,100 subscriptions.
>
> The problem of exchanges—that is, when a subscriber is unable to attend on one of his scheduled dates and would like to exchange his tickets for another performance of the same presentation—is one that vexes many box office employees. . . . The exchange privilege, when it can be offered, is highly prized by subscribers. . . . Many box office employees tend to become annoyed by the traffic in exchanges and their resentment is felt by the subscribers who are, after all, only asking for what has been promised them—that our theatre will exchange for another performance of the same play if tickets are available on the requested date. It should be pointed out to the box office crews of theatres where the bulk of the season's tickets are subscribed (meaning that the amount of work they have to do in selling single tickets is minimal) that once the season is in progress, they will have precious little to do but handle the subscriber's exchange requests, and that this procedure should be carried out with grace.[24]

A recurrent cause of organizational distress is a basic management failure to define and instill in others a powerful, shared theme, a vision of "what the agency does and how" with regard to marketing.

> Where there is no theme, it is most difficult for management to arrange a marketing *culture* which encourages closeness to the customer, careful analysis of buyer needs, and a shared zeal of satisfying their wants.
>
> Whether a strong theme and culture were arranged by top management example, the personal charisma of one manager, or through formal policy directives seemed irrelevant. The critical question was whether these intangibles existed as a powerful but unquantifiable feeling that imposed itself on an observer in the same way they inundated marketing acts.[25]

An art museum deciding to appeal only to well-educated, knowledgeable collectors should set a very different theme than another museum that wants to appeal to the general public. Opening hours, signs, the role of staff, the reaction to inquiries, and many other operating features would differ markedly across the two museums. Either approach could be successful, but less likely to prosper would be a museum that is unclear as to its theme and ends up with conflicting procedures and confused personnel. One church, for instance, recognized that it was losing membership as new, younger households with children moved into its local neighborhood, replacing the older members who were moving away to apartments. Although the church tried to appeal to these new residents, at first it had little success. Older members and the minister still preferred the traditional services and looked askance when children made noise and moved around or when parents came in the middle of the service. Only when a new minister was installed and succeeded in changing norms within the church service in particular—and established a family orientation throughout the church's entire range of activities—did membership and attendance start to increase.

Excellence in marketing execution first requires a clear theme. Success also requires high competence in carrying out the marketing-mix functions—advertising, pricing, and distributing the product. The suggested questions on activity analysis in Table 3.4 of Chapter 3, "Conducting a Marketing Audit," indicate specific areas of concern. The failure of a new one dollar coin to achieve widespread circulation and usage in the United States—except, perhaps, in gambling casinos—was largely a result of poor execution in product design, distribution, and communication.[27] The dollar coin offered substantial savings to the U.S. Treasury in manufacturing and distribution costs as well as benefits to consumers in terms of convenience and to retailers in reducing cash-handling costs. However, a product design that led to confusion with the quarter (the Susan B. Anthony dollar being only 9 percent greater in diameter), a distribution activity that assumed that merely sending coins to banks would be sufficient, and a minimal budget for consumer advertising all revealed subfunction inadequacies. Repeated failures by the U.S. Treasury to introduce new coins and bills into widespread circulation—the $2 bill and Kennedy half dollar have also largely become collector's curiosities—result not from a lack of need for new money forms (a 1988 dollar buys less than a quarter did in 1950) but from weak implementation. A striking contrast is provided by the British success in the much more difficult task of introducing a decimal currency in 1971.[28] As a later section indicates, government marketers operate under some constraints that private-sector marketers do not face, but weak execution has plagued the U.S. Treasury's introduction of new monetary forms. Without good execution, the results of a sound strategy are never brought to bear on the consumer.

In addition to skills in the marketing-mix functions themselves, there needs to be a program to coordinate the functions. In other words, management must make sure the elements operate as an integrated marketing mix, not as individual components. For example, as described in Chapter 18, a mail-order campaign by the National Trust to sell Christmas gifts was enormously successful in generating orders but produced huge embarrassment when stocks were exhausted early in the campaign.

Good implementation requires the development of a monitoring system to measure and control the results of marketing activities. In Chapter 5, "Building a Marketing Plan," we showed how the marketing plan can be the basis of a management-control system. In the first instance, an action plan can detail the specific activities that need to be carried out and assign responsibilities by name or functional area. By stating these activities in milestone format, everyone knows what has to be accomplished by when if the goals of the marketing strategy are to be achieved. In turn, the established targets become the basis for control so that deviations in performance are identified and corrective action, when necessary, is taken. By monitoring against these targets on a continuing basis, usually monthly or quarterly, time is available to make changes before the situation deteriorates to a crisis condition. It would seem easy for managers to get information to keep track of how well they are doing. Nevertheless, many marketing departments "are weak at constructing simple, reliable, and understandable monitoring mechanisms which do not get corrupted by the politics of the situation or mired in incomprehensible complexities."[29] The marketing strategy may set the direction and excellent execution may carry the organization along, but a reliable, timely monitoring and control system is needed to make sure the program is on the right path.

Finally, good practice in marketing requires that the organization constantly and consistently maintain a market orientation, not a product orientation. The realities of the market and the pressure of competition must be reflected in all that the organization does. As we have shown throughout this book, marketing is a demanding discipline and even successful organizations face the danger of slipping back into a product orientation. Chapter 1 discussed seven key indicators of a product-oriented instead of market-focused management, such as not tailoring marketing strategies to meet segment needs and seeing the product (good, service, or idea) as being inherently desirable for the target market. Consequently, the organization blames lack of consumer interest in the offering on ignorance or lack of motivation; places too much emphasis on communication strategies; and uses research not to understand consumer needs but to confirm management beliefs. Generic competition is largely ignored in a product-oriented agency, and product skills rather than marketing skills become the dominant criterion in hiring and promotion. Excellence in implementation requires that an institution maintain a market orientation at all levels of the agency and throughout all functional and management areas that interact directly or indirectly with users and other publics.

Distinctive Characteristics of Public and Nonprofit Marketing

Successful implementation of nonbusiness marketing requires that strategy and tactics recognize the distinctive characteristics of public and nonprofit marketing, which are summarized in Table 17.4.

Political pressures, public scrutiny, often conflicting expectations, and other factors all serve to make effective implementation in nonbusiness organizations difficult and complex. For example, at just about the same time that one U.S. congressman was protesting too great a use of government advertising in his district in 1980 (labeling it "propaganda" and calling it "disgraceful"), another representative was complaining because the Census Bureau had decided to use only public service advertisements for the 1980 census of the U.S. population. Fearing an undercount of minorities in his state, he wanted the Census Bureau to use paid advertising and spend more money.[30] In the private sector, neither comment would be made by people outside the organization.

Marketing management in the public and nonprofit sectors is not *uniquely* different from marketing practice in business firms. Nor should it be so. However, successful

Table 17.4 Distinctive Characteristics of Nonbusiness Marketing

Nature of the Products

Emphasizes not physical goods, but services and social behaviors, an area in which there is less theory and practice to draw on

Dominance of nonfinancial objectives

Makes objective setting and performance measurement more difficult

Need for resource attraction

Devotes resources to attract funds from donors or governments and/or to generate tax-derived revenues

Multiple constituencies

Needs to appeal to more than the immediate user

Tension between mission and consumer satisfaction

Requires a long-term view as social-behavior programs (e.g., obey speed laws) often offer long-term benefits to society as a whole at the expense of short-term costs to the individual

Public scrutiny

Attracts public attention to both its strategy and tactics and may be subject to journalistic review and political attack

Nonmarket pressures

Operates under political directives and regulatory bodies that constrain an agency from taking some actions and force it to take others (e.g., federal and state policies in the U.S. limit a hospital's authority to change the number of beds in different specialties; other policies mandate that universities provide facilities for handicapped people)

Suffers under restrictions by professional associations that accredit services (as in education), limit the use of marketing communication strategies (as in medicine), and define service standards (as in the role of paraprofessionals in providing legal service)

Availability of free or inexpensive support

Draws on donated labor, facilities, and services to help leverage efforts

Management in duplicate or triplicate

Needs to deal with tensions created by board members, volunteers, managers, and professionals (such as doctors or academics) sometimes pulling in different directions

marketing implementation must recognize the distinctive nature of nonbusiness marketing in general and the characteristics of each individual organization. Not all nonbusiness marketing managers need cope with all the complexities listed in Table 17.4, but few face none of them. Simplistic generalizations from private-sector practice need to be avoided, but excellence in marketing implementation will result from the creative combination of the best of business marketing and the challenge of the public and nonprofit organization's complex environment.

Looking to the Future

In the past decade, marketing has moved from a topic known to only a few public and nonprofit managers and an activity practiced by even fewer organizations to a management function employed by a growing number of agencies. Not all implementations of marketing have been successful, but growing recognition of the distinctive features of nonbusiness marketing and the development of strategies and tactics to deal with these unique characteristics have markedly improved the success rate.

Increasing competition in all sectors of the economy, heightened public demand for improved effectiveness in service delivery, and economic pressures compelling nonbusiness organizations to improve their revenue position have all been catalysts in the adoption of marketing. These forces are likely to accelerate in their intensity in future years, thereby making marketing even more vital in helping a public or nonprofit organization to meet its goals.

Marketing provides the link or bridge between the organization and its environment. Marketing helps an institution to move away from bureaucratic inertia and move toward responsiveness to and anticipation of changing needs. As such, it helps an organization to fulfill its mission by keeping the institution relevant in a dynamic environment.

As we have seen throughout this book, it is a mistake to view marketing simply as an "add-on" management function. On the contrary, marketing represents an orientation that should permeate all elements of organizational practice, starting at the level of the most senior executives and running through to the most junior members of the organization. All can have an impact on user satisfaction and competitive performance. Maintaining an external orientation is a demanding discipline, but in the long-run complacency and indifference to the environment lead to failure in a dynamic world. Marketing, of course, is not a panacea for all of an organization's ills, but a thoroughgoing marketing orientation backed with sound strategy and good execution makes a powerful contribution to organizational success.

SUMMARY

Implementation is concerned with transforming marketing plans into specific actions that will achieve the desired results. A necessary prerequisite is the existence of an appropriate marketing function within the organization.

When establishing or expanding a marketing function, managers often face resistance from other administrators who dislike change or feel threatened. It's important to establish marketing's value and credibility quickly by choosing early assignments which are neither central nor peripheral to the organization's mission, use a limited portion of available resources, are visible to key decision makers, offer a high probability of success, can be completed reasonably quickly, and will have results that can be readily evaluated.

Many people have negative views of marketing, partly because they have heard about tasteless, manipulative, or unethical marketing activities (which often receive wide publicity). Managers must be very sensitive to ethical concerns in their use of marketing and recognize that the potential for abuse exists in all elements of the marketing mix— not just advertising and sales. At the same time, they should emphasize that marketing itself is ethically neutral: it's how an organization *uses* marketing tools and strategies that matters.

Public and nonprofit organizations are often short on resources, but they may be able to leverage their efforts, at little or no cost, by working jointly with companies or other institutions. Government agencies sometimes supplement their marketing efforts with laws, rules, and regulations that can help to reinforce marketing programs by shaping behavior in socially desirable ways.

Outside assistance in developing and implementing marketing programs is available from a wide array of suppliers, including advertising agencies, market research firms, and consultants. But for best results, it's essential to specify the problem or project clearly, to take care in selecting suppliers, and to manage the relationship with the chosen supplier.

Finally, marketers need to coordinate and integrate their eforts with those of managers in other functional areas—especially, operations and human resources. A challenging aspect of this task is to ensure that a strong customer orientation pervades the entire organization, starting at the top with the chief executive. It's especially important that managers of service delivery facilities and other personnel who have direct contact with customers possess such an orientation. Internal marketing efforts (within the organization) may be necessary to build support for customer-driven strategies.

REFERENCES

1. Example is based on a speech given by John R. Modisett, vice-president of corporate relations, Evanston Hospital, on May 13, 1982, in Columbus, Ohio.
2. Paul N. Bloom and William K. Novelli, "Problems and Challenges in Social Marketing," *Journal of Marketing,* 45 (Spring 1981), pp. 79–88.
3. As in reference 2, p. 83.
4. Christopher H. Lovelock and Charles B. Weinberg, "The Role of Marketing in Improving Postal Service Effectiveness," in Joel Fleishman (ed.), *The Future of the Postal Service,* New York: Praeger, 1983.
5. As in reference 1.
6. Edward S. McKay, *The Marketing Mystique,* New York: American Management Association, 1972, p. 22.
7. Philip Kotler and Alan R. Andreasen, *Strategic Marketing for Nonprofit Organizations,* third edition, Englewood Cliffs, N.J.: Prentice-Hall, 1987, p. 276.
8. An insightful discussion of marketing implementation may be found in Thomas V. Bonoma, *Managing Marketing,* New York: The Free Press, 1984. Some of the ideas in this section are drawn from that book. See also the section "Accomplishing the Task" later in this chapter.
9. A.R. Krachenberg, "Bringing the Concept of Marketing to Higher Education," *Journal of Higher Education,* 43 (May 1972), p. 380. For a recent review, see Philip Kotler and Karen F. A. Fox, *Strategic Marketing for Educational Institutions,* Englewood Cliffs, N.J.: Prentice-Hall, 1985.
10. As in reference 7, p. 8.
11. Roger Ricklefs, "High-Class Hoopla, A Cultural Institution Succeeds by Marketing Its Wares Aggressively," *The Wall Street Journal,* January 23, 1979. Reprinted by permission of *The Wall Street Journal,* © Dow Jones & Company Inc. 1979. All rights reserved.
12. As reported in Christopher H. Lovelock and Michael L. Rothschild, "Uses, Abuses, and Misuses of Marketing in Higher Education," in *Marketing in College Admissions: A Broadening of Perspectives,* New York, College Entrance Examination Board, 1980, p. 54. See also reference 7, pp. 15–17.
13. Some organizations show scandalously little concern for users. One Chicago public food-stamp office had no sign indicating the existence of a food-stamp office on the outside of the building, on the door leading to the stairs, or on the office door itself. The only sign was a handwritten one on the door at the top of the stairs. Furthermore, the office was closed from March 10 to

April 8, 1980. See Bill Grady, "This Food Stamp Office is Hiding," *Chicago Tribune,* May 22, 1980, as quoted in reference 7. We hope such occurrences are rare.

14. Jeff Goldsmith, *Can Hospitals Survive?* Homewood, Ill.: Dow Jones-Irwin, 1981.

15. An excellent discussion is found in H. C. Kelman, "Manipulation of Human Behavior: An Ethical Dilemma for the Social Scientist," *Journal of Social Issues,* 21, No. 2 (April 1965). pp. 31–46. See also Jerry I. Porras and Charles B. Weinberg, "A Framework for Analyzing the Ethics of Marketing Inventions," in M. P. Mokwa and S. E. Permut (eds.), *Government Marketing: Theory and Practice,* New York: Praeger, 1981, pp. 356–375. An incisive, broader view may be found in Sissela Bok, *Lying: Moral Choice in Public and Private Life,* New York, Pantheon, 1978.

16. Robert M. Prowda, "Leveraging Marketing Efforts through Third Parties," in R. K. Robinson and C. H. Lovelock (eds.), *Marketing Public Transportation,* Chicago: American Marketing Association, 1981, p. 81.

17. As another example, banks have developed "affinity group" marketing in which, for instance, Sierra Club members apply for a credit card bearing the Sierra Club's name. The Chase Lincoln Bank of Rochester, N.Y., the actual issuer of the card, pays the Sierra Club 0.5 percent of the gross dollar amount charged to the card. Six months after the start of the program in August, 1986, 5 percent of Sierra Club members had joined the program and the Sierra Club was receiving $40,000 monthly from the bank. See Martin Mittelstaedt, "Credit Card Issuers Take Aim at Groups," *The Globe and Mail,* March 7, 1987, p. B7.

18. A well-written, helpful guide to the use of outside advisers is Antony Jay, "Rate Yourself as a Client," *Harvard Business Review* (July–August 1977), pp. 84–92.

19. As in reference 18, p. 85.

20. Michael Useem and Paul DiMaggio, "A Critical Review of the Content, Quality, and Use of Audience Studies," in David M. Cwi (ed.), *Research in the Arts,* Baltimore: Walters Art Gallery, 1977, pp. 30–32.

21. Reprinted by permission of the *Harvard Business Review.* "Rate Yourself as a Client," by Antony Jay (July–August 1977). Copyright © 1977 by the President and Fellows of Harvard College; all rights reserved.

22. Edward M. Tauber, "Consultants: How to Pick Them," *Advertising Age* (October 26, 1981), pp. 5, 28.

23. See Linda M. Lash, The Complete Guide to Customer Service. New York: John Wiley & Sons, 1989.

24. As in reference 8, p. 1.

25. From Danny Newman, *Subscribe Now!* Published by the Theatre Communications Group/ TCG, 355 Lexington Ave, New York, NY 10017.

26. As in reference 8, pp. 6–7.

27. For a further discussion see Claude R. Martin, Jr., "The Situation Confronting the Introduction of the Susan B. Anthony Dollar," in M. P. Mokwa and S. E. Permut (eds.), *Government Marketing: Theory and Practice,* New York, Praeger, 1981, pp. 186–198.

28. Christopher H. Lovelock, "Marketing National Change—Decimalization in Britain," in C. H. Lovelock and C. B. Weinberg (eds.), *Public and Nonprofit Marketing: Cases and Readings,* New York: John Wiley & Sons, 1984.

29. As in reference 8, p. 12.

30. This example is drawn from Dean L. Yarwood and Ben J. Enis, "Advertising and Publicity Programs in the Executive Branch of the National Government. Hustling or Helping the People?" *Public Administration Review* (January–February 1982), pp. 37–46.

PART 7

Resource Attraction

Chapter 18

Attracting Donations & Gifts-In-Kind

Diversity is one of the hallmarks of nonbusiness institutions—diversity in size, goals, ethos, and end products. Although the output of such organizations varies widely, the basic kinds of input have much more in common. Virtually all public agencies and nonprofit organizations require money and labor, office space and equipment, fuel and supplies; some also require land or raw materials. This much they have in common with private firms. The difference lies in how they finance these resource inputs.

Private firms finance their capital requirements—purchase of buildings, equipment, land, and working capital—either by generating funds internally, by borrowing the money (through bank loans, bond issues, and other credit arrangements), or by selling stock in the business. The expectation is that costs—including depreciation, debt interest, and loan repayments—will be more than covered by operating revenues derived from sale of the goods and services produced by the firm.

The situation for public and nonprofit organizations, however, is often sharply different. Some, such as the American Automobile Association, are closely akin to private firms in that they are self-supporting, selling their services at prices sufficient to result in a break-even position or a modest surplus (which is typically reinvested in the operation).* Although such organizations do not raise extra capital by selling equity in the business, their solid financial position usually makes it fairly easy to obtain loans from financial institutions (or from the government).

Most public and nonprofit organizations cannot be completely self-supporting simply by selling their products; indeed, many social-change or social-service organizations either cannot sell their output or else have as their mission to give their services away to those in need. Consequently, they must depend on donated resources—funds, volunteer labor, and gifts-in-kind—to cover both capital needs and operating expenditures. As Table 18.1 makes clear, all organizations periodically need to engage in marketing efforts to attract capital resources and labor input, but only public and nonprofit organizations normally engage in marketing activities to attract volunteer labor (as opposed to paid employees), tax or donated funds, and gifts-in-kind. For marketing managers, these important resource-attraction tasks are likely to be just as demanding as the work involved in producing and marketing the organization's end products. Moreover, a fine juggling act may be required to balance the needs and interests of the donors against those of the end users.

---

*In the case of profitable public corporations, the government sometimes receives a share of the profits, much as investors in a private business would receive dividends an their investments.

Table 18.1 Comparing Resource-Attraction Tasks for Private, Public, and Nonprofit Organizations

Type of Organization	Marketing Tasks for Attraction of:		
	Capital Resources	**Labor Resources**	**Operating Revenues**
Private firms	• Sell stocks or bonds • Persuade banks or other sources to make loans	• Recruit employees	• Sell goods and services
Public agencies or government departments	• Persuade elected officials to approve investment of tax-derived funds • Sell bonds to investors (public corporations) • Persuade banks or other sources to make loans	• Recruit employees • Recruit volunteers	• Sell core goods and services at a price • Sell supplementary goods and services at a price • Persuade elected officials or voters to approve direct taxation for operating revenues • Persuade elected officials to approve allocation of indirect taxes for operations support
Nonprofit organizations	• Persuade donors (individuals, corporations, or foundations) to give donations • Persuade government agencies to give capital grants or cheap loans • Persuade banks or other sources to make loans • Persuade governments, individuals, or corporations to give land, equipment, materials, or buildings	• Recruit employees at market rates and at below market rates • Recruit volunteers	• Sell core services or goods at a price • Sell supplementary goods and services at a price • Persuade donors to give periodic donations to help cover operating expenses • Persuade government agencies to give operating grants • Persuade individuals or corporations to give materials or equipment (for direct use or resale)

Scope of the Chapter

In many respects this chapter provides a good recapitulation of the marketing tools, concepts, and strategies discussed throughout the previous 17 chapters. Issues such as the exchange process, understanding customer behavior, market segmentation, the elements of the marketing mix, and marketing planning and strategy will be emphasized here in a new context.

The chapter begins with a review of resource attraction tasks for nonbusiness organizations and a typology of resources. These resources include: (1) voluntary donations of money, (2) tax-derived revenues, (3) volunteers' time, and (4) gifts of goods and services. Next is a discussion of how to go about planning a resource-attraction strategy. The balance of the chapter addresses, in turn, fund raising, attraction and management of volunteers, and attraction of gifts-in-kind. In each instance research has an important role to play in planning, not only as it relates to documentation of prior efforts (and their results), but also as an aid to competitive analysis, assessment of market potential, and identification of opportunities for market segmentation.

RESOURCE ATTRACTION TASKS FOR NONBUSINESS ORGANIZATIONS

Rising costs and the advent of conservative fiscal policies in government have placed numerous public and nonprofit organizations in a difficult financial situation. It is easy to understand why public agencies should be affected by cuts in government spending, but many nonprofit organizations in the United States are also affected because they have come to be heavily dependent on government funds distributed through purchase-of-service agreements, grants, and contracts. Others have experienced increased demand for their services as a result of cutbacks in government programs in health and human services.[1] This situation requires a search for new or enlarged sources of assistance (the topic of this chapter), consideration of increased prices (see Chapter 11), introduction of potentially profitable new product lines (see Chapters 10 and 20), and vigorous attempts to keep costs under control.

There are three basic resource-attraction options: attracting funds, attracting gifts-in-kind (both discussed in this chapter), and attracting volunteers (the topic of Chapter 19). These are not necessarily "either-or" strategies. Wise managers will want to investigate all three categories (and some of the subcategories within these, such as government grants versus corporate gifts). Moreover, the strategies available vary somewhat according to whether the organization in question is public or nonprofit in nature; nonprofit organizations tend to have the wider array of options.

Criteria for Developing a Resource-Attraction Strategy

The primary objective for any organization should be to develop a resource-attraction strategy that uses a complementary mix of all approaches and sources that seem appropriate for its needs and situation. Hence an important responsibility for the chief executive is to ensure that the organization develops a portfolio of donated resources that meets the following criteria.

1. Recognizes both the monetary and nonmonetary needs of the organization.

2. Emphasizes those sources that offer the best giving potential relative to the solicitation effort required.

3. Avoids the risk of becoming overreliant on a single source.

4. Offers prospective donors alternative ways of making a gift.

We will look briefly at each criterion in turn.

Monetary versus Nonmonetary Needs. In the last analysis, money can probably be used to pay for almost anything—buildings and equipment, labor, art objects for a collection, printing services, office rent, and so forth. In many instances, however, it may be economically more efficient (for everyone involved) for the donor to volunteer time or make gifts-in-kind than to make a financial gift that must then be converted into one of the necessary inputs, purchased on the open market. The basic task is to get the right mix of resources to fit the organization's needs. Developing an inventory of such needs up front will ensure that monetary gifts are directed to where they will have the greatest impact.

Efficiency of Solicitation Effort. Soliciting money, volunteers, or gifts-in-kind not only takes time and effort but can also be quite expensive. By definition, *resource attraction is a profit-seeking activity.* It is not worth doing unless the value of the results exceeds the costs of obtaining them over the long-run. In fund raising, a high net yield is very important. Inefficiency in fund raising discourages prospective donors, who may be dismayed if they learn that (say) 30 cents or more out of every dollar they give is consumed by fund-raising expenses. Making proposals to foundations, corporations, or government granting agencies is often a time-consuming and costly activity that offers no guarantee of a successful outcome. Clearly, the costs associated with making a specific proposal or soliciting a gift from a specific donor should be related to the probability attached to receiving a given value of grant or donation. As in many areas of marketing, gathering advance information about the marketplace for grants, gifts, or other types of donated resources will help a fund raiser to focus on the better prospects.

Avoidance of Overreliance on a Single Source. An organization that relies on just one or two sources for the bulk of its funding runs the risk of losing a substantial portion of its revenues if one funding source decides to pull out. A number of nonprofit organizations that expanded their activities sharply on receiving significant funding from a single donor, foundation, or government granting agency were subsequently left high and dry when these revenues were cut back or even eliminated. A related problem is the loss of control that may result when an organization becomes overly dependent on a single funding source. Consider the following example.

> The members of one local Alcoholics Anonymous group in America rented a small, rather dilapidated house, which they wanted as an informal "club house" and place where they could provide temporary lodging for recovering or unemployed alcoholics. This small operation prospered and so a few of the A.A. group members bought a larger house, independently incorporated it and built on the original activities of the smaller house. At this point, the local office of the State Department of Mental Health offered funds to help finance this expanded operation, and the process of further funding and expansion went on until there were five houses employing a dozen or so staff. Then, the

Department of Mental Health, which had encouraged and fostered the development of similar facilities in other communities, began to talk about "operating standards" and "accreditation requirements." The principles and policies of A.A. and people who had found sobriety by following them were no longer considered to be sufficient for running the agency and so various staff positions were created that could only be filled by suitable professionals. As a result A.A. staff members resigned, local A.A. support disappeared and the agencies were left in the hands of members of the various professions for whom, until A.A. came along, alcoholism was "incurable."[2]

Alternative Giving Formats. If prospective donors are unable to give money, they may still be willing to donate their time as volunteers or to offer some gift-in-kind. On the other hand, a busy individual (or corporate donor) may find it simpler to make a financial gift than to donate goods and services or to organize employees to work on a volunteer project. An important task for fund raisers in organizations where volunteer labor or gifts-in-kind have real value for the recipient institution is to offer donors alternative formats for giving. This may require setting priorities—"If you can't afford to give money, do you have any old clothes or furniture you could give us? Alternatively, could you spare any time to work with us on this project as a volunteer?" Occasionally, of course, donors may be able to help by making two or three different types of gifts. The key thing is to determine organizational needs in advance and then evaluate prospects' giving potential along several different dimensions.

In the balance of this chapter, we look at each of the three basic resource-attraction alternatives, beginning with strategies for attracting funds and then moving in turn to attracting volunteers and attracting gifts-in-kind. Although we consider these approaches separately, we want to emphasize again the importance of taking a portfolio approach to resource-attraction programs. Our primary emphasis will be on nonprofit organizations, but we refer to public agencies when appropriate.

ATTRACTING FUNDS

Relative to other countries, the extent of charitable giving in the United States is remarkable and exceeded $93 billion in 1987.[3] A national survey found that Americans claimed to give an average of 2.4 percent of their household incomes to charities in 1984.[4] (The American Association of Fund Raising Council estimates the figure at closer to 2.0%). While more than half of all Americans gave less than one percent of their incomes, the survey found that more than one-fourth gave 3 percent or more.

The survey also found that giving behavior varied with the age of the donor, as shown below:

Age	Average Annual Donations	Percent of Income
Under 30	$380	1.6
30–34	500	1.7
35–49	910	2.6
50–64	880	3.0
65+	400	2.7
All Ages	650	2.4

Other factors influencing or related to giving behavior are presented in the box "Giving Behavior in the U.S.A. and Its Determinants."

Although much is made of the roles of corporations and foundations as funding sources, over 88% of the value of gifts to nonprofit organizations in the United States comes from individuals and bequests. Where does all the money go? In 1987, 46.5% of the total was donated to churches and other religious organizations—not only to support the clergy and to construct or maintain houses of worship, but also for human service programs sponsored by religious groups.[5] Other major recipients were hospitals and other health-related activities (14.5%), educational institutions (11.6%), the arts and humanities (6.8%), human services (10.5%) and civic and public institutions (2.6%). In total, more than 300,000 charitable organizations and agencies receive donations in the U.S. each year.

Fund-Raising Techniques

A wide array of fund-raising techniques are available to nonbusiness organizations in their efforts to attract donated funds. These range from making proposals for government or foundation grants, possibly worth millions and requiring painstaking solicitation over months or even years, to "membership" programs conducted annually by direct mail and entitling the donor to specific benefits in return for, say, a $15 gift, down to streetcorner collections such as the "flag days"* organized by many charities in Britain which are designed to attract impulse giving of small donations from a broad cross section of the population. Although most gifts are made outright, some nonprofit organizations, notably churches, accept pledges from donors to give a certain amount on a weekly or monthly basis—donating on the installment plan, as it were.

One popular category of fund-raising techniques that goes beyond altruism in its appeal consists of lotteries, raffles, and sweepstakes. The primary appeal, of course, lies in the prizes that a few lucky participants stand to win. Lotteries are increasingly popular with government agencies as a revenue supplement to taxation. France was one of the pioneers with its national lottery, and the concept has been copied and adapted in many other places, including a number of states and provinces in the United States and Canada. (Of course, some critics feel that governments should not be in the gambling business.) Many nonprofit organizations make active use of raffles and sweepstakes (where legal) to raise funds not only from active supporters but also from individuals who would not normally be interested enough to make an outright donation. The downside is that selling raffle tickets is very labor intensive and the average purchase quite small.

Perhaps a better publicity generator is the charitable "benefit," typically a news-worthy entertainment, sporting, or social event honoring a specific cause or organization, which receives a portion of the ticket proceeds. Promoting the event also serves to promote the work of the organization in question. Further publicity opportunities come during the benefit itself and in subsequent news reports describing the event. Benefits are also very labor intensive, however, and run the risk of losing rather than making money if ticket sales for the event fall below expectations.

Some organizations use a mix of fund-raising techniques; others prefer to focus on a single approach. A large membership base provides a potential source of volunteers who

---

*So called because donors receive a little flag or other motif to pin on their clothing as a sign that they have already given.

GIVING BEHAVIOR IN THE U.S.A. AND ITS DETERMINANTS
FINDINGS FROM A NATIONAL SURVEY

Demographic characteristics are associated with making donations. Persons who are married or widowed, have higher education, are Protestants, are in professional occupations, are between 50 and 64 years of age, and have higher incomes are the most generous givers to religion and other charities. Persons with less than high school education and lower incomes give less and most of their contributions go to religion. Persons over 65 years of age are among the most generous of givers as a percentage of income, and they give most of their contributions to religious charities.

Attitudinal and behavioral factors may be more important than demographics. The five major indicators for all respondents who gave 2 percent or more of their incomes to charity were, in rank order:

- attend religious services

- perceive that they have a moderate amount or a lot of discretionary income

- have no worries about having enough money in the future

- volunteered in the last year

- worried only moderately or a little more about money.

While 42 percent of respondents reported pledging a dollar amount to their church or synagogue each week and 30 percent of respondents reported pledging a proportion of their incomes to their church or synagogue, less than one out of ten Americans reported pledging either a dollar amount or a proportion of their incomes to other charities.

Those who pledged a certain dollar amount each week to their church or synagogue on average gave almost twice as much ($880) to religious charities compared to those who did not pledge ($460).

When donors who gave more than $500 to charities in 1984 were asked which type of solicitation they were most likely to respond to, more than three out of four reported that they were most likely to give when asked by a person they knew well.

Source: *The Charitable Behavior of Americans.* Yankelovich, Skelly, and White, Inc., 1988.

can participate in phone or personal solicitation programs, sell tickets for raffles, and help organize benefits. In situations where individual members are not available for such tasks—either because the organization has no membership program or because these supporters are geographically scattered—the preferred approach to fund raising may be using professional staff to write proposals for foundation grants or government fee-for-service programs and to organize large-scale direct-mail fund-raising appeals. Some large organizations, such as the Scouts or the Red Cross, use a combination of such approaches, with national staff responsible for soliciting major gifts and local units (troops or chapters), engaging in such activities as benefits, raffles, and cookie sales.

A Marketing Framework for Fund Raising

Like all forms of resource attraction, effective fund raising requires a focused effort, based on a good understanding of the market for giving and the techniques for reaching that market. Both a sound strategy and good execution are required for success. Planning for a fund-raising effort requires that answers be obtained to the following questions.

1. How will we be using the funds we raise? What benefits will result that might not otherwise occur? Who will be the principal beneficiaries?

2. Which individuals, corporations, foundations, and government granting agencies are most likely to be interested in our organizations and, specifically, in the activities we seek to fund? Who are they and where are they located?

3. What motivations do prospective donors and granters have for giving? Do they expect to benefit directly as a result of our efforts, or do they anticipate broader societal benefits? What are the net financial costs (after tax) to them of making a gift? And what other costs or barriers to gift giving are involved?

4. Which institutions compete with us for donations and grants toward broadly similar ends? What is distinctive about our organization?

5. How much money might prospective donors and granters potentially give to our organization?

6. What communication channels might be used to reach these prospects? Which would be the most cost-effective way to reach them, given our assessment of their giving potential and the probability of receiving a gift or grant from them?

7. What appeals would be most likely to motivate prospects to make a gift or grant?

8. When is the most appropriate time and what is the most appropriate place to contact prospective donors and granters?

9. If no initial commitment is received from a prospect, is it cost effective to follow up with one or more reminders? In such instances should the nature of the appeal be changed or simply restated?

Application of Funds. The way in which donated funds and grants are employed serves to define the "product" of fund-raising efforts from the recipient's perspective. Some funds are earmarked for specific purposes; others represent unrestricted funds that can be used as deemed appropriate by the institution. In general, donors prefer to give funds for specific purposes, but managers of nonprofit organizations frequently need the flexibility of being able to direct funds to wherever they are most needed; this is particularly true of fund-raising efforts conducted on an annual (or more frequent) basis that are designed to raise money to cover operating deficits. In the latter instance, it often helps to provide illustrations of "giving opportunities"—possible ways in which gifts of, say, $50, $500, or $5000 might be used. It is particularly important that donors of small amounts are made aware of the usefulness of their gifts.

Identification of Prospects. Perhaps the most important task for the fund raiser is to identify target markets for solicitation efforts. Some organizations have natural constituencies, such as individuals who have used their services in the past and are known to be able to afford at least a modest gift. Examples include graduates of a university, past patients of a hospital, or previous attenders at a museum. In some instances, names and addresses are collected as part of the process of doing business. The task here is to develop a complete set of records and then keep them up to date. When the association is relatively brief (as in a museum visit) or even at arms' length (as in receiving radio and television broadcasts from a noncommercial station), it may be somewhat more difficult to obtain such data.

Where no direct relationship exists, fund-raising organizations have to use common sense and research insights in focusing their search for prospective donors. The example of the Drinan campaign in Chapter 7, "Market Segmentation," emphasized solicitation of votes, but the segmentation principles employed to focus efforts on the right individuals could also have been modified to provide the basis for a fund-raising campaign. Purchasing, borrowing, or swapping mailing lists sometimes provides a shortcut to developing a list of prospects. Personal interests, as expressed by magazine subscriptions or membership in other organizations, income and educational level (often closely correlated with location of residence), and a past history of giving to related organizations all represent useful indicators. The main difficulty lies in obtaining access to good, up-to-date lists. The small, locally based organization is often well placed to develop a list of good prospects based on the personal knowledge of its managers and the recommendations of board members and other supporters.

Information on corporations, foundations, and granting agencies is relatively easier to obtain, since many institutional donors now publish guidelines to their giving philosophies. One comprehensive publication in the United States is *The Foundation Directory.*[6] In larger cities, there is frequently a foundation or grant-makers resource center, which will supply both published data and advice on possible sources of funds for a particular purpose.

Benefits and Costs for Prospective Donors. What do donors get in return for giving? Among individual donors, the benefits may simply be internally generated feelings, such as a sense of satisfaction from helping a worthy cause; in other instances, donors may expect some favor directly from the recipient—such as priority seating at events sponsored by the organization, receipt of a publication, discounts on goods or services, or public recognition. Understanding these motivations can be helpful in developing messages to prospects and recognition strategies for donors. Costs may also be associated with making a donation that go beyond the financial outlays involved and thus act as a barrier to giving. Even a small gift, for instance, requires a little time and effort of the donor for writing the check and mailing it. The nature and impact of these benefits and costs are likely to vary significantly from one fund-raising situation to another, and even from one donor to another (thereby suggesting possibilities for segmentation strategies). Table 18.2 provides a useful starting point by suggesting a broad list of both motivations for and barriers to individual giving.

Corporate givers often develop formalized philanthropic programs, employing criteria that emphasize the potential social benefit of the gift to the company or its employees, or to the region in which its plants or offices are located. One study found evidence that some firms use corporate giving as a supplement to—or, at the margin, alternative to—advertising; it also found that firms with a high level of public contact spend more on advertising and contributions than do those with little public contact.[7]

Sometimes corporate support for a worthy cause is closely tied to the firm's own product-marketing campaign. During the past decade, Procter & Gamble has mailed out literally billions of coupons for its products that also help to promote the Special Olympics

Table 18.2 Factors Affecting Individual Donation Behavior

Motivations for Giving	Barriers to Giving
• Desire to help others; show sense of responsibility	• Self-centered; prefer to spend money on self
• Gratitude for past good experience or benefits received from institution	• Had bad past experience with institution or have received no benefits
• Have vested interest in preserving existence of institution or maintaining its quality	• No vested interest in future of institution
• Develop or maintain sense of involvement with institution or cause	• Disapprove of (or disinterested in) institution or cause
• Habit—have given for years	• Set higher priority on giving to other organizations
• Alleviate guilt at not investing more time and effort in the organization (giving is an easy way out and takes minimal effort)	• No tradition of giving
	• Feeling that cannot give enough to help the institution meaningfully
• Seek to gain influence and control over institution	• Ignorant or poorly informed of organization and its activities
• Get rid of ''nuisance'' solicitation	• Never asked
• Yield to peer pressure	• Asked by wrong person or in wrong way
• Inspired by opportunities to leverage value of gift through matched giving and tax deductions	• Cannot afford to give
• Desire for personal recognition (memorialize name if big donor)	• Solicited at wrong time (temporarily short of funds, distracted by other concerns)
• Wish to receive specific favors reserved for donors	• Willing but forgot (nobody followed up)

for retarded children. American Express coined the term *cause-related marketing* to describe its practice of tying donations to use of its credit cards—a practice that gained considerable coverage with the restoration of the Statue of Liberty, completed in 1986. American Express contributed one cent toward the restoration fund each time any of its credit cards were used in a transaction.

Johnson & Johnson's Personal Products Company has contributed one million dollars annually to a national hotline and network of shelters for victims of domestic violence. Much of the money for this program, known as "Shelter-Aid," is raised through coupon redemptions on the company's products. In 1988 Campbell's Soup Co. sponsored a walkathon for the March of Dimes Birth Defects Foundation, guaranteeing $150,000 in donations, creating grocery store displays, and distributing 40 million coupons.

Critics of cause-related marketing worry that these promotional campaigns will undercut philanthropy's independence and make companies less willing to give no-strings donations or to assist less popular or potentially controversial charities.[8] Support for this concern comes from a 1988 survey of 225 chief executive officers and 100 next-generation CEOs. The study was conducted for the Council on Foundations by the

Daniel Yankelovich Group. It found that substantial numbers of respondents—who were drawn from samples of large, medium, and small companies—agreed with statements that corporate giving was "good for PR," "enhances the company image with customers," "enhances the climate for doing business," and "helps in selling your product." Commenting on these findings, one observer remarked:

> Today's CEOs and CEOs-to-be, while as committed to giving as they were in the early 1980s, are more likely to tie it to community needs and to keep the company's self-interest foremost in mind. . . . What [the CEOs] search for is an effective way of aligning corporate self-interest with corporate giving.[9]

Among examples of corporate giving that reflect both corporate interests and community needs are:

- Interest-free loans by the Xerox Corporation to provide money for low-income housing in its headquarters town of Stamford, Connecticut, thereby promoting the company's image as a good neighbor.
- A program to match employees' charitable contributions offered as a fringe benefit to help attract and retain employees.
- Gifts to the arts or educational institutions donated as a means of impressing opinion leaders among customers, suppliers, and legislators.
- Donations made to a local college that educates prospective employees.

Few companies are motivated strictly by self-interest; many are also concerned to help society in broader ways. Philanthropic funds are limited, however, and as more and more demands are made on corporate givers by fund raisers, there is a natural tendency to define philanthropic goals in terms of set guidelines (usually available to fund raisers on request), and to apply sometimes rigid screening criteria. Many fund raisers fail to recognize the extent of the competition for corporate gifts, as emphasized by the comments of one slightly frustrated executive in charge of his company's giving program (see the accompanying box, "A Corporate Support Administrator's Lament").

Identifying the Competition. The idea of numerous nonprofit organizations competing for a limited supply of gifts and grants may not be a particularly attractive notion, but it is often a reality. Most corporations, foundations, and government granting agencies have a fixed amount of funds to give away. Personal bequests are obviously limited by the size of the deceased individual's estate. Even individual donors probably have an implicit limit as to how much of their income they are willing to give away.

Institutional donors and granters frequently evaluate fund-raising proposals on a competitive basis. It is not enough to run a worthwhile organization or have a worthy cause; the fund raiser must also submit an explicit and well-reasoned strategy for using the funds sought. Appeals to individual donors may be couched in more emotional terms (if that is what motivates the donor), but many donors have become sophisticated in their giving and wish to know about the efficiency of fund-raising efforts and the precise uses to which organizations with broadly similar goals put their funds. This situation may require not only an efficient and well-managed solicitation effort, but also development and communication of a distinctive positioning statement for the organization, as discussed in Chapter 4, "Competitive Strategy."

A CORPORATE SUPPORT ADMINISTRATOR'S LAMENT*

For eight years now, I have been in charge of allocating funds to charities, civic, cultural, health, educational causes, and assorted works on behalf of my company, a large midwestern manufacturing concern. And while corporate giving decidedly has its blessings, let me tell you it is no rose garden. Corporate philanthropy is a full-time, frustrating, finger-twisting job. You'd be amazed at how many hats and hands are stretched out to me every day, how many social injustices my company is expected to correct, how many of society's afflicted we are called upon to feed, clothe, and house, and how many diseases remain to be conquered by our dollars. From the relentless pressures brought to bear on us by organized charities and fund-raising groups—which are positively ingenious at putting the arm on potential corporate donors—one would think that the forward thrust of American philanthropy rests solely on the size of our annual check.

I get them all—the Little League team in dire need of uniforms, the city symphony that wants us for a patron, the new neighborhood day-care center that lacks the funds to open, and the local drug-rehabilitation center, that, without support, will have to close its doors. Each day my office is inundated with about two dozen different requests for money from charities. And at some big companies the annual cry for help has been known to approach as many as 15,000 separate pleas.

As a result, I have become rather cold and objective about the entire business. I deal with the organized charities that call on me like manufacturer to supplier. I demand to know how their work will directly benefit our employees, where they work, and where they live. I put their requests for funds through a heartless 45-point checklist that asks such questions as: Is the soliciting organization efficiently and honestly managed, with only a small percentage of funds raised spent on solicitation costs and administrative overhead? Will the contribution advance the community and public relations of our company?

Local impact and a sense of self-serving determine the course of most corporate giving today. When I decide that the appeal does not meet the objectives of my corporate contributions program, I let them down with thanks-but-no-thanks letters that are masterpieces of the diplomat's art.

It is not so much the endless stream of phone calls from fund raisers that bugs the corporate support administrator, but the countless requests for time in which to make their formal presentations. There are not enough hours in my week to schedule a flip-chart and slide show for every charity eager to set up its easel in my office.

At our company, we still think philanthropy is worthwhile. We want to see the killer diseases conquered, scholars educated, and the arts flourishing. We want all these things, and we are willing to put a fair-share portion of our pretax earnings where our corporate mouth is. But there is not enough money in our company treasury to make even a dent in the quotas of all the appeals that come to our door. I once figured out that if we granted every single request for money put to us in a single year, our total revenues would be insufficient for the demand.

*Condensed from "I Hate Charities," *Dun's Review,* September 1973. Reprinted with the special permission of *Duns Business Month* (formerly *Dun's Review*), copyright 1973, Dun & Bradstreet Publications Corporation.

Identifying Potential for Giving. Identifying a donor's potential for giving can be a difficult task, particularly where individual donors are concerned. Yet if a fund-raising organization does not understand a prospect's giving potential, it is hard to know how much effort to put into solicitation. Moreover, a wealthy person who is asked for a modest gift will rarely volunteer to make a much larger one. Many nonprofit organizations suggest a "menu" of alternative giving levels in fund-raising appeals sent by mail, leaving it to donors to select the most appropriate level for their circumstances and level of commitment. One advantage of this approach is that the suggested amounts can be adjusted upward periodically to take account of inflation or increased needs for funds.

Personal solicitation is, of course, more flexible than direct mail, in that the solicitor can tailor the amount of the appeal to the individual prospect. Successful fund raisers frequently devote considerable research efforts to evaluating the giving potential of prospective donors; a few even retain newspaper and magazine clipping services to track the financial situation of major prospects. In membership and college alumni organizations, other members and alumni are often good sources of information about their peers; they know which prospects are doing well financially and which ones are not well placed for charitable giving (perhaps on account of other commitments). When raising funds from donors who have given repeatedly in the past, it is important to assess their potential for increased giving, yet not to ask for too much, or make them feel that their previous gifts were inadequate or unappreciated (see next section).

Selection of Communication Channels. The same principles of communication apply to fund-raising campaigns as to other marketing programs. Solicitation of corporations, foundations, and government granting agencies is similar to industrial marketing in that it involves a relatively small number of high-value transactions and usually requires dealing with a decision-making unit of several executives rather than a single decision maker. Although initial contact may be by mail or telephone, most such solicitation efforts involve personal contact if the fund raiser succeeds in passing the initial screen.

Solicitation efforts directed at individuals can be divided into two broad categories (although there may also be an element of overlap). One category consists of membership organizations such as university alumni associations, where good record keeping should ensure that prospects and their past giving history are already known to the organization. Performing-arts organizations often use their subscription list as a source of prospects. Even with natural constituencies, fund raising is not easy; for instance, most universities receive gifts from only a fraction of their alumni. Personal solicitation (which is relatively expensive and time consuming) may be the best approach for prospects with a substantial giving potential, with personal or telephone contact being used for those with moderate potential, and mail or telephone contact for prospects with the lowest potential. For instance, telephone solicitation is often seen by universities as a particularly effective way to get recent graduates to start giving. Although this method is more time consuming than mail solicitation, it provides a more personal touch at less cost than face-to-face meetings.

In the second category are organizations that have no well-developed constituency or membership base. Determining a prospect's giving potential—and hence the appropriate type of solicitation procedure—is, of course, more difficult when his or her past giving history is not known. Organizations that cannot identify prospects by name may wish to consider buying mailing lists. Direct mail is widely used for fund raising when the target audience is relatively segmented (for instance, subscribers to certain types of periodicals, members of professional associations, or residents of upper-income areas). Those organizations with a strong outreach component to their mission often find it useful to employ house-to-house canvassing. This approach serves a dual purpose: fund raising and public education. Because it entails personal selling instead of an impersonal medium such as direct mail, there is a better opportunity to tailor the appeal—and the supporting arguments underlying this appeal—to the household in question. (For an example of canvassing in a political context, see the Drinan case history in Chapter 7.) Other communication channels, such as advertising on television, radio, or in the newspapers, are relatively less important in fund raising, although sometimes public-service advertising spots may be made available free of charge to a nonprofit organization for this purpose.

Determination of Appeals. What should the content of the solicitation message be? Table 18.2 suggested a broad list of motivations for and barriers to giving. More specific research is usually needed to determine bases for appeals and to develop messages for a particular fund-raising program. For instance, the nature of the prospect's affiliation with a university—such as a degree in music, law, or engineering—may suggest messages tailored to the person's interest in the institution. Similarly, political candidates often emphasize different platform planks to different groups of electors, based on their known or projected political concerns. The use of personal, telephone, or direct mail solicitation makes it quite easy to tailor messages in this way.

In addition to suggesting reasons for giving and emphasizing the organization's need for funds, the appeal may also include suggestions for leveraging the size of the gift—such as checking whether or not the donor's employer will match gifts to selected charities. Tax deductions offer another form of leveraging, although the mechanism varies from country to country.

Several aspects of leveraging are illustrated by the combined fundraising efforts of the Vancouver Symphony Orchestra, the Vancouver Bach Choir, and the Vancouver Chamber Choir in their "Orpheum Seat Sale" (see Figure 18.1). The City of Vancouver, owner of the beautifully restored Orpheum Theatre, allowed the Orpheum's three major users to "sell" seats (actually engraved plaques affixed to the arms) in order to raise money for their endowment funds. By launching the campaign just before Christmas time, the seats could be positioned not only as gifts for those so inclined, but also as a tax deduction for those doing end-of-the-year tax planning.

Timing and Location of Solicitation. The distribution aspects of fund raising are of interest for several reasons. Decisions on the scheduling and location of benefit events must obviously be made with reference to the convenience of the target audience. Decisions on timing solicitation efforts may also be vital because people's ability or willingness to give varies by season. The period prior to Christmas is often favored, not only because many people are traditionally in a generous mood during this season, but also for tax reasons. In the United States, where each year's charitable donations can be deducted against income for tax purposes, individuals in higher income brackets may wish to choose between gaining deductions in the tax year ending December 31 or in the new tax year, depending on their estimated tax liability.

Where major gifts are concerned, timing may be critical in terms of the individual (or institutional) donor's access to disposable funds. Thus someone who has just sold a large block of stock or liquidated capital assets may be well placed to give immediately once

A GIFT THAT'S UNIQUE, LASTING & TAX DEDUCTIBLE!

TO SOMEONE SPECIAL IN YOUR LIFE
Dedicate a Seat in
Vancouver's Historic Orpheum
A brass plaque on the arm of the seat and a duplicate
plaque on a handsome certificate of recognition will
bear testimony to your gift for years and years to come.
FOR INFORMATION CALL:
The Orpheum Theatre Foundation, 875-1661

Figure 18.1 Leveraging donations through income tax deductions.
Reprinted by permission of the Orpheum Theatre Foundation, Vancouver, Canada.

this transaction is completed, but not before. For tax reasons, some donors may find it less costly to make a direct donation of assets that have appreciated in value significantly than to make the sale and then donate the proceeds. Similarly, someone who is about to draw up a new will may be willing at that time to insert a bequest to a nonprofit organization. One task for fund raisers is to know when such events are about to occur. This is one reason why long-term cultivation of prospects can be worthwhile, since a good relationship may encourage the sharing of such confidences. Sophisticated fund raisers regularly scan financial and investment publications to gain information about mergers and sales of companies that may yield substantial cash disbursements to particular prospects.

Although some fund-raising programs, especially those emphasizing bequests or major gifts, operate on an ad hoc basis as far as timing of solicitation is concerned, organizations with an established base of members, friends, or alumni are more likely to operate annual fund drives extending over a period of several months. In addition to the money they raise, such annual drives often serve as a seedbed for major capital-fund drives. They help to develop an experienced volunteer operation and a base of regular donors with a sustained interest in the organization who may later be prepared to make a significant gift or bequest.

Another distribution decision is whether to solicit donations directly or to participate in collective efforts with other charities through an intermediary, such as the United Way, Combined Jewish Philanthropies, or the Black United Fund. Many organizations, of course, do both. The advantages and disadvantages of participating in a collective fund-raising effort are similar to those of distributing a product through a large retailing organization. The fund raiser gains access to a much broader market and enjoys cost efficiencies, but suffers loss of control and cannot easily develop direct relationships with donors who

Table 18.3 Segmentation of Prospective Donors to Provide Guidelines for Solicitation Reminders

Group Characteristics	Maximum Number of Mailings Sent
Last-year, first-time donors of $25 or more	Up to 5
Last-year, first-time donors of less than $25	Up to 5
Last-year, donors of $25 or more with a previous history of giving	Up to 5
Last-year donors of less than $25 with a previous giving history	Up to 5
Prospects who did not give a gift last year but gave the previous year	Up to 4
Prospects who had given at some time in the past but whose last gift was more than two years ago	Up to 4
Prospects who had never given a gift	Up to 2

Source: Christopher H. Lovelock, "Stanford University: The Annual Fund," in C. H. Lovelock and C. B. Weinberg, *Public and Nonprofit Marketing: Cases and Readings,* New York: John Wiley & Sons with The Scientific Press, 1984.

make gifts through the intermediary. Furthermore, many collective fund-raising operations are quite selective about which charities they will agree to include and may decline to accept an application from an organization with a controversial mission (such as advocating birth control.) Another reason for the popularity of collective fund-raising operations is that they minimize demands on an individual donor's time; this is particularly appealing to employers who are faced with a host of fund raisers wishing to solicit from employees at a particular plant or office. Unfortunately, some employers become so enthusiastic about helping a fund-raising intermediary that employees may feel unduly pressured to give. Furthermore, concentrating fund-raising efforts in the hands of a single intermediary risks development of an actual or perceived monopoly position in which new, small, or controversial organizations find it hard to reach "mass-market" donors, or else feel obliged to adapt their mission and operating procedures to the requirements of the intermediary.

Appropriateness of Reminders. How many times should a fund-raising organization recontact a prospect who has not responded to earlier appeals? Two issues are paramount: cost effectiveness and intrusiveness. In theory, it is worth making a renewed appeal if the cost of the solicitation is less than the expected value of the gift. For instance, if the fund raiser believes that 10 percent of the prospects on a mailing list will respond to a second appeal with a gift averaging $25 each, then theoretically any expenditure below $2.50 per prospect will result in a net gain. Experience suggests that the up-front efforts required to get donors into the habit of giving to a particular organization can pay dividends over an extended period, since repeat gifts are usually easier to obtain than first-time or second-time gifts. While it is hard to make judgments on an individual basis, experience may suggest rules of thumb for large groups of prospects, based on their past giving history, as shown in the mail solicitation guidelines presented in Table 18.3.

Evaluating Performance in Fund Raising

How do fund raisers know when they have done a good job? What performance measures are useful in helping to evaluate and refine strategies for future solicitation efforts? The most commonly used measures are:

- Total funds raised relative to target.

- Fund-raising expenses as a proportion of total funds raised.
- Value of average gift received.
- Percentage of prospects solicited who actually gave.
- Percentage change in all performance measures relative to previous campaign by the same organization.
- Performance relative to equivalent campaigns by similar organizations.

Each of these measures is useful, but the grand total of funds raised is more valuable for external publicity purposes and motivation of volunteers than for internal control and evaluation. Efficiency of solicitation is key, since net revenues after expenses are what is available to assist the institution in question. Furthermore, cost efficiency may be a positive characteristic to emphasize in solicitation messages. The level of fund-raising costs expressed as a percentage of donations varies widely from one type of campaign and institution to another, but an experienced fund raiser can usually offer guidelines for what constitutes a good percentage target to aim for in a particular situation. A study of fund-raising expenses as a percentage of contributions among 920 New York nonprofit organizations showed an average expense of 16.5 percent for voluntary health and social-welfare organizations and 12.4 percent for all others (including civic, cultural, fraternal, and United Way). However, more than one organization in eight had expenses in excess of 30 percent of contributions.[10]

Average gift size is useful for making comparisons between segments. Thus recent graduates of a college give less on average than older graduates, and former patients of a hospital give more than donors who have not been patients there. Evaluation of the percentage of prospects who were solicited and actually gave provides an important index of market penetration; it is feasible only if the institution solicits in person, by telephone, or by direct mail. Some foundations and corporate donors look carefully at the breadth of individual giving to a nonprofit organization, regarding a high ratio of donors to prospects as a measure of support for the institution's mission, programming, and services. Low participation rates, by contrast, may be perceived as evidence of a lack of interest, raising the question of why the corporation or foundation being solicited should be interested either. In the case of direct-mail fund-raising appeals using purchased lists of addresses, the response rates (in both percentage and revenue terms) provide a good index of the relative effectiveness of each list. Appeals employing broadcast or print media can only be evaluated in terms of numbers and size of donation, since no true estimate of market penetration can be computed.

Before expressing satisfaction or dismay at the results of a fund-raising campaign, those responsible should evaluate their performance against the organization's own past fund-raising efforts and against those of comparable campaigns by similar institutions. Thus state colleges and universities do not usually match the results of similarly sized private schools, and institutions serving different cultural (or national) groups may perform very differently depending on the competitive fund-raising environment, the personal values of prospects, and their potential for giving.

Clearly, careful evaluation requires excellent record keeping. But computerization has made this relatively simple and is usually well worth the front-end costs of installation, especially for larger institutions. Computerized records also allow organizations to make in-depth analyses of the donation performance of different market segments within the overall prospect pool. The fund raiser's task is to ensure that the right data are collected and readily accessible, and then to analyze them intelligently.

Success in upgrading existing donors to making larger gifts requires both segmentation and personalization—the ability to address prospects by name and with reference in written communications to such personal factors as the individual's giving history, areas of interest, and perhaps geographic location. Similar data is also essential, of course, for effective personal or telephone solicitation.

John Groman, who has had many years of experience in computer-based direct-response fundraising for nonprofit clients, argues that a good database must include the right information stored in specific ways.[11] Three elements should be incorporated in the database:

1. *Master mailing data*
   - name of individual
   - address, including postal code
   - sex, title, and suffix (if any)

2. *Individual donor history*
   - date and amount of each gift
   - whether acknowledgement and/or premium was sent in response to each gift received
   - number of fund account
   - appeal code
   - type of package mailed

3. *Donor background data*
   - personal salutation
   - nickname
   - spouse's name
   - telephone number
   - personal areas of interest

Storing the data, says Groman, should be done according to certain principles to allow easy access.

1. *Store separately:* each item of information, including each line in the address, should be stored independently to permit personalization as well as selection according to a variety of segmentation variables (e.g., size of last gift, area of interest, postal code).

2. *Store transactionally:* Storing data in its simplest (most disaggregated) form gives the manager unlimited ability to analyze details, trends, and results.

3. *Store historically:* The true value of a donor only becomes clear over a long period. The more is known of a donor's giving history, the more the fundraiser can seek to upgrade the donor and prevent attrition by varying the nature of the appeals and maintaining the donor's interest in the organization and its work.

4. *Store accurately:* data entry procedures should be designed to capture data correctly, promptly and in standardized form. Inaccurate, outdated, or missing

information may turn off donors as well as weaken planning and evaluation efforts.

Attracting Funds for Public Agencies

In an era of cutbacks in government expenditures, public agencies responsible for such services as public transportation, education, health care, the arts, parks, and other civic amenities are finding it difficult to fund them. Given the government's reluctance to provide financing from general tax revenues, the revenue-generating options for managers of such agencies include:

- Lobbying to rescind the proposed cuts or to obtain the additional financing needed for improvements.
- Instituting new user charges, or raising existing fees.
- Seeking assistance from corporations or other private donors.
- Issuing bonds to generate new capital.
- Seeking to institute new direct taxes whose proceeds can be allocated directly to cover capital and operating costs.

Lobbying. Cost cutting or freezing of budgets at current levels is being forced on many agencies. Sometimes there is significant fat and inefficiency to be removed. More often, freezing or reducing the level of government funding leads to reductions in the scale or quality of operations and thereby in the benefits to society that might potentially be generated by the agency. Managers seeking to build support for rescinding proposed cuts, adding needed supplementary funds, or raising new funds from alternative sources should begin by identifying the nature and extent of the benefits that will otherwise be lost. This task requires a good understanding of the agency's product line, the benefits created by each product, and the identity of both direct and indirect beneficiaries—now and in the future. Such understanding forms the basis for developing an effective lobbying and public-relations campaign designed to improve the agency's financial posture.

Lobbying, to be effective, must be directed at opinion leaders and at constituencies with an interest in the outcome. Although lobbying has—deservedly in some instances—acquired a bad reputation, it is a legitimate form of political activity provided the tactics employed are ethical.

Instituting or Raising User Charges. As noted in Chapter 11, "Developing Monetary Pricing Strategies," many public agencies have responded to loss of tax funds by instituting or raising user charges. While the level of such charges can be thought of as a pricing decision instead of a fund-raising activity, lobbying and public-relations efforts may be required to obtain legislative approval for the change and win public acceptance for it.

Seeking Assistance from Private Sources. Sometimes it may be possible to persuade corporations or other institutional donors to pick up all or part of the increased costs for a specific segment of the population—such as employees of a local company or residents of a certain area. For example, a number of firms now offer to pay a portion of the cost of their employees' monthly transit passes as an employee benefit. Similarly, retailers seeking to build patronage at their stores will sometimes refund the cost of a bus ticket to shoppers traveling by that mode. In such instances, employers and retailers have come to recognize that their organizations benefit from the availability of public transportation and are willing to support it. Another example concerns firms that volunteer to pay for the upkeep of small public parks near their offices. It generally takes some personal selling effort by the public agency in question to convince these companies of the benefits of making such subsidy payments and to help institute the necessary procedures.

Issuing Bonds. Bonds used to be a popular method of financing capital improvements for a wide range of local or regional government services. Payment of the interest and repayment of the capital was usually tied either to local property taxes or to revenues generated by sale of the agency's services (such as bridge or highway tolls). In many instances, the law required approval by a public referendum. As a result of increased public opposition to higher taxes of any sort, such referenda have become very difficult to pass. Particularly affected by this attitude have been bond issues designed to improve public education. Voters without school-aged children of their own often see little benefit to themselves in voting for such measures. In the current climate, only when a severe problem exists, whose resolution will quickly benefit a large cross section of the voting population, is it still feasible to develop a political campaign that will result in passage of the referendum.

Instituting or Raising Direct Taxes. One route that has often been followed in the past, especially in the United States, is to institute new direct taxes (or raise existing taxes) and earmark the revenues for a specific purpose. Examples include taxes on those who benefit directly (as when gasoline taxes are allocated to highway construction and repair) or a systematic cross-subsidy (such as using gasoline taxes to finance public transportation or the suggestion that liquor and tobacco tax revenues be earmarked for health-care purposes). In many states, such taxes require voter approval in a referendum. Because the law often prohibits public agencies from taking an advocacy position in political campaigns, the actual task of organizing and financing the campaign has to be assumed by a citizens' committee formed for that purpose. Referenda to raise new taxes are likely to be opposed by groups advocating lower taxation, with both sides seeking to raise money for public-opinion studies and extensive advertising campaigns, and to recruit volunteers for canvassing and getting voters to the polls on election day. Los Angeles, for instance, has been the site of several keenly fought but unsuccessful campaigns to increase property-tax funding to pay for improved and less expensive public-transportation services.

ATTRACTING GIFTS-IN-KIND

Offering gifts-in-kind is really a much older form of charity than donating funds, since it predates the widespread use of money. In modern society, giving money tends to be simpler both for the individual and for the recipient organization, with the result that relatively less attention is paid to improving procedures for attracting such gifts, even though many nonprofit organizations are highly dependent on them. Art museums sometimes purchase new acquisitions for cash, but most art objects in their collections have been gifts from generous private collectors. Among hospitals and health organizations the practice of paying donors for their blood is increasingly discouraged in favor of entirely voluntary blood donations (this is done more out of quality control than financial considerations). Churches, schools, and day-care centers regularly hold rummage sales (or "jumble sales" as they are called in Britain), reselling donated clothes, furniture, kitchen utensils, and other items as a way of raising money. Public broadcasting stations in the United States have become famous—some would say notorious—for their on-air fund-raising auctions of donated goods and services. A more common fund-raising device among nonprofit organizations is raffling valuable goods (such as a car or television) or services (such as a free vacation, theater tickets, or beauty treatment) that have been donated by business firms.

Much giving-in-kind comes from institutional donors. One of the world's largest recipients of donated goods and services is CARE, which distributes free clothing, food, and medicine to disaster victims or other needy individuals throughout the globe. In 1981, CARE reported that it received reimbursements of ocean-freight shipping charges worth $62.7 million, donations of surplus agricultural commodities by the U.S. government valued at $136.1 million, and corporate or individual gifts of food, clothes, and medicines worth $5.7 million.[12]

Certain gifts-in-kind are more likely to be made posthumously than during the donors' lifetimes. These include many gifts to libraries and museums from private collectors, gifts of buildings or land from an estate, and gifts of human organs such as eyes or kidneys. The task of the gift seeker in such cases is a sensitive one. In many instances the gift is indivisible, or at least worth more collectively than in several pieces. Other institutions may also be seeking the object in question, and the donor may be reluctant or unable to part with it during his or her lifetime.

Encouraging donation of human body parts present a special problem in that a major source of certain organs is from healthy young people who have died in accidents that left some or all of these organs intact. Permission for such donations must either be authorized after death by close family members or be given in advance by the prospective donor. Not surprisingly, this is an emotion-fraught issue for many people, although research suggests that the population can be segmented along various demographic and attitudinal factors that are correlated with willingness to give.[13]

As with recruitment of volunteers, the development of strategies for attracting gifts-in-kind shares some basic characteristics in common with fund raising. The nonprofit organization may also find itself cast in the role of broker—attracting goods and services and then redistributing them—or acting as a kind of "reverse retailer"—first attracting the gifts from sellers and then converting them into cash to fund its other activities.

Nonprofit managers should not overlook the potential for attracting gifts-in-kind from corporations. Many manufacturing and retailing companies need to dispose of surplus inventory or of slightly defective goods that are still quite serviceable. Food growers and processors deal with bulky, perishable items whose supply sometimes exceeds demand; instead of flooding the market and thus driving prices down, they may prefer to give away surplus items or destroy them. Service firms also have a perishable product that cannot always be fully sold during periods of low demand; hence donating airline seats or hotel rooms (to cite just two examples) may involve little out-of-pocket expense.

Enormous potential also exists for attracting gifts-in-kind from middle-class households in affluent societies. Used furniture, old clothes, and other goods are frequently thrown away long before they wear out. Unfortunately, it appears that only a small fraction of surplus personal or household items is donated to organizations such as the Salvation Army or Goodwill Industries; the bulk of the balance just gets thrown away.

Under U.S. tax law, both corporate and individual gifts-in-kind may qualify for a tax deduction equal to the value of the gift. Many individuals are probably unaware of this opportunity and might be motivated by this benefit if better informed.

A "Miracle" at the Salvation Army

"I don't know if you believe in miracles," said the Salvation Army officer from the large seaport city, "but let me tell you about something that happened to us a couple of years ago." He continued with his story.

> It was a bitterly cold March and a lot of older people just couldn't get out of their homes. One Monday, a fish processor called us and offered us two tons of frozen fish—the largest contribution in kind I've ever heard of. We went and got it and began cooking up about 100 gallons of fish chowder a day and distributing it. Then on the Thursday, we got a call from a local bakery telling us that they had gone out of business and had four walk-in freezers full of bread that they wanted us to come and get. We put the two together and called it our "loaves and fishes" program.[14]

The officer, a deeply religious man, talked quietly and matter-of-factly about the Lord taking care of them. Certainly, gifts of such magnitude, occurring together at a time of real need, do have a miraculous element to them. It is often said, though, that "the Lord helps those who help themselves." Consider these points.

- Both the fish processor and the baker knew enough about the Salvation Army to recognize this organization as an appropriate and worthwhile outlet for their surplus products.
- Each donor was able to find the Army's phone number and reach a responsible individual at the local Salvation Army Citadel.
- The Salvation Army was able to arrange truck transportation and labor at short notice to pick up the fish and bread and to find space in which to store them.
- Salvation Army personnel and facilities were available for cooking the food and serving it at local hostels as well as for arranging delivery to needy people in their homes.

Visible and well-prepared organizations stand the best chance of being chosen as the recipient of surplus foodstuffs or merchandise—and of being able to take advantage of such opportunities at short notice. By publicizing fortuitous gifts (if the donors are agreeable), and the uses to which they are put, nonprofit managers may further enhance their organizations' chances of receiving needed gifts in the future.

Soliciting Gifts of Goods and Services

Although unexpected gifts are often very welcome, they are the exception rather than the rule. In practice, most gifts-in-kind have to be solicited on a programmatic basis. There are basically four categories of such programs, reflecting the different ways in which the resulting gifts will be used.

1. Donations of materials or services that will help the organization run its basic operation. These might include buildings or the use of office space, fuel and supplies, use of office or transportation equipment, or free professional advice.

2. Gifts of goods or services that can be supplied directly to the organization's clients, such as food, clothing, medicines, blood and human body organs, toys, use of recreational facilities, entertainment, medical testing, and educational programs.

3. Gifts of communications and marketing services that can be used to develop and implement fund-raising programs, membership drives, or efforts to attract more customers. For instance, an advertising agency might volunteer the use of its creative and production personnel to develop a campaign, or a television station might offer free time for airing public-service messages.

4. Donations of items that the organization can resell through thrift shops, auctions, or special-event sales, thereby generating funds to support its core activities. Thus Goodwill Industries, which serves the handicapped and other disadvantaged groups, appeals for donations of clothes and housewares that can be processed by its clients and then offered for sale in its chain stores. The net proceeds go to support its programs.

As shown in Figure 18.2, developing a formal program to attract gifts-in-kind requires decisions and actions in a number of areas, starting with specification of the types of goods and services required. Lack of clarity on this point will result in having to reject (or dispose of) gifts that are not wanted. As in any marketing activity, it pays to focus communication efforts on those target segments (individuals, organizations, or groups) that offer the best potential for responding in the desired way. A combination of common sense and research may be needed to identify the best prospects and their motivation for giving.

Developing Reverse Distribution Channels

Before gifts of food, furniture, clothing, medicines, or other physical items are solicited, a system for collecting, transporting, and storing the goods needs to be designed. In a sense, the task is the opposite of developing channels to distribute goods from a manufacturer to retail outlets and thence to customers. Instead, donors must either bring their gifts to a collection center or make arrangements for them to be picked up. The process is not unlike establishing a recycling system. Just as in normal retailing, catering to customers' needs for convenience and simplicity is very important. If direct pickup is not feasible, collection stations must be established in convenient locations and kept open at convenient hours.

Organizations that operate on a large scale, such as Goodwill Industries, have experimented with unattended collection boxes, but have discovered that the merchandise deposited in some locations is vandalized, stolen, or damaged by bad weather. Instead, they prefer to set up attended trailers, parked in high-traffic locations such as shopping centers, where donors can drop off their gifts and receive a receipt that estimates the value of the gift for tax-reporting purposes. The resulting gifts then need to be transported to a central location for sorting, cleaning, repair, and (if they are to be resold) pricing. Smaller organizations, such as an individual church, may have a ready-made constituency in their congregation and can usually use their own facilities for drop-off and sorting purposes, so the logistics for them are a great deal simpler.

Some operations, such as Red Cross blood drives, use other organizations as intermediaries in a cooperative effort. Thus a company or college may agree to participate in a

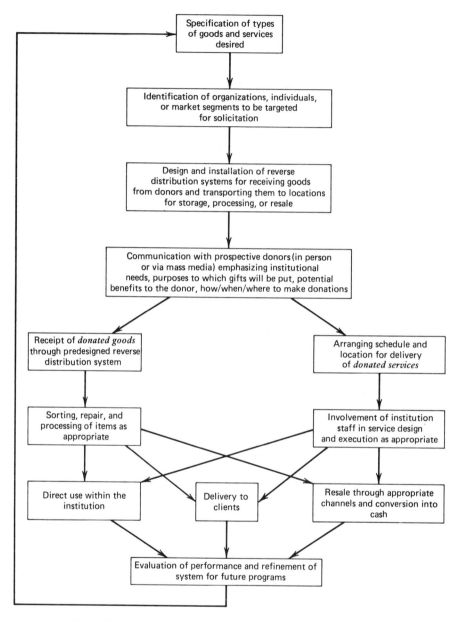

Figure 18.2 A programmatic approach to attracting gifts-in-kind.

blood drive, publicizing the event to employees or students, giving the former group free time off from work to make a donation, and letting the blood-collecting organization use on-site facilities such as a large meeting room or gymnasium.

Whatever the situation, careful attention should be given in advance to the design of these reverse distribution channels with an eye to both efficiency and donor convenience.

It is also important to publicize well the location and scheduling of collection centers. Such forethought increases the chances that donors will be prepared to make a repeat gift.

SUMMARY

Only a minority of public and nonprofit organizations can cover their operating expenses and finance future growth strictly from internally generated funds. Most need to devote significant marketing efforts to attracting donations of money and gifts of goods and services. Some nonbusiness organizations actively solicit both.

In each instance, the gift entails costs and benefits for the donor. Hence managers responsible for resource-attraction programs need to understand donor motivation and barriers to giving. Managers also need to recognize the opportunity costs entailed: donors could give money to other deserving causes or spend it on themselves, and those who donate goods and services could give them to another organization, attempt to sell them, or simply discard the goods and allow service-related personnel and equipment to remain idle.

Although there are important commonalities between these two forms of resources, there are also a few key differences. First, donated money is a commodity and can be used for any purpose unless earmarked for a specific project. By contrast, gifts-in-kind tend to vary widely in character and must be carefully matched to institutional needs. Hence marketing programs to attract volunteers and gifts-in-kind may need to be quite specific about what types of gifts are needed.

Finally, managing programs designed to attract gifts-in-kind requires attention to the procedures entailed in getting the gifts from the donor to the recipient. This may pose problems relating to both location and scheduling. Where physical goods are concerned, there is a need to set up and manage reverse distribution channels, possibly using intermediary organizations to help in the task.

A number of marketing tools and concepts can be helpful in managing a resource-attraction program. Segmentation of prospects and development of specific campaigns targeted at specific prospects not only help provide focus but are also likely to improve efficiency. Careful thinking about motivations for giving will be useful in developing a communications strategy for each segment, so that the most appropriate appeals and most cost-effective communication channels are used in each instance. The use of marketing research is particularly important, both for planning purposes—to determine attitudes toward the organization and its programs—and for later evaluations of how well the resource-attraction program is going. The key to getting existing donors to give more is excellent record-keeping and a computerized database that enables management to evaluate donor responsiveness to specific requests over time.

Perhaps the key factor underlying success in resource attraction is planning. Without clear objectives, it is difficult to develop a well-thought-out strategy and to give careful attention to all aspects of implementation. Most public and nonprofit organizations, especially smaller ones, are resource constrained. Attempts to attract new resources require investment of existing financial and human resources. An unsuccessful effort has a high opportunity cost, with potential negative impacts on existing programs. Further, a poorly planned and managed campaign may discourage donors and volunteers from participating in resource-attraction efforts by that organization in the future.

REFERENCES

1. Carol Hymowitz, "Helping Hand: Reagan's Welfare Cuts Shift Charity Burden to Religious Groups," *The Wall Street Journal* (March 15, 1982), pp. 1, 20.
2. D. Robinson and S. Henry, *Self-Help and Health: Mutual Aid for Modern Problems,* Oxford: Martin Robertson & Co. Ltd, 1977. Reprinted by permission of Martin Robertson, Oxford.
3. Source: *Giving U.S.A.* New York: American Association of Fundraising Council, 1988.
4. Virginia Hodgkinson and Murrary Weitzman, *The Charitable Behavior of Americans,* Washington, D.C., Independent Sector, 1986.
5. As reference 3.
6. Loren Renz and Stan Olson (eds,), *The Foundation Directory,* 11th edition. New York: The Foundation Center, 1987; and *Supplement to the 11th Edition,* 1988.
7. Louis W. Fry, Gerald D. Keim, Roger E. Meiners, " Corporate Contributions: Altruistic or For-Profit?" *Academy of Management Journal,* 25, No. 1 (1982), pp. 94–106.
8. "Doing Well by Doing Good," *Business Week* (December 5, 1988), pp. 53, 57; P. Rajan Varadarajan and Anil Menon, "Cause-Related Marketing: A Coalignment of Marketing Strategy and Corporate Philanthropy," *Journal of Marketing,* 52 (July 1988), pp. 58–74.
9. Roger M. Williams, "Change at the Top," *Foundation News,* November–December 1988, pp. 67–69.
10. Malvern J. Gross, Jr., "A New Study of the Cost of Fund Raising in New York," *The Philanthropy Monthly* (April 1976).
11. John E. Groman, "Designing Your Database for Successful Upgrading," *Nonprofit World,* January/February 1987, pp. 13–14.
12. CARE, *Annual Report 1981,* New York, 1982.
13. Edgar A. Pessemier, Albert C. Bemmaor, and Dominique M. Hanssens, "Willingness to Supply Human Body Parts: Some Empirical Results," *Journal of Consumer Research,* 4 (December 1977), pp. 131–140.
14. Interview with a Salvation Army officer who prefers to remain anonymous, 1982.

Chapter 19

Recruiting & Managing Volunteers & Boards of Directors

Volunteers are the lifeblood of many nonprofit organizations. In some instances, the organization literally could not function without unpaid labor and administrative help. In other instances, volunteers complement the work of paid managers and staff, performing vital tasks as board members, fund raisers, and providers of supplementary services.

Why do people volunteer their time and effort, especially when there are many other demands on their time? How does a nonprofit organization set about recruiting the right sort of volunteers for its own situation? And having recruited them, how does it get the best out of them? A significant problem facing nonprofit managers is how to direct volunteers: since they are not employees, can they be managed?

These questions become even more pointed when they concern what are arguably the most important volunteers of all: the members of the board of directors or trustees.

Scope of the Chapter

This chapter begins with a discussion of some of the differences between getting people to give money and getting them to give their time. We examine some of the motivations for volunteering, noting how they may vary according to age and job status. Research findings from studies of volunteer behavior in the United States provide additional perspective on the types of organizations to which people are willing to volunteer their time.

We then turn to the issue of how to manage volunteers. What are the key success factors in managing volunteers? An effective approach to volunteer management is particularly vital when the task involves fundraising. We'll discuss the case of a large university which has volunteer leaders manage a large corps of volunteer fundraisers, with support from a paid staff.

The final section of the chapter is devoted to recruiting and managing the board of directors. As nonprofit organizations continue to adopt a stronger marketing orientation, they need board members who understand marketing concepts, can develop mission statements that reflect current market needs and realities, and can develop—in concert with the staff—marketing strategies that will help their organizations achieve their missions.

ATTRACTING VOLUNTEERS

The tasks performed by volunteers vary widely, from assisting at religious services to staffing suicide-avoidance hotlines, from working on social advocacy programs to running retail operations in museum shops, and from participating in fund raising efforts to serving as teachers or companions to the disadvantaged. Some volunteer-staffed programs require specific skills in addition to the volunteer's time and enthusiasm. These talents include the professional skills offered by medical personnel working in health clinics, lawyers working in legal aid programs, and executives serving on boards of directors. Other volunteer jobs emphasize possession of necessary personal traits, augmented by careful training—as in such sensitive tasks as counselling and assisting victims of rape.

Attracting and managing volunteers successfully requires a marketing orientation somewhat similar to that employed in fund raising. Volunteers incur an opportunity cost in terms of forgoing alternative uses of their time; many forgo chances of earning additional income. Hence it's very important for managers to understand volunteer's motivations as well as their skills. There are some important parallels between marketing strategies for fund raising and those for recruiting volunteers. The list of questions in the previous chapter could easily be adapted for use in a volunteer recruitment program. Yet there are also some key differences between attracting volunteers and raising money:

- Money is a commodity and unrestricted gifts can be used for any purpose. By contrast, individual volunteers vary widely in skills, personalities, and motivations. Hence they must be carefully matched to appropriate jobs.
- Whereas money is ready to be used as soon as it is received, volunteers may need a period of training and familiarization before they become effective performers.
- Volunteers are in much closer contact with the recipient organization than are most donors of funds. Hence personal relationships and experiences play a stronger role in determining the amount and quality of a volunteer's work—and whether that person's commitment to the organization will be renewed in the future.

The traditional stereotype of a volunteer was that of a middle-class suburban woman who devoted her time to voluntary organizations for altruistic and social reasons, in between looking after husband and children. Never entirely accurate—for instance, men have always been involved in sports-related activities, scouting, and serving on boards of directors—this stereotype is even less true today, when a broad cross-section of people is volunteering.

In a very real sense, the recruiter of volunteers is like a broker, trying to find the right individual for the position available or looking to see if a position can be found for a volunteer with a particular set of skills and interests. To be an effective broker requires skills in identifying job requirements, evaluating individuals' capabilities, and bringing the two together in a matching process.[1]

Understanding why people volunteer and what they hope to get out of the experience is one of the keys to successful recruitment and retention. Volunteers' motivations may vary according to an individual's age and current job status. As suggested in Table 19.1

Table 19.1 How Self-Interested Motivations for Volunteering Vary by Age and Job Status

Group	Possible Motivations
Young people aged 16–25 already employed or about to enter the labor market	Obtain career insights and guidance, develop skills, help decide on vocation, make friends
Underemployed younger people, including but not limited to liberal arts college graduates	Find intellectual stimulation and interesting colleagues (who are missing from current job), while searching for better job
Women and men aged 25–50 with discretionary time (including those who are returning to the labor force after a period of absence)	Substitute for challenging full-time job, gain experience, work in positions of responsibility, obtain job-related recommendation, make people contacts/friends
Individuals aged 25–60 who are already in full-time jobs	Advance community or political issues by engaging in grass-roots work
Retired people (typically but not exclusively aged 60+)	Make productive use of time, use skills, socialize

Source: Interviews with experts in volunteer recruitment, 1984/87.

below, certain motivations reflect self-interest rather than pure altruism. For a series of extensive checklists on factors leading individuals to volunteer, decline to volunteer, continue in a voluntary capacity, or discontinue volunteering, readers should consult Eva Schindler-Raiman's work.[2]

Research Findings on Voluntary Behavior in the United States[3]

In a typical year, almost half the total adult and teenage population of the United States devotes time to some form of voluntary service. A 1981 study by the Gallup Organization for Independent Sector estimated that the average volunteer donated about 100 hours of time each year and valued these services nationwide at $64.5 billion, based on the average hourly rate for each individual's educational group. A 1984 study by Yankelovich, Skelly and White (also published by Independent Sector), estimated an average time commitment per volunteer of over three hours per week, but made no attempt to value this time.

One research finding of particular interest is that those who volunteer their time are also more likely than non-volunteers to make financial donations to nonprofit organizations. According to the 1981 study, 91 percent of active volunteers said that they made charitable contributions as compared to just 66 percent of non-volunteers. Only one respondent in six admitted to neither volunteering nor making charitable contributions. The 1984 study also found a relationship between giving time and giving money: volunteers donated an average of $830 per year (2.8 percent of their total income) versus an average of $510 (2.0 per cent of income) for non-volunteers. A partial explanation for this latter finding may be that volunteers had higher household incomes on average than did non-volunteers ($29,500 versus $25,400).

Two other correlates of volunteer behavior are the extent to which the individual is involved in community activities and—to a lesser extent—frequency of attendance at religious services.

What kinds of voluntary activity receive the most volunteer time? Table 19.2 shows the proportion of adults and 14–17 year-olds in the Gallup survey who stated that they

Table 19.2 Americans Engaging in Different Types of Voluntary Activities
(includes multiple responses)

Field of Activity	Adults (%)	Teens (14–17) (%)	Average No. Hours Volunteered in Past 3 Months
Religion Ushering, choir, Sunday School, fund raising, etc.	19	20	28
Health Fund raising, hospital work, rescue squad, elderly care, nursing homes, etc.	12	16	26
Education PTA, school board, room parent, teaching/tutoring, fund raising, etc.	12	16	22
Recreation (including coaching)	7	12	28
General fund raising	6	7	12
Citizenship (including Scouts)	6	5	25
Community action	6	5	18
Political Office holder, poll watcher, campaign worker, etc.	6	2	21
Work-related	6	1	28
Social and welfare	5	4	23
Arts and culture	3	2	31
Justice	1	0	27
Informal or alone (only volunteer in this area)	23 (5)	19 (6)	27
No voluntary activities	48	47	—

Source. Americans Volunteer, 1981. Based on responses from a nationally representative sample of 1601 adults and 152 teenagers conducted by the Gallup Organization, Inc., for Independent Sector, March 13–23, 1981. Reprinted by permission.

donate their time to specific activities, as well as the average amount of time donated in the previous three months. Among adults who volunteer, the largest portion (44 percent of adults and 53 percent of teens) learned of their chosen activity when asked if they would volunteer for it. Other key sources of information included having a family member or friend engaged in the activity—or benefiting from it—and prior participation. These responses demonstrate the power of both personal selling and word-of-mouth, as well as the importance of satisfying past experiences as a volunteer. Of particular interest is the fact that a quarter of all volunteers had sought out the activity on their own, and only six percent had seen an advertisement.

Of course, not everybody continues to volunteer indefinitely for the same activity. As people's interests and commitments change, so does the extent of their voluntary efforts. When asked whether they had been involved three years earlier with any voluntary activities that they no longer performed, 21 percent said yes. The principal reasons given included competition from other demands (too busy; went to paid job or school; went into other volunteer work that was more important) and reduced motivation (lost interest; child/ relative/friend no longer involved; had problem or bad experience with the organization).

Thus far we have addressed issues in volunteer recruitment and management from a broad perspective. To provide insights into some of the tasks entailed in specific contexts, we now look at the task of managing volunteers effectively, especially for undertaking personal solicitation efforts in fund raising.

MANAGING VOLUNTEERS EFFECTIVELY

In conducting research on volunteer behavior, we were struck by how often managers of nonprofit organizations made negative comments about volunteers. The adjective "unreliable" was used most frequently, especially in connection with failure to show up for work on schedule. Interviews with volunteers suggested that many of them found that their skills were not being utilized and that much of their time was spent milling around waiting for assignments. Discussing his own volunteer efforts, a high-earning consultant remarked: "I'm happy to volunteer for these organizations, but I drop out if I'm mainly doing envelope stuffing and other tasks that anyone could do."

On the other hand, those organizations with successful volunteer programs tended to disagree with such assessments, seeing them as a reflection of poor recruitment policies, lack of understanding of volunteer motivations, and failure to offer jobs that included at least some rewarding and challenging elements relative to the volunteer's skill and experience. As one professional recruiter of volunteers observed tartly, "Organizations that criticize volunteers as unreliable haven't figured out how to support and manage them properly."[4]

In situations where the basic job is inherently uninteresting, nonprofit managers will either have to lower their sights in terms of the types of volunteers they seek to recruit or else add frills to the job—perhaps by rotating volunteers through more interesting tasks. The alternatives are to hire paid employees, contract out the work to a specialist organization, or leave the job undone.

Table 19.3 lists a series of steps that managers of volunteers need to take if they want voluntary labor and expertise to be a resource that is worth getting and keeping. As in so many areas of activity, an initial investment of time and effort may pay handsome dividends later. Prior to taking these steps, the organization must clearly define the role of the volunteer program in the organization and the tasks and responsibilities to be assigned to volunteers.

Managing Volunteers in Fund-Raising Activities

Any form of fund raising that involves personal solicitation tends to be very labor intensive. Large numbers of solicitors are required to contact prospects in person or by telephone. To hire individuals for this work can be prohibitively expensive, so volunteers are much in demand for the task. There are other advantages to volunteers besides the fact that they do not expect to be paid.

One important principle of personal selling is that better results are usually achieved when the salesperson can empathize with the prospect. To the extent that volunteer fund

Table 19.3   Key Tasks in Effective Use of Volunteers

- Invest time in identifying and evaluating prospective volunteers to determine their capabilities, interests, expectations, and possible shortcomings.

- Be selective in recruitment and tactfully discourage those who would be a poor fit with the volunteer positions available.

- Pay special attention to the enlistment process, stating clearly and emphatically what the institution —and in particular the supervisor—expects of the volunteer; do not understate the demands of the job.

- Develop special orientation sessions to capitalize on new volunteers' interest and enthusiasm; inform them about the organization, clarify the nature of their role (both the scope and limits of their responsibilities), expose them to the problems and opportunities they will encounter, and introduce them to staff members and other volunteers; provide any necessary advance training required for specific jobs.

- Ensure that professional staff members encourage sharing and implementation of useful new ideas proposed by volunteers.

- Make a point of determining the benefits that each volunteer hopes to obtain from his or her work for the institution, and try to ensure that reasonable expectations are actually met.

- Ensure that professional staff members keep good volunteers in the public view.

- Seek to leverage volunteers' enthusiasm and expertise by minimizing their involvement in trivial and time-consuming issues; ensure that they receive an appropriate level of staff support for the task in question so that they can focus their efforts effectively.

- Develop a formal system for regular appraisal of volunteer's performance, preferably involving more experienced volunteers in the process; be prepared to promote, retrain, reassign, demote, or tactfully dismiss volunteers on the basis of these assessments. (Note: setting fixed terms to volunteers' appointments in specific positions facilitates reassignment or dismissal without undue hard feelings.)

- Remember that volunteers have other interests and activities competing for their attention; within the constraints of the situation in question, professional staff should seek to maximize the rewards that volunteers derive from their voluntary activities and to minimize frustrations and other barriers to personal commitment and effective performance.

raisers are also donors themselves and can be matched with prospects from similar backgounds and with similar giving potential, they should achieve greater success. For instance, alumni of a university may be asked to solicit donations from individuals who were in the same class as themselves. Not only does this offer conversational entrees, but it may mean that solicitors understand prospective donors' interests, motivations, and even their capacity for giving.

Volunteer-based fund raising programs still need coordination and direction. In large programs, this is usually achieved through the assistance of full-time professional staff working with experienced volunteers. Consider the systematic approach used at Stanford University in recent years to manage and motivate volunteers assisting in its annual fund-raising program, as described in a case study:

An annual Leadership Conference was held on campus each autumn for volunteers, as a way of updating them on the University's activities, involving them in fund raising planning and coordination, and providing an opportunity to revisit Stanford. The conference also served as a means of rewarding deeply involved volunteers for their hard work and included a banquet at which awards were presented to outstanding volunteer fund raisers.

Staff members were responsible for helping volunteer leaders coordinate their activities, including such important tasks as recruiting and training new workers. Working with the staff, experienced volunteers helped evaluate ongoing performance, provided suggestions for new approaches, assisted in the development of communications appeals and reviewed all printed materials for content and tone before mailing. Coordination and regular contact with all volunteers was viewed as a particularly important task. Particular efforts [were made] to ensure that volunteers, at all levels, were properly briefed.

[At year end], debriefing sessions were held with as many volunteers as possible, to ascertain what had worked well and what had not. [Alternatively] evaluation forms [might be used] for the same purpose. Supervisory volunteers provided staff members with assessments of the performance of those directly under them. In this way, a promising worker or captain might be promoted to a more responsible position or assigned more difficult prospects. Likewise, a worker who had been unsuccessful might be given different assignments next year or else tactfully discouraged from participating in the solicitation effort the following year. Additionally, further information might be received about existing or potential donors with significant giving capacity, which would facilitate the solicitation effort next year.[5]

This approach is not unique to Stanford, but it is particularly well implemented at that institution. Note the importance given to training, staff assistance, and evaluation. Note also the existence of a volunteer hierarchy paralleling that of the professional staff. Unlike volunteers in some organizations, Stanford fund raisers are not assigned the "scut work" at the behest of the staff; instead, the staff is there to provide coordination and to leverage the efforts of the volunteers. Moreover, although volunteers tend to start with entry-level jobs as "workers," they can expect, if successful, to progress to more responsible positions as supervisors and trainers of inexperienced or less proficient volunteers.

Of course, not every voluntary organization is as large as the one just described; further, some cannot afford paid staff, and more than a few would consider a strongly hierarchical volunteer organization inconsistent with their values and mission. Nevertheless, the fact remains that successful use of volunteers requires a clear statement of each volunteer's responsibilities, a transfer of expertise from experienced individuals to new recruits, and coordination of efforts to avoid duplication, waste, or failure to achieve key tasks.

THE BOARD OF DIRECTORS

Not all voluntary work, of course, involves assignments at the bottom or middle of the organization. All nonprofit organizations (and many public agencies) have a need for members of the board who will provide leadership and direction.

Defining the Role of the Board

In most nonprofit organizations, the board of directors (or trustees) is the final governing body. In membership organizations, directors are elected (or re-elected) by the membership. In others, board members are appointed by fellow board members or, in some cases, by sponsoring organizations.

Since there is so much diversity among nonprofit organizations, it's not surprising that there should be wide variations in the size, structure, and functions of their boards of directors. In those nonprofit organizations that are heavily dependent on donated funds, there is usually an expectation that board members will be active in fund raising, especially in personal solicitation of large gifts. Indeed, many directors are themselves among the most generous donors to the organizations on whose boards they sit. But what should be the board's involvement in other forms of marketing activity?

We've argued previously that no organization can be truly marketing oriented unless its chief executive is strongly supportive of marketing efforts. Now we'll expand on that point by arguing that both board members and the chief executive must work together to articulate a mission for the organization, formulate marketing strategy, attract the necessary resources (including new board members with needed expertise and connections), and oversee implementation of that strategy.

Miriam Wood studied college and university boards and looked at the interactions between the board, the chief executive, and the operating departments of the institution. She identified three operating patterns that can probably be generalized to most other nonprofit boards.[6]

The first type of board, associated mainly with larger organizations, has a *ratifying style,* also known as "rubber stamp." Here, the board sees its role as simply choosing a chief executive officer (CEO) and then placing itself and the institution in the CEO's hands. Board members rely almost totally on the chief executive's advice and have only superficial relationships with other managers and personnel.

Second, there is the increasingly common *corporate style,* in which board members and CEO try to run the board as if the institution were a business corporation. Here, the governing board receives briefing papers and plays an active role in dealing with such financial and managerial issues as capital expenditures, property acquisition, and asset management. However, the board expects the CEO to assume executive authority.

Finally, there is a *participatory style* where board members are more likely to work directly with staff members and program heads, and to gather information through formal and informal contacts. This approach is most likely to be found among small organizations, although it occurs in larger ones, too. Board members have a highly personal stake in the institution's success, but CEOs are sometimes discomforted by what they see as interference in administrative matters.

Wood notes that although the rhetoric of the boardroom is that trustees (or directors) make policy and rely on the chief executive to implement it, this canon is frequently violated. She adds:

> Particularly on corporate and participatory boards, trustees have in effect become senior partners to the vice presidents, and the short-term problems of the functional areas have become the primary focus of the energies and interests of key board members. This focus is not necessarily bad, except that it becomes a substitute for hard strategic thinking from an institutionwide perspective.[7]

In our view, the style that evolves is, in part, related to the size of the organization. The rubber stamp board really contributes very little to strategic direction; in between occasional searches for a new chief executive, it is managerially moribund. Its members may, however, be successful as fund raisers. But a fund raising role is probably insufficient for a small, leanly staffed organization which urgently needs advice on strategy.

The corporate board has historically been active in financial planning and fundraising but has had only limited involvement in marketing strategy; nevertheless, this corporate model lends itself well to extending the board's work to include active involvement in mission definition and strategic market planning. The participatory board, however, runs the risk of enfeebling the management team by usurping the latter's responsibilities; if such a board gets involved in marketing— especially within a large, well-staffed organization—it is likely to immerse itself in implementation and lose its strategic vision in a sea of tactical minutiae.

Paul Firstenberg argues that the primary role of the board should be to set strategic direction, in consultation with the chief executive, and then to delegate execution to an able staff working under the CEO's direction. Hence, the board's duty is not to undertake day-to-day managerial tasks but to ensure that a competent staff is in place to handle these tasks. However, such a role in no way precludes board members from providing consultative advice in their areas of expertise, attracting external resources, and heading up task forces or ad hoc committees.

When board members become active in implementing programs, they need to recognize that they are serving now as task volunteers, not as board members. Thus an advertising executive should not use her power as a board member to insist that the organization adopt a particular copy theme that she had developed.

Unfortunately, most boards of directors have yet to make a significant contribution to improving the marketing effectiveness of their organizations. This situation is surprising when one considers how many nonprofit boards are largely composed of successful business executives. As Firstenberg observes:

> The board of a not-for-profit institution, with its traditional business membership, ought to be well positioned to press management to think and act in a businesslike fashion as well as to insist that the staff of the organization has the professional competence to conduct the business of the enterprise. But business executives serving on such boards are often hesitant in their role as trustees to be assertive in suggesting that business practices have a place in the management of not-for-profit organizations. As the general manager of a major public broadcasting station put it: "When my trustees come to a board meeting, they seem to check all their business expertise at the door."[8]

Other executives of nonprofits voice similar complaints. How does such a problem arise? Two basic reasons suggest themselves. One may be that the wrong people are being recruited as board members—an issue that we'll address later in this chapter. A second explanation may be that the role of the board as a whole, and the responsibilities of its individual members, have not been made explicit when it comes to marketing. Many boards lack a clear mandate or lack agreement on how that mandate is to be interpreted. An analysis of various arts groups in the Philadelphia area concluded that most of their problems stemmed from the fact that their "boards have, over the years, translated [their] mandate with as much variety as husbands and wives interpret the vows to love, honor, and obey."[9]

While some boards may be guilty of abandoning their business sense, it would be a mistake for directors to assume that the organization should be managed just like a business. At the start of the book, we discussed some of these differences. To illustrate, Isaac Adizes argues for the following view of an artistic organization:

> The purpose of the not-for-profit artistic institution is to enable artists to create and communicate their output to the society at large according to their artistic consciences. The organization should develop the needs of the audience so that the audience will be able to absorb its product, rather than developing a product that is dictated by needs of the existing market.[10]

A board member must be able to recognize that the cost of producing and promoting an activity may far exceed the revenue obtained from it and still be appropriate for the organization. On the other hand, the board member still needs to ask if such an activity represents the best use of available funds, whether the project makes strategic sense, and if the monies are being spent efficiently.

At the beginning of this book, we described marketing as a bridging function that helps link the organization to its environment. In Melissa Middleton's view, the board, too, has the potential to play a vital bridging role:

> Boards are part of *both* the organization and its environment. . . . Boards of directors are part of the organization because they are responsible in the broadest sense for its well-being and for ensuring that it fulfills its stated purpose. They are part of the external environment in the sense that their members are drawn from and often have primary affiliations to other groups in the community. In its position as part of the organization and part of the environment, the board becomes a resource for each to use.[11]

All too often, board members lack a clear understanding of the organization that they are supposedly directing, and of the environment in which it is operating. Without such an understanding, it's unrealistic to assume that board members will feel comfortable in establishing marketing policies, let alone overseeing the execution of existing strategies. We will now turn to a discussion of how to develop greater marketing expertise among board members, and then follow with a look at how to target and attract board members with specific marketing knowledge and/or access to relevant marketing resources.

Developing Marketing Expertise Among Board Members

Assume for the moment that you are the executive director of a nonprofit organization that seeks to develop (or further strengthen) its marketing expertise. Yet few of your board members appear to think in marketing terms when it comes to making policy decisions for your organization, even though several of them are successful business executives. Most of your board members, in fact, seem to perceive marketing as a tactical activity centered on advertising and public relations. Other than giving them this book to read, what can you do to enhance their understanding of marketing?

For starters, it might be unwise to assume that all board members lack expertise in marketing: perhaps they are simply "checking" that expertise at the boardroom door. If a board member works in business, perhaps he or she has had some exposure to marketing at work (or in an educational setting) and has simply not made the connection between a for-profit and a nonprofit setting. Simply drawing some parallels in terms of competition, the elements of the marketing mix, and market segmentation may suffice to encourage such a person to see the potential contribution that marketing can make to your own organization.

Some boards periodically hold a retreat or seminar designed to enhance their knowledge of a particular issue, bringing in outside experts or staff members to lead an educational session. Dedicating such a meeting to the topic of marketing is a good way to build the board's collective understanding of marketing, but the leader needs to be knowledgeable about the types of activity in which the organization is engaged. Board members are not likely to be impressed by a presentation built around illustrations of packaged goods marketing!

If the organization has not conducted a marketing audit previously (or recently), then such a project provides an excellent opportunity to build the board's understanding of key marketing concepts and their relevance to strategic decision-making. Involving them selectively in each of the key stages of the marketing audit and subsequent planning process (see chapters 3 and 5), should help board members recognize the value of a marketing orientation in clarifying the organizational mission, formulating objectives, establishing priorities, and developing specific marketing strategies to achieve those objectives.

Many boards make use of standing or ad hoc committees to help them divide up their work. A growing number of boards are forming marketing committees designed to focus on specific marketing topics or on the broader issue of developing a stronger marketing orientation within the organization. In selecting members to serve on such a committee, the board president and the chief executive should pick individuals who are either knowledgeable about marketing or demonstrate an empathy toward customer concerns.

Attracting the Right Individuals to the Board

What types of marketing skills should a board possess? The answer is going to vary widely with the nature of the organization and the specific situation in which it finds itself.

The board's work in marketing is, of course, only part of its responsibilities. Andrew Swanson recommends creation of a board profile grid, comprising a list of needed skills and connections down the vertical axis and a list of all board members along the horizontal axis.[12]

In Table 19.4, we show sample board profile criteria as these might apply to marketing; not all of these criteria would be relevant for each organization and other criteria might have to be added. Certain needs would undoubtedly be more important than others and should be identified as such. For instance, organizations that emphasize strategic management and consultative advice at the board level should focus on skills in these areas.

By evaluating all current board members against the chosen criteria and rating each member (say on a three-point scale) according to how well he or she met each criterion, gaps or weaknesses in the current board would quickly become apparent.

If significant gaps exist, then new board members with the necessary skills and contacts will have to be sought. Limitations on the size of the board as well as other needs may limit the opportunity to close all the gaps. An alternative is to create an advisory panel to assist the board, recruiting individuals to the former panel with the expectation that they might later be elected to vacant board positions.

Once the gaps have been identified, how does the organization find prospective new board members who meet the relevant profiles? A distinction needs to be made between (1) *personal characteristics* (such as demographics or association with a specific community, market segment, or geographic area), (2) *personal skills* in marketing, and (3) *personal contacts* with organizations or individuals possessing needed expertise. For example, a

Table 19.4 Checklist of Marketing Criteria to be Included in a Board Profile Grid

Potential Criteria	Individual	Rating of Current/Prospective Board Members				
		A	B	C	D	E
1. Technical Skills						
Marketing research		☐	☐	☐	☐	☐
Market/competitive analysis		☐	☐	☐	☐	☐
Marketing information systems		☐	☐	☐	☐	☐
Product design and evaluation		☐	☐	☐	☐	☐
Retail facility design		☐	☐	☐	☐	☐
Pricing		☐	☐	☐	☐	☐
2. Strategic/Executional Skills						
Managing retail outlets		☐	☐	☐	☐	☐
Catalog sales		☐	☐	☐	☐	☐
Personal selling/sales management		☐	☐	☐	☐	☐
Advertising and promotion		☐	☐	☐	☐	☐
Public Relations/publicity		☐	☐	☐	☐	☐
Telemarketing		☐	☐	☐	☐	☐
Direct mail		☐	☐	☐	☐	☐
Customer service		☐	☐	☐	☐	☐
Fund raising and gift solicitation		☐	☐	☐	☐	☐
Recruiting volunteers		☐	☐	☐	☐	☐
3. Market Knowledge and Contacts						
Demographic segments (e.g., youth, elderly, ethnic)		☐	☐	☐	☐	☐
Geographic areas (e.g., regions, cities, neighborhoods)		☐	☐	☐	☐	☐
Business community		☐	☐	☐	☐	☐
Prospective donors (by category)		☐	☐	☐	☐	☐

bank president may not be a marketing expert yet may still be able to volunteer expert assistance from the bank's strategic planning, marketing research, and corporate communications departments.

Once a short list of prospective new directors has been prepared, the next task is that of recruitment. Although the same basic approach applies here as to any type of volunteer, it must be recognized that individuals of board caliber are often busy and successful people who are much sought after by other organizations. Understanding the prospect's needs and expectations is critically important. When a prospective director or trustee is deciding whether or not to join a specific board, he or she may even be evaluating a similar invitation from a competing organization. Arthur Frantzreb describes the recruiting approach used by one highly regarded manager.

> Perhaps the greatest and most successful volunteer manager was the general secretary [executive director] of a downtown division of the Chicago YMCA. The institution was housed in a disadvantaged area largely leveled by attempts at urban modernization.

Yet some four to five hundred guest rooms had to be occupied for budgetary reasons, an enormous cafeteria service had to be profitable, and community outreach services and needs were enormous.

The secretary prepared a four-foot by four-foot photo album of activities and functions of his institution, which he kept up-to-date. He studied the newspapers carefully to learn who the principal leaders of Chicago were and what they were doing, and he asked questions about leadership all the time. He designed the type of board committees he needed to address forty-four issues threatening the institution's financial survival. He used existing board members in all these planning functions to upgrade membership and to expand functional capabilities.

When he decided to visit a new volunteer prospect with a present board member . . . they took the album. At the appropriate time the album was opened on the floor. It was designed to be too big to put on any table. The prospect, the present trustee, and the secretary had to get down on their hands and knees to "get into the Y itself." It always worked.

Across the desk from the secretary, on the opposite wall conveniently covered by a curtain when necessary, were two things: the list of committees by member and forty four issues assigned to respective committees. Each member, each committee, and each issue were constantly visible to the secretary. Each day or at least once a week he was in telephone communication with each chairman. He was careful not to harass or embarrass any of them. The Y prospered. The board of trustees was the envy of every organization. The trustees were involved, constructive, highly motivated; they addressed real issues, and were well staffed to ensure that their time was used well.[13]

SUMMARY

Virtually all incorporated nonprofit organizations, as well as many public agencies, are served by a volunteer board of directors. Many nonprofits and a few public institutions (notably schools) also make extensive use of volunteers at all levels in the organization. Indeed, many nonprofits could not survive without volunteers' services.

Marketing direction must come from the top. Hence success in marketing efforts requires a board and a chief executive who recognize the competitive nature of the marketplace and are committed to understanding and meeting customer needs. Indeed, without this necessary marketing orientation at the top, it's unlikely that the organization can articulate a market-centered mission statement, develop a strategic marketing plan, or implement marketing strategies effectively.

The make-up of the board should reflect the need to include some individuals with marketing skills and others with connections to expert suppliers of marketing services, such as advertising, marketing research, and conducting marketing audits. But all members of the board, regardless of background, need to be sensitized to marketing issues. Retreats, internal seminars, and involvement in outside programs are all potential ways for board members to develop the necessary orientation.

Recruiting and managing board members and other volunteers has much in common with fundraising, in that management must understand what each prospective volunteer hopes to gain from donating time and effort to the organization. The difference, of course, between attracting volunteers and attracting contributions is that donated time requires an ongoing interaction with the organization.

Managers should never assume that individuals who donate their time will automatically be motivated by the mere fact of participation in the organization's activities. Participation alone is not sufficient to motivate a volunteer's best efforts nor to retain his or her interest. Careful definition of volunteers' responsibilities and tasks in the first instance, followed by sensitive direction of their performance, are two prerequisites for a successful volunteer program.

REFERENCES

1. For a broader discussion of brokerage management, see David H. Maister and Christopher H. Lovelock, "Managing Facilitator Services," *Sloan Management Review* (Summer 1982).
2. Eva Schindler-Rainman, "Volunteers: An Indispensable Human Resource in a Democratic Society," in T. D. Connors (ed), *The Nonprofit Organization Handbook,* New York: McGraw-Hill, 1980, p. 3.3–3.59.
3. This section is based on findings reported in *Americans Volunteer,* prepared by the Gallup Organization, Inc. for Independent Sector, Washington, DC, 1981; and *The Charitable Behavior of Americans,* conducted by Yankelovich, Skelly and White, Inc. for the Rockefeller Brothers Fund, Washington, DC: Independent Sector, 1986.
4. Interview with Betty Baker, Career and Volunteer Advisory Service, Boston, 1983.
5. Condensed from Christopher H. Lovelock, "Stanford University: The Annual Fund," in C. H. Lovelock and C. B. Weinberg, *Public and Nonprofit Marketing: Cases and Readings,* New York: John Wiley & Sons with the Scientific Press, 1984.
6. Miriam M. Wood, "What Role for College Trustees?" *Harvard Business Review,* May–June 1983, pp. 52–62.
7. Wood, as reference 6, p. 58.
8. Paul B. Firstenberg, *Managing for Profit in the Nonprofit World,* New York: The Foundation Center, 1986, p. 205.
9. Quoted in Melissa Middleton, "Nonprofit Boards of Directors: Beyond the Governance Function," in Walter W. Powell (ed.) *The Nonprofit Sector: A Research Handbook,* New Haven, CT: Yale University Press, 1987, pp. 141–153.
10. Isaac Adizes, "The Cost of Being an Artist," *California Management Review* (Summer 1975).
11. Middleton, as reference 9, p. 141.
12. Andrew Swanson, "Put Some Life Into Your Board!," *Nonprofit World,* January–February 1987, p. 32.
13. Arthur C. Frantzreb, "Management of Volunteers," in A. W. Rowland (ed.), *Handbook of Institutional Advancement,* 1977, pp. 140–141. Copyright by Jossey-Bass Inc., San Francisco. Reprinted by permission.

Chapter 20

Managing Retail &
Catalog Sales Operations

Retail operations, once regarded as alien or inappropriate activities by managers of public and nonprofit organizations, are now generating more and more interest. Museum shops have expanded from so-called sales desks selling cards and posters to large, carefully laid out stores offering a range of distinctive products often unavailable elsewhere. Hospital shops provide one-stop shopping for magazines, flowers, sundries, cards, small gifts, and other products serving the needs of patients and their visitors. Even a subsidized public transportation service such as London Transport sells postcards, tea towels, mugs, and tote bags with a transit theme, as well as a wide selection of books and posters. Many nonprofit organizations without their own shops have begun selling merchandise through the mail; others use direct-mail sales to extend and supplement on-site shops. As shown in Table 20.1, a wide range of public and nonprofit organizations are now engaged in the retail sale of ancillary products.

The principal reason for this growing participation in retail operations is economic. As operating costs continue to rise, while former mainstays of support such as endowment income and government allocations shrink or remain almost stagnant, new revenue sources become imperative. Hence increasing emphasis is being placed on user charges (see Chapter 11, "Developing Monetary Pricing Strategies") and on the income generated from such ancillary activities as educational programs, publishing, merchandise operations, rental of facilities to outside groups, restaurants, garages, royalties, advertising revenues, and other fees.

In 1986, gross revenues from merchandise and ancillary services at Boston's Museum of Fine Arts amounted to $12.5 million, or 43 percent of total support and revenue, up from $4.7 million (34 percent of income) in 1982.

Several other factors have also contributed to nonprofit managers' growing interest in retail activity. Sales of products connected to an organization's history or collection contribute to its educational mission and allow it to reach a wider public. From the consumer standpoint, such products can add beauty or interest to the home environment and serve as pleasant souvenirs of a museum visit or an afternoon at a historic home. High-quality reproductions may be treated like artwork in the home of the purchaser. The

Table 20.1 Examples of Retail and Catalog Sales Operations

Organization	Products and/or Markets	Example of Scope
National postal services	Stamps for philatelists	Amounts to $100+ million in sales to U.S. Postal Service, with a high gross profit margin
National government mints	Proof or uncirculated coins and medals for numismatists	Royal Canadian Mint sells coins struck on behalf of 11 nations (including Canada)
Planned Parenthood Federation and other family planning organizations	Contraceptives	Planned Parenthood has 189 affiliated clinics throughout the United States that supply contraceptives at or below cost, depending on the client's ability to pay
London Transport retail shops	Books, posters, postcards, and a variety of transit-related souvenirs	London Transport operates two retail stores and a large catalog sales business
Government printing office bookstores	Books, pamphlets, reports, maps, etc.	Sales for U.S. Superintendent of Documents exceed $50 million
University campus bookstores	Books, stationery, art supplies, souvenirs, records, etc.	Range from stores selling primarily course-related books and associated supplies to large-scale retail operations (e.g., U. of British Columbia, Stanford University)
Performing-arts organizations	Posters, souvenirs, books, records, films related to the organization or the particular event	National Theatre store in London serves all three theaters in NT complex
Behavioral-change organizations	T-shirts, bumper stickers, banners, publications	Action on Smoking and Health sells by mail a variety of products emblazoned with provocative slogans; Sierra Club publishes high-quality books and calendars on environmental topics sold direct or through retail stores
Museums, stately homes, zoos, aquariums, wildlife refuges	Museum shops and catalogs	Varies from an on-site shop selling a few limited items (e.g., Massachusetts Audubon Society) to extensive wholesale or mail-order operations as at the Metropolitan Museum in New York

Sierra Club book and calendar program, with its emphasis on fine photographs, enhances appreciation for the environment and the Sierra Club's cause. Some products, such as "Save the Whales" T-shirts, call public attention to a political or social position supported by the wearer. By keeping an organization's identity before the eyes of the public and occasionally attracting the attention of the media, retail operations can reinforce the image and aid the larger marketing effort of the entire institution.

On the other hand, engaging in retail activities is no panacea for an organization that is in financial difficulties because of insufficient support for its core service. Nor may this be an appropriate step even for a healthy organization. Running a retail operation involves risks. In the private sector, the turnover among small retailers is high—not least among arts and crafts shops and theme restaurants. Even large chains have fallen into bankruptcy in recent years. Moreover, building up and maintaining an effective retail store or mail catalog operation requires both money and time. Managers of nonbusiness organizations who are tempted by the profit potential of ancillary activities should ask themselves: "Can we afford the opportunity cost involved in diverting resources from our core activity?"

Scope of the Chapter

In this chapter, we will discuss the most important issues in managing and marketing retail operations on behalf of a public or nonprofit institution. Many ancillary activities—including licensing, wholesaling, holding classes, and operating restaurants and bars—also offer opportunities to generate significant revenues. Because a comprehensive treatment of these subjects would require examination of management issues outside the specific focus of this book, we will restrict our discussion to retailing. Our approach concentrates on common concerns and insights most readily transferable among a wide range of nonbusiness organizations. Drawing from recent interviews with retail managers, we will discuss the implementation as well as the conception of retailing strategy.

We begin our discussion with a look at the Mystic Seaport Museum Store, whose revenues more than quadrupled in six years, even as attendance at the museum itself declined. Consideration of the advantages and disadvantages of Mystic's highly commercial approach leads to an examination of the often controversial task of establishing appropriate commercial objectives for a nonbusiness organization. Then we consider direct involvement by management in retail operations. A series of strategic issues follow, beginning with the problem of selecting merchandise. Should an organization conduct a small retail operation offering only a limited range of products, or operate a major retail establishment serving a wide range of consumers with an extensive product line? One complication is the liability for taxes; in order for profits from the sale of merchandise to remain tax-exempt, the nature of the products sold must be closely related to an organization's mission. How can this relationship be defined? Within this restriction, what kind of products should be offered? Pricing, a central concern for many nonbusiness organizations, is particularly important to the success of a retailing operation. Under what circumstances should an organization price its merchandise at, above, or below private-sector competition?

Perhaps the biggest decision may be whether to conduct retail operations on site, in separate shops, or through the mail. In either case, a host of secondary questions arise. For example, how does a museum (or similar visitor attraction) decide where to locate its shop? When and where should "branch" satellite sales desks be set up? Should a postal service set up separate counters for philatelists? Should a family-planning clinic sell its products to people who are not its clients? if so, should the clinic open retail shops outside of clinic premises and/or sell by mail?

Finally, we consider the communication strategies most useful in bringing a retail operation to the attention of the public. Further communication is imperative if curators, administrators, and other internal personnel are to accept, understand, and appreciate an organization's retail activities.

As this brief overview indicates, successful management of retail operations is a complex and demanding responsibility, requiring an understanding of the entire marketing mix, as well as skills in such other managerial functions as labor relations, accounting and control, and operations management. It is unwise to assign this responsibility to an unskilled volunteer or to an employee who has dabbled in sales, but that practice has been the rule, not the exception, in the past.

THE MYSTIC SEAPORT MUSEUM STORE[1]

The Mystic Seaport Museum is a nonprofit maritime museum whose 40 outdoor exhibits occupy 17 acres along Connecticut's Mystic River. The local community, also known as Mystic, is a small seacoast settlement about 100 miles northeast of New York City. Easily accessible via interstate highway and Amtrak rail service, the Mystic area also contains the Mystic Marinelife Aquarium. Together, the aquarium and the museum attracted about 800,000 paying visitors in 1980, making Mystic the most popular tourist destination in the state. Over 100 retail shops are also located in Mystic, about 70 of them clustered in Old Mystic Village, a mall near the museum designed to resemble a small colonial town.

The museum defines its mission as "to preserve materials, artifacts, vessels, and skills relating to maritime history in order to enhance man's knowledge of the sea's influence on American life." The museum's collection is frequently visited by academic researchers from around the world and is recognized as one of the leading North American maritime museums. The collection includes 200 small boats and three larger ships open to visitors. Exhibits range from collections of scrimshaw and ship figureheads to a restored schoolhouse, a ship's chandlery, and a collection of navigational instruments. The library's collection numbers over 40,000 original manuscripts and volumes; and the museum's members, distributed through all 50 states and 15 foreign countries, total about 16,000.

The Mystic Seaport Museum Store is a wholly owned, for-profit subsidiary of the museum that competes actively with other local retailers. All after-tax profits go to the museum. "We do not hide our competitive activities under a nonprofit umbrella," explained Thomas Aageson, the store's president. "We pay taxes to the town, the state, and the federal government, just like our competitors. We're successful because we're good—not because we have a tax advantage."

The main Mystic store includes 8900 square feet of selling area spread over two floors in a colonial-style building located just outside the museum's south gate. The major traffic route from Interstate 95 into the town of Mystic is a few hundred feet away, bordered by a large parking lot. (A satellite 1700-square-foot store is operated inside the museum grounds, carrying postcards, candy, T-shirts, and inexpensive collectibles.)

Aageson believes that a museum shop located in a small community "can be dedicated to the museum visitor alone, or to the local community as well. If the latter, it must be more diversified and offer a wider range of goods" than the specifically service-related or education-related merchandise declared exempt by tax authorities. The Mystic Seaport Museum Store's merchandise ranges from inexpensive souvenirs to original paintings and ship models costing several thousand dollars. Articles carried are grouped in 12 "environments" or thematic areas, including apparel, a bakeshop, dolls and toys, crystal, a Victorian Christmas shop, home furnishings, and an extensive maritime bookstore. Many of the products are not specifically related to a maritime theme, but to New England, which is part of the purpose. According to Aageson, "Poor merchandising is one of the most common mistakes a museum store can make. You go in and it's junky—no sense of theme or order. The buying is done by committee, and it shows. Our gate charges for the museum are $7.50 adult, $3.50 children. If people pay that kind of money, they've been in the best of shops; we have to have the products and the merchandising to compete." Mystic's prices, too, are competitive, with markups comparable to those in leading retail stores.

Between 1975 and 1980, while sales in the Mystic Museum Store rose from $800,000 to over $3 million, annual attendance at the museum declined from 504,000 to 404,000. Nevertheless, Aageson believes his operation enjoys much support from the curatorial staff. "They're very supportive," he remarked, "and think we have a terrific bookstore." Aageson's plans include expanding the store's mail-order sales. The store's catalog mailings are received by more than half-a-million households. He rents mailing lists from other organizations, including private-sector retailers such as L. L. Bean, but will not make Mystic's own list available to competitors. Aageson also plans to continue improving the skills of his sales staff, having earlier invested in a sales-training program for two key personnel, who then trained the remainder of the museum's 34-person paid sales staff. Aageson's management strategy is to pay employees well and keep them highly motivated.

An Appraisal

The Mystic Museum Store—a retail operation that has taken on a corporate, for-profit life of its own—has achieved high profits while maintaining a strongly commercial approach that may not be acceptable to many nonprofit institutions. The real key to Mystic's success lies in management's ability to:

- Set distinct objectives, supported by the institution as a whole.
- Establish a level of institutional involvement that falls within the museum's capacities.
- Develop merchandising, pricing, and distribution strategies through which the central objectives may be achieved.

In the balance of this chapter we will consider an array of retail operations of widely differing sizes, with many varying objectives. Despite these differences, *all* share the same fundamental marketing and management problems. One of the most important common issues is how to balance the conflicting claims of commerce and education or service. Whether it be a large bookstore operated by a city art museum or a small gift shop run by a branch of a national wildlife protection agency, each retail operation managed by a nonprofit organization must constantly assess the nature of its relationship to the organization's mission. At no time is this more important than during the start of retail operations and the process of setting objectives.

DETERMINING INSTITUTIONAL OBJECTIVES AND INVOLVEMENT

The first step in beginning a retail operation is to establish a set of objectives. This task should involve senior management, since it raises the question: to what extent should the retail operation attempt to advance the mission of the institution? As noted in Chapter 9,

"Product Offerings," management should strive for consistency and synergy between the various products—goods, services, and social-behavior programs—contained in the organization's product portfolio. Managers initiating new retail operations can use Figure 20.1 to address the question of objectives by locating their operation on a grid, depending on the extent to which their retail objective is to make profits and the extent to which the nature of the products offered is expected to advance the institution's educational or service mission.

Profit-oriented strategies can lead to one of two extremes, neither of which may be compatible with the organization's overall goals. One approach is to offer a limited range of high-price (high-margin) merchandise that will appeal to only a small subset of consumers. The organization conducts a limited retail operation, saving on costs, and relying on the exclusivity and inherent quality of its merchandise. The national mints of several countries do this when they offer to sell collectors special proof-coin sets. At the other extreme is a strategy oriented toward volume sales of mass-produced items, some of which are only tangentially related to the organization's overall purpose. Museums and exhibitions that are tourist attractions, such as the Mystic Seaport, often see this as a viable option, relying on selling to partially "captive" consumers who may be more susceptible to point-of-sale merchandising at the end of a pleasant visit. Such an approach may not be acceptable to museums and other organizations dedicated to educating public taste. Moreover, the broader the product line, the more likely it is to draw the ire of private-sector competition and the investigation of local and national tax authorities.

The critical issue is to make an explicit choice about profit orientation, and then to develop a product line and retailing philosophy to support the chosen orientation. This choice should reflect not just a desire for profits, but also organizational mission and market factors, including product-market fit and product-organization fit.

Managers should recognize that a line of high-quality, expensive, and specialized merchandise may not generate many sales. Although an exclusive strategy may sometimes be profitable, it often results in financial loss because the merchandise range is too narrow to generate the necessary volume. In some instances, taking a loss on such an operation may be regarded as an investment in advancing the institutional mission. In practice, few nonprofit managers can afford to operate a shop or produce a catalog that loses money or barely breaks even, no matter how closely it appears to conform to an educational mission. If profits are important, the money spent on any retail operation returning less than market

	Monetary Goals		
Product—Mission Fit	Profit Oriented	Break Even	Loss as "Investment"
Retail products actively advance institutional mission			
Retail products compatible with institutional mission			
Retail products unrelated to institutional mission			

Figure 20.1 Alternate objectives for retail operations.

rates might be better invested in the organization's endowment. Managers should also recognize that retailing strategies that only appeal to upper-income segments of patrons or enthusiasts risk generating ill will among the bulk of the institution's users and supporters.

Setting objectives for a retail operation clearly requires a good understanding of an organization's customers—their income, age, sex, geographic distribution, values, and expectations. For instance, in selecting merchandise for the store at a zoo, aquarium, or museum visited by large numbers of schoolchildren, it would be appropriate to assume that a good deal of teaching would take place during the visit and that children shopping for souvenirs of their trip would prefer inexpensive posters, jewelry, or collectibles. The objective for this market segment might be to stock articles that provide a pleasant reminder of the visit, priced at levels that will yield a profit yet remain within a school-child's budget.

Finally, at least some of the objectives set for a retail operation should be quantifiable. As we noted earlier, because of the noncommercial nature of public and nonprofit organizations, their managers often find it difficult to set quantifiable goals and measure performance objectively. In retail operations, this kind of goal setting is not only possible but also imperative. What net income is needed to satisfy immediate operating needs? What percentage markup (gross profit margin) is financially and philosophically best for the organization? What gross sales level should be targeted? Frequently, managers will be able to set reasonable financial goals for their retail operations by drawing on the experience of other nonprofit organizations. In New England, for example, museum-shop managers gather annually to share and compare operating data from the previous year. Statistics kept include sales, sales per square foot, sales per visitor, gross profit margins, inventory turn, sales per transaction, and sales by mail order and through wholesale intermediaries.

While total museum store sales in the United States now exceed $200 million annually, sales for individual stores may range from less than $5000 to the $34.5 million reported in a recent year by the Smithsonian Institution in Washington, D.C.[2] The type of merchandise sold in museum stores varies as much as the institutions themselves: the Mystic Seaport Museum in Connecticut sells a wooden ship model for $10,000, but the most popular item at the Smithsonian is a $1.25 bar of freeze-dried ice cream, similar to what space shuttle passengers might eat. The size of the retail facility can vary, too. Some museums have minimal shops; the Smithsonian has nine stores and a mail-order catalogue. Operating data from other organizations can help shop managers establish targets for their own stores, although managers must be careful to select data from a comparable institution, operating under broadly similar conditions to their own. Aided by such guidelines, as well as by reliable sales forecasting, the task of setting quantifiable objectives becomes less intimidating. Good record keeping will identify sales trends, out-of-stock problems, and other important operating data, and also facilitate objective setting. Even if explicit guidelines are unavailable, objectives must still be set in advance as a guide to planning, execution, and performance appraisal.

Level of Involvement in Retail Operations

Having determined their retailing objectives, managers must then decide how deeply involved in retail operations they wish the organization to become. As Figure 20.2 shows, the level of involvement, like objective setting, can range widely. In the top left-hand box can be found large organizations such as New York City's Metropolitan Museum of Art

Channels of Distribution	Nature of Merchandise				
	Produce to Own Design	Commission Production to Own Design	Select Products, then Add Own Label	Select Other Branded Products	Delegate Selection to Outside Firm
Own shop					
Own catalog					
Concession shop					
Concession catalog					

Figure 20.2 Levels of institutional involvement in merchandise selection and sale.

and the United States Postal Service, with a good deal of working capital and considerable retailing expertise. These institutions produce most or all of their merchandise and sell it themselves in their own shops (or retail post offices) or through direct mail. Organizations with somewhat smaller but still well-capitalized retail operations often design much of their own merchandise, but usually commission its manufacture, then sell the finished goods themselves. A number of smaller countries produce commemorative stamps in just this way; some leave the marketing of proof coin sets outside their country to major mints such as the Royal Canadian Mint or British Royal Mint.

On the right side of the horizontal axis of Figure 20.2 are organizations that sell a relatively small number of articles directly identifiable with the institution (such as tote bags stamped with a name or logo), but offer numerous other articles, such as books, that are related to the institution's mission or collection interests. Washington's Folger Shakespeare Library, for example, sells only a few items immediately associated with the Folger name but offers a wide variety of articles pertaining to Shakespeare and Elizabethan drama, history, and culture, including a series of posters produced by the *Times* of London, depicting Shakespeare's characters, and a do-it-yourself model of an Elizabethan theater. In addition to organizations running their own stores, the vertical axis shows organizations that sell products through their own mail-order catalogs, preferring to avoid on-site retail involvement—or to obtain a broader market by adding a distribution channel with a wider reach.

The most limited form of involvement in distribution activities is represented in Figure 20.2 by organizations that delegate retail responsibilities almost entirely to outside agencies. Many souvenir shops in the U.S. national parks, for example, are managed by for-profit concessionaires. As we discuss in detail later, the Washington-based Center for Environmental Education (CEE), sponsor of well-known campaigns to save whales, seals, and sea turtles from extinction, decided to turn over its catalog operation to a consulting firm that specializes in managing direct-mail sales for nonprofit organizations. CEE's subsequent royalties from catalog sales exceeded the net income it took in while managing the catalog singlehandedly. Moreover, CEE is also free of many of the headaches involved in direct-mail retailing, such as maintaining inventory and running a packing and shipping operation.

Many considerations enter into an organization's discussion of the problem of institutional involvement. Some organizations, eager to augment income but reluctant to take on a new enterprise, may choose to follow CEE's course. Others that prefer to manage their own retailing operations may find that their size and working capital limit the type and number of specially commissioned products they can obtain, It is important to keep in mind that a decision to minimize or relinquish day-to-day institutional involvement must never lead to a relinquishment or loss of institutional control over retail sales. CEE still reviews and approves every article sold in the "Whale Gifts" catalog, well aware that this merchandise will be instrumental in helping to shape the public's perception of the organization. Managers who have delegated primary responsibility for decisions on merchandise selection, pricing, distribution, and similar strategic questions to outside agents should keep abreast of those decisions and maintain final veto power at all times.

MERCHANDISE ISSUES

Having set satisfactory objectives and determined the desired degree of institutional involvement in retailing, managers face a number of strategic decisions. The first is determining what articles their shop or catalog will carry.

Proximity of Merchandise to Mission

The key task in selecting retail merchandise is to decide how closely such merchandise should reflect the institution's mission. An art museum opting for close proximity of merchandise to mission might decide to sell only cards, prints, posters, and art reproductions, all drawn from its own collection. A more commercial, yet still mission-related, strategy would be to augment these offerings by "translating" items or designs in the collection into apparel, decorative objects, and other goods. Boston's Museum of Fine Arts (MFA), for example, sells a popular cast-iron trivet (pot rest) whose design was taken from a decorative brass adorning a Grecian couch. These products could be augmented even further by cards and prints reproducing works of art in the collection of another museum, ordered from that museum at wholesale rates.

Moving further from products unique to the institution, a museum might choose to carry products related to its mission or collection, but also available in competing private-sector shops. The MFA, like many other nonprofit institutions, has pursued this strategy by carrying a large selection of books. Indeed, with over 3000 titles in stock, the MFA museum store considers itself the best-equipped art bookstore in Boston. Similarly, the Smithsonian's National Air and Space Museum, located in Washington, D.C., carries a wide selection of do-it-yourself airplane models, many of which are also sold in local hobby shops.

The next step along the merchandise continuum is a risky one, but it has been taken by several institutions. This strategy is to sell functional or decorative merchandise such as ashtrays, keyrings, dish towels, hats, and T-shirts unrelated to the institutional mission, but emblazoned with the institutional name or logo. Additional products may be items that fit the general retail orientation of the store and round out the array of merchandise available there. These products, which can hardly be called educational, are essentially a way to make money for an institution and—in the case of souvenirs—to promote it.

The risks in carrying an overtly commercial line of retail products are threefold. First, the profits the activity produces may be judged taxable. Second, the image of the core institution may be blurred, demeaned, or obscured. Third, there is an opportunity cost attached to the time spent by senior management in planning and supervising the retail operation—time that could otherwise have been devoted to fund raising or advancing the central mission of the organization.

The Problem of Taxable Revenue

In the United States, the federal income tax code requires that all articles sold by a public or nonprofit organization must be substantially related to the charitable or educational purpose constituting the basis for the organization's federal income tax exemption (the so-called primary-purpose test). Income from unrelated trade or business activities is taxable, even though the institution itself may remain exempt.

The primary purpose of this "unrelated-business" income tax (UBIT) is to eliminate what might be perceived as unfair competition with nonexempt businesses (i.e., private enterprise). Private-sector competitors may not be selling copies of an obscure pre-Raphaelite painting, but they are certainly selling ashtrays, keyrings, and T-shirts whose aesthetic quality is the equivalent of those sold in a museum. Thus, although a nonprofit organization may be exempt from taxation on any revenue-generating activities related to its primary purpose, it cannot use this exemption as an umbrella to protect unrelated activities that are carried on, like those of any business, mainly to earn a profit. The criteria employed by the tax authorities in deciding whether or not to tax the profits of these ancillary activities should be reviewed at regular intervals, since they may be subject to change.

Quality, Price, and Design Issues

Determining the proximity of merchandise to mission involves further dilemmas outside the tax question. Most managers of historic sites would agree that a slide set depicting the site's attractions would be appropriate to the institution's mission, and popular with consumers as well, but how good should the quality of the slides be? At one nationally known historic site, this question aroused a good deal of conflict between the merchandising and audiovisual departments of the organization responsible for its administration. Merchandising obtained a slide and cassette package, including 40 slides plus a 25-minute cassette, from an outside supplier. According to the audiovisual department, these slides were made on motion picture stock and would fade in five years. Audiovisual's own slides were of archivist quality, with a 15–20-year life expectancy; at more than double the price, however, they were much less popular with consumers. As nonprofit retail operations continue to grow, many managers will be confronted by such dilemmas and should anticipate them in determining how closely the objectives of retail operations should mesh with those of the core institution.

The range of prices represented by a store or catalog's merchandise should reflect the nature of the market served. There is little point in carrying goods priced beyond the budgets of most visitors, no matter how much they may appeal to curators or trustees. One major aquarium originally offered very high-priced, high-quality merchandise (such as 14-karat gold charms) in its shop, much of it selected by the institution's trustees and their families. Even if such articles had been desired by the middle-class families, tourists, and school groups that composed most of the aquarium's visitors, their prices placed them beyond reach. When the product mix was changed to emphasize inexpensive collectibles, sales rose substantially and the shop has since become very successful.

Even after reviewing the considerations outlined here, managers will still find themselves left with a large field of potential offerings from which to choose. *Uniqueness,* many such retailers believe, is the key to high sales. By reproducing articles in their collections or using these articles as the inspiration for a design, many nonprofit institutions have developed unique, profitable, highly creative merchandise available nowhere else. The New York Botanical Garden, for example, sells an umbrella representing the glass dome of the garden's conservatory, as well as a quilted canvas tote bag decorated with reproductions of medieval floral prints. Pittsburgh's Carnegie Institute adapted a silk-screened scarf from a work by French artist Henri Matisse. The shop at the Heard Museum of Anthropology in Phoenix sells handmade Navajo rugs.

Art museums, of course, are particularly fortunate in possessing a wealth of "translatable" designs. Other institutions should not feel limited to cards and posters. The Henry Francis Du Pont Winterthur Museum of early American decorative arts in Delaware, which has successfully sold cards, books, posters, and art reproductions, has developed a profitable plant shop, selling shrubs and plants identical to those cultivated in the estate's extensive gardens. The Metropolitan Transit Authority in New York has received royalties from licensing its colorful subway map for reproduction on T-shirts and jigsaw puzzles, but some other U.S. transit authorities have missed this opportunity due to failure to copyright their subway maps. London Transport (LT) runs an extensive retail operation, with products reflecting its own transit services and other transport-related themes. The great majority of the items incorporate visual themes based on current or historical LT vehicles, posters, maps, and signs. LT operates two retail stores, one outside an underground station in central London and another at the London Transport Museum. A mail-order department sells to both individuals and bulk purchasers. Table 20.2 summarizes the scope of this operation.

Display

The display of merchandise within a store is a creative art as well as an operational function. A prolonged discussion of display is outside the province of this book, but managers of retail stores operated by public and nonprofit organizations should realize the extent to which marketing objectives can be achieved through display. Chief among these objectives are serving customers' needs (thereby generating sales), and communicating the desired image of the institution.

In developing their display of goods (a process known in retailing as "merchandising" a store), managers will frequently find that the needs of customers, as discerned through marketing research, do not coincide with those of the store or its personnel. In other words, displays and stocking arrangements that may be convenient in operating the store

Table 20.2 Scope of London Transport Retail Products

1. Reproductions of LT poster designs

   - Full size
   - Postcard size
   - Table mats

2. Picture postcards

   - Color photos of modern LT equipment
   - Sepia photos of antique LT equipment

3. Books about LT

   - Historical
   - Current system
   - Visitor's guides to places accessible by LT
   - Detailed bus and train schedules

4. Linen tea towels

5. Tote bags and carrier bags

6. T-shirts and sweatshirts

7. Lapel badges and buttons

8. Playing cards with LT map on the back

9. Jigsaw puzzles

10. Aprons in cotton and vinyl

11. Souvenir serving trays and mugs depicting LT buses or the underground map

12. Drink coasters depicting station signs and historical LT vehicles

13. Wall plaques depicting historical LT vehicles

14. Stickers reproducing the LT symbol or the LT "No Smoking" sign

15. Stationery, drawing books, and scrapbooks

Source. As described in London Transport retail catalog, "Memories Are Made Like This."

may prove inconvenient or even displeasing to those who shop in it. A decision to resolve this dilemma by emphasizing the needs of the institution rather than its customers will frequently result in a loss of good will, a loss of sales, or both.

During the 1970s, for example, the U.S. Postal Service decided that three-tiered, four-sided philatelic display units would increase the sale of commemorative stamps. Accordingly, these displays were sent to local post offices with instructions for use. Unfortunately, many local postmasters and personnel thought the displays cluttered the post office when placed a few feet into the lobby area (as instructed) and decided to place them against the wall, thereby blocking at least 25 percent of the stamps from public view.

The Metropolitan Museum of Art, on the other hand, made customer concerns a key issue in designing the display area of its new bookstore, a five-floor structure comprising over 15,000 square feet of space. Bradford D. Keller, vice president and publisher of museum publications, explained as follows.

We studied the design of lots of bookstores before deciding we would strive for a feeling of lightness. Working with another management firm that understands bookstore merchandising, we opted for the see-through fixtures and display cubes that invite the customer to browse rather than wall fixtures and gondolas that create barriers. Bookstores, we think, can be deadly if they are set up like big barns without architecture that effectively disperses traffic. We wanted good traffic flow and lots of small intimate areas.[3]

By inviting customers to browse freely—that is, to experience the books without buying them—the Metropolitan may also be fulfilling educational objectives. At the other extreme, a museum that shows customers only a single display copy of each book—a copy that may be inconvenient to examine or even inaccessible—is perhaps simplifying its operational chores (storage, maintenance, loss prevention) but is neither serving nor educating customers as much as it could.

Sometimes, of course, operational and marketing needs will coincide. Museum shops that rely heavily on volunteer labor find it useful to place large printed price tags next to every item displayed. Sales transactions are expedited because the volunteer salespeople do not have to keep checking prices; from their side of the counter, customers can also discern prices at a glance.

Special Requirements for Mail-Order Sales

Choosing merchandise to be sold through the mail presents a few special problems. Thomas Hoving, the former director of the Metropolitan Museum of Art, suggested that the following points are of particular note in developing the mail-order catalog.[4]

- Diversity of product—the beauty of color prints and postcards, the glowing aura of porcelain, the strength of sculpture, the warmth of needlepoint, the richness of jewelry.
- Superior photography—mostly color, but not all. Black and white can enhance many things.
- Clarity and romance of description—particularly true of museum items.
- Ease of obtaining the catalog. Not only the mailings, but catalogs sent to new members, handed out in shops, and available at exhibitions. One effective approach used at the Metropolitan has been to advertise the catalog in newspapers for a nominal price—say, half a dollar. This covers much of the cost of mailing and cuts out people who are more interested in collecting catalogs than in purchasing the items featured in them.
- Continual quality control.

To generate catalog sales, an item must photograph well, particularly if only black and white film is used. The problem of attractively photographing items of clothing is often best solved by displaying them on models. Sometimes, especially where a unique design has been employed, a detail of this design may usefully be enlarged for close inspection. Unless the organization is highly skilled in photography and layout, it is probably best to employ the services of a firm that specializes in development of gift catalogs for this type of work.

Merchandise sold through the mail should resist breakage (otherwise, it will require more packing matter and thus incur more cost to the institution). It should also be easy to keep in stock, since sellouts and delays in handling often result in a loss of customer goodwill. Some managers may not initially realize the inventory task involved in selling, say, a T-shirt through the mail. At the very least, the shirt will have to be stocked in three sizes—small, medium, and large. Children's sizes, a range of colors, and a choice of "cuts" add even more stock-keeping units (SKUs) to keep track of. Frequently, it is also necessary to decide whether all T-shirt "messages" or slogans will be carried in all sizes.

Finally, and most important, managers should realize that in choosing merchandise for a mail-order catalog, they are building an institutional image that may reach thousands of people who have never visited the institution itself. In this situation it is tempting to bypass cheaper, less prestigious merchandise in favor of expensive items that reflect a more lofty positioning. As long as the catalog meets the needs of existing customers and offers products priced at a markup that reflects institutional objectives, a decision to forego cheaper merchandise may in fact be wise. As noted later, mail order is an expensive form of retail distribution, and an organization inviting cheap single-item catalog sales may be courting disaster.

PRICING STRATEGY

To what extent should prices be set at levels that recover all related costs? The director of audiovisual programs at a large national historic foundation declared:

> There should be no relationship between cost and income generated in making decisions about what we do. When the day comes that we produce films only if we expect to get our costs back, I'll resign. Our concern is to reach the largest number of people we can.[5]

By contrast, the merchandising manager of a museum store took a different point of view.

> We're in business, and we can't afford to sell things at or near cost. On the other hand, we don't take an unusually high markup just because we're offering museum reproductions and unique goods.[6]

These two comments are indicative of the controversies to be anticipated in pricing items sold by a nonprofit institution. As Chapter 11 has shown, most businesses in the private sector develop their prices within boundaries set by production costs (or cost of goods, for retailers), competitors' prices, and consumer demand.

Most nonprofit institutions lack the capital to manufacture their own retail inventory, and thus begin their pricing considerations by looking at the cost of goods obtained from outside suppliers. Fewer and fewer nonprofit managers today can afford to agree completely with the comments of the foundation administrator quoted here. Pricing below cost is equivalent to giving money away at a time when such funds are usually badly needed elsewhere within the institution. Costs, then, usually serve as a floor for setting price.

When the product offered is similar to competitive offerings, then an upper limit on price is set by the competitive range. The organization may be able to charge slightly more because of the captive nature of its audience. More often, prices may be set slightly below comparable market offerings to reflect such overall objectives as education and public awareness of the institution. It is not necessarily true, however, that buyers *expect* to pay lower prices for merchandise just because it is bought during a visit to a nonprofit organization. Managers should be wary of imposing their preconceptions of consumer expectations on the pricing policy of a retail outlet. Market research can often be helpful here. What are comparable nonprofit organizations in other cities charging for similar products? Do prospective customers expect to pay more, less, or about the same for a similar product purchased from a commercial retailer?

A number of nonprofit organizations have adopted a strategy of offering discounts on their ancillary activities as a way of stimulating membership in the organization. For instance, members of the DeCordova Museum in Lincoln, Massachusetts, receive not only free admission to all exhibitions but also a discount on tuition for enrollment in highly regarded classes offered at the Museum School. Since family membership in a recent year was $40 and the discount for most classes was $15 for adults and $10 for children, a family could quickly recoup its initial membership investment. This membership discount strategy can easily be extended to retail store purchase. The Centennial Museum in Vancouver, British Columbia, offers members a 10 percent discount on artwork purchased from the museum store. This includes some merchandise that is also available from other retailers.

More difficult, of course, is the task of setting prices for unique items. By definition, competition becomes less of a direct factor. If a museum is selling reproductions of its works in a limited edition or scarves imprinted with its logo, there is no direct competitor. There is indirect competition from other museums selling reproductions of their own work, however, or from any organization marketing scarves of comparable quality and styling. The nature of consumer demand thus becomes a critical concern in situations where the uniqueness of the product makes demand-price elasticity particularly difficult to estimate. The organization must estimate demand and net revenues at varying pricing levels and then choose an appropriate price. That price should be based on profit goals, degree of risk the organization is willing to take, institutional objectives, and relationship to other products being sold in a retail shop or by mail order.

The cost of goods and the value added by uniqueness are only two of the factors considered by retail managers in establishing prices. Other costs, such as freight charges, wholesale and volume discounts, and the fees charged by credit-card companies for credit sales, must also be figured in. The size of any membership discount should be determined early, during the process of setting objectives; the decision will be made easier if the shop has kept records of the number and amount of members' transactions in the past, and knows the retail markups currently taken on different categories of merchandise.

Markdowns and Psychological Price Points

Markdowns (reductions from original purchase price) are a fact of life to private-sector retailers wishing to "turn" their inventory and keep new merchandise moving into the store. For many managers of nonprofit retail operations, the very word *markdown* conveys hair-raising images of "Mona Lisa, 20 percent off through Saturday only" and "While they last—two mummy models for the price of one." Managers sharing this reaction should realize that the carrying costs of unsold inventory can be considerable and that a fresh look is vital in attracting consumers back to the store. Moreover, merchandise can be marked down without evoking the atmosphere of a bargain basement. Slow-moving goods can be grouped together in a single area and labeled "reduced" or "specially priced." One strategically located sign will usually suffice to show customers where the special buys are. Marking down goods is not only a commercial effort to move inventory but also, for a nonprofit institution, a chance to bring those goods within the budget of a larger segment of the institution's customers.

Psychological price points—for example, $4.95 and $5.95 instead of $5 and $6—are also used by many private-sector retailers in the belief that they sell merchandise faster by creating the impression of a less expensive price. Even after some research, the validity of this rule of thumb has remained difficult to prove. Managers wishing to convey a less commercial image—and to simplify the process of making change at the cash register— may want to experiment with pricing in round numbers.

DISTRIBUTION STRATEGIES

As indicated earlier, the most important distribution decision confronting managers of nonprofit retail operations is whether to sell merchandise in retail shops or through the mail. Many institutions use both channels; others, having established a successful shop, are now considering direct mail. We begin this discussion by bringing up some issues to be considered in establishing the site of a store or sales desk, then review some of the rewards and risks of selling merchandise through the mail.

On-Site Retail Operations

The location of an institution's retail store is a key marketing decision. The space assigned to accommodate the store should be chosen because it meets customer needs, not because it happens to be vacant at the moment. The most important of these needs is easy access. Ideally, the store should be located in the institution's "free zone," the area just inside the front door, where customers can enter without paying to enter the museum or facility itself. Some institutions whose shops are located inside the admission gate allow customers planning only a shopping visit to pass through free of charge. This policy is better than charging to shop, of course, but it still means that shoppers must waste time waiting in line to enter. Particularly during the Christmas rush, when many people may be trying to shop during their lunch hour, frustrating delays may lead to lost tempers and lost sales.

Some managers locate their major shop at the end of the visitor's path through the institution, so that it is impossible to exit without going through the shop. Although space constraints occasionally make such a decision unavoidable, it may arouse resentment, especially among families with limited budgets who would prefer that they not be forced to expose their children to the merchandise. Moreover, such a location may discourage sales of expensive products. The publications manager of London's National Portrait Gallery, for example, recalled that when that institution's shop was remodeled,

> No one was forced to go through the shop to get anywhere else. This was a bit worrying at first, as obviously we might lose a great deal of trade by not "forcing" people to pass through. An interesting fact emerged: we made slightly fewer sales, but the "take" in each case was higher. People don't like buying high-priced goods in an "open" heavy traffic area.[7]

As large, highly promoted traveling exhibits become more common, several museums are having great success with small satellite shops or sales desks set up at the end of the exhibit and stocked with cards, posters, prints, books, and even jewelry or sculpture—all tied to the exhibit's theme. These sales desks are most profitable when they offer small, relatively high-margin items (such as boxed notecards) that are easy to keep in stock in the immediate area. For the convenience of those entering the museum only to shop, a selection of the articles tied to special exhibits should also be available in the main store.

Several nonprofit institutions operating in more than one location have established chains of retail shops. One of these is Britain's National Trust, dedicated to preserving the country's architectural and landscape heritage by maintaining stately homes, other historically or environmentally significant properties, and stretches of open countryside of outstanding natural beauty. The Trust's retailing activities in England and Wales began in 1970 with a few shops, approved by a hesitant board of trustees who hoped not so much to generate revenue as to convince visitors to join the organization. (Trust memberships were sold in the shops in addition to retail goods.) By 1988 the Trust operated 157 shops within its properties. The National Trust shops sell a variety of merchandise such as books, food items, and apparel, focusing on exclusive Trust-commissioned items yielding a high markup. Regional administrators have some flexibility in the choice of merchandise sold in each store and may include compatible high-quality items produced in the local area. A special push is made each year during the Christmas season, with merchandise sold through a mail order catalog as well as in 91 of the "property" shops, 40 free-standing "town" shops, and 26 boutiques in major department stores. In 1987, net profits from NT shops, catalogs, and food service totaled almost $6 million (at prevailing exchange rates), as compared to some $9 million in admission fees and $33 million in subscriptions.

Management of Retail Personnel

The staffing decision most likely to determine the success or failure of a nonprofit organization's retail operation is the selection of its manager. The importance of assigning responsibility for retail management to someone with retail experience can hardly be overemphasized. Operation of a retail shop is neither a hobby for curators nor a diversion for volunteers but a demanding business assignment. Many current museum-shop managers might echo the words of one manager in Boston, who recalled: "I almost fell into this job. I had no retail experience; I was just the only one around to do it. My only education was a liberal arts degree. It took me at least a year to figure out how to run the place." Today's nonprofit institutions can rarely afford to let employees learn on the job. Managing a retail shop requires merchandising flair, sharp buying instincts, hardheaded negotiations with vendors, pricing expertise, and a knack for quantitative analysis and paperwork. To assign these tasks to a former sales clerk or inexperienced volunteer is almost as risky as sending the same person on a major acquisitions trip for a museum.

The manager of a nonprofit organization's store, moreover, faces several problems in managing other retail personnel. Many applicants for sales jobs in museum stores, particularly those located in a large city, are overqualified for the work and become disgruntled when they find it has no direct tie to the collection. Many have an art background and expect a "job," but there is not much glamour in running a cash register. Consequently, most nonprofit organizations' shops share in the high staff turnover (often 100 percent or more annually) that plagues their private-sector competitors.

Staff management problems can be magnified when the shop relies on volunteers instead of employing a paid staff. As we noted in earlier, volunteers can be difficult to recruit and motivate. The problem most frequently mentioned by retail store managers is failure to appear for work. Volunteers are also frequently reluctant to work during summer, when many institutions achieve some of their highest monthly sales.

Many nonprofit organizations lacking the resources to pay salaries to their retail staff have little choice but to use volunteers. To do so successfully requires careful recruitment and selection, as well as continuous motivation and reinforcement—topics discussed in depth in Chapter 19.

Direct-Mail Selling

Direct-mail selling through a catalog is a tempting distribution channel for many nonprofit institutions today, especially those already operating a retail store. What could be easier than giving customers a chance to mail in orders for products with proven sales appeal? The success of such experienced mail-order merchants as the Metropolitan Museum of Art has received wide press coverage in recent years. Recently, the Met mailed over 1.5 million Christmas catalogs to its customers, each containing 116 pages of gifts and cards. Additional mailings included a spring catalog, a 32-page catalog of books and prints, and a 32-page catalog of gifts for children. Prices range from boxes of cards at $6.75 to limited-edition sculpture reproductions at $3800; most fall into the $30–85 range.

A modest mail-order operation, perhaps more instructive to small nonprofit institutions than the activities of the Metropolitan Museum, is carried out by Action on Smoking and Health (ASH). ASH, based in Washington, D.C., began selling bumper stickers, buttons, stickers, and T-shirts in response to requests from its donors. These articles, priced to break even, not raise money, carry messages such as "I don't spit in your face—please don't blow smoke in mine," "Kissing a smoker is like licking out a dirty old ashtray," and similar spirited slogans. "Some people feel more comfortable with some slogans than with others and a few find some of them in questionable taste," a spokesman for the organization commented, "but ASH feels it is appropriate to help people speak out across the broad spectrum of this problem." Other messages include the well-known "Cancer cures smoking" and "The brightest people don't need to light up." Many slogans are suggested by ASH's donors. All printed materials, such as bumper stickers, sold by ASH are manufactured for the agency at a generous discount by a Midwestern printer staunchly opposed to smoking.

ASH publicizes its products twice a year through an 8-1/2 by 11-inch advertisement inserted into solicitation letters mailed to past and prospective donors. The organization has had little luck with rented mailing lists and generates its highest number of responses (about 1 percent) by exchanging lists with other nonprofit organizations, such as Planned Parenthood and the National Wildlife Fund. Staff and space limitations made it infeasible to expand the program; the T-shirts were a particular problem because they required such a large inventory. "We had three kinds of T-shirts carrying different messages, available in three adult sizes and four children's," an ASH spokesman observed. "Add to that the fact that we could only buy in lots of one dozen, and the stock-keeping problem made it impossible to break even, even at $5 and $3.75." ASH solved these difficulties by switching to the sale of iron-on decals, letting people buy whatever size and style of T-shirt they wanted from a store and then apply the decals themselves. In response to the continued growth of its retail operation, ASH contracted out the task of maintaining inventory and filling orders to another organization which bills them on a cost basis.[9]

As the ASH experience shows, managers considering setting up a direct-mail operation should realize that this type of selling involves much more than compiling a mailing list and selecting products that photograph well. Competition in mail-order retailing is keen. Over 10,000 businesses use mail order in the U.S. to market their products. In contrast to a visitor to a museum, who sees only one shop on the site—the institution's own—consumers opening their mail at home may receive any of over 1000 catalogs published annually by a wide range of private-sector, public, and nonprofit organizations. Only a highly professional, well-produced catalog will stand out amid this barrage of solicitation. Other risks include the following.

- Catalogs are very expensive, especially when produced in full color for small runs. A large run is essential to amortize costs.
- Mail-order selling requires efficiently managed and well-staffed packing and shipping services. As discussed earlier, it also demands extensive inventory, particularly if products are offered in a choice of colors, designs, or sizes.
- Postal rates, delivery costs, and list-rental charges are rising steadily.
- As retail activities by nonprofit organizations proliferate, their favored postal status may be increasingly challenged.
- The low-ticket items that often appeal most to shop visitors are usually insufficient to support successful mail-order operations. Many nonprofits hope to sell low-cost, low-inventory items such as calendars and cards through the mail. As the cost of producing a catalog goes up, the average order must also increase, and the items are insufficient.

Reliable sales forecasting, an important technique for any retailer, is vital in mail-order sales. When an item is out of stock in a nonprofit organization's retail shop, it's simply not displayed, and many customers are not aware of its existence. An item that falls out of stock after being included in a catalog, on the other hand, may be ordered by scores of customers; the resulting backlog of orders and correspondence will strain the operating capabilities of the institution and can create much ill will among customers, particularly during the Christmas season.

The early experience of Britain's National Trust is a case in point. The Trust's 32-page Christmas 1977 mail-order catalog measured 9 by 6 inches and offered 105 items for sale (ranging from cards at 50 cents per packet to Irish linen sheets at $199.90 a pair).* It generated $800,000 in sales. Encouraged by this success, the Trust published a 24-page, 11 by 8 inch catalog the next year containing almost 200 stock-keeping units, several of which were color or design variations of each other. Among these were 16 varieties of bath products and 15 miniature toys. Prices ranged from 70 cents for a packet of cards to $20 for a book on life in the English country house. The catalog was sent to an enlarged mailing list and generated an enormous backlog of orders. Many orders were filled late, others not at all.

In light of this experience, the Trust took a very cautious approach in 1979. Its Christmas catalog that year consisted of a single sheet measuring 8 by 4 inches as mailed and 8 by 32 inches when fully unfolded. It offered only 13 products (two calendars, a

---

*Prices converted to dollars at the rate £1.00 = U.S. $2.00.

fruitcake, five packets of cards, two boxes of soap, a box of handkerchiefs, and a desk diary). A prominent headline drew attention to the following "message to members."

> Last year, a lot of people were disappointed because we were overwhelmed by the response to a large catalogue and many items were sold out, many orders were dispatched late, and we were unable to answer customer enquiries promptly. We apologised at the time and apologise again to everyone who was affected by that poor service.
>
> A detailed and intensive study is now taking place to determine how the Trust should organize its mail order operation to give full and efficient service which will be profitable to the Trust.
>
> In the meantime, we offer this very limited choice of essential Christmas items, confident that we can meet orders for such a small range quickly and efficiently, so long as orders are placed in time.
>
> A much wider choice of the National Trust's goods suitable as Christmas presents will be available in the shops listed overleaf.[10]

The time for such a "detailed and intensive study" is *before,* not after, mail-order operations begin. Fortunately, the National Trust has learned from past problems and now operates a professionally managed subsidiary, the National Trust (Enterprises) Ltd., which exercises tight control over the organization's expanding retail activity. The Trust's 1988 Christmas catalog featured 332 items.

In the mail-order area of retailing more than any other, expert advice is essential to success, and employing the services of consultants is a virtual necessity for nonprofit organizations. In order to avoid the tremendous waste of money incurred by sending catalogs to people who may not even look at them, the mail-order market must be segmented with extreme accuracy, a task requiring extensive analytic and quantitative skills. Consultants can also offer advice on proper merchandising of catalog goods and help an organization build and manage its mailing list. Obtaining productive lists is becoming more and more difficult in today's saturated market, and the lists of a fellow nonprofit organization are usually available only through an exchange arrangement. This is particularly true in the United States, where the Internal Revenue Service has ruled that the regular sale of membership mailing lists by an exempt educational organization constitutes unrelated trade or business and thus taxable revenue.[11]

Organizations unwilling or unable to launch a full-scale mail-order operation might consider the experience of the Center for Environmental Education (CEE), a Washington, D.C., organization founded to develop public awareness of environmental problems.[12] CEE, which is especially concerned with the protection of whales, seals, and sea turtles, began direct-mail activity in 1976, selling T-shirts, tote bags, stickers, and other articles. The enthusiastic public response was completely unexpected; managing the mail-order sales began to demand so much staff time that senior administrators decided that CEE's more important educational objectives were being threatened.

Mail-order operations were contracted out to a private firm that now handles complete day-to-day administration of the "Whale Gifts" catalog—selecting merchandise (subject to CEE's approval), dealing with vendors, writing copy, creating designs, and coordinating production. In return, CEE collects a royalty, which is taxable. This royalty income, which exceeds CEE's previous net profit on catalog sales, is not burdened by any expense; the specialist firm bears all costs, including those of carrying inventory. The contractor, of course, also realizes income from management of the catalog, which contains no direct reference to this arrangement.

Although merchandise selected for the 32-page, full-color catalog, issued three times yearly, is designed to appeal to an affluent, sophisticated audience, CEE's mission and objectives are central in production selection. The catalog contains no articles made in Japan, a country where whaling is officially sanctioned. All merchandise, ranging from window transparencies at $3 to a copper weather vane at $172, is related to marine animals, and several pages of educational toys, books, and games for children are included.

The implications of CEE's decision to delegate its mail-order activities in this way are potentially controversial. Certainly, as senior administrators began to complain, the organization was not founded to run a mail-order business. Because that business has proved itself a rich source of income, it's understandable that management was reluctant to forego catalog sales entirely.

In many ways, delegating the management of the catalog operation to a competent outside agency makes sense. On the other hand, not all nonprofits employing such an approach inform catalog readers of the specifics of this arrangement, rarely making reference to the fact that a for-profit firm is performing most of the work involved in the catalog operation, and also collecting most of the revenue.

COMMUNICATION STRATEGIES

Many nonprofit organizations prefer to avoid advertising their retail operations, since any advertisement that appears to solicit visits to a shop, as opposed to visits to the institution, may be considered unrelated business activity by tax authorities. Catalog advertisements, which could be construed as an effort to promote mission-related merchandise such as art reproductions to a geographically distant audience, are more common. Advertisements for Boston's Museum of Fine Arts gift catalog, for instance, draw attention to the museum, not the products. Readers are also encouraged to "subscribe" to the catalog. By charging a nominal fee of $1.00 for this subscription, the museum attempts to discourage "catalog collectors" unlikely to make a purchase.

It is important for nonprofit retail stores to realize the promotion potential of other tools besides media advertising. One of the most obvious is the name of the store, which is often the first part of the store's image to reach the public. "Museum store" or "museum shop" does nothing to differentiate a specific store from its competitors. But consider the distinct images evoked by "The Explore Store" of the Science Museum of Minnesota or "Artworks" at the Loch Haven Art Center in Orlando, Florida. Signs within the museum can also be a marketing tool. Directional signs are important, but a sign may help to remind visitors coming to a special exhibit sales desk that a wider variety of articles are on sale in the main store. Creatively designed shopping bags provide a good way to promote the institution to potential customers who have never even seen it. Free bookmarks, attractively designed and carrying the institution's name or logo, are often used as promotional tools. Organizations engaged in both retail and catalog sales can also use the catalog to stimulate interest in the larger selection of products available at the retail store.

Internal marketing is also an important task for a nonprofit organization's retail operations. Store managers and employees have traditionally been looked down on by many curators and professional personnel. Even today, when the income generated by a shop may be enough to pay the year's capital-construction expenses, vestiges of this attitude sometimes remain. The wise retail manager, realizing that all the institution's administrators share in its mission and objectives, will stress this common interest to colleagues. It is important that senior administrators share in the communications effort by publicizing, to trustees and staff alike, the achievements of the retail operation and the importance of retail income to the institution.

By establishing good relations with curators, in particular, retail managers can not only build the morale of their own staff, but possibly augment their merchandise mix as well. Curators' assistance in calling potential product ideas to a retail manager's attention and writing captions and other explanatory material can be very important in the success of nonprofit retail operations.

SUMMARY

Retailing operations, once a minor and even somewhat neglected function for many public and nonprofit organizations, are assuming more and more importance today. Not only do they represent a significant source of potential income; they also constitute a vital channel of communication with the public. By selling merchandise closely related to its institutional mission, an organization can serve or educate people whom it might not otherwise ever reach.

The appropriate commercial objectives for a noncommercial organization are widely debated and are likely to remain so in the future. Each organization must establish its own retailing positioning—a decision in which all seniors managers should participate and, eventually, support. As part of this process, certain key questions must be addressed.

- To what extent should the retail operation be charged with advancing the institutional mission? How important, comparatively, is profitability? What quantifiable sales objectives are appropriate?

- How involved in retailing does the organization wish to become? Should it commission products? Sell by mail only? Delegate operating tasks to an outside agency?

- How clearly should an organization's merchandise reflect its mission? Are the profits derived from sales of unrelated merchandise worth the risk of conflict with tax authorities? What impact might this merchandise have on the institution's image?

- What pricing strategy is most appropriate? Should a nonprofit organization necessarily aim for a lower gross profit margin than that sought by private-sector competitors?

- What are the risks and advantages of direct-mail selling? Should inexpensive items be sold through the mail, even though small orders may not cover allocated catalog production costs?

- What are the risks and advantages of employing volunteers, as opposed to paid sales staff? How hard is the organization willing to try to provide the intellectual stimulation that volunteers may demand in place of salary?

- What communication strategies are most useful, particularly if advertising is not an option? How can the retail operation best communicate its objectives and importance to other personnel within the institution?

As this chapter has shown, retail operations within nonprofit organizations today are growing increasingly complex. More than ever, proper management of stores and mail-order operations requires formal business education and experience. Mail-order retailing, a specialty in itself, will require the use of paid outside consultants for the majority of nonprofit institutions. As retail activity among the tax-exempt organizations expands, it has attracted increasing attention from tax authorities, and tax restrictions have grown more complex. Periodic review of retail operations—particularly merchandise selection and advertising—by professional legal counsel is strongly recommended. Revenues from retailing are greater today than many organizations would have thought possible a decade ago, but only careful planning and management, augmented by external expertise as necessary, will produce a retail operation that satisfies an organization's commercial, as well as philosophical, goals.

REFERENCES

1. Information on the Mystic Seaport Museum Store was based on personal interviews with Thomas H. Aageson, president, in August 1981.
2. Barbara Rudolph, "Mixing Class and Cash," *Time* (December 9, 1985), p. 56.
3. "Old Lean-to at Metropolitan Yields to Elegant, New Museum Bookshop," *Publishers Weekly* (January 18, 1980), p. 108.
4. Thomas Hoving, unpublished speech, London 1980. Used with permission.
5. Personal communication with an art director at a national historic foundation, February 1979.
6. Personal communication with a museum executive, August 1981.
7. Roger Sheppard, "Portrait Gallery Bookshop: Operation Shoestring," *News from the Museum Store Association* (Spring 1981), p. 25.
8. Information on the National Trust based on personal interviews with National Trust managers, most recently in November 1988.
9. Information on Action on Smoking and Health based on telephone interviews and correspondence with an ASH spokesperson, August 1981.
10. National Trust Christmas Catalogue, 1979.
11. IRS Rev. Rul. 72-431, IRS *Cumulative Bulletin,* 1972–2 (July–December). More generally, see Bruce R. Hopkins, "Nonprofits Facing Wide Range of Tax Controversies," *Nonprofit World* (November–December 1986), pp. 30–31.
12. Information on the Center for Environmental Education based on correspondence and a telephone interview with a CEE spokesperson, August 1981.

Glossary

Selected Marketing & Management Terms*

Advertising   any paid form of nonpersonal presentation and promotion of a product or organization by an identified sponsor

Affinity group   a group of individuals who share a specific relationship in common (e.g., alumni of a university, members of a club or association)

Attitudes   enduring systems of positive or negative evaluations of, or emotional feelings toward, an object

Augmented product   the core product plus any additional services and benefits that may be supplied

Backward integration   obtaining ownership or increased control of an organization's supply systems (see also *Forward integration* and *Vertical integration*)

Benefit segmentation   dividing the population into different groups on the basis of the benefits they want or require and the costs they wish to avoid

Bottom-up planning   programs are developed and implemented by middle-level and lower-level managers and other employees or volunteers who work out the details and follow through on them (see also *Top-down planning*)

Brand   a name, term, sign, symbol, design, or combination of these that seeks to identify the product of an organization and differentiate it from those of competitors

Branding   the process of creating, assigning, and publicizing a brand name, term, sign, symbol, etc., to one or more products

Breakeven   the volume of sales necessary, at a specific price, for a seller to recover all relevant financial costs of a product

Catchment area   the geographic region or area from which the bulk of an organization's customers are drawn

Cause-related marketing   collaborative arrangements between a company and a non-profit organization in which the former promotes both its own product and the nonprofit cause; often ties corporate donations to sales of its product

Centralized management   decision-making power is concentrated among a relatively small number of managers at the head office (see also *Decentralized management*)

Channels of distribution   see *Distribution or delivery system*

---

*Many more terms are defined in the course of the book and can be found by looking at the index.

Cognitive dissonance   perceived inconsistency within an individual's own beliefs or attitudes or between these and one's behavior. A person will attempt to reduce the dissonance through changes in either behavior or cognition

Communication   the transmission of a message from a sender (or source) to a receiver (or recipient)

Communication medium   the personal or impersonal channel through which a message is transmitted to an audience or individual (see also *Mass* media)

Communication mix   the combination of communication elements (personal selling, media advertising, signage, public relations, publicity, and on-site display) used by an organization to communicate its message(s) to its target market(s)

Competition   see *Direct competitor* and *Generic competitor*

Concentrated marketing strategy   in a segmented market, the organization focuses its efforts on one target group and designs its marketing strategy specifically to reach that group, rather than trying to be all things to all people

Contingency budget   funds set aside in advance to finance contingency plans and responses to unanticipated events

Contingency plans   plans outlining a course of action, prepared in advance to deal with situations that might potentially arise

Contribution   the difference between total sales revenues (gross income) and variable expenses (see also *Unit contribution margin*)

Convenience products   products the consumer usually purchases frequently, immediately, and with a minimum of effort in comparison and shopping (see also *Shopping products and Specialty products*)

Core product   the central elements of a product that serve a basic consumer or societal need (see also *Augmented product*)

Cost-per-thousand   the cost of advertising for each 1000 homes reached in TV or radio, or for each 1000 circulated copies of a publication (often abbreviated as CPM)

Crisis management   a situation created by the occurrence of an unexpected event for which management has not prepared and that requires immediate action (see also *Contingency plans*)

Cross-sectional data or study   research information gathered from a whole population (or a representative sample of that population) at a single point in time (see also *Longitudinal data*)

Customer service   a collective term that describes all the supplementary services provided by an organization to satisfy consumers and combat competitors, such as technical aid, information, order taking, complaint handling, refunds, or substitutions

Decentralized management   the power to make decisions is dispersed to relevant personnel at lower levels within an organization (see also *Centralized management*)

Demographic segmentation   categorizing or differentiating people based on demographic variables such as age, sex, religion, income, etc.

Differentiated marketing strategy   developing different products and/or marketing programs for each market segment that the organization plans to serve

Direct competitor   an organization offering a product that meets similar consumer needs and is broadly similar in substance or process to one's own product (see also *Generic competitor*)

Dissonance   see *Cognitive dissonance*

Distribution or delivery system   the combination of internal organizational resources and external intermediaries employed to move a product from production or creation to the final consumer. Goods necessarily move through physical distribution channels, involving transportation, storage, and display. Services may be delivered to the customer directly at the production site or, in certain instances, transmitted electronically

Diversification   the process of entering new markets with one or more products that are new to the organization

Elasticity of demand (to price)   The responsiveness of sales volume to a change in price. Demand is said to be *price inelastic* when raising (or lowering) price by a certain percentage has a proportionately smaller impact on sales volume, and *price elastic* when the impact on volume is proportionately greater than the price change

Fixed cost   a cost that remains unchanged in total for a given time period despite wide fluctuations in activity, such as property taxes, executive salaries, rent, insurance, and depreciation (see also *Variable cost*)

Focus-group interviews   a small-group-discussion method of obtaining qualitative information from individuals who are broadly representative of the target market

Forward integration   seeking ownership or increased control of the means by which an organization distributes its products to end users (see also *Backward integration* and *Vertical integration*)

Four Ps   see *Marketing mix*

Franchise   the licensing of a complete business format where one organization authorizes a number of independent outlets to market a product and engage in a business using the franchisor's trade names and methods of operation

Generic competitor   an organization offering a product that, while possibly different in substance or process, is capable of satisfying the same general consumer needs as one's own product (see also *Direct competitor*)

Horizontal integration   the process of obtaining ownership or increased control of one's competitors (see also *Vertical integration*)

Identifiers   printed words, symbols, or designs that communicate a message

Intermediary   an organization or individual that serves as a go-between or facilitator between producer, marketer, and/or customer

Longitudinal data or study   research information gathered over time (usually at periodic intervals) from the same population or sample; this allows the researcher to monitor individual changes among members of the study

Loss leaders   a product of known or accepted quality priced at a loss or no profit for the purpose of attracting consumers who may then purchase other regularly priced products

Market   the set of all current and potential consumers of a particular product

Market aggregation   see *Undifferentiated marketing strategy*

Market definition   an attempt by the organization to determine which segment of the market its operations are or should be serving

Market development   an organization marketing its current line of products to new markets or segments

Market niche   a segment of a market where there is demand for a product with specific attributes distinguishing it from competing offerings

Market penetration   an organization attempts to increase consumption of its current products in its current markets

Market potential   a calculation of maximum possible sales (in units or currency values) or usage opportunities in a defined territorial area for all marketers of a product during a stated period of time

Market segment   a homogeneous subset of the target market that may require a marketing plan tailored to the segment's distinctive characteristics

Market segmentation   the process of identifying homogeneous submarkets or segments within the target market

Market share   the ratio of an organization's sales volume for a particular product category to total market volume on either an actual or a potential basis

Marketing audit   a systematic, critical, unbiased, and comprehensive review and appraisal of an organization's or subunit's marketing objectives, strategies, policies, and activities

Marketing mix   the four basic ingredients (or elements) in a marketing program that influence consumers' decisions on whether or not to patronize the organization. These four elements are product, price, distribution or delivery systems, and communication. (Note: Some people use the phrase *the four Ps*—product, price, place, and promotion—to describe the elements of the marketing mix, but we regard the terms *place* and *promotion* as too narrow and potentially misleading)

Marketing planning   the tasks of setting up objectives for marketing activity and of determining and scheduling the steps necessary to achieve such objectives

Marketing research   the systematic gathering, recording, and analyzing of data to provide information for marketing decision making

Mass media   informational networks reaching large numbers of people that carry news, features, editorial opinion, and advertising—specifically newspapers, magazines, radio, and television; the term can also be applied to other communication vehicles, such as billboards, poster sites, and mail service, that can be used to convey marketing messages to large numbers of people

Members   individuals who join an organization and pay dues or support it on a periodic basis with funds, services, or their time and efforts

Merchandising   Selecting, displaying, and promoting products in a retail store or other distribution outlet

Noise or clutter   conflicting, counter, or unrelated communications that distract from an advertiser's message to members of a target audience

Opinion leader   an individual who influences other people's purchase and consumption behavior

Opportunity cost   the maximum benefit foregone by using scarce resources (e.g., money, management time, physical facilities) for one purpose instead of the next best alternative

Personal selling   personal interaction between the representative of an organization and one or more prospective purchasers with a view of making a sale or developing a favorable attitude toward the organization and its products

Price   defined narrowly as the monetary cost to the purchaser of obtaining a product; more broadly it includes other monetary outlays associated with purchasing and using the product, as well as all nonmonetary costs associated with purchase and use of a good or service (or adoption of a social behavior), such as time, and physical and psychological effort

Price elasticity   the extent to which an increase or decrease in the price of a product results in a corresponding fall or rise in demand for that product

Pricing strategy   the mix of monetary price level charged to the final purchaser, terms and methods of payment (e.g., checks, credit cards, exact change), and discounts offered to both intermediaries and final purchasers

Primary data   information the researcher collects through observation, experimentation, or survey research (see also *Secondary data*)

Primary demand   the current level of demand from all sources for the entire product class in question

Proactive selling   actively seeking out prospective consumers (see also *Reactive selling*)

Product   what the organization creates or sponsors and then offers to prospective customers for their acquisition, use, consumption, or adoption; the term includes physical goods, services, and social behaviors or causes

Product class   a group of products that serve the same general function or fulfill the same basic need

Product development   the process of developing or acquiring new or improved products for an organization's current markets (see also *Diversification*)

Product differentiation   to change or modify a product so that it is perceived by consumers as being different from the other offerings on the market

Product line   all the products marketed by a given organization, sometimes subdivided into sets of product lines

Profit center   an organizational unit whose revenues and costs are clearly identifiable and whose management is held responsible for controlling both sides of the income statement

Promotional activities   various nonrecurrent selling efforts, usually of a short-term nature, such as contests, discount coupons, special displays, and introductory offers

Psychographic segmentation   dividing the market into segments using variables such as people's life-styles, values, attitudes, personalities, and interests

Public relations   the managing of public perceptions of an organization and its products by making available news about the organization to the media, or by interacting directly with opinion leaders

Public service advertising   advertising who production and distribution is donated by agencies and media; usually confined to noncontroversial messages and issues

Publicity   staging and publicizing special events and activities to attract community attention, often via the news media

Reactive selling   letting consumers take the initiative in seeking out the vendor, who then tries to complete the transaction (see also *Proactive selling*)

Secondary data   existing information in an accessible form that can be used to provide insights for management decision making or serve as inputs to new primary-data-collection efforts (see also *Primary data*)

Shopping products products that the consumer, in the process of selection and purchase, characteristically compares on such bases as suitability, quality, price, and style (see also *Convenience products* and *Specialty products*)

Specialty products products with unique characteristics and/or brand identification for which a significant group of buyers are habitually willing to make a special purchasing effort (see also *Convenience products* and *Shopping products*)

Strategic business or management unit (SBU/SMU) a unit within a larger organization that is essentially treated as a separate entity and established as an independent profit center, usually with a distinct mission, objectives, competitive environment, and managerial requirements (see also *Profit center*)

Target market that portion of the total market the organization has selected to serve

Target marketing focusing the marketing efforts on specific segments within the total market

Third-party payers persons or organizations that provide the funding for projects, products, or services that benefit the user or consumer

Time-series data see *Longitudinal data*

Top-down planning programs are implemented by top-level management, and participation filters down to the lower levels (see also *Bottom-up planning*)

Trademark a brand or part of a brand that is given legal protection and whose use is restricted to its owners

Undifferentiated marketing strategy the organization treats the market as an aggregate and designs its products and marketing program to appeal to the greatest number of consumers possible

Unit contribution margin the difference between the price at which an item is sold by the marketer and the costs directly associated with producing and selling it (sometimes expressed as a percentage of the selling price received by the marketer)

Usage segmentation subdividing the total consumer market on the basis of where, when, and why the product is used

Variable cost a cost that changes in direct proportion to changes in activity, such as materials and parts, sales commissions, and certain labor and supplies (see also *Fixed cost*)

Vertical integration the process of purchasing or acquiring control over one's suppliers (see *Backward integration*) and/or one's distributors (see *Forward integration*) (see also *Horizontal integration*)

Index